D1877933

HUMAN RIGHTS
Acts, Statutes and Constitutional Provisions

HUMAN RIGHTS

Acts, Statutes and Constitutional Provisions

(Volume II)

D.N. Gupta
Chandrachur Singh

KALPAZ PUBLICATIONS
Delhi–110 052

HUMAN RIGHTS
Acts, Statutes and Constitutional Provisions
(Human Rights, Law)

Rs. 1800 (Set)

© D.N. Gupta, Chandrachur Singh

ISBN: 81-7835-098-X (Set)
ISBN: 81-7835-157-9 (Vol. II)

All rights reserved. No part of this book may be reproduced in any manner without written permission

Published in 2003 in India by
Kalpaz Publications
C–30, Satyawati Nagar
Delhi–110 052

e-mail: kalpaz@hotmail.com

Lasertypesetting at: Varsha Graphics, Delhi
Printed at: Mehra Offset Printers, Delhi

Contents

Preface

In this Volume, Acts, Statutes and Constitutional provisions that are concerned with environmental issues, protection of the rights of the Indian citizens vis-à-vis the illegal migrants, the rights of disabled persons, juveniles, prisoners/criminals, citizens' right to information and many other important subjects have been assimilated.

Providing economic and social security is the main task of the State. However, there is a paradox involved. Increasing economic prosperity involves technological upgradation and building new structures such as dams, bridges, township etc. Doing so leads to environmental problems such as pollution, degradation of common property resources, threat to biological diversity, etc. Development comes at a cost. Increasing deforestation, industrialization, urbanization, all lead to displacement. The Indian Constitution mentions about the protection of environment in the Directive Principles of State Policy and in the section on Fundamental Duties. The main awareness however came after 1972 Stockholm Conference. The Rio Declaration gave the slogan of 'sustainable development'. Government's efforts are towards integrating environmental imperatives with developmental aspirations. A set of documents concerning these issues have been included in Chapter Six.

Physical or mental disability is a silent crisis that not only affects the disabled persons and their families but also the entire civil society. There are approximately 500 million disabled in the world of which nearly 350 million come from developing countries. India also has a sizeable number (1.9% of the total population) of disabled persons. To draw the world's attention towards the plight of the disabled and recognise that disability is first and foremost a human rights issue, the United Nations declared the 1981 as the International Year of Disabled Persons. The UN defines disabled persons as those who are unable to ensure themselves, wholly or partly, the necessities of a normal individual/social life as a result of deficiency, either congenital or not, in their physical or mental capabilities; or persons with restrictions or lack of ability to perform an activity in the manner or within the range considered normal for a human being. The Indian Constitution protects the rights of disabled, under Schedule VII. Article 41 directs the State 'to make effective provisions for securing the right to work, education and public assistance in case of unemployment, old age, sickness, disablement and other cases of undeserved wants' The basic policy framework is enshrined in Equal Opportunities, Protection of Rights and Full Participation Act 1992; India has also made several attempts to make life better for the disabled. These efforts alongwith laws that have been enacted against illegal migrants in order to protect the rights of Indian citizens are included in Chapter Seven.

Delinquency is defined as a form of antisocial behaviour involving personal and social disorganisations. It involves a pattern of behaviour which deviates from the normal, is forbidden by law and is not sanctioned by society. "Juvenile Delinquency" refers to the offences committed by individuals who are too young to be called adults and too old to be called children. According to the Juvenile Justice Act, 1986, the age groups of 7-16 for boys and 7-18 for girls are considered Juveniles. Broken family, poverty, adverse impact of media, etc. are all attributed as reasons behind this problem. In order to protect the innocent children from the inhuman atmosphere in Indian prisons and other criminal activities that they are forced to undertake, a number of steps have been taken by the Government of India over the years.

With the development and progress of civil society, conditions in prisons and treatment meted out to prisoners have also become important tests of a civilized society and humane content of a nation. Article 21 of the Indian Constitution has laid down that no person 'shall be deprived of his life or personal liberty except according to procedure established by law'. This Article is applicable even to convicts, prisoners and criminals. Being a prisoner does not *ipso facto* amount to the fact that the concerned person has lost all his rights as a human being. Right to have interviews with family members and friends, speedy trials even in murder cases, assurance that criminal prosecution do not operate as engines of oppression are some of the rights that any prisoner | criminal is entitled to. Moreover, it is the duty of the State to ensure that basic facilities that a human being requires are also provided to the prisoners.

Acts concerning juveniles and prisoners / criminals form parts of Chapters Eight and Nine respectively.

It is believed that a nation progresses better only if it has an open society. Scholars have coined different words for this. In the contemporary times, the concept of civil society has gained prominence as an alternative to state simply because civil society gives opportunities of interaction among its members. The State is seen as an instrument of coercion. Transparency and accountability on the part of the State is the main ingredient of a civil society. This restores human dignity, ensures liberty and curbs arbitrariness and abuse of power. The attempts made by Indian Government over the years in this regard are the subject matter of Chapter Ten.

Thus, in the present collection of documents on human rights, an attempt has been made to place before all concerned the basic Acts, Statutes and Constitutional provisions on various issues concerning human rights.

D.N. Gupta
Chandrachur Singh

1

Environment and Human Rights

THE ENVIRONMENT (PROTECTION) RULES, 1986

In exercise of powers conferred by sections 6 and 25 of the Environment (Protection) Act, 1986 (29 of 1986), the Central Government hereby makes the following rules namely:

1. *Short title and commencement*

(i) These rules may be called the Environment (Protection) Rules, 1986.

(ii) They shall come into force on the date of their publication in the Official Gazette.

2. *Definitions.* In these rules, unless the context otherwise requires,—

(a) "Act" means the Environment (Protection) Act, 1986 (29 of 1986);

[(aa) "areas means all the areas where the hazardous substances are handled;]

(b) "Central Board" means the Central Board for the Prevention and Control of Water Pollution constituted under Section 3 of the Water (Prevention and Control of Pollution) Act, 1974 (6 of 1974);

(c) "form" means a form set forth in Appendix A to these rules;

(d) "Government Analyst" means a person appointed or recognized as such under Section 13;

(e) "person" in relation to any factory or premises means a person or occupier or his agent who has control over the affairs of the factory or premises and includes in relation to any substance, the person in possession of the substance;

(ee) "prohibited substance" means the substance prohibited for handling;

(f) "recipient system" means the part of the environment such as, soil, water, air or other which receives the pollutants;

(ff) "restricted substance" means the substance restricted for handling;]

(g) "Section" means a section of the Act;

(h) "schedule" means a schedule appended to these rules;

(i) "standards" means standards prescribed under these rules;

(j) "State Board" means a State Board for the Prevention and Control of Water Pollution constituted under Section 4 of the Water (Prevention and Control of Pollution) Act, 1974 (6 of 1974), or as a State Board for the Prevention and Control of Air Pollution constituted under Section 5 of the Air (Prevention and Control of Pollution) Act, 1981 (14 of 1981).

3. Standards for emission or discharge of environmental pollutants. 1. For the purposes of protecting and improving the quality of the environment and preventing and abating environmental pollution, the standards for emission or discharge of environmental pollutants from the industries, operations or processes shall be as specified in [Schedules I to IV]

2. Notwithstanding anything contained in sub-rule (1), the Central Board or a State Board may specify more stringent standards from those provided in [Schedules I to IV] in respect of any specific industry, operation or process depending upon the quality of the recipient system and after recording reasons, therefor, in writing.

3. The standards for emission or discharge of environmental pollutants specified under sub-rule (1) or sub-rule (2) shall be complied with by an industry, operation or process within a period of one year of being so specified.

[(3A) (i) Notwithstanding anything contained in sub-rules (1) and (2), on and from the 1st day of January, 1994, emission or discharge of environmental pollutants from the [industries, operations or processes other than those industries, operations or processes for which standards have been specified in Schedule I shall] not exceed the relevant parameters and standards specified in Schedule VI:

Provided that the State Boards may specify more stringent standards for the relevant parameters with respect to specific industry or locations after recording reasons therefor in writing;

(ii) The State Board shall while enforcing the standards specified in Schedule VI follow the guidelines specified in Annexures I and II in that Schedule.]

[(3B) Any emission or discharge of environmental pollutants

from the industries, operations or processes shall not exceed the relevant concentration in ambient air as indicated and set out against each pollutants in (3) to (5) of the Schedule VII.].

4. Notwithstanding anything contained in sub-rule (3)

(a) the Central Board or a State Board, depending on the local conditions or nature of discharge of environment pollutants, may, by order, specify a lesser period than a period specified under sub-rule (3) within which the compliance of standards shall be made by an industry, operation or process;

(b) the Central Government in respect of any specified industry, operation or process, by order, may specify any period other than a period specified under sub-rule (3) within which the compliance of standards shall be made by such industry, operation or process.

5. Notwithstanding anything contained in sub-rule (3), the standards for emission or discharge of environmental pollutants specified under sub-rule (1) or sub-rule (2) in respect of an industry, operation or process before the commencement of the Environment (Protection) Amendment Rules, 1991, shall be complied with by such industry, operation or process by the 31st day of December, 1991.]

[6. Notwithstanding anything contained in sub-rule (3), an industry, operation or process which has commenced production on or before 16th May, 1981 and has shown adequate proof of at least commencement of physical work for establishment of facilities to meet the specified standards within a time-bound programme, to the satisfaction of the concerned, State Pollution Control Board, shall comply with such standards latest by the 31st day of December, 1993.

7. Notwithstanding anything contained in sub-rule (3) or sub-rule (6) an industry, operation or process which has commenced production after 16th day of May, 1981 but before 31st day of December, 1991 and has shown adequate proof of at least commencement of physical work for establishment of facilities to meet the specified standards within a time-bound programme, to the satisfaction of the concerned State Pollution Control Board, shall comply with such standards latest by the 31st day of December, 1992.]

4. Directions. 1. Any direction issued under Section 5 shall be in writing.

2. The direction shall specify the nature of action to be taken and the time within which it shall be complied with by the person, officer or the authority to whom such direction is given.

[3-a]. The person, officer or authority to whom any direction is sought to be issued shall be served with a copy of the proposed direction and shall be given an opportunity of not less than fifteen days from the date of service of a notice to file with an officer designated in this behalf the objections, if any, to the issue of the proposed direction.]

[3-b]. Where the proposed direction is for the stoppage or regulation of electricity or water or any other service affecting the carrying on any industry, operation or process and is sought to be issued to an officer or an authority, a copy of the proposed direction shall also be endorsed to the occupier of the industry, operation or process, as the case may be, and objections, if any, filed by the occupier with an officer designated in this behalf shall be dealt with in accordance with the procedure under sub-rules (3-a) and (4) of this rule:

Provided that no opportunity of being heard shall be given to the occupier if he had already been heard earlier and the proposed direction referred to in sub-rule (3-b) above the stoppage or regulation of electricity or water or any other service was the resultant decision of the Central Government after such earlier hearing.]

4. The Central Government shall within a period of 45 days from the date of receipt of the objections, if any, or from the date up to which an opportunity is given to the person, officer or authority to file objections whichever is earlier, after considering the objections, if any, received from the person, officer or authority sought to be directed and for reasons to be recorded in writing, confirm, modify or decide not to issue the proposed direction.

5. In a case where the Central Government is of the opinion that in view of the likelihood of a grave injury to the environment it is not expedient to provide an opportunity to file objections against the proposed direction, it may, for reasons to be recorded in writing, issue directions without providing such an opportunity.

6. Every notice or direction required to be issued under this rule shall be deemed to be duly served:

(a) where the person to be served is a company, if the document is addressed in the name of the company at its registered office or at its principal office or place of business and is either,—

(i) sent by registered post; or
(ii) delivered at its registered office or at the principal office or place of business;

(b) where the person to be served is an officer serving Government, if the document is addressed to the person and a copy thereof is endorsed to the Head of the Department and also to the Secretary to the Government, as the case may be, incharge of the Department in which for the time being the business relating to the Department in which the officer is employed is transacted and is either,—

(i) sent by registered post; or
(ii) is given or tendered to him;

(c) in any other case, if the document is addressed to the person to be served and
(i) is given or tendered to him; or
(ii) if such person cannot be found, is affixed on some conspicuous part of his last known place of residence or business or is given or tendered to some adult member of his family or is affixed on some conspicuous part of the land or building, if any, to which it relates; or
(iii) is sent by registered post to that person.

Explanation. For the purpose of this sub-rule,

(a) "company" means any body corporate and includes a firm or other association of individuals;
(b) "a servant" is not a member of the family.

5. ***Prohibition and restriction on the location of industries and the carrying on processes and operations in different areas.*** 1. The Central Government may take into consideration the following factors while prohibiting or restricting the location of industries and carrying on of processes and operations in different areas:

(i) Standards for quality of environment in its various aspects laid down for an area.

(ii) The maximum allowable limits of concentration of various environment pollutants (including noise) for an area.

(iii) The likely emission or discharge of environmental pollutants from an industry, process or operation proposed to be prohibited or restricted.

(iv) The topographic and climatic features of an area.

(v) The biological diversity of the area which, in the opinion of the Central Government, needs to be preserved.

(vi) Environmentally compatible land use.

(vii) Net adverse environmental impact likely to be caused by an industry, process or operation proposed to be prohibited or restricted.

(viii) Proximity to a protected area under the Ancient Monuments and Archaeological Sites and Remains Act, 1958 or a sanctuary, National Park, game reserve or closed area notified, as such under the Wild Life (Protection) Act, 1972, or places protected under any treaty, agreement or convention with any other country or countries or in pursuance of any decision made in any international conference, association or other body.

(ix) Proximity to human settlements.

(x) Any other factors as may be considered by the Central Government to be relevant to the protection of the environment in an area.

2. While prohibiting or restricting the location of industries and carrying on of processes and operations in an area, the Central Government shall follow the procedure hereinafter laid down.

3. (a) Whenever it appears to the Central Government that it is expedient to impose prohibition or restrictions on the location of an industry or the carrying on of processes and operations in an area, it may, by notification in the Official Gazette and in such other manner as the Central Government may deem necessary from time to time, given notice of its intention to do so.

(b) Every notification under clause (a) shall give a brief description of the area, the industries, operations processes in that area about which such notification pertains and also specify the reasons for the imposition of prohibition or restrictions on the location of the industries and carrying on of processes or operations in that area.

(c) Any person interested in filing an objection against the imposition of prohibition or restriction on carrying on of processes or operations as notified under clause (a) may do so in writing to the Central Government within sixty days from the date of publication of the notification in the Official Gazette.

(d) The Central Government shall, within a period of one hundred and twenty days from the date of publication of the notification in the Official Gazette, consider all the objections received against such notification and may [within three hundred and sixty-five days] from such date of publication.] impose prohibition or restrictions on location of such industries and the carrying on of any process or operation in an area.

[4.Notwithstanding anything contained in sub-rule (3), whenever it appears to the Central Government that it is in public interest to do so, it may dispense with the requirement of notice under clause (a) of sub-rule (3).]

[6. Procedure for taking samples. The Central Government or the officer empowered to take samples under Section 11 shall collect the sample in sufficient quantity to be divided into two uniform parts and effectively seal and suitably mark the same and permit the person from whom the sample is taken to add his own seal or mark to all or any of the portions so sealed and marked. In case where the sample is made up in containers or small volumes and is likely to deteriorate or be otherwise damaged if exposed, the Central Government or the officer empowered shall take two of the said samples without opening the containers and suitably seal and mark the same. The Central Government or the officer empowered shall dispose of the samples so collected as follows:

(i) one portion shall be handed over to the person from whom the sample is taken under acknowledgement; and

(ii) the other portion shall be sent forth with to the environmental laboratory for analysis.]

7. Service of notice. The Central Government or the officer empowered shall serve on the occupier or his agent or person in charge of the place a notice then and there in Form I of his intention to have the sample analysed.

8. Procedure for submission of samples for analysis, and the form of laboratory report thereon. 1. Sample taken for analysis shall be sent by the Central Government or the officer empowered to the environmental laboratory by registered post or through special messenger along with Form II.

2. Another copy of Form II together with specimen impression of seals of the officer empowered to take samples along with the seals/marks, if any, of the person from whom the sample is taken shall be sent in a sealed cover by registered post or through a special messenger to the environmental laboratory.

3. The findings shall be recorded in Form III in triplicate and signed by the Government Analyst and sent to the Officer from whom the sample is received for analysis.

4. On receipt of the report of the findings of the Government Analyst, the officer shall sent one copy of the report to the person from whom the sample was taken for analysis, the second copy shall be retained by him for his records and the third copy shall be kept by him to be produced in the Court before which proceedings, if any are, instituted.

9. Functions of environmental laboratories. The following shall be the functions of environmental laboratories:

(i) to evolve standardised methods for sampling and analysis of various types of environmental pollutants;

(ii) to analyse samples sent by the Central Government or the officers empowered under sub-section (1) of Section 11;

(iii) to carry out such investigations as may be directed by the Central Government to lay down standards for the quality of environment and discharge of environmental pollutants, to monitor and to enforce the standards laid down;

(iv) to send periodical reports regarding its activities to the Central Government;

(v) to carry out such other functions as may be entrusted to it by the Central Government from time to time.

10. Qualifications of Government Analyst. A person shall not be qualified for appointment or recognised as a Government Analyst unless he is a—

(a) graduate in science from a recognised university with five years' experience in a laboratory engaged in environmental investigations, testing or analysis; or

(b) post-graduate in science or a graduate in engineering or a graduate in medicine or equivalent with two years' experience in a laboratory engaged in environmental investigations, testing or analysis; or

(c) post-graduate in environmental science from a recognized university with two years' experience in a laboratory engaged in environmental investigations, testing or analysis.

11. Manner of giving notice. The manner of giving notice under clause (b) of Section 19 shall be as follows, namely:

1. The notice shall be, in writing in Form IV.
2. The person giving notice may send notice to,

(a) if the alleged offence has taken place in a Union territory

(A) the Central Board; and

(B) the Ministry of Environment and Forests (represented by the Secretary of the Government of India);

(b) if the alleged offence has taken place in a State:

(A) the State Board; and

(B) the Government of the State (represented by the Secretary to the State Government incharge of environment); and

(C) the Ministry of Environment and Forests (represented by the Secretary to the Government of India).

3. The notice shall be sent by registered post-acknowledgement due.

4. The period of sixty days mentioned in clause (b) of Section 19 of the Environment (Protection) Act, 1986 shall be reckoned from the date it is first received by one of the authorities mentioned above.

[12. ***Furnishing of informulion to authorities and agencies in certain cases.*** Where the discharge of environmental pollutant in excess of the prescribed standard occurs or is apprehended to occur due to any accident or other unforeseen act or event, the person in charge of the place at which such discharge occurs or is apprehended to occur shall forthwith intimate the fact of such occurrence or apprehension of such occurrence to all the following authorities or agencies, namely:

(i) The officer in-charge of emergency or disaster relief operations in a district or other region of a State or Union Territory specified by whatever designation, by the Government of the said State or Union territory, and in whose jurisdiction the industry, process or operation is located;

(ii) The Central Board or a State Board, as the case may be, and its regional officer having local jurisdiction who have been delegated powers under Sections 20, 21, 23 of the Water (Prevention and Control of Pollution) Act, 1974 (6 of 1974), and Section 24 of the Air (Prevention and Control of Pollution) Act, 1981 (14 of 1981);

(iii) The Statutory authorities or agencies specified in column 3 in relation to places mentioned in column 2 against thereof of.] [Schedule V]

*[13. **Prohibition and restriction on the handling of hazardous substances in different areas*** 1. The Central Government may take into consideration the following factors while prohibiting or restricting the handling of hazardous substances in different areas:

(i) the hazardous nature of the substance (either in qualitative or quantitative terms) as far as may be in terms of its damage causing potential to the environment, human beings, other living creatures, plants and property;

(ii) the substances that may be or likely to be or readily available as substitutes for the substances proposed to be prohibited or restricted;

(iii) the indigenous availability of the substitute, or the state of technology available in the country for developing a safe substitute;

(iv) the gestation period that may be necessary for gradual introduction of a new substitute with a view to bringing about a total prohibition of the hazardous substance in question; and

(v) any other factor as may be considered by the Central Government to be relevant to the protection of environment.

2. While prohibiting or restricting the handling of hazardous substances in an area including their imports and exports the Central Government shall follow the procedure hereinafter laid down:

(i) Whenever it appears to the Central Government that it is expedient to impose prohibition or restriction on the handling of hazardous substances in an area, it may, by notification in the Official Gazette and in such other manner as the Central

Government may deem necessary from time to time, give notice of its intention to do so.

(ii) Every notification under clause (i) shall give a brief description of the hazardous substances and the geographical region or the area to which such notification pertains and also specify the reasons for the imposition of prohibition or restriction on the handling of such hazardous substances in that region or area.

(iii) Any person interested in filing an objection against the imposition of prohibition or restrictions on the handling of hazardous substances as notified under clause (i) may do so in writing to the Central Government within thirty days from the date of publication of the notification in the Official Gazette.

(iv) The Central Government shall within a period of sixty days from the date of publication of the notification in the Official Gazette consider all the objections received against such notification and may impose prohibition or restrictions on the handling of hazardous substances in a region or an area.]

[14. Submission of environment [statement]. Every person carrying on an industry, operation or process requiring consent under Section 25 of the Water (Prevention and Control of Pollution) Act, 1974 (6 of 1974) or under Section 21 of the Air (Prevention and Control of Pollution) Act, 1981 (14 of 1981) or both or authorisation under the Hazardous Waters (Management and Handling) Rules. 1989 issued under the Environment (Protection) Act, 1986 (29 of 1986) shall submit an environmental [statement] for the financial year ending on the 31st March in Form V to the concerned State Pollution Control Board on or before the [thirtieth day of Scptember] every year, beginning 1993.]

APPENDIX
STANDARDS OF POLLUTION

SCHEDULE [I]
(See Rule 3)

S. No.	*Industry*	*Parameter*	*Standards*
(1)	*(2)*	*(3)*	*(4)*
1.	Caustic Soda Industry		Concentration not to exceed, milligram per litre (except for pH and flow)
		Total concentration of mercury in the final effluent*	0.01
		Mercury bearing waste-water generation (flow)	10 kilolitres/tonne of caustic soda produced
		pH	5.5 to 9.0
		* Final effluent is the combined effluent from (a) cell house, (b) brine plant, (c) chlorine handling, (d) hydrogen handling, (e) hydrochloric acid plant.	
2.	Man-made fibres (synthetic)		Concentration not to exceed, milligram per litre (except for pH)
		Suspended solids	100
		[22][Bio-chemical oxygen demand, (3-days at 27°C)]	30
		pH	5.5 to 9.0

(1)	(2)	(3)	(4)	
3.	Oil-refinery industry	Concentration, not to exceed, milligram per litre (except for pH)		
		Oil and grease	10	7
		Phenol	1	0.7
		Sulphide	0.5	0.35
		[22][Bio-chemical oxygen demand, (3-days at 27°C)]	0.15	10.5
		Suspended solids	20	14
		pH	6 to 8.5	
4.	Sugar industry		Concentration not to exceed, milligram per litre	
		[22] [Bio-chemical oxygen demand (3-days at 27°C)]	100 for disposal on land 30 for disposal in surface waters	
		Suspended solids	100 for disposal on land 30 for disposal in surface waters	
5.	Thermal power plants		Maximum, limiting concentration, milligram per litre (except for pH and temperature)	
	Condenser cooling waters (once through cooling system)	pH	6.5–8.5	
		Temperature	Not more than 5°C higher than the intake water temperature	
		Free available chlorine	0.5	
	Boiler blowdowns	Suspended solids	100	
		Oil and grease	20	
		Copper (total)	1.0	
		Iron (total)	1.0	
	Cooling-tower blowdown	Free available chlorine	0.5	

(1)	(2)	(3)	(4)
		Zinc	1.0
		Chromium (total)	0.2
		Phosphate	5.0
		Other corrosion inhibiting material	Limit to be established on case by case basis by Central Board in case of Union territories and State Boards in case of States
	Ash-pond effluent	pH	6.5—8.5
		Suspended solids	100
		Oil and grease	20
6.	Cotton textile industries (composite and processing)		Concentration not to exceed, milligram per litre (except for pH and bio-assay)
	Common:		
		pH	5.5 to 9
		Suspended solid	100
		[Bio-chemical oxygen demand, (3 days at 27°C)]	150
		Oil and grease	10
		Bio-assay test	90% survival of fish after 96 hours
	Special		
		Total chromium (as Cr)	2
		Sulphide (as S)	2
		Phenolic compounds (as C_6H_5OH)	5

The special parameters to be stipulated by the Central Board in case of Union territories and State Boards in case of States depending upon the dye used in the industry. Where the industry uses chrome dyes, sulphur dyes and/or phenolic compounds in the dyeing/printing process, the limits on chromium of 2 mg/litre, sulphides of 2 mg/litre, and phenolic compounds of 5 mg/litre, respectively shall be imposed.

Where the quality requirements of the recipient systems so warrants, the limit of BOD should be lowered up to 30 according to the requirement by the State Boards for States and the Central Board for the Union territories.

A limit on sodium absorption ratio 26 should be imposed by the State Boards for the States and the Central Board for the Union territories if the disposal of effluent is to be made on land.

(1)	(2)	(3)	(4)
7.	Composite woollen mills		Concentration not to exceed, milligram per litre (except for pH and bio-assay)
	Common:	Suspended solids	100
		pH	5.5 to 9.0
		[Bio-chemical oxygen demand, (3-days at 27°C)]	100
		Oil and Grease	10
		Bio-assay	90% survival of fish after 96 hours
	Special	Total chromium (as Cr)	2
		Sulphide (as S)	2
		Phenolic compound (as C_6H_5OH)	5

The special parameters to be stipulated by the Central Board in case of Union Territories and State Boards in case of States depending upon the dye used in the industry. Where the industry uses chrome dyes, sulphur dyes and/or phenolic compounds in the dyeing/printing process, the limits on chromium of 2mg/litre, sulphides of 2 mg/litre, and phenolic compounds of 5 mg/litre, respectively shall be imposed.

Where the quality requirements of the recipient system so warrants, the limit of BOD should be lowered up to 30 according to the requirement by the State Boards for States and the Central Board for the Union Territories.

A limit on sodium absorption ratio of 26 should be imposed by the State Boards for the States and the Central Board for the Union territories if the disposal of effluent is to be made on land.

[8. Dye and Dye Intermediate		
		Concentration not to exceed miligrams per litre (except for pH, temperature and bio-assay)
	Suspended Solids	100
	pH	6 to 8.5
	Temperature	Shall not exceed 5°C above the ambient temperature of the receiving body
	Mercury (as Hg)	0.01
	Hexavalent Chromium (as Cr)	0.1
	Total Chromium (as Cr)	2.0
	Copper (as Cu)	3.0
	Zinc (as Zn)	5.0
	Nickel (as Ni)	3.0
	Cadmium (ad Cd)	2.0
	Chloride (as Cl)	1000

(1)	(2)	(3)	(4)
		Sulphate (as SO_4)	1000
		Phenolic Compounds (as C_6H_5OH)	
		Oil and Grease	10
		Bio-assay Test (with 1 : 8 dilution of effluents	90 per cent survival of test animals after 96 hours

The standards of chlorides and sulphates are applicable for discharge into inland and surface water-courses. However, when discharged on land for irrigation, the limit for chloride shall not be more than 600 milligrams per litre and the sodium absorption ratio shall not exceed 26.

(1)	(2)	(3)	(4)
9.	Electroplating		Concentration not to exceed, milligram per litre (except for pH and temperature)
		pH	6.0 to 9.0
		Temperature	Shall not exceed 5°C above, the ambient temperature of the receiving body
		Oil and Grease	10
		Suspended Solids	100
		Cyanides (as CN)	0.2
		Ammonical Nitrogen (as N)	50
		Total Residual Chloride (as Cl)	1.0
		Cadmium (as Cd)	2.0

(1)	(2)	(3)	(4)
		Nickel (as Ni)	3.0
		Zinc (as Zn)	5.0
		Hexavalent Chromium (as Cr)	0.1
		Total Chromium (as Cr)	2.0
		Copper (as Cu)	3.0
		Lead (as Pb)	0.1
		Iron (as Fe)	3.0
		Total metal	10.0
10.	Cement Plants		Not to exceed—milligrams per normal cubic metre
	Plant Capacity:		
	200 tonnes per day	Total dust (All sections)	400
	Greater than 200 tonnes per day	Total dust (All sections)	250

The Central and State Pollution Control Boards may fix stringent standards, not exceeding 250 milligrams per normal cubic metre for smaller plants and 150 milligrams per normal cubic metre for larger plants if the industry is located in an area which, in their opinion, requires more stringent standards.

Where continuous monitoring integrates are provided on dust emission lines, the integrated average values over a period, to be fixed by the Central and State Boards for not exceeding 72 hours shall be considered instead of momentary dust emission values for conformity to standards.]

(1)	(2)	(3)	(4)
[11.	Stone crushing unit	Suspended particulate matter	The suspended particulate matter measured between 3 metres and 10 metres from any process equipment of a stone-crushing unit shall not exceed 600 micro-grams per cubic metre.]
[12.	Coke ovens		Concentrations in the effluents when discharged into inland surface waters not to exceed milligram per litre (except for pH)
		pH	5.5 —9.0
		[Biochemical Oxygen Demand (3 days at 27°C)]	30
		Suspended Solids	100
		Phenolic Compounds (as C_6H_5OH)	5
		Cyanides (as CN)	0.2
		Oil and Grease	10
		Ammonical Nitrogen (as N)	50
13.	Synthetic Rubber		Concentrations in the effluents when discharged into inland surface waters not to exceed milligram per litre (except for colour, and pH)
		Colour	Absent
		pH	5.5 — 9.0
		[Biochemical Oxygen Demand (3 days at 27°C)]	50

(1)	(2)	(3)	(4)
		Chemical Oxygen Demand	250
		Oil & Grease	10.0
14.	Small Pulp and Paper Industry		Concentrations not to exceed milligramme per litre (except for pH and Sodium absorption ratio)
	Dischage into inland surface water	pH	5.5—9.0
		Suspended Solids	100
		BOD	30
	Disposal on land	pH	5.5—9.0
		Suspended Solids	100
		BOD	100
		Sodium absorption Ratio	26
15.	Fermentation Industry (Distilleries, Maltries and Beweries)		Concentration in the effluent not to exceed milligramme per litre (except for pH and colour & odour)
		pH	5.5—9.0
		Colour & odour	[All efforts should be made to remove colour and unpleasant odour as far as practicable)
		Suspended Solids	100
		[BOD (3 days at 27°C)]	
		—disposal into inland surface water/river/stream	30 mg/l.

(1)	(2)	(3)	(4)
		—disposal on land or for irrigation	100 mg/l

[**Notes**—*(1) Waste water generation shall not exceed 250 cubic metre per tonne of paper product.]

[* * *]

			Concentration in the effluents not to exceed milligram per litre (except for pH and per cent Sodium)			
			Inland Surface Waters	Public Sewers	Land for Irrigation	Marine Coastal areas
			(a)	(b)	(c)	(d)
16.	Leather Tanneries	Suspended Solids	100	600	200	100
		[BOD (3 days at 27°C)]	30	350	100	100
		pH	6.0–9.0	6.0–9.0	6.0–9.0	6.0–9.0
		Chlorides (as Cl)	1000	1000	600	—
		Hexavalent Chromium (Cr + 6)	0.1	0.2	0.1	1.0
		Total Chromium (as Cr)	2.0	2.0	2.0	2.0
		Sulphides (as S)	2.0	5.0	—	5.0
		Sodium per cent	—	60	60	—
		Boron (as B)	2.0	2.0	2.0	—
		Oil and Grease	10	20	10	20

(1)	(2)	(3)	(4)	
17.	Fertilizer Industry		Concentrations in the effluents not to exceed milligram per litre (except for pH)	
	Effluents—Straight Nitrogenous Fertilizers excluding the Calcium Ammonium Nitrate and Ammonium Nitrate Fertilizer		Plants Commissioned January 1, 1982 onwards	Plants Commissioned prior to January 1, 1982
			(a)	(b)
		pH	6.5—8.0	6.5—8.0
		Ammonical Nitrogen	50	75
		Total Kjeldahl Nitrogen	100	150
		Free Ammonical Nitrogen	4	4
		Nitrate Nitrogen	10	10
		Cyanide as CN	0.2	0.2
		Vanadium as V	0.2	0.2
		Arsenic as As	0.2	0.2
		Suspended Solids	100	100
		Oil and Grease	10	10
		*Hexavalent Chromium as Cr	0.1	0.1
		*Total Chromium as Cr	2.0	2.0

* To be complied with at the outlet of Chromate removal unit

Straight
Nitrogenous Fertilizers

(1)	(2)	(3)	(4)	
	including Calcium Ammonium Nitrate and Ammonium Nitrate Fertilizers		Plants Commissioned January 1, 1982 onwards	Plants Commissioned prior to January 1, 1982
			(a)	(b)
		pH	6.5—8.0	6.5—8.0
		Ammonical Nitrogen	50	75
		Total Kjeldahl Nitrogen	100	150
		Free Ammonical Nitrogen	4	4
		Nitrate Nitrogen	20	20
		Cyanide as CN	0.2	0.2
		Vanadium as V	0.2	0.2
		Arsenic as As	0.2	0.2
		Suspended Solids	100	100
		Oil and Grease	10	10
		*Hexavalent Chromium as Cr	0.1	0.1
		*Total Chromium as Cr	2.0	2.0

*To be complied with at the outlet of Chromate removal unit.

(1)	(2)	(3)	(4)	
	Complex Fertilizers, excluding Calcium Ammonium Nitrate, Ammonium Nitrate & Ammonium Nitrophosphate Fertilizers		Plants Commissioned January 1, 1982 onwards	Plants Commissioned prior to January 1, 1982
			(a)	(b)
		pH	6.5—8.0	6.5—8.0
		Ammonical Nitrogen	50	75
		Free Ammonical Nitrogen	4	4
		Total Kjeldhal Nitrogen	100	150
		Nitrate Nitrogen	10	10
		Cyanide as CN	0.2	0.2
		Vanadium as V	0.2	0.2
		Arsenic as As	0.2	0.2
		Phosphate as P	5	5
		Oil and Grease	10	10
		Suspended Solids	100	100
		*Fluoride as F	10	10
		**Hexavalent Chromium as Cr	0.1	0.1
		**Total Chromium as Cr	2.0	2.0

* To be complied with at the outlet of fluoride removal unit. If the recipient system so demand, Fluoride as F shall be limited to 1.5 mg/l.

** To be complied with at the outlet of Chromate removal unit.

(1)	(2)	(3)	(4)	
	Complex Fertilizers, including Calcium Ammonium Nitrate, Ammonium Nitrate and Ammonium Nitrophosphate Fertilizers		Plants Commissioned January 1, 1982 onwards	Plants Commissioned prior to January 1, 1982
			(a)	(b)
		pH	6.5—8.0	6.5—8.0
		Ammonical Nitrogen	50	75
		Free Ammonical Nitrogen	100	100
		Nitrate Nitrogen	20	20
		Cyanide as CN	0.2	0.2
		Vanadium as V	0.2	0.2
		Arsenic as As	0.2	0.2
		Phosphate as P	5	5
		Oil and Grease	10	10
		Suspended Solids	100	100
		*Fluoride as F	10	10
		**Hexavalent Chromium as Cr	0.1	0.1
		**Total Chromium as Cr	2.0	2.0
	Straight Phosphatic Fertilizers			
		pH	7.0—9.0	
		Phosphate as P	5	

(1)	(2)	(3)	(4)
		Oil and Grease	10
		Suspended Solids	100
		*Fluoride as F	10
		**Hexavalent Chromium as Cr	0.1
		*Total Chromium as Cr	2.0
	Emissions		
	—Phosphatic Fertilizers (Fluoride and particulate matter emission)	Phosphoric acid manufacturing	25 milligram per normal cubic metre as total Fluoride
		Granulation, mixing and grinding of rock phosphate	150 milligramme per normal cubic metre of particulate matter
	—Urea (particulate matter emission)	Prilling Tower Commissioned prior to 1-1-1982	150 milligram per normal cubic metre or 2 kilogram per tonne of product
		Commissioned after 1–1–1982	50 milligram per normal cubic metre or 0.5 kilogram per tonne of product

* To be complied with at the outlet of Fluoride removal unit. If the recipient system so demand, Fluoride as F shall be limited to 1.5 mg/l.

** To be complied with at the outlet of Chromate removal unit.

18.	Aluminium	Particulate Matter Emissions:	
		—Calcination	250 milligram per normal cubic metre of particulate matter
		—Smelting	150 milligram per normal cubic metre of particulate matter

(1)	(2)	(3)	(4)
19.	Calcium Carbide	Particulate Matter Emissions:	
		—Kiln	250 milligram per normal cubic metre
		—Arc Furnace	150 milligram per normal cubic metre
20.	Carbon Black	Particulate Matter Emission:	150 milligram per normal cubic metre
21.	Copper, Lead and Smelting	Particulate Matter Emission in Concentrator	150 milligram per normal cubic metre
		Emission of Oxides of Sulphur in Smelter & Convertor	Off-gases must be utilised for sulphuric acid manufacture. The limits of sulphur dioxide emission from stock shall not exceed 4 kilogram per tonne of concentrated (one hundred per cent) acid produced.
22.	Nitric Acid (emission of oxides of nitrogen)	Emission of Oxides of Nitrogen	3 kilogram of oxides of nitrogen per tonne of weak acid (before concentration) produced
23.	Sulphuric Acid (emission of Sulphur dioxide and acid mist)	Sulphur dioxide Emissions	4 kilogram per tonne of concentrated (one hundred per cent) acid produced
		Acid Mist	50 milligram per normal cubic metre
24.	Iron & Steel (Integrated)	Particulate Matter Emission	
		—Sintering Plant	150 milligram per normal cubic metre
		—Steel making	

(1)	(2)	(3)	(4)
		—during normal operations	150 milligram per normal cubic metre
		—during oxygen lancing	400 milligram per normal cubic metre
		—Rolling Mill	150 milligram per normal cubic metre
		—Carbon monoxide from coke oven	3 kilogram per tonne of coke produced]
[25.	Thermal Power Plants	*Particulate Matter Emissions:	

*Depending upon the requirement of local situation, such as protected area, the State Pollution Control Board and other implementing agencies under the Environment (Protection) Act, 1986, may prescribe a limit of 150 milligram per normal cubic metre, irrespective of generation capacity of the plant.

(1)	(2)	(3)	(4)
		—generation capacity 210 MW or more	150 milligram per normal cubic metre
		—generation capacity less than 210 MW	350 milligram per normal cubic metre
26.	Natural rubber industry		Concentration in the effluents to exceed milligram per (except for pH)
	—Discharge into inland surface waters	Colour and Odour	Absent
		pH	6.0—9.0
		BOD	50
		COD	250

(1)	(2)	(3)	(4)
		Oil and Grease	10
		Sulphides	2
		Total Kjeldhal Nitrogen	100
		Dissolved phosphate (as P)	5
		Suspended solids	100
		Dissolved solids (inorganic)	2100
		Ammonical nitrogen (as N)	50
		Free Ammonia (as NH_3)	5
	—Disposal on land for irrigation	Colour and Odour	Absent
		pH	6.0—8.0
		BOD	100
		COD	250
		Oil and Grease	10
		Suspended solids	200
		Dissolved solids	2100]
[27.	All types of Asbestos manufacturing units: (including all processes involving the use of Asbestos)	Emissions —Pure asbestos material —total dust	 4 fibre*/cc 2 mg/m^3 (normal)

* Fibre of length more than 5 micrometre and diameter less than 3 micrometre with an aspect ratio of 3 or more.

28.	Chlor Alkali (Caustic soda)	Emissions	Concentration in mg/m^2 (normal)

(1)	(2)	(3)	(4)
	(a) Mercury Cell	Mercury (from hydrogen gasholder stack)	0.2
	(b) All Processes	Chlorine (from hypo tower)	15.0
	(c) All Processes	Hydrochloric acid vapour and mist (from hydrochloric acid plant)	35.0
29.	Large pulp and paper	Emissions	Concentration in mg/m^3 (normal)
		Particulate matter	250**
		H_2S	10

**This standard of 250 mg/m^3 (normal) shall apply only for period of 3 years with effect from the date on which the Environment (Protection) Second Amendment Rules, 1989, came into force. After three years the standard to be applicable is 15 mg/m^3 (normal).

(1)	(2)	(3)	(4)
30.	Integrated Iron and Steel Plants:		
		I. Emissions	
	(a) Coke oven	Particulate matter	50
	(b) Refractory material plant:	Particulate matter	150
		II. Effluents	Concentration in mg/litre (except for pH)
	(a) Coke Oven By product plant	pH	6.0—8.5
		Suspended solids	100
		Phenol	1.0
		Cyanide	0.2
		[BOD (3 days at 27°C)	30
		COD	250
		Ammonical nitrogen	50
		Oil and Grease	10

(1)	(2)	(3)	(4)
	(b) Other plants such as sintering plant, blast furnace, steel melting and rolling mill:	pH	6.0—9.0
		Suspended solids	100
		Oil and Grease	10
31.	Reheating (Reverberatory Furnaces:	Emissions	Concentration in mg/m^3 (normal)
	Capacity: All sizes		150
	Sensitive area	Particulate matter	
	Other area	Particulate matter	450]
[32.	Foundries:		
	(a) Cupola		
	Capacity (melting rate):		
	Less than 3 MT/hr.	Particulate Matter	450
	3 MT/hr. and above	Particulate matter	150

Note—It is essential that the stack is constructed over the cupola beyond the charging door and the emissions are directed through the stack which should be at least six times the diameter of the cupola.

	(b) Arc Furnaces Capacity: All sizes	Particulate Matter	150
	(c) Induction furnaces Capacity:		
	All sizes	Particulate Matter	150

Note—In respect of arc furnaces and induction furnaces, provision has to be made for collecting the fumes before discharging the emissions through the stack.

(1)	(2)	(3)	(4)
33.	Thermal Power Plants	Stack height/limits	
		Power generation capacity:	
		—500 MW and above	215
		—275 MV/210 MW and above to less than 500 MW	220
		Less than 200 MW/210 MW	H = $14(Q)^{0.3}$ where Q is emission rate of SQ_2 in kg/hr. and H is stack height in metres.
		Steam generating capacity:	
		Less than 2 ton/hr.	2-1/2 times the neighbouring building height or 9 metres (whichever is more)
		—More than 2 ton/hr. to 5 ton/hr.	12
		—More than 5 ton/hr. to 10 ton/hr.	15
		—More than 10 ton/hr.	18
		—More than 15 ton/hr. to 20 ton/hr.	15
		—More than 26 ton/hr to 25 ton/hr.	24
		—More than 25 ton/hr. to 30 ton/hr.	27
		—More than 30 ton/hr.	30 or using formula H = $14 (Q)^{0.3}$ (whichever is more) where Q is emission rate of SQ_2 in kg/hr. and H is stack. Height in metres.
34.	Small boilers	Emissions	
	Capacity of boilers	Particulate Matter	
	—Less than 2 ton/hr.		1600
	—2 to 15 ton/hr.		1200
	—More than 15 ton/hr.		150

*All emissions normalized to 12 per cent carbon dioxide

(1)	(2)	(3)	(4)
35.	Oil refineries	Emissions	
	(Sulphur dioxide)		
		—Distillation (Atmospheric plus vacuum)	0.25 kg/MT of feed**
		—Catalytic cracker	2.5 kg/MT of feed
		—Sulphur recovery unit	120 kg/MT of sulphur in the feed
	**Feed indicates the food for that part of the process under consideration only.		
36.	Aluminium plants	Emissions	
	(a) Aluminium plant:		
	(i) Raw material handling	Primary and secondary crusher	150
		Particulate Matter	
	(ii) Precipitation area	Particulate Matter	250
	—Calcination	Carbon monoxide	1% max.
		Stack height	$H = 14 (Q)^{0.3}$ where Q is emission rate of SO_2 in kg/hr. and H is stack height in metres.
	(b) Smelter plant		
	(i) Green anode shop	Particulate Matter	150
	(ii) Anode bake oven	Particulate Matter	150
		Total fluoride (F)	0.3 kg/MT of Aluminium
	(iii) Potroom	Particulate Matter	
		Total fluoride (F)	150
		VSS	4.7 kg/MT of Aluminium produced

S. No.	*Industry*	*Parameter*	*Standards (Concentrations in mg/l except for pH temperature specific pesticides and Bio-assay test*
(1)	*(2)*	*(3)*	*(4)*
		HSS PBSW PBCW Stack height	6.0 kg/MT of Aluminium produced 2.5 kg/MT of Aluminium produced 1.0 kg/MT of Aluminium produced $H = 14 (Q)^{0.3}$ where Q is emission rate of SO_2 in kg/hr and H is stack height in metres.
Note: VSS = Vertical stud soderberg HSS = Horizontal stug soderberg PBSW = Prebacked side worked PBCW = Prebacked centre worked			
37.	Stone crushing Unit	Suspended Particulate Matter (SPM)	The standard consist of two parts: *(i) Implementation of the following pollution control measures:* (a) Dust containment cum suppression system of the equipment (b) Construction of wind breaking walls (c) Construction of the metalled roads within the premises (d) Regular cleaning and wetting of the ground within the premises (e) Growing of a green belt along the periphery

(1)	(2)	(3)	(4)
			(ii) *Quantitative standard for the SPM:* The Suspended Particulate Matter contribution value at a distance of 40 metres from a controlled isolated as well as from a unit located in a cluster should be less than 600 mg/Nm^3. The measurements are to be conducted at least twice a month for all the 12 months in a year.
38.	Petrochemical (Basic and Effluents Intermediates)	pH	6.5—8.5
		[*BOD (3 days at 27°C)]	50
		**Phenol	5
		Sulphide (as S)	2
		COD	250
		Cyanide (as CN)	0.2
		***Fluoride (as F)	15
		Total suspended solids	1000
		Hexavalent Chromium (as CR)	0.1
		****Total Chromium (as CR)	2.0

* State Boards may prescribe the BOD value of 30 mg/l if the recipient system so demands.

** The limit for phenol shall be conformed to at the outlet of effluent treatment of phenol plant. However, at the final disposal point, the limit shall be less than 1 mg/l.

*** The limit for fluoride shall be conformed to at the outlet of fluoride removal unit. However, at the disposal point fluoride concentration shall be lower than 5 mg/l.

**** The limits for total hexavalent chromium shall be conformed to at the outlet of the chromate removal unit. This implies that in the final treated effluent, total hexavalent chromium shall be lower than prescribed herein.

(1)	(2)	(3)	(4)
39.	Pharmaceutical manufacturing and formation industry	Effluents	
		1. pH	5.5—9.0
		2. Oil and Grease	10
		3. Total suspended solids	100
		4. [BOD (3 days at 27°C)]	30
		5. Bio-assay test	90% survival of fish after 96 hrs. in 100% effluent
		6. Mercury	0.01
		7. Arsenic	0.20
		8. Chromium (Hexavalent)	0.10
		9. Lead	0.10
		10. Cyanide	0.10
		11. Phenolics (as C_6H_5OH)	1.00
		12. Sulphides (as S)	2.00
		13. Phosphates (as P)	5.00

Notes—

1. Parameters listed as 1 to 13 are compulsory for formulators. However, the remaining parameters (6 to 13) will be optional for others.
2. State Board may prescribe limit for chemical oxygen demand (COD) correlated with BOD limit.
3. State Board may prescribe limit for total dissolved solids depending upon uses of recipient water body.
4. Limits should be complied with at the terminal of the treatment unit before letting out of the factory boundary limits.
5. For the compliance of limits, analysis should be done in the composite sample collected every hour for a period of 8 hours.

(1)	(2)	(3)	(4)
40.	Pesticide Manufacturing and Formulation Industry		
		Effluents	
		1. Temperature	Shall not exceed 5°C above the receiving water temperature
		2. pH	6.5—8.5
		3. Oil and Grease	10
		4. [BOD (3 days at 27°C)]	30
		5. Total suspended solids	100
		6. Bio-assay test	90% survival of fish after 96% hrs. in 100% effluent
		7.(a) Specific pesticides:	
		Benzene hexachloride	10
		Carboryl	10
		DDT	10
		Endosulfan	10
		Diamethoate	450
		Fenitrothion	10
		Malathion	10
		Phorate	10
		Methyl parathion	10
		Phenthoate	10
		Pyrethrums	10
		Copper oxychloride	9600
		Copper sulphate	50
		Ziram	1000
		Sulphur	30
		Paraquat	2300

(1)	(2)	(3)	(4)
		Proponil	7300
		Nitrogen	780
		(b) Heavy metals:	
		Copper	1.00
		Manganese	1.00
		Zinc	1.00
		Mercury	0.01
		Tin	0.10
		Any other metal like Nickel, etc.	Shall not exceed 5 times the drinking water standards of BIS
		(c) Organics:	
		Phenol and phenolic compounds as C_6H_5OH	1.0
		(d) Inorganics:	
		Arsenics (as As)	0.2
		Cyanide (as CN)	0.2
		Nitrate (as NO_3)	50.0
		Phosphate (as P)	5.0

Notes—

1. Limits should be complied with at the end of the treatment Plant before any dilution.
2. Bio-assay test should be carried out with available species of fish in receiving water.
3. State Boards may prescribe limits of total dissolved solids (TDS), sulphates and chlorides depending on the use of recipient water body.
4. State Board may prescribe COD limit correlated with BOD limits.
5. Pesticides are known to have metabolites and isomers. If they are found in significant concentration, standards may be prescribed for those in the list by Central or State Board.
6. Industries are required to analyse pesticides in waste water by advanced analytical method such as GLC/HPLC.
7. All the parameters will be compulsory for formulators, for others, the 7th will be optional.

(1)	(2)	(3)	(4)
41.	Tannery (after primary treatment) Disposal: Channel/Conduit Carrying waste waters to secondary treatment plants Type of tanneries —Chromo tanneries/combined chrome and vegetable tanneries.	Effluents	
		pH	6.5—9.0
		SS	Not to exceed 600
		Chromium concentration after treatment in the chrome waste water stream	45
	—Vegetable tanneries	pH	6.5—9.0
		SS	Not to exceed 600

Note—The above standards will apply to those tannery units which have made full contribution to a Common Effluent Treatment Plant (CETP) comprising secondary treatment. Those who have not contributed will be governed by earlier Notification No. S.O. 64 (E), dated January 13, 1988:

(1)	(2)	(3)	(4)
42.	Paint industry (Waste-water discharge)	Effluents	
		pH	6.0—8.5
		Suspended solids	100
		$BOD_5$20°C	50
		Phenolics as C_6H_5OH	1.0
		Oil and Grease	10.0
		Bio-assay test	90% survival in 96 hrs.
		Lead as Pb	0.1

(1)	(2)	(3)	(4)
		Chromium as Cr	
		Hexavalent	2.0
		Total	2.0
		Copper as Cu	2.0
		Nickel as Ni	2.0
		Zinc as Zn	5.0
		Total heavy metals	7.0
43.	Inorganic chemical industry (Waste-water discharge) Part I (metal compounds of Chromium, Manganese, Nickel, Lead and Mercury	Effluents	
		pH	6.0—8.5
		Chromium as Cr	0.1
		Hexavalent	
		Total	2.0
		Magnanese as Mn	2.0
		Nickel as Ni	2.0
		Copper as Cu	2.0
		Zinc as Zn	5.0
		Cadmium as Cd	0.2
		Lead as Pb	0.1
		Mercury as Hg	0.01
		Cyanide as CN	0.2
		Oil and Grease	10.0
		Suspended solids	30.0

In addition to the above, total metals are to be limited to 7 mg/l.

(1)	(2)	(3)	(4)
44.	Bullion Refining (Waste-water discharge)	Effluents	
		pH	6.5—8.5
		Cyanide as CN	0.2
		Sulphide as S	0.2

		Nitrate as N	10.00
		Free Cl_2 and Cl	1.0
		Zinc as Zn	5.0
		Copper as Cu	2.0
		Nickel as Ni	2.0
		Arsenic as As	0.1
		Cadmium as Cd	0.2
		Oil and Grease	10.0
		Suspended solids	100
45.	Dye and Dye Intermediate Industry (Waste-water discharge)	Effluents	
		pH	6.0—8.5
		Colour, Hazen Unit	400.0
		Suspended solids	100.0
		BOD_5 20°C	100.0
		Oil and Grease	10.0
		Phenolies as C_6H_5OH	1.0
		Cadmium as Cd	0.2
		Copper as Cu	2.0
		Manganese as Mn	2.0
		Lead as Pb	0.1
		Mercury as Hg	0.01
		Nickel as Ni	2.0
		Zinc as Zn	5.0
		Chromium as Cr	0.1
		Hexavalent	
		Total	2.0
		Bio-assay test	90% survival in 96 hrs.

Sl. No.	Category	Standards, Db (A)
1	2	3
46.	Noise limits for automobiles (free field at one metre in dB (A) at the manufacturing stage) to be achieved by the year 1992	
	(a) motorcycles, scooters and three wheelers	80
	(b) Passenger cars	82
	(c) Passenger or commercial vehicles up to 4 MT	85
	(d) passenger of commercial vehicles about 4 MT and up to 12 MT	89
	(e) Passenger or commercial vehicles exceeding 12 MT	91
47.	Domestic appliances and construction equipments at the manufacturing stage to be achieved by the year 1993	
	(a) Window air-conditioners of 1 ton to 1.5 ton	68
	(b) Air-coolers	60
	(c) Refrigerators	46
	(d) Diesel generators for domestic purposes	85—90
	(e) Compactors (rollers) front loaders, concrete mixers, cranes (movable) vibrators and saws	75]

S. No.	*Industry*	*Parameter*	*Standards*
1.	2	3	4
[48.	GLASS INDUSTRY	Emissions	
	A. Sodalime and Borosilicate and other special glass (other than lead)		

(1)	(2)	(3)	(4)
	(a) Furnace: Capacity		
	(i) Up to a product draw capacity of 60 Mt/Day	Particulate matter	20 kg/hr.
	(ii) Product draw capacity more than 60 Mt/Day	Particulate matter	0.8 kg/Mt. of product drawn
	(iii) For all capacities	Stack height	H = 14 $(Q)^{0.3}$ where Q is the emission rate of SQ_2 in kg./hr. and H is stack height in metres.
		Total fluorides Nox	5.0 mg/NM^3 Use of low nox burners in plants.
	(b) Implementation of the following measures for fugitive emission control from other sections:		
	(i) Raw materials should be transported in leak proof containers		
	(ii) Cullet preparation should be dust-free using water spraying.		
	(iii) Batch preparation section should be covered.		
B.	Lead glass		
	(a) Furnaces: All capacities	Participate matter	50 mg/NM^3
		Lead	20 mg/NM^3
	(b) Implementation of the following		

(1)	(2)	(3)	(4)
	measures for fugitive emission .control from other sections:		
	(i) Batch mixing, proportioning section and transfer points should be covered and it should be connected to control equipments to meet following standards :	Particulate matter	50 mg/NM^3
		Lead	20 mg/NM^3
	(ii) Minimum stack height should be 30 metre in lead glass units.		
	(c) Pot Furnace at Firozabad Furnace:	Particulate matter 1200 mg/NM^3	

Note—Depending upon local environmental conditions; State/Central Pollution Control Board can prescribe more stringent standards than those prescribed above.

(1)	(2)	(3)	(4)
	Glass Industry (for all categories)	Effluents:	
		pH	6.5–8.5
		Total suspended solids	100 mg/l
		Oil and Grease	10 mg/l
49.	Lime Kiln	Stack Height	
	Capacity	Stack Height	
	Up to 5T/Day		A hood should be provided with a stack of 30 metre height from ground level (including kiln height).
	Above 5T/Day	Stack Height	$H = 14(Q)^{0.3}$ where Q is the emission rate of SO_2 in kg./hr and H = stack height in metres.
	More than 5T/day and up to 40T/Day.	Particulate Matter	500 mg/NM^3

(1)	(2)	(3)	(4)
	Above 49T/Day	Particulate matter	150 mg/NM^3
50.	*Slaughter House, Meat and Sea Food Industry	Effluents	Concentration in mg/l
	A. Slaughter House		
	(a) Above 70 TL WK	BOD_5 at 20°C	100
		Suspended solids	100
		Oil and Grease	10
	(b) 70 TLWK and below	BOD_5 at 20°C	500
	B. Meat processing		
	(a) Frozen Meat	BOD_5 at 20°C	30
		Suspended solids	50
		Oil and Grease	10
	(b) Raw Meat from own slaughter house	BOD_5 at 20°C	30
		Suspended solids	50
		Oil and Grease	10
	(c) Raw Meat from other sources		Disposal via screen and septic tank
	C. Sea Food Industry	BOD_5 at 20°C	30
		Suspended solids	50
		Oil and Grease	10

Notes—(i) TLWK—Total Live Weight Killed. (ii) In case of disposal into municipal sewer where sewage is treated the industries shall install screen and oil and grease separation units. (iii) The industries having slaughter house along with meat processing units will be considered in meat processing category as far as standards are concerned.

(1)	(2)	(3)	(4)	
51.	Food and Fruit Processing Industry	Effluents	Concentration not to exceed mg/l except pH	Quantum gm/MT of product
Category				
A.	Soft Drinks			
	(a) Fruit based/synthetic (More than 0.4 MT/Day) bottles and tetrapack	pH	6.5—8.5	
		Suspended solids	100	
		Oil and Grease	10	
		BOD_5 at 20°C	30	

*The emission standards from Boiler House shall conform to the standards already prescribed under E(P) Act, 1986, vide notification No. GSR 742 (E), dated 30-8-1990: See [1991] 70 Comp. Cas. (St.) 5.

(1)	(2)	(3)	(4)	
	(b) Synthetic (Less than 0.4 MT/Day)		Disposal via septic tank	
B.	Fruit and vegetables			
	(a) Above 0.4 MT/Day	pH	6.5—8.5	
		Suspended solids	50	
		Oil and Grease	10	
		BOD_5 at 20°C	30	
	(b) 0.1—0.4 MT/Day (10MT/Yr)		Disposal via septic tank	
C.	Bakery			
	(a) Bread and Biscuit			

(1)	(2)	(3)	(4)	
	(i) Continuous process (more than 20T/Day)	pH	6.5—8.5	
		BOD_5 at 20°C	200	25
	(ii) Non continuous process (less than 20 MT/Day)		Disposal via septic tank	
	(b) Biscuit Production			
	(i) 10T/Day and above	pH	6.5—8.5	
		BOD_5 at 20°C	300	35
	(ii) Below 10 T/Day		Disposal via septic tank	
D.	Confectioneries	Effluents		
	(a) 4T/Day and above	pH	6.5—8.5	
		Suspended solids	50	
		Oil and Grease	10	
		BOD_5 at 20°C	30	
	(b) Below 4T/Day and above		Disposal via septic tank	

Note—

To ascertain the category of 'unit fails' the average of daily production and waste water discharge for the preceding 30 operating days from the date of sampling shall be considered.

*The emission from the boiler house shall conform to the standards already prescribed under the Environment (Protection) Act, 1986, *vide* Notification No. GSR 742 (E), dated 30–08–1990: See [1991] 70 Comp. Cas. (St.) 5.

52. *Jute Processing Industry:	Effluents	Concentration in Mg/l except pH and water consumption
	pH	5.5—9.0
	BOD_5 at 20°C	30
	Suspended solids	100

(1)	(2)	(3)	(4)
		Oil and Grease	10
		Water consumption	1.60 Cum/Ton of product produced

Note—

1. Water consumption for the jute processing industry will be 1.5 Cum/Ton of product from January, 1992.
2. At present no limit for colour is given for colour is liquid effluent. However, as far as possible, colour should be removed.

* Stack emissions from boiler house shall conform to the standards already prescribed under Environment (Protection) Act, 1986, *vide* Notification No. GSR 742 (E), dated 30-8-90.

(1)	(2)	(3)	(4)
53.	Large Pulp and Paper/news print/rayon Grade Plants of Capacity Above 24,000 mt/annum	Effluents	Concentration in mg/l except pH and TOCL
		pH	7.0—8.5
		BOD_5 at 20°C	30
		COD	350
		Suspended solids	50
		*TOCL	2.0 Kg/Ton of product
		Flow (Total waste water discharge)	
		**(i) Large pulp and paper	200 Cum/Ton of paper produced
		(ii) Large Rayon grade/ News print	150 Cum/Ton of paper produced

Note—

* The Standards for Total Organic Chloride (TOCL) will be applicable from January, 1992.

** The standards with respect to total waste water discharge for the large pulp and paper mills to be established from 1992, will meet the standards of 100 Cum/Ton of paper produced.

(1)	(2)	(3)	(4)
54.	Small Pulp and Paper, Paper Plant of Capacity Upto 24,000 MT/Annum Category	Effluent	
	A. *Agro-based	Total waste-water discharge	200 Cum/Ton of paper produced
	B. **Waste-paper based	-do-	75 Cum/Ton of paper produced

Note—

* The agro-based mills to be established from January, 1992 will meet the standards of 150 Cum/Ton of paper produced.

** The waste-paper mills to be established from January, 1992 will meet the standards of 50 Cum/Ton of paper produced.

(1)	(2)	(3)	(4)
55.	Common Effluent Treatment Plants: A. Primary Treatment	Effluents (inlet effluent quality for CETP)	(Concentration in mg/l)
		pH	5.5—9.0
		Temperature°C	45
		Oil and Grease	20
		Phenolic compounds (as C_6H_5OH)	5.0
		Ammonical Nitrogen (as N)	50
		Cyanide (as CN)	20
		Chromium (hexavalent) (as Cr + 6)	2.0
		Chromium (Total) (as Cr)	2.0
		Copper (as Cu)	3.0

(1)	(2)	(3)	(4)
		Lead (as Pb)	1.0
		Nickel (as Ni)	3.0
		Zinc (as Zn)	15
		Arsenic (as As)	0.2
		Mercury (as Hg)	0.01
		Cadmium (as Cd)	1.0
		Selenium (Se)	0.05
		Fluoride (as F)	15
		Boron (as B)	2.0
		Radioactive Materials	
		Alpha emitters, Hc/mL	10.7
		Beta emitters, Hc/mL	10.8

Note—

1. These standards apply to the small scale industries, i.e. total dischage upto 25 KL/day.
2. For each CETP and its constituent units, the State Board will prescribe standards as per the local needs and conditions; these can be more stringent than those prescribed above. However, in case of clusters of units, the State Boards with the concurrence of CPCB in writing, may prescribe suitable limits.

		Into inland surface waters	On land for Irrigation	Into Marine Coastal area
		(a)	(b)	(c)
Treated Effluent	Quality of common effluent Treatment plant	Concentration in mg/l except pH and Temperature		
	pH	5.5—9.0	5.5—9.0	5.5—9.0
	BOD_5 at 20°C	30	100	100

(1)	(2)	(3)	(4)		
		Oil and Grease	10	10	20
		Temperature	Shall not exceed 40°C in any section of the stream within 15 metres downstream from the effluent outlet.		45°C at the point of discharge
			Into inland surface	On land for waters	Into Marine Coastal area Irrigation
			(a)	(b)	(c)
		Suspended solids	100	200	(a) For process waste waters -100 (b). For cooling water effluents 10 per cent above total suspended matter of ineffluent cooling water

(1)	(2)	(3)	(4)		
		Dissolved solids (Inorganic)	2100	2100	—
		Total residual chlorine	1.0	—	1.0
		Ammonical Nitrogen (as N)	50	—	50
		Total Kjeldahl Nitrogen (as N)	100	—	100
		Chemical Oxygen Demand	250	—	250
		Arsenic (as As)	0.2	0.2	0.2
		Mercury (as Hg)	0.01	—	0.01
		Lead (as Pb)	0.1	—	1.0
		Cadmium (as Cd)	1.0	—	2.0
		Total Chromium (as Cr)	2.0	—	2.0
		Copper (as Cu)	3.0	—	3.0
		Zinc (as Zn)	5.0	—	15
		Selenium (as Se)	0.05	—	0.05
		Nickel (as Ni)	3.0	—	5.0
		Boron (as B)	2.0	2.0	—
		Per cent Sodium	—	60	—
		Cyanide (as CN)	0.2	0.2	0.2
		Chloride (as Cl)	1000	600	—
		Fluoride (as F)	2.0	—	15
		Sulphate (as SO_4)	1000	1000	—
		Sulphide (as S)	2.8	—	5.0
		Pesticides	Absent	Absent	Absent
		Phenolic Compounds (as C_6H_5OH)	1.0	—	5.0

Note—All efforts should be made to remove colour and unpleasant odour as far as possible.]

(1)	(2)	(3)		(4)
56.	Dairy	Effluents	Concentration in mg/l. except	Quantum per product processed
		pH	6.5—8.5	—
		*BOD_5 at 20°C	100	—
		**Suspended solids	150	—
		Oil and Grease	10	—
		Waste water generation	—	$3m^3$/Kl of milk

Note—*BOD may be made stringent upto 30 mg/l if the recipient fresh water body is a source for drinking water supply. BOD shall be setup to 350 mg/l for the chilling plant effluent for applying on land provided the land is designed and operated as a secondary treatment system with suitable monitoring facilities. The drainage water from the land after secondary treatment has to satisfy a limit of 30 mg/l of BOD and 10 mg/l of nitrate expressed as "N". The net addition to the ground water quality should not be more than 3 mg/l of BOD and 3 mg/l of nitrate expressed as "N". This limit for applying on land is allowed subject to the availability of adequate land for discharge under the control of the industry, BOD value is relaxable up to 350 mg/l, provided the waste water is discharged into a town sewer leading to secondary treatment of sewage.

**Suspended solids limit is relaxable upto 450 mg/l, provided waste water is discharged into a town sewer leading to secondary treatment of the sewage.

(1)	(2)	(3)		(4)
57.	Tanneries	Effluents	Concentration in mg/l. except	Quantum per raw hide processed
		pH	6.5—9.0	—
		*BOD_5 at 20°C	100	—
		Suspended solids	100	—
		Sulphides (as S)	1	—
		Total Chromium (as Cr)	2	—

(1)	(2)	(3)		(4)
		Oil and Grease	0.1	—
		Waste water generation	—	$28m^3/T$

Note—*For effluent discharge into inland surface waters BOD limit shall be made stricter to 30 mg/l by the concerned State Pollution Control Board.

		Centrifuging and creaming units		Crape and crumb units	
***58.	Natural rubber processing industry	for disposal into inland surface water	for disposal on land for irrigation	for disposal into inland surface water	for disposal on land for irrigation
		(a)	(b)	(a)	(b)
		(concentration in mg/l, except pH and quantum of waste water generation		(Concentration in mg/l, except pH and quantum of waste water generation)	
	pH	6–8	6–8	6–8	6–8
	Total Kjeldahl Nitrogen (as N)	200 (100*)	***	50	***
	Ammonical	100 (50*)	***	25	***
	Nitrogen (as N)	50	100	30	100
	BOD_5 at 20°C	250	***	250	***
	COD	10	20	10	20
	Oil and Grease	2	***	2	***

(1)	(2)		(3)		(4)	
		Sulphide	2100	NP**	2100	NP**
		TDS	100	200	100	200
		SS	5 lit/kg. of product processed	8 lit/kg. of product processed	40 lit/kg. of product processed	40 lit/kg. of product processed
		Quantum of Waste water generation				

* To be achieved in three years.

** Not prescribed in case of effluent is used for rubber plantations of their own, in other cases suitable limit, as necessary may be prescribed by the State Board.

*** Not specified

**** These standards supercede the standards notified at serial No. 26, *vide* Notification No. S.O. 8(E), dated 3rd January, 1989.

59.	Bagasse-fired boilers	Emissions	(Concentration in mg/l)
	(a) Step grate	Particulate matter	250
	(b) Horse shoe/pulsating grate	Particulate matter	500 (12% CO_2)
	(c) Spreader stroker	Particulate mater	800 (12% CO_2)

Note—In the case of horse shoe and spreader stroker boilers, if more if more than one boiler is attached to a single stack, the standard shall be fixed based on added capacity of all the boilers connected with the stack.

60.	Man-made fibre industry (semi-synthetic)	Effluents	(Concentration in mg/l except for pH)
		pH	5.5—9.0
		Suspended solids	100
		BOD_5 at 20°C	30
		Zinc (as Zn)	1
61.	Ceramic industry	Emissions	(Concentration in mg/Nm^3)

(1)	(2)	(3)	(4)
	A. Kilns		
	(a) Tunnel, Top Hat Chamber	Particulate matter	150
		Fluoride	10
		Chloride	100
		Sulphur dioxide	**
	(b) Down-draft	Particulate matter	1200
		Fluoride	10
		Chloride	100
		Sulphur dioxide	**
	(c) Shuttle	Particulate matter	150
		Fluoride	10
		Chloride	100
		Sulphur dioxide	**
	(d) Vertical shaft kiln	Particulate matter	250
		Fluoride	10
		Sulphur dioxide	**
	(e) Tank furnace	Particulate matter	150
		Fluoride	10
		Sulphur dioxide	**
B.	Raw material handling, processing and operations		
	(a) Dry raw materials handling and processing operations	Particulate matter	150
	(b) Basic raw materials and processing operations	Particulate matter	*
	(c) Other sources of air pollution generation	Particulate matter	*

(1)	(2)	(3)	(4)
C.	Automatic spray unit		
	(a) Dryers		
	(i) Fuel fired dryers	Particulate matter	150
	(ii) For heat recovery dryers	Particulate matter	*
	(b) Mechanical finishing operation	Particulate matter	*
	(c) Lime/plaster of paris manufacture Capacity	Stack height	
	Up to 5T/day	–do–	A. Hood should be provided with a stack of 30 metre height from ground level (including kiln height)
	Above 5T/day	–do–	$H = 14 (Q)^{0.3}$ Where Q is emission rate SO_2 in kg/hr and H-Stack Height in metres
	More than 5T/day and up to 40T/day	Particulate matter	500 mg/NM^3
		–do–	150 mg/NM^3

Note—Oxygen reference level for particulate matter concentration calculations for kilns mentioned at A (c) is 18 per cent for those at A (b) and A (c) is 8 per cent.

* All possible preventive measures should be taken to control pollution as far as possible.

** The standard for sulphur dioxide in terms of stack height limits for kilns with various capacities of coal consumption shall be as indicated below:

Coal consumed per day	Stack height
Less than 8.5 mt	9 m
More than 8.5 to 21 mt	12 m
More than 21 to 42 mt	15 m

(1)	(2)	(3)	(4)
More than 42 to 64 mt		18 m	
More than 64 to 104 mt		21 m	
More than 104 to 105 mt		24 m	
More than 105 to 126 mt		27 m	
More than 126 mt.		30 m or using formula H-14 $(Qg)^{0.3}$ (whichever is more)	

Note—In this notification, H-Physical height of the stack, Qg-Emission of sulphur dioxide in kg/hr, MT-Metric tonnes and m-metres].

(1)	(2)	(3)	(4)
[62. Viscose-Filament Yarn Effluents (sub-sector of man-made fibres semi-synthetic industry)			(Concentration in mg/l except for pH)
		pH	5.5—9.0
		Suspended solids	100
		BDD, at 20°C	30
		Zinc (as Zn)	5]
["63. Starch Industry (Maize products)		Effluents	Concentration not to exceed mg/l (except pH and waste water discharge)
		pH	6.5—8.5
		BOD (3 days at 27°C)	100
		Suspended Solids	150
		Waste water discharge	8 m^3/tonne of maize processed

Notes—The prescribed limits for BOD and suspended solids shall be

(1)	(2)	(3)	(4)
		made more stringent or less stringent depending upon the conditions and local requirements as mentioned below: (i) BOD shall be made stringent upto 30 mg/l if the recipient fresh water body is a source for drinking supply. (ii) BOD shall be allowed upto 350 mg/l for applying on land, provided the land is designed and operated as a secondary treatment system with the requisite monitoring facilities The drainage water from the land after secondary treatment has to satisfy a limit of 30 mg/l of BOD and 10 mg/l of nitrate expressed as "N". The net addition to ground water quality should not be more than 3 mg/l of BOD and 10 mg/l of nitrate expressed as "N". (iii) BOD shall be allowed upto 350 mg/1 for discharge into a town sewer, if such sewer leads to a secondary biological treatment system. (iv) Suspended solids shall be allowed upto 450 mg/l for discharge into a town sewer, if such sewer leads to a secondary biological treatment system. (v) In the event of bulking of sludge, the industry shall immediately apprise the respective Pollution Control Board.	
64.	Beehive hard coke oven	Emissions	
	(i) New unit	Particulate matter (corrected to 6% CO_2)	150 mg/Nm^3
		Hydrocarbons	25 ppm
	(ii) Existing units	Particulate matter (corrected to 6% CO_2)	350 mg/Nm^3
		Notes—For control of emissions and proper dispensation of pollutants the following guidelines shall be followed:	

(1)	(2)	(3)	(4)
		(i) **Units set up after the publication of this notification shall be treated as new units.** (ii) A minimum stack height of 20 metres shall be provided by each unit. (iii) Emissions from coke ovens shall be channelised through a tunnel and finally emitted through a stack. Damper adjustment techniques shall be used to have optimum heat utilisation and also to control the emission of unburnt carbon particles and combustible flue gases. (iv) Wet scrubbing system or waste heat utilisation for power generation or byproduct recovery systems should be installed preferably to achieve the prescribed standards. (v) After four years from the date of this notification, all the existing units shall comply with the standards prescribed for the new units.	
65.	Briquette Industry (Coal) (a) Units having capacity less than 10 tonnes (b) Units having capacity 10 tonnes or more	Emissions Particulate matter (corrected to 6 per cent CO_2) Particulate matter (corrected to 6 per cent CO_2) **Notes**—For control of emissions/proper dispersal of pollutants, the following guidelines shall be followed by the industry: (i) A minimum stack height of 20 metres shall be provided. (ii) All ovens shall be modified to single chimney multi-oven systems. (iii) Emissions from ovens shall be channelised through inbuilt draft stack. Optimum heat utilisation technique shall be used. (iv) In case of units having capacity 10 tonnes and above, wet scrubbing system shall be provided to control air pollution.	 350 mg/Nm^3 150 mg/Nm^3
66.	Soft Coke Industry	Particulate matter	350 mg/Nm^3

(1)	(2)	(3)	(4)
		(corrected to 6 per cent CO_2)	
		Note: Wet scrubbing systems alongwith by-product recovery system shall be provided.	
		Guidelines for Emissions Control to Improve Work Zone Environment (applicable for industries at serial number 64, 65, and 66):	
		(a) Water used for quenching and wet scrubbing shall be recirculated and reused through catch-pits.	
		(b) Leakages in the oven shall be sealed by bentonite or by any suitable paste and by proper maintenance to avoid fugitive emission.	
		Guidelines for Coal Handling and Crushing Plant (applicable to industries at serial numbers 64, 65 and 66):	
		(a) Unloading of coal trucks shall be carried out with proper care avoiding dropping of the materials from height. It is advisable to moist the material by sprinkling water while unloading.	
		(b) Pulverisation of coal shall be carried out in an enclosed place and water sprinkling arrangement shall be provided at coal heaps, crushing area and on land around the crushing unit.	
		(c) Work area surrounding the plant shall be asphalted or concreted.	
		(d) Green belt shall be developed along the boundary of the industry.	
		(e) Open burning of coal to manufacture soft coke shall be stopped.	
67.	Edible oil & *Vanaspati* Industry	Effluents Temperature	Not more than 5°C above ambient temperature of the recipient waterbody.
		pH	6.5—8.5
		Suspended solids	150 mg/l
		Oil & Grease	20 mg/l
		BOD (3 days at 27°C)	100 mg/l
		COD	200 mg/l

(1)	(2)	(3)	(4)
		Waste water discharge	
		(i) Solvent extraction	2.0 cum/tonne of product (oil)
		(ii) Refinery/*Vanaspati*	2.0 cum/tonne of product (refined oil/*Vanaspati*)
		(iii) Integrated unit of solvent extraction and refinery/*vanaspati*	4.0 cum/tonne of refined oil/*Vanaspati* produced
		(iv) Barometric cooling water/De-odoriser water	15.0 cum/tonne of refined oil/*Vanaspati*

Notes—

(i) The above standards shall be applicable to wastewater from processes and cooling.

(ii) BOD shall be made stringed upto 30 mg/l if the recipient fresh water body is source of drinking water supply.

(iii) The standards for boiler emissions shall be applicable as prescribed under Schedule I of these rules.

(1)	(2)	(3)	(4)
	68. Organic Chemicals manufacturing industry	Effluents	
	(a) Compulsory parameters	pH	6.5–8.5
		BOD (3 days at 27°C)	100 mg/l
		Bio-assay test	Minimum 90% survival after 96 hours with fish at 100% effluent)
	(b) Additional parameters		(mg/l)
		Nitrate (as N)	10
		Arsenic	0.2
		Hexavalent Chromium	0.1

(1)	(2)	(3)	(4)
		Total Chromium	1.0
		Lead	0.1
		Cyanide as CN	0.2
		Zinc	0.5
		Mercury	0.01
		Copper	2.0
		Nickel	2.0
		Phenolics as C_6H_5OH	5.0
		Sulphide	2.0

Notes

(i) No limit for COD is prescribed but it shall be monitored. If the COD in a treated effluent is persistently greater than 250 mg/l, such industrial units are required to identify chemicals causing the same. In case these are found to be toxic as defined in Hazardous Chemicals Rules, 1989 in Part I of Schedule–I, the State Boards in such cases may direct the industries to install tertiary treatment system stipulating time limit. This may be done on case-to-case basis.

(ii) These standards for boiler are not applicable to small scale detergent (formulating units).

(iii) The standards for boiler emissions shall be applicable as per the existing emission regulations.

(iv) Industry covered under this group are halo-aliphatics, plasticizers, aromatics (alcohols, phenols, esters, acids and salts, aldehydes, and ketone), substituted aromatics, aliphatic (alcohols, esters, acids, aldehydes, ketones, amines and amides) and detergents.

(1)	(2)	(3)	(4)
	69. Flour Mills	Effluents	
		pH	6.5—8.5

(1)	(2)	(3)	(4)
		BOD (3 days at 27°C)	100 mg/l
		Total Suspended solids	100 mg/l
		Oil and Grease	10 mg/l
		Waste water discharge	2 cubic metre per tonne of wheat processed.

Notes—

(i) BOD shall be made stringent upto 30 mg/l if the recipient fresh water body is source for drinking water supply.

(ii) BOD shall be allowed upto 350 mg/l for applying on land, provided the land is designed and operated as a secondary treatment system with the requisite monitoring facilities. The drainage water from the land after secondary treatment has to satisfy a limit of 30 mg/l of BOD and 10 mg/l of nitrate expressed as "N". The net addition to ground water quality should not be more than 3 mg/l of BOD and 10 mg/l of nitrate expressed as "N".

(iii) BOD shall be allowed upto 350 mg/l for discharge into a town sewer, if such sewer leads to a secondary biological treatment system.

(iv) Suspended solids shall be allowed upto 450 mg/l for discharge into a town sewer, if such sewer leads to a secondary biological treatment system.

(1)	(2)	(3)	(4)
70.	Boilers (small)	Steam generation capacity (ton/hour)	Particulate emission matter (mg/Nm^3)
		less than 2	1200*
		2 to less than 10	800*
		10 to less than 15	600*
		15 and above	150*

(1)	(2)	(3)	(4)
		* to meet the respective standards, cyclone/multicyclone is recommended as control equipment with the boiler. ** To meet the standard, bag filter/ESP is recommended as control equipment with the boiler.	
		Notes— (i) 12% of CO_2 correction shall be the reference value for particulate matter emission standards for all categories of boilers. (ii) These limits shall supersede the earlier limits notified under Schedule I at serial number 34 of Environment (Protection) Act, 1986 *vide* notification GSR 742 (E), dated 30th August, 1990. (iii) Stack Height for small Boilers. For the small boilers using coal or liquid fuels, the required stack height with the boiler shall be calculated by using the formula $H = 14\ Q^{0.3}$ Where H = Total stack height in metres from the ground level. Q = SO_2 emission rate in kg/hr In no case the stack height shall be less than 11 metres. Where providing all stacks are not feasible using above formula the limit of 400 mg/Nm^3 for SO_2 emission shall be met by providing necessary control equipment with a minimum stack height of 11 metres.	
71.	**Pesticide Industry**	(i) Compulsory Parameters	mg/l except pH
		pH	6.5–8.5
		BOD (3 days at 27°C)	100
		Oil & Grease	10
		Suspended solids	100

(1)	(2)	(3)	(4)
		Bio-assay test:	Minimum 90 per cent survival of fish after 96 hours with 90 per cent effluent and 10 per cent dilution water. Test shall be carried out as per IS: 6502–1971.
		(ii) Additional Parameters	m/gl
		(a) Heavy metal	
		Copper	1.0
		Manganese	1.0
		Zinc	1.0
		Mercury	0.01
		Tin	0.1
		Any other like Nickel	Shall not exceed 5 times the drinking water standards (BIS) individually
		(b) Organics Phenol and Phenolic Compounds as C_6H_5OH	1.0
		(c) Inorganics	
		Arsenic as As	0.2
		Cyanide as CN	0.2
		Nitrate as NO_3	50
		Phosphate as P	5.0
		(d) Specific pesticide	(microgram/litre)
		Benzene hexachloride	10
		DDT	10
		Dimethoate	450

(1)	(2)	(3)	(4)
		Copper oxychloride	9600
		Ziram	1000
		2, 4D	400
		Paraquat	23000
		Propanil	7300
		Nitrofen	780
		Other/below mentioned pesticides individually)	100
Other pesticides:			
(i)	Insecticides:		
	Aluminium Phosphide	Lindane	Pyrethrum extract
	Dichlorovos	Malathion	Quinalphos
	EDTC Mixer	Methyl Bromide	Monocrotophos
	Ethylene Dibromide	Nicotine Sulphate	Carbaryl
	Ethion	Oxydemeton Methyl	Endosulfan
	Fenitrothion	Methyl Parathion	Fenvalerate
	Lime-sulphur	Phosphamidon	Phorate
	Temephos		
(ii)	Fungicides:		
	Aureofungin	Organomercurials (MEMC & PMA)	
	Barium Polysulphide	Sulphur (Colloidal, Wettable & Dust)	
	Cuprous Oxide	Streptocycline	
	Ferbam	Thiram	

(1)	(2)	(3)	(4)
	Mancozeb	Zineb	
	Manab	Carbendazim	
	Nickel Chloride	Tridemorph	
(iii)	Rodenticides:		
	Comafuryl		
	Warfarin		
	Zinc Phosphide		
(iv)	Nematicides:		
	Metham N-Sodium		
(v)	Weedicides:		
	Fluchloralin		
	Isoproturon		
	Butachlor		
	Anilphos		
(vi)	Plant Growth Regulants:		
	Chloromequat Chloride		
	Nemphalene Acetic Acid		
(vii)	Any other pesticide not specified above		

Notes:

(1) Limits shall be complied with at the end of the treatment plant before any dilution.

(2) From the 'Additional Parameters' specified in 71 (ii), only the relevant parameters (based on the raw-materials used and products manufactured) may be prescribed by the concerned State Board on a case-to-case basis.

(3) No limit for COD is prescribed. If the COD in a treated effluent is persistently more than 250 mg/l, such industrial units are required to identify the chemicals causing the same. In case, these are found to be toxic as defined in Schedule I of the Hazardous Chemicals Rules, 1989, the State Boards in such cases may direct the industries to install tertiary treatment, stipulating time limit. This may be done on a case-to-case basis.

(4) Solar evaporation followed by incineration is a recognised practice, provide the guidelines of solar evaporation as given below are followed.

Guidelines on solar evaporation system or waste water from pesticide industry.

(i) Solar evaporation pans shall be constructed in such a way that the bottom is at least one metre above the ground level.

(ii) Solar evaporation pans shall be leak proof and of impervious construction and designed as per IS:7290.

(iii) The solar evaporation pans shall be designed on the basis of evaporation rate matching to the output of waste-water.

(iv) Waste water must be pre-treated as below before subjecting to solar evaporation:

(a) Oil and grease and floating organics shall be removed so that the rate of evaporation is not effected.

(b) Acidic/Alkaline waste must be neutralised before solar evaporation to maintain pH in the range of 6.5 to 8.5.

(c) Toxic volatile matter shall be removed so as not to cause air pollution.

(v) During the rainy season, storm water shall not be allowed to mix with process waste and enter the pans. The waste-water shall in no case outflow from the evaporation pans. Alternative arrangements shall be made to hold the waste water in proper impervious tanks and if necessary, force evaporated.

(vi) In no circumstances, the liquid effluent shall be discharged without conforming to the minimal national standards or stored in a holding arrangement which is likely to cause pollution.

(vii) The sludge from the solar evaporation pans shall be incinerated or disposed as per the guidelines for management and handling of hazardous waste, published by the Ministry of Environment and Forests, Government of India, after obtaining authorization from the State Pollution Control Board under the Hazardous Wastes (Handling and Management) Rules, 1989.

(viii) The facility shall be protected from flood and storm to prevent embankments from erosion or any other damage which may render any portion inoperable.

(ix) Facilities shall have protective enclosure to keep wildlife, domestic animals, unauthorised persons, etc., away.

72. Oil Drilling and Gas Extraction Industry

A. Standards for Liquid Effluent

1.0 On-Shore facilities
(For Marine Disposal)

Parameter	Standard
pH	5.5–9.0
Oil & Grease	10 mg/l
Suspended solids	100 mg/l
BOD (3 days at 27°C)	30 mg/l

Notes—

For on-shore discharge of effluents, in addition to the standards prescribed above, proper marine outfall has to be provided to achieve the individual pollutant concentration level in sea water below their toxicity limits as given below, within a distance of 50 metre from the discharge point, in order to protect the marine aquatic life:

Parameter	Toxicity limit, mg/l
Chromium as Cr	0.1
Copper, as Cu	0.05
Cyanide, as CN	0.005
Fluoride, as F	1.5
Lead, as Pb	0.05
Mercury, as Hg	0.01
Nickel, as Ni	0.1
Zinc, as Zn	0.1

(ii) Oil and gas drilling and processing facilities, situated on land and away from saline water sink, may opt either for disposal of treated water by onshore disposal or by reinjection in abandoned well, which is allowed only below a depth of 1000 metres from the ground level. In case of re-injection in abandoned well the effluent have to comply with respect to suspended solids and oil and grease at 100 mg/l and 10 mg/l, respectively. For on-shore disposal, the permissible limits are given below:

S.No.		*Parameter On-Shore discharge Standards (Not to exceed)*
1.	2	3
1.	pH	5.5–9.0
2.	Temperature	40°C
3.	Suspended Solids	100 mg/l
4.	Zinc	2 mg/l

1.	2	3
5.	BOD	30 mg/1
6.	COD	100 mg/1
7.	Chlorides	600 mg/1
8.	Sulphates	1000 mg/1
9.	TDS	2100 mg/1
10.	% Sodium	60 mg/1
11.	Oil and Grease	10 mg/1
12.	Phenolics	1.2 mg/1
13.	Cyanides	0.2 mg/1
14.	Fluorides	1.5 mg/1
15.	Sulphides	2.0 mg/1
16.	Chromium (Cr + 6)	0.1 mg/1
17.	Chromium (Total)	1.0 mg/1
18.	Copper	0.2 mg/1
19.	Lead	0.1 mg/1
20.	Mercury	0.01 mg/1
21.	Nickel	3.0 mg/1

2.0 Off-shore facilities:

For off-shore discharge of effluents, the oil content of the treated effluent without dilution shall not exceed 40 mg/1 for 95 per cent of the observation and shall never exceed 100 mg/l. Three 8-hourly grab samples are required to be collected daily and the average value of oil and grease content of the three samples shall comply with these standards.

B. Guidelines for Discharge of Gaseous Emission:

1.0 DG Sets

1.1 DG sets at drill site as well as production station shall conform with the norm notified under the Environment (Protection) Act, 1986.

2.0 Elevated/ground flares

2.1 Cold Venting of gases shall never be restored to and all the gaseous emissions are to be flared.

2.2 All flaring shall be done by elevated flares except where there is any effect on crop production in adjoining areas due to the flaring. In such cases, one may adopt ground flaring.

2.3 In case of ground flare, to minimise the effects of flaring, the flare pit at Group Gathering Station (GGS) Oil Collecting Station (OCS) and Group Collection Station (GCS) shall be made of RCC surrounded by a permanent wall (made of refractory brick) of minimum 5 m height to reduce the radiation and glaring effects in the adjoining areas.

2.4 A green belt of 100 m width may be developed around the flare after the refractory wall in case of ground flaring.

2.5 If the ground flaring with provision of green belt is not feasible, enclosed ground flare system shall be adopted, and be designed with proper enclosure height, to meet the ground level concentration (GLC) requirement.

2.6 In case of elevated flaring, the minimum stack height shall be 30 m. Height of the stack shall be such that the maximum GLC never exceeds the prescribed ambient air quality limit.

3.0 Burning of effluent in the pits shall not be carried out at any stage.

C. Guidelines for Disposal of Solid Waste:

1.0 Disposal of drill cuttings.

1.1 The drill cutting shall be conveyed through a conveyor system to the disposal pit after proper washing.

1.2 No drill cuttings (of any composition) shall be disposed off-shore. For off-shore installation, drill cuttings separated from mud, shall be transported on-shore through supply vessels for secured land-fill disposal as per Ministry of Environment and Forests' guidelines. The site shall be approved by the concerned authority (State Government/State Pollution Control Board).

1.3 The disposal of drill cuttings (on-shore/off-shore) shall conform to the guidelines provided by the Ministry of Environment and Forests.

1.4 The secured land-fill pit shall be covered with a thick layer of local top soil provided with proper top slope, after drilling operation is over.

2.0 Disposal of drilling mud.

2.1 The unusable portion of the drilling mud (of any composition); after reclamation shall be disposed of only at a secured land-fill site approved by the concerned authority (State Government/State Pollution Control Boards). The disposal of mud shall conform to the guidelines provided by the Ministry of Environment and Forests under the Hazardous Wastes (Management and Handling) Rules, 1989.

2.2	No mud of any composition) shall be disposed off-shore. For off-shore installation, the unusable portion of the mud shall be brought back to the shore for disposal in a secured land-fill.		
2.3	Only water-based mud system shall be used. Where oil-based muds are used, the muds, after they become unusable, shall be properly treated/incinerated, in a centralised treatment facility. In case of off-shore installation, these may be brought to the shore and treated.		
3.0	Production stage solid waste disposal.		
3.1	The dried sludge from wastewater treatment plant and other solid wastes at production stage shall be disposed in a secured land-fill.		
3.2	In case oil content in the sludge is high, it shall be properly treated/incinerated and ash shall be disposed of in a secured land fill.		
73.	Pharmaceuticals industry (Bulk Drugs)		
		(i) Compulsory Parameters	(mg/l except pH)
		pH	6.5–8.5
		Oil & Grease	10
		BOD (3 days at 27°C)	100
		Total suspended solids	100
		Bioassay test	90 per cent survival after 96 hours in 100 per cent effluent test shall be carried out As per IS: 6582–1971
		(ii) Additional parameters	mg/l
		Mercury	0.01
		Arsenic	0.2
		Chromium (Hexavalent)	0.1
		Lead	0.1

7	Cyanide	0.1
	Phenolics (C_6H_5OH)	1.0
	Sulphides (as S)	2.0
	Phosphate (as P)	5.0

Note—

(i) The limit of BOD (3 days at 27°C) shall be 30 mg/l if effluent is discharged directly to a fresh water body.

(ii) The additional parameters are applicable to bulk drug manufacturing units depending upon the process and product.

(iii) No limit for COD is prescribed, but it shall be monitored. If the COD of the treated effluent is greater than 250 mg/l, such industrial units are required to identify chemicals causing the same. In case these are found to be toxic, as defined in the Hazardous Chemicals Rules, 1989 (Schedule I), the State Boards in such cases shall direct the industries to instal tertiary treatment system within the stipulated time limit. This may be done on a case-to-case basis.

74. Emission Standards for brick kilns:

1. Minimal National Emission for Brick Kilns:

Size	*Kiln Capacity*	*Maximum limit for the concentration of particulate matter (mg/N cu.m)*
1	2	3
Small	Less than 15,000 bricks per day (less than 15 ft trench width)	1000
Medium	15,000–30,000 bricks per day (15–22 ft trench width)	750
Large	More than 30,000 bricks per day (more than 22 ft trench width)	750

Note: The above particulate matter emission limits are achievable by installing fixed chimney high draught kilns and/or settling chamber.

II. Stack Height Regulation:

The following stack heights are recommended for optional dispersion of particular matter:

Kiln Capacity	*Stack Height*
Less than 15,000 bricks per day (less than 15 ft trench width)	Minimum stack height of 22 m or,
	Induced draught fan operating with minimum draught of 50 mm Water Gauge with 12 m stack height.
15,000–30,000 bricks per day (15–22 ft trench width)	Minimum stack height of 27 m with gravitational settling chamber or
	Induced draught fan operating with minimum draught of 50 mm Water Gauge with 15 m stack height.
More than 30,000 bricks per day (more than 22 ft. trench width)	Minimum stack height of 30 m with gravitational settling chamber or,
	Induced draught fan operating with minimum draught of 50 mm Water Gauge with 17 m stack height.

III Existing moving chimney Bull's trench kilns shall be dispensed with by December 31, 1997 and no new moving chimney kilns shall be allowed to come up.

IV Considering the immediate need to protect the top soil and to find ways for safe disposal/utilisation of flyash, it is provided that from the 1st January 1997, all brick manufacturing units within a radius of 50 kms from any thermal power plant, shall utilise flyash in optimal proportion for making bricks.

75. Soda Ash Industry (Solvay Process)

Parameter	MINAS (Recipient body specified)		
	Marine	*Brackish*	*Inland surface water*
pH	6.5–9	6.5–9	6.5–9
Temperature	45°C or less	45°C or less	45°C or less
Oil & Grease	2 mg/l	20 mg/l	10 mg/l
Suspended solids (SS)	500 mg/l	200 mg/l	100 mg/l
Ammoniacal nitrogen	5 mg/l	50 mg/l	30 mg/l
Bio-assay	96 hours 30 per cent survival	96 hours 90 per cent survival	96 hours 90 per cent survival

Note—Mains for disposal in brackish and inland surface water are without any dilution. Standards for Dual Process Soda Ash Plants.

Parameter	*MINAS (Inland Surface Water)*
pH	6.5–8.0
Ammoniacal nitrogen as N (mg/l)	50
Nitrate nitrogen, as N (mg/l)	10
Cyanide, as CN (mg/l)	0.2
Hexavalent Chromium (mg/l)	0.1
Total Chromium (mg/l)	2.0
Suspended solids, (mg/l)	100
Oil and grease (mg/l)	10

Note—The standards are to be implemented by the industry in a time targetted schedule within two years. The progress on the time targetted implementation schedule shall be periodically submitted by the industry to the State Pollution Control Board and Central Pollution Control Board.

76. Emission Standard for SO_2 from Cupola furnace
Standard for Sulphur Dioxide emission from Cupola Furnace:

Characteristics	*Emission limit*
Sulphur dioxide (SO_2) emission	300 mg/Nm^3 at 12 per cent CO_2 correction

To achieve the standard, foundries may install scrubber, followed by a stack of height six times the diameter of the Cupola beyond the charging door.

Note—In case due to some technical reasons, installation of scrubber is not possible, then value of SO_2 to the ambient air has to be effected through the stack height.

77. Specification of Motor Gasoline for Emission Related Parameter:

Sl. No.	*Characteristics*	*Requirement*	*Method of Test ref, to P: of IS: 1448*
(i)	Reid Vapour Pressure at 38°C, KPa	35 to 70	P : 39
(ii)	Benzene, per cent by volume, Max	5.0[(1)]	P : 104
(iii)	Lead Content (as Pb) g/l, Max	0.15 (low leaded)[(2)] 0.013 (unleaded)	P : 38
(iv)	Sulphur, per cent by mass, Max	0.10 (unleaded) 0.20 (leaded)	P : 34
(v)	Potential Gum, g/m^3, Max	50	ASTM 873 : 8
(vi)	Gum (Solvent Washed) g/m^3 Max	40	P : 29
(vii)	Oxygenates Content Ether (MTBE, ETBE) Alcohol, per cent by volume, Max	 15	
(viii)	Phosphorus	See Foot Note (3)	ASTMD 3231

(1) 3.0 per cent by volume maximum in metro cities by 2000 AD.

(2) 0.15 g/l by 31st December, 1996 (for entire country).
0.013 g/l by 1st April, 1995 (in four metro cities);
by 1st December, 1998 (for all State capitals/UTs and major metro cities) and
by 1st April, 2000 for the entire country.

(3) Phosphorous containing additives shall be absent.

Note:

(a) Above specifications applies to leaded as well as unleaded petrol except lead content.

(b) For new refineries coming up during or after 1997 the specification applicable by 2000 for existing refineries shall be applicable by 1997.

78. Specification of Diesel Fuel for Emission Related Parameters:

Sl. No.	*Characteristics*	*Requirement*	*Method of Test ref. to P : of IS : 1448*
(i)	Density at 15°C, kg/m^3	820 to 880[(1)]	P : 32
(ii)	Cetane Number, Min	45.0[(2)]	P : 9
(iii)	Distillation 85 per cent by volume recovery at °C Max	350	P : 18
	95 per cent volume recovery at °C, Max	350	P : 18
(iv)	Sulphur, per cent by mass	0.50[(3)]	P : 33

(1) 820 to 860 by 2000 AD

(2) 48 by 31st December, 1998 (except in the refineries–Digboi, Gauhati and Bongaigaon Refineries and Petrochemicals Ltd.)

(3) (i) 0.50 per cent by mass by 1st April, 1996 in four metros and Taj Trapezium
(ii) 0.25 per cent by mass by 1st October, 1996 in Taj Trapezium.
(iii) 0.25 per cent by mass by 1st April, 1999 throughout the country.

Notes:

(a) Above specifications apply to HSD only.

(b) For new refineries coming during or after 1997 specification applicable by 2000 for existing refineries shall be applicable by 1997.

(c) 'P' refers to parts of IS : 1448.]

SCHEDULE II

[* * *]

[Schedule III]

(See Rule 3)

Ambient Air Quality Standards in Respect of Noise

Area Code	*Category of Area*	*Limits in dB (A)*	*Leg.*
		Day Time	*Night Time*
(A)	Industrial area	75	70
(B)	Commercial area	65	55
(C)	Residential area	55	45
(D)	Silence Zone	50	40

Note 1 Day time is reckoned in between 6 a.m. and 9 p.m.

Note 2 Night time is reckoned in between 9 p.m. and 6 a.m.

Note 3 Silence zone is defined as areas upto 100 metres around such premises as hospitals, educational institutions and courts. The Silence zones are to be declared by the Competent Authority.

Use of vehicular horns, loudspeakers and bursting of crackers shall be banned in these zones.

Note 4 Mixed categories of areas should be declared as one of the four above-mentioned categories by the Competent Authority and the corresponding standards shall apply.]

Schedule IV
(See Rule 3)

Standards for Emission of Smoke, Vapour, etc. from Motor Vehicles

(1) Every motor vehicle shall be manufactured and maintained in such condition and shall be so driven that smoke, visible vapour, grit, sparks, ashes, cinders or oily substance do not emit therefrom.

(2) On and from the 1st day of March, 1990, every motor vehicle in use shall comply with the following standards:

(a) Idling CO (Carbon monoxide) emission limit for all four wheeled petrol driven vehicles shall not exceed 3 per cent by volume;

(b) Idling CO emission limit for all two and three wheeled petrol driven shall not exceed 4.5 per cent by volume;

(c) Smoke density for all diesel driven vehicles shall be as follows:

	Method of Test	*Maximum smoke density*		
		Light absorption coefficient (m–1)	*Bosch Units*	*Harride Units*
(a)	Full load at a speed of 60% to 70% of maximum engine rated speed declared	3.1	5.2	75
(b)	Free acceleration	2.3		65

(3) On and from the 1st day of April, 1991, all petrol driven vehicles shall be so manufactured that they comply with the mass emission standards as specified at Annexure 'I'. The breakdown of the operating cycle used for the test shall be as specified at Annexure 'II' and the reference fuel for all such tests shall be as specified in Annexure 'III' to this Schedule.

(4) On and from the 1st day of April, 1991 all diesel driven vehicles shall be so manufactured that they comply with the mass emission standards based on exhaust gas opacity as specified at Annexure 'IV' to this Schedule.

(5) On and from the 1st day of April, 1992, all diesel driven vehicles shall be so manufactured that they comply with the following levels of emissions under the Indian driving cycle:

Mass of Carbon Monoxide (CO) Maxm. Grams per KWH	*Mass of Hydro Carbons (HC) Maxm. Grams per KWH*	*Mass of Nitrogen Oxides (NO) Maxm. Grams per KWH*
14	3.5	18

(6) Each motor vehicle manufactured on and after the dates specified in paragraphs (2), (3), (4) and (5) shall be certified by the manufacturers to be conforming to the standards specified in the said paragraphs and the manufactures shall further certify that the components liable to effect the emission of gaseous pollutants are so designed, constructed and assembled as to enable the vehicle, in nominal use, despite the vibration to which it may be subjected, to comply with the provision of the said paragraphs.

(7) Test for smoke emission level and Carbon Monoxide level for motor vehicles—

(a) Any officer not below the rank of a Sub-inspector of police or an Inspector of motor vehicles, who has reason to believe that a motor vehicle is by virtue of smoke emitted from it or other pollutants like Carbon Monoxide emitted from it, is likely to cause environmental pollution, endangering the health or safety of any other user of the road or the public, may direct the driver or any person incharge of the vehicle to submit the vehicle for undergoing a test to measure the standard of black smoke or the standard of any other pollutants.

(b) The driver or any person incharge of the vehicle shall upon demand by any officer referred to in sub-paragraph (a), submit the vehicle for testing for the purpose of measuring the standard of smoke or the levels of other pollutants or both.

(c) The measurement of standard of smoke shall be done with a smoke meter of a type approved by the State Government and the measurement of other pollutants like Carbon Monoxide shall be done with instrument of a type approved by the State Government.

ANNEXURE I

(See paragraph 3)

Mass Emission Standards for Petrol driven Vehicles

1. Type Approval Tests:
   Two and Three Wheeler Vehicles

Reference Mass, R (kg)	*CO (g/km)*	*HC (g/km)*
R ≤ 150	12	8
150 R ≤ 150	$12+\frac{18(R-150)}{200}$	$8+\frac{4(R-150)}{200}$
R > 350	30	12

Light Duty Vehicles:

Reference Mass, rw (kg)	*CO (g/km)*	*HC (g/km)*
rw ≤ 1020	14.3	2.0
1020 < rw ≤ 1250	16.5	2.1

1250 < rw ≤ 1470	18.8	2.1
1470 < rw ≤ 1700	20.7	2.3
1700 < rw ≤ 1930	22.9	2.5
1930 < rw ≤ 2150	24.9	2.7
rw ≤ 2150	27.1	2.9

1. Conformity of Production Tests:
   Two and Three Wheeler Vehicles

Reference Mass, R (kg)	*CO (g/km)*	*HC (g/km)*
R < 150	15	8
150R < 350	$15+\frac{25(R-150)}{200}$	$10+\frac{5(R-150)}{200}$
R > 350	40	15
rw ≤ 1020	17.3	2.7
1020 ≤ rw ≤ 1250	19.7	2.7
1250 ≤ rw ≤ 1470	22.5	2.8
1470 ≤ rw ≤ 1700	24.9	3.0
1700 ≤ rw ≤ 1930	27.9	3.3
1930 ≤ rw ≤ 2150	29.9	3.5
rw ≤ 2150	32.6	3.7

For any of the pollutants referred to above of the three results obtained may exceed the limit specified for the vehicle by not more than 10 per cent.

Explanation: Mass emission standards refers to the gm of pollutants emitted per km run of the vehicle, as determined by a chassis dynamometer test using the Indian Driving Cycle.

ANNEXURE II

(See paragraph 3)

Breakdown of the Operating Cycle used for the Tests

	No. of Operation	*Acceleration (m/sec^2)*	*Speed (km/h)*	*Duration of each operation (s)*	*Cumulative Time (s)*
01.	Idling	—	—	16	16
02.	Acceleration	0.65	0–14	6	22
03.	Acceleration	0.56	14–22	4	26
04.	Deceleration	– 0.63	22–13	4	30
05.	Steady speed	—	13	2	32
06.	Acceleration	0.56	13–23	5	37
07.	Acceleration	0.44	23–31	5	42
08.	Deceleration	– 0.56	31–25	3	45
09.	Steady speed	—	25	4	49
10.	Deceleration	– 0.56	25–21	2	51
11.	Acceleration	0.45	21–34	8	59
12.	Acceleration	0.32	34–42	7	66
13.	Deceleration	– 0.46	42–37	3	69
14.	Steady speed	—	37	7	76
15.	Deceleration	– 0.42	34–34	2	78
16.	Acceleration	0.32	34–42	7	85
17.	Deceleration	– 0.46	42–47	9	94
18.	Deceleration	– 0.52	27–14	7	101
19.	Deceleration	– 0.56	14–00	7	108

ANNEXURE III

(See paragraph 3)

Reference Fuel for Type and Production Conformity Tests

S. No.	*Characteristic*	*Requirement*		*Method of Test (ref. of P : or IS : 1448*)*
		87 Octane	*93 Octane*	
1.	Colour, visual	Orange	Red	—
2.	Copper-strip corrosion for 3 hours at 50°C	Not worse than No.1		P: 15 (1968)
3.	Density at 15°C	Not limited but to be reported		P: 16 (1967)
4.	Distillation:			P: 18 (1967)
	(a) Initial boiling point	Not limited but to be reported		P: 16 (1967)
	(b) Recovery upto 20°C per cent by volume, Min.	10	10	
	(c) Recovery upto 125°C 50 per cent by volume	50	50	
	(d) Recovery upto 130°C per cent by volume, Min.	90	90	
	(e) Final boiling point, Max.	215°C	215°C	
	(f) Residue per cent by volume, Max.	2	2	
5.	Octane number (Research method) Max.	87	94	P: 27 (1960)
6.	Oxidation stability in minutes, Min	360	360	P: 28 (1966)
7.	Residue on evaporation mg/100 ml, Max.	4.0	4.0	P: 29 (1960) Air-jet solvent washed)
8.	Sulphur, total, per cent by weight Max.	0.25	0.20	P: 34 (1966)
9.	Lead content (as Pb), g/l Max.	0.56	0.80	P: 37 (1967) or P: 38 (1967)
10.	Reid vapour pressure at 38 degree C, kg/cm^3, Max.	0.70	0.70	P: 39 (1967)

* Methods of test for petroleum and its products

ANNEXURE IV

(See paragraph 4)

Limit Values of Exhaust Gas Opacity applicable for Diesel Driven Vehicles. The engine tests at steady speed

Normal Flow G (l/s)	*Absorption Coefficient K (m^{-1})*	*Nominal Flow G (l/s)*	*Absorption Coefficient (Km^{-1})*
42	2.00	120	1.20
45	1.91	125	1.17
50	1.82	130	1.15
55	1.75	135	1.31
60	1.68	140	1.11
65	1.61	145	1.09
70	1.56	150	1.07
75	1.50	155	1.05
80	1.46	160	1.04
85	1.41	165	1.02
90	1.38	170	1.01
95	1.34	175	1.00
100	1.31	180	0.99
105	1.27	185	0.97
110	1.25	190	0.96
115	1.22	195	0.95
		< 200	0.93

SCHEDULE [V]
(See Rule 12)

Sl. No.	*Place at which the discharge of any environment pollutant in excess of prescribed standards occurs or is apprehended to occur*	*Authorities or agencies to be intimated*	*Appointed under*
1	2	3	4
1.	Factories as defined under the Factories Act 1948:		
	(a) Owned by the Central Government and engaged in carrying out the purposes of the Atomic Energy Act, 1962	(i) Atomic Energy Regulatory Board (AERB).	The Atomic Energy Act, 1962
		(ii) The Ministry of Environment and Forests	
	(b) Factories other than those mentioned in para (a)	(i) The Chief Inspector of Factories	The Factories Act, 1948
		(ii) The Inspector of Factories having local jurisdiction	-do-
		(iii) The Ministry of Environment and Forests	
2.	Mine as defined under the Mines and Minerals (Regulation and Development) Act, 1957	[(i) Controller-General of Mines	The Mines and Minerals (Regulation and Development) Act, 1957
		[(ii) Regional Controller	-do-

			of Mines having local jurisdiction	
		(iii)	The Ministry of Environment and Forests	
3.	Port as defined under the Indian Ports Act, 1908	(i)	Conservator of Ports	The Indian Ports Act, 1908
		(ii)	The Ministry of Environment and Forests	-do-
4.	Plantation as defined under the Plantations Labour Act, 1951	(i)	The Chief Inspector of Plantations	The Plantations Labour Act, 1951
		(ii)	The Inspector of Plantations having local jurisdiction	-do-
		(iii)	The Ministry of Environment and Forests	
5.	Motor Vehicle as defined under the Motor Vehicles Act, 1939	(i)	State Transport Authority	The Motor Vehicles Act, 1939
		(ii)	Regional Transport Authority having regional jurisdictions	-do-
		(iii)	The ministry of Environment and Forests	
6.	Ship as defined under the Merchant Shipping Act, 1958	(i)	Director-General of Shipping	The Merchant Shipping Act, 1958
		(ii)	Surveyor having jurisdiction	-do-

(iii)	The Ministry of Environment and Forests	–do–

[Schedule VI]

(See Rule 3-A)

General standards for discharge of environmental pollutants Part-A Effluents

Sl. No.	Parameter	Standards			
		Inland surface water	Public Sewers	Land of irrigation	Marine coastal areas
1.	2	3(a)	3(b)	3(c)	3(d)
1.	Colour and odour	Sec 6 of Annexure-I	—	Sec 6 of Annexure I	Sec 6 of Annexure I
2.	Suspended solids mg/l, Max.	100	600	200	(a) For process waste water-100 (b) For cooling water effluent 10 per cent above total suspended matter of influent.
3.	Particle size of Suspended solids	shall pass 850 micron IS Sieve	—	—	(a) Floatable solids, max. 3 mm. (b) Settleable solids, max 850 microns.
4.	[***]				
5.	pH value.	5.5 to 9.0	5.5 to 9.0	5.5 to 9.0	5.5 to 9.0
6.	Temperature	shall not exceed 5°C above the receiving water temperature	—	—	shall not exceed 5°C above the receiving water temperature

1.	2	3(a)	3(b)	3(c)	3(d)
7.	Oil and grease mg/l, Max.	10	20	10	20
8.	Total residual chlorine mg/l Max.	1.0			1.0
9.	Ammonical nitrogen (as N), mg/l, Max.	50	50	—	50
10.	Total Kjeldhal nitrogen [N]; mg/l, Max.	100	—	—	100 —
11.	Free ammonia [NH_3] mg/l, Max.	5.0	—	—	5.0
12.	Biochemical oxygen demand (5 days at 20°C) [mg/l, Max.]	30	350	100	100
13.	Chemical Oxygen demand, mg/l, Max.	250	—	—	250
14.	Arsenic (as As.) [mg/l], Max.	0.2	0.2	0.2	0.2
15.	Mercury (as Hg), mg/l, max.	0.01	0.01	—	0.01
16.	Lead (as Pb) mg/l, Max.	0.1	1.0	—	2.0
17.	Cadmium (as Cd) mg/l, Max.	2.0	1.0	—	2.0
18.	Hexavalent chromium (as Cr + 6), mg/l, Max.	0.1	2.0	—	1.0

1.	2	3(a)	3(b)	3(c)	3(d)
19.	Total chromium (as Cr) mg/l, Max.	2.0	2.0	—	2.0
20.	Copper (as Cu) mg/l, Max.	3.0	3.0	—	3.0
21.	Zinc (as Zn) mg/l, Max.	5.0	15	—	15
22.	Selenium (as Se) mg/l, Max.	0.05	0.05	—	0.05
23.	Nickel (as Ni) mg/l, Max. [***]	3.0	3.0	—	5.0
27.	Cyanide (as CN) mg/l, Max. [***]	0.2	2.0	0.2	0.2
29.	[Fluoride] (as F) mg/l, Max.	2.0	15	—	15
30.	Dissolved phosphates (as P), mg/l, max. [***]	5.0	—	—	—
32.	Sulphide (as S) mg/l, Max.	2.0	—	—	5.0
33.	Phenolic compounds [as C_6H_5OH] mg/l, Max.	1.0	5.0	—	5.0
34.	Radioactive materials:				
	(a) Alpha emitters [micro-curie/ml] Max.	10^{-7}	10^{-7}	[10^{-8}]	10^{-7}
	(b) Beta emitters [micro-curie/ml] M	10^{-6}	10^{-6}	10^{-7}	[10^{-6}]

1.	2	3(a)	3(b)	3(c)	3(d)
35.	Bio-assay test	90 per cent survival of fish after 96 hours in 100 per cent effluent	90% survival of fish after 96 hours in 100 per cent effluent	90 per cent survival of fish after 96 hours in 100 per cent effluent	90 per cent survival of fish after 96 hours in 100 per cent effluent
36.	Manganese (as Mn)	2 mg/l	2 mg/l		2 mg/l
37.	Iron (as Fe)	3 mg/l	3 mg/l		3 mg/l
38.	Vanadium (as V)	0.2 mg/l	0.2 mg/l		0.2 mg/l
39.	Nitrate Nitrogen	10 mg/l	—	—	20 mg/l
40.	Pesticides: (microgm per lit. maximum)				
(i)	Benzene hexa chloride	10	—	10	10
(ii)	Carboryl	10	—	10	10
(iii)	DDT	10	—	10	10
(iv)	Endosulfan	10	—	10	10
(v)	Diamethoate	450	—	450	450
(vi)	Penitrothion	10	—	10	10
(vii)	Malathion	10	—	10	10
(viii)	Phorate	10	—	10	10
(ix)	Methyl Parathion	10	—	10	10
(x)	Phenthoate	10	—	10	10
(xi)	Pyrethrums	10	—	10	10
(xii)	Copper Oxychloride	9600	—	9600	9600
(xiii)	Copper Sulphate	50	—	50	50
(xiv)	Ziram	1000	—	1000	1000
(xv)	Sulphur	30	—	30	30
(xvi)	Paraouat	2300	—	2300	2300
(xvii)	Proponil	7300	—	7300	7300
(xviii)	Nitrogen	780	—	780	780

PART B

Waste Water Generation Standards

Sl. No.	Industry	Quantum
1.	Integrated Iron & Steel	16 [m^3/tonne] of finished steel
2.	Sugar	0.4 [m^3/tonne] of cane crushed
3.	Pulp & Paper Industries	
	(a) Larger pulp & paper	
	(i) Pulp & paper	175 [m^3/tonne] to paper produced
	[(ii) Viscose Staple Fibre	150 m^3/tonne of product
	(iii) Viscose Filament Yarn	500 m^3/tonne of product
	(b) Small pulp & paper:	
	(i) Agro-residue based	150 [m^3/tonne] of paper produced
	(ii) Waste paper based	50 [m^3/tonne] of paper produced
4.	Fermentation Industries	
	(a) Maltry	3.5 [m^3/tonne] of paper produced
	(b) Brewery	0.25 M^3/KL of beer produced
	(c) Distillery	12 M^3/KL of alcohol produced
5.	Caustic Soda	
	(a) Membrane cell process	[m^3/tonne] of caustic soda produced excluding cooling tower blow down
	(b) Mercury cell process	4 [m^3/tonne] of caustic soda produced (mercury bearing), 10 per cent blow down permitted for cooling tower
6.	Textile Industries:	
	Man-made fibre	
	(i) Nylon & Polyster	12 [m^3/tonne] of fibre produced
	(ii) Viscose rayon	150 [m^3/tonne] of product
7.	Tanneries 28 [m^3/tonne] of raw hide	

8.	Starch, Glucose and related products	8 [m^3/tonne] of maize crushed
9.	Dairy	3M^3/KL of Milk
10.	Natural rubber processing industry	4 [m^3/tonne] of rubber
11.	Fertiliser	
	(a) Straight nitrogenous fertiliser	5 [m^3/tonne] of urea or equivalent produced
	(b) Straight phosphatic fertiliser (SSP & TSP) excluding manufacture of any acid	0.5 [m^3/tonne] of SSP/TSP
	(c) Complex fertiliser	Standards of nitrogenous and phosphatic fertiliser are applicable depending on the primary product.

PART C
Load Based Standards

	Parameter	*Quantum in [kg]/100 tonnes of of crude processed*
1.	Oil Refinery Industry	
	Oil & Grease	10.00
	Phenol	0.70
	BOD	10.50
	Suspended solids	14.00
	Sulphide	0.35
2.	Large Pulp & Paper, News Print/Rayon grade plants of capacity above 24000 [tonne]/Annum	
	Parameter	Quantum
	Total organic Chloride (TOCI)	2 [kg/tonne] of product

PART D
General Emission Standards

I. Concentration Based Standards:

Sl. No.	*Parameter*	*Standard* Concentration not to exceed (in mg/NM^3)
(1)	(2)	2. (3)
1	[Particulate Matter (PM)]	150
2	[Total Fluoride]	[25]
3.	Asbestos	[4 Fibres/cc and dust should not be more than 2 mg/Nm^3]
4.	Mercury	0.2
5.	Chlorine	15
6.	Hydrochloric acid vapour and mist	35
	[***]	
8.	Sulphuric acid mist	50
9.	Carbon monoxide	[1% max (v/v)]
	[***]	
10.	Lead	
	[***]	[10 mg/Nm^3]
II.	Equipment Based Standards	
	[For dispersal of sulphur dioxide, a minimum stack height limit is accordingly prescribed as below:]	

Sl. No.	*Parameter*	*Standard*
1.	Sulphur dioxide	Stack-height limit in [metre]
	(i) Power generation capacity	
	—500 MW and more	275
	—200/210 MW and	

	above to less than 500 MW	220
	—less than 200/210 MW	$H = 14 (Q)^{0.3}$
(ii)	Steam generation capacity	Coal consumption per day
	—Less than 2 [tonne/hr]	[***]
	—2 to 5 [tonne/hr]	
	—5 to 10 [tonne/hr]	
	—10 to 15 [tonne/hr]	
	—15 to 20 [tonne/hr]	
	—20 to 25 [tonne/hr]	
	—25 to 30 [tonne/hr]	
	—More than 30 T/hr	

Note—H—Physical height of the stack in [metre]
Q—Emission rate of SO_2 in kg/hr. [***]

III Load/Mass-based Standards:

Sl. No.	*Industry*	*Parameter*	*Standard*
1.	[Fertiliser] (Urea)		
	Commissioned prior to 1–1–1982	[Particulate Matter (PM)]	14 [kg/tonne] of product
	Commissioned after 1–1–1982	[Particulate Matter (PM)]	0.5 [kg/tonne] of product
2.	Copper, Lead and [Zinc Smelter Converter]	Sulphur dioxide	4 [kg/tonne] of concentrated [100 per cent and acid produced]
3.	Nitric Acid	Oxides of Nitrogen	3 [kg/tonne] of weak acid (before concentration) produced
4.	Sulphuric Acid	Sulphur dioxide	4 [kg/tonne] of concentrated (100 per cent) acid produced
5.	Coke Oven	Carbon Monoxide	3 (kg/tonne) of coke produced
6.	Oil Refineries		

(a) [For the oil refineries the following standards shall be applicable:]

Process	Parameter	Standard
Distillation [Atmospheric plus Vacuum)]	Sulphur dioxide	0.25 [kg/tonne] of feed in this process
Catalytic cracker	-do-	2.5 [kg/tonne] of feed in this process
Sulphur Recovery Unit	-do-	120 [kg/tonne] of Sulphur in the feed

[***]

7. Aluminium Plants:		
(i) Anode Bake Oven	Total Fluoride	0.3 kg/MT of Aluminium
(ii) Pot room		
(a) VSS	-do-	4.7 kg/MT of Aluminium
(b) HSS	-do-	6 kg/MT of Aluminium
(c) PBSW	-do-	2.5 kg/MT of Aluminium
(d) PBCW	-do-	1.0 kg/MT of Aluminium

Note—

VSS = Vertical Stud Soderberg

HSS = Horizontal Stud Soderberg

[PBSW = Pre Backed Side Work]

[PBCW = Pre Backed Centre Work]

8. Glass Industry		
(a) Furnace Capacity		
(i) Up to the product draw capacity of 60 MT/day	Particulate mater	2 kg/hr
(ii) Product draw capacity more than 60 MT/Day	-do- Drawn	0.8 kg/MT of Product

PART E

Noise Standards

A. Noise Limits for Automobiles [Free Field Distance at 7.5 Metre] in dB (A) at the manufacturing Stage

(a)	Motorcycle, Scooter & Three-wheelers	80
(b)	Passenger Cars	82
(c)	Passenger or Commercial Vehicles up to 4 MT	85
(d)	Passenger or Commercial vehicles above 4 MT and up to 12 MT	89
(e)	Passenger or Commercial vehicles exceeding 12 MT	91

B. Domestic appliances and Construction equipments at the manufacturing stage to be achieved by 31st December, 1993

(a)	Window Air Conditioner of 1 ton to 1.5 ton	68
(b)	Air [coolers]	60
(c)	Refrigerators	46
(d)	Diesel generator for domestic purposes	85–90
(e)	Compactors (rollers), Front loaders, Concrete mixers, Cranes (movable), Vibrators and Saws	75

ANNEXURE I

(For the purposes of Parts A, B and C)

The State Boards shall follow the following guidelines in enforcing the standards specified under Schedule VI:

1. The waste waters and gases are to be treated with the best available technology [(BAT)] in order to achieve the prescribed standards.
2. The industries need to be encouraged for recycling and reuse of waste materials as far as practicable in order to minimise the discharge of wastes into the environment.

3. The industries are to be encouraged for recovery of biogas, energy and reusable materials.
4. While permitting the discharge of effluents and omissions into the environment, State Boards have to take into account the assimilative capacities of the receiving bodies, especially water bodies so that quality of the intended use of the receiving water is not affected. Where such quality is likely to be affected, discharges should not be allowed into water bodies.
5. The Central and State Boards shall put emphasis on the implementation of clean technologies by the industries in order to increase fuel efficiency and reduce the generation of environmental pollutants.
6. All efforts should be made to remove colour and unpleasant odour as far as practicable.
7. The standards mentioned in this Schedule [shall also apply to all other [effluents] discharged such as] mining and mineral processing activities and sewage.
8. The limit given for the total concentration of mercury in the final effluent of caustic soda industry, is for the combined effluent from (a) Cell house, (b) Bribe plant (c) Chlorine handling, (d) Hydrogen handling, and (e) Hydrochloric acid plant.

[Omitted]

10. All effluents discharged including from the industries such as cotton textile, composite woollen mills, synthetic rubber, small pulp and paper, natural rubber, petrochemicals, tanneries, paint, dyes, slaughter houses, food & fruit processing and dairy [industries] into surface waters shall conform to the BOD limits specified above, namely, 30 mg/l. For discharge of an effluent having a BOD more than 30 mg/l, the standards shall conform to those given above for other receiving bodies, namely, sewers, coastal waters and land for irrigation.

[***]

12. In case of fertilizer industry the limits in respect of chromium and [fluoride] shall be complied with at the outlet of chromium and [fluoride] removal units respectively.
13. In case of pesticides:

(a) The limits should be complied with at the end of treatment plant before dilution.
(b) Bio-assay test should be carried out with the available species of fish in the receiving water, the COD limits to be specified in the consent conditions should be correlated with the BOD limits.
(c) In case metabolites and isomers of the Pesticides in the given list are found in significant concentrations, standards should be prescribed for these also in the same concentration as the individual pesticides.
(d) Industries are required to analyse pesticides in waste water by advanced analytical methods such as GLC/HPLC.

[14. The chemical oxygen demand (COD) concentration in a treated effluent, if observed to be persistently greater than 250 mg/l before disposal to any receiving body (public sewer, land for irrigation, inland surface water and marine coastal areas), such industrial units are required to identify chemicals causing the same. In case these are found to be toxic as defined in the Schedule I of the Hazardous Wastes (Management and Handling) Rules, 1989 the State Boards in such cases shall direct the industries to install tertiary treatment stipulating time limit.

15. Standards specified in Part A of Schedule VI for discharge of effluents into the public sewer shall be applicable only if such sewer lead to a secondary treatment including biological treatment system, otherwise these discharge into sewers shall be treated as discharge into inland surface waters.]

ANNEXURE II

(For the purpose of Part D)

1. The State Boards shall follow the following guidelines in the standards specified under Schedule VI:

   (a) In case of cement plants, the total dust (from all sections) shall be within 400 mg/ [Nm^3] and 250 mg/[Nm^3] for the plants up to 200 t/d and more than 200 t/d capacities respectively.

(b) In respect of calcination process (e.g. aluminium plants), Kilns and Step Gate Bagasse-fired Boilers. Particulate Matter (PM) emissions shall be within 250 mg/[Nm^3].

(c) In case of thermal power plants commissioned prior to 1–1–1982 and having generation capacity less than 62.5 MW, the PM emission shall be within 350 mg/[Nm^3].

(d) In case of Lime Kilns of capacity more than 5t/day and up to 40 t/day, the PM emission shall be within 500 mg/[Nm^3].

(e) In case of horse shoe/Pulsating Grate and Spreader Stroker Bagasse-fired-Boilers, the PM emission shall be within 500 (12 per cent CD_2) and 800 (12 per cent CO_2) mg/[Nm^3] respectively. In respect of these boilers, if more than attached to a single stack, the emission standard shall be fixed, based on added capacity of all the boilers connected with the stack.

(f) In case of asbestos dust, the same shall not exceed 2 mg/[Nm^3].

(g) In case of the urea plants commissioned after 1-1-1982, coke ovens and lead glass units, the PM emission shall be within 50 mg/[Nm^3].

(h) In case of small boilers of capacity less than 2 tonnes/hr and between 2 to 5 tonnes/hr the PM emissions shall be within 1600 and 1200 mg/[Nm^3].

(i) In case of integrated Iron and Steel Plants, PM emission up to 400 mg/ [Nm^3] shall be allowed during oxygen lancing.

(j) In case of stone crushing units, the suspended PM contribution value at a distance of 40 metres from a controlled, isolated as well as from a unit located in the cluster should be less than 600 [micrograms/Nm^3].

These units must also adopt the following pollution control measures:

(i) Dust containment cum suppression system for the equipment;
(ii) Construction of wind breaking walls;
(iii) Construction of the metalled roads within the premises;
(iv) Regular cleaning and wetting of the ground within the premises;
(v) Growing of a green belt along the periphery.
(k) In case of Ceramic industry, form the other sources of pollution, such as basic raw material and processing operations, heat recovery dryers, mechanical finishing operation, all possible preventive measures should be taken to control PM emissions as far as practicable.

2. The total fluoride emissions in respect of Glass and Phosphatic Fertilizers shall not exceed 5 mg/NM^3 and 25 mg/NM^3 respectively.

3. [In case of copper, lead and zinc smelting, the off-gases may, as far as possible, be utilized for manufacturing sulphuric acid.]

[4. In case of cupolas (Foundries) having capacity (melting rate) less than 3 tonne/per hour, the particulate matter emission shall be within 450 mg/Nm^3. In these cases it is essential that stack is constructed over the cupola beyond the charging door and the emissions are directed through the stack, which should be at least six times the diameter of cupola. In respect of Arc Furnaces and Induction Furnaces, provision has to be made for collecting the fumes before discharging the emissions through the stack.

[SCHEDULE VII[

[See Rule (3B)]

National Ambient Air Quality Standards (NAAQS)

Pollutant	*Time Weighted Average*	*Concentration in Ambient Air*			
		Industrial Area	*Residential Rural and other area*	*Sensitive Area*	*Method of measurement*
1	2	3	4	5	6
Sulphur Dioxide	Annual Average*	80 ug/m^3	60 ug/m^3	15 ug/m^3	–Improved West and Gaeke method
$(SO)_2$	24 hours**	120 ug/m^3	80 ug/m^3	30 ug/m^3	–Ultraviolet Fluorescence
Oxides of nitrogen as NO_2	Annual Average*	80 ug/m^3	60 ug/m^3	15 ug/m^3	–Jacab and Hochheiser modified (Na-Arsenite) method
	24 hours**	120 ug/m^3	80 ug/m^3	30 ug/m^3	–Gas Phase Chemiluminescence
Suspended Particulate Matter (SPM)	Annual Average*	360 ug/m^3	140 ug/m^3	70 ug/m^3	–High Volume Sampling
	24 hours**	500 ug/m^3	200 ug/m^3	100 ug/m^3	–Average Flow rate not less than 1.1 m^3/minute]

Respirable Particulate Matter (size less than 10 um) (RPM)	Annual Average*	120 ug/m^3	60 ug/m^3	50 ug/m^3	–Respirable particulate matter Sampler.
	24 hcurs**	150 ug/m^3	100 ug/m^3	75 ug/m^3	
Lead (Pb)	Annual Average*	1.0 ug/m^3	0.75 ug/m^3	0.50 ug/m^3	AAS method after sampling using EMP 200 or equivalent-filter paper.
	24 hours**	1.5 ug/m^3	1.00 ug/m^3	0.75 ug/m^3	
Carbon Monoxide	8 hours**	5.0 mg/m^3	2.0 mg/m^3	1.0 mg/m^3	–Non disbersive, infra-red spectroscopy
	1 hour	10.0 mg/m^3	4.0 mg/m^3	2.0 mg/m^3	

* Annual Arithmetic mean of minimum 104 measurements in a year taken twice a week 24 hourly at uniform interval.

** 23 hourly/8 hourly values shall be met 98 per cent of the time in a year, 2 per cent of the time, it may exceed but not on two consecutive days.

Note—

1. National Ambient Air Quality Standard: The levels of an air quality necessary with an adequate margin of safety, to protect the public health, vegetation and property.
2. Whenever and wherever two consecutive values exceeds the limit specified above for the respective category, it shall be considered adequate, reason to institute regular/continuous monitoring and further investigations.]

2

Illegal Migrants, Disabled Persons and Human Rights

THE ILLEGAL MIGRANTS (DETERMINATION BY TRIBUNALS) ACT, 1983

(Act No. 39 of 1983)

25th December, 1983

An Act to provide for the establishment of Tribunals for the determination, in a fair manner, of the question whether a person is an illegal migrant to enable the Central Government to expel illegal migrants from India and for matters connected therewith or incidental thereto.

Whereas a good number of the foreigners who migrated into India across the borders of the eastern and north-eastern regions of the country on and after the 25th day of March, 1971, have, by taking advantage of the circumstances of such migration and their ethnic similarities and other connections with the people of India and without having in their possession any lawful authority so to do, illegally remained in India:

And whereas the continuance of such foreigners in India is detrimental to the interests of the public of India.

And whereas on account of the number of such foreigners and the manner in which such forcigners have clandestinely been trying to pass off as citizen of India and all other relevant circumstances, it is necessary for the protection of the citizens of India to make special provisions for the detection of such foreigners in Assam and also in any other part of India in which such foreigners may be found to have remained illegally;

Be it enacted by Parliament in the Thirty-fourth Year of the Republic of India as follows:

PRELIMINARY

1. Short title, Extent and Commencement. 1. This Act may be called the Illegal Migrants (Determination by Tribunals) Act, 1983.

2. It extends to the whole of India.

3. It shall be deemed to have come into force in the State of Assam on the 15th day of October, 1983 and in any other State on such date as the Central Government may, by notification in the Official Gazette, appoint and different dates may be appointed for different States and references in this Act to the commencement of this Act shall be construed in relation to any State as references to the date of commencement of this Act in such State.

2. ***Application.*** Nothing in this Act shall apply to or in relation to:

(a) any person who was in any State and who had been expelled from that State or India before the commencement of this Act in that state or in relation to whose expulsion from such State or India any order made before such commencement under any other law is in force;

(b) any person detected as a foreigner at the time of his entry across any border of India;

(c) any foreigner who, having entered into India under a valid passport or travel document, continued to remain therein after the expiry of the period of which he was authorised to remain in India under such passport or travel document.

3. ***Definitions and construction of references.*** 1. In this Act, unless the context otherwise requires:

(a) "Appellate Tribunal" means an Appellate Tribunal established by the Central Government under sub-section(i) of Section 15;

(b) "foreigner" has the same meaning as in the Foreigners Act, 1946 (31 of 1946);

(c) "illegal migrant" means a person in respect of whom each of the following conditions is satisfied, namely:

 (i) he has entered into India on or after the 25th day of March, 1971;

 (ii) he is a foreigner;

 (iii) he has entered into India without being in possession of a valid passport or other travel document or any other lawful authority in that behalf;

(d) "notification" means a notification published in the Official Gazette;

(e) "prescribed" means prescribed by rules made under this Act;

(f) "Tribunal" means a Tribunal established by the Central Government under sub-section(1) of Section 5.

2. Any reference in this Act to any law which is not in force in any area shall, in relation to that area, be construed as a reference to the corresponding law, if any, in force in that area.

4. *Overriding effect of the Act.* 1. The provisions of this Act or of any rule or order made thereunder shall have, effect notwithstanding anything contained in the Passport (Entry into India) Act, 1920 (34 of 1920) or the Foreigners Act, 1946 (31 of 1946) or the Immigrants (Expulsion from Assam) Act, 1950 (10 of 1950) or the Passports Act, 1967 (15 of 1967) or any rule or order made under any of the said Acts and in force for the time being.

2. In particular and without prejudice to the generality of the provisions of sub-section(1), nothing in the provision to Section 2 of the Immigrants (Expulsion from Assam) Act, 1950 (10 of 1950) shall apply to or in relation to an illegal migrant as defined in clause (c) of sub-section(1) of Section 3.

ESTABLISHMENT OF TRIBUNALS

5. *Establishment of Illegal Migrants (Determination) Tribunals.* 1. The Central Government may, by notification, establish, for the purposes of this Act, as many Illegal Migrants (Determination) Tribunals as it may deem necessary and specify the principal place of sitting of, and the territorial limits within which, each such Tribunal shall exercise its jurisdiction.

2. No person shall be appointed as a member of any such Tribunal unless he is or has been a District Judge or an Additional District Judge in any State.

3. Each Tribunal shall consist of [two members.]

4. On the establishment of a Tribunal, the Central Government shall appoint one of the members thereof as the Chairman of such Tribunal.

5. Each Tribunal shall sit in its principal place of sitting and in such other place or places as its Chairman may, from time to time, appoint.

6. *Filling of vacancies.* If, for any reason, any vacancy occurs in the office of the Chairman or [the member] of a Tribunal, the Central Government may fill the vacancy by appointing any person who fulfils the qualifications specified in sub-section(2) of Section 5, as the Chairman, or, as the case may be, member of such Tribunal.

7. Staff of the Tribunals. The Central Government shall make available to every Tribunal such staff as may be necessary for the discharge of its functions under this Act.

8. References or applications to Tribunals. 1. If any question arises as to whether any person is or is not an illegal migrant, the Central Government may, whether such question has arisen on a representation made by such person against order under the Foreigners Act, 1946 (31 of 1946) requiring him not to remain in India or to any other effect or has arisen in any other manner whatsoever, refer such question to a Tribunal for decision.

2. [xxx], any person may make an application to the Tribunal, for its decision, as to whether the person whose name and other particulars are given in the application, is or is not an illegal migrant:

[Provided that no such application shall be entertained by the Tribunal unless the person in relation to whom the application is made is found, or resides, within the jurisdiction of the same police station wherein the applicant has his place of residence;]

3. Every application made under sub-section(2) shall be made in such form and in such manner as may be prescribed and shall be accompanied by affidavits sworn by not less than [two persons residing within the jurisdiction of the same police station] in which the person referred to in the application is found, or residing, corroborating the averments made in the application, and shall also be accompanied by such fee, being not less than [ten], and not more than one hundred rupees, as may be prescribed.

4. [Every reference under sub-section(1) shall be made to the Tribunal within the territorial limits of whose jurisdiction the place of residence of the person named in such reference is, at the time of making such reference, situated:

Provided that where such person has no place of residence, the reference shall be made to the Tribunal within the territorial limits of whose jurisdiction such person is, at the time of making such reference, found.

5. Every application under sub-section(2) shall be made to the tribunal within the territorial limits of whose jurisdiction the person named in such application is found or, as the case may be,

has his place of residence, at the time of making such application].

[8-A. *Application to the Central Government for reference.* 1. Any person may make an application to the Central Government, for decision by a Tribunal, as to whether the person whose name and other particulars are given in the application, is or is not an illegal migrant, and where any such application is received by the Central Government, it may, on the basis of any information on its possession or after making such inquiry as it deems fit, reject the application on the ground that the application is frivolous or vexatious or it does not comply with the requirements of this Section or refer such application to Tribunal for decision.

2. Every application made under sub-section(1) shall be made in such form and in such manner as may be prescribed and shall be accompanied by a declaration by another person residing within the jurisdiction of the same revenue sub-division in which the applicant resides in such form as may be prescribed to the effect that the particulars, mentioned in the application are true to his knowledge, information and belief:

Provided that no person shall make more than ten such applications or more than ten such declarations.

3. Every reference under sub-section(1) shall be made to the Tribunal within the territorial limits of whose jurisdiction the place of residence of the person named in such reference is at the time of making such reference situated:

Provided that where such person has no place of residence, the reference shall be made to the Tribunal within the territorial limits of whose jurisdiction such person is at the time of making such reference, found."

Commentary

9. Powers of the Tribunal. Every Tribunal shall have the same powers as are vested in a civil court under the Code of Civil Procedure, 1908 (5 of 1908) while trying a suit, in respect of the following matters, namely:

(a) summoning and enforcing the attendance of witnesses and examining them on oath;
(b) discovery and production of any document;
(c) reception of evidence on affidavits;
(d) requisitioning of public records from any court or office;

(e) issuing of any commission for the examination of witnesses.

10. Procedures with respect to references under sub-section(1) of Section 8. On receipt of reference under sub-section(1) of Section 8 [or sub-section(1) of Section 8-A], the Tribunal shall serve on the person named in such reference, in a notice, accompanied by a copy of such reference, calling upon him to make, within a period of thirty days from the date of receipt such notice, such representation with regard to the averments made in the reference, and to produce such evidence as he may think fit in support of his defence:

Provided that if the Tribunal is satisfied that the person aforesaid was prevented by sufficient cause from making his representation and from producing evidence in support of his defence within the said period of thirty days, it may permit him to make his representation and to produce evidence in support of his defence, within such further period, not exceeding thirty days, as it may, by order, specify.

11. Procedures with respect to applications under sub-section(2) of Section 8. 1. On receipt of an application under sub-Section (2) of Section 8, the Tribunal shall issue a notice, accompanied by a copy of the application, to the prescribed authority calling upon it to furnish, after making such inquiry as that authority may deem fit, a report to the Tribunal with regard to the averments made in the application.

2. If, on consideration of the report made by the prescribed authority, the Tribunal is satisfied that:

(a) the person named in the application is not an illegal migrant or that the application is frivolous or vexatious, or has not been made in good faith, the Tribunal shall, after giving the applicant an opportunity to be heard, reject the application;

(b) there are reasonable grounds to believe that the person named in the application is an illegal migrant, the Tribunal shall issue a notice accompanied by a copy of application, to the person named in application calling upon him to make, within thirty days from the date of receipt of the notice, such representation with regard to the averments made in the application and to produce such evidence as he may think fit in support of his defence.

Provided that if the Tribunal is satisfied that the person aforesaid was prevented by sufficient cause from making his representation and from producing evidence in support of his defence within the said period of thirty days, it may permit him to make his representation and to produce evidence in support of his defence, within such further period, not exceeding thirty days, as it may, by order, specify.

12. ***Determination of the question as to whether a person is illegal migrant.*** 1. The Tribunal to which a reference has been made under Section 8 or [Section 8-A] or to which an application has been made under Section 8, shall, after taking such evidence as may be adduced before it and after making such inquiry as it may think fit and after hearing such persons as it may deem appropriate, by order, decide the question as to whether the person named in such reference or application, as the case may be, is or is not an illegal migrant:

Provided that where for the determination of such question in any case decision on any issue renders any decision on any other issue or issues unnecessary, the Tribunal may not decide such other issue or issues.

2. "[Where the members of the Tribunal differ in their opinion on any point, the Chairman of the Tribunal shall state the point or points on which they differ and make a reference to the President of the Appellate Tribunal which exercises jurisdiction in relation to the Tribunal who shall refer the case for hearing on such point or points by a member of another Tribunal under its jurisdiction and such point or points by a member of another Tribunal under its jurisdiction and such point or points shall be decided according to the opinion of that member and such decision shall be deemed to be the decision of the Tribunal."]

3. The Tribunal shall send a copy of every order passed by it to the prescribed authority [or authorities] and to the parties to the reference, or the application, as the case may be.

4. Every order passed under sub-section(1) shall, subject to the decision of the Appellate Tribunal, be final and shall not be called in question in any court.

13. ***Reference and application to be disposed of within six months.*** Every reference made to a Tribunal under [Section or Section 8-A or application made to a Tribunal under Section 8] shall be inquired into as expeditiously as possible and every endeavour shall be made to conclude such inquiry within a period of six months from the date of the service, on the person concerned, of a copy of such reference or application.

14. Appeal. The Central Government, or any person, named on a reference or an application under Section 8, or any person named in a reference under sub-section(2) of that Section [or any person named in a reference under Section 8-A] or applicant under sub-section(2) of that Section may, if it or he is not satisfied with any order made by a Tribunal under Section 12, prefer an appeal to the Appellate Tribunal against such order.

15. Appellate Tribunal. 1. The Central Government may, by notification, establish for each State in which this Act is in force an Appellate Tribunal to be known as the Illegal Migrants (Determination) Appellate Tribunal for deciding appeals preferred under Section 14 against orders made by Tribunals in the State and specify the principal place of sitting of such Appellate Tribunal.

2. No person shall be appointed as a member of an Appellate Tribunal unless he is or has been a Judge of a High Court.

3. An Appellate Tribunal shall consist of as many members, not being less than [two] and more than six, as the Central Government may think fit.

4. The Central Government shall appoint one of the members of an Appellate Tribunal to be the President thereof.

5. An Appellate Tribunal shall sit in its principal place of sitting or any such other place or places as the President thereof may, from time to time, appoint.

6. The powers and functions of an Appellate Tribunal may be exercised and discharged by benches constituted by the President thereof from amongst members thereof [which may either be single Member Benches consisting of not less than two members].

7. The Central Government shall make available to every Appellate Tribunal such staff as may be necessary for the discharge of its functions under this Act.

8. Every memorandum of appeal to an Appellate Tribunal shall be made in such form and in such manner as may be prescribed, and, in the case of an appeal preferred by an applicant under sub-section(2) of Section 8, shall also be accompanied by

such fee, not being less than twenty-five and more than one hundred rupees, as may be prescribed.

9. Every appeal shall be preferred within thirty days from the date on which the order sought to be appealed against was communicated to the appellant:

Provided that the Appellate Tribunal may, if it is satisfied that the appellant was prevented by sufficient cause from preferring the appeal within the said period, admit an appeal after the expiry of the aforesaid period of thirty days.

10. [Every Appellate Tribunal shall have the same powers as are vested in an appellate court under the Code of Civil Procedure, 1908 (5 of 1908) while hearing an appeal.]

16. Order of the Appellate Tribunal. 1. The Appellate Tribunal may, after giving the parties to the appeal a reasonable opportunity of being heard, pass such orders thereon as it may think fit, confirming, modifying or annulling the order appealed against or may remand the case to the Tribunal which had passed such order with such directions to that Tribunal as the Appellate Tribunal may think fit, for fresh determination after taking additional evidence, if necessary.

2. Where an appeal had been heard by the Appellate Tribunal and the members thereof differ in their opinion on any point, the decision on such point shall, where there is a majority, be according to the opinion of such majority, and where there is no majority and the members are equally divided in their opinion, they shall draw up a statement of the facts of the case and the point or points on which they differ in their opinion and make a reference of the point or points or of the appeal, as the case may be, to the President of such Tribunal, and on receipt of such reference, the President of the Tribunal shall arrange for the hearing of point or points, or the appeal by one or more of the members of the Appellate Tribunal, and point or points, or the appeal, as the case may be, shall be decided according to the opinion of the majority of the members of the Appellate Tribunal, who have heard the appeal, including those who had first heard it.

3. The Appellate Tribunal shall send a copy of every order passed by it under sub-section(1) to the parties to the appeal, to the Tribunal concerned and to the prescribed authority or authorities].

4. [xxx] Every order passed under sub-section(1), other than

an order remanding the case, shall be final and no order passed under that sub-section shall be called in question in any court.

17. Power of superintendence by Appellate Tribunals. 1.Every Appellate Tribunal shall have superintendence over all the Tribunals in the State.

2. Without prejudice to the generality of the foregoing provisions the Appellate Tribunal may—

(a) call for returns from any Tribunal;
(b) make general rules and specify forms for regulating the practice and proceedings of Tribunals; and
(c) specify the forms in which books, entries and accounts shall be kept by the officers of Tribunals].

Burden placed on the Petitioner to Establish Commentary that They are Citizens of India

As held in the case of Md. Sahid Ali Fakir v. Union of India, 1992 (1) GLJ 110, both the learned Tribunal and Appellate Tribunal have committed manifestos of law apparent on the face of the record in placing burden on the petitioners to establish that they are citizens of India. When the State came with the complaint that the petitioners migrated into India in 1973 onus was on the complainant to prove the allegation.

Provisions Applicable to All Tribunals

18. Procedure. Subject to the provisions of this Act and the rules made thereunder, every Tribunal and every Appellate Tribunal shall have the power to regulate its own procedure in all matters arising out of the exercise of its powers or for the discharge of its functions.

19. Proceeding before every Tribunal to be judicial proceeding for certain purposes. Every proceeding before a Tribunal or the Appellate Tribunal shall be deemed to be a judicial proceeding within the meaning of Sections 193 and 228, and for the purpose of Section 196 of the Indian Penal Code, 1860 (45 of 1860) and every such Tribunal or Appellate Tribunal, as the case may be, shall be, deemed to be a civil court for the purpose of Section 195 and Chapter XXVI of the Code of Criminal Procedure, 1973 (2 of 1974).

ENFORCEMENT OF THE ORDERS MADE BY THE TRIBUNALS

20. Expulsion of illegal migrant. 1. Where a person has been determined by a Tribunal, or, as the case may be, by the Appellate Tribunal, to be an illegal migrant, the Central Government shall, by order served on such person, direct such person to remove himself from India within such time and by such route as may be specified in the order and may give such further directions in regard to his removal from India as it may consider necessary or expedient.

2. Any police officer not below the rank of a Superintendent of Police shall have such powers as may be necessary, including the power to obtain a bond from any person for the due compliance of an order under sub-section(1) and to arrest such person in the event of his failure to furnish such bond to the satisfaction of such police officer].

MISCELLANEOUS

21. Delegation of Powers. The Central Government may, by notification, direct that the powers and duties conferred or imposed on it by this Act, other than the powers conferred by Section 28, and the powers conferred by this Section, may, subject to such conditions as may be specified in the notification, be exercised or discharged also by—

(a) any officer subordinate to the Central Government;
(b) any State Government or any officer subordinate to that Government.

21A. Power to bind certain persons against whom complaint is made under the Act. Notwithstanding anything contained in any other law for the time being in force, it shall be lawful for a police officer not below the rank of a Superintendent of Police, if he is satisfied that the circumstances so require and for reasons to be recorded in writing, to direct any person against whom a reference or an application has been made under this Act to enter into a bond with or without sureties for making himself available for the inquiry and observance of such restrictions or conditions as may be specified by such police officer.

Provided that if such person fails to enter into such bond he may be arrested and detained in such manner as may be prescribed.

22. Power to give effect to the orders, etc. Any authority empowered by or in pursuance of the provisions of this Act to exercise any power, may, in addition to any other action expressly provided for in this Act, take, or cause to be taken, such steps, and use, or cause to be used; such force, as may in its opinion be reasonably necessary for the effective exercise of such power.

23. *Bar of jurisdiction of civil courts.* Where a Tribunal or Appellate Tribunal has been established for any area for the purpose of determining whether a person is or is not an illegal migrant, no civil court shall have jurisdiction to entertain any question relating to that matter in that area and no injunction or any other order in respect of any action taken by, or before, the Tribunal or Appellate Tribunal in respect of that matter shall be granted or made by any civil court.

24. *Transitory provision.* Where in any suit or other legal proceeding pending, whether in a civil court or in any Tribunal established under any other law for the time being in force, immediately before the commencement of this Act, a question arises as to whether a person is not an illegal migrant, such court or Tribunal shall, without deciding such question, make an order transferring such suit or other legal proceeding to the Tribunal under this Act within the territorial limits of whose jurisdiction such court or other Tribunal is situated and on each transfer such question shall be dealt with by such Tribunal in accordance with the provisions of this Act.

25. *Penalties.* Any person who:

(a) contravenes or attempts to contravene, or abets the contravention of, any order made under Section 20; or

(b) fails to comply with any direction given by any such order; or

(c) harbours any person who has contravened any order made under Section 20 or has failed to comply with any direction given by any such order.

[shall be punishable with imprisonment for a term which shall not be less than one year but which may extend to three years and with fine which shall not be less than two thousand rupees:

Provided that the court may, for adequate and special reasons to be mentioned in the judgement, impose a sentence of imprisonment for a term of less than one year or a fine of less than two thousand rupees].

26. Protection of action taken in good faith. No suit, prosecution or other legal proceeding shall lie against any person for anything which is in good faith done or intended to be done under this Act.

27. Power to remove difficulties. 1. If any difficulty arises in giving effect to the provisions of this Act, the Central Government may, by order to be published in the Official Gazette, make such provisions, not inconsistent with the provisions of this Act, as appear to it to be necessary or expedient for removing the difficulty:

Provided that no such order shall be made after the expiry of a period of two years from the commencement of this Act.

2. Every order made under this section shall, as soon as may be after it is made, be laid before each House of Parliament.

28. Power to make rules. 1. The Central Government may, by notification, make rules to carry out the provisions of this Act.

2. In particular and without prejudice to the generality of the foregoing powers, such rules may provide for all or any of the following matters, namely:

(a) the form and the manner in which an application may be made and the fee which shall accompany such application, as required by sub-section(3) of Section 8;

[(aa) the form and the manner in which an application, and the form in which a declaration, may be made under sub-section(2) of Section 8-A;"]

[(b) the authority or authorities to be prescribed under Sections 11, 12 and 16;]

(c) the form and the manner in which an appeal to the Appellate Tribunal may be preferred and the fee which shall accompany such appeal, as required by sub-section(8) of Section 15;

[(ca) the manner of arrest and detention under the proviso to Section 21-A.]

(d) any other matter which is required to be, or may be, prescribed.

3. Every rule made by the Central Government under this Act shall be laid, as soon as may be after it is made, before each House of Parliament, while it is in session, for a total period of thirty days which may be comprised in one session or in two or more successive sessions, and if, before the expiry of the session immediately following the session or the successive sessions

aforesaid, both Houses agree in making any modification in the rule or both Houses agree that the rule should not be made, the rule shall thereafter have effect only in such modified form or be of no effect, as the case may be, so, however, that any such modification or annulment shall be without prejudice to the validity of anything previously done under that rule.

29. Repeal and saving. 1. The Illegal Migrants (Determination by Tribunals) Ordinance, 1983 (8 of 1983) is hereby repealed.

2. Notwithstanding such repeal, anything done or any action taken under the said Ordinance shall be deemed to have been done or taken under the corresponding provisions of this Act.

Commentary

The object of this Act is to establish Tribunals for determination of persons who are illegal migrants and to expel the illegal migrants from India who has entered into India on or after the 25th of March, 1971, without being in possession of a valid passport or other travel documents or any other lawful authority in that behalf.

THE ILLEGAL MIGRANTS (DETERMINATION BY TRIBUNALS) RULES, 1984

G.S.R. 52 (E).—In exercise of the powers conferred by Section 28 of the Illegal Migrants (Determination by Tribunals) Act, 1983 (39 of 1983) and of all other powers enabling it this behalf, the Central Government hereby makes the following rules, namely:

1. Short title and commencement. 1. These rules may be called the Illegal Migrants (Determination by Tribunals) Rules, 1984.

2. They shall come into force on the date of their publication in the Official Gazette.

2. Definitions. In these rules, unless the context otherwise requires,

(i) "Act" means the Illegal Migrants (determination by Tribunals) Act, 1983 (39 of 1983);
(ii) "Competent authority" means the Central Government and includes, where a State Government or any officer subordinate to the Central Government or a State Government is empowered by notification under Section 21 to exercise and discharge the powers and duties of the Central Government under the sub-section (1) of Section 8, [and sub-section 1 of Section 8-A] such State Government or Officer;
(iii) "Diary" means a diary specified in rule 6;
(iv) "Form" means a form appended to these rules;
(v) "Inquiry Officer" means the officer directed to make inquiry under rule 3;
(vi) "Section" means a section of the Act;
(vii) "State Government" means the Government of a State in which the Act is in force.
(viii) "Superintendent of Police" means a Superintendent of Police under the State Government concerned.

3. Preliminary Inquiry. For the purpose of making a reference in relation to any person under sub-section(1) of [Section 8 and sub-section(1) of Section 8-A] to the Tribunal (including consideration as to whether a question such as is referred to in that Section has arisen in relation to such person:

(a) the competent authority seized of the matter shall require the Superintendent of Police to direct, or
(b) where such competent authority is the Superintendent of

Police himself, the Superintendent of Police shall direct any officer not below the rank of a sub-inspector of Police to make an inquiry.

4. ***Inquiry Officer to proceed with the inquiry.*** An Inquiry Officer, who is directed to make an inquiry under rule 3 in relation to a person as referred to therein, shall call upon that person to give information as regards the particulars in Form I.

5. ***Power to elicit information.*** An inquiry Officer may elicit information from any person who, in his opinion appears to be acquainted with the facts and circumstances of the case in relation to which he is making inquiry.

6. ***Diary to be kept by an Inquiry Officer.*** Every Inquiry Officer making inquiry under the rules shall day by day enter details of his inquiry in a diary kept for the purpose setting forth the time at which any information reached him, or as the case may be ascertained by him, the time at which he began and closed his inquiry, the place or places, visited by him and the statement of the circumstances ascertained through such inquiry.

Note: Every diary kept under this rule shall be in the form of a diary as is referred to in sub-section(1) of Section 172, the Code of Criminal Procedure, 1973 (2 of 1974).

7. ***Submission of Report.*** On completion of the inquiry, the Inquiry Officer shall submit the report in Form II along with the diary to the immediate superior officer who shall endorse the comments thereon and submit it to the Screening Committee referred to in Rule 8.

8. ***Recommendation of the Screening Committee.*** 1. There shall be a Screening Committee at every sub-division level where the Tribunals are established and shall consist of two members one of whom shall be Sub-Divisional Magistrate, the other a Police Officer not below the rank of Deputy Superintendent of Police, in the sub-division concerned.

2. The Screening Committee shall after solemnising the information contained in Form II and diary, make its recommendations to the Superintendent of Police as to whether the person mentioned in the report is or is not an illegal migrant.

3. The recommendations of the Screening Committee shall be signed by both the members of the Committee.

9. ***Procedure for making reference to Tribunals.*** If, on the

recommendation of the Screening Committee and such further information as the competent authority may call for, it appears to that authority that a question arises as to whether any person is or is not on illegal migrant, that authority shall make a reference to the Tribunal for its decision thereon, alongwith the following material namely:

(i) The Diary;
(ii) Report of the Inquiry Officer containing the endorsement of his immediate superior officer;
(iii) Recommendations of the Screening Committee;
(iv) Such further information as that authority may consider necessary.

10. Applications to the Tribunals. Every application to the Tribunal under sub-section(2) of Section 8 shall be made in form III.

[10-A. Application to the Central Government. Every application to the Central Government under sub-section(2) of Section 8-A shall be made in Form V.

10-B. Every declaration under sub-section(2) of Section 8-A shall be made in Form VI.]

11. Application Fee. Every application shall be accompanied by a fee of (ten) rupees to be paid in the form of court fee stamp.

12. Prescribed Authority under Section 11. The Superintendent of Police shall be the authority for the purposes of Section 11.

[12-A. Prescribed Authority. The Chief Election Officer of the State and the District Election Officer and the Superintendent of Police having jurisdiction in the area shall be the authorities for the purposes of sub-section(3) of Section 12 and sub-section(3) of Section 16.]

13. Procedure to be followed in respect of notices issued under Section 11. 1. The Superintendent of Police may without prejudice to the powers conferred on him under sub-section(1) of Section 11 so far as may be, follow the procedure specified in rules 3 to 8 while making an inquiry in respect of a notice issued to him by the Tribunal under that sub-section.

14. Procedure for filing Appeals. 1. An appeal to the Appellate Tribunal shall be made in Form IV.

2. The particulars and grounds of appeal and the form of verification appended thereto shall be signed:

(a) in the case of Central Government, by any officer subordinate to the Central Government or any officer subordinate to the State Government to whom the Central Government has delegated its powers:

(b) in the case of any person named in a reference or an application under sub-section(2) of Section 8, by the person himself; and

(c) in the case of a person referred to in sub-section(2) of Section 8, by the person himself.

15. Fee for Appeals. Every memorandum of appeal to the Appellate Tribunal shall be accompanied by a fee of twenty-five to be paid in the form of court fee stamp.

16. Date of presentation of Appeals. The duly authorised officer of the Appellate Tribunal shall endorse on every copy of the memorandum of appeal the date on which it is presented and shall sign the endorsement.

17. Contents of Memorandum of Appeal. Every appeal shall set forth, concisely and under distinct heads, the grounds of appeal without any argument or narrative; and such grounds shall be numbered consecutively.

18. What to Accompany Memorandum of Appeal. Every memorandum of appeal shall be submitted in duplicate and shall be accompanied by two copies (at least one of which shall be a copy certified by the officer authorised by the Tribunals) of the order appealed against.

19. Rejection or Amendment of Memorandum of Appeal. The Appellate Tribunal may reject a memorandum of appeal, if it is not in the prescribed form or return it for being amended within such time as it is not in the prescribed form or return it for being amended within such time as it may allow and on presentation after such amendment, the memorandum shall be endorsed in the manner specified in Rule 16.

[***20. The manner of arrest and detention under Section 21-A.*** 1. The person who fails to enter into a bond with or without sureties or making himself available for the inquiry and observance of such restrictions or conditions as may be specified by a Police Officer not below the rank of Superintendent of Police shall be arrested in accordance with the provisions of Section 46 and 49 of Code of

Criminal Procedure 1973 (2 of 1974). The arrest may be made by any Police officer on the orders of the Superintendent of Police in writing.

2. After arrest, as soon as possible but not later than 24 hours exclusive of the time necessary for the journey from the place of arrest to the place of Tribunal the person shall be forwarded in custody to the Tribunal having jurisdiction in the case who may authorise the detention of the person till the reference or an application filed against him Section 8 or Section 8-A is disposed of:

Provided that he shall be released if at any time he is prepared to and does furnish bond with or without sureties as directed by the Tribunal.]

FORM I

(See Rule 4)

Particulars in relation to which information may be ascertained under Rule 4 by the Inquiry Officer.

1. Name of the person
2. Father's name
3. Marital status
4. Particulars of spouse
5. Address in the country of origin:
   Village........................ Police Station........................
   District....................... Country.................................
6. Address in India:
   Village........................ Police Station........................
   District....................... State ....
7. Physical description
   (i) Age
   (ii) Sex
   (iii) Height
   (iv) Identity mark
   (v) Complexion etc.
8. Profession/occupation, if any, with details,
9. Name(s) and age, date of birth and place of birth of other member (s) of the family:
   (i) Wife/wives/husband
   (ii) Son(s)
   (iii) Daughter(s)
   (iv) Brother(s)/Sister(s)

(v) Other(s)/Dependent(s)

10. Does the person hold any passport issued by any foreign country? If so furnish particulars.
11. What are the reasons for leaving the person's country of origin.
12. If the person has entered into India without a passport, how the person entered India?
(Name of Village, District from which the person entered), Date of entry
13. Does the person own any land/house in India?
    (a) If so, since when and where?
    (Furnish particulars of Public records).
14. Does the person claim to be a share cropper?
If the person is a share cropper, please mention details of the places, landlord, etc.
    (a) Is there any evidence in support of the person's claim that the person is a share cropper under any of the Croppers Tenancy Act?
    (b) Is the person an agricultural labourer?
    If so, in whose land or house he/she is staying now? Furnish particulars).
15. Is the person an employee of the Government/Private company etc.
16. If the answer to question 15 is yes, then give the name and address of the employer.

Date: Signature of the Inquiry Officer.
Place:

FORM II

(See Rules 7 and 8)

REPORT OF THE INQUIRY OFFICER

1. Name of the person
2. Father's name
3. Marital status
4. Particulars of spouse
    (a) Name
    (b) Nationality
5. Address in the country of origin:
Village........................ Police Station........................
District........................ Country...................................

6. Address in India:
   Village........................ Police station........................
   District........................ Country..................................
7. Physical description
   - (i) Age
   - (ii) Sex
   - (iii) Height
   - (iv) Identity mark
   - (v) Complexion etc.
8. Profession/occupation, if any, with details.
9. Name(s) and age, date of birth and place of birth of other member(s) of the family:
   - (i) Wife/wives/husband
   - (ii) Son(s)
   - (iii) Daughter(s)
   - (iv) Brother(s)/Sister(s)
   - (v) Other(s)/Dependent(s)
10. Does the person hold any passport issued by any foreign country? If so, furnish particulars.
11. What are the reasons for leaving the person's country of origin?
12. If the person has entered into India without a passport, how the person entered India?
    (Name of Village, District from which the person entered),
    Date of entry
13. Does the person own any land/house in India?
    If so, since when and where?
    (Furnish particulars of Public records).
14. Does the person claim to be a share cropper?
    If the person is a share cropper, please mention details of the places, landlord, etc.
    - (a) Is there any evidence in support of the person's claim that the person is a share cropper under any of the Croppers Tenancy Act?
    - (b) Is the person an agricultural labourer?
      (if so, in whose land or house he is staying now? Furnish particulars).

15. Is the person an employee of the Government/Private company etc.
16. Does the person's name appear in the electoral rolls prepared prior to 25th day of March, 1971?
(When did it appear? Furnish particulars)
17. Does the person's name appear in any public records, such as Panchayat Family Registers, Refugees Register, etc.*
(*The list is only illustrative and not exhaustive).
18. Is the person an 'illegal migrant' within the meaning of Section 3 (c) of the Illegal Migrants (Determination by Tribunals) Act, 1983, that is, does the person satisfy each of the following conditions, namely:

    (i) Person has entered into India on or after the 25th day of March, 1971;
    (ii) Person is a foreigner;
    (iii) Person entered into India without being in possession cf a valid passport or other travel documents or any other lawful authority in that behalf.

19. What are the pleas of the person? Does the person—

    (a) admit that he is an illegal migrant.
    (b) claim to be an Indian citizen.
    (c) a foreigner but entered into India after prior to 25th day of March, 1971?

20. What is the evidence on which the person seeks to rely in support of plea (Furnish particulars).
21. Names with addresses of persons from whom information in respect of person(s) interrogated is received.
22. Details of the documentary, oral and other evidence (list to be attached).
23. Finding of the Inquiry Officer (with his recommendations)
Date........................ (Signature and designation of the Inquiry Officer)
Place......................
24. Comments of the Immediate Superior Officer (Signature and designation of the Immediate Superior Officer)

25. Recommendations of the Screening Committee
    Date........................ (Signature of SDM and
    Place...................... DSP)
26. Conclusion of the Superintendent of Police
    Date........................ (Signature of the Superintendent
    Place...................... of Police)

FORM III

(See Rule 10)

APPLICATION TO THE TRIBUNAL UNDER SECTION 8 (2)

1. Name of the applicant
2. Address
3. Place of birth, with date, month and year
4. Profession/Occupation with details
5. Name and address of the person in relation to whom the application is made
6. Did the person, in relation to whom the application is made, enter into India on or after the 25th day of March, 1971? If so,

    (a) the date of his entry into India as per knowledge of the applicant.
    (b) whether he/she is a foreigner?
    (c) whether he/she entered India without being in possession of a valid passport or travel document or any lawful authority in that behalf.
    [(d) Whether he/she is staying at place within the jurisdiction of the same police station in which the place of residence of applicant is situated.
    (e) Since when and where he/she has been staying in the above place.

7. Names of person who have sworn the affidavits accompanying the application.
8. Full addresses of the persons swearing the affidavits.

Sd/-......................

Designation

Name of the applicant

I declare that what is stated in the application is true to the best of my information and belief.

I, therefore, request for decision as to whether Shri/ Smt.................... whose particulars are given in this application, is or is not an illegal migrant.

Sd/-

FORM IV

(See Rule 14)

MEMORANDUM OF APPEAL TO THE APPELLATE TRIBUNAL UNDER SECTION 14

Before the Illegal Migrants (Determination) Appellate Tribunal, ... (Name of the Headquarter of the Appellate Tribunal).

Particulars

1. Name and full address of the appellant
2. Full details including the name of the Tribunal, number and date of communication of the order appealed against.
3. Address to which notice may be sent to the appellant.
4. Relief claimed in appeal.

GROUNDS OF APPEAL

1.
2.
3.
4.
5.

(Signed)
Authorised representative of
appellant, if any.

(Signed)
Appellant

VERIFICATION

I, ..., the appellant, do hereby declare that what is stated above is true to the best of my information and belief verified today, the .... day of .... 200 .

Signed
(Appellant)

FORM V

(See Rule 10A)

APPLICATION TO THE CENTRAL GOVERNMENT UNDER SECTION 8-A (2)

1. Name of the applicant.
2. Full address.
3. Place of birth with date, month and year.
4. Profession/Occupation with details.
5. Name and address of the person in relation to whom the application is made.
6. Did the person, in relation to whom the application is made, enter into India on or after the 25th day of March, 1971? If so,
   - (a) the date of his entry into India as per knowledge of the applicant
   - (b) whether he/she is a foreigner?
   - (c) whether he/she entered India without being in possession of a valid passport or travel documents or any lawful authority in that behalf?
   - (d) what is the approximate distance between the place of residence of the applicant and the place of residence of the person named in column 5 above.
   - (e) since when and where he/she has been staying in the above place.
7. Evidence in possession of applicant.
   - (a) Documentary (i)
(ii)
(iii)
   - (b) Oral (i)
(ii)
(iii)
8. Name of the person who has given the declaration accompanying the application.
9. Full address of the person making the declaration.
10. The number and details of applications under Section 8-A made by the applicant till to date:

Sl. No.	Date of application	Name and addresses of	To whom made

the person named in
column 5 of the
application

I declare that what is stated in the application is true to the best of my information and belief.

I further declare that including this application I have not made more than 10 such applications to the Central Government or authorities duly empowered in this behalf.

I am aware that in the event of this application being found as false or made with a view to cause vexation to the person named in this application or any member of his family, I am liable to be proceeded against in accordance with law for giving false evidence.

I, therefore, request that my application may be referred to the Tribunal for decision as to whether Shri/Smt........................., whose particulars are given in this application is or is not on illegal migrant. I would be willing to produce the evidence in my possession during any inquiry that may be undertaken by the Central Government or authority duly empowered by it as well as depose on oath before the Tribunal as to the facts stated in the application.

Place.........................
Date..........................
Made before me
....
(Gazetted Officer
Executive Magistrate
Judicial Magistrate) Signature/T.I. of the applicant.
Name of the applicant.................

FORM VI

(See Rule 10-B)

DECLARATION TO BE MADE UNDER SUB-SECTION(2) OF SECTION 8-A

I .... , son of ...., resident of .... (Village .... (Police Station) do hereby declare as follows:

That the particulars mentioned in this application dated ...., by Shri ...., son of Shri ...., resident of .... are true to my knowledge, information and belief and that I am residing within the jurisdiction of .... (name of revenue sub-division) revenue sub-division in which the applicant also resides.

That including this, I have to date made .... (state number) such declarations.

I am aware that in the event of this declaration being found as false or made with a view to cause vexation to the person named in this application or any member of his family, I am liable to be proceeded against in accordance with the law for giving false evidence.

I would be willing to produce the evidence in my possession during any inquiry that may be undertaken by the Central Government or authority duly empowered by it as well as depose on oath before the Tribunal as to the facts stated in the application.

Place.........................

Date..........................

Made before me

....

(Gazetted Officer
Executive Magistrate
Judicial Magistrate)

Signature/T.I. of the declarant.
Name in full ....
Full postal address...................
....
....
....

THE PERSONS WITH DISABILITIES (EQUAL OPPORTUNITIES, PROTECTION OF RIGHTS AND FULL PARTICIPATION) ACT, 1995

Ministry of Law, Justice and Company Affairs (Legislative Department)

(No. 1 of 1996)

[New Delhi, Pausa 11, 1917 (Saka)]

1st January, 1996

An Act to give effect to the Proclamation on the Full Participation and Equality of the People with Disabilities in the Asian and Pacific Region.

Whereas the Meeting to Launch the Asian and Pacific Decade of Disabled Persons 1993–2002 convened by the Economic and Social Commission for Asia and Pacific held at Beijing on 1st to 5th December 1992, adopted the Proclamation on the Full Participation and Equality of the People with Disabilities in the Asian and Pacific Region;

And Whereas India is a signatory to the said Proclamation;

And Whereas it is considered necessary to implement the Proclamation aforesaid.

Be it enacted by Parliament in the Forty-sixth Year of the Republic of India as follows:

PRELIMINARY

1. Short title, extent and commencement. 1. This Act may be called the Persons With Disabilities (Equal Opportunities, Protection of Rights and Full Participation) Act 1995.

2. It extends to the whole of India except the State of Jammu and Kashmir.

3. It shall come into force on such date as the Central Government may, by notification, appoint.

2. *Definitions.* In this Act, unless the context otherwise requires:

(a) "appropriate Government" means

(i) in relation to the Central Government or any establishment wholly or substantially financed by that Government, or any local authority, other than a Cantonment Board constituted under the Cantonment Act, 1924, the Central Government; 2 of 1924

(ii) in relation to State Government or any establishment

wholly or substantially financed by that Government, or any local authority, other than a Cantonment Board, the State Government;

(iii) in respect of the Central Coordination Committee and the Central Executive Committee, the Central Government;

(iv) in respect of the State Coordination Committee and the State Executive Committee, the State Government;

(b) "blindness" refers to a condition where a person suffers from any of the following conditions, namely:

(i) total absence of sight; or

(ii) visual acuity not exceeding 6/60 or 20/200 (Snellen) in the better eye with correcting lenses; or

(iii) limitation of the field of vision subtending an angle 20 degree or worse;

(c) "Central Coordination Committee" means the Central Coordination Committee constituted under sub-section(1) of Section 3;

(d) "Central Executive Committee" means the Central Executive Committee constituted under sub-section(1) of Section 9;

(e) "cerebral palsy" means a group of non-progressive conditions of a person characterised by abnormal motor control posture resulting from brain insult or injuries occurring in the pre-natal, peri-natal or infant period of development.

(f) "Chief Commissioner" means the Chief Commissioner appointed under sub-section(1) of Section 57;

(g) "Commissioner" means the Commissioner appointed under sub-section(1) of Section 60;

(h) "competent authority" means the authority appointed under Section 50;

(i) "disability means:

(i) blindness;

(ii) low vision;

(iii) leprosy-cured;

(iv) hearing impairment;

(v) locomotor disability;

(vi) mental retardation;

(vii) mental illness;

(j) "employer" means,

(i) in relation to Government, the authority notified by the Head of the Department in this behalf or where no such authority is notified, the Head of the Department; and

(ii) in relation to an establishment, the chief executive officer of that establishment;

(k) "establishment" means a corporation established by or under a Central, Provincial or State Act, or an authority or a body owned or controlled or aided by the Government or a local authority or a Government company as defined in Section 617 of the Companies Act, 1956 and includes Departments of a Government;

(l) "hearing impairment" means loss of sixty decibels or more in the better year in the conversational range of frequencies;

(m) "institution for persons with disabilities" means an institution for the reception, care, protection, education, training, rehabilitation or any other service of persons with disabilities;

(n) "leprosy cured person" means any person who has been cured of leprosy but is suffering from:

(i) loss of sensation in hands or feet as well as loss of sensation and paresis in the eye and eye-lid with no manifest deformity;

(ii) manifest deformity and paresis but having sufficient mobility in their hands and feet to enable them to engage in normal economic activity;

(iii) extreme physical deformity is well as advanced age which prevents him from undertaking any gainful occupation and the expression "leprosy cured" shall be construed accordingly;

(o) "locomotor disability" means disability of the bones, joints or muscles leading to substantial restriction of the movement of the limbs or any form of cerebral palsy;

(p) "medical authority" means any hospital or institution specified for the purposes of this Act by notification by the appropriate Government;

(q) "mental illness" means any mental disorder other than retardation;

(r) "mental retardation" means a condition of arrested or incomplete development of mind of a person which is specially characterised by subnormality of intelligence;

(s) "notification" means a notification published in the Official Gazette;

(t) "person with disability" means a person suffering from not less than forty per cent of any disability as certified by a medical authority;

(u) "person with low vision" means a person with impairment of visual functioning even after treatment or standard refractive correction but who uses or is potentially capable of using vision for the planning or execution of a task with appropriate assistive device;

(v) "prescribed" means prescribed by rules made under this Act;

(w) "rehabilitation" refers to a process aimed at enabling persons with disabilities to reach and maintain their optimal, physical, sensory, intellectual, psychiatric or social functional levels;

(x) "Special Employment Exchange" means any office or place established and maintained by the Government for the collection and furnishing of information, either by keeping of registers or otherwise, respecting

  (i) persons who seek to engage employees from amongst the persons suffering from disabilities;

  (ii) persons with disability who seek employment;

  (iii) vacancies to which person with disability seeking employment may be appointed;

(y) "State Coordination Committee" means the State Coordination Committee constituted under sub-section(1) of Section 13;

(z) "State Executive Committee" means the State Executive Committee constituted under sub-section(1) of Section 19.

THE CENTRAL COORDINATION COMMITTEE

3. ***The Central Coordination Committee.*** 1. The Central Government shall by notification constitute a body to be known as the Central Coordination Committee to exercise the powers conferred on, and to perform the functions assigned to it, under this Act.

2. The Central Coordination Committee shall consist of

(a) The Minister in charge of the Department of Welfare in the Central Government, Chairperson, *ex officio;*

(b) The Minister of State in-charge of the department of Welfare in the Central Government, Vice-Chairperson, *ex-officio;*

(c) Secretaries to the Government of India in-charge of the Departments of Welfare, Education, Woman and Child Development, Expenditure, Personnel, Training and Public Grievances, Health, Rural Development, Industrial Development, Urban Affairs and Employment, Science and Technology, Legal Affairs, Public Enterprises, Members, *ex officio;*

(d) Chief Commissioner, Member, *ex officio*

(e) Chairman Railway Board, Member, *ex officio;*

(f) Director General of Labour, Employment and Training, Member *ex officio;*

(g) Director, National Council for Educational Research and Training, Member, *ex officio;*

(h) three Members of Parliament, of whom two shall be elected by the House of the People and one by the Council of States, Members;

(i) three persons to be nominated by the Central Government to represent the interests, which in the opinion of that Government ought to be represented, Members;

(j) Directors of the—

 (i) National Institute for the Visually Handicapped, Dehradun;

 (ii) National Institute for the Mentally Handicapped, Secunderabad;

 (iii) National Institute for the Orthopaedically Handicapped, Kolkata;

 (iv) Ali Yavar Jung National Institute for Hearing Handicapped, Mumbai, Members, *ex office;*

(k) four Members to be nominated by the Central Government by rotation to represent the States and the Union territories in such manner as may be prescribed by the Central Government;

Provided that no appointment under this clause shall be made except on the recommendation of the State Government or, as the case may be, the Union territory.

(l) five persons as far as practicable, being persons with disabilities, to represent non-governmental organisations or associations which are concerned with disabilities, to be nominated by the Central Government, one from each area of disability, Members:

Provided that while nominating persons under this clause, the Central Government shall nominate at least one woman and one person belonging to Scheduled Castes or Scheduled Tribes;

(m) Joint Secretary to the Government of India in the Ministry of Welfare dealing with the welfare of the handicapped, Member-Secretary, *ex-officio*.

3. The Office of the Member of the Central Coordination Committee shall not disqualify its holder for being chosen as or for being a Member of either House of Parliament.

4. *Term of Office of Members.* 1. Save as otherwise provided by or under this Act a Member of Central Coordination Committee nominated under clause (i) or clause (1) of sub-section(2) of Section 3 shall hold office for a term of three years from the date of his nomination;

Provided that such a Member shall, notwithstanding the expiration of his term, continue to hold office until his successor enters upon his office.

2. The term of office of an *ex-officio* Member shall come to an end as soon as he ceases to hold the office by virtue of which he was so nominated.

3. The Central Government may if it thinks fit remove any Member nominated under clause (i) or clause (1) of sub-section(2) of Section 3, before the expiry of his term of office after giving him a reasonable opportunity of showing cause against the same.

4. A Member nominated under clause (i) or clause (1) of sub-section(2) of Section 3 may at any time resign his office by writing under his hand addressed to the Central Government and the seat of the said Member shall thereupon become vacant.

5. A casual vacancy in the Central Coordination Committee shall be filled by a fresh nomination and the person nominated to fill the vacancy shall hold office only for the remainder of the term for which the Member in whose place he was so nominated.

6. A Member nominated under clause (i) or clause (1) sub-section(2) of Section 3 shall be eligible for renomination.

7. Members nominated under clause (i) or clause (1) of sub-section(2) of Section 3 shall receive such allowances as may be prescribed by the Central Government.

5. Disqualifications. 1. No person shall be a Member of the Central Coordination Committee, who:

(a) is, or at any time has been, adjudged insolvent or has suspended payment of his debts or has compounded with his creditors, or
(b) is of unsound mind and stands so declared by a competent court, or
(c) is or has been convicted of an offence which, in the opinion of the Central Government, involves moral turpitude, or
(d) is or at any time has been convicted of an offence under this Act, or
(e) has so abused in the opinion of the Central Government his position as a Member as to render his continuance in the Central Coordination Committee detrimental to the interests of the general public.

2. No order of removal shall be made by the Central Government under this Section unless the Member concerned has been given a reasonable opportunity of showing cause against the same.

3. Notwithstanding anything contained in sub-section(1) or sub-section(6) of Section 4, a Member who has been removed under this Section shall not be eligible for renomination as a Member.

6. Vacation of seats by Members. If a Member of the Central Coordination Committee becomes subject to any of the disqualifications specified in Section 5, his seat shall become vacant.

7. Meetings of the Central Coordination Committee. The Central Coordination Committee shall meet at least once in every six months and shall observe such rules of procedure in regard to the transaction of business at its meetings as may be prescribed by the Central Government.

8. Functions of the Central Coordination Committee. 1. Subject to the provisions of this Act, the function of the Central Coordination Committee shall be to serve as the national focal point on disability matter and facilitate the continuous evolution of a comprehensive policy towards solving the problems faced by persons with disabilities.

2. In particular and without prejudice to the generality of the foregoing, the Central Coordination Committee may perform all or any of the following functions, namely:

(a) review and coordinate the activities of all the Departments of Government and other Governmental and non-Governmental Organisations which are dealing with matters relating to persons with disabilities;
(b) develop a national policy to address issues faced by persons with disabilities;
(c) advise the Central Government on the formulation of policies, programmes, legislation and projects with respect to disability;
(d) take up the cause of persons with disabilities with the concerned authorities and the international organisations with a view to provide for schemes and projects for the disabled in the national plans and other programmes and policies evolved by the international agencies;
(e) review in consultation with the donor agencies their funding policies from the perspective of their impact on persons with disabilities;
(f) take such other steps to ensure barrier free environment in public places, work places, public utilities, schools and other institutions;
(g) monitor and evaluate the impact of policies and programmes designed for achieving equality and full participation of persons with disabilities;
(h) to perform such other functions as may be prescribed by the Central Government.

9. Central Executive Committee 1. The Central Government shall constitute a Committee to be known as the Central Executive Committee to perform the functions assigned to it under this Act.

2. The Central Executive Committee shall consist of

(a) the Secretary to the Government of India in the Ministry of Welfare, Chairperson, *ex-officio;*
(b) the Chief Commissioner, Member, *ex-officio;*
(c) the Director-General for Health Services, Member, *ex-officio;*

(d) the Director-General for Employment and Training, Member, *ex-officio;*

(e) six persons not below the rank of a Joint Secretary to the Government of India, to represent the Ministries or Departments of Rural Development, Education, Welfare, Personnel Public Grievances and Pension and Urban Affairs and Employment, Science and Technology, Members, *ex-officio;*

(f) the Financial Advisor, Ministry of Welfare in the Central Government, Member, *ex-officio;*

(g) Advisor (Tariff) Railway Board, Member, *ex-officio;*

(h) four members to be nominated by the Central Government, by rotation, to represent the State Governments and the Union Territories in such manner as may be prescribed by the Central Government;

(i) one person to be nominated by the Central Government to represent the interest, which in the opinion of the Central Government ought to be represented, Member;

(j) five persons, as far as practicable, being persons with disabilities, to represent non-governmental organisations or associations which are concerned with disabilities, to be nominated by the Central Government, one from each area of disability, Member:

Provided that while nominating persons under this clause, the Central Government shall nominate at least one woman and one person belonging to Scheduled Castes or Scheduled Tribes;

(k) Joint Secretary to the Government of India in the Ministry of Welfare dealing with the welfare of the handicapped, Member-Secretary, *ex-officio.*

3. Members nominated under clause (i) and clause (j) of sub-section(2) shall receive such allowances as may be prescribed by the Central Government.

4. A Member nominated under clause (i) or clause (j) of sub-section(2) may at any time resign his office by writing under his hand addressed to the Central Government and the seat of the said Member shall thereupon become vacant.

10. Functions of the Central Executive Committee 1. The Central Executive Committee shall be the executive body of the

Central Coordination Committee and shall be responsible for carrying out the decisions of the Central Coordination Committee.

2. Without prejudice to the provisions of sub-section(1), the Central Executive Committee shall also perform such other functions as may be delegated to it by the Central -Coordination Committee.

11. Meetings of the Central Executive Committee. The Central Executive Committee shall meet at least once in three months and shall observe such rules of procedure in regard to the transaction of business at its meetings as may be prescribed by the Central Government.

12. Temporary association of persons with Central Executive Committee for particular purposes. 1. The Central Executive Committee may associate with itself in such manner and for such purposes as may be prescribed by the Central Government any person whose assistance or advice it may desire to obtain in performing any of its functions under this Act.

2. A person associated with the Central Executive Committee under sub-section(1) for any purpose shall have the right to take part in the discussions of the Central Executive Committee relevant to that purpose, but shall not have a right to vote at a meeting of the said Committee, and shall not be a member for any other purpose.

3. A person associated with the said Committee under sub-section(1) for any purpose shall be paid such fees and allowances, for attending meetings and for attending to any other work of the said Committee, as may be prescribed by the Central Government.

THE STATE COORDINATION COMMITTEE

13. State Coordination Committee. 1. Every State Government shall, by notification, constitute a body to be known as the State Coordination Committee to exercise the powers conferred on and to perform the function assigned to it, under this Act.

2. The State Coordination Committee shall consist of:

(a) The Minister in-charge of the Department of Social Welfare in the State Government, Chairperson, *ex-officio;*

(b) The Minister of State in-charge of the Department of Social Welfare, if any, Vice-Chairperson, *ex-officio;*

(c) Secretaries to the State Government in-charge of the Departments of Welfare, Education, Woman and Child Development, Expenditure, Personnel Training and Public Grievances, Health, Rural Development, Industrial Development, Urban Affairs and Employment, Science and Technology, Public Enterprises, by whatever name called, Members, *ex officio;*

(d) Secretary of any other Department which the State Government considers necessary, Member, *ex officio;*

(e) Chairman Bureau of Public Enterprises (by whatever name called) Member, *ex officio;*

(f) Five persons, as far as practicable, being persons with disabilities, to represent non-governmental organisations or associations which are concerned with disabilities, to be nominated by the State Government, one from each area of disability, Members:

Provided that while nominating persons under this clause, the State Government shall nominate at least one woman and one person belonging to Scheduled Castes or Scheduled Tribes;

(g) three Members of State Legislature, of whom two shall be elected by the Legislative Assembly and one by the Legislative Council, if any;

(h) three persons to be nominated by that State Government to represent agriculture, industry or trade or any other interest, which in the opinion of State Government ought to be represented, Members, *ex officio;*

(i) the Commissioner, Member, *ex officio;*

(j) Secretary to the State Government dealing with the welfare of the handicapped, Member-secretary, *ex-officio.*

3. Notwithstanding anything contained in this Section, no State Coordination Committee shall be constituted for a Union Territory and in relation to a Union Territory, the Central Coordination Committee shall exercise the functions and perform the functions of a State Coordination Committee for the Union Territory:

Provided that in relation to a Union Territory, the Central Coordination Committee may delegate all or any of its powers and functions under this sub-section to such person or body of persons as the Central Government may specify.

14. Terms and Conditions of Service of Members. 1. Save as otherwise provided by or under this Act, a Member of a State Coordination Committee nominated under clause (f) or clause (h) of sub-section(2) of Section 13 shall hold office for a term of three years from the date of his nomination:

Provided that such a Member shall, notwithstanding the expiration of his term, continue to hold office until his successor enters upon his office.

2. The term of office of an *ex-officio* Member shall come to an end as soon as he ceases to hold the office by virtue of which he was so nominated.

3. The State Government may, if it thinks fit, remove any Member nominated under clause (f) or clause (h) of sub-section(2) of Section 13 before the expiry of his term of office after giving him a reasonable opportunity of showing cause against the same.

4. A Member nominated under clause (f) or clause (h) of sub-section(2) of Section 13 may, at any time, resign his office by writing under his hand addressed to the State Government and the seat of the said Member shall thereupon become vacant.

5. A casual vacancy in the State Coordination Committee shall be filled by a fresh nomination and the person nominated to fill the vacancy shall hold office only for the remainder of the term for which the Member in whose place he was so nominated.

6. A Member nominated under clause (f) and clause (h) of sub-section(2) of Section 13 shall be eligible for renomination.

7. Members nominated under clause (f) and clause (h) of sub-section(2) of Section 13 shall receive such allowances as may be prescribed by the State Government.

15. Disqualifications. 1. No person shall be a Member of the State Coordination Committee, who:

(a) is, or at any time, has been adjudged insolvent or has suspended payment of his debts or has compounded with his creditors, or

(b) is of unsound mind and stands so declared by a competent court, or

(c) is or has been convicted of an offence which in the opinion of the State Government involves moral turpitude, or

(d) is or at any time has been convicted of an offence under this Act, or

(e) has so abused, in the opinion of the State Government, his position as a member as to render his continuance in the State Coordination Committee detrimental to the interests of the general public.

2. No order of removal shall be made by the State Government under this Section unless the Member concerned has been given a reasonable opportunity of showing cause against the same.

3. Notwithstanding anything contained in sub-section(1) or sub-section(6) of Section 14, a member who has been removed under this Section shall not be eligible for renomination as a Member.

16. Vacation of Seats. If a Member of the State Coordination Committee becomes subject to any of the disqualifications specified in Section 15, his seat shall become vacant.

17. Meetings of the State Coordination Committee. The State Coordination Committee shall meet at least once in every six months and shall observe such rules of procedure in regard to the transaction of business at its meetings as may be prescribed.

18. Functions of the State Coordination Committee. 1. Subject to the provisions of this Act, the function of the State Coordination Committee shall be to serve as the state focal point on disability matters and facilitate the continuous evolution of a comprehensive policy towards solving the problems faced by persons with disabilities.

2. In particular and without prejudice to the generality of the foregoing function the State Coordination Committee may, within the state perform all or any of the following functions, namely:

(a) review and coordinate the activities of all the departments of Government and other Governmental and non-Governmental Organisations which are dealing with matters relating to persons with disabilities;
(b) develop a State policy to address issues faced by persons with disabilities;
(c) advise the State Government on the formulation of policies, programmes, legislation and projects with respect to disability;
(d) review, in consultation with the donor agencies, their funding policies from the perspective of their impact on persons with disabilities;

(e) take such other steps to ensure barrier free environment in public places, work places, public utilities schools and other institutions;

(f) monitor and evaluate the impact of policies and programmes designed for achieving equality and full participation of persons with disabilities:

(g) to perform such other functions as may be prescribed by the State Government.

19. State Executive Committee. 1. The State Executive Committee shall constitute a committee to be known as the State Executive Committee to perform the functions assigned to it under this Act.

2. The State Executive Committee shall consist of:

(a) the Secretary, Department of Social Welfare, Chairperson, *ex officio;*

(b) the Commissioner, Member, *ex officio;*

(c) nine persons not below the rank of a Joint Secretary to the State Government, to represent the Departments of Health, Finance, Rural Development, Education, Welfare, Personnel Public Grievances, Urban Affairs, Labour and Employment, Science and Technology, Members, *ex-officio;*

(d) one person to be nominated by the State Government to represent the interest, which in the opinion of the State Government ought to be represented, Member;

(e) five persons, as far as practicable being persons with disabilities, to represent non-governmental organisations or associations which are concerned with disabilities, to be nominated by the State Government, one from each area of disability, Members:

Provided that while nominating persons under this clause, the State Government shall nominate at least one woman and one person belonging to Scheduled Castes or Scheduled Tribes;

(f) Joint Secretary dealing with the disability division in the Department of Welfare, Member-secretary, *ex-officio.*

3. Members nominated under clause (d) and clause (e) of sub-section(2) shall receive such allowances as may be prescribed by the State Government.

4. A Member nominated under clause (d) or clause (e) may

at any time resign his office by writing under his hand addressed to the State Government and the seat of the said Member shall thereupon become vacant.

20. *Functions of the State Executive Committee.* 1. The State Executive Committee shall be the executive body of the State Coordination Committee and shall be responsible for carrying out the decisions of the State Coordination Committee.

2. Without prejudice to the provisions of sub-section(1), the State Executive Committee shall also perform such other functions as may be delegated to it by the State Coordination Committee.

21. *Meetings of the State Executive Committee.* The State Executive Committee shall meet at least once in three months and shall observe such rules of procedure in regard to the transaction of business at its meetings as may be prescribed by the State Government.

22. *Temporary Association of Persons with State Executive Committee for Particular Purposes.* 1. The State Executive Committee may associate with itself in such manner and for such purposes as may be prescribed by the State Government any person whose assistance or advice it may desire to obtain in performing any of its functions under this Act.

2. A person associated with the State Executive Committee under sub-section(1) for any purpose shall have the right to take part in the discussions of the State Executive Committee relevant to that purpose, but shall not have a right to vote at a meeting of the said Committee, and shall not be a member for any other purpose.

3. A person associated with the said Committee under sub-section(1) for any purpose shall be paid such fees and allowances, for attending its meetings and for attending to any other work of the said Committee, as may be prescribed by the State Government.

23. *Power to give directions.* In the performance of its functions under this Act:

(a) the Central Coordination Committee shall be bound by such directions in writing, as the Central Government may give to it; and

(b) the State Coordination Committee shall be bound by such directions in writing, as the Central Coordination Committee or the State Government may give to it:

Provided that where a direction given by the State Government is inconsistent with any direction given by the Central Coordination Committee, the matter shall be referred to the Central Government for its decision.

24. No act or proceeding of the Central Coordination Committee, the Central Executive Committee, a State Coordination Committee, or a State Executive Committee shall be called in question on the ground merely on the existence of any vacancy in or any defect in the constitution of such Committees.

PREVENTION AND EARLY DETECTION OF DISABILITIES

25. ***Approved Government and local authorities to take certain steps for the prevention of occurrence of disabilities.*** Within the limits of their economic capacity and development, the appropriate Governments and the local authorities, with a view to preventing the occurrence of disabilities, shall:

(a) undertake or cause to be undertaken surveys, investigations and research concerning the cause of occurrence of disabilities;
(b) promote various methods of preventing disabilities;
(c) screen all the children at least once in a year for the purpose of identifying "at-risk" cases;
(d) provide facilities for training to the staff at the primary health centres;
(e) sponsor or cause to be sponsored awareness campaigns and disseminate or cause to be disseminated information for general hygiene, health and sanitation;
(f) take measures for pre-natal, perinatal and post-natal care of mother and child;
(g) educate the public through the pre-schools, primary health centres, village level workers and *anganwadi* workers;
(h) create awareness amongst the masses through television, radio and other mass media on the causes of disabilities and the preventive measures to be adopted.

EDUCATION

26. ***Appropriate Governments and local authorities to provide children with disabilities free education, etc.*** The appropriate Governments and the local authorities shall:

(a) ensure that every child with a disability has access to free education in an appropriate environment till he attains the age of eighteen years;
(b) endeavour to promote the integration of students with disabilities in the normal schools;
(c) promote setting up of special schools in Government and private sector for these in need of special education, in such a manner that children with disabilities living in any part of the country have access to such schools;
(d) endeavour to equip the special schools for children with disabilities with vocational training facilities.

27. The appropriate Governments and the local authorities shall by notification make schemes for:

(a) conducting part-time classes in respect of children with disabilities who having completed education up to class fifth and could not continue their studies on a whole time basis;
(b) conducting special part-time classes for providing functional literacy for children in the age group of sixteen and above;
(c) imparting non-formal education by utilizing the available manpower in rural areas after giving them appropriate orientation;
(d) imparting education through open schools or open universities;
(e) conducting class and discussions through interactive electronic or other media;
(f) providing every child with disability free of cost special books and equipment needed for his education.

28. *Research for designing and developing new assistive devices, teaching aids, etc.* The appropriate Governments shall initiate or cause to be initiated research by official and non-governmental agencies for the purpose of designing and developing new assistive devices, teaching aids, special teaching materials or such other items as are necessary to give a child with disability equal opportunities in education.

29. *Appropriate Governments to set up teachers' training institutions to develop trained manpower for schools for children with disabilities.* The appropriate Governments shall set up adequate number of teachers' training institutions and assist the

national institutes and other voluntary organisations to develop teacher's training programmes specialising in disabilities so that requisite trained manpower is available for special schools and integrated schools for children with disabilities.

30. Appropriate Governments to prepare a comprehensive education scheme providing for transport facilities, supply of books, etc. Without prejudice to the foregoing provisions, the appropriate Governments shall by notification prepare a comprehensive education scheme which shall make provision for:

(a) transport facilities to the children with disabilities or in the alternative financial incentives to parents or guardians to enable their children with disabilities to attend schools;
(b) the removal of architectural barriers from schools, colleges or other institutions imparting vocational and professional training.
(c) the supply of books, uniforms and other materials to children with disabilities attending school;
(d) the grant of scholarship to students with disabilities;
(e) setting up of appropriate fora for the redressal of grievances of parents regarding the placement of their children with disabilities;
(f) suitable modification in the examination system to eliminate purely mathematical questions for the benefit of blind students and students with low vision;
(g) restructuring of curriculum for the benefit of children with disabilities;
(h) restructuring the curriculum for the benefit of students with hearing impairment to facilitate them to take only one language as part of their curriculum.

31. Educational institutions to provide amanuensis to students with visual handicap. All educational institutions shall provide or cause to be provided amanuensis to blind students and students with or low vision.

EMPLOYMENT

32. Identification of posts which can be reserved for persons with disabilities. Appropriate Governments shall

(a) identify posts, in the establishments, which can be reserved for the persons with disability;

(b) at periodical intervals not exceeding three years, review the list of posts identified and up-date the list taking into consideration the developments in technology.

33. ***Reservation of posts.*** Every appropriate Government shall appoint in every establishment such percentage of vacancies not less than three per cent, for persons or class of persons with disability of which one per cent, each shall be reserved for persons suffering from

(i) blindness or low vision;

(ii) hearing impairment;

(iii) locomotor disability or cerebral palsy, in the posts identified for each disability:

Provided that the appropriate Government may, having regard to the type of work carried on in any department or establishment, by notification subject to such conditions, if any, as may be specified in such notification, exempt any establishment from the provisions of this Section.

34. ***Special Employment Exchange.*** 1. The Appropriate Government may, by notification, require that from such date as may be specified, by notification, the employer in every establishment shall furnish such information or return as may be prescribed in relation to vacancies appointed for persons with disability that have occurred or are about to occur in that establishment to such Special Employment Exchange as may be prescribed and the establishment shall thereupon comply with such requisition.

2. The form in which and the intervals of the time for which information or returns shall be furnished and the particulars, they shall contain shall be such as may be prescribed.

35. ***Power to inspect record or document in possession of any establishment.*** Any person authorised by the Special Employment Exchange in writing, shall have access to any relevant record or document in the possession of any establishment and may enter at any reasonable time and premises where he believes such record or document to be, and inspect or take copies of relevant records or documents or ask any question necessary for obtaining any information.

36. Vacancies not filled up to be carried forward. Where in any recruitment year any vacancy under Section 33, cannot be filled up due to non-availability of a suitable person with disability, or, for any other sufficient reason, such vacancy shall be carried forward in the succeeding recruitment year and if in the succeeding recruitment year also suitable person with disability is not available, it may first be filled by interchange among the three categories and only when there is no person with disability available for the post in that year, the employer shall fill up the vacancy by appointment of a person, other than a person with disability;

Provided that if the nature of vacancies in an establishment is such that a given category of person cannot be employed, the vacancies may be interchanged among the three categories with the prior approval of the appropriate Government.

37. Employers to maintain records. 1. Every employer shall maintain such record in relation to the person with disability employed in his establishment in such form and in such manner as may be prescribed by the appropriate Government.

2. The records maintained under sub-section(1) shall be open to inspection at all reasonable hours by such persons as may be authorised in this behalf by general or special order by the appropriate Government.

38. Schemes for ensuring employment of persons with disabilities. The appropriate Governments and local authorities shall by notification formulate schemes for ensuring employment of persons with disabilities, and such schemes may provide for:

(a) the training and welfare of persons with disabilities;
(b) the relaxation of upper age limit;
(c) regulating the employment;
(d) health and safety measures and creation of a non-handicapping environment in places where persons with disabilities are employed;
(e) the manner in which and the persons by whom the cost of operating the schemes is to be defrayed; and
(f) constituting the authority responsible for the administration of the scheme.

39. All educational institutions to reserve seats for persons with disabilities. All Government educational institutions and other educational institutions receiving aid from the Government, shall reserve not less than three per cent, seats for persons with disabilities.

40. Vacancies to be reserved in poverty alleviation schemes. The appropriate Governments and local authorities shall reserve not less than three per cent, in all poverty alleviation schemes for the benefit of persons with disabilities.

41. Incentives to employers to ensure five per cent of the work force is composed of persons with disabilities. The appropriate Governments and local authorities shall, within the limits of their economic capacity and development, provide incentives to employers both in public and private sectors to ensure that at least five per cent, of their work force is composed of persons with disabilities.

AFFIRMATIVE ACTION

42. Aids and appliances to persons with disabilities. The appropriate Governments shall by notification make schemes to provide aids and appliances to persons with disabilities.

43. Schemes for preferential allotment of land for certain purposes. The appropriate Governments and local authorities shall by notification frame schemes in favour of persons with disabilities, for the preferential allotment of land at concessional rates for:

(a) house;
(b) setting up business;
(c) setting up of special recreation centres;
(d) establishment of special schools;
(e) establishment of research centres;
(f) establishment of factories by entrepreneurs with disabilities.

NON-DISCRIMINATION

44. Non-discrimination in transport. Establishments in the transport sector shall, within the limits of their economic capacity and development for the benefit of persons with disabilities, take special measures to:

(a) adapt rail compartments, buses, vessels and aircrafts in such a way as to permit easy access to such persons;

(b) adapt toilets in rail compartments, vessels, aircrafts and waiting rooms in such a way as to permit the wheel chair users to use them conveniently.

45. *Non-discrimination on the road.* The appropriate governments and the local authorities shall, within the limits of their economic capacity and development, provide for:

(a) installation of auditory signals at red lights in the public roads for the benefit of persons with visually handicap;
(b) causing curb cuts and slopes to be made in pavements for the easy access of wheel chair users;
(c) engraving on the surface of the zebra crossing for the blind or for persons with low vision;
(d) engraving on the edges of railway platforms for the blind or for persons with low vision;
(e) devising appropriate symbols of disability;
(f) warning signals at appropriate places.

46. *Non-discrimination in the built environment.* The appropriate Governments and the local authorities shall, within the limits of their economic capacity and development, provide for:

(a) ramps in public buildings;
(b) adaptation of toilets for wheel chair users;
(c) braille symbols and auditory signals in elevators or lifts;
(d) ramps in hospitals, primary health centres and other medical care and rehabilitation institutions.

47. *Non-discrimination in Government employment.* 1. No establishment shall dispense with, or reduce in rank, an employee who acquires a disability during his service;

Provided that, if an employee after acquiring disability is not suitable for the post he was holding, could be shifted to some other post with the same pay scale and service benefits;

Provided further that if it is not possible to adjust the employee against any post, he may be kept on a supernumerary post until a suitable post is available or he attains the age of superannuation, which is earlier.

2. No promotion shall be denied to a person merely on the ground of his disability:

Provided that the appropriate government may, having regard to the type of work carried on in any establishment, by notification and subject to such conditions, if any, as may be specified in such notification exempt any establishment from the provisions of this Section.

RESEARCH AND MANPOWER DEVELOPMENT

48. Research. The appropriate Governments and local authorities shall promote and sponsor research, *inter alia*, in the following area:

(a) prevention of disability;
(b) rehabilitation including community based rehabilitation;
(c) development of assistive devices including their psycho-social aspects;
(d) job identification;
(e) on site modifications in offices and factories.

49. Financial incentives to Universities to enable them to undertake research. The appropriate Governments shall provide financial assistance to universities, other institutions of higher learning, professional bodies and non-governmental research-units or institutions, for undertaking research for special education, rehabilitation and man-power development.

RECOGNITION OF INSTITUTIONS FOR PERSONS WITH DISABILITIES

50. Competent authority. The State Government shall appoint any authority as it deems fit to be a competent authority for the purposes of this Act.

51. No person to establish or maintain an institution for persons with disabilities except in accordance with a certificate of registration. Save as otherwise provided under this Act, no person shall establish or maintain any institution for persons with disabilities except under and in accordance with a certificate of registration issued in this behalf by the competent authority:

Provided that a person maintaining an institution for persons with disabilities immediately before the commencement of this Act, may continue to maintain such institution for a period of six months from such commencement and if he has made an application for such certificate under this Section within the said period of six months, till the disposal of such application.

52. ***Certificate of registration.*** 1. Every application for certificate of registration shall be made to th competent authority in such form and in such manner as may be prescribed by the State Government.

2. On receipt of an application under sub-section(1), the competent authority shall make such enquiries as it may deem fit and where it is satisfied that the applicant has complied with the requirements of this Act and the rules made thereunder it shall grant a certificate of registration to the applicant and where it is not so satisfied the competent authority shall, by order, refuse to grant the certificate applied for:

Provided that before making any order refusing to grant a certificate the competent authority shall give to the applicant a reasonable opportunity of being heard and every order of refusal to grant a certificate shall be communicated to the applicant in such manner as may be prescribed by the State Government.

3. No certificate of registration shall be granted under-Section (2) unless the institution with respect to which an application has been made is in a position to provide such facilities and maintain such standards as may be prescribed by the State Government.

4. A certificate of registration granted under this Section—

(a) shall, unless revoked under Section 53, remain in force for such period as may be prescribed by the State Government.
(b) may be renewed from time to time for a like period; and
(c) shall be in such form and shall be subject to such conditions as may be prescribed by the State Government.

5. An application for renewal of a certificate of registration shall be made not less than sixty days before the period of validity.

6. The Certificate of registration shall be displayed by the institution in a conspicuous place.

53. ***Revocation of certificate.*** 1. The competent authority may, if it has reasonable cause to believe that the holder of the certificate of registration granted under sub-section(2) of Section 52 has:

(a) made a statement in relation to any application for the issue of renewal of the certificate which is incorrect or false in material particulars; or

(b) committed or has caused to be committed any breach of rules or any conditions subject to which the certificate was granted, it may, after making such inquiry, as it deems fit, by order, revoke the certificate:

Provided that no such order shall be made until an opportunity is given to the holder of the certificate to show cause as to why the certificate should not be revoked.

2. Where a certificate in respect of an institution has been revoked under sub-section(1), such institution shall cease to function from the date of such revocation:

Provided that where an appeal lies under Section 54 against the order of revocation, such institution shall cease to function—

(a) where no appeal has been preferred immediately on the expiry of the period prescribed for the filing of such appeal, or

(b) where such appeal has been preferred, but the order of revocation has been upheld, from the date of the order of appeal.

3. On the revocation of a certificate in respect of an institution, the competent authority may direct that any person with disability who is an inmate of such institution on the date of such revocation, shall be:

(a) restored to the custody of her or his parent, spouse or lawful guardian, as the case may be, or

(b) transferred to any other institution specified by the competent authority.

4. Every institution which holds a certificate of registration which is revoked under this session shall, immediately after such revocation, surrender such certificate to the competent authority.

54. Appeal. 1. Any person aggrieved by the order of the competent authority refusing to grant a certificate or revoking a certificate may, within such period as may be prescribed by the State Government, prefer an appeal to that Government against such refusal or revocation.

2. The order of the State Government on such appeal shall be final.

55. ***Act not to apply to institutions established or maintained by the Central or State Government.*** Nothing contained in this chapter shall apply to an institution for persons with disabilities established or maintained by the Central Government or a State Government.

INSTITUTION FOR PERSONS WITH SEVERE DISABILITIES

56. ***Institutions for persons with severe disabilities.*** 1. The appropriate Government may establish and maintain institutions for persons with severe disabilities at such places as it thinks fit.

2. Where the appropriate government is of opinion that any institution other than an institution, established under sub-section(1), is fit for the rehabilitation of the persons with severe disabilities, the Government may recognise such institution as an institution for persons with severe disabilities for the purposes of this Act:

Provided that no institution shall be recognised under this Section unless such institution has complied with the requirements of this Act and the rules made thereunder.

3. Every institution established under sub-section(1) shall be maintained in such manner and satisfy such conditions as may be prescribed by the appropriate government.

4. For the purposes of this Section "person with severe disability" means a person with eighty per cent, or more of one or more disabilities.

THE CHIEF COMMISSIONER AND COMMISSIONERS FOR PERSONS WITH DISABILITIES

57. ***Appointment of Chief Commissioner for persons with disabilities.*** 1. The Central Government may, by notification, appoint a Chief Commissioner for persons with disabilities for the purposes of this act.

2. A person shall not be qualified for appointment as the Chief Commissioner unless he has special knowledge or practical experience in respect of matters relating to rehabilitation.

3. The salary and allowances payable to and other terms and conditions of service (including pension, gratuity and other retirement benefits) of the Chief Commissioner shall be such as may be prescribed by the Central Government.

4. The Central Government shall determine the nature and categories of officers and other employees required to assist the Chief Commissioner in the discharge of his functions and provide the Chief Commissioner with such officers and other employees as it thinks fit.

5. The officers and employees provided to the Chief Commissioner shall discharge their functions under the general superintendence of the Chief Commissioner.

6. The salaries and allowances and other conditions of service of officers and employees provided to the Chief Commissioner shall be such as may be prescribed by the Central Government.

58. Functions of the Chief Commissioner. The Chief Commissioner shall:

(a) coordinate the work of the Commissioners;
(b) monitor the utilisation of funds disbursed by the Central Government;
(c) take steps to safeguard the rights and facilities made available to persons with disabilities;
(d) submit reports to the Central Government on the implementation of the act at such intervals as that Government may prescribe.

59. Chief Commissioner to look into complaints with respect to deprivation of rights of persons with disabilities. Without prejudice to the Provisions of Section 58 the Chief Commissioner may of his own motion or on the application of any aggrieved person or otherwise look into complaints with respect to matters relating to:

(a) deprivation of rights of persons with disabilities;
(b) non-implementation of laws, rules, bye-laws, regulations, executive orders, guidelines or instructions made or issued by the appropriate Governments and the local authorities for the welfare and protection of rights of persons with disabilities, and take up the matter with the appropriate authorities.

60. Appointment of Commissioners for persons with disabilities. 1. Every State Government may, by notification appoint a Commissioner for persons with disabilities for the purposes of this Act.

2. A person shall not be qualified for appointment as a Commissioner unless he has special knowledge or practical experience in respect of matters relating to rehabilitation.

3. The salary and allowances payable to and other terms and conditions of service (including pension, gratuity and other retirement benefits) of the Commissioner shall be such as may be prescribed by the State Government.

4. The State Government shall determine the nature and categories of officers and other employees required to assist the Commissioner in the discharge of his functions and provide the Commissioner with such officers and other employees as it thinks fit.

5. The officers and employees provided to the Commissioner shall discharge their functions under the general superintendence of the Commissioner.

6. The salaries and allowances and other conditions of officers and employees provided to the Commissioner shall be such as may be prescribed by the State Government.

61. Powers of the Commissioner. The Commissioner within the State shall:

(a) coordinate with the departments of the State Government for the programmes and schemes for the benefit of persons with disabilities;

(b) monitor the utilisation of funds disbursed by the State Government;

(c) take steps to safeguard the rights and facilities made available to persons with disabilities;

(d) submit reports to the State Government on the implementation of the Act at such intervals as that Government may prescribe and forward a copy thereof to the Chief Commissioner.

62. Commissioner to look into complaints with respect to matters relating to deprivation of rights of persons with disabilities. Without prejudice to the provisions of Section 61 the Commissioner may of his own motion or on the application of any aggrieved person or otherwise look into complaints with respect to matters relating to:

(a) deprivation of rights of persons with disabilities;

(b) non-implementation of laws, rules, bye-laws, regulations, executive orders, guidelines or instructions made or issued by the appropriate Governments and the local authorities for the welfare and protection of rights of persons with disabilities, and up the matter with the appropriate authorities.

63. Authorities and officers to have certain powers of civil court. 1. The Chief Commissioner and the Commissioners shall, for the purpose of discharging their functions under this Act, have the same powers as are vested in a court under the Code of Civil Procedure, 1908 while trying a suit, in respect of the following matters, namely:

(a) summoning and enforcing the attendance of witnesses;
(b) requiring the discovery and production of any document(5 of 1908);
(c) requisitioning any public record or copy there of from any court or office;
(d) receiving evidence on affidavits; and
(e) issuing commissions for the examination of witnesses or documents.

2. Every proceeding before the Chief Commissioner and Commissioners shall be a judicial proceeding within the meaning of Sections 193 and 228 of the Indian Penal Code (45 of 1860) and the Chief Commissioner, the Commissioner, the competent authority, shall be deemed to be a civil court for the purposes of Section 195 and Chapter XXVI of the Code of Criminal Procedure, 1973 (2 of 1974).

64. Annual report to be prepared by the Chief Commissioner. 1. The Chief Commissioner shall prepare such form and at such time for each financial year as may be prescribed by the Central Government an annual report giving a full account of his activities during the previous financial year and forward a copy thereof to the Central Government.

2. The Central Government shall cause the annual report to be laid before each House of Parliament along with the recommendations explaining the action taken or proposed to be taken on the recommendation made therein in so far as they relate

to the Central Government and the reasons for non-acceptance, if any, of any such recommendation or part.

65. Annual report to be prepared by the Commissioner. 1. The Commissioner shall prepare in such form and at such time for each financial year as may be prescribed by the State Government an annual report giving a full account of his activities during the previous financial year and forward a copy thereof to the State Government.

2. The State Government shall cause the annual report to be laid before each State Legislature along with the recommendations explaining the action taken or proposed to be taken on the recommendation made therein in so far as they relate to the State Government and the reasons for non-acceptance, if any, of any such recommendation or part.

SOCIAL SECURITY

66. Appropriate Governments and local authorities to undertake rehabilitation. 1. The appropriate Governments and the local authorities shall within the limits of their economic capacity and development undertake or cause to be undertaken rehabilitation of all persons with disabilities.

2. For purposes of sub-section(1), the appropriate Governments and local authorities shall grant financial assistance to non-governmental organisations.

3. The appropriate Government and local authorities while formulating rehabilitation policies shall consult the non-governmental organisations working for the cause of persons with disabilities.

67. Insurance scheme for employees with disabilities. 1. The appropriate Government shall by notification frame an insurance scheme for the benefit of its employees with disabilities.

2. Notwithstanding anything contained in this Section, the appropriate Government may instead of framing an insurance scheme frame an alternative security scheme for its employees with disabilities.

68. Unemployment allowance. The appropriate Governments shall within the limits of their economic capacity and development shall by notification frame a scheme for payment of an unemployment allowance to persons with disabilities registered with the Special Employment Exchange for more than two years and who could not be any gainful occupation.

MISCELLANEOUS

69. *Punishment for fraudulently availing any benefit meant for persons with disabilities.* Whoever, fraudulently avails or attempts to avail, any benefit meant for persons with disabilities, shall be punishable with imprisonment for a term which may extend to two years or with fine which may extend to twenty thousand rupees or with both.

70. *Chief Commissioners, Commissioners, Officers and other staff to be public servants.* The Chief Commissioner, the Commissioners and other officers and staff provided to them shall be deemed to be public servants within the meaning of Section 21 of the Indian Penal Code. (45 of 1860)

71. *Protection of action taken in good faith.* No suit, prosecution of other legal proceeding shall lie against the Central Government, the State Government or the local authority or any officer of the Government in respect of anything which is done in good faith or intended to be done in pursuance of this Act and any rules or orders made thereunder.

72. *Act to be in addition to and not derogation of any other law.* The provisions of this Act, or the rules made thereunder shall be in addition to, and not in derogation of any other law for the time being in force or any rules, order or any instructions issued thereunder, enacted for and issued for the benefit of persons with disabilities.

73. *Power of appropriate Government to make rules.* 1. The appropriate Government may, by notification, make rules for carrying out the provisions of this Act.

2. In particular, and without prejudice to the generality of the foregoing powers, such rules may provide for all or any of the following matters, namely:

(a) the manner in which a State Government or a Union Territory shall be chosen under clause (k) of sub-section (2) of Section 3.

(b) allowances which members shall receive under sub-section(7) of Section 4;

(c) rules or procedure which the Central Coordination Committee shall observe in regard to the transaction of business in its meetings under Section 7;

(d) such other functions which the Central Coordination Committee may perform under clause (h) of sub-section(2) 8;

(e) the manner in which a State Government or a Union Territory shall be chosen under clause (h) of sub-section(2) of Section 9:

(f) the allowances which the Members shall receive under sub-section(3) of Section 9;

(g) rules of procedure which the Central Executive Committee shall observe in regard to transaction of business at its meetings under Section 11;

(h) the manner and purposes for which a person may be associated under sub-section(1) of Section 12;

(i) fees and allowances which a person associated with the Central Executive Committee shall receive under sub-section(3) of Section 12;

(j) allowances which members shall receive under sub-Section (7) of Section 14;

(k) rules of procedure which a State Coordination Committee shall observe in regard to transaction of business in its meetings under Section 17;

(l) such other functions which a State Coordination Committee may perform under clause (g) of sub-Section (2) of Section 18;

(m) the allowances which Members shall receive under sub-section(3) of Section 19;

(n) rules of procedure which a State Executive Committee shall observe in regard to transaction of business at its meetings under Section 21;

(o) the manner and purposes for which a person may be associated under sub-section (1) of Section 22;

(p) fees and allowances which a person associated with the State Executive Committee may receive under sub-section(3) of Section 22;

(q) information or return which the employer in every establishment should furnish and the Special Employment

Exchange to which such information or return shall be furnished under sub-section(1) of Section 34;

(r) the form and the manner in which record shall be maintained by an employer under sub-section(1) of Section 37;

(s) the form and manner in which an application shall be made under sub-section(1) of Section 52;

(t) the manner in which an order of refusal shall be communicated under sub-section(2) of Section 52;

(u) facilities or standards required to be provided or maintained under sub-section(3) of Section 52;

(v) the period for which a certificate of registration shall be valid under clause (a) of sub-section(4) of Section 52;

(w) the form in which and conditions subject to which a certificate of registration shall be granted under clause (c) of sub-section(4) of Section 52;

(x) period within which an appeal shall lie under sub-section(1) of Section 54;

(y) the manner in which an institution for persons with severe disabilities shall be maintained and conditions which have to be satisfied under sub-section(3) of Section 56;

(z) the salary, allowances and other terms and conditions of service of the Chief Commissioner under sub-section(3) of Section 57;

(za) the salary, allowances and other conditions of service of officers and employees under sub-section(6) of Section 57;

(zb) intervals at which the Chief Commissioner shall report to the Central Government under clause (d) of Section 58;

(zc) the salary, allowances and other terms and conditions of service of the Commissioner under sub-Section (3) of Section 60;

(zd) the salary, allowances and other conditions of service of officers and employees under sub-section(6) of Section 60;

(ze) intervals within which the Commissioner shall report to the State Government under clause (d) of Section 61;

(zf) the form and time in which annual report shall be prepared under sub-section(1) of Section 64;

(zg) the form and time in which annual report shall be prepared under sub-section(1) of Section 65;

(zh) any other matter which is required to be or may be prescribed.

3. Every notification made by the Central Government under the proviso to Section 33, proviso to sub-section(2) of Section 47, every scheme framed by it under Section 27, Section 30, sub-section(1) of Section 38, Section 42, Section 43, Section 67, Section 68 and every rule made by it under sub-section(1), shall be laid, as soon as may be after it is made, before each House of Parliament, while it is in session for a total period of thirty days which may be comprised in one session or in two or more successive sessions, and if, before the expiry of the session immediately following the session or the successive sessions aforesaid, both houses agree in making any modification in the rule, notification or scheme, both Houses agree that the rule, notification or scheme should not be made, the rule, notification or scheme shall thereafter have effect only in such modified form or be of no effect, as the case may be; so, however, that any such modification or annulment shall be without prejudice to the validity of anything previously done under that rule, notification or scheme, as the case may be.

4. Every notification by the State Government under the proviso to Section 33, proviso to sub-Section (2) of Section 47, every scheme made by it under Section 27, Section 30, sub-Section (1) of Section 38, Section 42, Section 43, Section 67, Section 68 and every rule made by it under sub-Section (1) shall be laid, as soon as may be after it is made, before each House of State Legislature, where it consists of two Houses or where such legislature consists of one House before that House.

71. Amendment of Act 39 of 1987. In Section 12 of Legal Services Authorities Act, 1987, for clause (d), the following clause shall be substituted, namely:

"(d) a person with disability as defined in clause (i) of Section (2) of the Persons with Disabilities (Equal Opportunities, Protection of Rights and Full Participation) Act, 1995."

THE PERSONS WITH DISABILITIES (EQUAL OPPORTUNITIES, PROTECTION OF RIGHTS AND FULL PARTICIPATION) RULES, 1996

S.O. 908(E), dated 31-12-1996. In exercise of the powers conferred by sub-sections (1) and (2) of Section 73 of the Persons with Disabilities (Equal Opportunities of Rights and Full Participation) Act, 1995 (1 of 1996), the Central Government hereby makes the following rules, namely—

PRELIMINARY

1. ***Short title and commencement.*** 1. These rules may be called the Persons with Disabilities (Equal Opportunities, Protection of Rights and Full Participation) Rules, 1996.

2. They shall come into force on date of their publication in the Official Gazette.

2. ***Definitions.*** In these rules unless the context otherwise requires:

(a) "Act" means the Persons with Disabilities (Equal Opportunities, Protection of Rights and Full Participation) Act, 1995 (1 of 1996);

(b) "Chairperson" means a Chairperson appointed under the Act;

(c) "Vice-Chairperson" means a Vice-Chairperson appointed under the Act;

(d) "Member" means a Member appointed under the Act;

(e) "Member-Secretary" means a Member-Secretary appointed under the Act;

(f) "Special Employment Exchange" means a Special Employment Exchange, Special cell in normal Employment Exchange and such Employment Exchanges which are notified Special Employment Exchanges by notification in the official Gazette.

(g) "Year" means the financial year commencing on first day of April.

GUIDELINES FOR EVALUATION AND ASSESSMENT OF VARIOUS DISABILITIES

3. The general guidance for evaluation and assessment of various disabilities issued by the Government of India in the Ministry of Welfare, vide No. 4-2/83-H.W. III, dated the 6th August,

1986 and as may be amended from time to time, shall be followed for evaluation of various disabilities specified in Sections 2(b), (e), (l), (n), (o), (q), (r), (t), and (u) of the Act.

4. *Authorities to give Disability Certificate.* 1. A Disability Certificate shall be issued by a Medical Board duly constituted by the Central and the State Governments.

2. The State Government may constitute a Medical Board consisting of at least three members out of which at least one shall be a specialist in the particular field for assessing locomotor/Visual including low vision/hearing and speech disability, mental retardation and leprosy cure, as the case may be.

5. 1. The Medical Board shall, after due examination, give a permanent Disability Certificate in cases of such permanent disabilities where there are no chances of variation in the degree of disability.

2. The Medical Board shall indicate the period of validity in the certificate, in cases where there is any chance of variation in the degree of disability.

3. No refusal of Disability certificate shall be made unless an opportunity is given to the applicant of being heard.

4. On representation by the applicant, the Medical Board may review its decision having regard to all the facts and circumstances of the case and pass such order in the matter as it thinks fit.

5. The certificate issued by the Medical Board under Rule 5 shall make a person eligible to apply for facilities, concessions and benefits admissible under schemes of the Government or Non-governmental Organisations, subject to such conditions as the Central or the State Government may impose.

THE CENTRAL CO-ORDINATION COMMITTEE

7. *Nomination of State Government representatives by rotation.* The Central Government shall nominate four members—three from the State and one from the Union Territories under clause (k) of sub-section(2) of Section 3 of the Act, by rotation, in such a manner so as to cover all the four regions of the country, every year.

8. *Membership Roll.* The Member Secretary shall keep a record of names of Members and their addresses.

9. *Change of Address.* If a Member changes his address, he shall notify his new address to the Member-Secretary, who shall thereupon enter his new address, in the official records (but if he fails to notify) his new address, the address in the official records shall for all purposes be treated as his correct address.

10. Daily and Travelling Allowances. 1. Non-official members of the Central Co-ordination Committee, resident in Delhi, shall be paid an allowance of rupees seventy-five per day for each day of the actual meetings of the Central Co-ordination Committee.

2. Non-official members of the Central Co-ordination Committee, not resident in Delhi, shall be paid daily and travelling allowances for each day of the actual meetings at the highest rates admissible to a Grade I Officer of the Central Government:

Provided that in the case of a Member of Parliament who is also a Member of the Central Co-ordination Committee, the said daily and travelling allowances shall be paid at the rates admissible to him as Member of Parliament, when the Parliament is not in session and on production of a certificate by the Member that he has not drawn any such allowance for the same journey and halts from any other Government source.

3. An official member of the Central Co-ordination Committee shall be paid daily and travelling allowances, at the rates admissible under the relevant rules of the respective Government under whom he is serving on production of a certificate by him that he has not drawn any such allowance for the same journey and halts from any other Government source.

11. Notice of Meetings. 1. The meetings of the Central Co-ordination Committee shall ordinarily be held in New Delhi on such dates as may be fixed by the Chairperson:

Provided that it shall meet at least once in every six months.

2. The Chairperson shall, upon the written request of not less than ten members of the Central Co-ordination Committee, call a special meeting of the Committee.

3. Fifteen clear days' notice of an ordinary meeting and five clear days' notice of a special meeting specifying the time and the place at which such meeting is to be held and the business to be transacted thereat, shall be given by Member-Secretary to the Members.

4. Notice of a meeting may be given to the members by delivering the same by messenger or sending it by registered post to his last known place of residence or business or in such other manner as the Chairperson, may, in the circumstances of the case thinks fit.

5. No member shall be entitled to bring forward for the consideration of the meeting any matter of which he has not given ten clear days' notice to the Member-Secretary, unless the Chairperson, in his discretion, permits him to do so.

6. (a) The Central Co-ordination Committee may adjourn its meeting from day to day or to any particular day.

(b) Where a meeting of the Central Co-ordination Committee is adjourned from day to day, notice of such adjourned meeting shall be given to the members available at the place where the meeting which is adjourned if held by messenger and it shall not be necessary to give notice of the adjourned to other members.

(c) Where a meeting of the Central Co-ordination Committee is adjourned not from day to day but from the day on which the meeting is to be held to another date, notice of such meeting shall be given to all the members as provided in sub-rule (4) of this rule.

12. Presiding Officer. The Chairperson shall preside at every meeting of the Board and in his absence, the Vice-Chairperson shall preside, but when both the Chairperson and the Vice-Chairperson are absent from any meeting, the members present shall elect one of the members to preside at the meeting.

13. Quorum. 1. One-third of the total members shall form the quorum for any meeting.

2. If any time fixed for any meeting or during the course of any meeting less than one-third of the total members are present, the Chairperson may adjourn the meeting to such hours on the following or on some other future date as he may fix.

3. No quorum shall be necessary for the adjourned meeting.

4. No matter which had not been on the agenda of the ordinary or the special meeting as the case may be, shall be discussed at adjourned meeting.

5. (a) Where a meeting of the Central Co-ordination Committee is adjourned under sub-rule (2) above for want of quorum to the following day, notice of such adjourned meeting shall be given to the members available at the place where the meeting which is adjourned is held by messenger and it shall not be necessary to give notice of the adjourned meeting to other members.

(b) Where a meeting of the Central Co-ordination Committee is adjourned under sub-rule (2) above for want of quorum not to the following date with sufficient gap, notice of such adjourned meeting shall be given to all the members as provided in sub-rule (4) of Rule 11.

14. Minutes. 1. Record shall be kept of the names of members who attend the meeting and of the proceedings at the meeting in a book to be maintained for that purpose by the Member-Secretary.

2. The minutes of the previous meeting shall be read at the beginning of the every succeeding meeting, and shall be confirmed and signed by the Presiding Officer at such meeting.

3. The proceedings shall be open to inspection by any member at the office of the Member-Secretary during office hours.

15. Maintaining order at meeting. The Presiding Officer shall maintain order at the meeting.

16. Business to be transacted at meeting. Except with the permission of the Presiding Officer, no business which is not entered in the agenda or of which notice has not been given by a member under sub-rule (5) of Rule 11, shall be transacted at any meeting.

17. 1. At any meeting, business shall be transacted in the order in which it is entered in the agenda, unless otherwise resolved in the meeting with the permission of the Presiding Officer.

2. Either at the beginning of the meeting or after the conclusion of the debate on a motion during the meeting, the Presiding Officer or a member may suggest a change in the order of business as entered in the agenda and if the Chairperson agrees, such a change shall take place.

18. Decision by majority. All questions considered at a meeting of the Committee shall be decided by a majority of votes of the members present and voting and in the event of equality of votes, the Chairperson, or in the absence of the Chairperson, the Vice-Chairperson or in the absence of both the Chairperson and the Vice-Chairperson, the Member presiding at the meeting, as the case may be, shall have a second or casting vote.

19. No Proceeding to be invalid due to vacancy or any defect. No proceeding of the Central Co-ordination Committee shall be invalid by reasons of existence of any vacancy in or any defect in the constitution of the Committee.

THE CENTRAL EXECUTIVE COMMITTEE

20. Nomination of State Government representatives by rotation. The Central Government shall nominate four members—

three from the States and one from the Union Territories under clause (h) of sub-section(2) of Section 9 of the Act, by rotation, in such a manner so as to cover all the four regions of the country, every year.

21. *Daily and Travelling Allowances.* 1. Non-official members of the Central Executive Committee, resident in Delhi, shall be paid an allowance of rupees seventy five per day for each day of the actual meetings of the Central Co-ordination Committee.

2. Non-official members of the Central Executive Committee, not resident in Delhi, shall be paid daily and travelling allowances for each day of the actual meetings at the highest rates admissible to a Grade I Officer of the Central Government.

3. Official members of the Central Executive Committee shall be paid daily and travelling allowances, at the rates admissible under the relevant rules of the respective Government under whom he is serving on production of a certificate by him that he has not drawn any such allowance for the same journey and halts from any other Government source.

22. *Notice of Meetings.* 1. The meetings of the Central Executive Committee shall ordinarily be held in New Delhi on such dates as may be fixed by the Chairperson:

Provided that it shall meet at least once in every three months.

2. The Chairperson shall, upon the written request of not less than ten members of the Central Executive Committee, call a special meeting of the Committee.

3. Fifteen clear days' notice of an ordinary meeting and five clear days' notice of a special meeting specifying the time and the place at which such meeting is to be held and the business to be transacted thereat, shall be given by the Member-Secretary to the members.

4. Notice of a meeting may be given to the members by delivering the same by messenger or sending it by registered post to his last known place of residence or business or in such other manner as the Chairperson, may, in the circumstances of the case, thinks fit.

5. No member shall be entitled to bring forward for the consideration of the meeting any matter of which has not given ten clear days' notice to the Member-Secretary, unless the Chairperson, in his discretion, permits him to do so.

6. (a) The Central Executive Committee may adjourn its meetings from day to day or to any particular day.

(b) Where a meeting of the Central Executive Committee is adjourned from day to day, notice of such adjourned meeting shall be given to the members available at the place where the meeting which is adjourned if held, by messenger and it shall not be necessary to give notice of the adjourned meeting to other members.

(c) Where a meeting of the Central Executive Committee is adjourned not from day to day but, from the day on which the meeting is to be held to another date, notice of such meeting shall be given to all the members as provided in sub-rule (4) of this Rule.

23. *Presiding Officer.* The Chairperson shall preside at every meeting of the Board and in his absence, the members present shall elect one of the members to preside at that meeting.

24. *Quorum.* 1. One third of the total members shall form the quorum for any meeting.

2. If at any time fixed for any meeting or during the course of any meeting less than one-third of the total members are present, the Chairperson may adjourn the meeting to such hours on the following or on some other future date as he may fix.

3. No quorum shall be necessary for the adjourned meeting.

4. No matter which had not been on the agenda of the ordinary or the special meeting, as the case may be, shall be discussed at adjourned meeting.

5. (a) Where a meeting of the Central Co-ordination Committee is adjourned under sub-rule (2) above for want of quorum to the following day, notice of such adjourned meeting shall be given to the members available at the place where the meeting which is adjourned is held by messenger and it shall not be necessary to give notice of the adjourned meeting to other members.

(b) Where a meeting of the Central Executive Committee is adjourned under sub-rule (2) above for want of quorum not to the following date with sufficient gap, notice of such adjourned meeting shall be given to all the members as provided in sub-rule (2) of Rule 22.

25. *Minutes.* 1. Record shall be kept of the names of members, who attend the meeting and of the proceedings at the meeting in a book to be maintained for that purpose by the Member-Secretary.

2. The minutes of the previous meeting shall be read at the beginning of the every succeeding meeting, and shall be confirmed and signed by the Presiding Officer at such meeting.

3. The proceedings shall be open to inspection by any member at the office of the Member-Secretary during office hours.

26. Maintaining order at meeting. The Presiding Officer shall maintain order at the meeting.

27. Business to be transacted at meeting. Except with the permission of the Presiding Officer, no business which is not entered in the agenda or of which notice has not been given by a Member under sub-rule (5) of Rule 22, shall be transacted at any meeting.

28. 1. At any meeting, business shall be transacted in the order in which it is entered in the agenda.

Either at the beginning of the meeting or after the conclusion of the debate on a motion during the meeting, the Presiding Officer or a member may suggest a change in the order of business as entered in the agenda and if the Chairperson agrees, such a change shall take place.

29. Decision by majority. All questions considered at a meeting of the Committee shall be decided by a majority of votes of the members present and voting and in the event of equality of votes, the Chairperson, or in the absence of the Chairperson, the member presiding at the meeting, as the case may be, shall have a second or casting vote.

30. No proceeding to be invalid due to vacancy or any defect. No proceeding of the Central Executive Committee shall be invalid by reasons of existence of any vacancy in or any defect in the constitution of the Committee.

31. Manner and purpose of association of persons with Central Executive Committee. 1. The Central Executive Committee may invite any person to participate in the deliberations of its meetings, whose assistance or advice, is considered useful in performing any of its function, under the Act.

2. If the person associated with the Central Executive Committee under sub-rule (1) happens to be a non-official resident in Delhi, he shall be entitled to get an allowance of rupees seventy-five per day for each day of actual meeting of the Committee in which he is so associated.

3. If such a person is not resident in Delhi, he shall be paid daily and travelling allowances for each day of the actual meeting at the highest rates admissible to Grade I Officer of the Central Government.

4. If such person is a Government servant, or an employee in a Government undertaking, he shall be entitled to travelling and daily allowances at the rates admissible under the relevant rules applicable to him on production of a certificate by him that he has not drawn any such allowance for the same journey and halts from any other Government source.

32. Fee for the associated person. Notwithstanding anything in Rule 31, the Central Executive Committee may pay the person associated with the Committee, with the prior approval of the Central Government such fees as the Central Government may determine depending on the nature of work assigned and the qualifications and experience of the associated person.

33. Tours by associated person. The associated person may, with the prior approval of the Chairperson, undertake tours within the country for the performance of the duties entrusted to him by the Central Executive Committee and in respect of such tours he shall be entitled to travelling and daily allowances at the rates admissible to a Grade I Officer of the Central Government.

34. Associated person not to disclose any information. The associated person shall not disclose any information either given by the Central Executive Committee or obtained during the performance of the duties assigned to him either from the Central Executive Committee or otherwise, to any person other than the Central Executive Committee without the written permission of the chairperson of the committee.

35. Duties and functions of the associated person. The associated person shall discharge such duties and perform such functions as are assigned to him, by the Central Executive Committee.

EMPLOYMENT

36. Computation of vacancies. For the purpose of computation of vacancies for persons with disabilities in Group A, B, C and D posts, the manner of computation of vacancies shall be such as may be determined by the Government by instructions or orders in this regard.

37. Notification of vacancies to the Special Employment Exchanges. 1. The following vacancies shall be notified to the Special Employment Exchanges, namely:

(a) Vacancies in posts of a technical and scientific nature carrying a basic pay of Rs. 1,400 or more per month occurring in establishments in respect of which the Central Government is the appropriate Government under the Act, and

(b) Vacancies which an employer may desire to be circulated to the Special Employment Exchanges outside the State or Union Territory in which the establishment is situated, shall be notified to such Special Employment Exchanges as may be specified by the Central Government by notification in the Official Gazette, in this behalf. A copy of the notification of vacancies shall also be sent to the Vocational Rehabilitation Centre for Handicapped concerned.

2. Vacancies other than those specified in sub-rule (1) shall be notified to the local Special Employment Exchange concerned. A copy of the notification of vacancies shall also be sent to the Vocational Rehabilitation Centre for Handicapped concerned.

38. Form and manner of notification of vacancies. The vacancies shall be notified in writing to the Special Employment Exchange concerned, and the following particulars shall be furnished in respect of each type of vacancy, namely:

1. Name and address of the employer
2. Telephone number of the employer, if any;
3. Nature of vacancy—

   (a) Type of workers required (Designation);

   (b) (i) Description of duties
   (ii) Physical requirements (i.e., job involves visual accuracy, frequent movement/ walking, continuous long hours sitting, etc.)

   (c) Qualification required—

   (i) Essential,
   (ii) Desirable

(d) Age-limits, if any
(e) Whether women are eligible?

4. Number of vacancies—

Reserved for Physically Handicapped Persons Orthopaedically

Handicapped Visually
Handicapped Hearing
Handicapped

(a) Regular
(b) Temporary

5. Pay and allowances.
6. Place of work (name of town/village and district in which it is situated).
7. Probable date by which the vacancy will be filled.
8. Particulars regarding interview/test of applicants—
   (a) Date of interview/test
   (b) Time of interview/test
   (c) Place of interview/test
   (d) Designation and address of the person to whom applicants should report.
9. Any other relevant information—

The vacancies shall be re-notified in writing to the concerned Special Employment Exchange if, there is any change in the particulars already furnished to the Special Employment Exchange and Vocational Rehabilitation Centre for Handicapped under this Rule.

39. Time-limit for the notification of vacancies. 1. Vacancies, required to be notified to the local Special Employment Exchange, shall be notified at least thirty days before the date on which applicants will be interviewed or tested where interviews or tests are held, or the date on which vacancies are intended to be filled, if no interviews or tests are held.

2. Vacancies, required to be notified to the Special Employment Exchange notified under sub-rule (1) of Rule 37 shall be notified at least three weeks before the date on which applicants will be interviewed or tested where interviews or tests are held, or the date on which vacancies are intended to be filled, if no interviews or tests are held.

3. An employer shall furnish to the concerned Special Employment Exchange, the results of selection within fifteen days from the date of selection.

40. Submission of returns. 1. An employer shall furnish to the local Special Employment Exchange quarterly returns in DPER-I and biennial returns in Form DPER-II, as may be amended from time to time.

2. Quarterly returns shall be furnished within thirty days of the due dates, namely, 31st March, 30th June, 30th September and 31st December.

3. Biennial returns shall be furnished within thirty days of the due date as notified in the Official Gazette.

41. Form in which record to be kept by an employer. An employer shall maintain the record of employees with disabilities in Form DPER-III, as may be amended from time to time.

CHIEF COMMISSIONER FOR PERSONS WITH DISABILITIES

42. Procedure to be followed by Chief Commissioner. 1. A complaint containing the following particulars shall be presented by the complainant in person or by his agent to the Chief Commissioner for Persons with Disabilities or be sent by registered post addressed to the Chief Commissioner:

(a) The name, description and the address of the complainant;
(b) The name, description and the address of the opposite party or parties, as the case may be, so far as they can be ascertained;
(c) The facts relating to complaint and when and where it arose;
(d) Documents in support of the allegations contained in the complaint;
(e) The relief which the complainant claims.

2. The Chief Commissioner on receipt of a complaint shall refer a copy of the complaint to the opposite party/parties mentioned in the complaint directing him to give his version of the case within a period of thirty days or such extended period not exceeding fifteen days as may be granted by the Chief Commissioner.

3. On the date of hearing or any other date to which hearing could be adjourned, it shall be obligatory on the parties or their agents to appear before the Chief Commissioner.

4. Where the complainant or his agent fails to appear before the Chief Commissioner on such days, the Chief Commissioner may in his discretion either dismiss the complaint on default or decide it on merits.

5. Where the opposite party or his agent fails to appear on the date of hearing the Chief Commissioner may take such necessary action under Section 63 of the Act as he deems fit for summoning and enforcing the attendance of the opposite party.

6. The Chief Commissioner may dispose of the complaint *ex parte*, if necessary.

7. The Chief Commissioner may on such terms as he deems fit and at any stage of the proceedings, adjourn the hearing of the complaint.

8. The complaint shall be decided, as far as possible, within a period of three months from the date of notice received by the opposite party.

43. *Salary and allowances of the Chief Commissioner.* The Chief Commissioner for persons with disabilities shall be entitled to salary, allowances and other perquisites as are available to the Secretary to the Government of India.

44. *Submission of Report of Central Government.* The Chief Commissioner shall submit report to the Central Government on the implementation of the Act at the interval of six months in such a manner that at least two reports are sent in one financial year.

45. *Submission of annual report* 1. The Chief Commissioner shall as soon as possible after the end of the financial year but not later than the 30th day of September in the next year ensuing prepare and submit to the Central Government an annual report giving a complete account of his activities during the said financial year.

2. In particular, the annual report referred to in sub-rule (1) shall contain information in respect of each of the following matters, namely:

(a) Names of officers, staff of the Board and a chart showing the organisational set-up;

(b) The functions which the Chief Commissioner has been empowered under Sections 58 and 59 of the Act and the highlights of the performance in this regard;

(c) The main recommendations made by the Chief Commissioner.

(d) Progress made in the implementation of the Act State-wise;

(e) Any other matter deemed appropriate for inclusion by the Chief Commissioner or specified by the Central Government from time to time.

FORM DPER-I

[Disabled Persons Employed Return]

[*See Rule 40*]

Quarterly return to be submitted to the Special Employment Exchange for the Quarter ended...

Name and Address of the Employer:...

Whether— Head Office:...

Branch Office:...

Nature of business/principal activity:...

1. (a) Employment: Total number of persons including working proprietors/partners/commission agents/contingent paid and contractual workers, on the pay rolls of establishment excluding part-time workers and apprentices. (Figures should include every person whose wage or salary is paid by the Establishment.)

	On the last working day of the previous quarter			On the last working day of the quarter under report		
	Orthopaedically Handicapped	Visually Handicapped	Hearing Impairment	Orthopaedically Handiccapped	Visually Handicapped	Hearing Impairment
Men with disability						
Women with disability						
Total						

(b) Please indicate the main reasons for any increase or decrease in employment if the increase is more than 5 per cent during the quarter.

2. ***Vacancies.*** Vacancies carrying total emoluments as per prevailing minimum wage per month and of over three months' duration.

(a) Number of vacancies occurred and notified during the quarter and the number filled during the quarter (separate figures may be given for men with disability and women with disability).

Number of vacancies which come within the purview of the Act:

Occurred	*Notified*	*Filled*	*Sources*	*(Describe the source from which filled)*
	Local Special Employment Exchange	*General Employment Exchange*		
1	2	3	4	5

(b) Reasons for not notifying all vacancies occurred during the quarter under report, vide 2(a) above.........

3. ***Manpower Shortage.*** Vacancies/posts unfilled because of shortage of suitable applicants.

Name of the occupation or designation of the post	*Number of unfilled vacancies/posts disability wise*		
	Essential qualification	*Essential experience*	*Experience not necessary*
1	2	3	4

Please list any other occupations for which this establishment had recently any difficulty in obtaining suitable applicants.

Signature of the employer

To

The Employment Exchange

....

....

Note: This return relates to quarters ending 31st March/30th June/30th September and 31st December and shall be rendered to the local Special Employment Exchange within thirty days after the end of the quarter concerned.

FORM DPER-II

[*See Rule 40*]

Occupational return to be submitted to the local Special Employment Exchange once in two years.

Name and address of the Employer.........

Nature of business.......

(describe what the establishment makes or does as its principal activity)

1. Total number of persons on the payrolls of the establishment on (specify date)....(This figure should include every person whose wage or salary is paid by the establishment) (Separate figures for men with disability and women with disability may be given.)

2. Occupational Classification of all employees as given in Item 1 above.

(Please give below the number of employees in each occupation separately)

Occupation	*Numbers of Employees*						
Use exact terms	*Men with Disability*			*Women with Disability*			*Total*
Such as engineer	O	V	H	O	V	H	
(Mechanical);	R	I	E	E	I		
teacher (domestic/	Y	S	A	T	S	A	
science); officer on duty	H	U	R	H	U	R	
(actuary) assistant							
director	O	A	I	O	A	I	Please give as far
(Metallurgist);	P	L	N	P	L	N	as possible approxi-
Scientific Assistant	A	L	G	A	L	G	mate number of
(chemist); Research							vacancies in each
Officer	E			E	Y		occupation you are

(economist); instructor	D	Y	D	likely to fill during
(Carpenter);	I		I	the next calendar
Supervisor (Tailor)				year due to retire-
fitter	C	C		ment.
(internal combustion	A	A		
engine); Inspector	Y	Y		
(sanitary); Superin-				
tendent				
(office); apprentice				
(electrician				
Total				

Dated.........

Signature of Employee

To

The Employment Exchange

(Please fill in here the address of your Local Special Employment Exchange)

Note: Total of Col. 8 under Item 2 should correspond to the figures given against Item 1.

Form DPER III

[*See Rule 41*]

1. Name and address of the employer...
2. Whether Head Office........................
   Branch Office.....................
3. Nature of business/principal activity.....
4. Total number of persons on the payroll of the establishment. (This figure should include every person whose wage or salary is paid by the establishment.)
5. Total number of disabled persons (disabilitywise) on the payroll of the establishment. (This figure should include every person with disability whose wage or salary is paid by the establishment.)
6. (a) Occupational qualification of all employees as given in Item 5 above (Please give below the number of employees in each occupation separately.)

Occupation	*Numbers of Employees*							
Use exact terms	*Men with Disability*			*Women with Disability*			*Total*	
Such as engineer (Mechanical); teacher (domestic/ science); officer on duty (actuary) assistant director (Metallurgist); Scientific Assistant (chemist); Research Officer (economist); instructor (Carpenter); Supervisor (Tailor) fitter (Internal Combustion engine); Inspector (sanitary); Superintendent (office); Apprentice (electrician)	ORTH OPAEDICA	VISU ALLY	HEAR ING	ORTH OPAEDICA	VISU ALLY	HEAR ING		Nature and extent of disability
	1	2	3	4	5	6	7	8
Total								

(c) Please indicate the main reasons for any increase or decrease in employment if the increase or decrease is more than 5 per cent during the quarter.........

7. Vacancies: Vacancies carrying total emoluments as per prevailing minimum wage per month and of over three months' duration.

(a) Number of vacancies occurred and notified during the quarter and the number filled during the quarter.

Number of vacancies which come within the purview of the Act.

Occurred/Notified	*Local Special Employment Exchange*	*Filled General Employment*	*Sources (Describe the source from which filled.)*	
1	*2*	*3*	*4*	*5*
Total				

(b) Reason for not notifying all vacancies occurred during the quarter under report, vide (a) 2.

4. Manpower Shortages:—Vacancies/posts unfilled because of shortage of suitable applicants

Name of the occupation or Designation of the posts	*Number of unfilled vacancies/posts*		
	essential qualification	*essential experience*	*experience not necessary*
1	2	3	4

Please list any other occupations for which this establishment had recently any difficulty in obtaining suitable applicants.

Signature of Employer

3

Juvenile Justice and Human Rights

THE JUVENILE JUSTICE ACT, 1986

An Act to provide for the care, protection, treatment and rehabilitation of neglected or delinquent juveniles and for the adjudication of certain matters relating to, and disposition of, delinquent juveniles.

Be it enacted by Parliament in the Thirty-seventh Year of the Republic of India as follows:

PRELIMINARY

1. Short title, extent and commencement. 1. This Act may be called the Juvenile Justice Act. 1986

2, It extends to the whole of India except the State of Jammu and Kashmir.

3. It shall come into force on such date as the Central Government may, by notification in the official Gazette, appoint, and different dates may be appointed for different provisions of this Act and for different States.

2. Definitions: In this Act, unless the context otherwise requires,

(a) "begging" means

(i) Soliciting or receiving alms in a public place or entering into any private premises for the purpose of soliciting or receiving alms, whether under the pretence of signing, dancing, fortunetelling, performing tricks or selling articles or otherwise;

(ii) exposing or exhibiting, with the object of obtaining or extorting alms, any sore, wound, injury, deformity or disease, whether of himself or of any other person or of an animal;

(iii) allowing oneself to be used as an exhibit for the purpose of soliciting or receiving alms;

(b) "Board" means a Juvenile Welfare Board constituted under Section

(c) "brothel", "prostitute", "prostitution" and "public place" shall have the meaning respectively assigned to them in the Suppression of Immoral Traffic in Women and Girls Act, 1956 (104 of 1956):

(d) "competent authority" means, in relation to neglected juveniles, a Board and, in relation to delinquent juveniles, a juvenile Court and where no such Board or juvenile Court has been constituted, includes any Court empowered under sub-section (2) of section 7 to exercise the powers conferred on a Board or juvenile Court

(e) "delinquent juvenile" means a juvenile who has been found to have committed an offence

(f) "fit person" or 'fit institution' means any person or institution found fit by the competent authority to receive and take care of a juvenile entrusted to his or its care and protection on the terms and conditions specified by the competent authority.

(g) "guardian", in relation to a juvenile, incudes any person who, in the opinion of the competent authority, having cognizance of any proceeding in relation to a juvenile, has, for the time being, the actual charge of or control over, that juvenile.

(h) "juvenile" means a boy who has not attained the age of sixteen years or a girl who has not attained the age of eighteen years;

(i) "Juvenile Court" means a Court constituted under section 5.

(j) "juvenile home" means an institution established or certified by the State Government under Section 9 as a juvenile home.

(k) "narcotic drug" and " psychotropic substance" shall have the meaning respectively assigned to them in the Narcotic Drugs and Psychotropic Substances Act, 1985 (61 of 1985)

(l) "neglected juvenile", means a juvenile who

- (i) is found begging; or
- (ii) is found without having any home or settled place of abode and without any ostensible means of subsistence and is destitute;
- (iii) has a parent or guardian who is unfit or incapacitated to exercise control over the juvenile; or
- (iv) lives in a brothel or with a prostitute or frequently goes to any place used for the purpose of prostitution, or is found to associate with any prostitute or any other person who leads an immoral drunken or depraved life;

(v) who is being or is likely to be abused or exploited for immoral or illegal purposes or unconscionable gain;

(m) "observation home", means any institution or place established or recognised by the State Government under Section 11 as an observation home;

(n) "offence", means an offence punishable under any law for the time being in force;

(o) "place of safety" means any place or institution, the person incharge of which is willing temporally to receive and take care of a juvenile and which, in the opinion of the competent authority may be a place of safety for the juvenile;

(p) "prescribed" means prescribed by rule made under this Act;

(q) "probation officer" means an officer appointed as a probation officer under this Act or under the probation of Offender Act, 1958 (20 of 1958)

(r) "special home "means an institution established or certified by the state Government under Section 10;

(s) "supervision", in relation to a juvenile placed under the care of any parent, guardian or other fit person or fit institution under this Act, means the supervision of that juvenile by a probation officer for the purpose of ensuring that the juvenile is properly looked after and that the conditions imposed by the competent authority are complied with;

(t) all words and expressions used but not defined in this Act and defined in the Code of Criminal Procedure, 1973 (2 of 1974), shall have the meanings respectively assigned to them in that Code.

3. *Continuation of Inquiry in respect of juvenile who has ceased to be a juvenile.* Where an inquiry has been initiated against a juvenile and during the course of such inquiry the juvenile ceases to be such, then notwithstanding anything contained in this Act or in any other law for the time being in force, the inquiry may be continued and orders may be made in respect of such person as if such person had continued to be a juvenile.

COMPETENT AUTHORITIES AND INSTITUTIONS FOR JUVENILES

4. Juvenile Welfare Boards. 1. The State Government may, by notification in the official Gazette, constitute for any area specified in the notification, one or more Juvenile Welfare Boards for exercising powers and discharging the duties conferred or imposed on such Board in relation to neglected juveniles under this Act.

2. A Board shall consist of a Chairman and such other members as the State Government thinks fit to appoint of whom not less than one shall be a woman; and every such member shall be vested with the powers of a Magistrate under the Code of Criminal Procedure, 1973 (2 of 1974).

3. The Board shall function as a Bench of Magistrates and shall have the powers conferred by the Code of Criminal Procedure, 1973 (2 of 1974) on a Metropolitan Magistrate or, as the case may be, a Judicial Magistrate of the first class.

5. Juvenile Courts. 1. Notwithstanding anything contained in the Code of Criminal Procedure, 1973 (2 of 1974), the State Government may, by notification in the official Gazette, constitute for any area specified in the notification, one or more Juvenile Courts for exercising the powers and discharging the duties conferred or imposed on such Court in relation to delinquent juveniles under this Act.

2. A Juvenile Court shall consist of such number of Metropolitan Magistrates or Judicial Magistrates of the first class, as the case may be, forming a Bench as the State Government thinks fit to appoint, of whom one shall be designated as the Principal Magistrate: and every such Bench shall have the powers conferred by the Code of Criminal Procedure, 1973 (2 of 1974) on a Metropolitan Magistrate or, as the case may be, a Judicial Magistrate of the first class.

3. Every Juvenile Court be assisted by a panel of two honorary social workers possessing such qualifications as may be proscribed of whom at least one shall be a woman, and such panel shall be appointed by the State Government.

6. Procedure, etc. in relation to Boards and Juvenile Courts. 1. In the event of any difference of opinion among the members of a Board or among the Magistrates of a Juvenile Court, the opinion of the majority shall prevail, but where there is no such majority the opinion of the Chairman or of the Principal Magistrate, as the case may be, shall prevail.

2. A Juvenile Court may act notwithstanding the absence of any member of the Board or, as the case may be, any Magistrate of the Juvenile Court, and no order be made by the Board or Juvenile Court shall be invalid by reason only of the absence of the member or Magistrate, as the case may be, during any stage of the proceeding.

3. No person shall be appointed as a member of the Board or as a Magistrate in the Juvenile Court unless he has, in the opinion of the State Government, special knowledge of child psychology and child welfare.

*7. **Powers of Board and Juvenile Court.*** 1. Where a Board or a Juvenile Court has been constituted for any area, such Board or Court, shall, notwithstanding any thing contained in any other law for the time being in force but save as otherwise expressly provided in this Act have power to deal exclusively with all proceedings under this Act relating to neglected juveniles or delinquent juveniles as the case may be:

Provided that a Board or a Juvenile Court may, if it is of the opinion that it is necessary so to do having regard to the circumstances of the case, transfer any proceedings to any Juvenile Court or Board, as the case may be:

Provided further that where there is any difference of opinion between a Board and a Juvenile Court regarding the transfer of any proceedings under the first proviso it shall be referred to the Chief Metropolitan Magistrate or, as the case may be, the Chief Judicial Magistrate for decision, and in a case where the District Magistrate is functioning as a Board or a Juvenile Court, such difference of opinion shall be referred to the Court of Session, and the decision of the Chief Metropolitan Magistrate or Chief Judicial Magistrate or as the case may be, the court of Session on such reference shall be final.

2. Where no Board or Juvenile Court has been constituted for any area, the Powers conferred on the Board or the Juvenile Court by or under this Act shall be exercised in that area, only by the following, namely

(a) the District Magistrate; or

(b) the Sub-Divisional Magistrate; or

any Metropolitan Magistrate or Judicial Magistrate of the first class, as the case may be.

3. The powers conferred on the Board of Juvenile Court by or

under this Act may also be exercised by the High Court and the Court of Session, when, the proceeding comes before them in appeal, revision or otherwise.

8. Procedure to be followed by a Magistrate not empowered under the Act. 1. When any Magistrate not empowered to exercise the powers of a Board or a Juvenile Court under this Act is of opinion that a person brought before him under any of the provisions of this Act is a juvenile, he shall record such opinion and forward the juvenile and the record of the proceeding to the competent authority having jurisdiction over the proceeding.

2. The competent authority to which the proceeding is forwarded under sub-section (1) shall hold the inquiry as if the juvenile had originally been brought before it.

9. Juvenile homes. 1. The State Government may establish and maintain as many juvenile homes as may be necessary for the reception of neglected juveniles under this Act.

2. Where the State Government is of opinion that any institution other than a home established or maintained under sub-section is fit for the reception, of the neglected to be sent there under this Act, it may certify such institution as a juvenile home for the purposes of this Act.

3. Every juvenile home to which a neglected; juvenile is sent under this Act shall not only provide the juvenile with accommodation; maintenance and facilities for education, vocational training and rehabilitation, but also provide him with facilities for the development of his character and abilities and give him necessary training for protecting himself against moral danger or exploitation and shall also perform such other functions as may be prescribed to ensure all round growth and development of his personality.

4. The State Government may, by rules made under this Act, provide for the management of juvenile homes, including the standards and the nature of services to be maintained by them and the circumstances under which, and the manner in which, the certification of a juvenile home may be granted or withdrawn.

10. Special homes. 1. The State Government may establish and maintain as many special homes as may be necessary for the reception of delinquent juveniles under this Act.

2. Where the State Government is of opinion that any institution other than a established or maintained under sub-section (1), is fit

for the reception of the delinquent juveniles to be sent there under No Act, it may certify such institution as a special home for the purposes of this Act.

3. Every special home to which a delinquent juvenile is sent under this Act shall not only provide the juvenile with accommodation, maintenance and facilities for education, vocational training and rehabilitation, but also provide him with facilities for, the development of his character and abilities and give him necessary training for his reformation and shall also perform such other functions as may be prescribed to ensure all round growth and development of his personality.

4. The State Government may, by rules made under this Act, provide for the management of special homes, including the standards and the nature of services to be maintained by them, and the circumstances under which, and the manner in which, the certification of a special home may be granted or withdrawn.

5. The rules made under sub-section (4) may also provide the classification and separation of delinquent juveniles on the basis of age and nature of offences committed by them.

11. Observation homes. 1. The State Government may establish and maintain as many observation homes as may be necessary for the temporary reception of juveniles during the pendency of any inquiry, regarding them under this Act.

2. Where the State Government is of opinion that any institution other than a home established or maintained under sub-section (1) is fit for the temporary reception of juveniles during the pendency of any inquiry regarding them under this Act, it may recognise such institution as an observation home for the purposes of this Act;

3. Every observation home to which a juvenile is sent under this Act shall not only provide the juvenile with accommodation, maintenance and facilities for medical examination and treatment, but also provide him facilities for useful occupation.

4. The State Government may, by rules made under this Act, provide for the management of observation homes, including the standards and the nature of services to be maintained by them and the circumstances under which, and the manner in which, an institution may be recognised as an observation home or the recognition may be withdrawn.

12. After-care organisations. The State Government may, by rules made under this Act, provide

(a) for the establishment or recognition of after-care organisations and the powers that may be exercised by them for effectively carrying out their functions under this Act.

(b) for a scheme of after-care programme to be followed by such after-care organisations for the purpose of taking care of juveniles after they leave juvenile homes or special homes and for the purpose of enabling them to lead an honest life.

(c) for the preparation or submission of a report by the probation officer in respect of each juvenile prior to his discharge from a juvenile home or special home, as the case may be regarding the necessity and nature of after-care of such juvenile, the period of such after-care, supervision thereof and for the submission of a report by the probation officer on the progress of each such juvenile.

(d) for the standards and the nature of services to be maintained by such after-care organisations.

(e) for such other matters as may be necessary for the purpose of effectively carrying out the scheme of aftercare programme of juveniles.

NEGLECTED JUVENILES

13. Production of neglected juveniles before Boards. 1. If any police officer or any other person or organisation authorised by the State Government in this behalf, by general or special order, is to opine that a person is apparently a neglected juvenile, such police officer or other person or organisation may take charge of that person for bringing him before a Board.

2. When information is given to an officer incharge of a police station about any neglected juvenile found with the limits of such station, he shall enter in a book to be kept for the purpose the substance of such information and take such action there on as he deems fit and if such officer does not propose take charge of the juvenile, he shall forward a copy of the entry made to the Board.

3. Every juvenile taken charge of under sub-section (1) shall be brought before the board without any loss of time but within a period of twenty-four hours of such charge taken excluding the time necessary for the journey from the place where the juvenile had been taken charge of to the Board.

4. Every juvenile taken charge of under sub-section (1) shall unless he is kept with his parent or guardian, be sent to an

observation home but not to a police station or jail until he can be brought before a Board.

14. Special procedure to be followed, when neglected juvenile has parents. 1. If a person, who is in the opinion of the police officer or the authorised person or organisation is a neglected juvenile, has a parent or guardian who has the actual charge of, or control over, the juvenile, the police officer or the authorised person or the organisation may, instead of taking charge of the juvenile, make report to the Board for initiating an inquiry, regarding that juvenile.

2. On receipt of a report under sub-section (1), the Board may call upon the parent or guardian to produce the juvenile before it and to show cause, why the juvenile should not be dealt with as neglected juvenile under the provisions of this Act and if it appears to the Board that the juvenile is likely to be removed from its jurisdiction or to be concealed, it may immediately order his removal to an observation home or a place of safety.

15. Inquiry by Board regarding neglected Juveniles. 1. When a person alleged to be a neglected juvenile is produced before a Board, it shall examine the police officer or the authorised person or, the organisation who brought the juvenile or made the report and record the substance of such examination and hold the inquiry in the prescribed manner and may make such orders in relation to the juvenile as it may deem fit.

2. Where a Board is satisfied on inquiry that a juvenile is a neglected juvenile and that it is expedient so to deal with him; the Board may make an order directing the juvenile to be sent to a juvenile home for the period until he ceases to be a juvenile.

Provided that the Board may, for reasons to be recorded, extend the period of such stay, but in no case the period of stay shall extend beyond the time when the juvenile attains the age of eighteen years, in the case of a boy, or twenty years, in the case of a girl.

Provided further that the Board may, if it is satisfied that having regard to the circumstances of the case it is expedient so to do, for reasons to be recorded, reduce the period of stay to such period as it thinks fit,

3. During the pendency of any inquiry regarding a juvenile, the juvenile shall, unless he is kept with his parent or guardian, be sent to an observation home or a place of safety for such period as may be specified in the order of the Board:

Provided that no juvenile shall be kept with his parent or guardian if, in the opinion of the Board, such parent or guardian is unfit or unable to exercise or does not exercise proper care and control over the juvenile.

16. Power to commit neglected juvenile to suitable custody: 1. If the Board so thinks fit, it may, instead of making an order under sub-section (2) of Section 15, for sending the juvenile to a juvenile home, make an order placing the juvenile under the care of a parent, guardian or other fit person, on such parent, guardian, or fit person executing a bond with or without surety to be responsible for the good behaviour and wellbeing of the juvenile and for the observance of such conditions as the Board may think fit to impose.

2. At the time of making an order under sub-section (1) or at any time subsequently the Board may, in addition, make an order that the juvenile be placed under supervision for any period not exceeding three years in the first instance.

3. Notwithstanding anything contained in sub-section (1) or sub-section (2), if at any time it appears to the Board, on receiving a report from the probation officer or otherwise, that there has been a breach of any of the conditions imposed by it in respect of the juvenile, it may, after making such inquiry as it deems fit, order the juvenile to be sent to a juvenile home.

17. Uncontrollable juveniles. Where a parent or guardian of a juvenile complains to the Board that he is not able to exercise proper care and control over the juvenile and the Board is satisfied on inquiry that proceedings under this Act should be initiated regarding the juvenile, it may send the juvenile to an observation home or a place of safety and make such further inquiry as it may deem fit and the provisions of Section 15 and Section 16 shall , as far as may be, apply to such proceedings.

DELINQUENT JUVENILES

18. Bail and custody of Juveniles. 1. When any person accused of a bailable or non-bailable offence and apparently a juvenile is arrested or detained or appears or is brought before a Juvenile Court, such person shall, notwithstanding anything contained in the Code of Criminal Procedure, 1973 (2 of 1974), or in any other law for the time being in force, be released on bail with or without surety but he shall not be so released if there appear reasonable grounds for believing that the release is likely to bring him into association with any known criminal or expose him to moral danger or that its release would defeat the ends of justice,

2. When such person having been arrested is not released or, bail under sub-section (1) by the officer-in-charge of the police station, such officer shall cause him to be kept in an observation home or a place of safety in the prescribed manner (but not in a police station or jail) until he can be brought before a Juvenile Court.

3. When such person is not released on bail under sub-section (1) by the Juvenile Court it shall, instead of committing him to prison, make an order sending him to an observation home or a place of safety for such period during the pendency of the inquiry regarding him as may be specified in the order.

19. Information to parent or guardian or probation officer. Where a juvenile is arrested, the officer incharge of the police station to which the juvenile is brought shall, as soon as may be after the arrest, inform

(a) the parent or guardian of the juvenile, if he can be found of such arrest and direct him to be present at the Juvenile Court before which the juvenile will appear; and

(b) the probation officer of such arrest in order to enable him to obtain information regarding the antecedents and family history of the juvenile and other material circumstances likely to be of assistance to the juvenile Court of making the inquiry.

20. Inquiry by Juvenile Court regarding delinquent Juveniles. Where a juvenile having been charged with an offence appears or is produced before a Juvenile Court, the Juvenile Court shall hold the inquiry in accordance with the provisions of Section 39 and may, subject to the provisions of this Act, make such order in relation to the juvenile as it deems fit.

21. Orders that may be passed regarding delinquent juveniles. 1. Where a Juvenile Court is satisfied on inquiry that a Juvenile has committed an offence, notwithstanding anything to the contrary contained in any such parent, guardian or other fit person executing a bond, with or without surety as that Court may require, for the good behaviour and well-being of the juvenile for any period not exceeding three years;

(c) direct the juvenile to be released on probation of good conduct and placed under the care of any fit institution for the good behaviour and wellbeing of the juvenile for any period no exceeding three years:

(d) make an order directing the juvenile to be sent to a special or ir default or furnishing security:
home,

(i) in the case of a boy over fourteen years of age or of a gir over sixteen years of age, for a period of not less thar three years;

(ii) in the case of any other juvenile, to the period until he ceases to be a juvenile:

Provided that the Juvenile Court may, if it is satisfied tha having regard to the nature of the offence and circumstances of th case it is expedient so to do, for reasons to be recorded, reduce th period of stay to such period as it thinks fit:

Provided further that the Juvenile Court may, for reasons to b recorded, extend the period of such stay, but in no case the period c stay shall extend beyond the time when the juvenile attains the ag of eighteen years, in the case of a boy, or twenty years, in the case c a girl;

(e) order the juvenile to pay a fine if he is over fourteen years of ag and earns money.

2. Where an order under clause (b), clause (c) or clause (e) c sub-section (1) is made, the Juvenile Court may, if it is of opinion tha in the interests of the juvenile and of the public it is expedient so t do, in addition make an order that the delinquent juvenile sha remain under the supervision of a probation officer named in th order during such period, not exceeding three years as may b specified therein, and may in such supervision order impose suc conditions as it deems necessary for, the due supervision for th delinquent juvenile.

Provided that any time afterwards it appears to the Juvenil Court on receiving a report from the probation officer or otherwis that the delinquent juvenile has not been of good behaviour durin the period of supervision or that the fit institution under whose cas the juvenile was placed is no longer able or willing to ensure th good behaviour and well-being of the juvenile it may after makin such inquiry as it deems fit, order the delinquent juvenile to be ser to special home.

3. The Juvenile Court making a supervision order under sub-section (2), shall explain to the Juvenile and the parent, guardian or other fit person or fit institution, as the case may be, under whose care the juvenile has been placed, the terms and conditions of the order and shall forthwith furnish one copy of the supervision order to the juvenile, the parent, guardian or other fit person or fit institution, as the case may be, the sureties, if any, and the probation officer.

4. In determining special home, or any person or institution to whose custody a juvenile is to be committed or entrusted under this Act, the court shall pay due regard to the religious denomination of the juvenile to ensure that religious instruction contrary to the religious persuasion of the juvenile is not imparted to him.

22. *Order that may not be passed against delinquent juveniles.* Notwithstanding anything to the contrary contained in any other law time being in force, no delinquent juvenile shall be sentenced to death or imprisonment, or committed to prison in default of payment of fine.

Provided that where a juvenile who has attained the age of fourteen years has committed an offence and the Juvenile Court is satisfied that the offence committed is of so serious a nature that his conduct and behaviour been such that it would not be in his interest or in the interest of Juvenile in a special home to send him to such special home and that none of the other measures provided under this Act is suitable or sufficient, or Juvenile Court, may order the delinquent juvenile to be kept in safe custody in such place and manner as it thinks fit and shall report the case for the orders of the State Government.

2. On receipt of a report from a Juvenile Court under, sub-section (1), the State Government may make such arrangement in respect of the juvenile as it deems proper and may order such delinquent juvenile to be detained at such place and on which conditions as it thinks fit.

Provided that the period of detention so ordered shall not exceed that maximum period of imprisonment to which the juvenile could have been sentenced for ft. offence committed.

23. *Proceeding under Chapter VIII of the Code of Criminal Procedure not competent against juvenile.* Notwithstanding anything to the contrary contained in the Code of Criminal Procedure, 1973 (2 of 1974) no proceeding shall be instituted and no order shall be passed against a juvenile under Chapter VIII of the said Code.

24. No joint trial of juvenile and person not a juvenile. 1. Notwithstanding anything contained in Section 223 of the Code of Criminal Procedure, 1973 (2 of 1974), or any other law for the time being in force, no juvenile shall be charged with or tried for; any offence together with a person who is not a juvenile.

2. If a person is accused of an offence for which under Section 223 of the Code of Criminal Procedure, 1973 (2 of 1974), or in any other law for the time being in force, such juvenile and any person who is not a juvenile, would, but for the prohibition contained in sub-section (1), have been charged and tried together, the court taking cognizance of that offence shall direct separate trials of the juvenile and the other person.

25. Removal of disqualification attaching to conviction. Notwithstanding anything contained in any other law, a juvenile who has committed an offence and has been dealt with under the provisions of this Act shall not suffer disqualification, if any attaching to a conviction of an offence under such law.

26. Special provision in respect of pending cases. Notwithstanding anything contained in this Act, all proceedings in respect of a juvenile pending in any court in any area on the date on which this Act comes into force in that area, shall be continued in that court as if this Act had not been passed and if the court finds that the juvenile has committed an offence, it shall record such finding and instead of passing any sentence in respect of the juvenile, forward the Juvenile to the Juvenile Court which shall pass orders in respect of that juvenile in accordance with the provisions of this Act as if it has been satisfied on inquiry under this Act that the juvenile has committed the offence.

PROCEDURE OF COMPETENT AUTHORITIES GENERALLY AND APPEALS AND REVISION FROM ORDERS OF SUCH AUTHORITIES

27. Sittings, etc., of Boards and Juvenile Courts. 1. A Board or a Juvenile Court shall hold its sittings at such place, on such day and in such manner, as may be prescribed.

2. A Magistrate empowered to exercise the powers of a Board or, as the case may be, a Juvenile Court under sub-section (2) of Section 7 shall, while holding any inquiry regarding a juvenile under this Act, as far as practicable, sit in a building or room different from that in which the ordinary sittings of Civil and Criminal Courts are

held, or on different days or at times different from those at which the ordinary sittings of such Courts are held.

3. An inquiry regarding a juvenile under this Act shall be held expeditiously and shall ordinarily be completed within a period of three months from date of its commencement, unless, for special reasons to be recorded in writing, the competent authority otherwise directs.

28. Persons who may be present before the competent authority. 1. Save as provided in this Act, no person shall be present at any sitting of a competent authority, except

(a) any officer of the competent authority, or
(b) the parties to the inquiry before the competent authority the parent or guardian of the juvenile and other persons directly concerned in the inquiry including officers and legal practitioners, and
(c) Such other persons as the competent authority may permit to be present.

2. Notwithstanding anything contained in sub-section (1), if at any stage during an inquiry a competent authority, considers it to be expedient in the interest of the juvenile or on grounds of, decency or morality that any person including the police officers, legal practitioners, the parent, guardian or the juvenile himself should withdraw, the competent authority may give such directions, and if any person refuses to comply with such direction, the competent authority may have him removed and may, for this purpose, cause to be used such force as may be necessary.

3. No legal practitioner shall be entitled to appear before a Board in any case or proceeding before it, except with the special permission of that Board.

29. Attendance of parent or guardian of juvenile. Any competent authority before which a juvenile is brought under any of the provisions of this Act may, whenever it so thinks fit, require any parent or guardian having the actual charge of, or control over, the juvenile to be present at any proceeding respect of the juvenile.

30. Dispensing with attendance of juvenile. If, at any stage during the course of an inquiry, a competent authority is satisfied that the attendance of the juvenile is not essential for the purpose of the inquiry, the competent authority may dispense with his attendance and proceed with the inquiry in the absence of the juvenile.

31. *Committal to approved place of juvenile suffering from dangerous disease and his future disposal.* 1. When a juvenile who has been brought before a competent authority under this Act is found to be suffering from a disease requiring prolonged medical treatment or physical or mental complaint that will respond to treatment, the competent authority may send the juvenile to any place recognised to be an approved place in accordance with the rules made under this Act for such period as it may think necessary for the required treatment.

2. Where a juvenile is found to be suffering from leprosy or is of unsound mind he shall be dealt with under the provisions of the Lepers Act, 1898 (3 of 1898), or the Indian Lunacy Act, 1912 (4 of 1912), as the case may be.

3. Where a competent authority has taken, action under sub-section (1) in the case of juvenile suffering from an infectious or contagious disease, the competent authority before resorting the said juvenile to his partner in marriage, if there has been such, or to the guardian, as the case may be, shall where it is satisfied that such action will be in the interest of the said juvenile call upon his partner in marriage or the guardian, as the case may be, to satisfy the competent authority by submitting to medical examination that such partner or guardian will not re-infect the juvenile in respect of whom the order has been passed.

32. *Presumption and determination of age.* 1. Where it appears to a competent authority that a person brought before it under any of the provisions of this Act is a juvenile, the competent authority shall make due inquiry as to the age of that person and for that purpose shall take such evidence as may be necessary and shall record a finding whether the person is a juvenile or not, stating his age as nearly as may be.

2. No order of a competent authority shall be deemed to have become invalid merely by any subsequent proof that the person in respect of whom the order has been made is not a Juvenile, and the age recorded by the competent authority to be the age of the person brought before it shall, for the purposes of this Act, be deemed to be the true age of that person.

33. *Circumstances to be taken into consideration in making orders under the Act.* In making any order in respect of a juvenile under this Act, a competent authority shall take into consideration the following circumstances, namely:

(a) the age of the juvenile,
(b) the state of physical and mental health of the juvenile:
(c) the circumstances in which the Juvenile was and is living;
(d) the reports made by the probation officer
(e) the religious persuasion of the juvenile
(f) such other circumstances as may, in the opinion of the competent authority, require to be taken into consideration in the interest of the welfare of the juvenile.

Provided that in the case of a delinquent juvenile, the above circumstances shall be taken into consideration after the Juvenile Court has recorded a finding against the juvenile that he has committed the offence:

Provided further that if no report of the probation officer is received within ten weeks of his being informed under Section 19, it shall be open in the Juvenile Court to proceed without it.

34. Sending a juvenile outside jurisdiction. In the case of a neglected or delinquent juvenile whose ordinary place of residence ties outside the jurisdiction of the competent authority before which he is brought, the competent authority may, if satisfied under due inquiry that it is expedient so to do, send the juvenile back to a relative or other person who is fit and willing to receive him at his ordinary place of residence and exercise proper care and control over him, notwithstanding that such place of residence is outside the jurisdiction of the competent authority; and the competent authority exercising jurisdiction over the place to which the juvenile is sent shall in respect of any matter arising subsequently have the same powers in relation to the juvenile as if the original order had been passed by itself.

35. Reports to be treated as confidential. The report of the probation officer or any circumstance considered by the competent authority under Section 33 shall be treated as confidential.

Provided that the competent authority may, if it so thinks fit communicate the substance thereof to the juvenile or his parent or guardian and may give such juvenile, parent or guardian an opportunity of producing such evidence as may be relevant to the matter stated in the report.

36. Prohibition of publication of names, etc., of juveniles involved in any proceeding under the Act. 1. No report in any newspaper, magazine or news-sheet or any inquiry regarding a juvenile under this Act shall disclose the name, address of school or any other particulars calculated to lead to the identification of the Juvenile nor shall any picture of any such juvenile be published.

Provided that for reasons to be recorded in writing, the authority holding inquiry may permit such disclosure, if in its opinion such disclosure is in the interest of the juvenile.

2. Any person contravening the provisions of sub-section (1) shall be punishable with fine which may extend to one thousand rupees.

37. Appeals. 1. Subject to the provisions of this section, any person aggrieved by an order made by a competent authority under this Act may, within thirty days from the date of such order, prefer an appeal to the Court of Session.

Provided that the Court of Session may entertain the appeal after the expiry of the said period of thirty days if it is satisfied that the appellant was prevented by sufficient cause from filing the appeal in time.

2. No appeal shall lie from:

(a) any order of acquittal made by the Juvenile Court in respect of a juvenile alleged to have committed an offence; or

(b) any order made by a Board in respect of a finding that a person is not a neglected juvenile.

3. No second appeal shall lie from any order of the Court of Session passed in appeal under this section.

38. Revision. The High Court may at any time, either of its own motion or on an application received in this behalf, call for the record of any proceeding in which any competent authority or Court of Session has passed an order for the purpose of satisfying itself as to the legality or propriety of any such order and may pass such order in relation thereto as it thinks fit:

Provided that the High Court shall not pass an order under this section prejudicial to any person without giving him a reasonable opportunity of being heard.

39. Procedure in inquiries, appeals and revision proceedings. 1. Save as otherwise expressely provided by this Act, a competent authority while holding any inquiry under any of the provisions of this Act, shall follow such procedure as may be prescribed and subject thereto shall follow, as far as may be the procedure laid down in the

Code of Criminal Procedure, 1973 (2 of 1974), for trials in summons cases.

2. Save as otherwise expressely provided by or under this Act, the procedure to be followed in hearing appeals or revision proceedings under this Act shall be, as far as practicable, in accordance with the provisions of the Code of Criminal Procedure, 1973 (2 of 1974).

40. Power to amend orders. 1. Without prejudice to the provisions for appeal and revision under this Act, any competent authority may, either on its own motion or on an application received in this behalf, amend any order as to the institution to which a juvenile is to be sent or as to the person under whose care or supervision a juvenile is to be placed under this act.

2. Clerical mistakes in orders passed by a competent authority or errors arising therein from any accidental slip or omission may, at any time be corrected by the competent authority either on its own motion or on an application received in this behalf.

SPECIAL OFFENCES IN RESPECT OF JUVENILES

41. Punishment for cruelty to juvenile. 1. Whoever, having the actual charge of, or control over a juvenile, assaults, abandons, exposes or wilfully neglects the juvenile or causes or procures him to be assaulted; abandoned, exposed or neglected in a manner likely to cause such juvenile unnecessary mental or physical suffering shall be punishable with imprisonment for a term which may extend to six months, or with fine or with both.

2. No court shall take cognizance of an offence punishable under sub-section (1) unless the complaint is filed with the previous sanction of the State Government or an officer authorised by it in this behalf.

42. Employment of juveniles for begging. 1. Whoever employs or uses any juvenile for the purposes of begging or causes any juvenile to beg shall be punishable with imprisonment for a term which may extend to three years and shall also be liable to fine.

2. Whoever, having the actual charge of, or control over, a juvenile abets the commission of the offence punishable under sub-section (1), shall be punishable with imprisonment for a term which may extend to one year and shall also be liable to fine.

3. The offence punishable under this section shall be cognizable.

43. Penalty for giving intoxicating liquor or narcotic drug or psychotropic substance to a juvenile. Whoever gives, or causes to be given, to any juvenile any intoxicating liquor in a public place or any narcotic drug or psychotropic substance except upon the order of a duly qualified medical practitioner or in case of sickness shall be punishable with imprisonment for a term which may extend to three years and shall also be liable to fine.

44. Exploitation of juvenile employees. Whoever ostensibly procures a juvenile for the purpose of any employment and withholds the earnings of the juvenile or uses such earnings for his own purposes shall be punishable with imprisonment for a term which may extend to three years and shall also be liable to fine.

45. Alternative punishments. Where an act or omission constitutes an offence punishable under this Act and also under any other Central or State Act, then notwithstanding anything contained in any law for the time being in force, the offender found guilty of such offence shall be liable to punishment only under such Act as provides for punishment which is greater in degree.

MISCELLANEOUS

46. Power of the State Government to discharge and transfer Juveniles. 1. The State Government may, notwithstanding anything contained in this Act, at any time, order a neglected or delinquent juvenile to be discharged from the juvenile home or special home, either absolutely or on such conditions as it may think fit to impose.

2. The State Government may, notwithstanding anything containing in this Act, order

(a) a neglected juvenile to be transferred from one juvenile home to another;

(b) a delinquent juvenile to be transferred from one juvenile home to another or from a special home to borstal school where such school exists or from a special home to juvenile home;

(c) a neglected or a delinquent juvenile to be transferred from a juvenile home or a special home to a fit person or a fit institution;

(d) a juvenile who has been released on licence which has been released on licence which has been revoked or forfeited, to be sent to the special home or juvenile home from which he was released or to any other juvenile home or special home or borstal school.

Provided that the total period of the stay of the juvenile in a juvenile home or a special home or a fit institution or under a fit person shall not be increased by such transfer.

3. The State Government may, notwithstanding anything contained in this Act at any time, discharge a juvenile from the care of any person under whom he was placed under this Act either absolutely or on such conditions as may think fit to impose.

47. Transfers between juvenile homes, etc., under the Act and juvenile homes, etc., of like nature in different parts of India. The Government of a State may direct any neglected juvenile or delinquent juvenile to be transferred from any juvenile home or special home within the State to any other juvenile home, special home or institution of a like nature in any other State with the consent of the Government of that State.

2. The Government of a State may, by general or special order provide for the reception in a juvenile home or special home within the State of a neglected juvenile or delinquent juvenile detained in a juvenile home or special home or institution of a like nature in any other State where the Government of that State makes an order for such transfer, and upon such transfer the provisions of this Act shall apply to such juvenile as if he had been originally ordered to be sent to such juvenile home or special home under this Act.

48. Transfer of juveniles of unsound mind or suffering from leprosy or addicted to drugs. 1. Where it appears to the State Government that any juvenile kept in a special home or a juvenile home or institution in pursuance of this Act is suffering from leprosy or is of unsound mind, or is addicted to any narcotic drug or psychotropic substance, the State Government may order his removal to a leper asylum or mental hospital or treatment centre for drug addicts or other place of safe custody for being kept there for such period not exceeding the period for which he is required to be kept in custody under the orders of the competent authority or for such further period as may be certified by the medical officer to be necessary for proper treatment of the juvenile.

2. Where it appears to the State Government that the juvenile is cured of leprosy or of unsoundness of mind or drug addiction it may, if the juvenile is still liable to be kept in custody, order the person having charge of the juvenile to send him to the special home or juvenile home or institution from which he was removed or, if the juvenile is no longer liable to be kept in custody, order him to be

discharged.

49. Placing out on licence. 1. When a juvenile is kept in a juvenile home or special home, the State Government may, if it so thinks fit, release the juvenile from the juvenile home or special home and grant him a written licence for such period and on such conditions as may be specified in the licence permitting him to live with, or under the supervision of, any responsible person named in the licence willing to receive and take charge of him with a view to educate him and train him for some useful trade or calling.

2. Any licence so granted under sub-section (1) shall be in force for the period specified in the licence or until revoked or forfeited by the breach of any of the conditions on which it was granted.

3. The State Government may, at any time, by order in writing revoke any such licence and order the juvenile to return to the juvenile home or special home from which he was released or to any other juvenile home or special home, and shall do so at the desire of the person with whom or under whose supervision the juvenile has been permitted to live in accordance with a licence granted under sub-section (1).

4. When a licence has been revoked or forfeited and the juvenile refuses or fails to return to the special home or juvenile home to which he was directed so to return the State Government may, if necessary, cause him to be taken charge and to be taken back to the special home or juvenile home.

5. The time during which a juvenile is absent from a special home or juvenile home in pursuance of a licence granted under this section shall be deemed to be a part of the time for which he is liable to be kept in custody in the special home or juvenile home.

Provided that when a juvenile has failed to return to the special home or juvenile home on the licence being revoked or forfeited, the time which elapses after his failure so to shall be excluded in computing the time during which he is liable to be kept in custody.

50. Provision in respect of escaped juveniles. Notwithstanding anything to the contrary contained in any other law for the time being in force, any police officer may take charge without warrant of a juvenile who has escaped from a special home or a Juvenile home or from the care of a person under whom he was placed under this Act and shall send the juvenile back to the special home or the juvenile home or that person, as the case may be, and no proceeding shall be instituted in respect of the juvenile by reason or such escape but the special home, juvenile home or the person may after giving the information to the competent authority which passed the order in respect of the juvenile, take such steps against the juvenile as may be deemed necessary.

51. *Contribution by parents.* 1. The competent authority which makes an order for sending a neglected juvenile or a delinquent juvenile home or a special home or placing the juvenile under the care of a fit person or fit institution may make an order requiring the parent or other person liable to maintain the juvenile to contribute his maintenance, is able to do so, in the prescribed manner.

2. The competent authority before making any order under sub-section (1) shall inquire into the circumstances of the parent or other person liable to maintain the juvenile and shall record evidence, if any, in the presence of the parent or such other person, as the case may be.

This person liable to maintain a juvenile shall, for the purposes to (1), include in the case of illegitimacy, his putative father.

Provided that where the juvenile is illegitimate and an order for his maintenance has been made under Section 125 of the Code of Criminal Procedure, 1973 (2 of 1974), the competent authority shall not ordinarily make an order for contribution against the putative father, but may order the whole or any part of the sums accruing due under the said order for maintenance to be paid to such person as may be named by the competent authority and such sum shall be paid by him towards the maintenance of the Juvenile.

4. Any order made under this section may be enforced in the same manner as an order under Section 125 of the Code of Criminal Procedure, 1973 (2 of 1974).

52. *Fund.* 1. The State Government may create a Fund under such name as it thinks fit for the welfare and rehabilitation of the juveniles dealt with under this Act.

2. There shall be credited to the Fund such voluntary donations, contributions or subscriptions as may be made by ay individual or organisation.

3. The Fund created under sub-section (1) shall be administered by such officers or authority, in such manner and for such purposes as may be prescribed.

53. *Advisory Board.* 1. The State Government may constitute an Advisory Board to advise it on matters relating to the establishment and maintenance of homes, mobilisation of resources, provision of facilities for education, training and rehabilitation of neglected and delinquent juveniles and coordination among the various official and non-official agencies concerned.

The Advisory Board shall consist of such number of officers and other persons as the State Government thinks fit and may also include experts and the representatives of voluntary organisations engaged in the relevant areas.

54. Visitors. (1) The State Government may nominate not more than three non-officials to be Visitors for each of the homes established under this Act.

A Visitor nominated for a home under sub-section (1) shall periodically visit such home and make a report to the State Government.

55. Control of custodian over juvenile. Any person in whose custody a juvenile is placed in pursuance of this Act shall, while the order is in force, have the like control over the juvenile as he would have if, he were his parent, and shall be responsible for his maintenance, and the juvenile shall continue in his custody for the period stated by the competent authority, notwithstanding that he is claimed by his parent or any other person.

Provided that no juvenile while in such custody shall be carried except with permission of the competent authority.

56. Delinquent juvenile undergoing sentence at commencement of the Act. In any area in which this Act is brought into force, the State Government may direct that a delinquent juvenile who is undergoing any sentence of imprisonment at the commencement of this Act shall, in lieu of undergoing such sentence, be sent to a special home or be kept in safe custody in such place and manner as the State Government thinks fit for the remainder of the period of the sentence I and the provisions of this Act shall apply to the juvenile as if he had been ordered by a Juvenile Court to be sent to such special home or, as the case may be, ordered to be detained under sub-section (2) of Section 22.

57. Appointment of officers. 1. The State Government may appoint as many probation officers, officers for the inspection of special homes, juvenile homes, observation homes or after-care organisations and such other officers as it may deem necessary for carrying out the purposes of this Act.

2. It shall be the duty of the probation officer

(a) to inquire, in accordance with the direction of a competent authority, into the antecedents and family history of any juvenile accused of an offence, with a view to assist the authority in making the inquiry.

(b) to visit neglected and delinquent juvenile at such intervals as the probation officer may think fit;

(c) to report to the competent authority as to the behaviour of any neglected or delinquent juvenile.

(d) to advice and assist neglected or delinquent juveniles and if necessary, endeavour to find them suitable employment

(e) where a neglected or delinquent juvenile is placed under the care of any person or institution on certain conditions, to see whether such conditions are being complied with; and

(f) to perform such other duties as may be prescribed.

3. Any officer empowered in this behalf by the State Government may enter new special home, juvenile home, observation home or aftercare organisation and make a complete inspection thereof in all its departments and of all papers, registers and accounts relating thereto and shall submit the report of such inspection to the State Government.

58. Officers appointed under the Act to be public servants. Probation officers and other officers appointed in pursuance of this Act shall be deemed to be public servants within the meaning of Section 21 of the Indian Penal Code (45 of 1860).

59. Procedure in respect of bonds. The provisions of Chapter XXXIII of the Code of Criminal Procedure, 1973 (2 of 1974), shall, as far as may be, apply to bonds taken under this Act.

60. Delegation of powers. The State Government may, by general or special order direct that any power exercisable by it under this Act shall, in such circumstances and under such conditions, if any, as may be specified in the order, be exercisable also by an officer subordinate to that Government.

61. Protection of action taken in good faith. No suit or other legal proceedings shall lie against the State Government or any probation officer or other officer appointed under this Act; In respect of anything which is in good faith done or intended to be done in pursuance of this Act or any rules or orders made thereunder.

62. Power to make rules. 1. The State Government may, by notification in the Official Gazette, make rules to carry out the purposes of this Act.

2. In particular, and without prejudice to the generality of the foregoing power, such rules may provide for all or any of the following matters, namely:

(a) the places at which, the days on which, the time at which, and the manner in which, a competent authority may hold its sittings.

(b) the procedure to be followed by a competent authority in holding inquiries under this Act, and the mode of dealing with juveniles suffering from dangerous diseases or mental complaints.

(c) the circumstances in which, and the conditions subject to which, an institution may be certified as a special home or a juvenile's home or recognised as an observation home, and the certification or recognition withdrawn;

(d) the internal management of special homes, juvenile homes and observation homes and the standards and the nature of services to be maintained by them;

(e) the functions and responsibilities of special homes, juvenile homes and observation homes;

(f) the inspection of special homes, juvenile homes, observation homes and aftercare organisations;

(g) the establishment, management and functions of aftercare organisations; the circumstances in which, and the conditions subject to which an institution may be recognised as an aftercare organisation and such other matters as are referred to in Section 12;

(h) the qualifications and duties of probation officers;

(i) the recruitment and training of persons appointed to carry out the purposes of this Act and the terms and conditions of their services;

(j) the conditions subject to which a girl who is a neglected or delinquent juvenile may be escorted from one place to another, and the manner in which a juvenile may be sent outside the jurisdiction of a competent authority;

(k) the manner in which, contribution for the maintenance of a juvenile may be ordered to be paid by a parent or guardian;

(l) the officers or authorities by whom, the manner in which and the purpose for which the Fund created under Section 52 shall be administered;

(m) the conditions under which a juvenile may be placed out on licence and the form and conditions of such licence;

(n) the conditions subject to which juveniles may be placed under the care of any parent, guardian or other fit person or fit institution under this Act and the obligations of such persons or institutions towards the juveniles so placed;

(o) any other matter which has to be, or may be prescribed.

3. Every rule made by a State Government under this Act shall be laid, as soon as may be after it is made, before the Legislature of that State.

63. *Repeal and savings.* If, immediately before the date on which this Act comes into force in any State, there is in force in that State, any law corresponding to this Act, that law shall stand repealed on the said date:

Provided that the repeal shall not affect:

(a) the previous operation of any law so repealed or anything duly done or suffered thereunder; or

(b) any right, privilege, obligation or liability, acquired or incurred under any law so repealed; or

(c) any penalty, forfeiture or punishment incurred in respect of any offence committed against any law so repealed; or

(d) any investigation, legal proceeding or remedy in respect of any such right, privilege, obligation, liability, penalty, forfeiture or punishment as aforesaid; and

any such investigation, legal proceeding or remedy may be instituted, continued or enforced and any such penalty, forfeiture or punishment may be imposed, as if this Act had not been passed.

4

Criminals, Prisoners and Human Rights

THE IDENTIFICATION OF PRISONERS ACT, 1920

An Act to authorize the taking of measurements and photographs of convicts and others.

Whereas it is expedient to authorise the taking of measurements and photographs of convicts and others; it is hereby enacted as follows.

*1. **Short title and extent.*** 1. This Act may be called the Identification of Prisoners Act, 1920; and

2. It extends to the whole of India except the territories which, immediately before the 1st November, 1956, were comprised in Part B States.

STATE AMENDMENTS

Andhra Pradesh

In its application to the areas in the former Part B State of Hyderabad, for sub-section (2) the following shall be substituted; namely;

"(2) It extends to the whole of the Hyderabad area of the State of Andhra Pradesh" (Vide Hyderabad Act 27 of 1956, Section 2 and Sch. as adopted APALO 1957).

Karnataka

In its application to the State of Karnataka in Section 1, sub-section (2) add the following after the "Part B States":

"Other than the territories specified in clause (a) and clause (b) of sub-section 7 of the State Reorganisation Act, 1956. (Vide Karnataka Act 29 of 1975 Section 4(1), (w.e.f. 12–8–1995).

Madhya Pradesh

In sub-section 2(2), after the words "Part B State", insert the words "other than Madhya Pradesh and Sironj regions of the State of Madhya Pradesh" [Vide M.P. Act 10 of 1961, Sec 3 and Soh., Pt. A (w.e. f 1–2–62).

Maharashtra

In sub-section after the words "Part B States", insert the words "other than the Hyderabad area of State of Maharashtra (Vide Maharashtra" Act 35 if 1970, Section 2 (w.e.f. 4-9-1956)

2. Definitions: In this Act, unless there is anything repugnant in the subject or context.

(a) "measurements" include finger-impressions and foot-print impressions;

(b) "police officer" means an officer in charge of a police station, a police officer making an investigation under Chapter XIV of the Code of Criminal Procedure, 1898 (5 of 1898) or any other police officer not below the rank of Sub-Inspector; and

(c) "prescribed" means prescribed by rules made under this Act.

STATE AMENDMENTS

Tamil Nadu

In its application to the state of Tamil Nadu in Section 2, clause (b), after the words 'Sub-Inspector, the words "and includes Finger Print Experts of the Finger Print Bureau, Madras and of the Single Digit Finger Print sections in the State of Tamil Nadu" inserted. (Vide T.N.Act 44 of 1981, Section 2).

3. *Taking of measurements, etc. of convicted persons.* Every person who has been:

(a) convicted of any offence punishable with rigorous imprisonment for a term of one year or upwards, or of any offence which would render him liable to enhanced punishment on a subsequent conviction; or

(b) ordered to give security for his good behaviour under Section 118 of the Code of Criminal Procedure, 1898 (5 of 1898), I shall, if so required, allow his measurements and photograph to be taken by a police officer in the prescribed manner.

STATE AMENDMENTS

Gujarat

In clause (b) of Section 3, add the following, shall be substituted namely:

"or under Section 93 of the Bombay Prohibition Act, 1949. (Vide

Bombay Act 58 of 1953, Section 2 (w.e.f. 2-11-1953); Act 11 of 1960, Section 87.

Maharashtra

For Section 3 substitute the following:

"3. *Taking of measurements, etc. of convicted persons.* Every person who has been

(a) convicted of any offence punishable with rigorous imprisonment for a term of one year or upwards, or of any offence punishable under Sec. 19 of the Dangerous Drugs Act, 1930, or of any offence which would render him liable to enhanced punishment on a subsequent conviction.

(b) ordered to give security for his good behaviour under Section 118 of the Code of Criminal Procedure, 1898, or under Section 93 of the Bombay Prohibition Act, 1949, or to give security for abstaining from commission, of certain offences under Section 18 of the Dangerous Drugs Act. 1930.

shall, if so required allow his measurements, and photographs to be taken by a police officer in the prescribed manner [vide Maharashtra Act 35 of 1970, Section 4 (w.e.f. 1-3-1971)].

4. *Taking of measurements etc, of non-convicted persons.* Any person who has been arrested in connection, "with an offence punishable with rigorous imprisonment for a term of one year or upwards shall, if so required by a police officer, allow his measurements to be taken in the prescribed manner.

STATE AMENDMENTS

Gujarat

In its application to the State of Gujarat for Section 4, the following shall be substituted, namely:

"4. Taking of measurements, etc., of non-convicted persons: Any person

(a) who has been arrested

(i) under Section 55 of the Code of Criminal Procedure, 1898, or under Section 4 of the Bombay Beggars Act, 1945.

(ii) in connection with an offence punishable under Section 122 of the Bombay Police Act, 1951, or under Section 6 or 9 of the Bombay Beggars Act, 1945, or in connection with an offence punishable with rigorous imprisonment for a term of one year or upwards, or

(b) in respect of whom a direction or order under Section 55 or 56 of the Bombay Police Act, 1951, or under sub-section (1) or (2) of Section 23 of the Bombay Beggars Act, 1945, or under Section 2 of the Bombay Public Security Measures Act, 1947, has been made,

shall, if so required by a police officer, allow his measurements or photograph to be taken in the prescribed manner. [Vide Bombay Acts, 15 of 1948, Section 2 (w.e.f. 24-3-1948) and 21 of 1954, Section 3 and Sch. II (w.e.f. 8-4-1954), Act 11 of 1960, Section 87]

Karnataka

In its application to the State of Karnataka, for Section 4 substitute the following:

(a) who has been arrested in connection with an offence punishable under Section 66 of the Karnataka Police Act, 1963, or in connection with an offence punishable with rigorous imprisonment for a term of one year or upward or in connection with an offence for the commission of which on a second or subsequent occasion enhanced penalties have been proved for under any law for the time being in force, or

(b) in respect of whom direction or order under Section 54 or 55 of the Karnataka Police Act, 1963, has been made,

shall if so required by a police officer, allow his measurement photographs to be taken in the prescribed manner".

Maharashtra

For Section 4, substitute the following

4. Any person arrested

(a) who has been convicted

(i) in connection with an offence punishable under Section 19 of the of the Dangerous Drugs Act, 1930, or Section 66, 69 or 85 of the Bombay Prohibition Act, 1949, or Section 122 of the Bombay Police Act, 1951, or Section of the Drugs and Magic Remedies Act, 1954, or Section 8 of the Suppression of the Immoral Traffic in Women and Girls

Act, 1958, or Section 6 or 11 of the Bombay Prevention of Begging Act, 1959, or any other offence punishable with rigorous imprisonment for a term of one year or upwards, or

(ii) under Section 54, 55 or 151 of the Code of Criminal Procedure 1898 or Section 4 of the Passport Act, 1920, or

(b) in respect of whom a direction or order under Section 5 of the Passport (Entry into India) Act, 1920 or under Sections 55, 56 or 57 of the Bombay Police Act, 1951, has been made, or

(c) to whom a pardon has been tendered. Under Section 337 or 338 or who has been acquitted under Section 339-A of the Code of Criminal Procedure, 1898,

shall it so required by a Police Officer, allow his measurements or photograph to be taken in the prescribed manner" [Vide Maharashtra Act 35 of 1970, Section 5 (w.e.f. 1-3-1971)].

4.A Taking of measurements, etc., of habitual offenders against whom restriction order is made. Any person against whom an order of restriction has been made under the Provisions of Karnataka Habitual Offenders Act, 1961, shall if so required by a police officer, allow his measurements or photograph to be taken in the prescribed manner.

Section 4-A

Gujarat : Maharashtra

In its application to the State of Bombay, after Section 4, insert the following:

"***4-A. Taking of measurements, etc., of habitual offenders against whom restriction order is made.*** Any person against whom an order of restriction has been made under the Provisions of the Bombay Habitual Offenders Act 1959, shall, if so required, allow his measurements and photographs to be taken by a police officer in the prescribed manner," [Vide Bombay Act 58 of 1953, Section 3 (w.e.f. 2-11-1953) and Maharashtra Act 35 of 1970 Section (w.e.f. 1-3-1971): Act 1 of 1960 Section 87].

Karnataka

In its application to the State of Karnataka after Section 4A (as inserted by Karnataka Act 29 of 1975) insert after Section 4A, the following

"**4-B. *Taking of measurements, etc., of beggars under the Karnataka Prohibition of Beggary Act, 1975.*** Any person who has been arrested and not released under sub-section (2) of Section 11 of the Karnataka Prohibition of Beggary Act, 1975 (Karnataka Act 27 of 1975) or against whom an order of detention has been made under sub-section (1) of Section 12 of the said Act, shall if so required by an officer incharge of receiving centre or relief centre allow his measurements and photographs to be taken in the prescribed manner." [Vide Karnataka Act I of 1987, Section 2 (w.e.f. 16-1-1982).

5. *Power of Magistrate to order a person to be measured or photographed.* If a Magistrate is satisfied that, for the purposes of any investigation or proceeding under the Code of Criminal Procedure, 1898 (5 of 1898) it is expedient to direct any person to allow his measurements or photograph to be taken, he may make an order to that effect, and in that case the person to whom the order relates shall be produced or shall attend at the time and place, specified in the order and shall allow his measurements or photograph to be taken, as the case may be, by a police officer.

Provided that no order shall be made directing any person to be photographed except by a Magistrate of the first class:

Provided further, that no order be made under this section unless the person has at some time been arrested in connection with such investigation or proceeding.

STATE AMENDMENTS

Gujarat : Maharashtra

In its application to these States, in Section 5

(a) In the first proviso, for the words "except by a Magistrate of the class" substitute the words "except by the District Magistrate, Sub-Divisional Magistrate, a Magistrate of the first class [Vide Bombay Act 8 of 1954, Section 2 and Schedule, Part II (w.e.f. 10-2-1954) and Maharashtra Act 35 of 1,970, Section 3 (w.e.f. 1-3-1971) Act 11 of 1960, Section 87.

(b) To the first proviso add the words of a Presidency Magistrate, now it has been replaced by the words metropolitan Magistrates, Besides Bombay, Calcutta and Madras, Ahmedabad has such Magistrates. See Criminal Procedure Code, 1973, Sections 8 and 16 [Vide Bombay Act 11 of 1922,

Section 3 (w.e.f. 14-12-1922) as amended by Bombay Act 17 of 1945, Maharashtra Act 35 of 1970, Section 3 (w.e.f. 1–3–1971), Act 11 of 1960, Section 87.

Karnataka

In its application to the State of Karnataka, in Section 5, substitute the following for first proviso

Provided that no order shall be made directing any person to be photographed except by a District Magistrate a Sub-Divisional Magistrate or a Magistrate of the First Class [vide Karnataka Act 29 of 1975, Section 4 (3) (w.e.f. 12-3-1975)

6. Resistance to the taking of, measurements, etc. 1. If any person who under this Act is required to allow his measurements or photograph to be taken resists or refuse to allow the taking of the same, it shall be lawful to use all means necessary to secure the taking thereof.

2. Resistance to or refusal to allow taking of measurement or photograph under this Act shall be deemed to be an offence under Section 186 of the Indian Penal Code (45 of 1860).

7. Destruction of photographs and records of measurements on acquittal. Where any person who not having been previously convicted of an offence punishable with rigorous imprisonment for a term of one year or upwards has had his measurements and all photographs so taken shall taken, unless the court or District Magistrate or Sub-Divisional Officer for reasons to be recorded in writing otherwise directs, be destroyed or made over to him.

STATE AMENDMENTS

Gujarat : Maharashtra

In Section 7, after the word "officer" insert the words or in any area for which a Commissioner of Police has been appointed the Commissioner of Police [Vide Bombay Act 11 of 1922, Section 4 (w.e.f. 14–12–1922) as amended by Bombay Acts 17 of 1945, 21 of 1954 and 56 of Maharashtra Act 35 of 1970, Section 3 (w.e.f. 1–3–1971) Act 11 of 1960. Section 87.]

Karnataka

In its application to the State of Karnataka for Section 7, substitute the following:

7. Destruction of photographs and records of measurements, etc., on acquittal. Where any person who not having been previously convicted of an offence punishable with rigorous imprisonment, for a term of one year or upwards, has had his measurements taken or has been photographed in accordance with the provisions of this Act, is released without trial or discharged or acquitted by any court, all measurement and all photographs so taken shall, unless the court or in a case where a person is released without trial, the District Magistrate or the Sub-Divisional Magistrate, or in any area where a Commissioner of Police, has been appointed, the Commissioner of Police, for reasons to be recorded in writing, otherwise directs, be destroyed or made over to him" [Vide Karnataka Act 29 of 1975, Section 4(4) (w.e.f. 12-8-1975)].

8. Power to make Rules. 1. The State Government may [by notification in Official Gazette] make rules for the purpose of carrying into affect the provisions of this Act.

2. In particular and without prejudice to the generality, of the foregoing provision such rules may provide for

(a) restrictions on the taking of photographs of persons under Section

(b) the places at which measurements and photographs; may be taken

(c) the nature of the measurements that may be taken

(d) the method in which any class or classes of measurements shall be class or taken:

(e) the dress to be worn by a person when being photographed under Section 3: and

(f) the preservation, safe custody, destruction and disposal of records of measurements and photographs.

3. Every rule made under this section shall be laid, as soon as may be after it is made before State Legislature.]

Gujarat: Maharashtra

In clause (e) of sub-section (2), for the words "under Section 3" substitute the words "in accordance with the provisions of this Act." [Vide Bombay Act 58 of 1953, Section 4 (w.e.f, 1–11–1953); Maharashtra Act 35 of 1970, Section 3 (w.e.f. 1.3.1971), Act 11 of 1960, Section 87.]

Karnataka

In its application to the State of Karnataka, in clause (a) of sub-section (2) of Section 8, for the words "under Sec. 3", substitute the words "in accordance with the provisions of this Act". (Vide Karnataka Act 29 of 1975, Section 4 (5) (w.e.f. 12–8–1975)

9. Bar of suits. No suit or other proceedings shall lie against any person for anything done, or intended to be done in good faith under this Act or under any rule made thereunder.

THE CRIMINAL LAW (AMENDMENT) ACT, 1932

An Act to supplement the criminal law. Whereas it is expedient to supplement the Criminal Law and to that end to amend the Indian Press (Emergency Powers) Act, 1931 (23 of 1931) and further to amend the Indian Criminal Law (Amendment) Act, 1908 (14 of 1908) for the purposes hereinafter appearing;

It hereby enacted as follows:

STATE AMENDMENTS

Goa, Daman and Diu

For Preamble substitute the following:

"Whereas it is expedient to supplement the Criminal Law for the purposes hereinafter appearing. It is hereby enacted as follows". [Vide G.S.R. 863, Gazette of India, 261966, Part 11 Section 3 (i), Ext. p. 389.]

Pondicherry

Same as that of Goa, Daman and Diu. [Vide G.S.R. 200, Gaz. of India, Pt II, Section 3 (i), dated 18–12–1967, p. 230].

1. Short title, extent, duration and commencement. 1. This Act may be called the Criminal Law (Amendment) Act, 1932.

2. It extends to the whole of India except the territories which immediately before the 1st November, 1956, were comprised in Part B States.

3. xxxx

4. The whole of the Act except xxx Section 7 shall come into force at once and the State Government may, by notification in the official Gazette direct that x,xx Section 7 shall come into force in any area on such date as may be specified in the notification.

STATE AMENDMENTS

Andhra Pradesh

In Section 1 (2) add at the end "other than those specified in sub-section (1) of Section 3 of S.R. Acts 1956 [Vide A.P. Act 25 of 1979, Section 3 (w.e.f. 9-10-1979)].

Gujarat

In sub-section (2) and (4) of Section 1, the words "State of Bombay" shall stand unmodified. [Vide Guj A.L, (8th Amendment) Order, 1961) (w.e.f. 1-5-1960)].

Karnataka

In sub-section (2) of Section 1, at the end add the following:

Other than the territories specified in clause (a) and clause (c) of sub-section (1) of Section 7 of the State Reorganisation Act, 1956 (C.A. 37 of 1956. [Vide Karnataka Act 29 of 1975, Section 2 and 3 (w.e.f. 1-8-1975)].

Madhya Pradesh

For sub-section (2) of Section 1, in its application to the State of Madhya Pradesh substitute the following:

"(2) It extends to the whole of India except the territories which immediately before the 1st November, 1956 were comprised in Part 6 State other than the Madhya Bharat and Sironj Regions of the State of Madhya Pradesh (Vide M.P. Act 10 of 1967, Section 2 (w.e.f. 2-5-1967)].

Maharashtra

(i) In sub-section (2), after the words and letter "comprised in Part B States", inserted the words "other than the Hyderabad and Saurashtra areas of the State of Bombay."

(ii) To sub-section (4), the following proviso shall be added, namely:

"Provided that in the Hyderabad and Saurashtra areas of the State of Bombay, this Act except Section 7 shall come into force on the date of commencement of the Criminal Law (Amendment) (Bombay Amendment and Extension) Act, 1959. [Vide Bom Act XXIV of 1959, 10 (27-4-1959) Maharashtra A.L.O. 1960].

2 to 4. *[Repealed by Section 2 of the Criminal law (Amendment) Act 1935).*

5. *Dissemination of contents of prescribed document.* 1. Whoever publishes, circulates or repeats in public any passage from a newspaper, book or other document, copies whereof have been declared to be forfeited to Government under any law for the time being in force, shall be punished with imprisonment for a term which may extend to six months, or with fine, or with both.

2. No court shall take cognizance of an offence punishable under this section unless the State Government has certified that the passage published, circulated or repeated contains in the opinion of the State Government, seditious or other matter of the nature referred to in sub-section (1) of Section 99–A of the Code of Criminal Procedure,

1898 (5 of 1898), or sub-section (1) of Section 4 of the Indian Press (Emergency Powers) Act, 1931 (23 of 1931).

Andhra Pradesh

For the words "Section 99-A of Cr.P.C. 1898" substitute "Section 95 of Code of Criminal Procedure, 1973" [Vide A.P. Act 25 of 1979, Section 4 (w.e.f. 9-10-1979)].

Goa, Daman and Diu

Same as that in Maharashtra. [Vide Act 11 of 1960, Section 87 and Gujarat A.L.O., 1960]

Maharashtra

In Section 5, in sub-section (2), delete the words, brackets and figures for sub-section (1) of Section 4 of the Indian Press (Emergency Powers) Act [Vide Bom Act XXIV of 1959, Section 5 (27-4-1969)].

Pondicherry

Same as in Maharashtra, [Vide GSR 200, Gazette of India, 18-2-1967 Pt. II Section 3 (i) P. 230

6. *Dissemination of false rumours.* [Repealed by Section 2 of the Criminal Law (Amendment) Act, 1935]

7. *Molesting a person to prejudice of employment or business.* 1. Whoever

(a) with intent to cause any person to obtain from doing or to do any act which such person has a right to do or to obtain from doing, obstructs or uses violence to or intimidates such person or any member of his family or person in his employ, or loiters at or near a place where such person or member or employed person resides or works or carries on business or happens to be, or persistently follows him from place to place or interferes with any property owned or used by him deprives him of or hinders him in the use thereof, or

(b) loiters or does any similar act at or near the place where a person carries on business, in such way and with intent that any person may thereby be deterred from entering or approaching or dealing at such place.

shall be punished with imprisonment for a term which may extend to six months, or with fine which may extend to five hundred rupees or with both.

Explanation. 1. Encouragement of indigenous industries of advocacy of temperance without the commission of any of the acts prohibited by this section is not an offence under this section.

2. No Court shall take cognizance of air offence punishable under this section except upon a report in writing of facts which constitute such offence made by a police officer not below the rank of officer in charge of a police station.

8. Power to order guardian to pay fine imposed on young person. [Repealed by Section 2 of the Criminal Law (Amendment) Act 1935]

9. Procedure in offences under the Act. Notwithstanding anything contained in the Code of Criminal Procedure 1898 (5 of 1898).

(i) no court inferior to that of presidency Magistrate or Magistrate of the first class shall try any offence under this Act.

(ii) an offence punishable under xxxx 5 or 7 shall be cognizable by the police;

2 (iii) xxxx and

(iv) an offence punishable under Section 7 shall be non-bailable.

STATE AMENDMENTS

Andhra Pradesh

1. For the Words "Code of Criminal Procedure, 1898" substitute the words "Code of Criminal Procedure 1973";

2. In clause (I) omit the words "Presidency magistrate or" (Vide A.P. Act 25 of 1979, Section 5 (w.e.f., 9-10-1979)].

Punjab, Haryana and Chandigarh

In clause (i) of Section 9, for the words "Magistrate of the first class substitute the words Judicial Magistrate of the first class". [Vide Punjab Act 25 of 1964, Section 2 and Schedule, Pt. 11 (2-10-64); Act 31 of 1966, Section 29 and 89: Haryana A.L.O., 1968].

10. Power of State Government to make certain offences cognizable and non-bailable. 1. The State Government may, by notification in the official Gazette declare that any offence punishable under Sections 186, 188, 189, 190, 228, 295-A, 298, 505, 606 or 507 of the Indian Penal Code 1860, (45 of 1860), when committed in any area specified in the notification shall, notwithstanding anything contained in the code of criminal procedure 1898 (5 of 1898), be cognizable and thereupon the Code of Criminal Procedure 1898, shall while such notification remains in force, be deemed to be amended accordingly.

2. The State Government may, in like manner and subject to the like conditions, and which the like effect, declare that an offence punishable under Section 188 or Section 506 of the Indian Penal Code (45 of 1860), shall be non-bailable.

11 to 14. [Repealed by Section 2 and Schedule of the Repealing Act, 1938 (1 of 1938)]

15. [Repealed by Section 2 and Schedule of the Repealing Act, 1938, 1935)

16. [Repealed by Section 2 of the Criminal Law (Amendment) Act, (1 of 1938)]

17. [Repealed by Section 2 of the Criminal Law (Amendment) Act, 1935]

18. Adoption and continuance of action taken under Ordinance 10 of 1932. Anything done or any proceeding commenced in pursuance of the provisions of Chapter VI of the Special Powers Ordinance, 1932 (10 of 1932) shall upon the commencement of this Act, be deemed to have been done or to have been commenced in pursuance of the corresponding provisions of the Indian Criminal Law (Amendment) Act, 1908 (45 of 1908), as amended by this Act, and shall have effect as if this Act, was already in force when such thing was done or such proceedings were commenced.

STATE AMENDMENTS

Andhra Pradesh

(i) For the words 'The State Government.... official Gazette', substitute 'if the State Government are satisfied, in the public interest it is necessary or expedient so to do, they may, by notification in the A.P. Gazette";

(ii) For the words 'Cr.P.C. 1898' substitute, 'Code of Criminal Procedure, 1973'; and

(iii) A notification issued under sub-section (2) shall be in force for six months only, but the State Government may, by a like notification, extend it for any period not exceeding six months if they are satisfied that in the public interest it is necessary or expedient so to do' [Vide A.P. Act 25 of 1979, Section 6 (w.e.f. 9-10-1979)].

Goa, Daman and Diu

Omit Section 18. [Vide Gaz, of India, Extra, Pt. 11, Section 3(i), dated 2–6–1996, (GSR 863)]

Gujarat

Delete Section 18, [Vide Act 11 of 1960, Section 87 and Gujarat ALO, 1960, Section 3 and Schedule (1-5-1960)].

Maharashtra

Delete Section 18, [Vide Bom Act XXIV of 1959, Section 6 (27–4–1959)]

Pondicherry

Same as in Goa, Daman and Diu, [Vide Gaz of India, Extg. Pt. 11, Section 3 (i), dated 18–2–1967 (GSR 200)],

19. Adoption and continuance of action taken under Act 23 of 1931 as amended by Ordinance 10 of 1932. Anything done or any proceedings commenced in pursuance of the provisions of the Indian Press (Emergency Powers) Act, 1931 (23 of 1931), as amended by Section 77 of the Special Powers Ordinance, 1932 (10 of 1932), shall upon the commencement of this Act, be deemed to have been done or to have been commenced in pursuance of the corresponding provisions of the Indian Press (Emergency Powers) Act, 1931 (23 of 1931), as amended by this Act, and shall have effect as if this Act was already in force when such thing was done or such proceedings were commenced.

STATE AMENDMENTS

Goa, Daman and Diu:

Omit Section 19, [Vide Gaz of India, Pt It, Section 3 (i), dated 2-6-1966 (GSR 863)].

Gujarat

Delete Section 19. {Vide Act 11 of 1920, Section 87 and Guj. ALO 1960, Section 3 and Sch. (1–5–1960)].

Maharashtra

Delete Section 19. (Vide Bom. Act XXIV of 1959, Section 9 (27-4-1959)]
Pondicherry:

Same as of Goa, Daman and Diu [Vide Gaz of India, Extra Pt 11, Section 3(i), dated 18-2-1967 (GSR 200)].

20. [Repealed by Section 2 of the Criminal Law (Amendment) Act, 1935].

THE CRIMINAL LAW (AMENDMENT) ACT, 1961

An Act to supplement the criminal law

Be it enacted by Parliament in the Twelfth year of the Republic of India as follows:

1. Short title and extent. This Act may be called the Criminal Law (Amendment) Act, 1961.

It extends to the whole of India except the State of Jammu and Kashmir.

2. Questioning the territorial integrity or frontiers of India in a manner prejudicial to the interest of safety and security of India. Whoever, by words either spoken or written, or by signs, or by visible representation or otherwise, questions its territorial integrity or frontiers of India in a manner which is, or is likely to be, prejudicial to the interests of the safety or security of India shall be punishable with imprisonment for a term which may extend to three years, or with fine or with both.

3. Statements, etc., in a notified area prejudicial to maintenance of public order, etc., therein or to safety or security of India and regulation of entry of persons in such area. 1. If the Central Government considers that in the interest of the safety or security of India or in the public interest, it is necessary or expedient so to do, it may by notification in the official Gazette, declare any area adjoining the frontiers of India to be a notified area; and thereupon, for so long as the notification is in force, such area shall be a notified area for the purpose of this Section.

2. Whoever makes, publishes or circulates in any notified area any statement, rumour or report which is or likely to be to the maintenance of public order or essential supplies or services in the said area or to the interests of the safety or security of India, shall be punishable with imprisonment for a term which may extend to three years, or with fine, or with both.

3. On and after such day as may be specified in and subject to any exemptions for which provision may be made by, a notification issued under sub-section (1), no person who was not immediately before the said day a resident in the area declared to be a notified area by the notification shall enter or attempt to enter that area or be therein except in accordance with the terms of a permit in writing granted to him by a person, not below the rank of a Magistrate of the first class specified in the said notification.

4. Any police officer, not below the rank of Sub-Inspector of Police, may search any person entering or attempting to enter, or being in, or leaving, a notified area and any vehicle, vessel, animal or article brought in by such person, and may, for the purpose of the search, retain such person vehicle, animal or article:

Provided that no person shall be searched in pursuance of this sub-section except by a woman authorised in this behalf by the police officer.

5. If any person is in a notified area in contravention of the provisions of sub-section (3) then, without prejudice to any other proceedings which may be taken, against him, he may be removed therefrom by or under the direction of any police officer on duty in the notified area not below the rank of sub-inspector of police.

6. If any person enters or attempts to enter a notified area or is therein in contravention of any of the provisions of sub-section (3) he shall be punishable with imprisonment for a term which may extend to one year, or with fine, or with both.

4. Power to declare certain publications forfeited and to issue search warrants for the same. 1. Where any newspaper or book as defined in the Press and Regulations of the Books Act, 1867 (25 of 1867), or any other document wherever printed, appears to the State Government to contain any matter the publication of which is punishable under Section 2 or sub-section 20 of Section 3, the State Government may, by notification in the official Gazette, stating the grounds of its opinion, declare every copy of the issue of the newspaper containing such matter and every copy of such book or other document to be forfeited to the Government, and thereupon any police officer may seize the same wherever found that any Magistrate may by warrant authorise any police officer not below the rank of sub-inspector to enter upon and search for the same in any premises where any copy of such issue or any copy of such book or other document may be or may be reasonably suspected to be.

2. The powers conferred by sub-section (1) on the State Government may also be exercised by the Central Government.

3. In sub-section (1), "document" includes also any painting, drawing or photograph, or other visible representation.

5. Application to High Court to set aside order of forfeiture. 1. Any person having any interest in any newspaper, book or other document in respect of which an order of forfeiture has been made under Section 4 may, within two months from the date of such order, apply to high Court to set aside such order on the ground that the issue of the newspaper, or the book or other document in respect of which the order was made did not contain any matter of such a nature as is referred to in sub-section (1) of Section 4.

2. The provisions of Section S. 96 (Cr. P.C. 1973) of the code of Criminal Procedure 1898 (5 of 1898), shall apply in relation to an application under sub-section (1) as they apply in relation to an application under Section 928 of that Code and the reference in Section 99-D to seditious or other matter of such a nature is referred to in sub-section (1) of Section 99-A of that Code shall be construed as a reference to any matter of such a nature as is referred to in sub-section (1) of Section 4 of this Act.

3. No order passed or action taken under Section 4 shall be called in question in any court otherwise than in accordance with the provisions of this section.

THE CRIMINAL LAW AMENDMENT (AMENDING) ACT, 1966

An Act to further amend the Criminal Law (Amendment) Act, 1952. Be it enacted by Parliament in the Seventeenth Year of the Republic of India as follows.

1. Short title. This Act may be called the Criminal Law Amendment (Amending) Act, 1966

2. Amendment of Section 8. (incorporated in the principal Act).

3. Insertion of new Section 11. (Incorporated in the principal Act).

4. Validation and indemnity. No trial or other proceeding held or taken before, and no sentence passed by a courtmartial or any other authority under any military, naval or air force law before the 30th day of June, 1966, shall be called in question in any court merely on the ground that the courtmartial or other authority had no jurisdiction by virtue of the provisions of the principal Act, and all such trials, proceedings and sentences shall, notwithstanding any judgment or order of any court, be as valid and operative as if they had been held, taken or passed in accordance with law, and accordingly no suit or other legal proceeding shall be maintained or continued against any person whatever on the ground that any such trial, proceeding or sentence was not held, taken or passed in accordance with law.

5. Pending cases. 1. Notwithstanding anything contained in this Act or in the principal Act as amended by this Act

(a) cases pending immediately before the 30th day of June, 1966 before a special judge in which one or more persons subject to military, naval or air force law is or are charged with and tried for an offence under the principal Act together with any other person or persons not so subject, and

(b) cases pending immediately before the said date before a special judge in which one or more persons subject to military, naval or air force law is or are alone charged with and tried for an offence under the principal Act and charges have already been framed against such person or persons.

shall be tried and disposed of by the special Judge.

2. Where in any case pending immediately before the 30th day of June, 1966, before a special judge, one or more persons subject to military, naval or air force law is or are alone charged with and tried

for an offence under the principal Act and charges have been framed against such person or persons before the said date or where, one appeal or on revision against any sentence passed by a special judge in any case in which one or more persons to subject was or were alone tried, the appellate court has directed that such person or persons be retried and on such retrial charges have not been framed against such person or persons before the said date, then, in either case, the special Judge shall follow the procedure laid down in Section 549 of the Code of Criminal Procedure 1898 (5 of 1898), as if the special Judge was a Magistrate.

6. Repeal and saving. (I) The Criminal Law (Amendment) Ordinance, 1966 (7 of 1966), is hereby repealed.

BODY OF PRINCIPLES FOR THE PROTECTION OF ALL PERSONS UNDER ANY FORM OF DETENTION OR IMPRISONMENT

Scope of the Body of Principles

These principles apply for the protection of all persons under any form of detention or imprisonment.

Use of Terms

For the purpose of the Body of Principles:

(a) "Arrest" means the act of apprehending a person for the alleged commission of an offence or by the action of an authority;

(b) "Detained person" means any person deprived of personal liberty except as a result of conviction for an offence;

(c) "Imprisoned person" means any person deprived of personal liberty as a result of conviction for an offence;

(d) "Detection" means the condition of detained persons as defined above;

(e) "Imprisonment" means the condition of imprisoned persons as defined above;

(f) The words "a judicial or other authority" means a judicial or other authority under the law whose status and tenure should afford the strongest possible guarantees of competence, impartiality and independence.

Principle 1

All persons under any form of detention or imprisonment shall be treated in a humane manner and with respect for the inherent dignity of the human person.

Principle 2

Arrest, detention or imprisonment shall only be carried out strictly in accordance with the provisions of the law and by competent officials or persons authorized for that purpose.

Principle 3

There shall be no restriction upon or derogation from any of the human rights of persons under any form of detention or imprisonment recognized or existing in any State pursuant to law, conventions, regulations or custom on the pretext that this Body of

Principles does not recognize such rights or that it recognizes them to a lesser extent.

Principle 4

Any form of detention or imprisonment and all measures affecting the human rights of a person under any form of detention or imprisonment shall be ordered by, or be subject to the effective control of, a judicial or other authority.

Principle 5

1. This principle shall be applied to all persons within the territory of any given State, without distinction of any kind, such as race, colour, sex, language, religion or religious belief, political or other opinion, national, ethnic or social origin, property, birth or other status.
2. Measures applied under the law and designed solely to protect the rights and special status of women, especially pregnant women and nursing mothers, children and juveniles, aged, sick or handicapped persons shall not be deemed to be discriminatory. The need for, and the application of, such measures shall always be subject to review by a judicial or other authority.

Principle 6

No person under any form of detention or imprisonment shall be subjected to torture or to cruel, inhuman or degrading treatment or punishment. No circumstances whatever may be invoked as a justification for torture or other cruel, inhuman or degrading treatment or punishment.

Principle 7

1. States should prohibit by law and any act contrary to the rights and duties contained in these principles, make any such act subject to appropriate sanctions and conduct impartial investigations upon complaints.
2. Officials who have reason to believe that a violation of this body of principles has occurred or is about to occur shall report the matter to the superior and, where ncecessary to other appropriate authorities or organs vested with reviewing or remedial powers.

3. Any other person who has ground to believe that a violation of this Body of Principles has occurred or is about to occur shall have the right to report the matter to the superiors of the officials involved as well as to other appropriate authorities or organs vested with reviewing or remedial powers.

Principle 8

Persons in detention shall be subject to treatment appropriate to their unconvicted status. Accordingly, they shall, whenever possible, be kept separate from imprisoned persons.

Principle 9

The authorities which arrest a person, keep him under detention or investigate the case shall exercise only the powers granted to them under the law and the exercise of these powers shall be subject to recourse to a judicial or other authority.

Principle 10

Anyone who is arrested shall be informed at the time of his arrest of the reason for his arrest and shall be promptly informed of any charges against him.

Principle 11

1. A person shall not be kept in detention without being given an effective opportunity to be heard promptly by a judicial or other authority. A detained person shall have the right to defend himself or to be assisted by counsel as prescribed by law.
2. A detained person and his counsel, if any, shall receive prompt and full communication of any order of detention, together with the reason therefor.
3. A judicial or other authority shall be empowered to review as appropriate the continuance of detention.

Principle 12

1. There shall be duly recorded:

   (a) The reasons for the arrest;
   (b) The time of the arrest and taking of the arrested person to a place of custody as well as that of his first appearance before a judicial or other authority.
   (c) The identity of the law enforcement officials concerned;

(d) Precise information concerning the place of custody.

2. Such records shall be communicated to the detained person, or his counsel, if any, in the form prescribed by law.

Principle 13

Any person shall, at the moment of arrest and at the commencement of detention or imprisonment, or promptly thereafter, be provided by the authority responsible for his arrest, detention or imprisonment, respectively with information on and an explanation of his rights and how to avail himself of such rights.

Principle 14

A person who does not adequately understand or speak the language used by the authorities responsible for his arrest, detention or imprisonment is entitled to receive promptly in a language which he understands the information referred to in principle 10, principle 11, paragraph 2, principle 12, paragraph 1, and principle 13 and to have the assistance, free of charge, if necessary, of an interpreter in connection with legal proceedings subsequent to his arrest.

Principle 15

Notwithstanding the exceptions contained in principle 16, paragraph 4, and principle 18, paragraph 3, communication of the detained or imprisoned person with the outside world, and in particular his family or counsel, shall not be denied for more than a matter of days.

Principle 16

1. Promptly after arrest and after each transfer from one place of detention or imprisonment to another, a detained or imprisoned person shall be entitled to notify or to require the competent authority to notify members of his family or other appropriate persons of his choice of his arrest, detention or imprisonment or of the transfer and of the place where he is kept in custody.
2. If a detained or imprisoned person is a foreigner, he shall also be promptly informed of his right to communicate by appropriate means with a consular post or the diplomatic mission of the

State of which he is a national or which is otherwise entitled to receive such communication in accordance with international law or with the representative of the competent international organization, if he is a refugee or is otherwise under the protection of an intergovernmental organization.

3. If a detained or imprisoned person is a juvenile or is incapable of understanding his entitlement, the competent authority shall on its own initiative undertake the notification referred to in the present principle. Special attention shall be given to notifying parents or guardians.
4. Any notification referred to in the present principle shall be made or permitted to be made without delay. The competent authority may however delay a notification for a reasonable period where exceptional needs of the investigation so require.

Principle 17

1. A detained person shall be entitled to have the assistance of a legal counsel. He shall be informed of his right by the competent authority promptly after arrest and shall be provided with reasonable facilities for exercising it.
2. If a detained person does not have a legal counsel of his own choice, he shall be entitled to have legal counsel assigned to him by a judicial or other authority in all cases where the interests of justice so require and without payment by him if he does not have sufficient means to pay.

Principle 18

1. A detained or imprisoned person shall be entitled to communicate and consult with his legal counsel.
2. A detained or imprisoned person shall be allowed adequate time and facilities for consultation with his legal counsel.
3. The right of a detained or imprisoned person to be visited by and to consult and communicate, without delay or censorship and in full confidentiality, with his legal counsel may not be suspended or restricted save in exceptional circumstances, to be specified by law or lawful regulations, when it is considered indispensable by a judicial or other authority in order to maintain security and good order.
4. Interviews between a detained or imprisoned person and his legal counsel may be within sight, but not within the hearing of a law enforcement official.

5. Communication between a detained or imprisoned person and his legal counsel mentioned in the present principle shall be inadmissible as evidence against the detained or imprisoned person unless they are connected with a continuing or contemplated crime.

Principle 19

A detained or imprisoned person shall have the right to be visited by and to correspond with, in particular, members of his family and shall be given adequate opportunity to communicate with the outside world, subject to reasonable conditions and restrictions as specified by law or lawful regulations.

Principle 20

If a detained or imprisoned person so requests, he shall if possible be kept in place of detention or imprisonment reasonably near his usual place of residence.

Principle 21

1. It shall be prohibited to take undue advantage of the situation of a detained or imprisoned person for the purpose of compelling him to confess, to incriminate himself otherwise or to testify against any other person.
2. No detained person while being interrogated shall be subject to violence, threats or methods of interrogation which impair his capacity of decision or his judgment.

Principle 22

No detained or imprisoned person shall, even with his consent, be subjected to any medical or scientific experimentation which may be detrimental to his health.

Principle 23

1. The duration of any interrogation of a detained or imprisoned person and of the intervals between interrogations as well as the identity of the officials who conducted the interrogations and other persons present shall be recorded and certified in such form as may be prescribed by law.

2. A detained or imprisoned person, or his counsel when provided by law, shall have access to the information described in paragraph 1 of the present principle.

Principle 24

A proper medical examination shall be offered to a detained or imprisoned person as promptly as possible after his admission to the place of detention or imprisonment, and thereafter medical care and treatment shall be provided whenever necessary. This care and treatment shall be provided free of charge.

Principle 25

A detained or imprisoned person or his counsel shall, subject only to reasonable conditions to ensure security and good order in the place of detention or imprisonment, have the right to request or petition a judicial or other authority for a second medical examination or opinion.

Principle 26

The fact that a detained or imprisoned person underwent a medical examination, the name of the physician and the results of such an examination shall be duly recorded. Access to such records shall be ensured. Modalities therefore shall be in accordance with relevant rules of domestic law.

Principle 27

Non-compliance with these principles in obtaining evidence shall be taken into account in determining the admissibility of such evidence against a detained or imprisoned person.

Principle 28

A detained or imprisoned person shall have the right to obtain within the limits of available resources, if from public sources, reasonable quantities of educational, cultural and informational material, subject to reasonable conditions to ensure security and good order in the place of detention or imprisonment.

Principle 29

1. In order to supervise the strict observance of relevant laws and regulations, places of detention shall be visited regularly by

qualified and experienced persons appointed by, and responsible to, a competent authority distinct from the authority directly in charge of the administration of the place of detention or imprisonment.

2. A detained or imprisoned person shall have the right to communicate freely and in full confidentiality with the persons who visit the places of detention or imprisonment in accordance with paragraph 1 of the present principle, subject to reasonable conditions to ensure security and good order in such places.

Principle 30

1. The types of conduct of the detained or imprisoned person that constitute disciplinary offences during detention or imprisonment, the description and duration of disciplinary punishment that may be inflicted and the authorities competent to impose such punishment shall be specified by law or lawful regulations and duly published.
2. A detained or imprisoned person shall have the right to be heard before disciplinary action is taken. He shall have the right to bring such action to higher authorities for review.

Principle 31

The appropriate authorities shall endeavour to ensure, according to domestic law, assistance when needed to dependent and, in particular, minor members of the families of detained or imprisoned persons and shall devote a particular measure of care to the appropriate custody of children left without supervision.

Principle 32

1. A detained person or his counsel shall be entitled at any time to take proceedings according to domestic law before a judicial or other authority to challenge the lawfulness of his detention in order to obtain his release without delay, if it is unlawful.
2. The proceedings referred to in paragraph 1 of the present principle shall be simple and expeditious and at no cost for detained persons without adequate means. The detaining authority shall produce without unreasonable delay the detained person before the reviewing authority.

Principle 33

1. A detained or imprisoned person or his counsel shall have the right to make a request or complaint regarding his treatment, in particular in case of torture or other cruel, inhuman or degrading treatment, to the authorities responsible for the administration of the place of detention and to higher authorities and, when necessary, to appropriate authorities vested with reviewing or remedial powers.
2. In those cases where neither the detained or imprisoned person nor his counsel has the possibility to exercise his rights under paragraph 1 of the present principle, a member of the family of the detained or imprisoned person or any other person who has knowledge of the case may exercise such rights.
3. Confidentiality concerning the request or complaint shall be maintained if so requested by the complainant.
4. Every request or complaint shall be promptly dealt with and replied to without undue delay. If the request or complaint is rejected or, in case of inordinate delay, the complainant shall be entitled to bring it before a judicial or other authority. Neither the detained or imprisoned person nor any complainant under paragraph 1 of the present principle shall suffer prejudice for making a request or complaint.

Principle 34

Whenever the death or disappearance of a detained or imprisoned person occurs during his detention or imprisonment, an inquiry into the cause of death or disappearance shall be held by a judicial or other authority, either on its own motion or at the instance of a member of the family of such a person or any person who has knowledge of the case. When circumstances so warrant, such an inquiry shall be held on the same procedural basis whenever the death or disappearance occurs shortly after the termination of the detention or imprisonment. The findings of such inquiry or a report thereon shall be made available upon request, unless doing so would jeopardize an ongoing criminal investigation.

Principle 35

1. Damage incurred because of acts or omissions by a public

official contrary to the rights contained in these principles shall be compensated according to the applicable rules or liability provided by domestic law.

2. Information required to be recorded under these principles shall be available in accordance with procedures provided by domestic law for use in claiming compensation under the present principle.

Principle 36

1. A detained person suspected of or charged with a criminal offence shall be presumed innocent and shall be treated as such until proved guilty according to law in a public trial at which he has had all the guarantees necessary for his defence.
2. The arrest or detention of such a person pending investigation and trial shall be carried out only for the purposes of the administration of justice on grounds and under conditions and procedures specified by law. The imposition of restrictions upon such a person which are not strictly required for the purpose of the detention or to prevent hindrance to the process of investigation or the administration of justice, or for the maintenance of security and good order in the place of detention shall be forbidden.

Principle 37

A person detained on a criminal charge shall be brought before a judicial or other authority provided by law promptly after his arrest. Such authority shall decide without delay upon the lawfulness and necessity of detention. No person may be kept under detention pending investigation or trial except upon the written order of such an authority. A detained person shall, when brought before such an authority, have the right to make a statement on the treatment received by him while in custody.

Principle 38

A person detained on a criminal charge shall be entitled to trial within a reasonable time or to release pending trial.

Principle 39

Except in special cases provided for by law, a person detained on a criminal charge shall be entitled, unless a judicial or other authority decides otherwise in the interest of the administration of justice, to release pending trial subject to the conditions that may be imposed in accordance with the law. Such authority shall keep the necessity of detention under review.

General Clause

Nothing in this Body of Principles shall be construed as restricting or derogating from any right defined in the International Covenant on Civil and Political Rights.

AN OUTLINE OF THE INDIAN PRISONS BILL, 1996
(as proposed by the National Human Rights Commission)

Never before in its history, prison administration was a subject of such a public criticism, judicial indignation and legislative scrutiny as at present. Since independence, several expert committees, appointed by the Government of India, have unequivocally emphasised an urgent need for a thorough reorganisation of the prison system to come in tune with the modern criminological and penological thinking and to effectively cater to the changed an changing demands, for the society in transition. In this context, the rationalization, revision and consolidation of prison laws in long overdue. The present outline of the proposed Indian Prisons Bill, 1996 is intended to achieve this purpose.

Taking up this issue, the National Human Rights Commission prepared an outline of the Indian Prisons Bill, 1995, which was circulated among State Governments and Union Territory Administrations for their comments, suggestions and observations. The outline was further discussed at the National Conference on Human Rights in Prisons, convened by the Commission on 14 November, 1995. The Conference recommended the setting up of a Core Group for the finalisation of the outline of the proposed Bill. In its meetings held on 30 and 31 January and on 22 and 23 February, 1996, the Core Group crystallised its views on various Chapters of the outline as given hereinafter.

Statement of Objective and Reasons

The proposed Prisons Bill, 1996 may have the following objects and reasons:

— to bring in a 'basic uniformity in matters relating to the administration of prisons and managements of prisoners in the country.

— to lay down the framework and criteria for a sound and safe custody and reformative treatment of prisoners.

— to rationalise prison system to cater effectively to various categories of prisoners.

— to provide for minimum standards of services for the care, protection, treatment, education, training and welfare of prisoners.

- to devise such procedures for the handling of prisoners as are compatible with human dignity and consistent with prison security, safe custody and maintenance of discipline.
- to differentiate institutional treatment of prisoners in keeping with their personality traits, behavioural patterns, and custodial and correctional requirements.
- to lay down mechanism for coordination between prison administration and other components of the criminal justice system.
- to ensure the availability of such services from other public departments as are essential for an effective management of prisons.
- to forge constructive linkages between prison programmes and community-based governmental and non-governmental resources for the rehabilitation and social reintegration of offenders.

'reamble

The preamble of the proposed Bill may be constructed as under:

- "to provide for the detention of persons committed to prison custody and for their reformation and rehabilitation".

hapterisation

The proposed Bill envisages the formulation of a basic legal ramework for the governance of persons in the country. Within a niform structure, the detailed rules and regulations may be ormulated by State Governments and Union Territory dministrations and incorporated in their respective Prison Manuals.

PRELIMINARY

This chapter may contain title, extent and commencement f proposed Bill, and definitions of various terms to be used herein. While the terms to be defined may be specified when the proposed Bill is finally drafted by the Legislative Department, he same may include the definitions of such terms, as, 'prison', prisoner', 'court', 'magistrate', 'offence', 'civil prisoner', undertrial prisoner', 'military prisoner', 'habitual offender', family', (for the purposes of stay in open camps), 'young offender', etc.

RIGHTS AND DUTIES OF PRISONERS

The All India Committee on Jail Reforms, 1980–83, had recommended that a separate chapter on rights and duties of prisoners may be contained in the ensuing law, as under:

— Right to human dignity; to be treated as 'person'; and non deprivation of fundamental rights other than what are taken away of restricted by incarceration, as spelt out in the relevant chapters

— Right to basic minimum needs; adequate diet; health and medical care; clean and hygienic living conditions; and proper clothing, bedding and equipment.

— Right to communication; contact with family members and authorised persons, subject to security requirements.

— Right to access to law, and speedy trial. Side by side, the following duties of prisoners were recommended by the Committee:

— to obey lawful orders and instructions.

— to abide by prison rules and regulations.

— to maintain prescribed standards of cleanliness, hygiene and prison discipline.

— to respect human dignity of fellow prisoners, prison staff and others.

— to refrain from making false or exaggerated allegations.

— to abstain from hurting religious feelings, beliefs, and faiths of others.

— to use government property with care and not to damage or destroy negligently or wilfully.

— to assist prison authorities in the performance of their duties

— to preserve and promote correctional environment and to be responsive to it.

INSTITUTIONAL FRAMEWORK

The proposed Bill may adequately provide for the diversification of institutional resources to cater to the differential requirements of prisoners in terms of custody and correction. The factors to be considered may include age, sex, legal status of the prisoner, nature of crime, length of sentence, security requirement, state of health and correctional needs. Such a course implies the setting up of separate institutional facilities for different categories of prisoners, such as:

- — prisons/annexcs/yards for undertrial prisoners.
- — maximum security prisons/annexes/yards for security risk prisoners and habitual or hardened offenders.
- — medium security prisons/annexes/yards for non-habitual adult offenders.
- — semi-open or open prisons and open camps.
- — prisons/annexes/yards for women prisoners.
- — prisons/annexes/yards for young offenders.
- — prisons/annexes/yards for those suffering from infectious diseases.
- — prisons/annexes/yards for mentally ill prisoners.
- — prisons/annexes/yards for drug addicts.
- — Mobile camps for prisoners sentenced for less than one year.
- — Prisons for those courting arrest during non-violent socio-political and economic agitations for a declared public cause.
- — Sub-jails.

State Government may be required to establish a mechanism for the classification of prisoners to be housed in various types of institutions as enumerated above and to lay down the procedure to be followed in their respective Prison Manuals. They may also specify the authorised population for each type of institution and norms with regard to area/space for prisoner as well as number of prisoners to be housed in an association barrack as suggested in Model Prison Manual. This may also include norms for the creation of facilities for education, vocational training, work programmes, socio-cultural activities, library and recreation both indoor and outdoor as also for the staff to be appointed in each type of institution. Apart from various types of prisons for specific categories of prisoners, State Government may be authorised in the proposed Bill to create temporary prisons to deal with emergent situation.

ORGANISATIONAL STRUCTURE

In this chapter, State Government may be required to set up the Directorate of Prisons and Correctional Services at the State Headquarters, under the Director-General/Inspector-General of Prisons and Correctional Services, with the provision of the following staff to assist him:

- — Such number of Additional/Deputy Inspectors-General of Prisons as the need be for administration, inspections, supervision, programme development, and staff training and welfare.

- Separate units for correctional programmes, prison industries and vocational training, agriculture/horticulture, planning, research and evaluation, probation and after care, and audit and accounts, each under a senior officer.
- A vigilance and public grievance cell under a senior officer,
- A legal cell under a senior law officer,
- A Public Relation Officer,
- A prison building cell under a senior engineer,
- A statistical officer for an on-going collection, interpretation and presentation of factual information and data with computer back-up.
- A Deputy/Assistant Inspector-General of Prisons for women, preferably a women officer.
- Supporting staff for various units and officers as per the requirements of the State.

Bigger states with heavy prison population may be provided with a regional set-up, as per requirements, consisting of:

- Deputy/Assistant Inspector General of Prisons,
- Probation and after care officer,
- Audit and Accounts officer,
- Engineer, Building
- Supporting staff.

The institutional organisation in the state may be based on the specific requirements of custody and correction, including:

- Superintendent of Prison to be assisted by Additional/Deputy/Assistant Superintendents of Prisons as per the requirements,
- Custodial staff including Chief Head Warders, Head Warders, Warders and other security personnel,
- Resident medical officer with supporting staff including that for deaddiction as per requirement,
- Correctional staff including specialists from various relevant disciplines,
- Law Officer with necessary subordinate officers and supporting staff,
- Adequate number of technical instructors,
- Adequate number of teachers,
- Accounts Officers/Assistant Account Officers/Accountants as per the requirement,

— Agriculture Officer/Assistant Agriculture Officer as per the requirement,
— Statistician for each jail having a population of 500 or more,
— Ministerial and other supporting staff including cooks, barbers, washermen, electricians, pump operators, etc., as per the requirements.

The probation and after care unit may be provided at the District level to be instrumental in the rehabilitation and social reintegration of prisoners, under a District Probation Officer with adequate number of Probation Officers and supporting staff.

Separate institutions for women prisoners may be run only by the female staff, while annexes and yards for women prisoners may be directly supervised by the female staff only.

The proposed Bill may provide for the Staff Governments to lay down norms for the provisions of staff at various levels for an effective discharge for their duties so as to secure an efficient functioning of prisons.

The chapter may also have specific provisions for the duties of various personnel including their responsibility towards the protection of the rights of prisoners.

MAINTENANCE OF PRISONERS

The proposed Bill may clearly specify that prison administration has to deal with prisoners in conditions compatible with human dignity. This would require the formulation of a set of minimum standards to be detailed out in the State Prison Manuals. The proposed Bill may accordingly make suitable provisions for a humane handling and upkeep of prisoners on the following lines:

— State Governments may be required to work out definite norms for accommodations of prisoners. Apart from determining the authorised population for each institutions, area/space per prisoner to be provided in living barracks, work sheds and hospitals may be indicated in the proposed Bill on the lines enunciated in the Model Prison Manual, as under.

In sleeping barracks, 50 square feet of ground area, 500 cubic feet of air space and 12 square feet of lateral ventilation.

In cells, 96 square feet of ground area, 966 cubic feet of air space and 21 square feet of lateral ventilation.

In hospitals, 70 square feet of ground area and 700 cubic feet of air space.

The Bill may further make it mandatory for State Governments to determine in their rules, norms for the provision of latrines, bathrooms, educational classes, vocational training centres, recreational activities, libraries, open spaces for games etc. As recommended by the All India Committee on Jail Reforms, 1980–83, the following provisions may be specifically made:

One latrine for every six prisoners.

One bathrooms for every ten prisoners.

Hospital accommodation on the basis of 5 per cent of the daily average inmate population in all Central and District Jails.

— State Governments may be required in the proposed Bill to formulate scales of clothing, bedding and equipment for men and women as well as for child dependents (upto 5 years of age) in keeping with the requirements of various seasons and geographical areas. The children of women prisoners may be provided clothing by the prison administration, they cannot afford from their own sources. Similarly, undertrial prisoners who cannot arrange their own clothing may have to be served by the prison administration.

— The proposed Bill may lay down the responsibility of the prison administration to create adequate facilities for medical care and treatment of prisoners. Besides establishing hospitals within prisons the proposed Bill may provide for the referral of seriously ailing prisoners including those suffering from infectious diseases, mental ailments or addiction to drugs, to outside governmental and non-governmental treatment centres. The proposed Bill may specifically provide or arrange, besides hospital beds within the prison, for an ambulance for every prison.

— While protecting the right of prisoners to communication, the proposed Bill may require State Governments to make rules for the number of letters and interviews to be granted to prisoners in a month, with a provision for the Superintendent of prison to allow as many letters and interviews as he may deem fit in the interest of prisoners. Interviews may be conducted with full respect to prisoners right to privacy by keeping them within sight but not within hearing, unless there are reasons to do otherwise. Prisoners may be allowed legal interviews with their lawyers. However, the Bill may uphold the power of the Superintendent of prison to impose in individual cases any restriction in these matters in the interest of security. The proposed Bill may also prescribe the procedure for taking searches of prisoners and their visitors.

- The proposed Bill should clearly lay down a ban on the confinement of non-criminal lunatics in prisons.
- The proposed Bill may provide the every prison having 10 children may establish a creche/nursery. Where the number of dependent children is less than 10, arrangements for a creche/nursery may be made in conjunction with some non-governmental organisations.
- As recommended by the All India Committee on Jail Reforms, 1980–83, only two scales of food in terms of labouring and non-labouring diet may be prescribed in the proposed Bill. However, special diet may be provided on medical ground and for pregnant mothers and dependent children (upto 5 years of age) in prisons.
- The proposed Bill may lay down the responsibility of the prison administration to ensure a proper management of the kitchen with modern equipment, ventilation and place to eat under hygienic conditions. The kitchen should be so equipped as to ensure that no person is subjected to any hazardous condition.
- The responsibility of the prison administration in ensuring an adequate water supply for drinking, bathing, washing, etc., may be made mandatory. Similarly, a continuous supply of electricity may also be ensured with a provision for an alternate arrangement in the event of its failure.
- The proposed Bill may require the prison administration to ensure a proper severage system to maintain the requisite level of sanitation and hygiene including arrangements for garbage collection and its removal. For every prison having an authorised population of more than 200 prisoners, there may be a provision for mechanized laundry.
- In every prison having an authorised population of 200 prisoners or more the provision of a canteen may be provided in the proposed Bill.
- The proposed Bill may empower the Director-General/

Inspector-General of Prisons to directly request in any emergen situation involving security of prisons as well as of prisoner any other department to provide facilities or services essentia for the maintenance and unkeep of prisoners. On receipt c such a request, it may be the duty of the department concernec to make all possible efforts. Similarly, the responsibility of th Superintendent of prison to seek assistance from othe department during any natural calamity such as flooc epidemic etc., may be laid down in the proposed Bill.

— The proposed Bill may require that every prison may hav upto five non-official visitors attached to it. The non-officia visitors may be appointed from amongst retired criminal justic functionaries, social scientists and eminent public-spirite individuals. Such prison visitors may be appointed by th Director-General/Inspector-General of Prisons on th recommendations of District Magistrates/Superintendents c Police.

UNDERTRIAL PRISONERS

An indiscriminate confinement in prisons of person accuse of various offences has emerged as a major issue of human rights i the recent years. Despite a new thrust having been given towards speedy disposal of cases in courts and the liberalisation of bail systen the proportion of undertrial prisoners has been increasing over th years. As persons undergoing trials in the courts are to be presume innocent till they are found guilty, their legal status warrants differential handling and treatment in jail. It is, therefore, necessar that the proposed Bill may contain specific provisions to protect th rights of undertrial prisoners, as under:

— It may be the responsibility of the prison administration t send a periodic report to the District Judge/District Magistrat on all cases of undertrial prisoners pending for 2 months i the prison.

— The proposed Bill may clearly lay down that for every ja adequate strength of police personnel with appropriate an sufficient transport facilities, be provided for escorting undertria prisoners during their production before courts, treatment i outside hospitals or transfer from one institution to another.

— The proposed Bill may provide that the cases of all suc

undertrial prisoners who have completed half of the maximum sentence to be awarded on possible conviction may, under intimation to the District Magistrate, be referred to the concerned Court for consideration of release on personal bond.

- Such cases of undertrial prisoners who were granted bail by courts but could not produce sureties for 2 months may be referred to the concerned Court for consideration of release on personal bond. For this purpose, the trial court may be required to send copies of the bail orders to the Superintendent of prison.
- The instrument of restraint such as handcuffs and irons may be used on undertrial prisoners only in exceptional circumstances in the interest of security on the ground to be recorded in writing by the officer concerned.
- It will be the responsibility of the prison administration to send the details of such cases of undertrial prisoners who need free legal aid to the Free Legal Aid Cell for necessary assistance.
- The proposed Bill may contain that no food or article other than wearing apparel may be allowed from outside to undertrial prisoners in accordance with the rules.
- For the purpose of quarterly review of undertrial cases pending in courts, a committee consisting of District Sessions Judge as Chairman, District Magistrate, Superintendent of Police, Prosecution Officer and Probation Officer as members and the Superintendent of Prison as Member-Secretary may be constituted in each District and the procedure to be followed may be prescribed the rules. The quorum will be three including the Chairman. The meeting shall be held in the jail premises or as decided by the Chairman.
- The proposed Bill may incorporate a provision to allow undertrial prisoners to receive vocational training or to engage in productive work as available in the prison, on a voluntary basis. Adequate incentive may be provided to them for productive work by way of remuneration as prescribed in the rules.

INSTITUTIONAL TREATMENT

The proposed Bill may provide for all the basic elements of and the procedure to be adopted for institutional treatment of prisoners in keeping with the objective of imprisonment. Within the overall framework of sound custody, the institutional programme is required to be geared towards the reformative and rehabilitative goal. In this respect, the Bill may contain the following provisions:

— The procedure to be followed on admission may include the placement of a prisoner in a Reception Unit with adequate facilities for study, orientation and induction into the institutional programme. Each prisoner on arrival may be medically examined and his state of health be duly recorded in case of a women by a lady doctor. Besides a detailed report, the file may include prisoner's photograph and background information from the police. During observation, the prisoner may be subjected to a programme of social education, some purposeful occupation and exercise and recreation.

— Each convict sentenced to one year or more may be thoroughly studied and diagnosed in terms of his/her personality traits, behavioural pattern and socio-economic background for the purposes of institutional treatment, with the help of specialists. Every central or district prison of class I or II may have on the staff Welfare Officer/Assistant Welfare Officer appointed on the basis one such officer for every 200 prisoners, so as to provide for a specialised input in the study and diagnosis process.

— Apart from the segregation of prisoners on the basis of their legal status, age, sex (male, female and eunuchs), health and security, all prisoners sentenced to imprisonment of one year or more may be scientifically classified into homogenous groups for the purposes of institutional treatment. Classification of prisoners may be based on a thorough study of the offender as an individual, understanding of the sequence of his/her criminal behaviour and the problems presented by him/her. A Classification committee may be set up in each prison with Superintendent of prison as Chairman and Medical Officer/Assistant Medical Officer and other specialists drawn on it. The initial classification may be followed by a periodic review of each case for reclassification as and when found necessary.

— Welfare officer/Assistant Welfare Officer with the assistance of other specialists may be responsible for providing individualised counselling and guidance to prisoners so as to secure their adjustment within the institutional setting and a positive participation on their part in various reformative and rehabilitative programmes. A differential approach may be adopted towards the adjustment problems and correctional requirements of women and young offenders.

— A diversified programme of education may be introduced in prisons to cater to the varied requirements of different categories of prisoners. The educational programme should cover all the aspects of physical, academic, socio-cultural and moral development. Besides imparting education with prisons, appropriate linkages may be established with the educational facilities in the outside community, so as to secure an integration of prison education into the mainstream of the educational system. The necessary manpower, facilities and equipment including libraries may be provided in prisons.

— A comprehensive programme of vocational training may be organised for prisoners. While in case of convicts sentenced to rigorous imprisonment work will be mandatory, it may be optimal for other categories. For this purpose, adequate staff, equipment and material may be provided by the State Government concerned. The Classification Committee may plan training projects for prisoners selected on the basis of aptitudes and vocational guidance. A set of minimum standards may be adopted to regulate training projects in conjunction with State Technical Education Departments'. All categories of convicts may be engaged in productive work. Undertrial prisoners may be encouraged to work through adequate incentives by way of wages/remunerations. While prison labour may not be allowed to be hired by private employees, appropriate linkages may be established with outside industries in developing vocational training and work programmes in prisons. The work programme may be diversified to meet the varied needs and abilities of prisoners and be adopted to the requirements of the labour market in the free community. A priority attention may be given to developing such work programmes as are directly conducive to the economic rehabilitation and self-reliance of prisoners when they return to the free community. All prisoners engaged in productive work may be provided incentive in the form of wages by way of reasonable remuneration. Work conditions may conform to the accepted safety measures, hours of work, exemptions, shifts, rest days, compensation, etc. Though prisoners have no right to wages, a uniform system may be evolved for the purpose as an incentiv for productive work and a rehabilitative device. Apart fron engaging prisoners in various industries and vocations prisoners may be employed in essential services anc maintenance work in prisons. Prisoners may be placed o extra-mural work at the discretion of the Superintendent.

— All prisons may undertake well-planned cultural an recreational activities for prisoners both as an incentive fo good behaviour and a means for the inculcation of health social values. Facilities for spiritual and moral developmen may also be uniformly provided. Both indoor and outdoo games may be organised in prisons with due regard to th requirements of security.

— The support of the community may be purposefully availed c in strengthening the correctional, reformative and rehabilitativ content of prison programmes. Appropriate linkages may b established with community-based governmental and nor governmental organisations concerned with the welfare c prisoners.

— Prisoners may be constructively involved in all measure pertain to their self-management and self-improvemen without passing on them such administrative responsibilitie as legitimately belong to the prison staff.

PRISON DISCIPLINE

Discipline in prisons has to be maintained with fairness an firmness. It has to cover every aspect of life in the prison. A punishmer for indiscipline has to be balanced in relation to the gravity of th violation. A positive approach towards prison discipline involve not only a strict adherence to rules and regulations but also a fair, jus and equitable handling of prisoners on the part of the staf Accordingly, the proposed Bill may clearly spell out the act constituting prison offences and the punishment against such act a well as a sound mechanism to deal with them, on the following line

— After their admission, all prisoners may be informed of thei rights, duties and disciplinary requirements in the prison in language understandable to them. This aspect may b displayed on a board accessible to prisoners.

The following and such other acts as may be specified fror time to time may be deemed as prison offences:

Endangering the security and custody of a prison in any way hrough a wilful or negligent act;

Doing any act calculated to create any unnecessary alarm in minds of other prisoners.

Doing or omitting to do any act with intent to cause to himself any illness, injury or disability;

Omitting to report any prison offence,

Offending against law and order and discipline,

Planning, instigating, abetting directly or indirectly in the commission of any prison offence,

Refusing or omitting or conniving to abide by standards of behaviour, rules and regulations, lawful instructions and orders;

Failing to assist in the maintenance of prison discipline,

Failing to give assistance to a prison official when called upon to do so,

Making any complaint against prison officials, written or oral which is proved to be false, malicious or groundless,

Committing nuisance or mischief or any sort,

Quarrelling with prisoners,

Smoking at places or at times other than appoint.

Attacking or assaulting or causing gross personal violence;

Participating in a riot or mutiny, abetting another prisoner to riot or mutiny,

Escaping or attempting to escape from prison or legal custody or falling to report prison officials about attempted escape,

Possessing, hiding, smuggling or attempting to smuggle, obtaining, giving, or receiving or bartering contraband articles, failing to report to prison officials about contraband articles;

Stealing, damaging, destroying, disfiguring misappropriating any prison property or prisoners' articles and property.

Failing to report at once any loss, breakage or injury which the prisoner may accidently have caused to prison property or implements.

Tampering with or defacing identity cards, records, or documents,

Breaches of the conditions of leave and special release;

Refusing to eat food or going on hunger-strike;

Eating or apportioning any food not assigned to him or taking from or adding to the portions assigned to other prisoners,

Wilfully or negligently destroying or spoiling food or throwing it away without orders,

Introducing into food or drink anything likely to render it unpalatable or unwholesome or dangerous for human consumption,

Cooking unauthorisedly,

Violating rules and regulations framed for the orderly running of canteen,

Bartering canteen articles,

Being idle, careless or negligent at work, refusing to work, malingering, disturbing other prisoner at work on in barracks,

Manufacturing any article without the knowledge or permission of a prison officer,

Performing any portion of the task allotted to another prisoner or obtaining unauthorized assistance of another prisoner in the performance of his task,

Apportioning to any prisoner any part of the task performed by another prisoner,

Mixing or adding any foreign substance to the materials issued for work. Wilfully disabling himself from labour.

Converting or attempting to convert a prisoner to a different religious faith, Wilfully hurting others' religious feelings, beliefs or faith.

Agitating or acting on the basis of caste or religious prejudices,

Having any communication, in writing or by word or by signs without permission with any outsider undertrial prisoners, prisoners of different class detenus, civil prisoners, approvers and other prisoners.

Sending messages surreptitiously by writing or speech.

Participating or organizing unauthorised activities like gambling, etc.

Using indecent, abusive, insolent, threatening or improper language; being disrespectful, making indecent or vulgar acts or gestures,

Soiling or befouling any place or article,

Loitering or lingering, leaving the appointed area or work-group without permission. Failing to assist or preventing other person from assisting prison officials in suppressing violence, assault, riot, mutiny, attack, gross personal violence or any other emergencies.

The proposed Bill may provide for the punishment of such offences in the following manner:

(i) **A formal Warning:** To be personally addressed to a prisoner by the Superintendent and to be recorded in the Punishment Book but it may not be treated as punishment.

(ii) **Forfeiture of remission:**

(a) The Director-General/Inspector-General may be empowered to:

Forfeit all earned remission except State Government remission,

Remove a prisoner from remission system for a specified period or during prisoner's whole term of imprisonment;

(b) The superintendent may be empowered to

Order forfeiture of remission upto a maximum period of thirty days at one time,

Remove a prisoner from the remission system upto a period of six months;

(c) When a prisoner escapes from legal custody, the total remission earned by him upto the date of escape may stand cancelled,

(d) When a prisoner attempts to escape from legal custody or plans or abets escape, the question of revoking his entire remission may be referred to the Inspector-General for orders,

(e) If a prisoner has been punished during the quarter otherwise than by a formal warning, following action should be taken.

If a prisoner is punished for bad conduct and if the violation was a minor one, one day may be cut from his monthly remission for good conduct; if the violation was of serious nature, he/she may not be awarded the remission for good conduct for that month.

If the prisoner has been punished for a minor violation related with work, one day's remission may be cut for each offence from his monthly remission for work. If the violation is serious, he/she may not be granted monthly remission for work for that month.

(iii) **Recreational facilities:** The superintendent may be empowered to award the punishment of stoppage of recreational facilities upto a maximum period of one month.

(iv) **Canteen facilities:** The Superintendent may be empowered to stop canteen facilities upto a maximum period of three months at a time.

(v) **Interviews:** The Superintendent may be empowered to stop interviews upto a period of one month.

(vi) **Wages:** Where a prisoner wilfully or negligently spoils production or damages Government property, the Superintendent may be empowered to:

(a) Cut the prisoner's wages upto a maximum of 50 per cent of wages earned during a month.

(b) Deny 50 per cent of the wages for the work done upto a maximum period of three months with the approval of Director-General/Inspector-General of Prisons.

(vii) **Transfer to special ward or another prison:** The Superintendent may with the approval of Director General/ Inspector-General of Prisons transfer a prisoner to special ward or another prison as a punishment. This punishment may be awarded to prisoners who are persistently violating prison discipline.

When the punishment of transfer to another prison is awarded, a Nominal Roll alongwith a statement of details of the offences and punishments may be sent to the Superintendent of the other prison and copy to the Director-General/Inspector-General for issuance for formal transfer order.

(viii) **Fatigue work:** Subject to medical advice, the Superintendent may order fatigue work for thirty minutes a day upto a maximum period of seven days.

(ix) **Forfeiture of unauthorised cash, currency, other articles, etc.:** The Superintendent may be authorised to forfeit to Government cash, currency, other articles, etc., found in the possession of the inmates.

(x) **Punishment for breaches in the conditions of leave:** The Superintendent may be authorised to inflict punishment for breaches and violations in the conditions of leave as shown below:

(a) Not counting leave period towards sentence and treating it as out-period,

(b) Cut in remission upto five days for each day of overstay, provided that where the prisoner has not sufficient remission to his credit, he/she may cease to earn remission in future for such period as the Superintendent may direct,

(c) Postponement of the next due leave upto a period of two years.

In case of armed forces prisoners, the orders of the concerned armed forces authority will be obtained.

(xi) **Segregation:** The Superintendent may be empowered to award this punishment for a maximum period of three months at one time. Under sanction of the Inspector-General, this punishment can be extended upto six months.

Prisoners kept in segregation yard may be confined in barracks/cells from lockup to opening. At other times, they may remain in earmarked places only,

They may work in the verandah in front of the cell/barrack during prescribed work hours,

Exercise for one hour in the morning and one hour before lockup may be allowed,

Letters, interviews, books and newspapers may be allowed as per rules,

Except soap and other hygienic requirements, all other canteen facilities may be withdrawn,

Grant of remission may be subject to close review of the prisoner's work and behaviour during the period of segregation,

Prisoners undergoing this punishment may not be released on leave during the period of this punishment.

(xii) **Separate confinement:** The Superintendent may be empowered to award the punishment of separate confinement upto one month at one time. Under the sanction of the Inspector-General this punishment can be extended upto three months.

Where a separate exercise area is attached to each cell, the inmate may be allowed exercise facilities for one hour each time in the morning and evening. If a separate exercise block is not attached to each cell, inmates undergoing this punishment may be taken out one by one at prescribed times for exercise, forty-five minutes in the morning and forty-five minutes in the evening.

If bath and w.c. facilities are not attached to the barrack/cell, inmates confined in the cells may be taken out one at a time for bathing and other purposes. They may not be allowed to communicate or congregate during such periods.

Except for periods as mentioned above, the prisoner may be confined in the cell. Food should be served in the cell.

The following concessions may be extended to prisoners undergoing this punishment:

(a) Letters as per rule,
(b) Interviews with family members and relatives may be granted in the discretion of the Superintendent provided he thinks that such interview will have a salutary effect on the conduct and behaviour of the inmate,
(c) Religious and moral books and religious pictures may be allowed as per rules.
(d) Work may be given in the cell at the discretion of the Superintendent.

Remission may not be granted for the period of separate confinement,

No prisoner may be punished unless he has been informed of the offence alleged against him and given a proper opportunity of presenting his defence. The competent authority may conduct an inquiry into the case. No prisoner may be punished except in accordance with the terms of law or regulation.

No prisoner may be punished twice for the same offence, provided that no security measure (separate confinement, fetters, etc.) taken for the safe custody of a refractory and dangerous prisoner or for preventing him from committing mischief or the stoppage of privileges which are otherwise admissible to well behaved prisoners only, may not be construed as prison punishment for this purpose.

The punishment of separate confinement or fatigue work may not be implemented unless the medical officer has examined the prisoner and certified in writing that he/she is fit to sustain it. The same rules may apply to any other punishment that may be prejudicial to the physical or mental health of a prisoner.

The Medical Officer may daily visit prisoners undergoing any such punishment and may advise the Superintendent, if he/she considers the termination or alteration of the punishment necessary on the ground of physical or mental health.

If a prisoner is guilty of an offence against prison discipline which, by reason of his having frequently committed such offences or otherwise, in the opinion of the Superintendent is not adequately punishable by infliction of any prison punishments, the Superintendent may send a statement of the circumstances, alongwith the prisoner concerned to the court of a Magistrate, having jurisdiction for being dealt with by way of summary trial and imprisonment upto six months.

In respect of offences committed or abetted by prisoners which are punishable both under the Indian Penal Code or the proposed Bill or any other criminal law, it may be discretionary with the Superintendent either to use his own powers of punishment as set forth in rules or to prosecute the offender before a Magistrate, provided that in the case of cognizable offences having a punishment above three years, a prosecution shall be initiated.

The proposed Bill may require the formulation of detailed rules for the holding of enquiries and for the segregation of the prisoner pending enquiry, medical examination in the case of an injury, informing the prisoner of the charge against him, conduct of the enquiry, recording of statements and the decision arrived at, and an opportunity for any appeal or revision.

If any condition on or subject to which a sentence has been suspended or remitted or release on leave or special leave is granted is in the opinion of the authority exercising such power, not fulfilled, such authority may cancel its order granting such suspension, remission or release on leave or special leave, and thereupon the person in whose favour such order was made may, if at large, be arrested by any Police Officer without warrant and remanded to undergo the unexpired portion of his/her sentence.

If any prisoner fails without sufficient cause to observe any of the conditions on or subject to which his/her sentence was suspended or remitted, or release on leave or special leave was granted to him/her, he/she may, on conviction, be punished (such punishment being in addition to any punishment which such prisoner was undergoing when he committed such offence) with imprisonment for a term which may extend to two years or with fine which may extend to one thousand rupees, or with both. No court may take cognizance of an offence under this provision except with the previous sanction of the State Government or the authority which granted suspension or remission of the sentence.

The Superintendent may be made responsible to undertake effective measures to ensure safe custody and security of prisoners, including the use of handcuffs and fetters in keeping with the directives of the Supreme Court of India. In an emergent situation the Superintendent may be empowered to use handcuffs and fetters for reasons to be recorded in writing under intimation to the Magistrate concerned within 48 hours. Similarly, the confinement of a prisoner in a separate cell may also be restored to in the interest of custody and security.

In order to evolve a suitable mechanism for grievance redressal, a Discipline Committee may be set up in the jail under the chairmanship of the Superintendent with Deputy Superintendent, Medical Officer/Assistant Medical Officer drawn on it. Such a committee may meet at least once a month to review grievances, petitions and representations from prisoners.

The proposed Bill may be required the formulation of detailed rules for maintenance of the physical and mental health of prisoners sentenced to death, facilities for appeal and petition for mercy and action to be taken on confirmation and execution of death sentence. It should be the responsibility of prison administration to provide for the necessary legal assistance to prisoners sentenced to death at various stages.

In view of the specific nature of the tasks to be performed by the prison staff, it is necessary that the proposed Bill clearly lays down their accountability towards the duties and responsibilities assigned to them. Every official of the prison who is found guilty of any violation of duty or wilfully breach or neglect of any rule or regulation or lawful order made by competent authority or who withdraws from the duties of his office without permission or without having given previous notices in writing of his intention or who wilfully overstays without permission any leave granted to him or who engages without authority in any employment other than a prison duty or who shows cowardice or who is found guilty of any cruel, inhuman or degrading treatment of the prisoner under his/her charge, may be made liable on conviction before a Magistrate to fine not acceding Rs. 1,000 or to imprisonment for a period not acceding 3 months or to both.

The proposed Bill may prohibit the formation of unions, strikes and agitations by prison personnel.

TRANSFER, REMOVAL AND ATTENDANCE IN COURTS

As the proposed Bill aims at consolidating various prison laws, the provisions of the Transfer of Prisoners Act, 1950, and the Prisoners (Attendance in Courts) Act, 1955, may be appropriately incorporated in this chapter. While transferring or removing prisoners from one prison to another whether within and outside the State or producing them before the concerned courts, the welfare interest of prisoners may be kept in view. In this respect the new provisions may clearly lay down that:

On arrival in the prison from police custody or on transfer, every prisoner, even if he/she comes after lockup, may be medically examined. The State Government may be required to make necessary arrangements for this purpose.

For the treatment of prisoners suffering from infectious diseases, mental ailments, addiction to drugs, serious sickness, injuries or sudden health problems, the proposed Bill may require State Governments to identify and declare referral hospital both in the governmental and non-governmental sectors.

A provision may be made for the transfer of a prisoner from one prison to another within the state on administrative, medical or humanitarian grounds. Such a transfer may be affected with the approval of the Inspector General of Prisons under intimation to the concerned court. The basis of transfer may be recorded in writing.

In order to facilitate the transfer of prisoners from a particular state to the State of his origin or on security grounds, the proposed Bill may lay down the procedure for consultation between the States at appropriate levels. In the case of a prisoner being transferred to the State of his origin, the Inspector-General of the Prisons may be authorised to ensure the consent of the receiving State. In case of a prisoner being transferred from one State to another on security grounds such consultation may take place at the level of Secretaries of Home Departments of the States concerned.

In respect of the prisoners to be transferred to the countries of their origin, the specific provisions of the bilateral agreements or treaties with the countries concerned may be followed by the prison departments.

While the Superintendent has to ensure the appearance of a prisoner for trial or evidence as and when required by the concerned Court, the existing provisions for the exemption from attendance of certain prisoners in courts may be appropriately incorporated in the proposed Bill. A provision may also be made for the high security prisoners within the prison in the interest of security and public order, on a selective basis.

LEAVE AND SPECIAL LEAVE

A variety of systems exist in States in regard to leave or special leave for prisoners during the period of imprisonment in the form of parole, ticket leave, furlough, etc. With a view to bringing in a basic uniformity in these matters, especially as an incentive for good behaviour and responsiveness to correctional treatment, the proposed Bill may provide for common framework for the release of a prisoner on leave or special leave on the following lines:

A prisoner may be entitled to leave of 21 days in one or two spells during a year on the completion of half of his/her sentence or a minimum period of 3 years of imprisonment, whichever is less. Such a leave may be earned by a prisoner on the basis of his/her good behaviour and conduct in the prison.

In the case of a prisoner to be granted leave, the application for leave may be sent to the concerned District Magistrate and the Superintendent of Police for comments before it is placed before the Inspector General of Prisons for consideration. If no comment is received from the District Magistrate and the Superintendent of Police within 3 weeks, it may be presumed that there is no adverse opinion to be offered by them and the recommendation of the Superintendent of Jail may be considered by the Inspector General of Prisons. For the subsequent leave, the Superintendent of Jail may be empowered to grant leave on the basis of the conduct of the prisoner during the previous leave without any consultation with the concerned District Magistrate or the Superintendent of Police. Leave availed of by a prisoner may be counted towards his/her imprisonment.

Special leave may be granted to a prisoner for a maximum period of 14 days on a specific ground of death, marriage, sickness or any other sufficient cause in his/her family. Special leave may be granted to a prisoner on the recommendation of the Superintendent of Jail by the Inspector General of Prisoners under intimation to the concerned District Magistrate and the Superintendent of Police, so as to facilitate the prisoner to attend the emergency in his/her family. Special leave granted to a prisoner may not count towards his/her imprisonment.

If the prisoner on leave or special leave fails to maintain good behaviour and peace and other conditions specified in relevant order, the order of leave or special leave may be revoked by the competent authority.

The following categories of prisoners may not be eligible for being released on leave:

(i) Prisoner whose presence is considered dangerous or otherwise prejudicial to public peace and order by the District Magistrate/ Superintendent of Police;
(ii) Prisoners who are considered dangerous, or who have been prosecuted for serious prison violation like assault, outbreak, riot, mutiny, escape, instigation to serious violations, strike, etc.;
(iii) Prisoners transferred to special prisons on disciplinary grounds for the period of their incarceration in such prisons;
(iv) Prisoners committed to prisons in default of furnishing security to keep the peace or be of good behaviour;
(v) Prisoners suffering from unsoundness of mind.

In case of prisoners government by any of the laws relating to armed forces of the Union and having separate mode of trial, these provisions of leave and special leave shall be subject to their laws.

REMISSION AND PREMATURE RELEASE

Remission is a concession granted to prisoners as an incentive for good behaviour and work. It is not a right as the same can be withdrawn forfeited or revoked by the competent authority. All prisoners undergoing a substantive sentence of 3 months or more may be entitled to the grant of remission. However, the grant of remission has to be based on an objective criteria for the assessment of prisoners' conduct. Accordingly, the system may be standardised on the following lines.

The types of remission may include ordinary remission, special remission and State Government remission. While ordinary remission is to be granted to all eligible prisoners for any special remission may be considered on a selective basis to deserving prisoners for any special service, achievement or conduct. The State remission may be awarded by the Government concerned to such prisoners or categories of prisoners as decided from time to time.

Prisoners eligible for earning ordinary remission may include:

(i) Prisoners having substantive sentence of three months or more.

(ii) Prisoners fulfilling the conditions as mentioned in (i) above, but who are unable to participate in institutional activities because of factors beyond their control such as court attendance or frequent transit from one prison to another or admission as indoor patients in a hospital, including mental-hospital, may be granted ordinary remission at the scale earned by the prisoners during the previous month, provided their conduct during the period in question has been good. If the inability referred to above arises soon after admission, ordinary remission at minimum scale should be given.

(iii) In case of prisoners who fulfil conditions mentioned at (i) above and who are admitted in hospital as indoor patients or during the periods of their convalescence, ordinary remission may be granted subject to certification by the Medical officer regarding their bona fides.

(iv) Prisoners fulfilling conditions mentioned in (i) above and who have been certified by the Medical Officer as invalid or infirm.

(v) Habitual prisoners should be granted remission under circumstances to be specified in rules.

(vi) Prisoners working on conservancy jobs irrespective of the length of their sentence.

(vii) Prisoners sentenced to simple imprisonment of three months and more and who volunteer to work.

(viii) Ordinary remission can be earned throughout a period of imprisonment in lieu of fine which immediately follows and is continued with a substantive sentence of not less than three months.

Ordinary remission may be granted at the following scale:

(i) for good behaviour, discipline, interest, effort and participation in institutional activities three days per completed calender month.

(ii) for performing allotted work at prescribed standards—three days per completed calender month.

(iii) for conservancy jobs—two days per month. This remission should be in addition to remission as stated in (i) and (ii) above.

(iv) any prisoner eligible for ordinary remission should be awarded fifteen days' annual good conduct ordinary remission in addition to any other remission provided that he/she has committed no prison offence whatever for a period of one year reckoned from the date of his/her sentence or the date on which he/she was last punished for a prison offence.

Special remission may be granted by the Inspector General of Prisons upto 60 days in a year and by the Remission Committee upto 30 days during a year. The Discipline Committee of the prison may function as the Remission Committee for this purpose.

The total remission to be granted to a prisoner may not exceed one-half of the sentence undergone for the purposes of getting released.

Remission may be forfeited by the State Government, the Inspector General of Prisons and the Superintendent under circumstances to be specified in rules.

The review of sentences provides the necessary flexibility to the determinate/definite sentencing system under the law. It serves as a mechanism for release of a prisoner at a stage considered appropriate for his/her reintegration into society. Pre-mature releases are effected under Section 432 of the Cr.P.C. which in certain states, is further spelt out under special laws. Under the Constitution of India the President and the Governor have an overriding power in this regard. There is, however, a need to bring in a basic uniformity and consistency in the operation of the relevant laws, rules and regulations governing premature releases, as under:

Review of sentences may be considered by a Review Board to be presided over by the Director-General/Inspector-General of Prisons with the District Magistrate, District Judge, the Superintendent of Police and two social workers/social scientists drawn on it. The recommendations of the Board may be sent to the State Government for orders. The procedure to be adopted may be prescribed in rules.

The case of a prisoner suffering from any serious disease and about whom civil surgeon and the prison medical officer certify that in all probability the prisoner is not likely to survive may be submitted to the Government for being reviewed for conditional or unconditional release.

RELEASE AND AFTER-CARE

From the viewpoint of his/her rehabilitation and social reintegration, the release of a prisoner has to be preceded by a careful planning for his/her smooth transition from the closed institution to the open community. The process involves prerelease preparation, after-care and follow-up of prisoners of an individualised basis. It certainly requires a systematic programme on the following lines:

A separate yard may be earmarked in each prison for the organisation of a pre-release programme to reorient those to be released shortly and to prepare them for their post-release adjustment. The programme may address the specific problems and challenges to be faced by individual prisoners in the communities they are expected to return to. This may require a variety of inputs including counselling, guidance and referral to appropriate agencies.

The Welfare Officer/Assistant Welfare Officer may have to play a key role in the assessment of individual needs and mobilisation of necessary resources both from inside and outside the prison to help prisoners to overcome situation likely to impede their social readjustment.

Each prison may set up a mechanism to maintain a regular contact with community-based after-care organisations and to draw upon them as per the individual needs of prisoners being released.

A periodic review of releases may be undertaken by the Superintendent of jail. The concerned Superintendent of Police and Probation Officer may be given adequate prior notice of the date and time of releases.

A scheme of rehabilitation assistance in deserving cases may be introduced by the prison department with adequate provision made in the jail budget. Side by Side, specific schemes with other departments which can help prisoners in availing training, equipment, capital, marketing facilities, etc., may be identified and utilised in individual cases.

The prison department may work closely with organisations offering after-care facilities, both in the governmental and non-governmental sectors. Deserving cases may be referred to them for such assistance as found necessary on an individualised basis.

Appropriate linkages may be established between the prison department and voluntary welfare organisations, to mobilise resources for the rehabilitation and social reintegration of prisoners, especially women and young offenders being released from prisons.

OPEN INSTITUTIONS

Experience has shown that many prisoners after undergoing certain period of their institutional treatment are fit to be placed in open, semi-open and community-based mobile camps. The success in the experimentation with open institutions has not only opened up an important avenue towards a progressive classification of prisoners but has also bridged the gap between the closed institution and the open community. However, the functioning of and operations in open institutions need to be standardised on a uniform basis as indicated below:

Only such prisoners whose behaviour and progress in closed institutions is found good and are fit for regime based upon trust, responsibility and self-discipline should be considered for transfer to open, semi-open or community-based mobile camps.

The Classification Committee may be used as a mechanism for the screening of cases for semi-open or open institutions or community-based mobile camps.

A set of minimum standards may be prescribed for a semi-open or open institutions or a community-based mobile camp in terms of accommodation, equipment, care, education, training and welfare of the inmates. The inmates of open institution or community-based mobile camps may be granted enhanced remission at the rate of one day spent therein. Similarly, the wages for inmates in open institutions or mobile camps may be fixed at par with wages in the open community with such deductions as considered necessary for their maintenance.

The work programmes in open institutions or community-based mobile camps may, as far as possible, be linked with national development projects or private industries, on a selective basis.

The inmates of open institutions or community-based mobile camps may be liberally allowed letters, interviews, family visits and stay of their families without undergoing institutional security and discipline.

A priority attention may be given to the welfare of inmates in open institutions in conjunction with community based-organisations.

If a prisoner transferred to an open institution or community-based mobile camp fails to abide by the requisite standard of discipline, self-management and work, he/she may be liable to be reverted back to the closed institution to undergo the remaining period of his/her sentence.

The staff for semi-open or open institutions or community-based mobile camps may be carefully selected in keeping with the aptitude, talent, commitment, initiative and dedication required to run such innovative projects. The State Government may provide adequate incentives to the staff employed in open institution or community-based mobile camp. Employment in such a setting may be considered as an added qualification for promotion to higher ranks.

The sale proceeds in a semi-open or open institution or community-based mobile camp may be allowed to be ploughed back into the development of prison industries with the necessary accounting procedure being introduced in the jail budget.

STAFF DEVELOPMENT

It is universally accepted that the success of institutional programmes depends mainly on the quality, calibre and competence of the staff. However, the staff position in most of the states, whether quantitatively and qualitatively, is reported to be unsatisfactory. Besides the need to attract the requisite talent to the prison service, it is essential to keep the prison staff abreast of new trends and patterns of criminality.

Therefore, a concerted approach towards staff development has to become an integral part of the legal framework that regulates prisons. In this context, the proposed Bill may provide as under:

The staffing pattern may be thoroughly restructured to cater effectively to the requirements of both custody and correction. This implies the provision of all the components of the staff at various levels as spelt out in the chapter on institutional organisation.

In order to maintain the necessity level of morale, discipline and efficiency of the prison staff, only persons possessing the requisite aptitude and attributes may be appointed on various posts in the prison department. Each State Government may be required to formulate a recruitment and selection policy that meets the demands of the jobs to be performed at various levels.

For the custodial staff at the Institutional level, the Superintendent may be empowered to serve as the appointing and promoting authority for Warders, Head Warders and Chief Warders. The Inspector General of Prisons may be the appointing and promoting authority for Assistant Superintendents, Deputy Superintendents and Superintendents. The correctional staff may be recruited and promoted by a Selection Board to be presided over by the Inspector General of Prisons with specialists from the relevant disciplines drawn on it.

No person may be placed on a job in the prison department without an intensive training of at least 6 months. Every State may be required to set up a training institution with the necessary staff and equipment for imparting initial training and in-service training. While the initial training of the Superintendent of Prison may spread over 9 months, the subordinate staff may be provided with a 6 months training.

All the categories of prison staff may be given in-service refresher training at least once in 5 years, so as to keep them abreast with the newly emerging problems and requirements of prison administration.

Each state may set up a mechanism for a periodic review of the service conditions of the prison staff, including their salaries, allowances, housing conditions, education of children, transport facilities, promotional avenues working hours, leave, etc. Apart from maintaining the principle of equal pay for equal work with the personnel of other governmental departments, the special nature and the hazards in the prison work may be kept in view. Each State may develop a cadre of prisons and correctional services at the appropriate level in keeping with the specialised nature of the jobs to be performed. A system of reward, recognition and appreciation for the meritorious services rendered by the prison personnel may be introduced in every State.

A welfare fund for prison personnel may be created in every state so as to maintain the requisite morale of the prison service as also to render a timely assistance to a member of the staff in the case of any calamity or distress.

SPECIAL CATEGORIES OF PRISONERS

Within the overall framework of institutional care, certain categories of prisoners are in need of a specialised treatment. These categories may include women offenders, military prisoners, adolescent offenders, if convicts, habitual offenders, simple imprisonment prisoners, military prisoners sentenced to death, civil prisoners and lunatics. A focussed attention on the correctional needs of such categories may be provided in the proposed Bill on the following lines:

Apart from ensuring a complete segregation and a differential management of women prisoners under the supervision of female staff, the proposed Bill may require State Governments to formulate a comprehensive scheme for the care, protection, treatment, education, training and development of women prisoners in keeping with their personal characteristics and rehabilitation needs.

Adolescents may be segregated from adults in prisons and given a concerted attention in terms of their educational, training and rehabilitation requirements. The State Government may work out a comprehensive scheme in this regard.

Life convicts may be subject to a programme of long term institutional treatment with an opportunity for their transfer to semi-open or open institutions or community-based mobile camps.

Habitual offenders may be classified to focus on a thorough study of their personality and correctional requirements and to provide them with a differential set of such programmes as are conducive to their mainstreaming.

Simple imprisonment prisoners may not only be separated from other prisoners and handled in a differential manner but may also be given adequate incentive to engage in productive work and healthy recreation.

While military prisoners may not ordinarily be admitted in prisons whenever received, may be confined in central prisons in segregated manner and be given such facilities as are necessary to maintain their physical and mental health.

Special precautions may be taken in ensuring adequate security and upkeep of prisoners sentenced to death, with a special consideration to their safety, health and legal rights.

Civil prisoners, as and when received in jails, may be segregated from other undertrials and sentenced prisoners and allowed to meet their basic requirements of food, clothing, bedding, etc., from their own sources, or from the decree holders and treated like undertrial prisoners with regard to other matters in the prison.

While non-criminal lunatics may not be lodged in jails, criminal lunatics may be sent to mental hospitals for treatment, as early as possible, as per the procedure to be prescribed in the rules. Pending their removal to mental hospitals, special care may be taken to maintain their human dignity and security.

MISCELLANEOUS

This chapter may cover general aspects of prison administration and its development. This may include, among others, the following:

An Advisory Board for the development of prisons and allied correctional services may be set up in each state under the Chief Secretary with members from various concerned governmental and non-governmental organisations and individual experts. Such a Board may meet half-yearly and advise the government on relevant issues.

Steps may be taken by State Governments to integrate correctional programmes in prisons with development schemes of the Central and State Governments as part of the national planning.

The educational and vocational training programmes in prisons may be periodically reviewed and updated in keeping with the standards adopted by the concerned state departments in the open community so as to ensure their recognition and continuation even after the release of prisoners, if necessary.

The State Governments may be required to formulate detailed rules to implement the provisions of the proposed law. The specific items of such rules may be indicated on the finalisation of the draft of the proposed Bill.

5

Official Secrecy and Right to Information and Human Rights

THE OFFICIAL SECRETS ACT, 1923

Wrongful communication, etc. of information

1. If any person having in his possession or control any secret official code or password or sketch, plan, model, article, note, document or information which relates to or is used in a prohibited place or related to anything in such a place, (or which is likely to assist, directly or indirectly, an enemy or which relates to a matter the disclosure of which is likely to affect that sovereignty and integrity of India, the security of the State or friendly relations with foreign States or which has been made or obtained in contravention of this Act, or which has been entrusted in confidence to him by any person holding office under Government, or which he has obtained or to which he has had access owing to his position as a person who holds or has held office under Government, or as a person who holds or has held a contract made on behalf of Government, or as a person who is or has been employed under a person who holds or has held such an office or contract Act.

(a) wilfully communicates the code or password, sketch, plan, model, article, note, document or information to any person other than person to whom he is authorised to communicate it, or a Court of Justice or a person to whom it is, in the interests of the State, his duty to communicate it; or

(b) uses the information in his possession for the benefit of any foreign power or in any other manner prejudicial to the safety of the State; or

(c) retains the sketch, plan, model, article, note or document in his possession or control when he has no right to retain it, or when it is contrary to his duty to retain it, or wilfully fails to comply with all directions issued by lawful authority with regard to the return or disposal thereof; or

(d) fails to take reasonable care of, or so conducts himself as to endanger the safety of the sketch, plan, model, article, note, document, secret official code or password or information;

he shall be guilty of an offence under this section

2. If any person voluntarily received any secret official code or password or any sketch, plan, model, article, note, document or information knowing or having reasonable ground to believe, at the time when he receives it, that the code, password, sketch, plan, model, article, note, document, or information is communicated in contravention of this Act, he shall be guilty of an offence under this section.

3. If any person having in his possession or control any sketch, plan, model, article, note, document or information, which relates to munitions of war, communicates it, directly or indirectly, to any foreign power or in any other manner prejudicial to the safety or interests of the State, he shall be guilty of an offence under this section.

4. A person guilty of an offence under this section shall be punishable with imprisonment for a term which may extend to three years, or with fine, or with both.

FREEDOM OF INFORMATION BILL, 1997

A Bill drafted by the Working Group on Right to Information and Promotion of Open and Transparent Government under the auspices of the Ministry of Personnel, Public Grievances and Pension, Government of India. No bill has yet been presented in Parliament.

A Bill to provide freedom to every citizen to secure access to information under the control of public authorities, consistent with public interest, in order to promote openness, transparency and accountability in administration and in relation to matters connected therewith or incidental thereto.

1. Short title and commencement. 1. The Act may be called the Freedom of Information Act, 1997.

2. It extends to the whole of India.

3. It shall come into force on such date as the Central Government may, by notification in the Official Gazette, appoint.

2. Definitions. In this Act, unless the context otherwise requires:

(a) "appropriate Government" means the Government of India or the Government of a State/Union Territory, as the case may be.

(b) "document" means a document in any form and includes any printed or written material, information stored or recorded by means of any devices and visual images which are reproducible, whether with or without the aid of any device.

(c) "freedom of information" means the freedom to seek information and includes inspection, taking notes and extracts and obtaining certified copies of documents or records of any public authority; and where the information is stored in computers or any other electromagnetic device, the facility of access to it through terminals or supply of printouts.

(d) "information" means any material relating to the affairs, administration or decision of a public authority and includes any document or record relating to the affairs of the public authority;

(e) "Public Information Officer" means the Public Information Officer appointed under the Act.

(f) "prescribed" means prescribed by rules under the Act.

(g) "public authority" includes:

(i) the Government of India, the Government of each of the States/Union Territories, local bodies and other bodies owned or substantially controlled or funded by the Government of India or Government of a State/Union Territory and the administrative offices of the Supreme Court, High Courts, subordinate Courts and of Parliament and the State Legislatures,

(ii) a company, corporation, trust, firm, society or a cooperative society shall have the same meaning as assigned to them in the respective Acts under which they are registered.

(h) "third party" means a person or an organisation other than the person making a request for access to information and a public authority.

3. ***Freedom of Information.*** Subject to the provisions of this Act, every citizen shall have the freedom to seek information from a public authority.

4. ***Obligations on Public Authorities.*** 1. Every public authority shall be under a duty to maintain all its records as per its operational requirements, duly catalogued and indexed and, subject to the provisions of sections 9 and 10, grant access to information to any citizen requesting for such access.

2. Each public authority shall public periodically, and keep updated, information indicating:

(i) particulars of its organisation, functions and responsibilities;

(ii) description of its decision making processes in terms of procedures and powers and responsibilities of its officers and employees;

(iii) norms for performance of activities such as prescribed periods for their processing and completion of physical and financial targets etc., and the actual achievements with reference to such norms;

(iv) classes of records under its control including the rules, regulations, instructions and list of manuals, etc. used by its employees for carrying out activities;

(v) the facilities provided for access to information; and

(vi) the name, designation and other relevant particulars of the Public Information Officer, to whom requests for information may be addressed.

3. It shall also be the duty of the concerned officers of a public authority to give reasons for decisions—whether administrative or adjudicative—to those affected and to disclose the relevant facts and analyses when major policies or decisions are announced.

5. Appointment of Public Information Officers. (i) Every public authority shall appoint officers to be called Public Information Officers in its offices.

(ii) It will be the responsibility of Public Information Officers to deal with requests for access to information and to render reasonable assistance to requesters seeking access to information.

6. Requests for Access to Information. A request under this Act shall be made to the appropriate Public Information Officer in writing and shall specify, as clearly as possible, the particulars of the information, document or records to which access is being sought.

Provided that where a requester cannot, for valid reasons, make a request in writing, the Public Information Officer may either accept an oral request or render reasonable assistance to the requester in making a written request.

7. Disposal of Requests. 1. Upon a request being made to him, the Public Information Officer shall provide access to the information, where it is decided not to refuse such access, as expeditiously as possible and in any case within 30 days of the receipt of the request.

Provided that where it is not possible to provide access within 30 days, the period may be extended upto a maximum of another 30 days, for reasons to be recorded, and communicated to the requester, in writing.

Provided further that where it is decided to grant access to information on payment of any additional fee, representing the cost of providing such access, the Public Information Officer shall send an intimation to the requester, accompanied by details of fees determined by him, requesting him to deposit the fees; and the period intervening between the dispatch of the said intimation and payment of fees shall be excluded for the purpose of calculating the period prescribed for grant of access to information.

2. Where the Public Information Officer decides to refuse access, such decision shall also be taken within 30 days of receipt of the request and it shall be communicated to the requester in writing, setting out the precise grounds and the relevant provisions of the Act, on which such refusal is based and mention the remedy open to

the requester.

3. Access to information shall ordinarily be provided in the form in which it is sought unless it would disproportionately divert the resources of a public authority or would be detrimental to the safety or preservation of the document in question.

8. Deemed Refusal of Request. Where the decision on a request for access to information is not communicated to the requester within 30 days, on within the extended period, the request shall be deemed to have been refused and the requester shall have the right to make a review application in accordance with the provisions of the Act.

9. Exemption from disclosure of Information. Information covered by any of the following categories shall be exempted from disclosure under the provisions of this Act.

(i) information disclosure of which would prejudicially affect the sovereignty and integrity of India, security of the State, conduct of international relations, including information received in confidence from foreign Governments, their agencies or international organizations;

(ii) information disclosure of which would prejudicially affect the conduct of Centre-State relations, including information exchanged in confidence between the Central and State Governments or any of their authorities/agencies:

(iii) information of the nature of Cabinet papers, including papers prepared for submission to Cabinet or submitted to Cabinet, other than the documents whereby such decision are published.

(iv) information in the nature of internal working papers such as interdepartmental/intra-departmental notes and correspondence, papers containing advice, opinions, recommendations or minutes for the purpose of deliberative processes in a public authority.

Provided that the exemption shall not apply to reports of scientific or technical experts, including their opinion or scientific or technical matters or information that is factual;

(v) information disclosure of which would prejudicially affect the enforcement of any law including detection, prevention, investigation or suppression of crime or contravention of any law; or would lead to incitement to an offence, or would prejudicially affect the operations of any intelligence organizations to be specified by the appropriate Government; or would prejudicially affect public safety or the safety of an individual; or would prejudicially affect fair trial or adjudication of a pending case; or would reveal the existence or identity of a confidential record or source of information; or would prejudice future supply of information relating to violation or contravention of any law;

(vi) information, the disclosure of which would prejudicially affect the Government's ability to manage the economy or would prejudicially affect the legitimate economic and commercial interests of a public authority; or would cause unfair gain or loss to any individual or organization;

Without prejudice to the generality of this provision such information may include premature disclosure of proposals relating to

(a) taxes, including duties of Customs and Excise;
(b) currency, exchange or interest rates;
(c) regulation of supervision of financial institutions.

(vii) information, the disclosure of which would prejudicially affect the management of services under, and operations of public authorities.

(viii) information in the nature of trade or commercial secrets or any information having a commercial value which is likely to be prejudicially affected by such disclosure, or information the disclosure of which is likely to prejudicially affect the competitive position of a third party:
Provided that, excepting in the case of a trade or commercial secrets projected by law, disclosure may be allowed if public interest in such disclosure outweighs in importance any possible harm of injury to the interests of any such third party;

(ix) information the disclosure of which would not subserve any public interest;

(x) information which would cause unwarranted invasion of the privacy of an individual;

(xi) information, the disclosure of which may result in the breach of Parliamentary privileges or would amount to violation of an order of a competent Court.

10. Ground for Refusal of Access in certain cases. Without prejudice to the provisions of Section 9, a Public Information Officer may refuse access to information where:

(i) the request is too general or is of such a nature that, having regard to the volume of information required to be retrieved or processed for fulfilling it, it would involve disproportionate diversion of the resources of a public authority or would "adversely interfere" with the functioning of such authority.
Provided that, where access is being refused on the ground that the request is too general, it would be the duty of the Public Information Officer to render help as far as possible, to the requester to reframe his request in such a manner as may facilitate compliance with it;

(ii) the request relates to information that is required by law or convention to be published at a particular time; or

(iii) the request relates to information that is contained in published material available for sale.

11. Fee. The appropriate Government may prescribe the fees to be charged for access to information, which may include an application fee and such additional fees as may represent the cost of providing access.

Provided that the fees may be waived where the disclosure of information can be said to be in the larger public interest.

12. Severability. If a request for access to information is refused on the ground that it is in relation to information which is exempted from disclosure, then notwithstanding anything contained in this Act, access may be given to that part of the document which does not contain any information that is exempted from disclosure under this Act and which can reasonably be severed from any part that contains exempted information.

13. Third Party Intervention. Where a public authority intends to disclose information which relates to, or has been supplied by a third party and has consistently been treated as confidential by such third party, a notice may be given to it of the intended disclosure inviting it to make a representation against the intended disclosure, within 14 days of such notice. The Public Information Officer shall take such representation, if any made, into consideration while taking a decision on the request for information in question.

Provided that, excepting in the cases of trade or commercial secrets protected by law, disclosure may be allowed if the public interest in disclosure outweighs in importance any possible harm or injury to the interests of such third party.

14. Internal Review. 1. A requester, whose request for access to information has been refused by the Public Information Officer, may make an application, within 30 days of the refusal, for review of the decision to the Head of Department, or such other authority as may be prescribed, having jurisdiction over the office of the public authority to which the request had been addressed.

2. The reviewing authority shall dispose of the application within 30 days.

Provided that, where the application for review is rejected, the grounds for rejection shall be communicated to the applicant in writing setting out the appellate remedy available to the applicant.

3. In the case of third party information, the reviewing authority shall also follow the procedure set out in Section 13 of the Act.

4. A review application may also be made as regards the fee proposed to be charged by the Public Information Officer for access to information.

15. Appeals. 1. An appeal against the decision of a reviewing authority may be made, within 30 days of such decision. The appeal shall be considered and disposed of as a complaint under the Consumer Protection Act, 1986.

2. It shall be disposed of by the District Forum, the State Commissioner or the National Commission, as the case may be, by a written order, within 30 days.

3. The concerned Forum or the Commission, as the case may be, on an application by the public authority, hold proceedings in camera.

Provided that no document or record shall be withheld from the perusal of the appellate authority.

16. Publication of Certain Matters by Public Authorities. Notwithstanding anything contained in this Act or in any other law for the time being in force, but subject to the provisions of Section 9, it shall be the duty of every public authority which proposes to initiate any project or activity, to appropriately publish, as soon as possible, and in any case well before the commencement of the project or activity, for the information of the general public and the persons to be affected, such matters within its knowledge and control as affect the general public.

17. Protection of action taken in good faith. No suit, prosecution or other legal proceedings shall lie against any public authority or any individual, for anything which is in good faith done or intended to be done under the provisions of this Act or any rule made thereunder.

18. The Act to have overriding effect. The provisions of this Act shall have effect notwithstanding anything inconsistent therewith contained in any other law for the time being in force.

19. National Council for Freedom of Information. 1. The Central Government may, by notification in the Official Gazette, establish with effect from such day as may be specified in the notification, a Council to be known as the National Council for Freedom of Information.

2. The National Council may consist of the following members:

(a) the Minister in charge of Department of Administrative Reforms in the Central Government, who shall be its Chairman, and
(b) such other official and non-official members representing such interests as may be prescribed;
(c) the Council may meet as and when necessary, with at least one meeting being held every year;
(d) the time and place of the meeting of Council shall be as the Chairman thinks fit and it shall observe such procedure as may be prescribed to transact its business.

20. Objects of the National Council. The object of the National Council shall be to promote freedom of information in the country and it shall deal with all matters related to freedom of information such as:

(a) review of the operation of the Act and rules made thereunder,
(b) review of the administrative arrangements and procedures to secure for citizens the fullest possible access to information,
(c) research and documentation as regards management of information with a view to improve the extent and accuracy of information being made available under the Act, and
(d) to advise the Government on all matters related to freedom of information, including training, development and orientation of employees to bring in a culture of openness and transparency.

21. State Councils for Freedom of Information. 1. The State Government may, by notification in the Official Gazette, establish with effect from such day as may be specified in the notification, a Council to be known as the State Council for Freedom of Information.

2. The State Council may consist of the following members:

(a) the Minister in charge of Department of Administrative Reforms in the State Government, who shall be its Chairman, and

(b) such other official and non-official members representing such interests as may be prescribed;

(c) the Council may meet as and when necessary, with at least one meeting being held every year;

(d) the time and place of the meeting of the Council shall be as the Chairman thinks fit and it shall observe such procedure as may be prescribed to transact its business.

22. *Objects of the State Council.* The object of the State Council shall be to promote the freedom of information within the State and it shall deal with the matters specified in Section 20 in respect of the State.

23. *Powers to make rules.* 1. The appropriate Government may, by notification in the Official Gazette, make rules to carry out the provisions of this Act.

2. Without prejudice to the generality of the foregoing power, such rules may provide for all matters in respect of which rules are required to be made by the appropriate Government under this Act.

24. *Laying of Rules.* 1. Every rule made under this Act by the Central Government shall be laid, as soon as may be after it is made, before each House of Parliament, while it is in session, for a total period of thirty days which may be comprised in one session or in two or more successive sessions and if, before the expiry of the session immediately following the session or the successive sessions aforesaid, both Houses agree in making any modification in the rule, or both Houses agree that the rule should not be made, the rule shall thereafter have effect only in such modified form or be of no effect, as the case may be; so, however, that any such modification or annulment shall be without prejudice to the validity of anything previously done under that rule.

2. Every rule made under this Act by a State Government shall be laid, as soon as may be after it is made before the State legislature.

RIGHT TO INFORMATION BILL, 1997

Bill favoured by the National Campaign for People's Right to Information.

A Bill to make provision for securing right to information which is a Fundamental Right being part of Article 19 (1) (a) of Constitution and for matters connected therewith or incidental thereto.

Be it enacted by Parliament in the forty-eighth year of the Republic of India as follows:

1.

1. The act may be called the Right to Information Act, 1997.
2. It extends to the whole of India.

It shall come into force on such date as Central Government may, by notification in the Official Gazette, appoint, which shall not be later than 6 months from the date of the passing of the Act.

2. ***Definitions.*** In this Act, unless the context otherwise requires,

(a) "information: means any material or information relating to the affairs, administration or conduct of public authority and includes any document or record relating to the affairs of the public authority;

(b) "prescribed" means prescribed by rules under the Act;

(c) "Public authority" includes,

  (i) the Government and Parliament of India and the Government and Legislature of each of the States and of a local or other authorities within the territory of India the control of the Government of India; and

  (ii) The Administrative Offices of the Courts

  (iii) a company, corporation, trust, firm, society, a cooperative society or associations whether owned or controlled by the Government or by private individuals and institutions;

The expressions company, corporation, trust, firm, society, cooperative society and association shall have the same meaning as assigned to them in the respective Acts under which they are registered.

(d) "right to information" means the right of access to information and includes the inspection, taking notes and extracts and obtaining certified copies of documents or records of any public authority;

(e) "State Government" includes the administrator of a Union Territory appointed by the President under Article 239 of the Constitution.

3. ***Right to Information.*** 1. Every citizen shall have a right to information from a public authority.

2. Every public authority shall be under a duty to maintain all its records duly catalogued and indexed and subject to the provisions of Section 4, to make available to any person requesting information from it, the information sought for including such information as it is under an obligation to obtain and furnish and shall not withhold any information or limit its availability;

4. ***Obligations on public authorities.*** 1. Each public authority shall publish periodically, and keep updated information indicating:

(i) particulars of its organisation, functions and responsibilities;
(ii) description of its decision making processes in terms of procedures and powers and responsibilities of its officers and employees;
(iii) norms form performance of activities such as prescribed periods for their processing and completion of physical and financial targets, etc., and the actual achievements with reference to such norms;
(iv) classes of records under its control including the rules, regulations, instructions and list of manuals etc. used by its employees for carrying its activities;
(v) the facilities provided for access to information; and
(vi) the name, designation and other relevant particulars of the Public Information Officer, to whom requests for information may be addressed.

2. It shall also be the duty of the concerned officer of a public authority to give reasons for decisions—whether administrative or adjudicative—to those affected and to disclose the relevant facts and analysis when major policies or decisions are announced.

3. Nothing in the foregoing provisions of this section shall preclude the right of any person to obtain such information as would affect life or liberty of any person in whom he is interested.

4. It shall be mandatory for each custodial establishment such as a police lock-up, jail mental asylum, remand house, women's

home, beggars home, etcetera to appoint a visitors' committee comprising independent citizens which shall have full access to them at all hours of the day and night and to their records and inmates.

5. Restrictions on Right to Information. The public authority may, for reasons to be recorded in writing, withhold

(a) information, the disclosure or contents of which will prejudicially affect the sovereignty and integrity of India, security for the State and friendly relations with foreign States, public order, investigation of an offence or which leads to incitement to an offence:

(b) information relating to personal or other information, the disclosure of which has no relationship to any public activity or in which the public has no interest and would constitute a clear and unwarranted invasion of personal privacy;

(c) trade and commercial secrets protected by law, provided that an appeal against the refusal of the information under clause (a) above, will lie to a Board headed by Cabinet secretary of the Government of India or the Chief Secretary of state Government as the case may be, and the Board shall dispose of the appeal within a period of 30 days from the receipt thereof.

Provided that information which cannot be denied to Parliament or State Legislature shall not be denied to any citizen.

6. Procedure for the supply of information. 1. A person desiring from a public authority under this Act shall make an application to the person who shall be designated by the public authority for the purpose. For the said purpose the Official may be allowed to inspect the concerned document(s).

2. The information asked for under sub-section (1) shall be furnished to the applicant by the public authority within thirty days of the application under sub-section (1), and where such information relates to the life or liberty of the individual, the information shall be supplied within forth-eight hours of the making of the application.

3. The information asked for under sub-section (1) shall be supplied in writing either in English or Hindi or in the language of the State in which the public authority is located.

Provided that where a requester cannot, for valid reasons, make a request in writing the Public Information Officer may either accept an oral request or render reasonable assistance to the requester in making a written request.

4. Every public authority shall have a right to charge fees for the supply of any document subject to the condition that such fees shall not exceed the cost of making and supplying the document.

7. Refusal to be given in writing. If the information asked for under sub-section (1) of Section 4 is refused by any public authority, the reasons for such refusal shall be given to such authority in writing.

8. Severability. If a request for access to information is refused on the ground that it is in relation to information which is withheld from disclosure, then notwithstanding anything contained in this Act, access may be given to that part of the document which does not contain any information that is withheld from disclosure under this Act and which can reasonably be severed from any part that contains withheld information. When only a part of the document is furnished, the reasons for withholding the rest of the document shall be given. If the information is refused, it shall be done so only with the approval of the higher Officer to be designated by the Public authority.

9. Appeal. An appeal against a refusal to furnish and document by a public authority under this Act shall lie to the District Judge or the Principle Civil Judge of the City Civil Court as the case may be of ordinary original civil jurisdiction of the area in which office of the public authority is located and any appeal shall be preferred within fifteen days of the date of refusal of the supply of information by the public authority and any appeal so preferred shall be disposed of by the Judge within thirty days of its filing, by a written order and giving reasons for its filing, by a written order and giving reasons for its decision which shall be final.

10. Penalties. 1. Any individual responsible for providing any information under this Act shall be personally liable for furnishing the information with the period specified therein.

2. Where the information asked for under this Act is not furnished with the time specified, the person responsible for supplying the information shall be punishable or liable to pay personally a fine of rupees fifty for every day of delay after the day which it is required to be supplied.

3. If any person responsible for providing any information under this Act, fails to furnish such information or furnishes any

information which is false in any material particular and which he knows or has reasonable cause to believe to be false or does not believe it to be true, he shall be punishable or liable to pay personally a fine which shall not be less than rupees one thousand and which may extend to rupees five thousand.

Provided that the Court may, for reasons to be recorded in writing, levy a fine of less than one thousand rupees.

11. Offences by Companies and Societies, etc. 1. Where an offence under this Act has been committed by a company, every person who, at the time the offence was committed, was in charge of and was responsible to the company for the conduct of the business of the company, shall be deemed to be guilty of the offence and shall be liable to be proceeded against and punished accordingly:

Provided that nothing contained in this section shall render any such person liable to any punishment provided in this Act if he proves that the offence was committed without his knowledge or that he had exercised all due diligence to prevent the commission of such offence;

2. Notwithstanding anything contained in sub-section (1) where an offence under this Act has been committed by a company and it is proved that the offence has been committed with the consent or connivance of or is attributable to any neglect on the part of any director, manager, secretary or other officer of the company, such director, manager, secretary or officer shall also be deemed to be guilty of that offence and shall be liable to be proceeded against and punished accordingly.

Explanation: For the purposes of this section,

(a) "company" means any body corporate, and includes a firm or association of individuals; and

(b) "director" in relation to a firm means a partner of the firm.

12. Offences to be cognizable. Notwithstanding anything contained in the Code of the Criminal Procedure 1973, every offence under this Act shall be cognizable.

13. Notwithstanding anything contained in this Act or in any other law for the time being in force, it shall be the duty of every public authority which proposes to initiate any project or activity, subject to the provisions of Section 4, to notify, as soon as possible, and in any case well before the commencement of the project or activity, for the information of the general public and the persons to be affected, such matters within its knowledge and control as affect the general public or are vital to life, health and livelihood.

14. Protection action taken in good faith. No suit, prosecution or other legal proceeding shall lie against the Central Government or a State Government or any individual, for anything which is in good faith done or intended to be done under the provisions of this Act or any rule made thereunder.

15. Act to have overriding effect. The provisions of this Act shall have effect notwithstanding anything inconsistent therewith contained in any other law for the time being in force.

16. National Council for Freedom of Information. 1. The Central Government may, by notification in the Official Gazette, establish with effect from such day as may be specified in the notification, a Council to be known as the National Council for Freedom of Information.

2. The National Council may consist of the following members:

(a) the Minister in charge of Department of Administrative Reforms in the Central Government, who shall be its Chairman, and

(b) Such other official and non-official members drawn from different disciplines such as Law, Education, Media, Science and Technology, Social Activities, Business.

3.(a) the Council may meet as and when necessary, with at least one meeting being held every four months;

(b) the time and place of the meetings of the Council shall be as the Chairman thinks fit and it shall observe such procedure as may be prescribed to transact its business.

17. Objects of the National Council. The object of the National Council shall be to promote freedom of information in the country and it shall deal with all matters related to freedom of information such as.

(a) review of the operation of the Act and rules made thereunder,

(b) review of the administrative arrangements and procedures to secure for citizens the fullest possible access to information,

(c) research and documentation as regards management of information with a view to improving the extent and accuracy of information being made available under the Act, and

(d) to advise the government on all matters related to freedom of information, including training, development and orientation of employees to bring in a culture of openness and transparency.

(e) there shall be a statutory Parliamentary Committee on the Right to Information to review the implementation of the Act.

18. State Councils for Freedom of Information 1. The State Government may, by notification in the Official Gazette, establish with effect from such day as may be specified in the notification, a Council to be known as the State Council for Freedom of Information.

2. The State Council may consist of the following members:

(a) the Minister in charge of Department of Administrative Reforms in the State Government, who shall be its Chairman, and

(b) such other official and non-official members drawn from different disciplines such as Law, Education, Science and Technology, Media, Social Activities and Business.

3.(a) the Council may meet as and when necessary, with at least one meeting being held every four months.

(b) the time and place of the meeting of the Council shall be as the Chairman thinks fit and it shall observe such procedure as may be prescribed to transact its business.

19. Objects of the State Council. The object of the State Council shall be to promote the freedom of information within the State and it shall deal with the matters specified in Section 18 in respect of the State. The State Council shall present its report annually to the State Legislature.

20. Powers of the Central Government to make rules. 1. The Central Government may, by notification in the Official Gazette, make rules to carry out the provisions of this Act.

2. Without prejudice to the generality of the foregoing power, such rules may provide for all matters in respect of which rules are required to be made by the Central Government under this Act.

21. Power of the State Government to Make Rules. A State Government may, by notification in the Official Gazette, make rules to provide for any matter in respect of which rules are required to be made by the State Government under this Act.

22. Laying of Rules. 1. Every rule made under this Act by the Central Government shall be laid, as soon as may be after it is made, before each House of Parliament, while it is in session, for a total period of thirty days which may be comprised in one session or in two or more successive sessions and if, before the expiry of the session immediately following the session or the successive sessions aforesaid, both Houses agree in making any modification in the rule, or both Houses agree that the rule should not be made, the rule shall thereafter have effect only in such modified form or be of no effect, as the case may be; so, however, that any such modification or annulment shall be without prejudice to the validity of anything previously done under the rule.

2. Every rule made under this Act by a State Government shall be laid, as soon as may be after it is made, before the State Legislature.

FORM I

(See Rule 7)

Notice of Intention to have Sample Analysed

To

....

....

Take notice that is intended to have analysed the sample of*...which has been taken today, the ....day of ....200...... from ....(Name and designation of the person who takes the sample)...

* Specify the place from where the sample is taken
(Seal)
Date.........................

FORM II

(See Rule 8)

Memorandum to Government Analyst

From

....

....

To

The Government Analyst

....

....

The portion of sample described below is sent herewith for analysis (under Rule 6 of the Environment (Protection) Rules, 1986.
The portion of the sample has been marked by me with the following mark: Details of the portion of samples taken.

Name and designation of person who sends the sample.

(SEAL)

Date...................

FORM III

(See Rule 8)

Report by Government Analyst

Report No...................
Date..............................
I hereby certify that I .... Government Analyst duly appointed under Section 13 of the Environment (Protection) Act, 1986, received on the ....
day of .... 200 ....
from ....
*..
a sample of ....
for analysis. The sample was in a condition fit for analysis as reported below.

I further certify that I have analysed the afore-mentioned sample on .... and declare that the result of the analysis to be as follows:

**..

....

The condition of seals, fastening of samples on receipt was as follows.

Signed this .... day of .... 200..........
Address ....

Signature
(Government Analyst)

To

....

....

....

* Here write the name of the officer/authority from whom the sample was obtained.

** Here write full details of analysis and method of analysis.

FORM IV

(See Rule 11)

Form of Notice

By registered post-acknowledgement due

From

Shri................................

....

....

To

....

....

Notice under Section 19(b) of the Environment (Protection) Act, 1986. Whereas an offence under the Environment (Protection) Act, 1986, has been committed/is being committed by .... (2) I/We hereby give notice of 60 days under Section 19(b) of Environment (Protection) Act, 1986, of my/our intention to file a complaint in the Court against .... (3) for violation of Section .... of the Environment (Protection) Act, 1986. In support of my/our notice, I am/we are enclosing the following documents (3) as evidence of proof of violation of the Environment (Protection) Act, 1986.

Place ....

Date .... Signature (s)

Explanation:

1. In case the notice is given in the name of a company, documentary evidence authorising the person to sign the notice on behalf of the company shall be enclosed to this notice.
   Company for this purpose means a company defined in the explanation to sub-rule (6) of Rule 4.
2. Here give the name and address of the alleged offender. In case of a manufacturing/processing/operating unit, indicate the name/location/nature of activity, etc.
3. Documentary evidence shall include photographs/technical reports/health reports to the area, etc., for enabling enquiry into the alleged violation/offence.

FORM V

(See Rule 14)

Environmental Statement for the financial year ending the 31st March..........

PART A

(i) Name and address of the owner/occupier of the industry or process.

(ii) Industry category Primary—(STC Code) Secondary—(STC Code).

(iii) Production capacity—Units—

(iv) Year of establishment.

(v) Date of the last environmental statement submitted.

PART B

Water and Raw Material Consumption

(1) Water consumption m^3/d

Process

Cooling

Domestic

Name of products	*Process water consumption per unit of product output*	
	During the previous financial year	*During the current financial year*
(1)		
(2)		
(3)		

(2) Raw material consumption

**Name of raw materials*	*Name of products*	*Consumption of raw material per unit*	
		During the previous financial year	*During the current financial year*

*Industry may use codes if disclosing details of raw material would violate contractual obligations, otherwise all industries have to name the raw materials used.

PART-C

Pollution discharged to environment/unit of output

(Parameter as specified in the consent issued)

(1) Pollution	Quantity of pollution discharged (mass/day)	Concentration of pollutions in discharges (mass/volume)	Percentage of variation from prescribed standards with reasons
(a) Water			
(b) Air			

PART D

Hazardous Wastes

[as specified under Hazardous Waste (Management and Handling) Rules, 1989]

Hazardous Wastes	Total Quantity	
	During the previous financial year	During the current financial year
(a) From process		
(b) From pollution control facilities		

PART E

Solid Wastes

	Total Quantity	
	During the previous financial year	During the current financial year
(a) From process		
(b) From Pollution control facility		
(c) (1) Quantity recycled or re-utilised within the unit		
(2) Sold		
(3) Disposed		

PART F

Please specify the characterisation (in terms of composition an quantum) of hazardous as well as solid wastes and indicate dispos practice adopted for both these categories of wastes.

PART G

Impact of the pollution abatement measures taken on conservati of natural resources and on the cost of production.

PART H

Additional measures/investment proposal for environmen protection abatement of pollution, prevention of pollution.

PART I

Any other particulars for improving the quality of environment.

HUMAN RIGHTS
Acts, Statutes and Constitutional Provisions

HUMAN RIGHTS
Acts, Statutes and Constitutional Provisions
(Volume I)

D.N. Gupta
Chandrachur Singh

KALPAZ PUBLICATIONS
Delhi–110 052

HUMAN RIGHTS
Acts, Statutes and Constitutional Provisions
(Human Rights, Law)

Rs. 1800 (Set)

© D.N. Gupta, Chandrachur Singh

ISBN: 81-7835-098-X (Set)
ISBN: 81-7835-156-0 (Vol. I)

All rights reserved. No part of this book may be reproduced in any manner without written permission

Published in 2003 in India by
Kalpaz Publications
C-30, Satyawati Nagar
Delhi–110 052

e-mail: kalpaz@hotmail.com

Lasertypesetting at: Varsha Graphics, Delhi
Printed at: Mehra Offset Printers, Delhi

Contents

Foreword

The Second World War (1939 – 1945) shook up mankind all over the globe. It turned the whole world into a battle field. The new concept of total war was a real menace. Millions of people were killed and crippled. Generations of *homo sapiens*, yet to be born were seriously affected by the atom bomb.

Right-thinking leaders started working on total elimination of war and ensuring a war-free world. Lasting peace for mankind was the dream.

The United Nations replaced the League. A new instrumentality – the Security Council was vested with the duty of maintaining peace. The U.N. Charter in its preamble emphasised upon the need of greater understanding among the people and the rights of the people to be recognized. It provided that a commission be set-up to enlist the rights of everyone and the same should be implemented. The General Assembly of the United Nations adopted the report of the Commission and on the 10th December, 1948, the Universal Declaration was made. In the preamble, the Declaration recognized the inherent dignity and the equal and inalienable rights of all members of the human family and declared that disregard and contempt for human which have resulted in barbarous acts and outraged the conscience of mankind must end.

The Universal Declaration has set out the inalienable human rights and has called upon mankind to be aware of them, to recognize and respect them and ensure their acceptance and performance by generation of a strong culture of human rights.

The United Nations in its fifty four years of operation has highlighted the concept of one human family, recognition of the rights specified in the Declaration and has looked for the generation of a strong human rights culture which alone would ensure a pro-uniform human-rights conduct in the *homo sapiens* society.

These fifty-four years have been a crucial period in the life and history of human rights. The literature created during this period through teaching and reading would provide the base on which the edifice of human rights would be strengthened.

I am happy that this compilation seeks to make the literature available to the reader in two exquisite volumes. I welcome this attempt and congratulate the authors.

Ranganath Misra
Formerly Chief Justice of India

14 August, 2002

Preface

Keeping in view the relevance and importance of human rights in our everyday life, this two-volume compilation of documents on human rights is being published. Ever since the formation of the United Nations (1945) the concept of civil liberties and human rights has been both institutionalized and universalized. However, the situation is quite paradoxical. It is a fact that with the increasing expansion of the scope of human rights and its relevance to the living process, their violation also continues unabated. As Justice Ranganath Misra, former Chief Justice of India and the first Chairman of the National Human Rights Commission, once remarked :

> As of now, violation of human rights is widely rampant. Violation of human rights is in the homes, the streets, the public offices [and] educational institutions.

How can such a paradox be resolved? Spread of awareness about, and promotion and protection of human rights, respect for each other's rights and fulfillment of our obligations/duties towards the society and fellow beings, are the only possible solutions. As Justice Misra has suggested :

> Promotion and protection of human rights are the only way by which the society can be saved in an effective way. We are degenerating and degenerating very fast, and unless there is first stoppage of the degenerating process and then an attempt for elevation, thereafter, we might lose our status of being *homo sapiens* and a group above animal life.

Unless we are adequately armed with the knowledge of our rights and the existing remedies available against their violations, it is not really possible to move in the direction suggested by Justice Mr. Misra. As such the basic purpose of the present work is to acquaint scholars working on various aspects of human rights, human rights activists and Non-Government Organizations (NGOs) engaged in the task of spreading awareness about human rights and particularly the citizens who are directly affected by the violations of their rights, with the Statutory and Constitutional provisions enacted to guarantee such rights. Moreover, inadequacies of the present machinery that exists for the protection and promotion of human rights can be removed only with its proper knowledge and understanding. Therefore, it is hoped that this two-volume collection of documents on human rights will be useful to all those who are either concerned with or affected by their violations.

The present study has been divided into two volumes, each containing five chapters. In every chapter, documents concerning a specific human rights issue have been presented.

As the United Nations Charter (1945) and the Universal Declaration of Human Rights (1948) introduced the concept of human rights at global level, these two world famous documents form the opening of Chapter One. India was not only a signatory to the Charter but also accepted the Universal Declaration of Human Rights in 1948. And consonant with the acceptance of these United Nations Declarations, India also gave her consent to the two International Covenants that had been adopted by the General Assembly of the United Nations in its resolution 2200 (XXI) of 16 December, 1966 and came into force in 1976. The basic purpose of these Covenants was to supplement the Charter and the Universal Declaration of Human Rights. However, it is noteworthy that India accepted these Covenants with certain reservations which have been spelt out in the Government of India's Declaration of 1979. India's Declaration and the two International Covenants are also included in Chapter One.

As this compilation is mainly concerned with human rights in India, the rest of the nine chapters are devoted to various aspects of human rights in India.

Much before the United Nations Charter and the Declaration laid the foundations of human rights globally, the Karachi Resolution of the Indian National Congress on Fundamental Rights and on Economic Equality (1931) had popularized the concept of civil liberties and human rights in India. In fact, the Karachi Resolution formed the basis of the Fundamental Rights and the Directive Principles of State Policy which were enshrined in the Indian Constitution (1950). The Karachi Resolution, the Fundamental Rights and the Directive Principles of State Policy are the subject matter of Chapter Two. It may be noted that the difference between the Fundamental Rights and the Directive Principles is due to the fact that whereas the State could straightway guarantee political and civil liberties, it could only strive to secure economic and social justice. Therefore, Fundamental Rights are judicially enforceable, but the Directive Principles are not justiciable. Nevertheless, the Apex Court of the Country has, from time to time, asserted that none of the two is subordinate to the other and also that while making laws, the two should be read together rather than in competition to each other.

The Ordinance of 1993 that created the National Human Rights Commission and provided for the formation of Human Rights Commissions in States was another milestone in the development of human rights in India. For many years, it was felt that India did not require such an organization because of the presence of Fundamental Rights in the Indian Constitution and the elaborate judicial system that stood guarantee for the protection and promotion of civil liberties and human rights. But with the passage of time, it became impossible for the Government of India to resist the increasing internal and external pressures for the formation of the National Human Rights Commission.

National Human Rights Commission, despite its many limitations, has emerged as a prominent institution for safeguarding the rights of Indian citizens. It not only looks into human rights violations but also recommends action against such violations to the appropriate authorities. It is an autonomous body under the Chairmanship of a former Chief Justice of India. It submits its annual report to the Indian Parliament.

As far as the formation of Human Rights Commissions in States is concerned, the record has not been that encouraging. Even after the passage of the Act (1993), only twelve states have formed such Commissions. These include Assam, Chhattisgarh, Himachal Pradesh, Jammu and Kashmir, Kerala, Madhya Pradesh, Manipur, Maharashtra, Punjab, Rajasthan, Tamil Nadu and West Bengal.

In Chapter Three the Ordinance and the subsequent Act (1993) for the formation of Human Rights Commission in India and such Commissions in Indian States have been included. Since the Ordinance is quite comprehensive, it does not require any elaboration.

The next two Chapters, i.e., Four and Five deal with the human rights of the weaker sections of India. Undoubtedly, Scheduled

Castes, Scheduled Tribes, Other Backward Classes (OBCs), *Safai Karamcharis*, Women and Children are certainly important segments of the weaker sections of India. These, in themselves, make over 70% of the Indian population. If their rights are not adequately safeguarded, the concept of human rights will have no meaning in the Indian context.

The specific constitutional provisions to safeguard the interests of the Scheduled Castes relate to the abolition of untouchability and the prohibition on its practice in any form (Article 17); prohibition of *begar* or forced labour (Article 23); consideration of the claims of the Scheduled Castes and Scheduled Tribes in appointments to services and posts in connection with the affairs of the Union or a state (Article 335); and reservations of seats in proportion to their numbers in the Lok Sabha (Article 330) and in the Vidhan Sabha (Article 332). Over a period of time, however, it was discovered that mere constitutional provisions will not improve the lot of these important segments of Indian society. Therefore, since independence and the promulgation of the Indian Constitution in 1950, successive governments have taken several steps to uplift the weaker sections. The Untouchability Act, 1955, Protection of Civil Rights Act, 1976, Bonded Labour System (Abolition) Act, 1976 and the Child Labour Prohibition and Regulation Act,1976, have been some of the steps taken to improve the position of the SCs/STs. Institutional structures for the upliftment of the SCs/STs, OBCs, *Safai Karamcharis* and Minorities in the form of the National Commissions for SCs/STs, OBCs, *Safai Karamcharis* and Minorities have been created. These Commissions are included in Chapter Four.

Indian society, like any other society, is also divided on the basis of gender. While sexual differences are biologically determined, gender differences are culturally constructed. It is a paradox that while Indian Women enjoyed an equal status with man during the early Vedic period, in contemporary India, they are discriminated against. They do not get the same access to healthcare, education and economic opportunities as men do. Violence against women in the form of rape, molestation, eve-teasing, sati and dowry deaths is quite common. Even though the Indian Constitution guarantees equal rights to women, the Indian Parliament has taken many further steps to enhance the status of women in India by enacting a number of laws including that which has constituted the National

Commission for Women. These Acts and Regulations are detailed in Chapter Five.

One of the most pressing social problems confronting Indian society is that of the working child. In Indian context, child labour is aptly described as 'children without childhood'. Children are employed both in formal and informal sectors of our economy. According to the 1991 census, child labour formed 1.34 per cent of the total population and 3.59 per cent of the total workforce. In spite of many provisions in the Indian Constitution regarding the upliftment of Indian Children (Articles 24, 39 (e), 39 (f) and 45), the Government of India announced the National Child Labour Policy only in 1987. In Chapter Five steps that the Government of India has taken to improve the lot of this 'tongueless' and 'speechless' segment of society have been included.

D.N. Gupta
Chandrachur Singh

Acknowledgements

We are indeed indebted to Justice Mr. Ranganath Misra, former Chief Justice of India and the first Chairman of National Human Rights Commission of India. Justice Misra not only initiated us into the human rights movement in India, but has also given us his paternal love and affection which has sustained us in the movement. He has been kind enough to have written the foreword to the present work. Words are inadequate to express our gratitude to honourable *Judge Saheb*.

We would never have ventured into the exciting arena of human rights but for the constant encouragement and support we have received from Prof. Bipan Chandra. Prof. Chandra has always been a source of inspiration to us. He has been gracious enough to give us permission to make liberal use of his writings on India's struggle for independence.

We are grateful to Shri P.C. Verma, former Principal, Hindu College, Delhi University, for supporting us through thick and thin.

We have benefitted immeasurably from the valuable discussions with Prof. Suhash Chakravarty which have sharpened our understanding of a complex, yet dynamic subject. We are indeed thankful to him.

We are grateful to Prof. Subrata Mukherjee for his continual help and encouragement. We also appreciate Shri Ratan Lal's co-operation and help.

We also acknowledge our sincere thanks to Mr. Rakesh Kumar Sharma and Ms. Rajesh Sharma for typesetting.

Uday, Shivani, Hena and Suchitra Gupta have given us their love and support. However, we do not think it necessary to thank them.

Last, but not the least, we express our gratitude to the editorial and production team of Kalpaz Publications, specially Shri Amit and Shalini Garg for associating us with this work and for doing a splendid and painstaking job in bringing out these volumes.

Delhi

D.N. Gupta
Chandrachur Singh

Introduction

The issue of human rights is of immense importance, as they are the corner-stone of civilisation, the alpha and omega of humanity's mission for a better life. The struggle for human rights is a part of the quest for collective happiness. It is believed that a civil society is only actualised by the fulfillment of rights. Modern society's prosperity and state are interlinked. But the state has the tendency of monopolizing power, thereby increasing the possibilities of coercion obstructing freedom of the individual.

Modern endeavour for human rights is an attempt to reconcile the opposite pulls of power of the state and the urge for social freedom which would result in human progress and prosperity. Even though the concept of human rights has got a new thrust in the contemporary times, its roots can be traced back to 1215 when the Magna Carta curtailed the power of the King John of England. After the King violated a number of ancient laws and customs, his subjects forced him to sign the Magna Carta, or Great Charter, which enumerates what later come to be known as human rights. Among them were the rights of church to be free from governmental interference, the right of all free citizens to own and inherit property and to be free from excessive tax. It established the right of widows who owned property to choose not to remarry and established principles of due process and equality before the law. It also contained provisions forbidding bribery and official misconduct.

I

The political and religious traditions in other parts of the world also proclaimed what have come to be called human rights, by calling on rulers to rule justly and compassionately and delineating limits on their power over the lives, property and activities of their citizens. The Hindu concept of Dharma explicitly maintains that all expressions are inter-related and bound in a visible unity; that no violence shall be done to a person by another except with the due process of law, which at all times must be free from anger and hatred; and that the political and legal governance of human relationship shall have as their chief aim enhancement of the individual and the progress of the people. It is from these that the principles of law and government must be derived, and it is in them that they shall have their ultimate validation.

In the eighteenth and the nineteenth centuries several philosophers in Europe proposed the concept of 'natural rights', i.e. belonging to a person by nature and because he/she was a human being, not by virtue of his/her citizenship in a particular country or membership in a particular religious or ethnic group. Though this conception was rejected by some philosophers such as Bentham, still it found its advocates in Thomas Paine and J.S. Mill. The late eighteenth century revolutions namely American War of Independence and the French Revolution drew heavily on this concept. In 1776 most of British colonies in North America proclaimed their independence from the British Empire in a document which still stirs feelings and debate. The World famous American Declaration of Independence maintained:

> We hold these truths to be self evident: That all men are created equal; that they are endowed by their Creator with certain unalienable rights; that among these are life, Liberty and the pursuit of happiness . . .;

In 1789 the people of France overthrew their monarchy and established the First French Republic. Out of the revolution came to the Declaration of Rights of Man.

Although the term natural right eventually fell into disfavour, the concept of universal rights took root. Philosophers such as Thomas Paine, John Stuart Mill and Henry David Thoreau expanded the concept. It is said that Thoreau was the first philosopher to use the word "Human Right" in his treatise, 'Civil Disobedience'. The work which was to influence people such as Leo Tolstoy, Mahatma Gandhi and Martin Luther King; Gandhi and King in particular, developed their ideas on non-violent resistance to unethical governmental actions.

II

The middle and the late 19th century saw a number of issues take centre stage, which later in 20th century are issues of human rights. They included i.e. slavery, serfdom, brutal working conditions, starvation, wages, child labour etc. In the United States a bloody war over slavery came close to destroying a country founded on the conception of equality. For the last part of 19th century and first decades of 20th century, human rights activism remained largely tied to political and religious groups and beliefs. Revolutionaries pointed to the atrocities of governments as proof of their ideology, which stressed violent action. The state on the other hand also resorted to violence and stern approach towards dissent. However, even then many specific civil rights and human rights movements managed to condition social change. Labour unions brought about laws granting workers the right to strike, establishing minimum working conditions, forbidding or regulating child labour, establishing forty hours a week working hours in USA. The women's rights movement succeeded in gaining for many women the right to vote. National liberation movements in many countries succeeded in driving out colonial powers. One of the most influential mass action was the Indian National Movement which, under the stewardship of Mahatma Gandhi, based itself on human dignity. As a matter of fact, the Indian Constitution which guarantees fundamental freedom and stresses on human dignity, draws inspiration from it.

III

However, the year 1914-18 saw immense brutalities. War crimes, violence and deaths devastated the World and human essence was lost. Immediately after the war, attempts were made to restore peace and establish universal principles acceptable to all, so that humanity could be saved.

The League of Nations (1918) was entrusted with the responsibility to administer certain provisions of the First World War; while peace treaties protected the rights of racial, religious and linguistic refugees and minorities. Thus, the League of Nations institutionalised two principles of humanism. Beyond this, the League had little involvement with human rights, and its Covenant did not mention them. The desire for peace was short-lived, and then came the Second World War—the most horrifying so far in human memory. A greater need for peace and human dignity was felt and this led to a search for an effective international alternative to guarantee peace and security. Protracted deliberations and mutual negotiations led to the inception of United Nations Organisation in 1945. The objectives of the United Nations Organisation clearly point out that it was an effort towards guaranteeing human rights. There were four major objectives:

1. To save the succeeding generations from the scourge of war.
2. To reaffirm faith in fundamental human rights, in the work and dignity of human persons and equal rights of men, women and nations large and small.
3. To establish conditions under which justice and respect for the obligations arising from treaties and other sources of international law can be maintained.
4. To promote social progress and better standards of life in larger freedom.

These objectives envisaged a better and peaceful life to the people of the world through living together in peace, tolerance and harmony with one another. The UN Charter thereby provided the foundation for a global approach to human rights.

IV

The UN lost no time in dealing with Human Rights. The third General Assembly (1948) adopted a Universal Declaration of Human Rights submitted by the UN Commission on human rights chaired by Eleanor Roosevelt. Several articles cover a wide range of basic human rights and fundamental freedoms. Article 29 imposes duties and restrictions upon those enjoying rights and freedoms. This was a proper recognition that individual duty and responsibilities go hand in hand with personal rights and privileges. The declaration runs:

> . . . a common standard of achievement for all peoples and all nations, to the end that every individual and every organ of society, keeping this declaration constantly in mind, shall strive by teaching and education to promote respect for these rights and freedoms and by progressive measures, national and International to secure their universal and effective recognition and observance, both among the peoples of member states themselves and among the peoples of territories under their jurisdiction.

Each year, the 10th December, is observed internationally

as Human Rights Day. The Universal Declaration included civil, economic, social and cultural freedom, justice and equality. It is a quest for a larger and broader base for social values. It is yet only a beginning because there is a great hiatus between word and deed. The march of human rights, however continued. In 1966 two Covenants were adopted to add meaning and volume to 1948 Declaration of Universal Human Rights. These came into force in 1976. The UN has been continuing its other efforts.

United Nations Treaties Concerning Human Rights

Treaties	*Year of Force*
Convention on prevention and punishment of the crime of Genocide	1951
Convention for the suppression of Traffic in persons and of the Exploitation of the prostitution of others	1951
Protocol Amending slavery convention	1953
Convention relating to status of Refugees	1954
Convention on Political Rights of Women	1954
Slavery convention of 25 September 1926 as Amended	1955
Supplementary convention on the abolition of slavery, the slave Trade, Institution and Practice, similar to slavery	1957
Convention on Nationality of married women	1958
Convention relating to status of stateless persons	1960
Convention on International Right of correction	1962
Convention on consent of marriage, minimum age for marriage, and Registration of marriage	1964
Convention on elimination of all forms of racial discrimination	1969
Convention on non-applicability of statutory limitation to War crimes and crimes against Humanity	1970
Convention on Reduction of statelessness	1975
International covenant on Economic, Social and Cultural rights	1976
International covenant on civil and political rights	1976
Optional protocol on complaints from individuals	1976

V

As the UN Charter (1945) and its Universal Declaration of Human Rights 1948 both universalised and institutionalised the concept of Human Rights, it has been argued that the sections of the Indian Constitution on Fundamental Rights and the Directive Principles of State Policy emulated the United Nations Declaration of Human Rights. Apart from the fact that the drafting of the Indian Constitution 1947-1948 coincided with the UN Declaration (1948), the remarkable similarities between the two documents have also been cited in favour of this theory. Also the fact that colonial India was an original signatory to the Charter and Independent India adopted the UN declaration in 1948, itself. However, the theory that the two Chapters on Fundamental Rights and the Directive Principles of State Policy in the Indian Constitution reflected the pitch of the UN Declaration seems to be an over-simplified view because of the fact that it was the anti-imperialist movement of Indian people that made it possible for them to recover their lost rights and dignity. The Indian liberation movement, apart from attaining political Independence, stood for the establishment of a democratic and liberal society that encompassed the essence of civil liberty. Therefore, in order to appreciate the adoption of the UN Declaration by India and the provisions for Fundamental Rights and Directive Principles of State Policy in the Indian Constitution, one has to comprehend and assess the nature, policy and programme and achievements of India's struggle for independence.

VI

It was due to the establishment and consolidation of the British imperialist rule during the period from 1757 to 1857 that the Indian people lost most of their human rights and dignity. The assault of the alien rulers on the basic human rights and dignity, though began with the establishment and consolidation of its strangle hold over India, it was only with the emergence of anti-imperialist sentiments and movement that it became increasingly threatening. For example, in order to counter the rising political consciousness in India, section 124A was incorporated in the Indian Penal Code 1870. According to section 124A 'Whomsoever attempts to excite feelings of dissatisfaction, to the Government established by law in British

India,' was to be punished by transportation for life or for any term or with imprisonment upto three years. The Vernacular Act (1878) provided for the confiscation of the printing press, paper and other materials of a newspaper if the Government believed that it was publishing 'seditious' materials and had flouted an official warning.

It was this kind of an authoritarian, undemocratic, and arbitrary regime that the Indian people were confronted with. Committed as they were to the rights and civil liberties of our people, politically conscious Indians led the struggle for the establishment of a rational social order based on civil liberties, human rights and dignity. This national struggle was a part of the political struggle against the subjugation of India and for the attainment of independence. Therefore, it was a long drawn out battle. Instead of implementing liberal ideas, the colonial rulers took the position that democracy was not suited to India. Hot and humid climate of India, the historical traditions of the Indian people, the nature of their religious and social structure, particularly the caste system and authoritarian and tyrannical nature of their pre-British political system were some of the arguments that were advanced against the introduction of democratic institutions in India. If this was the nature of colonial mindset, how could they think of introducing freedoms of speech, association and the press?

The struggle for the establishment of civil liberties and human rights and dignity began with the struggle for the freedom of the press. In the absence of mass meetings and other means of reaching the people like a powerful political party, the leaders of our liberation movement realised that the press could play an instrumental role in arousing, training and mobilizing nationalist public opinion in India. That was the reason why a large number of newspapers like the *Hindu, Swadeshmitran, Kesari, Maratha, Bengalee, Amrit Bazar Patrika, Sudharak, Indian Mirror, Voice of India* and *Hindustani* were started by the nationalist leaders— G. Subramaniya Iyer, B.G. Tilak, Surendranath Banerjee, Sisir Kumar and Motilal Ghosh, G.K. Gokhale, N.N. Sen, Dadabhai Naoroji and G.P. Verma. *Tribune* and *Akhbar-I-Aam* in Punjab, *Indu Prakash, Dhyan Prakash, Kal* and *The Gujrati* in Western India, *Som Prakash, Banganivasi* and *Sadharni* in Bengal also played significant role of opposition to the Government. The important role that the Vernacular Press played in opposing the authoritarianism of the colonial regime can be gauged from Lord Dufferin's following observation:

> Day after day, hundreds of sharp-witted Babus pour forth their indignation against their oppressors in a very pungent and effective diatribe. In this way there can be no doubt there is generated in the minds of those who read these papers a sincere conviction that we are all of us the enemies of mankind in general and of India in particular.

VII

Even though Raja Ram Mohan Roy started the struggle for the freedom of the press and Surendranath Banerjee was the first national leader who was sent to jail in 1883, for performing his duty as a journalist, it was Tilak who really launched the movement for a free press. A great champion of civil liberties and human dignity, Tilak often remarked that 'liberty of the press and liberty of speech (and association) gave birth to a nation and nourish it'. When in 1897 Lokmanya was arrested under Section 124 A of the Indian Penal Code on the charge of spreading dissatisfaction and hatred against the Government and sent to rigorous imprisonment for eighteen months and some of his friends tried to pressurise him to apologize, Tilak's reply was:

> My position (as a leader) amongst the people entirely depends on my character . . . Their (Governments') object is to humiliate the Poona leaders, and I think in me they will not find kutcha (weak) reed . . . Then you must remember that beyond a certain stage we are all servants of the people. You will be betraying and disappointing them if you show a lamentable want of courage at a critical time.

With the emergence of the Swadeshi and Boycott Movement in Bengal in 1905, there started a new wave of official repression in India. Hundreds of political workers were imprisoned for making so called seditious speeches, many newspapers were either closed down or their editors imprisoned and Tilak was again arrested in 1908 and sent to prison for six years. Just a few days before his arrest, a friendly police officer warned him of the impending arrest and suggested him to take precautionary steps, Tilak's reply to the friendly advice was:

> The Government has converted the entire nation into a prison and we are all prisoners. Going to prison only means that from a big cell one is confined to a smaller one.

And when there were demonstrations, closures of markets, strikes of textile mills workers and railway workshops and resistance to the police and the army broke the strike leaving sixteen workers dead, it simply meant that it was a protest against the Government attack on the civil liberties and human dignity.

VIII

Therefore, it is not at all surprising that the first all India mass movement was organised on the issue of civil liberties in 1918-1919. In January 1919 the Government of India presented two bills to the Imperial Legislative Council. These Bills are known as Rowlatt Bills. The second of the two Bills was designed to invest the Government of India with the discretionary power to keep a person in prison without trial in a court of law. But despite the unanimous opposition of the Indian members of the Council, the new legislation was rushed through the legislature with indecent haste. Having failed in the Council to stop the passage of the Bills, the nationalist leaders particularly Gandhi took up the challenge and organised the first all India Rowlatt Satyagraha because the Rowlatt Bills, as Professor Ravindra Kumar has opined, reflected a deep rooted distrust of the common man. These acts demonstrated the British Governments' reluctance to part with its arbitrary powers, and, invalidated the impact of the reforms (Montagu-Chelmsford Act 1919) which were meant to hold out the prospect of self-determination to the peoples of India.

IX

It is an axiomatic truth that Gandhiji made most outstanding contribution to the establishment of rights, dignity and self-respect of the Indian people. From the days of his struggle in South Africa where he fought against the denial of basic human rights and racial discrimination for nearly twenty years, till the end of his life, he waged a struggle against all sorts of existing social inequalities and denial of civil liberties. That was the reason why he was pained at General Dyer's action at Jallianwala Bagh leaving 379 innocent and peaceful marchers dead, but more so at the proceedings in the House of Lords that ultimately exonerated General Dyer and endorsed his inhuman action.

Gandhiji was of the firm view that the two basic human rights, i.e., rights of free speech and association, must be available to the Indians. One could not talk about other rights if these were not available to the people. Emphasizing the significance of these rights in human life, he wrote in January 1922:

> We must first make good the rights of free speech and free association before we can make any further progress towards our goal. We must defend these elementary rights with our lives. Liberty of speech means that it is unassailed even when the speech hurts, liberty of the Press can be said to be truly respected when the Press can comment in the severest terms upon and even misrepresent matters. Freedom of association is truly respected when assemblies of people can discuss even revolutionary projects.

Irrespective of their political and ideological differences, nationalist leaders of different orientations defended each others' civil liberties and human dignity. For example, Shaheed Bhagat Singh and his comrades being tried in Lahore Conspiracy case and the Communists and others in the Meerut conspiracy case, were defended by Motilal Nehru, M.C. Chagla and C.B. Gupta, who, otherwise did not endorse their political line. Similarly, the Public Safety Bill and the Trade Disputes Bill, aimed at suppressing the industrial workers, the left wing and the communists were opposed not only by Motilal Nehru but also by Madan Mohan Malaviya and M.R. Jayakar.

X

Alongwith Gandhiji, Nehru was a great adherent and champion of civil liberties and human rights. His assertion that: "If Civil Liberties are suppressed, a nation loses all its vitality and becomes impotent for anything substantial', was the basis of his position on human rights and dignity. That was the reason why he took initiative in forming the Indian Civil Liberties Union. In 1936, Nehru wrote a letter to 160 prominent intellectuals of the country explaining the need for an all-India organisation for the protection of civil liberties and human rights of the Indian people. His efforts led to the formation of the Indian Civil Liberties Union in August 1936 at Bombay with Rabindranath Tagore as the President, Sarojini Naidu as the Chairperson and Head of its National Council and K.B. Menon as General Secretary.

The Civil Liberties Union was formed on non party, non sectarian lines to collect and publish data and to mobilise public opinion against all enroachment on civil liberties. The Civil Liberties Union investigated cases of political imprisonment and harassment, police brutalities, bans and restrictions on citizens' rights imposed not only by the British but also by the rulers of the princely states and published and lodged complaints on the basis of its investigations.

Nehru was also of the opinion that press could play an instrumental role in popularising the concepts of civil liberties and human rights. Therefore, commenting on the desirability of the freedom of the press, he observed in 1940;

> The freedom of the press does not consist in our permitting such things as we like to appear. Even a tyrant is agreeable to this type of freedom. Civil liberties and freedom of the press consist in our permitting what we do not like, in our putting up with criticism of ourselves.

Even though struggle for civil liberties and human rights was made a part of India's liberation struggle, Nehru attached importance as an end in itself. For example, Nehru took up the case of Rani Gaidinliu, the young Naga girl, sponsored in the Indian Liberties Union and also placed it before the British Civil Liberties Union in London. Professor S. Gopal has described Nehru's position on civil liberties as follows:

> The struggle for civil liberties is obviously part and parcel of any national movement but Nehru attached importance to it even in itself and was insistent that civil liberties to the utmost extent possible should be promoted even in such a blatantly colonial society as India was

before 1947. Take for example, the case of Rani Gaidinliu, the young Naga girl who later became the leader of the Nagas. In the early thirties, she was arrested and placed in prison for many years without trial on a charge which was only remotely connected with politics. But Nehru took it up when he heard about it, sponsored a case in the Indian Civil Liberties Union, also placed it before the British Civil Liberties Union in London, wrote to people to whom he normally would not have bothered to write to, like Lady Astor and Eleanor Rathbone. He also wrote to the British Press so that finally everybody was so stirred up in England that the British Government had to take action, hold a trial and release her. The case of Rani Gaidinliu has been a cause celebre and has integrated the Nagas with the rest of India.

XI

As Nehru was committed to the cause of civil liberties and human rights and dignity of the Indian people, he had sponsored the Karachi Resolution on fundamental rights in 1931. The Karachi Resolution (1931) on the Fundamental Rights, was the climax of the commitment of the nationalist leaders to the basic human rights of our countrymen. The Karachi Resolution is a landmark in the history of Indian liberation movement not only because it included important fundamental rights but also because of the safeguards it guaranteed to the rights of the minorities. While fighting against the mightiest of imperialisms for political independence, restoration of human rights and dignity and for the establishment of a new value system, the nationalist leaders were confronted with a serious issue, the problem of minorities rights. Their rights had to be protected—a cause that was inherent in the pluralistic nature of the Indian society. That was the reason why the rights of the minorities were protected in the Karachi Resolution. Emphasis on free profession and practice of religion, subject to public order and morality, protection of the culture, language and scripts of the minorities and religious neutrality on the part of the state, were some of the guarantees for the minority rights.

XII

From the beginning, the nationalist leaders were also conscious of the multi-lingual, multi-caste, multi-community and multi-religious nature of the Indian society alongwith the existence of many ethnic groups. The unity in diversity or diversity in unity could not be ignored if a joint all-India front had to be organised against British imperialism. Taking a serious note of these complexities, as early as 1888, the Indian National Congress passed the following resolution:

> That no subject shall be passed for discussion by the subject committee, or allowed to be discussed at any Congress by the president thereof, to the introduction of which the Hindu or Mohammadan Delegates as a body object unanimously or nearly unanimously.

The Lucknow Pact (1916) that put up the Congress-League Joint Charter of Demands was again a nationalist policy to protect the minority rights. The Lucknow Pact was certainly motivated by a sincere desire to allay minority fears about majority domination. And when the Pact was criticised in certain quarters on the ground that too much had been conceded to the Muslims by accepting separate Electorates, Tilak defended the Pact and said:

> When we have to fight against a third party—it is very important that we stand on this platform United, United in race, United in religion, United as regards all different shades of political creed.

Thus, as Professor Bipan Chandra pointed out:

> It was the national movement and not the bureaucratic, authoritarian colonial state that indigenised, popularised and rooted parliamentary democracy and civil liberties in India. The grass-roots level nationalist workers carried the national movement to the remotest of villages. In the speeches that they made, simultaneously with the idea of nationalism, they talked about democracy and civil liberties.

Over the years, the nationalist movement successfully created an alternative political culture based on respect for dissent, freedom of expression, the majority principle and the right of minority opinions to exist and grow.

XII

In short, by the time India attained independence in 1947, the Indian peoples' anti-imperialist struggle had already laid the foundations of a socio-cultural and politico-economic system based on the philosophy of civil liberties and human dignity. Therefore, it is not surprising that the framers of the Indian Constitution included chapters on the Fundamental Rights and the Directive Principles of State Policy. Adoption of the United Nations Charter and the Universal Declaration of Human Rights by India was not a sudden decision. It was indeed rooted in the principle that was inherent in the Indian peoples' struggle against the British imperialism. That explains why India has been also a willing party to the two Covenants that the United Nations General Assembly adopted in 1966 and which came into force in 1976.

D.N. Gupta
Chandrachur Singh

1

United Nations and Human Rights

CHARTER OF THE UNITED NATIONS, 1945

WE THE PEOPLES OF THE UNITED NATIONS, DETERMINED

to save succeeding generations from the scourge of war, which twice in our lifetime has brought untold sorrow to mankind, and

to reaffirm faith in fundamental human rights, in the dignity and worth of the human person, in the equal rights of men and women and of nations large and small, and

to establish conditions under which justice and respect for the obligations arising from treaties and other sources of international law can be maintained, and

to promote social progress and better standards of life in larger freedom.

AND FOR THESE ENDS

to practice tolerance and live together in peace with one another as good neighbours, and

to unite our strength to maintain international peace and security, and

to ensure, by the acceptance of principles and the institution of methods, that armed force shall not be used, save in the common interest, and

to employ international machinery for the promotion of the economic and social advancement of all peoples.

HAVE RESOLVED TO COMBINE OUR EFFORTS TO ACCOMPLISH THESE AIMS

Accordingly, our respective Governments, through representatives assembled in the city of San Francisco, who have exhibited their full powers found to be in good and due form, have agreed to the present Charter of the United Nations and do hereby establish an international organization to be known as the United Nations.

Purposes and Principles

Article 1

The Purposes of the United Nations are:

1. To maintain international peace and security, and to that end: to take effective collective measures for the prevention and removal of threats to the peace, and for the suppression of acts of aggression or other breaches of the peace, and to bring about by peaceful means, and in conformity with the principles of justice and international law, adjustment or settlement of international disputes or situations which might lead to a breach of the peace;

2. To develop friendly relations among nations based on respect for the principles of equal rights and self-determination of peoples, and to take other appropriate measures to strengthen universal peace;

3. To achieve international co-operation in solving international problems of an economic, social, cultural, or humanitarian character, and in promoting and encouraging respect for human rights and for fundamental freedoms for all without distinction as to race, sex, language, or religion; and

4. To be a centre for harmonizing the actions of nations in the attainment of these common ends.

Article 2

The Organization and its members, in pursuit of the purposes stated in Article 1, shall act in accordance with the following Principles:

1. The organization is based on the principle of the sovereign equality of all its Members.

2. All members, in order to ensure to all of them the rights and benefits resulting from membership, shall fulfil in good faith the obligations assumed by them in accordance with the present Charter.

3. All members shall settle their international disputes by peaceful means in such a manner that international peace and security, and justice, are not endangered.

4. All members shall refrain in their international relations from the threat or use of force against the territorial integrity or political independence of any state, or in any other manner inconsistent with the Purposes of the United Nations.

5. All members shall give the United Nations every assistance in any action it takes in accordance with the present Charter, and shall refrain from giving assistance to any state against which the United Nations is taking preventive or enforcement action.

6. The organization shall ensure that states which are not members of the United Nations act in accordance with these Principles so far as may be necessary for the maintenance of peace and security.

7. Nothing contained in the present Charter shall authorize the United Nations to intervene in matters which are essentially within the domestic jurisdiction of any state or shall require the members to submit such matters to settlement under the present Charter, but this principle shall not prejudice the application of enforcement measures under Charter VII.

Membership

Article 3

The original members of the United Nations shall be the states which, having participated in the United Nations Conference on International Organization at San Francisco, or having previously signed the Declaration by United Nations on 1 January 1942, sign the present Charter and ratify it in accordance with Article 110.

Article 4

1. Membership in the United Nations is open to all other peace-loving states which accept the obligations contained in the present Charter and, in the judgment of the Organization, are able and willing to carry out these obligations.

2. The admission of any such state to membership in the United Nations will be effected by a decision of the General Assembly upon the recommendation of the Security Council.

Article 5

A member of the United Nations against which preventive or enforcement action has been taken by the Security Council may be suspended from the exercise of the rights and privileges of membership by the General Assembly upon the recommendation of the Security Council. The exercise of these rights and privileges may be restored by the Security Council.

Article 6

A member of the United Nations which has persistently violated the Principles contained in the present Charter may be expelled from the Organization by the General Assembly upon the recommendation of the Security Council.

ORGANS

Article 7

1. These are established as the principal organs of the United Nations: a General Assembly, a Security Council, an Economic and Social Council, a Trusteeship Council, an International Court of Justice, and a Secretariat.

2. Such subsidiary organs as may be found necessary may be established in accordance with the present Charter.

Article 8

The United Nations shall place no restrictions on the eligibility of men and women to participate in any capacity and under conditions of equality in its principal and subsidiary organs.

THE GENERAL ASSEMBLY

Composition

Article 9

1. The General Assembly shall consist of all the members of the United Nations.

2. Each member shall have not more than five representatives in the General Assembly.

Functions and Powers

Article 10

The General Assembly may discuss any questions or any matters within the scope of the present Charter or relating to the powers and functions of any organs provided for in the present Charter, and, except as provided in Article 12, may make recommendations to the members of the United Nations or to the Security Council or to both on any such questions or matters.

Article 11

1. The General Assembly may consider the general principles of co-operation in the maintenance of international peace and security, including the principles governing disarmament and the regulation of armaments, and may make recommendations with regard to such principles to the members or to the Security Council or to both.

2. The General Assembly may discuss any question relating to the maintenance of international peace and security brought before it by any member of the United Nations, or by the Security Council, or by a state which is not a member of the United Nations in accordance with Article 35, paragraph 2, and, except as provided in Article 12, may make recommendations with regard to any such questions to the state or states concerned or to the Security Council or to both. Any such question on which action is necessary shall be referred to the Security Council by the General Assembly either before or after discussion.

3. The General Assembly may call the attention of the Security Council to situations which are likely to endanger international peace and security.

4. The powers of the General Assembly set forth in this Article shall not limit the general scope of Article 10.

Article 12

1. While the Security Council is exercising in respect of any dispute or situation the functions assigned to it in the present Charter, the General Assembly shall not make any recommendation with regard to that dispute or situation unless the Security Council so requests.

2. The Secretary-General, with the consent of the Security Council, shall notify the General Assembly at each session of any matters relative to the maintenance of international peace and security which are being dealt with by the Security Council and shall similarly notify the General Assembly, or the members of the United Nations if the General Assembly is not in session, immediately the Security Council ceases to deal with such matters.

Article 13

1. The General Assembly shall initiate studies and make recommendations for the purpose of:

(a) promoting international co-operation in the political field and encouraging the progressive development of international law and its codification;

(b) promoting international co-operation in the economic, social, cultural, educational, and health fields, and assisting in the realization of human rights and fundamental freedoms for all without distinction as to race, sex, language or religion.

2. The further responsibilities, functions and powers of the General Assembly with respect to matters mentioned in paragraph 1 (b) above are set forth in Chapters IX and X.

Article 14

Subject to the provisions of Article 12, the General Assembly may recommend measures for the peaceful adjustment of any situation, regardless of origin, which it deems likely to impair the general welfare or friendly relations among nations, including situations resulting from the violation of the provisions of the present Charter setting forth the Purposes and Principles of the United Nations.

Article 15

1. The General Assembly shall receive and consider annual and special reports from the Security Council; these reports shall include an account of the measures that the Security Council has decided upon or taken to maintain international peace and security.

2. The General Assembly shall receive and consider reports from the other organs of the United Nations.

Article 16

The General Assembly shall perform such functions with respect to the international trusteeship system as are assigned to it under Chapters XII and XIII, including the approval of the trusteeship agreements for areas not designated as strategic.

Article 17

1. The General Assembly shall consider and approve the budget of the Organization.

2. The expenses of the Organization shall be borne by the members as apportioned by the General Assembly.

3. The General Assembly shall consider and approve any financial and budgetary arrangements with specialized agencies referred to in Article 57 and shall examine the administrative budgets of such specialized agencies with a view to making recommendations to the agencies concerned.

Voting

Article 18

1. Each member of the General Assembly shall have one vote.

2. Decisions of the General Assembly on important questions shall be made by a two-thirds majority of the members present and voting. These questions shall include: recommendations with respect to the maintenance of international peace and security, the election of the non-permanent members of the Security Council, the election of the members of the Economic and Social Council, the election of members of the Trusteeship Council in accordance with paragraph 1(c) of Article 86, the admission of new members to the United Nations, the suspension of the rights and privileges of membership, the expulsion of members, questions relating to the operation of the trusteeship system, and budgetary questions.

3. Decisions on other questions, including the determination of additional categories of questions to be decided by a two-thirds majority, shall be made by a majority of the members present and voting.

Article 19

A member of the United Nations which is in arrears in the payment of its financial contributions to the Organization shall have no vote in the General Assembly if the amount of its arrears equals or exceeds the amount of the contributions due from it for the preceding two full years. The General Assembly may, nevertheless, permit such a member to vote if it is satisfied that the failure to pay is due to conditions beyond the control of the member.

Procedure

Article 20

The General Assembly shall meet in regular annual sessions and in such special sessions as occasion may require. Special sessions shall be convoked by the Secretary-General at the request of the Security Council or of a majority of the members of the United Nations.

Article 21

The General Assembly shall adopt its own rules of procedure. It shall elect its President for each session.

Article 22

The General Assembly may establish such subsidiary organs as it deems necessary for the performance of its functions.

THE SECURITY COUNCIL

Composition

Article 23

1. The Security Council shall consist of fifteen members of the United Nations. The Republic of China, France, the Union of Soviet Socialist Republics, the United Kingdom of Great Britain and Northern Ireland, and the United States of America shall be permanent members of the Security Council. The General Assembly shall elect ten other members of the United Nations to be non-permanent members of the Security Council, due regard being specially paid, in the first instance to the contribution of members of the United Nations to the maintenance of international peace and security and to the other purposes of the Organization, and also to equitable geographical distribution.

2. The non-permanent members of the Security Council shall be elected for a term of two years. In the first election of the non-permanent members after the increase of the membership of the Security Council from eleven to fifteen, two of the four additional members shall be chosen for a term of one year. A retiring member shall not be eligible for immediate re-election.

3. Each member of the Security Council shall have one representative.

Functions and Powers

Article 24

1. In order to ensure prompt and effective action by the United Nations, its members confer on the Security Council primary responsibility for the maintenance of international peace and security, and agree that in carrying out its duties under this responsibility the Security Council acts on their behalf.

2. In discharging these duties the Security Council shall act in accordance with the Purposes and Principles of the United Nations. The specific powers granted to the Security Council for the discharge of these duties are laid down in Chapters VI, VII, VIII and XII.

3. The Security Council shall submit annual and, when necessary, special reports to the General Assembly for its consideration.

Article 25

The members of the United Nations agree to accept and carry out the decisions of the Security Council in accordance with the present Charter.

Article 26

In order to promote the establishment and maintenance of international peace and security with the least diversion for armaments of the world's human and economic resources, the Security Council shall be responsible for formulating, with the assistance of the Military Staff Committee referred to in Article 47, plans to be submitted to the Members of the United Nations for the establishment of a system for the regulation of armaments.

Voting

Article 27

1. Each member of the Security Council shall have one vote.

2. Decisions of the Security Council on procedural matters shall be made by an affirmative vote of nine members.

3. Decisions of the Security Council on all other matters shall be made by an affirmative vote of nine members including the concurring votes of the permanent members; provided that, in

decisions under Chapter VI, and under Paragraph 3 of Article 52, a party to a dispute shall abstain from voting.

Procedure

Article 28

1. The Security Council shall be so organized as to be able to function continuously. Each member of the Security Council shall for this purpose be represented at all times at the seat of the Organization.

2. The Security Council shall hold periodical meetings at which each of its members may, if it so desires, be represented by a member of the government or by some other specially designated representative.

3. The Security Council may hold meetings at such places other than the seat of the Organization as in its judgment will best facilitate its work.

Article 29

The Security Council may establish such subsidiary organs as it deems necessary for the performance of its functions.

Article 30

The Security Council shall adopt its own rules of procedure, including the method of selecting its President.

Article 31

Any member of the United Nations which is not a member of the Security Council may participate, without vote, in the discussion of any question brought before the Security Council whenever the latter considers that the interests of that Member are specially affected.

Article 32

Any member of the United Nations which is not a member of the Security Council or any state which is not a member of the United Nations, if it is a party to a dispute under consideration by the Security Council, shall be invited to participate, without vote, in the discussion relating to the dispute. The Security Council shall lay down such conditions as it deems just for the participation of a state which is not a member of the United Nations.

PACIFIC SETTLEMENT OF DISPUTES

Article 33

1. The parties to any dispute, the continuance of which is likely to endanger the maintenance of international peace and security, shall, first of all, seek a solution by negotiation, enquiry, mediation, conciliation, arbitration, judicial settlement, resort to regional agencies or arrangements, or other peaceful means of their own choice.

2. The Security Council shall, when it deems necessary, call upon the parties to settle their dispute by such means.

Article 34

The Security Council may investigate any dispute, or any situation which might lead to international friction or give rise to a dispute, in order to determine whether the continuance of the dispute or situation is likely to endanger the maintenance of international peace and security.

Article 35

1. Any member of the United Nations may bring any dispute, or any situation of the nature referred to in Article 34, to the attention of the Security Council or of the General Assembly.

2. A state which is not a Member of the United Nations may bring to the attention of the Security Council or of the General Assembly any dispute to which it is a party if it accepts in advance, for the purposes of the dispute, the obligations of pacific settlement provided in the present Charter.

3. The proceedings of the General Assembly in respect of matters brought to its attention under this Article will be subject to the provisions of Articles 11 and 12.

Article 36

1. The Security Council may, at any stage of a dispute of the nature referred to in Article 33 or of a situation of like nature, recommend appropriate procedures or methods of adjustment.

2. The Security Council should take into consideration any procedures for the settlement of the dispute which have already been adopted by the parties.

3. In making recommendations under this Article the Security Council should also take into consideration that legal disputes should as a general rule be referred by the parties to the International Court of Justice in accordance with the provisions of the Statute of the Court.

Article 37

1. Should the parties to a dispute of the nature referred to in Article 33 fail to settle it by the means indicated in that Article, they shall refer it to the Security Council.

2. If the Security Council deems that the continuance of the dispute is in fact likely to endanger the maintenance of international peace and security, it shall decide whether to take action under Article 36 or to recommend such terms of settlement as it may consider appropriate.

Article 38

Without prejudice to the provisions of Articles 33 to 37, the Security Council may, if all the parties to any dispute so request, make recommendations to the parties with a view to a pacific settlement of the dispute.

ACTION WITH RESPECT TO THREATS OF THE PEACE, BREACHES OF THE PEACE, AND ACTS OF AGGRESSION

Article 39

The Security Council shall determine the existence of any threat to the peace, breach of the peace, or act of aggression and shall make recommendations, or decide what measures shall be taken in accordance with Articles 41 and 42, to maintain or restore international peace and security.

Article 40

In order to prevent an aggravation of the situation, the Security Council may, before making the recommendations or deciding upon the measures provided for in Article 39, call upon the parties concerned to comply with such provisional measures as it deems necessary or desirable. Such provisional measures shall be without prejudice to the rights, claims, or position of the parties concerned. The Security Council shall duly take account of failure to comply with such provisional measures.

Article 41

The Security Council may decide what measures not involving the use of armed forces are to be employed to give effect to its decisions, and it may call upon the members of the United Nations to apply such measures. These may include complete or partial interruption of economic relations and of Rail, Sea, Air, Postal, Telegraphic, Radio, and other means of communication, and the severance of diplomatic relations.

Article 42

Should the Security Council consider that measures provided for in Article 41 would be inadequate or have proved to be inadequate, it may take such action by Air, Sea, or Land forces as may be necessary to maintain or restore international peace or security. Such action may include demonstrations, blockade, and other operations by Air, Sea, or Land forces of Members of the United Nations.

Article 43

1. All Members of the United Nations, in order to contribute to the maintenance of international peace and security, undertake to make available to the Security Council, on its call and in accordance with a special agreement or agreements, Armed forces, assistance, and facilities, including rights of passage, necessary for the purpose of maintaining international peace and security.

2. Such agreement or agreements shall govern the numbers and types of forces, their degree of readiness and general location, and the nature of the facilities and assistance to be provided.

3. The agreement or agreements shall be negotiated as soon as possible at the initiative of the Security Council. They shall be concluded between the Security Council and Members or between the Security Council and groups of Members and shall be subject to ratification by the signatory states in accordance with their respective constitutional processes.

Article 44

When the Security Council has decided to use force it shall, before calling upon a Member not represented on it to provide armed forces in fulfilment of the obligations assumed under Article 43, invite that member, if the member so desires, to participate in the decisions of the Security Council concerning the employment of contingents of that Members's Armed forces.

Article 45

In order to enable the United Nations to take urgent military measures, Members shall hold immediately available national Airforce contingents for combined international enforcement action. The strength and degree of readiness of these contingents and plans for their combined action shall be determined, within the limits laid down in the special agreement or agreements referred to in Article 43, by the Security Council with the assistance of the Military Staff Committee.

Article 46

Plans for the application of Armed force shall be made by the Security Council with the assistance of the Military Staff Committee.

Article 47

1. There shall be established a Military Staff Committee to advise and assist the Security Council on all questions relating to the Security Council's military requirements for the maintenance of international peace and security, the employment and command of forces placed at its disposal, the regulation of armaments, and possible disarmament.

2. The Military Staff Committee shall consist of the Chiefs of Staff of the permanent members of the Security Council or their representatives. Any Member of the United Nations not permanently represented on the Committee shall be invited by the Committee to be associated with it when the efficient discharge of the Committee's responsibilities requires the participation of that member in its work.

3. The Military Staff Committee shall be responsible under the Security Council for the strategic direction of any armed forces placed at the disposal of the Security Council. Questions relating to the command of such forces shall be worked out subsequently.

4. The Military Staff Committee, with the authorization of the Security Council and after consultation with appropriate regional agencies, may establish regional sub-committees.

Article 48

1. The action required to carry out the decisions of the Security Council for the maintenance of international peace and security shall be taken by all the Members of the United Nations or by some of them, the Security Council may determine.

2. Such decisions shall be carried out by the Members of the United Nations directly and through their action in the appropriate international agencies of which they are members.

Article 49

The Members of the United Nations shall join in affording mutual assistance in carrying out the measures decided upon by the Security Council.

Article 50

If preventive or enforcement measures against any state are taken by the Security Council, any other state, whether a Member of the United Nations or not, which finds itself confronted with special economic problems arising from the carrying out of those measures shall have the right to consult the Security Council with regard to a solution of those problems.

Article 51

Nothing in the present Charter shall impair the inherent right of individual or collective self-defence if an armed attack occurs against a Member of the United Nations, until the Security Council has taken measures necessary to maintain international peace and security. Measures taken by Members in the exercise of this right of self-defence shall be immediately reported to the Security Council and shall not in any way affect the authority and responsibility of the Security Council under the present Charter to take at any time such action as it deems necessary in order to maintain or restore international peace and security.

REGIONAL ARRANGEMENTS

Article 52

1. Nothing in the present Charter precludes the existence of regional arrangements or agencies for dealing with such matters

relating to the maintenance of international peace and security as are appropriate for regional action, provided that such arrangements or agencies and their activities are consistent with the purpose and Principles of the United Nations.

2. The Members of the United Nations entering into such arrangements or constituting such agencies shall make every effort to achieve pacific settlement of local disputes through such regional arrangements or by such regional agencies before referring them to the Security Council.

3. The Security Council shall encourage the development of pacific settlement of local disputes through such regional arrangements or by such regional agencies either on the initiative of the states concerned or by reference from the Security Council.

4. The Article in no way impairs the application of Articles 34 and 35.

Article 53

1. The Security Council shall, where appropriate, utilize such regional arrangements or agencies for enforcement action under its authority. But no enforcement action shall be taken under regional arrangements or by regional agencies without the authorization of the Security Council, with the exception of measures against any enemy state, as defined in paragraph 2 of this Article, provided for pursuant to Article 107 or in regional arrangements directed against renewal of aggressive policy on the part of any such state, until such time as the organization may, on request of the Governments concerned, be charged with the responsibility for preventing further aggression by such a state.

2. The term enemy state as used in Paragraph 1 of this Article applies to any state which during the Second World War has been an enemy of any signatory of the present Charter.

Article 54

The Security Council shall at all times be kept fully informed of activities undertaken or in contemplation under regional arrangements or by regional agencies for the maintenance of international peace and security.

INTERNATIONAL, ECONOMIC AND SOCIAL CO-OPERATION

Article 55

With a view to the creation of conditions of stability and well-being which are necessary for peaceful and friendly relations among nations based on respect for the principle of equal rights and self-determination of peoples, the United Nations shall promote:

(a) higher standards of living, full employment, and conditions of economic and social progress and development;

(b) solutions of international economic, social, health, and related problems; and international cultural and educational co-operation; and

(c) universal respect for, and observance of, human rights and fundamental freedoms for all without distinction as to race, sex, language, or religion.

Article 56

All Members pledge themselves to take joint and separate action in co-operation with the Organization for the achievement of the purposes set forth in Article 55.

Article 57

1. The various specialized agencies, established by inter-governmental agreement and having wide international responsibilities, as defined in their basic instruments, in economic, social, cultural, educational, health, and related fields, shall be brought into relationship with the United Nations in accordance with the provisions of Article 63.

2. Such agencies thus brought into relationship with the United Nations are hereinafter referred to as specialized agencies.

Article 58

The Organization shall make recommendations for the co-ordination of the policies and activities of the specialized agencies.

Article 59

The Organization shall, where appropriate, initiate negotiations among the states concerned for the creation of any new specialized agencies required for the accomplishment of the purpose set forth in Article 55.

Article 60

Responsibility for the discharge of the functions of the Organization set forth in this Chapter shall be vested in the General Assembly and, under the authority of the General Assembly, in the Economic and Social Council, which shall have for this purpose the powers set forth in Chapter X.

THE ECONOMIC AND SOCIAL COUNCIL

Composition

Article 61

1. The Economic and Social Council shall consist of fifty-four Members of the United Nations elected by the General Assembly.

2. Subject to the provisions of paragraph 3, eighteen members of the Economic and Social Council shall be elected each year for a term of three years. A retiring member shall be eligible for immediate re-election.

3. At the first election after the increase in the membership of the Economic and Social Council from twenty-seven to fifty-four members, in addition to the members elected in place of the nine members whose term of office expires at the end of that year, twenty-seven additional members shall be elected. Of these twenty-seven additional members, the term of office of nine members so elected shall expire at the end of one year, and of nine other members at the end of two years, in accordance with arrangements made by the General Assembly.

4. Each member of the Economic and Social Council shall have one representative.

Functions and Powers

Article 62

1. The Economic and Social Council may make or initiate studies and reports with respect to international economic, social, cultural, educational, health and related matters and may make recommendations with respect to any such matters to the General

Assembly, to the Members of the United Nations, and to the specialized agencies concerned.

2. It may make recommendations for the purpose of promoting respect for, and observance of, human rights and fundamental freedoms for all.

3. It may prepare draft conventions for submission to the General Assembly, with respect to matters falling within its competence.

4. It may call, in accordance with the rules prescribed by the United Nations, international conferences on matters falling within its competence.

Article 63

1. The Economic and Social Council may enter into agreements with any of the agencies referred to in Article 57, defining the terms on which the agency concerned shall be brought into relationship with the United Nations. Such agreements shall be subject to approval by the General Assembly.

2. It may co-ordinate the activities of the specialized agencies through consultation with and recommendations to such agencies and through recommendations to the General Assembly and to the Members of the United Nations.

Article 64

1. The Economic and Social Council may take appropriate steps to obtain regular reports from the specialized agencies. It may make arrangements with the Members of the United Nations and with the specialized agencies to obtain reports on the steps taken to give effect to its own recommendations and to recommendations on matters falling within its competence made by the General Assembly.

2. It may communicate its observations on these reports to the General Assembly.

Article 65

The Economic and Social Council may furnish information to the Security Council and shall assist the Security Council upon its request.

Article 66

1. The Economic and Social Council shall perform such functions as fall within its competence in connection with the carrying out of the recommendations of the General Assembly.

2. It may, with the approval of the General Assembly, perform services at the request of Members of the United Nations and at the request of specialized agencies.

3. It shall perform such other functions as are specified elsewhere in the present Charter or as may be assigned to it by the General Assembly.

Voting

Article 67

1. Each Member of the Economic and Social Council shall have one vote.

2. Decisions of the Economic and Social Council shall be made by a majority of the members present and voting.

Procedure

Article 68

The Economic and Social Council shall set up commission in economic and social fields and for the promotion of human rights, and such other commissions as may be required for the performance of its functions.

Article 69

The Economic and Social Council shall invite any Member of the United Nations to participate, without vote, in its deliberations on any matter of particular concern to that Member.

Article 70

The Economic and Social Council may make arrangements for representatives of the specialized agencies to participate, without vote, in its deliberations and in those of the commissions established by it, and for its representatives to participate in the deliberations of the specialized agencies.

Article 71

The Economic and Social Council may make suitable arrangements for consultation with non-governmental organizations which are concerned with matters within its competence. Such arrangements may be made with international organization and, where appropriate, with national organizations after consultation with the Member of the United Nations concerned.

Article 72

1. The Economic and Social Council shall adopt its own rules of procedure, including the method of selecting its President.

2. The Economic and Social Council shall meet as required in accordance with its rules, which shall include provision for the convening of meetings on the request of a majority of its members.

DECLARATION REGARDING NON-SELF-GOVERNING TERRITORIES

Article 73

Members of the United Nations which have or assume responsibilities for the administration of territories whose peoples have not yet attained a full measure of self-government recognize the principle that the interests of the inhabitants of these territories are paramount, and accept as a sacred trust the obligation to promote to the utmost, within the system of international peace and security established by the present Charter, the well-being of the inhabitants of these territories, and, to this end:

(a) to ensure, with due respect for the culture of the peoples concerned, their political, social, and educational advancement, their just treatment, and their protection against abuses;

(b) to develop self-government, to take due account of the political aspirations of the peoples, and to assist them in the progressive development of their free political institutions, according to the particular circumstances of each territory and its peoples and their varying stages of advancement;

(c) to further international peace and security;

(d) to promote constructive measures of development, to encourage research, and to co-operate with one another and, when and where appropriate, with specialized international bodies with a view to the practical achievement of the social, economic, and scientific purposes set forth in this Article; and

(e) to transmit regularly to the Secretary-General for information purposes, subject to such limitation as security and constitutional considerations may require, statistical and other information of a technical nature relating to economic, social, and educational conditions in the territories for which they are respectively responsible other than those territories to which Chapters XII and XIII apply.

Article 74

Members of the United Nations also agree that their policy in respect of the territories to which this Chapter applies, no less than in respect of their metropolitan areas, must be based on the general principle of good-neighbourliness, due account being taken of the interests and well-being of the rest of world, in social, economic, and commercial matters.

INTERNATIONAL TRUSTEESHIP SYSTEM

Article 75

The United Nations shall establish under its authority an international trusteeship system for the administration and supervision of such territories as may be placed thereunder by subsequent individual agreements. These territories are hereinafter referred to as trust territories.

Article 76

The basic objectives of the trusteeship system, in accordance with the Purposes of the United Nations laid down in Article 1 of the present Charter, shall be:

(a) to further international peace and security;

(b) to promote the political, economic, social, and educational advancement of the inhabitants of the trust territories, and their progressive development towards self-government or independence as may be appropriate to the particular circumstances of each territory and its peoples and the freely expressed wishes of the peoples concerned, and as may be provided by the terms of each trusteeship agreement;

(c) to encourage respect for human rights and for fundamental freedoms for all without distinction as to race, sex, language, or religion, and to encourage recognition of the interdependence of the peoples of the world; and

(d) to ensure equal treatment in social, economic, and commercial matters for all Members of the United Nations and their nationals, and also equal treatment for the latter in the administration of justice, without prejudice to the attainment of the foregoing objectives and subject to the provisions of Article 80.

Article 77

1. The trusteeship system shall apply to such territories in the following categories as may be placed thereunder by means of trusteeship agreements:

(a) territories now held under mandate;
(b) territories which may be detached from enemy states as a result of the Second World War; and
(c) territories voluntarily placed under the system by states responsible for their administration.

2. It will be a matter for subsequent agreement as to which territories in the foregoing categories will be brought under the trusteeship system and upon what terms.

Article 78

The trusteeship system shall not apply to territories which have become Members of the United Nations, relationship among which shall be based on respect for the principle of sovereign equality.

Article 79

The terms of trusteeship for each territory to be placed under the trusteeship system, including my alteration or amendment, shall be agreed upon by the states directly concerned, including the mandatory powers in the case of territories held under mandate by a Member of the United Nations, and shall be approved as provided for in Articles 83 and 85.

Article 80

1. Except as may be agreed upon in individual trusteeship agreements, made under articles 77, 79, and 81, placing each territory under the trusteeship system, and until such agreements have been concluded, nothing in this Chapter shall be construed in or of itself

to alter in any manner the rights whatsoever of any states or any peoples or the terms of existing international instruments to which Members of the United Nations may respectively be parties.

2. Paragraph 1 of this Article shall not be interpreted as giving grounds for delay or postponement of the negotiation and conclusion of agreements for placing mandated and other territories under the trusteeship system as provided for in Article 77.

Article 81

The trusteeship agreement shall in each case include the terms under which the trust territory will be administered and designate the authority which will exercise the administration of the trust territory. Such authority, hereinafter called the administering authority, may be one or more states or the Organization itself.

Article 82

There may be designated, in any trusteeship agreement, a strategic area or areas which may include part or all of the trust territory to which the agreement applies, without prejudice to any special agreement or agreements made under Article 43.

Article 83

1. All functions of the United Nations relating to strategic areas, including the approval of the terms of the trusteeship agreements and of their alteration or amendment, shall be exercised by the Security Council.

2. The basic objectives set forth in Article 76 shall be applicable to the people of each strategic area.

3. The Security Council shall, subject to the provisions of the trusteeship agreements and without prejudice to security considerations, avail itself of the assistance of the Trusteeship Council to perform those functions of the United Nations under the trusteeship system relating to political, economic, social, and educational matters in the strategic areas.

Article 84

It shall be the duty of the administering authority to ensure that the trust territory shall play its part in the maintenance of international peace and security. To this end the administering authority may make use of volunteer forces, facilities, and assistance from the trust territory in carrying out the obligations towards the Security Council undertaken in this regard by the administering authority, as well as for local defence and the maintenance of law and order within the trust territory.

Article 85

1. The functions of the United Nations with regard to trusteeship agreements for all areas not designated as strategic, including the approval of the terms of the trusteeship agreements and of their alteration or amendment, shall be exercised by the General Assembly.

2. The Trusteeship Council, operating under the authority of the General Assembly, shall assist the General Assembly in carrying out these functions.

THE TRUSTEESHIP COUNCIL

Composition

Article 86

1. The Trusteeship Council shall consist of the following Members of the United Nations:

(a) those Members administering trust territories;
(b) such of those Members mentioned by name in Article 23 as are not administering trust territories; and
(c) as many other Members elected for three-year terms by the General Assembly as may be necessary to ensure that the total number of members of the Trusteeship Council is equally divided between these Members of the United Nations which administer trust territories and those which do not.

2. Each member of the Trusteeship Council shall designate one specially qualified person to represent it therein.

Functions and Powers

Article 87

The General Assembly and, under its authority, the Trusteeship Council, in carrying out their functions, may:

(a) consider reports submitted by the administering authority;

(b) accept petitions and examine them in consultation with the administering authority;
(c) provide for periodic visits to the respective trust territories at times agreed upon with the administering authority; and
(d) take these and other actions in conformity with the terms of the trusteeship agreements.

Article 88

The Trusteeship Council shall formulate a questionnaire on the political, economic, social and educational advancement of the inhabitants of each trust territory, and the administering authority for each trust territory within the competence of the General Assembly shall make an annual report to the General Assembly upon the basis of such questionnaire.

Voting

Article 89

1. Each member of the Trusteeship Council shall have one vote.

2. Decisions of the Trusteeship Council shall be made by a majority of the members present and voting.

Procedure

Article 90

1. The Trusteeship Council shall adopt its own rules of procedure, including the method of selecting its President.

2. The Trusteeship Council shall meet as required in accordance with its rules, which shall include provisions for the convening of meetings on the request of a majority of its members.

Article 91

The Trusteeship Council shall, when appropriate, avail itself of the assistance of the Economic and Social Council and of the specialized agencies in regard to matters with which they are respectively concerned.

THE INTERNATIONAL COURT OF JUSTICE

Article 92

The International Court of Justice shall be the principal judicial organ of the United Nations. It shall function in accordance with the annexed Statute, which is based upon the Statute of the Permanent Court of International Justice and forms an integral part of the present Charter.

Article 93

1. All Members of the United Nations are *ipso facto* parties to the Statute of the International Court of Justice.

2. A state which is not a member of the United Nations may become a party to the Statute of the International Court of Justice on conditions to be determined in each case by the General Assembly upon the recommendation of the Security Council.

Article 94

1. Each member of the United Nations undertakes to comply with the decision of the International Court of Justice in any case to which it is a party.

2. If any party to a case fails to perform the obligations incumbent upon it under a judgment rendered by the Court, the other party may have recourse to the Security Council, which may, if it deems necessary, make recommendations or decide upon measures to be taken to give effect to the judgment.

Article 95

Nothing in the present Charter shall prevent Members of the United Nations from entrusting the solution of their difference to other tribunals by virtue of agreements already in existence or which may be concluded in the future.

Article 96

1. The General Assembly or the Security Council may request the International Court of Justice to give an advisory opinion on any legal question.

2. Other organs of the United Nations and specialized agencies, which may at any time be so authorized by the General Assembly, may also request advisory opinions of the Court on legal questions arising within the scope of their activities.

THE SECRETARIAT

Article 97

The Secretariat shall comprise a Secretary-General and such staff as the Organization may require. The Secretary-General shall be appointed by the General Assembly upon the recommendation of the Security Council. He shall be the chief administrative officer of the Organization.

Article 98

The Secretary-General shall act in that capacity in meetings of the General Assembly, of the Security Council, of the Economic and Social Council and of the Trusteeship Council, and shall perform such other functions as are entrusted to him by these organs. The Secretary-General shall make an annual report to the General Assembly on the work of the Organization.

Article 99

The Secretary-General may bring to the attention of the Security Council any matter which in his opinion may threaten the maintenance of international peace and security.

Article 100

1. In the performance of their duties the Security-General and the staff shall not seek or receive instructions from any government or from any other authority external to the Organization. They shall refrain from any action which might reflect on their position as international officials responsible only to the Organization.

2. Each Member of the United Nations undertakes to respect the exclusively international character of the responsibilities of the Secretary-General and the staff and not to seek to influence them in the discharge of their responsibilities.

Article 101

1. The staff shall be appointed by the Secretary-General under regulations established by the General Assembly.

2. Appropriate staff shall be permanently assigned to the Economic and Social Council, the Trusteeship Council, and, as required, to other organs of the United Nations. These staffs shall form a part of the Secretariat.

3. The paramount consideration in the employment of the staff and in the determination of the conditions of service shall be the necessity of securing the highest standards of efficiency,

competence, and integrity. Due regard shall be paid to the importance of recruiting the staff on as wide a geographical basis as possible.

MISCELLANEOUS PROVISIONS

Article 102

1. Every treaty and every international agreement entered into by any Member of the United Nations after the present Charter comes into force shall as soon as possible be registered with the Secretariat and published by it.

2. No party to any such treaty or international agreement which has not been registered in accordance with the provisions of paragraph 1 of this Article may invoke that treaty or agreement before any organ of the United Nations.

Article 103

In the event of a conflict between the obligations of the Members of the United Nations under the present Charter and their obligations under any other international agreement, their obligations under the present Charter shall prevail.

Article 104

The Organization shall enjoy in the territory of each of its Members such legal capacity as may be necessary for the exercise of its functions and the fulfilment of its purposes.

Article 105

1. The Organization shall enjoy in the territory of each of its Members such privileges and immunities as are necessary for the fulfilment of its purposes.

2. Representatives of the Members of the United Nations and officials of the Organization shall similarly enjoy such privileges and immunities as are necessary for the independent exercise of their functions in connection with the Organization.

3. The General Assembly may make recommendations with a view to determining the details of the application of paragraphs 1 and 2 of the Article or may propose conventions to the Members of the United Nations for this purpose.

TRANSITIONAL SECURITY ARRANGEMENTS

Article 106

Pending the coming into force of such special agreements referred to in Article 43 as in the opinion of the Security Council enable it to begin the exercise of its responsibilities under Article 42, the parties to the Four-Nation Declaration, signed at Moscow, 30 October 1943, and France, shall, in accordance with the provisions of paragraph 5 of that Declaration, consult with one another and as occasion requires with other Members of the United Nations with a view to such joint action on behalf of the Organization as may be necessary for the purpose of maintaining international peace and security.

Article 107

Nothing in the present Charter shall invalidate or preclude action, in relation to any state which during the Second World War has been an enemy of any signatory to the present Charter, taken or authorized as a result of that war by the Governments having responsibility for such action.

AMENDMENTS

Article 108

Amendments to the present Charter shall come into force for all Members of the United Nations when they have been adopted by a vote of two thirds of the members of the General Assembly and ratified in accordance with their respective constitutional processes by two thirds of the Members of the United Nations, including all the permanent members of the Security Council.

Article 109

1. A General Conference of the Members of the United Nations for the purpose of reviewing the present Charter may be held at a date and place to be fixed by a two-thirds vote of the members of the General Assembly and by a vote of any nine members of the Security Council. Each Member of the United Nations shall have one vote in the conference.

2. Any alteration of the present Charter recommended by a two-thirds vote of the conference shall take effect when ratified in accordance with their respective constitutional processes by two

thirds of the Members of the United Nations including all the permanent members of the Security Council.

3. If such a conference has not been held before the tenth annual session of the General Assembly following the coming into force of the present Charter, the proposal to call such a conference shall be placed on the agenda of that session of the General Assembly, and the conference shall be held if so decided by a majority vote of the members of the General Assembly and by a vote of any members of the Security Council.

RATIFICATION AND SIGNATURE

Article 110

1. The present Charter shall be ratified by the signatory states in accordance with their respective constitutional processes.

2. The ratifications shall be deposited with the Government of the United States of America, which shall notify all the signatory states of each deposit as well as the Secretary-General of the Organization when he has been appointed.

3. The present Charter shall come into force upon the deposit of ratifications by the Republic of China, France, the Union of Soviet Socialist Republics, the United Kingdom of Great Britain and Northern Ireland, and the United States of America, and by a majority of the other signatory states. A protocol of the ratifications deposited shall thereupon be drawn up by the Government of the United States of America which shall communicate copies thereof to all the signatory states.

4. The states signatory to the present Charter which ratify it after it has come into force will become original Members of the United Nations on the date of the deposit of their respective ratifications.

Article 111

The present Charter, of which the Chinese, French, Russian, English, and Spanish texts are equally authentic, shall remain deposited in the archives of the Government of the United States of America, Duly certified copies thereof shall be transmitted by that Government to the Governments of the other signatory states.

IN FAITH WHEREOF the representatives of the Governments of the United Nations have signed the present Charter.

Done at the city of San Francisco the twenty-sixth day of June, one thousand nine hundred and forty-five.

UNIVERSAL DECLARATION OF HUMAN RIGHTS, 1948

Adopted and proclaimed by General Assembly resolution 217 A (III) of 10 December 1948

Preamble

Whereas recognition of the inherent dignity and of the equal and inalienable rights of all members of the human family is the foundation of freedom, justice and peace in the world.

Whereas disregard and contempt for human rights have resulted in barbarous acts which have outraged the conscience of mankind, and the advent of a world in which human beings shall enjoy freedom of speech and belief and freedom from fear and want has been proclaimed as the highest aspiration of the common people,

Whereas it is essential, if man is not to be compelled to have recourse, as a last resort, to rebellion against tyranny and oppression, that human rights should be protected by the rule of law,

Whereas it is essential to promote the development of friendly relations between nations,

Whereas the peoples of the United Nations have in the Charter reaffirmed their faith in fundamental human rights, in the dignity and worth of the human person and in the equal rights of men and women and have determined to promote social progress and better standards of life in larger freedom,

Whereas Member states have pledged themselves to achieve, in co-operation with the United Nations, the promotion of universal respect for and observance of human rights and fundamental freedoms.

Whereas a common understanding of these rights and freedoms is of the greatest importance for the full realisation of this pledge,

Now, therefore

The General Assembly,

Proclaims this Universal Declaration of Human Rights as a common standard of achievement for all peoples and all nations, to the end that every individual and every organ of society, keeping this Declaration constantly in mind, shall strive by teaching and education to promote respect for these rights and freedoms and by progressive measures, national and international, to secure their universal and effective recognition and observance, both among the peoples of Member States themselves and among the peoples of territories under their jurisdiction.

Article 1

All human beings are born free and equal in dignity and rights. They are endowed with reason and conscience and should act towards one another in a spirit of brotherhood.

Article 2

Everyone is entitled to all the rights and freedoms set forth in this Declaration, without distinction of any kind, such as race, colour, sex, language, religion, political or other opinion, national or social origin, property, birth or other status.

Furthermore, no distinction shall be made on the basis of the political jurisdiction or international status of the country or territory to which a person belongs, whether it be independent, trust, non-self-governing or under any other limitation of sovereignty.

Article 3

Everyone has the right to life, liberty and security of person.

Article 4

No one shall be held in slavery or servitude; slavery and the slave trade shall be prohibited in all their forms.

Article 5

No one shall be subjected to torture or to cruel, inhuman or degrading treatment or punishment.

Article 6

Everyone has the right to recognition everywhere as a person before the law.

Article 7

All are equal before the law and are entitled without any discrimination to equal protection of the law. All are entitled to equal protection against any discrimination in violation of this Declaration and against any incitement to such discrimination.

Article 8

Everyone has the right to an effective remedy by the competent national tribunals for acts violating the fundamental rights granted him by the constitution or by law.

Article 9

No one shall be subjected to arbitrary arrest, detention or exile.

Article 10

Everyone is entitled in full equality to a fair and public hearing by an independent and impartial tribunal, in the determination of his rights and obligations and of any criminal charge against him.

Article 11

1. Every one charged with a penal offence has the right to be presumed innocent until proved guilty according to law in a public trial at which he has had all the guarantees necessary for his defence.

2. No one shall be held guilty of any penal offence on account of any act or omission which did not constitute a penal offence, under national or international law. at the time when it was committed. Nor shall a heavier penalty be imposed than the one that was applicable at the time the penal offence was committed.

Article 12

No one shall be subjected to arbitrary interference with his privacy, family, home or correspondence, nor to attacks upon his honour and reputation. Everyone has the right to the protection of the law against such interference or attacks.

Article 13

1. Everyone has the right to freedom of movement and residence within the borders of each state.

2. Everyone has the right to leave any country, including his own, and to return to his country.

Article 14

1. Everyone has the right to seek and to enjoy in other countries asylum from persecution.

2. This right may not be invoked in the case of prosecutions genuinely arising from non-political crimes or from acts contrary to the purposes and principles of the United Nations.

Article 15

1. Everyone has the right to a nationality.

2. No one shall be arbitrarily deprived of his nationality nor denied the right to change his nationality.

Article 16

1. Men and women of full age, without any limitation due to race, nationality or religion, have the right to marry and to found a family. They are entitled to equal rights as to marriage, during marriage and at its dissolution.

2. Marriage shall be entered only with the free and full consent of the intending spouses.

3. The family is the natural and fundamental group unit of society and entitled to protection by society and the state.

Article 17

1. Everyone has the right to own property alone as well as in association with others.

2. No one shall he arbitrarily deprived of his property.

Article 18

Everyone has the right to freedom of thought, conscience and religion; this right includes freedom to change his religion or belief, and freedom, either alone or in community with others and in public or private, to manifest his religion or belief in teaching, practice, worship and observance.

Article 19

Everyone has the right to freedom of opinion and expression; this right includes freedom to hold opinions without interference and to seek, receive and impart information and ideas through any media and regardless of frontiers.

Article 20

1. Everyone has the right to freedom of peaceful assembly and association.

2. No one may be compelled to belong to an association.

Article 21

1. Everyone has the right to take part in the government of his country, directly or through freely chosen representatives.

2. Everyone has the right to equal access to public service in his country.

3. The will of the people shall be the basis of the authority of government; this will shall be expressed in periodic and genuine elections which shall be by universal and equal suffrage and shall be held by secret vote or by equivalent free voting procedures.

Article 22

Everyone, as a member of society, has the right to social security and is entitled to realisation, through national effort and international co-operation and in accordance with the organisation and resources of each State, of the economic, social and cultural rights indispensable for his dignity and the free development of his personality.

Article 23

1. Everyone has the right to work, to free choice of employment, to just and favourable conditions of work and to protection against unemployment.

2. Everyone, without any discrimination, has the right to equal pay for equal work.

3. Everyone who works has the right to just and favourable remuneration ensuring for himself and his family an existence worthy of human dignity, and supplemented, if necessary, by other means of social protection.

4. Everyone has the right to form and to join trade unions for the protection of his interests.

Article 24

Everyone has the right to rest and leisure, including reasonable limitation of working hours and periodic holidays with pay.

Article 25

1. Everyone has the right to a standard of living adequate for the health and well-being of himself and of his family, including food, clothing, housing and medical care and necessary social services, and the right to security in the event of unemployment, sickness, disability, widowhood, old age or other lack of livelihood in circumstances beyond his control.

2. Motherhood and childhood are entitled to special care and assistance. All children, whether born in or out of wedlock, shall enjoy the same social protection.

Article 26

1. Everyone has the right to education. Education shall be free, at least in the elementary and fundamental stages. Elementary education shall be compulsory. Technical and professional education shall be made generally available and higher education shall be equally accessible to all on the basis of merit.

2. Education shall be entitled to the full development of the human personality and to the strengthening of respect for human rights and fundamental freedoms. It shall promote understanding, tolerance and friendship among all nations, racial or religious groups, and shall further the activities of the United Nations for the maintenance of peace.

3. Parents have a prior right to choose the kind of education that shall be given to their children.

Article 27

1. Everyone has the right freely to participate in the cultural life of the community, to enjoy the arts and to share in scientific advancement and its benefits.

2. Everyone has the right to the protection of the moral and material interests resulting from any scientific, literary or artistic production of which he is the author.

Article 28

Everyone is entitled to social and international order in which the rights and freedoms set forth in this Declaration can be fully realised.

Article 29

1. Everyone is entitled to the community in which alone the free and full development of his personality is possible.

2. In the exercise of his rights and freedoms, everyone shall be subject only to such limitations as are determined by law solely for the purpose of securing due recognition and respect for the rights and freedoms of others and the general welfare in a democratic society.

3. These rights and freedoms may in no case be exercised contrary to the purposes and principles of the United Nations.

Article 30

Nothing in this Declaration may be interpreted as implying for any State, group or person any right to engage in any activity or to perform any act aimed at the destruction of the rights and freedoms set forth herein.

DECLARATION BY THE GOVERNMENT OF INDIA, 1979

WHEREAS the International Covenant on Economic, Social and Cultural Rights and the International Covenant on Civil and Political Rights were adopted by the General Assembly of the United Nations in Resolution 2200 (XXI) of 16 December 1966, which Covenants are reproduced in the Annexure to this Document;

AND WHEREAS it is fit and expedient to accede to the aforesaid covenants subject to the following Declarations:

Declarations

I. With reference to Article I of the International Covenant on Economic, Social and Cultural Rights and Article I of the International Covenant on Civil and Political Rights, the Government of the Republic of India declares that the words "the right of self-determination" appearing in those articles apply only to the peoples under foreign dominations and that these words do not apply to sovereign independent States or to a Section of a people or nation—which is the essence of national integrity.

II. With reference to Article 9 of the International Covenant on Civil and Political Rights, the Government of the Republic of India takes the position that the provisions of the article shall be so applied as to be in consonance with the provisions of clauses (3) to (7) of Article 22 of the Constitution of India. Further under the Indian Legal System, there is no enforceable right to compensation for persons claiming to be victims of unlawful arrest or detention against the State.

III. With respect to Article 13 of the International Covenant on Civil and Political Rights, the Government of the Republic of India reserves its right to apply its law relating to foreigners.

IV. With respect to Articles 4 and 8 of the International Covenant on Economic, Social and Cultural Rights, and Articles 12, 19(3), 21 and 22 of the International Covenant on Civil and Political Rights, the Government of the Republic of India declares that the provisions of the said articles shall be so applied as to be in conformity with the provisions of Article 19 of the Constitution of India.

V. With reference to Article 7(c) of the International Covenant on Economic, Social and Cultural Rights, the Government of the Republic of India declares that the provisions of the said Article shall be so applied as to be in conformity with the provisions of

Article 16(4) of the Constitution of India.

NOW, THEREFORE, BE IT KNOWN that the Government of the Republic of India, having seen and considered the said Covenants, do hereby accede to the same, subject to the aforementioned Declarations.

IN TESTIMONY WHEREOF I, NEELAM SANJIVA REDDY, PRESIDENT OF INDIA, have signed these Presents and affixed hereunto my Seal at New Delhi this the sixth day of Chaitra of the Saka year one thousand nine hundred and one corresponding to the twenty-seventh day of March of the year one thousand nine hundred and seventy-nine A. D. in the Thirtieth year of the Republic of India.

Sd/-

(Neelam Sanjiva Reddy)

President of India

Deposited with the U. N. on
10.4.79

INTERNATIONAL COVENANT ON CIVIL AND POLITICAL RIGHTS, 1966

Adopted and opened for signature, ratification and accession by General Assembly resolution 2200 A (XXI) of 16 December 1966

Entry into Force: 23 March 1976, in accordance with Article 49

Preamble

The State Parties to the present Covenant,

Considering that, in accordance with the principles proclaimed in the Charter of the United Nations, recognition of the inherent dignity and of the equal and inalienable rights of all members of the family is the foundation of freedom, justice and peace in the world,

Recognising that these rights derive from the inherent dignity of the human person,

Recognising that, in accordance with the Universal Declaration of Human Rights, the idea of free human beings enjoying civil and political freedom and freedom from fear and want can only be achieved if conditions are created whereby everyone may enjoy his civil and political rights, as well as his economic, social and cultural rights.

Considering the obligation of States under the Charter of the United Nations to promote universal respect for, and observance of, human rights and freedoms,

Realising that the individual, having duties to other individuals and to the community to which he belongs, is under a responsibility to strive for the promotion and observance of the rights recognised in the present Covenant.

Agree upon the following articles:

Article 1

1. All peoples, have the right of self-determination. By virtue of that right they freely determine their political status and freely pursue their economic, social and cultural development.

2. All peoples may, for their own ends, freely dispose of their natural wealth and resources without prejudice to any obligations arising out of international economic co-operation, based upon the

principle of mutual benefit, and international law. In no case may a people be deprived of its own means of subsistence.

3. The States Parties to the present Covenant, including those having responsibility for the administration of Non-Self-Governing and Trust Territories, shall promote the realisation of the right of self-determination, and shall respect that right, in conformity with the provisions of the Charter of the United Nations.

Article 2

1. Each State Party to the present Covenant undertakes to respect and to ensure to all individuals within its territory and subject to its jurisdiction the rights recognised in the present Covenant, without distinction of any kind, such as race, colour, sex, language, religion, political or other opinion, national or social origin, property, birth or other status.

2. Where not already provided for by existing legislative or other measures, each State Party to the present Covenant undertakes to take necessary steps, in accordance with its constitutional processes and with the provisions of the present Covenant, to adopt such legislative or other measures as may be necessary to give the rights recognised in the present Covenant.

3. Each State party to the present Covenant undertakes:

(a) To ensure that any person whose rights or freedoms as herein recognised are violated shall have an effective remedy, notwithstanding that the violation has been committed by person acting in an official capacity;

(b) To ensure that any person claiming such a remedy shall have his right thereto determined by competent judicial, administrative or legislative authorities, or by any other competent authority provided for by the legal system of the State, and to develop the possibilities of judicial remedy;

(c) To ensure that the competent authorities shall enforce such remedies when granted.

Article 3

The States Parties to the present Covenant undertake to ensure the equal right of men and women to the enjoyment of all civil and political rights set forth in the present Covenant.

Article 4

1. In time of public emergency which threatens the life of the nation and the existence of which is officially proclaimed, the States Parties to the present Covenant may take measures derogating from their obligations under the present Covenant to the extent strictly required by the exigencies of the situation, provided that such measures are not inconsistent with their other obligations under international law and do not involve discrimination solely on the ground of race, colour, sex, language, religion or social origin.

2. No derogation from articles 6, 7, 8 (paragraphs 1 and 2), 11, 15, 16 and 18 may be made under this provision.

3. Any State Party to the present Covenant availing itself of the right of derogation shall immediately inform the other States Parties to the present Covenant, through the intermediary of the Secretary-General of the United Nations, of the provisions from which it has derogated and of the reasons by which it was actuated. A further communication shall be made, through the same intermediary, on the date on which it terminates such derogation.

Article 5

1. Nothing in the present Covenant may be interpreted as implying for any State, group or person any right to engage in any activity or perform any act aimed at the destruction of any of the rights and freedoms recognised herein or at their limitation to a greater extent than is provided for in the present Covenant.

2. There shall be no restriction upon derogation from any of the fundamental human rights recognised or existing in any State Party to the present Covenant pursuant to law, conventions, regulations or custom on the pretext that the present Covenant does not recognise such rights or that it reognises them to a lesser extent.

Article 6

1. Every human being has the inherent right to life. This right shall be protected by law. No one shall be arbitrarily deprived of his life.

2. In countries which have not abolished the death penalty, sentence of death may be imposed only for the most serious crimes in accordance with the law in force at the time of the commission of the crime and not contrary to the provisions of the present Covenant

and to the Convention on the Prevention and Punishment of Crime of Genocide. This penalty can only be carried out to a final judgement rendered by a competent court.

3. When deprivation of life constitutes the crime of genocide, it is understood that nothing in this article shall authorise any State Party to the present Covenant to derogate in any way from any obligation assumed under the provisions of the Convention on the Prevention and Punishment of the Crime of Genocide.

4. Anyone sentenced to death shall have the right to seek pardon or commutation of the sentence. Amnesty, pardon or commutation of the sentence of death may be granted in all cases.

5. Sentence of death shall not be imposed for crimes committed by persons below eighteen years of age and shall not be carried out on pregnant women.

6. Nothing in this article shall be invoked to delay or to prevent the abolition of capital punishment by any State Party to the present Covenant.

Article 7

No one shall be subjected to torture or to cruel, inhuman or degrading treatment or punishment. In particular, no one shall be subject without his free consent to medical or scientific experimentation.

Article 8

1. No one shall be held in slavery; slavery and the slave-trade in all their forms shall be prohibited.

2. No one shall be held in servitude.

3. (a) No one shall be required to perform forced or compulsory labour;

(b) Paragraph 3 (a) shall not be held to preclude, in countries where imprisonment with hard labour may be imposed as a punishment for a crime, the performance of hard labour in pursuance of a sentence to such punishment by a competent court;

(c) For the purpose of this paragraph the term "forced or compulsory labour" shall not include:

(i) Any work or service, not referred to in subparagraph (b), normally required of a person who is under detention in consequence of a lawful order of a court, or of a person during conditional release from such detention;

(ii) Any service of a military character and, in countries where conscientious objection is recognised, any national service required by law of conscientious objectors;

(iii) Any service exaced in cases of emergency or calamity threatening the life or well-being of the community;

(iv) Any work or service which forms part of normal civil obligations.

Article 9

1. Everyone has the right to liberty and security of person. No one shall be subjected to arbitrary arrest or detention. No one shall be deprived of his liberty except on such grounds and in accordance with such procedure as are established by law.

2. Anyone who is arrested shall be informed, at the time of arrest, of the reasons for his arrest and shall be promptly informed of any charges against him.

3. Anyone arrested or detained on a criminal charge shall be brought promptly before a judge or other officer authorised by law to exercise judicial power and shall be entitled to trial within a reasonable time or to release. It shall not be the general rule that persons awaiting trial shall be detained in custody, but release may be subject to guarantees to appear for trial, at any other stage of the judicial proceedings, and, should occasion arise, for execution of the judgement.

4. Anyone who is deprived of his liberty by arrest or detention shall be entitled to take proceedings before a court, in order that court may decide without delay on the lawfulness of his detention and order his release if the detention is not lawful.

5. Anyone who has been the victim of unlawful arrest or detention shall have an enforceable right to compensation.

Article 10

1. All persons deprived of their liberty shall be treated with humanity and with respect for the inherent dignity of the human person.

2. (a) Accused persons shall, save in exceptional circumstances, be segregated from convicted persons and shall be subject to separate treatment appropriate to their status as unconvicted persons;

(b) Accused juvenile persons shall be separated from adults and brought as speedily as possible for adjudication.

3. The penitentiary system shall comprise treatment of prisoners the essential aim of which shall be their reformation and social rehabilitation. Juvenile offenders shall be segregated from adults and be accorded treatment appropriate to their age and legal status.

Article 11

No one shall be imprisoned merely on the ground of inability to fulfil a contractual obligation.

Article 12

1. Everyone lawfully within the territory of a state shall, within that territory, have the right to liberty of movement and freedom to choose his residence.

2. Everyone shall be free to leave any country, including his own.

3. The above-mentioned rights shall not be subject to any restrictions except those which are provided by law, are necessary to protect national security, public order *(ordre public)*, public health or morals or the rights and freedoms of others, and are consistent with the other rights recognised in the present Covenant.

4. No one shall be arbitrary deprived of the right to enter his own country.

Article 13

An alien lawfully in the territory of a State Party to the present Covenant may be expelled therefrom only in pursuance of a decision reached in accordance with law and shall, except where compelling reasons of national security otherwise require, be allowed to submit the reasons against his expulsion and to have his case reviewed by, and be represented for the purpose before, the competent authority or a person or persons especially designated by the competent authority.

Article 14

1. All persons shall be equal before the courts and tribunals. In the determination of any criminal charge against him, or of his rights and obligations in a suit at law, everyone shall be entitled to a fair and public hearing by a competent, independent and impartial tribunal established by law. The press and the public may be excluded from all or part of a trial for reasons of morals, public order

(*ordre public*) or national security in a democratic society, or when the interest of the private lives of the parties so requires, or to the extent strictly necessary in the opinion of the court in special circumstances where publicity would prejudice the interests of justice; but any judgement rendered in a criminal case or in a suit at law shall be made public except where the interest of juvenile persons otherwise requires or the proceedings concern matrimonial disputes or the guardianship of children.

2. Everyone charged with a criminal offence shall have the right to be presumed innocent until proved guilty according to law.

3. In the determination of any criminal charge against him, everyone shall be entitled to the following minimum guarantees, in full equality:

(a) To be informed promptly and in detail in a language which he understands of the nature and cause of the charge against him;

(b) To have adequate time and facilities for the preparation of his defence and to communicate with counsel of his own choosing;

(c) To be tried without undue delay;

(d) To be tried in presence, and to defend himself in person or through legal assistance of his own choosing; to be informed, if he does not have legal assistance, of this right; and to have legal assistance assigned to him, in any case where the interests to justice so require, and without payment by him in any such case if he does not have sufficient means to pay for it;

(e) To examine, or have examined, the witnesses against him and to obtain the attendance and examination of witnesses on his behalf under the same conditions as witnesses against him;

(f) To have the free assistance of an interpreter if he cannot understand or speak the language used in court;

(g) Not to be compelled to testify against himself or to confess guilt.

4. In the case of juvenile persons, the procedure shall be such as will take account of their age and the desirability of promoting their rehabilitation.

5. Everyone convicted of a crime shall have the right to his conviction and sentence being reviewed by a higher tribunal according to law.

6. When a person has by a final decision been convicted of a criminal offence and when subsequently his conviction has been reversed or he has been pardoned on the ground that a new or newly discovered fact shows conclusively that there has been a miscarriage of justice, the person who has suffered punishment as a result of such conviction shall be compensated according to law, unless it is proved that the non-disclosure of the unknown fact in time is wholly or partly attributable to him.

7. No one shall be liable to be tried or punished again for an offence for which he has already been finally convicted or acquitted in accordance with the law and penal procedure of each country.

Article 15

1. No one shall be held guilty of any criminal offence on account of any act or ommission which did not constitute a criminal offence, under national or international law, at the time when it was committed. Nor shall a heavier penalty be imposed than the one that was applicable at the time when the criminal offence was committed. If, subsequent to the commission of the offence, provision is made by law for the imposition of the lighter penalty, the offender shall benefit thereby.

2. Nothing in this article shall prejudice the trial and punishment of any person for any act or omission which, at the time when it was committed, was criminal according to the general principles of law recognised by the community of nations.

Article 16

Everyone shall have the right to recognition everywhere as a person before the law.

Article 17

1. No one shall be subjected to arbitrary or unlawful interference with his privacy, family, home or correspondence, nor to unlawful attacks on his honour and reputation.

2. Everyone has the right to the protection of the law against such interference or attacks.

Article 18

1. Everyone shall have the right to freedom of thought, conscience and religion. This right shall include freedom to have or

to adopt a religion or belief of his choice, and freedom, either individually or in community with others and in public or private, to manifest his religion or belief in worship, observance, practice and teaching.

2. No one shall be subject to coercion which would impair his freedom to have or to adopt a religion or belief of his choice.

3. Freedom to manifest one's religion or beliefs may be subject only to such limitations as are prescribed by law and are necessary to protect public safety, order, health, or morals or the fundamental rights and freedoms of others.

4. The State Parties to the present Covenant undertake to have respect for the liberty of parents and, when applicable, legal guardians to ensure the religious and moral education of their children in conformity with their own convictions.

Article 19

1. Everyone shall have the right to hold opinions without interference.

2. Everyone shall have the right to freedom of expression; this right shall include freedom to seek, receive and impart information and ideas of all kinds, regardless of frontiers, either orally, in writing or in print, in the form of art, or through any other media of his choice.

3. The exercise of the rights provided for in Paragraph 2 of this article carries with it special duties and responsibilites. It may therefore be subject to certain restrictions, but these shall only be such as are provided by law and are necessary:

(a) For respect of the rights or reputations of others;
(b) For the protection of national security or of public order (*ordre public*), or of public health or morals.

Article 20

1. Any propaganda for war shall be prohibited by law.

2. Any advocacy of national, racial or religious hatred that constitutes incitement to discrimination, hostility or violence shall be prohibited by law.

Article 21

The right of peaceful assembly shall be recognised. No restrictions may be placed on the exercise of this right other than those imposed in conformity with the law and which are necessary in a democratic society in the interests of national security or public safety, public order *(ordre public)*, the protection of public health or morals or the protection of the rights and freedoms of others.

Article 22

1. Everyone shall have the right to freedom of association with others, including the right to form and join trade unions for the protection of his interests.

2. No restrictions may be placed on the exercise of this right other than those which are prescribed by law and which are necessary in a democratic society in the interests of national security or public safety, public order *(ordre public)*, the protection of public health or morals or the protection of the rights and freedoms of others. This article shall not prevent the imposition of lawful restrictions on members of the armed forces and of the police in their exercise of this right.

3. Nothing in this article shall authorise States Parties to the International Labour Organisation Convention of 1948 concerning Freedom of Association and Protection of the Right to Organise to take legislative measures which would prejudice, or to apply the law in such a manner as to prejudice, the guarantees provided for in that Convention.

Article 23

1. The family is the natural and fundamental group unit of society and is entitled to protection by society and the state.

2. The right of men and women of marriageable age to marry and to found a family shall be recognised.

3. No marriage shall be entered into without the free and full consent of the intending spouses.

4. States Parties to the present Covenant shall take appropriate steps to ensure equality of rights and responsibilities of spouses as to marriage, during marriage and at its dissolution. In the case of dissolution, provision shall be made for the necessary protection of any children.

Article 24

1. Every child shall have, without any discrimination as to race, colour, sex, language, religion, national or social origin,

property or birth, the right to such measures of protection as are required by his status as a minor, on the part of his family, society and the State.

2. Every child shall be registered immediately after birth and shall have a name.

3. Every child has the right to acquire a nationality.

Article 25

Every citizen shall have the right and the opportunity, without any of the distinctions mentioned in Article 2 and without unreasonable restrictions:

(a) To take part in the conduct of public affairs, directly or through freely chosen representatives;
(b) To vote and to be elected as genuine periodic elections which shall be by universal equal suffrage and shall be held by secret ballot, guaranteeing the free expression of the will of the electors;
(c) To have access, on general terms of equality, to public service in his country.

Article 26

All persons are equal before the law and are entitled without any discrimination to the equal protection of the law. In this respect, the law shall prohibit any discrimination and guarantee to all persons equal and effective protection against discrimination on any ground such as race, colour, sex, language, religion, political or other opinion, national or social origin, property, birth or other status.

Article 27

In those States in which ethnic, religious or linguistic minorities exist, persons belonging to such minorities shall not be denied the right, in community with the other members of their group, to enjoy their own culture, to profess and practise their own religion, or to use their own language.

Article 28

1. There shall be established a Human Rights Committee (hereafter referred to in the present Covenant as the Committee). It shall consist of eighteen members and shall carry out the functions hereinafter provided.

2. The Committee shall be composed of nationals of the States Parties to the present Covenant who shall be persons of high moral character and recognised competence in the field of human rights, consideration being given to the usefulness of the participation of some persons having legal experience.

3. The members of the Committee shall be elected and shall serve in their personal capacity.

Article 29

1. The members of the Committee shall be elected by secret ballot from a list of persons possessing the qualifications prescribed in article 28 and nominated for the purpose by the State Parties to the present Covenant.

2. Each State Party to the present Covenant may nominate not more than two persons. These persons shall be nationals of the nominating State.

3. A person shall be eligible for renomination.

Article 30

1. The initial election shall be held no later than six months after the date of entry into force of the present Covenant.

2. At least four months before the date of each election to the Committee, other than an election to fill a vacancy declared in accordance with article 34, the Secretary-General of the United Nations shall address a written invitation to the States Parties to the present Covenant to submit their nominations for membership of the Committee within three months.

3. The Secretary-General of the United Nations shall prepare a list in alphabetical order of all the persons thus nominated, with an indication of the States Parties which have nominated them, and shall submit it to the States Parties to the present Covenant no later than one month before the date of each election.

4. Election of the members of the Committee shall be held at a meeting of the States Parties to the present Covenant convened by the Secretary-General of the United Nations at the Headquarters of the United Nations. At that meeting, for which two thirds of the States Parties to the present Covenant shall constitute a quorum, the persons elected to the Committee shall be those nominees who obtain the largest number of votes and an absolute majority of the votes of the representatives of States Parties present and voting.

Article 31

1. The Committee may not include more than one national of the same State.

2. In the election of the Committee, consideration shall be given to equitable geographical distribution of membership and to the representation oif the different forms of civilisation and of the principal legal systems.

Article 32

1. The members of the Committee shall be elected for a term of four years. They shall be eligible for re-election if renominated. However, the terms of nine of the members elected at the first election shall expire at the end of two years; immediately after the first election, the names of these nine members shall be chosen by lot by the Chairman of the meeting referred to in Article 30, Paragraph 4.

2. Elections at the expiry of office shall be held in accordance with the preceding articles of this part of the present Covenant.

Article 33

1. If, in the unanimous opinion of the other members, a member of the Committee has ceased to carry out his functions for any cause other than absence of a temporary character, the Chairman of the Committee shall notify the Secretary. General of the United Nations, who shall then declare the seat of that member to be vacant.

2. In the event of the death or the resignation of a member of the Committee, the Chairman shall immediately notify the Secretary-General of the United Nations, who shall declare the seat vacant from the date of death or the date on which the resignation takes effect.

Article 34

1. When a vacancy is declared in accordance with Article 33 and if the term of office of the member to be replaced does not expire within six months f the declaration of the vacancy, the Secretary-General of the United Nations shall notify each of the State Parties to the present Covenant, which may within two months submit nominations in accordance with Article 29 for the purpose of filling the vacancy.

2. The Secretary-General of the United Nations shall prepare a

list in alphabetical order of the persons thus nominated and shall submit it to the States Parties to the present Covenant. The election to fill the vacancy shall then take place in accordance with the relevant provisions of this part of the present Covenant.

3. A member of the Committee elected to fill a vacancy declared in accordance with Article 33 shall hold office for the remainder of the term of the member who vacated the seat on the Committee under the provisions of that article.

Article 35

The members of the Committee shall, with the approval of the General Assembly of the United Nations, receive emoluments from United Nations resources on such terms and conditions as the General Assembly may decide having regard to the importance of the Committee's responsibilities.

Article 36

The Secretary-General of the United Nations shall provide the necessary staff and facilities for the effective performance of the functions of the Committee under the present Covenant.

Article 37

1. The Secretary-General of the United Nations shall convene the initial meeting of the Committee at the Headquarters of the United Nations.

2. After its initial meeting, the Committee shall meet at such times as shall be provided in its rules of procedure.

3. The committee shall normally meet at the Headquarters of the United Nations or at the United Nations Office at Geneva.

Article 38

Every member of the Committee shall, before taking up his duties, make a solemn declaration in open committee that he will perform his functions impartially and conscientiously.

Article 39

1. The Committee shall elect its officers for a term of two years. They may be re-elected.

2. The Committee shall establish its own rules of procedure, but these rules shall provide, *inter alia*, that:

(a) Twelve members shall constitute a quorum;
(b) Decisions of the Committee shall be made by a majority vote of the members present.

Article 40

1. The States Parties to the present Covenant undertake to submit reports on the measures they have adopted which give effect to the rights recognised herein and on the progress made in the enjoyment of those rights:

(a) Within one year of the entry into force of the present Covenant for the States Parties concerned;
(b) Thereafter whenever the Committee so requests.

2. All reports shall be submitted to the Secretary-General of the United Nations, who shall transmit them to the Committee for consideration. Reports shall indicate the factors and difficulties, if any, affecting the implementation of the present Covenant.

3. The Secretary-General of the United Nations may, after consultation with the Committee, transmit to the specialised agencies concerned copies of such parts of the reports as may fall within their field of competence.

4. The Committee shall study the reports submitted by the State Parties to the present Covenant. It shall transmit its reports, and such general comments as it may consider appropriate, to the States Parties. The Committee may also transmit to the Economic and Social Council these comments alongwith the copies of the reports it has received from States Parties to the present Covenant.

5. The States Parties to the present Covenant may submit to the Committee observations on any comments that may be made in accordance with Paragraph 4 of this Article.

Article 41

1. A State Party to the present Covenant may at any time declare under this Article that it recognises the competence of the Committee to receive and consider communications to the effect that a State Party claims that another State Party is not fulfilling its obligations under the present Covenant. Communications under this Article may be received and considered only if submitted by a State Party which has made a declaration recognising in regard to itself the competence of the Committee. No communication shall be received

by the Committee if it concerns a State Party which has not made such a declaration. Communications received under this Article shall be dealt with in accordance with the following procedure:

(a) If a State Party to the present Convenant considers that another State Party is not giving effect to the provisions of the present Covenant, it may, by written communication, bring the matter to the attention of that State Party. Within three months after the receipt of the communication the receiving State shall afford the State which sent the communication an explanation, or any other statement in writing clarifying the matter which should include, to the extent possible and pertinent, reference to domestic procedures and remedies taken, pending, or available in the matter;

(b) If the matter is not adjusted to the satisfaction of both States Parties concerned within six months after the receipt by the receiving State of the initial communication, either State shall have the right to refer the matter to the Committee, by notice given to the Committee and to the other State;

(c) The Committee shall deal with a matter referred to it only after it has ascertained that all available domestic remedies have been invoked and exhausted in the matter, in conformity with the generally recognised principles of international law. This shall not be the rule where the application of the remedies is unreasonably prolonged;

(d) The Committee shall hold closed meetings when examining communications under this article.

(e) Subject to the provisions of subparagraph (c), the Committee shall make available its good offices to the States Parties concerned with a view to a friendly solution of the matter on the basis of respect for human rights and fundamental freedoms as recognised in the present Covenant;

(f) In any matter referred to it, the Committee may call upon the States Parties concerned, referred to in subparagraph (b), to supply any relevant information;

(g) The States Parties concerned, referred to in subparagraph (b), shall have the right to be represented when the matter is being considered in the Committee and to make submissions orally and/or in writing;

(h) The Committee shall, within twelve months after the date of receipt of notice under subparagraph (b), submit a report:

(i) If a solution within the terms of subparagraph (e) is reached, the Committee shall confine its report to a brief statement of facts and of the solution reached;

(ii) If a solution within the terms of subparagraph (e) is not reached, the Committee shall confine its report to a brief statement of the facts; the written submissions and record of the oral submissions made by the States Parties concerned shall be attached to the report.

In every matter, the report shall be communicated to the State Parties concerned.

2. The provisions of this article shall come into force when ten State Parties to the present Covenant have made declarations under paragraph 1 of this article. Such declarations shall be deposited by the States Parties with the Secretary-General of the United Nations, who shall transmit copies thereof to the other States Parties. A declaration may be withdrawn at any time by notification to the Secretary-General. Such a withdrawal shall not prejudice the consideration of any matter which is the subject of a communication already transmitted under this article; no further communication by any State Party shall be received after the notification of withdrawal of the declaration has been received by the Secretary General, unless the State Party concerned has made a new declaration.

Article 42

1. (a) If a matter referred to the Committee in accordance with Article 41 is not resolved to the satisfaction of the States Parties concerned, the Committee may, with he prior consent of the States Parties concerned, appoint an *ad hoc* Conciliation Commission (hereinafter referred to as the Commission). The good offices of the Commission shall be made available to the States Parties concerned with a view to an amicable solution of the matter on the basis of respect for the present Covenant;

(b) The Commission shall consist of five persons acceptable to the States Parties concerned. If the States Parties concerned fail to reach agreement within three months on all or part of the composition of the Commission, the members of the Commission concerning whom no agreement has been reached shall be elected by secret ballot by a two-thirds majority vote of the Committee from among its members.

2. The members of the Commission shall serve in their personal

capacity. They shall not be nationals of the States Parties concerned, or of a State not Party to the present Covenant, or of a State Party which has not made a declaration under Article 41.

3. The Commission shall elect its own Chairman and adopt its own rules of procedure.

4. The meetings of the Commission shall normally be held at the Headquarters of the United Nations or at the United Nations Office at Geneva. However, they may be held at such other convenient places as the Commission may determine in consultation with the Secretary-General of the United Nations and the States Parties concerned.

5. The secretariat provided in accordance with Article 36 shall also service the commissions appointed under this article.

6. The information received and collected by the Committee shall be made available to the Commission and the Commission may call upon the States Parties concerned to supply any other relevant information.

7. When the Commission has fully considered the matter, but in any event not later than twelve months after having been seized of the matter, it shall submit to the Chairman of the Committee a report for communication to the State Parties concerned.

(a) If the Commission is unable to complete its consideration of the matter within twelve months, it shall confine its report to a brief statement of the status of its consideration of the matter;

(b) If an amicable solution to the matter on the basis of respect for human rights as recognised in the present Covenant is reached, the Commssion shall confine its report to a brief statement of the facts and of the solution reached;

(c) If a solution within the terms of subparagraph (b) is not reached, the Commission report shall embody its findings on all questions of fact relevant to the issues between the States Parties concerned, and its views on the possibilities of an amicable solution of the matter. This report shall also contain the written submissions and a record of the oral submissions made by the States Parties concerned.

(d) If the Commission's report is submitted under subparagraph (c), the States Parties concerned shall, within three months of the receipt of the report, notify the Chairman of the Committee whether or not they accept the contents of the report of the Commission.

8. The provisions of this article are without prejudice to the responsibilities of the Committee under Article 41.

9. The States Parties concerned shall share equally all the expenses of the members of the Commission in accordance with estimates to be provided by the Secretary-General of the United Nations.

10. The Secretary-General of the United Nations shall be empowered to pay the expenses of the members of the Commission, if necessary, before reimbursement by the States Parties concerned, in accordance with paragraph 9 of this article.

Article 43

The members of the Committee, and of the *ad hoc* conciliation commissions which may be appointed under Article 42, shall be entitled to the facilities, privileges, and immunities of experts on mission for the United Nations as laid down in the relevant sections of the Convention on the Privileges and Immunities of the United Nations.

Article 44

The provisions of the implementation of the present Covenant shall apply without prejudice to the procedures prescribed in the field of human rights by or under the constituent instruments and the conventions of the United Nations and of the specialized agencies and shall not prevent the States Parties to the present Covenant from having recourse to other procedures for settling a dispute in accordance with general or special international agreements in force between them.

Article 45

The Committee shall submit to the General Assembly of the United Nations, through the Economic and Social Council, an annual report on its activities.

Article 46

Nothing in the present Covenant shall be interpreted as impairing the provisions of the Charter of the United Nations and of the Constitutions of the specialised agencies which define the respective responsibilities of the various organs of the United Nations and of the specialized agencies in regard to the matters dealt with in the present Covenant.

Article 47

Nothing in the present Covenant shall be interpreted as impairing the inherent right of all peoples to enjoy and utilise full and freely their natural wealth and resources.

Article 48

1. The present Covenant is open for signature by any State Member of the United Nations or member of any of its specialised agencies, by any State Party to the Statute of the International Court of Justice, and by any other State which has been invited by the General Assembly of the United Nations to become a Party to the present Covenant.

2. The present Covenant is subject to ratification. Instruments of ratification shall be deposited with the Secretary-General of the United Nations.

3. The present Covenant shall be open to accession by any State referred to in paragraph 1 of this article.

4. Accession shall be effected by the deposit of an instrument of accession with the Secretary-General of the United Nations.

5. The Secretary-General of the United Nations shall inform all States which have signed this Covenant or acceded to it of the deposit of each instrument of ratification or accession.

Article 49

1. The present Covenant shall enter into force three months after the date of the deposit with the Secretary-General of the United Nations of the thirty-fifth instrument of ratification or instrument of accession.

2. For each State ratifying the present Covenant or acceding to it after the deposit of the thirty-fifth instrument of ratification or instrument of accession, the present Covenant shall enter into force three months after the date of the deposit of its own instrument of ratification or instrument of accession.

Article 50

The provisions of the present Covenant shall extend to all parts of federal States without any limitations or exceptions.

Article 51

1. Any State Party to the present Covenant may propose an amendment and file it with the Secretary-General of the United Nations. The Secretary-General of the United Nations shall thereupon communicate any proposed amendments to the States Parties to the present Covenant with a request that they notify him whether they favour a conference of States Parties for the purpose of considering and voting upon the proposals. In the event that at least one third of the States Parties favours such a conference, the Secretary-General shall convene the conference under the auspices of the United Nations. Any amendment adopted by a majority of the States Parties present and voting at the conference shall be submitted to the General Assembly of the United Nations for approval.

2. Amendments shall come into force when they have been approved by the General Assembly of the United Nations and accepted by a two-thirds majority of the States Parties to the present Covenant in accordance with their respective constitutional processes.

3. When amendments come into force, they shall be binding on those States Parties which have accepted them, other States Parties still being bound by the provisions of the present Covenant and any earlier amendment which they have accepted.

Article 52

Irrespective of the notifications made under article 48, paragraph 5, the Secretary-General of the United Nations shall inform all States referred to in paragraph 1 of the same article of the following particulars:

(a) Signatures, ratifications and accessions under Article 48;
(b) The date of the entry into force of the present Covenant under Article 49 and the date of the entry into force of any amendments under Article 51.

Article 53

1. The present Covenant, of which the Chinese, English, French, Russian and Spanish texts are equally authentic, shall be deposited in the archives of the United Nations.

2. The Secretary-General of the United Nations shall transmit certified copies of the present Covenant to all States referred to in Article 48.

INTERNATIONAL COVENANT ON ECONOMIC, SOCIAL AND CULTURAL RIGHTS, 1966

Adopted and opened for signature, ratification and accession by General Assembly resolution 2200 A (XXI) of 16 December 1966

Entry into Force: 3 January 1976, in Accordance with Article 27

Preamble

THE STATES PARTIES TO THE PRESENT COVENANT,

Considering that, in accordance with the principles proclaimed in the Charter of the United Nations, recognition of the inherent dignity and of the equal and inalienable rights of all members of the human family is the foundation of freedom, justice and peace in the world,

Recognizing that these rights derive from the inherent dignity of the human person,

Recognizing that, in accordance with the Universal Declaration of Human Rights, the ideal of free human beings enjoying freedom from fear and want can only be achieved if conditions are created whereby everyone may enjoy his economic, social and cultural rights, as well as his civil and political rights,

Considering the obligation of State under the Charter of the United Nations to promote universal respect for, and observance of, human rights and freedoms,

Realising that the individual, having duties to other individuals and to the community to which he belongs is under a responsibility to strive for the promotion and observance of the rights recognised in the present Covenant,

Agree upon the following articles:

Article 1

1. All peoples have the right of self-determination. By virtue of that right they freely determine their political status and freely pursue their economic, social and cultural development.

2. All peoples may, for their own ends, freely dispose of their natural wealth and resources without prejudice to any obligations arising out of international economic cooperation, based upon the principle of mutual benefit, and international law. In no case may a people be deprived of its own means of subsistence.

3. The States Parties to the present Covenant, including those having responsibility for the administration of Non-Self-Governing and Trust Territories, shall promote the realisation of the right of self-determination, and shall respect that right, in conformity with the provisions of the Charter of the United Nations.

Article 2

1. Each State Party to the present Covenant undertakes to take steps, individually and through international assistance and cooperation, especially economic and technical, to the maximum of its available resources, with a view to achieving progressively the full realisation of the rights recognised in the present Covenant by all appropriate means, including particularly the adoption of legislative measures.

2. The State Parties to the Covenant undertake to guarantee that the rights enunciated in the present Covenant will be exercised without discrimination of any kind as to race, colour, sex, language, religion, political or other opinion, national or social origin, property, birth or other status.

3. Developing countries, with due regard to human rights and their national economy, may determine to what extent they would guarantee the economic rights recognised in the present Covenant, to non-nationals.

Article 3

The State Parties to the present Covenant undertake to ensure the equal right of men and women to the enjoyment of all economic, social and cultural rights set forth in the present Covenant.

Article 4

The States Parties to the present Covenant recognise that, in the enjoyment of those rights provided by the State in conformity with the present Covenant, the State may subject such rights only to such limitations as are determined by law only in so far as this may be compatible with the nature of these rights and solely for the purpose of promoting the general welfare in a democratic society.

Article 5

1. Nothing in the present Covenant may be interpreted as

implying for any State, group or person any right to engage in any activity or to perform any act aimed at the destruction of any of the rights or freedoms recognised herein, or at their limitation to a greater extent than is provided for in the present Covenant.

2. No restriction upon or derogation from any of the fundamental human rights recognised or existing in any country in virtue of law, conventions, regulations or custom shall be admitted on the pretext that the present Covenant does not recognise such rights or that it recognises them to a lesser extent.

Article 6

1. The State Parties to the present Covenant recognise the right to work, which include the right of everyone to the opportunity to gain his living by work which he freely chooses or accepts, and will take appropriate steps to safeguard this right.

2. The steps to be taken by a State Party to the present Covenant to achieve the full realisation of this right shall include technical and vocational guidance and training programmes, policies and techniques to achieve steady economic, social and cultural development and full and productive employment under conditions safeguarding fundamental political and economic freedoms to the individual.

Article 7

The State Parties to the present Covenant recognise the right of everyone to the enjoyment of just and favourable conditions of work which ensure, in particular:

(a) Remuneration which provides all workers, as a minimum, with:

 (i) Fair wages and equal remuneration for work of equal value without distinction of any kind, in particular women being guaranteed conditions of work not inferior to those enjoyed by men, with equal pay for equal work;

 (ii) A decent living for themselves and their families in accordance with the provisions of the present Covenant;

(b) Safe and healthy working conditions;

(c) Equal opportunity for everyone to be promoted in his employment to an appropriate level, subject to no consideration other than those of seniority and competence;

(d) Rest, leisure and reasonable limitation of working hours and periodic holidays with pay, as well as remuneration for public holidays.

Article 8

1. The States Parties to the present Covenant undertake to ensure:

(a) The right of everyone to form trade unions and join the trade union of his choice, subject only to the rules of the organisation concerned, for the promotion and protection of his economic and social interests. No restrictions may be placed on the exercise of this right other than those prescribed by law and which are necessary in a democratic society in the interests of national security or public order or for the protection of the rights and freedoms of others;

(b) The right of trade unions to establish national federations or confederations and the right of the latter to form or join international trade union organisations;

(c) The right of trade unions to function freely subject to no limitations other than those prescribed by law and which are necessary in democratic society in the interests of national security or public order or for the protection of the rights and freedoms of others;

(d) The right to strike, provided that it is exercised in conformity with the laws of the particular country.

2. This article shall not prevent the imposition of lawful restrictions on the exercise of these rights by members of the armed forces or of the police or of the administration of the State.

3. Nothing in this article shall authorise State Parties to the International Labour Organisation Convention of 1948 concerning Freedom of Association and Protection of the Right to Organise to take legislative measures which would prejudice, or apply the law in such a manner as would prejudice, the guarantees provided for in that Convention.

Article 9

The State Parties to the present Covenant recognise the right of everyone to social security, including social insurance.

Article 10

The State Parties to the present Covenant recognise that :

1. The widest possible protection and assistance should be accorded to the family, which is the natural and fundamental group unit of society, particularly for its establishment and while it is responsible for the care and education of dependent children. Marriage must be entered into with the free consent of the intending spouses.

2. Special protection should be accorded to mothers during a reasonable period before and after childbirth. During such period working mothers should be accorded paid leave or leave with adequate social security benefits.

3. Speical measures of protection and assistance should be taken on behalf of all children and young persons without any discrimination for persons of parentage or other conditions. Children and young persons should be protected from economic and social exploitation. Their employment in work harmful to their morals or health or dangerous to life or likely to hamper their normal development should be punishable by law. States should also set age limits below which the paid employment of child labour should be prohibited and punishable by law.

Article 11

1. The States Parties to the present Covenant recognise the right of everyone to an adequate standard of living for himself and his family, including adequate food, clothing and housing, and to the continuous improvement of living conditions. The States Parties will take appropriate steps to ensure the realisation of this right, recognising to this effect the essential importance of international cooperation based on free consent.

2. The State Parties to the present Covenant, recognising the fundamental right of everyone to be free from hunger, shall take, individually and through international cooperation the measures, including specific programmes, which are needed:

(a) To improve methods of production, conservation and distribution of food by making full use of technical and scientific knowledge, by disseminating knowledge of the principles of nutrition and by developing or reforming agrarian systems in such a way as to achieve the most efficient development and utilisation of natural resources;

(b) Taking into account the problems of both food-importing and food-exporting countries, to ensure an equitable distribution of world food supplies in relation to need.

Article 12

1. The State Parties to the present Covenant recognise the right of everyone to the enjoymemt of the highest attainable standard of physical and mental health.

2. The steps to be taken by the State Parties to the present Covenant to achieve the full realisation of this right shall include those necessary for:

(a) The provision for the reduction of the stillbirth rate and of infant mortality and for the healthy development of the child;

(b) The improvement of all aspects of environmental and industrial hygiene;

(c) The prevention, treatment and control of epidemic, endemic, occupational and other diseases;

(d) The creation of conditions which would assure ot all medical service and medical attention in the event of sickness.

Article 13

1. The State Parties to the present Covenant recognise the right of everyone to education. They agree that education shall be directed to the full development of the human personality and the sense of its dignity, and shall strengthen the respect for human rights and fundamental freedoms. They further agree that education shall enable all persons to participate effectively in a free society, promote understanding, tolerance and friendship among all nations and all racial, ethnic or religious groups, and further the acitivities of the United Nations for the maintenance of peace.

2. The States Parties to the present Covenant recognise that, with a view to achieving the full realisation of this right:

(a) Primary education shall be compulsory and available free to all;

(b) Secondary education in its different forms, including technical and vocational secondary education, shall be made generally available and accessible to all by every appropriate means, and in particular by the progressive introduction of free education;

(c) Higher education shall be made equally accessible to all, on the basis of capacity, by every appropriate means, and in particular by the progressive introduction of free education;

(d) Fundamental education shall be encouraged or intensified as far as possible for those persons who have not received or completed the whole period of their primary education;

(e) The development of a system of schools at all levels shall be actively pursued, an adequate fellowship system shall be established, and the material conditions of teaching staff shall be continuously improved.

3. The State Parties to the present Covenant undertake to have respect for the liberty of parents and, when applicable, legal guardians to choose for their children schools, other than those established by the public authorities, which conform to such minimum educational standards as may be laid down or approved by the State and to ensure the religious and moral education of their children in conformity with their own convictions.

4. No part of this article shall be construed so as to interfere with the liberty of individuals and bodies to establish and direct educational institutions, subject always to the observance of the principles set forth in paragraph 1 of this article and to the requirement that the education given in such institutions shall conform to such minimum standards as may be laid down by the State.

Article 14

Each State Party to the present Covenant which, at the time of becoming a Party, has not been able to secure in its metropolitan territory or other territories under its jurisdiction compulsory primary education, free of charge, undertakes, within two years, to work out and adopt a detailed plan of action for the progressive implementation, within a reasonable number of years, to be fixed in the plan, of the principle of compulsory education free of charge for all.

Article 15

The States Parties to the present Covenant recognise the right of everyone:

(a) To take part in cultural life;
(b) To enjoy the benefits of scientific progress and its applications;
(c) To benefit from the protection of the moral and material interests resulting from any scientific, literary or artistic production of which he is the author.

2. The steps to be taken by the State Parties to the present Covenant to achieve the full realisation of this right shall include those necessary for the conservation, the development and the diffusion of science and culture.

3. The States Parties to the present Covenant undertake to respect the freedom indispensable for scientific research and creative activity.

4. The States Parties to the present Covenant recognise the benefits to be derived from the encouragement and development of international contacts and co-operation in the scientific and cultural fields.

Article 16

1. The States Parties to the present Covenant undertake to submit in conformity with this part of the Covenant reports on the measures which they have adopted and the progress made in achieving the observance of rights recognised herein.

2. (a) All reports shall be submitted to the Secretary-General of the United Nations, who shall transmit copies to the Economic and Social Council for consideration in accordance with the provisions of the present Covenant;

(b) The Secretary-General of the United Nations shall also transmit to the specialised agencies copies of the reports, or any relevant parts therefrom, from States Parties to the present Covenant which are also members of these specialised agencies insofar as these reports, or parts therefrom, relate to any matters which fall within the responsibilities of the said agencies in accordance with their constitutional instruments.

Article 17

1. The States Parties to the present Covenant shall furnish their reports in stages, in accordance with a programme to be established by the Economic and Social Council within one year of the entry into force of present Covenant after consultation with the State Parties and the specialised agencies concerned.

2. Reports may indicate factors and difficulties affecting the degree of fulfilment of obligations under the present Covenant.

3. Where relevant information has previously been furnished to the United Nations or to any specialised agency by any State Party to the present Covenant, it will not be necessary to reproduce that information, but a precise reference to the information so furnished will suffice.

Article 18

Pursuant to its responsibilities under the Charter of the United Nations in the field of human rights and fundamental freedoms, the Economic and Social Council may make arrangements with the specialised agencies in respect of their reporting to it on the progress made in achieving the observance of the provisions of the present Covenant falling within the scope of their activities. These reports may include particulars of decisions and recommendations on such implementation adopted by their competent organs.

Article 19

The Economic and Social Council may transmit to the Commission on Human Rights for study and general recommendation or, as appropriate, for information the reports concerning human rights submitted by States in accordance with articles 16 and 17, and those concerning human rights submitted by the specialised agencies in accordance with Article 18.

Article 20

The States Parties to the present Covenant and the specialised agencies concerned may submit comments on the Economic and Social Council on any general recommendation under Article 19 or reference to such general recommendation in any report of the Commission on Human Rights or any documentation referred to therein.

Article 21

1. The Economic and Social Council may submit from time to time to the General Assembly reports with recommendations of a general nature and a summary of the information received from the States Parties to the present Covenant and the specialised agencies on the measures taken and the progress made in achieving general observance of the rights recognised in the present Covenant.

Article 22

The Economic and Social Council may bring to the attention of other organs of the United Nations, their subsidiary organs and specialised agencies concerned with furnishing technical assistance any matters arising out of the reports referred to in this part of the present Covenant which may assist such bodies in deciding, each within its field of competence, on the advisability of international measures likely to contribute to the effective progressive implementation of the present Covenant.

Article 23

The States Parties to the present Covenant agree that international action for the achievement of the rights recognised in the present Covenant includes such methods as the conclusion of conventions, the adoption of recommendations, the furnishing of technical assistance and the holding of regional meetings and technical meetings for the purpose of consultation and study organised in conjunction with the Governments concerned.

Article 24

Nothing in the present Covenant shall be interpreted as impairing the provisions of the Charter of the United Nations and of the constitutions of the specialised agencies which define the respective responsibilities of the various organs of the United Nations and of the specialised agencies in regard to the matters dealt within the present Covenant.

Article 25

Nothing in the present Covenant shall be interpreted as impairing the inherent right of all peoples to enjoy and utilise fully and freely their natural wealth and resources.

Article 26

1. The present Covenant is open for signature by any State Member of the United Nations or member of any of its specialised agencies, by any State Party to the Statute of the International Court of Justice and by any other State which has been invited by the General Assembly of the United Nations to become a party to the present Covenant.

2. The present Covenant is subject to ratification. Instruments of ratification shall be deposited with the Secretary-General of the United Nations.

3. The present Covenant shall be open to accession by any State referred to in paragraph 1 of this article.

4. Accession shall be effected by the deposit of an instrument of accession with the Secretary-General of the United Nations.

5. The Secretary-General of the United Nations shall inform all States which have signed the present Covenant or acceded to it of the deposit of each instrument of ratification or accession.

Article 27

1. The present Covenant shall enter into force three months after the date of the deposit with the Secretary-General of the United Nations of the thirty-fifth instrument of ratification or instrument of accession.

2. For each State ratifying the present Covenant or acceding to it after the deposit of the thirty-fifth instrument of ratification or instrument of accession, the present Covenant shall enter into force three months after the date of the deposit of its own instrument of ratification or instrument of accession.

Article 28

The provisions of the present Covenant shall extend to all parts of federal States without any limitations or exceptions.

Article 29

1. Any State Party to the present Covenant may propose an amendment and file it with the Secretary-General of the United Nations. The Secretary-General shall thereupon communicate any proposed amendments to the State Parties to the present Convenant

with a request that they notify him whether they favour a conference of States Parties for the purpose of considering and voting upon the proposals. In the event that at least one-third of the State Parties favour such a conference, the Secretary-General shall convene the conference under the auspices of the United Nations. Any amendment adopted by a majority of the State Parties present and voting at the conference shall be submitted to the General Assembly of the United Nations for approval.

2. Amendments shall come into force what they have been approved by the General Assembly of the United Nations and accepted by a two-thirds majority of the States Parties to the present Covenant in accordance with their respective constitutional processes.

3. When amendments come into force they shall be binding on those States Parties which have accepted them, other States Parties still being bound by the provisions of the present Covenant and any earlier amendment which they have accepted.

Article 30

Irrespective of the notification made under Article 26, Paragraph 5, the Secretary-General of the United Nations shall inform all States referred to in Paragraph 1 of the same article of the following particulars:

(a) Signatures, ratifications and accessions under Article 26;

(b) The date of the entry into force of the present Covenant under article 27 and the date of the entry into force of any amendments under Article 29.

Article 31

1. The present Covenant, of which the Chinese, English, French, Russian and Spanish texts are equally authentic, shall be deposited in the archives of the United Nations.

2. The Secretary-General of the United Nations shall transmit certified copies of the present Covenant to all States referred to in Article 26.

2

Indian Constitution and Human Rights

INDIAN NATIONAL CONGRESS—KARACHI RESOLUTION, 1931

In order to end the exploitation of the masses, political freedom must include real economic freedom of the starving millions. The Congress, therefore, declares that any constitution which may be agreed to on its behalf should provide, or enable the Swaraj Government to provide, for the following:

1. Fundamental rights of the people, including:

   (i) freedom of association and combination;
   (ii) freedom of speech and of the press;
   (iii) freedom of conscience and the free profession and practice of religion, subject to public order and morality;'
   (iv) protection of the culture, language, and scripts of the minorities;
   (v) equal rights and obligations of all citizens, without any bar on account of sex;
   (vi) no disability to attach to any citizen by reason of his or her religion, caste or creed or sex in regard to public employment, office of power or honour, and in the exercise of any trade or calling;
   (vii) equal right to all citizens in regard to public roads, wells, schools and other places of public resort;
   (viii) right to keep and bear arms in accordance with regulations and reservations made in that behalf;
   (ix) no person shall be deprived of his liberty nor shall his dwelling or property be entered, sequestered or confiscated, save in accordance with law.

2. Religious neutrality on the part of the State.

3. Adult suffrage.
4. Free primary education.
5. A living wage for industrial workers, limited hours of labour, healthy conditions of work, protection against the economic consequences of old age, sickness and unemployment.
6. Labour to be freed from serfdom or conditions bordering on serfdom.
7. Protection of woman workers, and, specially, adequate provisions for leave during maternity period.
8. Prohibition against employment of children of school going age in factories.
9. Right of labour to form unions to protect their interests with suitable machinery for settlement of disputes by arbitration.
10. Substantial reduction in agricultural rent or revenue paid by the peasantry and in case of uneconomic holdings exemption from rent for such period as may be necessary, relief being given to small zamindars wherever necessary by reason of such reduction.
11. Imposition of a progressive income tax on agricultural income above a fixed minimum.
12. A graduated inheritance tax.
13. Military expenditure to be reduced by at least one half of the present scale.
14. Expenditure and salaries in civil department to be largely reduced. No servant of the State, other than specially employed expects and the like, to be paid above a certain fixed figure which should not ordinarily exceed Rs. 500 per month.
15. Protection of indigenous cloth by exclusion of foreign cloth and foreign yarn from the country.
16. Total prohibition of intoxicating drinks and drugs.
17. No duty on salt manufactured in India.
18. Control, over exchange and currency policy so as to help Indian industries and bring relief to the masses.
19. Control by the State of key industries and ownership of mineral resources.
20. Control of usury—direct or indirect.

THE CONSTITUTION OF INDIA

Preamble

WE THE PEOPLE OF INDIA

having solemnly resolved to constitute India into a

[SOVEREIGN SOCIALIST SECULAR DEMOCRATIC REPUBLIC]

and to secure to all its citizens:

JUSTICE, social, economic and political:

LIBERTY of thought, expression, belief, faith and worship:

EQUALITY of status and of opportunity:

and to promote among them all

FRATERNITY assuming the dignity of the individual and the [unity and integrity of the Nation]:

IN OUR CONSTITUENT ASSEMBLY

this twenty-sixth day of November, 1949, do

HEREBY ADOPT, ENACT AND GIVE TO OURSELVES THIS CONSTITUTION.

FUNDAMENTAL RIGHTS, 1950

General

12. Definition. In this Part, unless the context otherwise requires, " the State" includes the Government and Parliament of India and the Government and the Legislature of each of the States and all local or other authorities within the territory of India or under the control of the Government of India.

13. Laws Inconsistent with or in Derogation of the Fundamental Rights. 1. All laws in force in the territory of India immediately before the commencement of this Constitution, in so far as they are inconsistent with the provisions of this Part, shall, to the extent of such inconsistency, be void.

2. The State shall not make any law which takes away or abridges the rights conferred by this Part and any law made in contravention of this clause shall, to the extent of the contravention, be void.

3. In this article, unless the context otherwise requires.—

(a) "law" includes any Ordinance, order, bye-law, rule regulation, notification, custom or usage having in the territory of India the force of law;

(b) "laws in force" includes laws passed or made by a Legislature or other competent authority in the territory of India before the commencement of this Constitution and not previously repealed, notwithstanding that any such law or any part thereof may not be then in operation either at all or in particular areas.

4. Nothing in this article shall apply to any amendment of this Constitution made under Article 368.

Right to Equality

14. Equality Before Law. The State shall not deny to any person equality before the law or the equal protection of the laws within the territory of India.

15. Prohibition of Discrimination on Grounds of Religion, Race, Caste, Sex or Place of Birth. 1. The State shall not discriminate against any citizen on grounds only of religion, race, caste, sex, place of birth or any of them.

2. No citizen shall, on grounds only of religion, race, caste, sex,

place of birth or any of them, be subject to any disability, liability, restriction or conditions with regard to—

(a) access to shops, public restaurants, hotels and places of public entertainment; or

(b) the use of wells, tanks, bathing ghats, roads and places of public resort maintained wholly or party out of State funds or dedicated to the use of the general public.

3. Nothing in this article shall prevent the State from making any special provision for women and children.

4. Nothing in this article or in clause (2) of Article 29 shall prevent the State from making any special provision for the advancement of any socially and educationally backward classes of citizens or for the Scheduled Castes and the Scheduled Tribes.]

16. Equality of Opportunity in Matters of Public Employment. 1. There shall be equality of opportunity for all citizens in matters relating to employment or appointment to any office under the State.

2. No citizen shall, on grounds only of religion, race, caste, sex, descent, place of birth, residence or any of them, be ineligible for, or discriminated against in respect of, any employment or office under the State.

3. Nothing in this article shall prevent Parliament from making any law prescribing, in regard to a class or classes of employment or appointment to an office [under the Government of, or any local or other authority within, a State or Union territory, any requirement as to residence within that State or Union territory] prior to such employment or appointment.

4. Nothing in this article shall prevent the State from making any provision for the reservation of appointments or posts in favour of any backward class of citizens which, in the opinion of the State, is not adequately represented in the services under the State.

5. Nothing in this article shall affect the operation of any law which provides that the incumbent of an office in connection with the affairs of any religious or denominational institution or any member of the governing body thereof shall be a person professing a particular religion or belonging to a particular denomination.

17. Abolition of Untouchability. "Untouchability" is abolished and its practice in any form is forbidden. The enforcement of any disability arising out of "Untouchability" shall be an offence punishable in accordance with law.

18. Abolition of Titles. 1. No title, not being a military or academic distinction, shall be conferred by the State.

2. No citizen of India shall accept any title from any title from any foreign State.

3. No person, who is not a citizen of India shall, while he holds any office of profit or trust under the State, accept without the consent of the President any title from any foreign State.

4. No person holding any office of profit or trust under the State shall, without the consent of the President, accept any present, emolument, or office of any kind from or under any foreign State.

Right to Freedom

19. Protection of Certain Rights Regarding Freedom of Speech, etc. 1. All citizens shall have the right—

(a) to freedom of speech and expression;
(b) to assemble peaceably and without arms;
(c) to form association or unions;
(d) to move freely throughout the territory of India;
(e) to reside and settle in any part of the territory of India; and,
(g) to practise any profession, or to carry on any occupation, trade or business.

[2. Nothing in sub-clause (a) of clause (1) shall affect the operation of any existing law, or prevent the State from making any law, insofar as such law imposes reasonable restrictions on the exercise of the right conferred by the said sub-clauses in the interests of [the sovereignty and integrity of India,] the security of the State , friendly relations with foreign States, public order, decency or morality, or in relation to contempt of court, defamation or incitement to an offence.]

3. Nothing in sub-clause (b) of the said clause shall affect the operation of any existing law insofar as it imposes, or prevent the State from making any law imposing, in the interests of [the sovereignty and integrity of India or] public order, reasonable restrictions on the exercise of the right conferred by the said sub-clause.

4. Nothing in sub-clause (c) of the said clause shall affect the operation of any existing law in so far as it imposes, or prevent the State from making any law imposing, in the interests of [the sovereignty and integrity of India or] public order or morality,

reasonable restrictions on the exercise of the right conferred by the said sub-clause.

5. Nothing in [sub-clauses (d) and (e)] of the said clause shall affect the operation of any existing law in so far as it imposes, or prevent the State from making any law imposing, reasonable restrictions on the exercise of any of the rights conferred by the said sub-clause either in the interests of the general public or for the protection of the interests of any Scheduled Tribe.

6. Nothing in sub-clause (g) of the said clause shall affect the operation of any existing law in so far as it imposes, or prevent the State from making any law imposing, in the interests of the general public, reasonable restrictions on the exercise of the rights conferred by the said sub-clause, and, in particular, [nothing in the said sub-clause shall affect the operation of any existing law in so far as it relates to, or prevent the State from making any law relating to.—

(i) the professional or technical qualifications necessary for practising any profession or carrying on any occupation, trade or business, or

(ii) the carrying on by the State, or by a corporation owned or controlled by the State, of any trade, business, industry or service, whether to the exclusion, complete or partial, of citizens or otherwise].

20. Protection in Respect of Conviction for Offences. 1. No person shall be convicted of any offence except for violation of a law in force at the time of the commission of the act charged as an offence, nor be subjected to a penalty greater than that which might have been inflicted under the laws in force at the time of the commission of the offence.

2. No person shall be prosecuted and punished for the same offence more than once.

3. No person accused of any offence shall be compelled to be a witness against himself.

21. Protection of Life and Personal Liberty. No person shall be deprived of his life or personal liberty except according to procedure established by law.

22. Protection Against Arrest and Detention in Certain Cases. 1. No person who is arrested shall be detained in custody without being informed, as soon as may be, of the grounds for such arrest nor shall he be denied the right to consult, and to be defended by, a legal practitioner of his choice.

2. Every person who is arrested and detained in custody shall be produced before the nearest magistrate within a period of twenty-four hours of such arrest excluding the time necessary for the journey from the place of arrest to the court of the magistrate and no such person shall be detained in custody beyond the said period without the authority of a magistrate.

3. Nothing in clauses (1) and (2) shall apply—

(a) to any person who for the time being is an enemy alien; or

(b) to any person who is arrested or detained under any law providing for preventive detention.

4. No law providing for preventive detention shall authorise the detention of a person for a longer period than three months unless—

(a) an Advisory Board consisting of persons who are, or have been, or are qualified to be appointed as, Judges of a High Court has reported before the expiration of the said period of three months that there is in its opinion sufficient cause for such detention:

Provided that nothing in this sub-clause shall authorise the detention of any person beyond the maximum period prescribed by any law made by Parliament under sub-clause (b) of clause (7); or

(b) such person is detained in accordance with the provisions of any law made by Parliament under sub-clauses (a) and (b) of clause (7).

5. When any person is detained in pursuance of an order made under any law providing for preventive detention, the authority making the order shall, as soon as may be, communicate to such person the grounds on which the order has been made and shall afford him the earliest opportunity of making a representation against the order.

6. Nothing in clause (5) shall require the authority making any such order as is referred to in that clause to disclose facts which such authority considers to be against the public interest to disclose.

7. Parliament may by law prescribe—

(a) the circumstances under which, and the class or classes of cases in which, a person may be detained for a period longer than three months under any law providing for preventive detention without obtaining the opinion of an Advisory Board in accordance with the provisions of sub-clause (a) of clause (4):

(b) the maximum period for which any person may in any class or classes of cases be detained under any law providing for preventive detention; and

(c) the procedure to be followed by an Advisory Board in an inquiry under sub-clause (a) of clause (4).

Right Against Exploitation

23. ***Prohibition of Traffic in Human Beings and Forced Labour.*** 1. Traffic in human beings and *begar* and other similar forms of forced labour are prohibited and any contravention of this provision shall be an offence punishable in accordance with law.

2. Nothing in this article shall prevent the State from imposing compulsory service for public purposes, and in imposing such service the State shall not make any discrimination on grounds only of religion, race, caste or class or any of them.

24. Prohibition of Employment of Children in Factories, etc. No child below the age of fourteen years shall be employed to work in any factory or mine or engaged in any other hazardous employment.

Right to Freedom of Religion

25. Freedom of Conscience and Free Profession, Practice and Propagation of Religion. 1. Subjcct to public order, morality and health and to the other provisions of this Part, all persons are equally entitled to freedom o. conscience and the right freely to profess, practise and propagate religion.

2. Nothing in this article shall affect the operation of any existing law or prevent the State from making any law—

(a) regulating or restricting any economic, financial, political or other secular activity which may be associated with religious practice;

(b) providing for social welfare and reform or the throwing open of Hindu religious institutions of a public character to all classes and sections of Hindus.

Explanation I.—The wearing and carrying of *kirpans* shall be deemed to be included in the profession of the Sikh religion.

Explanation II.—In sub-clause (b) of clause (2), the reference to Hindus shall be construed as including a reference to persons professing the Sikh, Jaina or Buddhist religion, and the reference to Hindu religious institutions shall be construed accordingly.

26. Freedom to Manage Religious Affairs. Subject to public order, morality and health, every religious denomination or any section thereof shall have the right—

(a) to establish and maintain institutions for religious and charitable purpose;
(b) to manage its own affairs in matters of religion;
(c) to own and acquire movable and immovable property; and
(d) to administer such property in accordance with law.

27. Freedom as to Payment of Taxes for Promotion of any Particular Religion. No person shall be compelled to pay any taxes, the proceeds of which are specifically appropriated in payment of expenses for the promotion or maintenance of any particular religion or religious denomination.

28. Freedom as to Attendance at Religious Instruction or Religious Worship in Certain Educational Institutions. 1. No religious instruction shall be provided in any educational institution wholly maintained out of State funds.

2. Nothing in clause (1) shall apply to an educational institutions which is administered by the State but has been established under any endowment or trust which requires that religious instruction shall be imparted in such institution.

3. No person attending any educational institution recognised by the State or receiving aid out of State funds shall be required to take part in any religious instruction that may be imparted in such institution or to attend any religious worship that may be conducted in such institution or in any premises attached thereto unless such person or, if such person is a minor, his guardian has given his consent thereto.

Cultural and Educational Rights

29. Protection of Interests of Minorities. 1. Any section of the citizens residing in the territory of India or any part thereof having a distinct language, script or culture of its own shall have the right to conserve the same.

2. No citizen shall be denied admission into any educational institution maintained by the State or receiving aid out of State funds on grounds only of religion, race, caste, language or any of them.

30. Right of Minorities to Establish and Administer Educational Institutions. 1. All minorities, whether based on religion or language, shall have the right to establish and administer educational institutions of their choice.

[(1A) In making any law providing for the compulsory acquisition of any property of an educational institution established and administered by a minority, referred to in clause (1), the State shall ensure that the amount fixed by or determined under such law for the acquisition of such property is such as would not restrict or abrogate the right guaranteed under that clause.]

2. The State shall not, in granting aid to educational institutions, discriminate against any educational institution on the ground that it is under the management of a minority, whether based on religion or language.

31. *[Compulsory acquisition of property] Rep. by the Constitution (Forty-fourth Amendment) Act, 1978,* s. 6 (w.e.f. 20-6-1979).

[Saving of Certain Laws]

[31A. Saving of Laws Providing for Acquisition of Estates, etc. [(1) Notwithstanding anything contained in Article 13, no law providing for—

(a) the acquisition by the State of any estate or of any right therein or the extinguishment or modification of any such rights, or
(b) the taking over of the management of any property by the State for a limited period either in the public interest or in order to secure the proper management of the property, or
(c) the amalgamation of two or more corporations either in the public interest or in order to secure the proper management of any of the corporations, or
(d) the extinguishment or modification of any rights of managing agents, secretaries and treasurers, managing directors, directors or mangers of corporations, or of any voting rights of shareholders thereof, or

(e) the extinguishment or modification of any rights accruing by virtue of any agreement, lease or licence for the purpose of searching for, or winning, any mineral or mineral oil, or the premature termination of cancellation of any such agreement, lease or licence.

shall be deemed to be void on the ground that it is consistent with, or takes away or abridges any of the rights conferred by [Article 14 or Article 19]:

Provided that where such law is a law made by the Legislature of a State, the provisions of this article shall not apply thereto unless such law, having been reserved for the consideration of the President, has received his assent:]

[Provided further that where any law makes any provision for the acquisition by the State of any estate and where any land comprised therein is held by a person under his personal cultivation, it shall not be lawful for the State to acquire any portion of such land as is within the ceiling limit applicable to him under any law for the time being in force or any building or structure standing, thereon or appurtenant thereto, unless the law relating to the acquisition of such land, building or structure, provides for payment of compensation at a rate which shall not be less than the market value thereof.]

(2) In this article—

[(a) the expression "estate" shall, in relation to any local area, have the same meaning as that expression or its local equivalent has in the existing law relating to land tenures in force in that area and shall also include—

(i) any *jagir*, *inam* or *muafi* or other similar grant and in the States of [Tamil Nadu] and Kerala, any *janman* right;
(ii) any land held under ryotwari settlement;
(iii) any land held or let for purposes of agriculture or for purposes ancillary thereto, including waste land, forest land, land for pasture or sites of buildings and other structures occupied by cultivators of land, agricultural labourers and village artisans;]

(b) the expression "rights", in relation to an estate, shall include any rights vesting in proprietor, sub-proprietor, under-proprietor, tenure-holder, *[raiyat, under-raiyat]* or other intermediary and any rights or privileges in respect of land revenue.]

[31B. Validation of Certain Acts and Regulations. Without prejudice to the generality of the provisions contained in Article 31 A. None of the Acts and Regulations specified in the Ninth Schedule nor any of the provisions thereof shall be deemed to be void, or ever to have become void, on the ground that such Act, Regulation or provision is inconsistent with, or takes away or abridge any of the rights conferred by, any provisions of this Part, and notwithstanding any judgment, decree or order of any court or tribunal to the contrary, each of the said Acts and Regulations shall, subject to the power of any competent Legislature to repeal or amend it, continue in force.]

[31C. Saving of Laws Giving Effect to Certain Directive Principles. Notwithstanding anything contained in Article 13, no law giving effect to the policy of the State towards securing [all or any of the principles laid down in Part IV] shall be deemed to be void on the ground that it is inconsistent with, or takes away or abridges any of the rights conferred by [Article 14 or Article 19]; *and no law containing a declaration that it is for giving effect to such policy shall be called in question in any court on the ground that it does not give effect to such policy:*

Provided that where such law is made by the Legislature of a State, lthe provisions of this article shall not apply thereto unless such law, having been reserved for the consideration of the President, had received his assent.]

31D. [*Saving of laws in respect of anti-national activities.*] *Rep. by the Constitution (Forty-third Amendment) Act,* 1977. s. 2 (w.e.f. 13-4-1978).

Right to Constitutional Remedies

32. Remedies for Enforcement of Rights Conferred by This Part. 1. The right to move the Supreme Court by appropriate proceedings for the enforcement of the rights conferred by this Part is guaranteed.

2. The Supreme Court shall have power to issue directions or orders or writs, including writs in the nature of *habeas corpus, mandamus, prohibition, quo warranto* and *certiorari*, whichever may be appropriate, for the enforcement of any of the rights conferred by this part.

3. Without prejudice to the powers conferred on the Supreme Court by clauses (1) and (2), Parliament may by law empower any

other court to exercise within the local limits of its jurisdiction all or any of the powers exercisable by the Supreme Court under clause (2).

4. The right guaranteed by this article shall not be suspended except as otherwise provided for by this Constitution.

32.A*[Constitutional validity of State laws not to be considered in proceedings under Article 32.] Rep. by the Constitution (Forty-third Amendment)* Act, 1977, s. 3 (w.e.f. 13-4-1978).

[33. Power of Parliament to Modify the Rights Conferred by this Part in Their Application to Forces, etc. Parliament may, by law, determine to what extent any of the rights conferred by this Part shall, in their application to—

(a) the members of the Armed Forces; or

(b) the members of the Forces charged with the maintenance of public order; or

(c) persons employed in any bureau or other organisation established by the State for purposes of intelligence or counter-intelligence; or

(d) persons employed in, or in connection with, the telecommunications system set up for the purposes of any Force, bureau or organisation referred to in clauses (a) to (c).

be restricted or abrogated so as to ensure the proper discharge of their duties and the maintenance of discipline among them.]

34. Restriction on Rights Conferred by this Part While Martial Law is in Force in Any Area. Notwithstanding anything in the foregoing provisions of this Part, Parliament may by law indemnify any person in the service of the union or of a State or any other person in respect of any act done by him in connection with the maintenance or restoration of order in any area within the territory of India where martial law was in force or validate any sentence passed, punishment inflicted, forfeiture ordered or other act done under martial law in such area.

35. Legislation to Give Effect to the Provisions of This Part—*Notwithstanding anything in this Consitution*—

(a) Parliament shall have, and the Legislature of a State shall not have, power to make laws—

 (i) with respect to any of the matters which under clause (3) of Article 16, clause (3) of Article 32, Article 33 and Article 34 may be provided for by law made by Parliament; and

(ii) for prescribing punishment for those acts which are declared to be offences under this Part;

and parliament shall, as soon as may be after the commencement of this Constitution, make laws for prescribing punishment for the acts referred to in sub-clause (ii);

(b) any law in force immediately before the commencement of this Constitution in the territory of India with respect to any of the matters referred to in sub-clause (i) of clause (a) or providing for punishment for any act referred to in sub-clause (ii) of that clause shall, subject to the terms thereof and to any adaptations and modifications that may be made therein under Article 372, continue in force until altered or repealed or amended by Parliament

Explanation.—In this article, the expression "law in force" has the same meaning as in Article 372.

DIRECTIVE PRINCIPLES OF STATE POLICY, 1950

36. Definition. In this part, unless the context otherwise requires, "the State" has the same meaning as in Part III.

37. Application of the Principles Contained in This Part. The provisions contained in this Part shall not be enforceable by any court, but the principles therein laid down are nevertheless fundamental in the governance of the country and it shall be the duty of the State to apply these principles in making laws.

38. State to Secure a Social Order for the Promotion of Welfare of the People. 1. The State shall strive to promote the welfare of the people by securing and protecting as effectively as it may a social order in which justice, social, economic and political, shall inform all the institutions of the national life.

[2. The State shall, in particular, strive to minimise the inequalities in income, and endeavour to eliminate inequalities in status, facilities and opportunities, not only amongst individuals but also amongst groups of people residing in different areas or engaged in different vocations.]

39. Certain Principles of Policy to be Followed by the State. The State shall, in particular, direct its policy towards securing—

(a) that the citizens, men and women equally, have the right to an adequate means of livelihood;

(b) that the ownership and control of the material resources of the community are so distributed as best to subserve the common good;

(c) that the operation of the economic system does not result in the concentration of wealth and means of production to the common detriment;

(d) that there is equal pay for equal work for both men and women;

(e) that the health and strength of workers, men and women, and the tender age of children are not abused and that citizens are not forced by economic necessity to enter avocations unsuited to their age or strength;

[(f) that children are given opportunities and facilities to develop in a healthy manner and in conditions of freedom and dignity and that childhood and youth are protected against exploitation and against moral and material abandonment.]

39A. Equal Justice and Free Legal Aid. The State shall secure that the operation of the legal system promotes justice, on the basis of equal opportunity, and shall, in particular. provide free legal aid, by suitable legislation or schemes or in any other way, to ensure that opportunities for securing justice are not denied to any citizen by reason of economic or other disabilities.]

40. Organisation of Village Panchayats. The State shall take steps to organise village panchayat and endow them with such powers and authority as may be necessary to enable them to function as units of self-government.

41. Right to Work, to Education and to Public Assistance in Certain Cases. The State shall, within the limits of its economic capacity and development, make effective provision for securing the right to work, to education and to public assistance in cases of unemployment, old age, sickness and to public assistance in cases of unemployment, old age, sickness and disablement, and in other cases of undeserved want.

42. Provision for Just and Human Conditions of Work and Maternity Relief. The State shall make provision for securing just and humane conditions of work and for maternity relief.

43. Living Wage, etc., for Workers. The State shall endeavour to secure by suitable legislation or economic organisation or in any other way, to all workers, agricultural, industrial or otherwise, work, a living wage, conditions of work ensuring a decent standard of life and full enjoyment of leisure and social and cultural opportunities and, in particular, the State shall endeavour to promote cottage industries on an individual or co-operative basis in rural areas.

[43A. Participation of Workers in Management of Industries. The State shall take steps, by suitable legislation or in any other way, to secure the participation of workers in the management of undertakings, establishments or other organisations engaged in any industry.]

44. Uniform Civil Code for the Citizens. The State shall endeavour to secure for the citizens a uniform civil code throughout the territory of India.

45. Provision for Free and Compulsory E ducation for Children. The State shall endeavour to provide, within a period of ten years from the commencement of this Constitution, for free and compulsory education for all children until they complete the age of fourteen years.

46. Promotion of Educational and Economic Interests of Scheduled Castes, Scheduled Tribes and Other Weaker Sections. The State shall promote with special care the educational and economic interests of the weaker sections of the people, and, in particular, of the Scheduled Castes and the Scheduled Tribes, and shall protect them from social injustice and all forms of exploitation.

47. Duty of the State to Raise the Level of Nutrition and the Standard of Living and to Improve Public Health. The State shall regard the raising of the level of nutrition and the standard of living of its people and the improvement of public health as among its primary duties and, in particular, the State shall endeavour to bring about prohibition of the consumption except for medicinal purposes of intoxicating drinks and of drugs which are injurious to health.

48. Organisation of Agriculture and Animal Husbandry. The State shall endeavour to organise agriculture and animal husbandry on modern and scientific lines and shall, in particular, take steps for preserving and improving the breeds, and prohibiting the slaughter, of cows and calves and other milch and draught cattle.

[***48A. Protection and Improvement of Environment and Safeguarding of Forests and Wildlife.*** The State shall endeavour to protect and improve the environment and to safeguard the forests and wild life of the country.]

49. Protection of Monuments and Places and Objects of National Importance. It shall be the obligation of the State to protect every monument or place or object of artistic or historic interest, [declared by or under law made by Parliament] to be of national importance, from spoilation, disfigurement, destruction, removal, disposal or export, as the case may be.

50. Separation of Judiciary from Executive. The State shall take steps to separate the judiciary from the executive in the public services of the State.

51. Promotion of International Peace and Security. The State shall endeavour to—

(a) promote international peace and security;
(b) maintain just and honourable relations between nations;
(c) foster respect for international law and treaty obligations in the dealings of organised peoples with one another; and
(d) encourage settlement of international disputes by arbitration.

FUNDAMENTAL DUTIES

51A. Fundamental Duties. It shall be the duty of every citizen of India—

(a) to abide by the Consitution and respect its ideals and institutions, the National Flag and the National Anthem;
(b) to cherish and follow the noble ideals which inspired our national struggle for freedom;
(c) to uphold and protect the sovereignty, unity and integrity of India;
(d) to defend the country and render national service when called upon to do so;
(e) to promote harmony and the spirit of common brotherhood amongst all the people of India transcending religious, linguistic and regional or sectional diversities; to renounce practices derogatory to the dignity of women;
(f) to value and preserve the right heritage of our composite culture;
(g) to protect and improve the natural environment including forests, lakes, rivers and wild life, and to have compassion for living creatures;
(h) to develop the scientific temper, humanism and the spirit of inquiry and reform;
(i) to safeguard public property and to abjure violence;
(j) to strive towards excellence in all spheres of individual and collective activity so that the nation constantly rises to higher levels of endeavour and achievement.

CONSTITUTION OF INDIA

(Extracts)

5. *Citizenship at the Commencement of the Constitution.* At the commencement of this Constitution, every person, who has his domicile in the territory of India and—

(a) who was born in the territory of India; or

(b) either of whose parents was born in the territory of India; or

(c) who has been ordinarily resident in the territory of India for not less than five years immediately preceding such commencement, shall be a citizen of India.

6. *Rights of Citizenship of Certain Persons who have Migrated to India from Pakistan.* Notwithstanding anything in Article 5, a person who has migrated to the territory of India from the territory now included in Pakistan shall be deemed to be a citizen of India at the commencement of this Constitution if—

(a) he or either of his parents or any of his grand-parents was born in India as defined in the Government of India Act, 1935 (as originally enacted); and

(b) (i) in the case, where such a person has so migrated, before the nineteenth day of July 1948, he has been ordinarily resident in the territory of India since the date of his migration, or

(ii) in the case, where such person has so migrated on or after the nineteenth day of July 1948, he has been registered as a citizen of India by an officer appointed in that behalf by the Government of the Dominion of India on an application made by him therefor to such officer before the commencement of this Constitution in the form and manner prescribed by that Government:

Provided that no person shall be so registered unless he has been resident in the territory of India for at least six months immediately preceding the date of his application.

7. *Rights of Citizenship of Certain Migrants to Pakistan.* Notwithstanding anything in Articles 5 and 6, a person who has after the first day of March 1947, migrated from the territory of India to the territory now included in Pakistan shall not be deemed to be a citizen of India:

Provided that nothing in this Article shall apply to a person who, after having so migrated to the territory now included in Pakistan, has returned to the territory of India under a permit for resettlement of permanent return issued by or under the authority of any law and every such person shall for the purposes of clause (b) of Article 6 be deemed to have migrated to the territory of India after nineteenth day of July, 1948.

8. Rights of Citizenship of Certain Persons of Indian Origin Residing Outside India. Notwithstanding anything in Article 5, any person who or either of whose parents or any of whose grandparents was born in India as defined in the Government of India Act, 1935, (as originally enacted) and who is ordinarily residing in any country outside India as so defined shall be deemed to be a citizen of India if he has been registered as a citizen of India by the diplomatic or consular representative of India in the country where he is for the time being residing on an application made by him therefor to such diplomatic or consular representative whether or after the commencement of this Constitution, in the form and manner prescribed by the Government of the Dominion of India or the Government of India.

9. Persons Voluntarily Acquiring Citizenship of a Foreign State not to be Citizens. No person shall be a citizen of India by virtue of Article 5, or be deemed to be a citizen of India by virtue of Article 6 and Article 8, if he has voluntarily acquired the citizenship of any foreign State.

10. Continuance of the Rights of Citizenship. Every person who is or is deemed to be a citizen of India under any of the foregoing provisions of this Part shall, subject to the provisions of any law that may be made by Parliament, continue to be such citizen.

11. Parliament to Regulate the Right of Citizenship by Law. Nothing in the foregoing provisions of this Part shall derogate from the power of Parliament to make any provision with respect to the acquisition and termination of citizenship and all other matters relating to citizenship.

12. Definition. In this Part, unless the context otherwise requires, "the State" includes the Government and Parliament of India and the Government and the Legislature of each of the States and all local or other authorities within the territory of India or under the control of the Government of India.

13. Laws Inconsistent with or in Derogation of the Fundamental Rights. 1. All laws in force in the territory of India immediately before the commencement of this Constitution, in so far as they are inconsistent with the provisions of this Part, shall, to the extent of such inconsistency, be void.

2. The State shall not make any law which takes away or abridge the rights conferred by this Part and any law made in contravention of this clause shall, to the extent of the contravention, be void.

3. In this Article, unless the context otherwise requires,—

(a) "law" includes any ordinance, order, by-law, rule, regulation, notification, custom or usage having in the territory of India, the force of law;

(b) "laws in force" includes laws passed or made by a Legislature or other competent authority in the territory of India before the commencement of this Constitution and not previously repealed, notwithstanding that any such law or any part thereof may not be then in operation either at all or in particular areas.

4. Nothing in this Article shall apply to any amendment of this Constitution made under Article 368.

15. Prohibition of Discrimination on Grounds of Religion, Race, Caste, Sex or Place of Birth. 1.The State shall not discriminate against any citizen on grounds only of religion, race, caste, sex, place of birth or any of them.

2. No citizen shall, on grounds only of religion, race, caste, sex, place of birth or any of them, be subject to any disability, liability, restriction or condition with regard to—

(a) access to shops, public restaurants, hotels and places of public entertainment; or

(b) the use of wells, tanks, bathing *ghats,* roads and places of public resort maintained wholly or partly out of State funds or dedicated to the use of the general public.

3. Nothing in this Article shall prevent the State from making any special provision for women and children.

4. Nothing in this Article or in clause (2) of Article 29 shall prevent the State from making any special provision for the

advancement of any socially and educationally backward classes of citizens or for the Scheduled Castes and the Scheduled Tribes.

16. Equality of Opportunity in Matters of Public Employment. 1. There shall be equality of opportunity for all citizens in matters relating to employment or appointment to any office under the State.

2. No citizen shall, on grounds only of religion, race, caste, sex, descent, place of birth, residence or any of them, be ineligible for, or discriminated against in respect of, any employment or office under the State.

3. Nothing in this Article shall prevent Parliament from making any law prescribing, in regard to a class or classes of employment or appointment to an office, under the Government of, or any local or other authority within a State or Union Territory, any requirement as residence within that State or Union Territory, prior to such employment or appointment.

4. Nothing in this Article shall prevent the State from making any provision for the reservation of appointments or posts in favour of any Backward Class of citizens which, in the opinion of the State, is not adequately represented in the services under the State.

4-A. Nothing in this Article shall prevent the State from making any provision for reservation in matters of promotion to any class or classes of posts in the service under the State in favour of the Scheduled Castes and the Scheduled Tribes which, in the opinion of the State, are not adequately represented in the services under the State.

5. Nothing in this Article shall affect the operation of any law which provides that the incumbent of an office in connection with the affairs of any religious or denominational institution or any member of the governing body thereof, shall be a person professing a particular religion or belonging to a particular denomination.

17. Abolition of Untouchability. "Untouchability" is abolished and its practice in any form is forbidden. The enforcement of any disability arising out of 'untouchability' shall be an offence punishable in accordance with law.

18. Abolition of Titles. 1. No title, not being a military or academic distinction, shall be conferred by the State.

2. No citizen of India shall accept any title from any foreign States.

3. No person, who is not a citizen of India shall, while he holds

any office of profit or trust under the State, accept without the consent of the President any title from any foreign State.

4. No person holding any office of profit or trust under the State shall without the consent of the President, accept any present, emolument, or office of any kind from or under any foreign State.

19. Protection of Certain Rights Regarding Freedom of Speech, etc. 1. All citizens shall have the right—

(a) to freedom of speech of expression;
(b) to assemble peaceably and without arms;
(c) to form associations of unions;
(d) to move freely throughout the territory of India;
(e) to reside and settle in any part of the territory of India; and
(f) [Omitted by Consitution (Forty-fifth Amendment) Act, 1978, Section 2 (w.e.f. 20-6-1979)].
(g) to practise any profession, or to carry on any occupation, trade or business.

2. Nothing in sub-clause (a) of clause (1) shall affect the operation of any existing law, or prevent the State from making any law, in so far as such law imposes reasonable restrictions on the exercise of the right conferred by the said sub-clause in the interests of (the sovereignty and integrity of India), the security of the State, friendly relations with foreign States, Public order, decency or morality, or in relation to contempt of Court, defamation or incitement to an offence.

3. Nothing in sub-clause (b) of the said clause shall affect the operation of any existing law in so far as imposes, or prevents the State from making any law imposing, the interests of, the sovereignty and integrity of India or, Public order, reasonable restrictions on the exercise of the right conferred by the said sub-clause.

4. Nothing in sub-clause (c) of the said clause shall affect the operation of any existing law in so far as it imposes, or prevent the State from making any law imposing, in the interests of the sovereignty and integrity of India, or public order or morality, reasonably restrictions on the exercise of the right conferred by the said sub-clause.

5. Nothing in [sub-clauses (d) and (ee)], of the said clause shall affect the operation of any existing law in so far as imposes, or prevent, the State from making any law imposing, reasonable restrictions of the exercise of any of the rights conferred by the said

sub-clause either in the interests of the general public or for the protection of the interests of any Scheduled Tribe.

6. Nothing in sub-clause (g) of the said clause shall affect the operation of any existing law in so far as it imposes, or prevent the State from making any law imposing, in the interests of the general public, reasonable restrictions on the exercise of the right conferred by the said sub-clause, and, in particular, (nothing in the said sub-clause shall affect the operation of any existing law in so far as it relates to, or prevent the State from making any law relating to,—

(i) the professional or technical qualification necessary for practising any profession or carrying on any occupation, trade or business, or

(ii) the carrying on by the State or by a Corporation owned or controlled by the state, or any trade, business, industry or service, whether to the exclusion, complete or partial, of citizens or otherwise.

20. Protection in Respect of Conviction for Offences. 1. No person shall be convicted of any offence except for violation of a law in force at the time of the commission of the act charged as an offence, nor be subjected to a penalty greater than that which might have been inflicted under the law in force at the time of the commission of the offence.

2. No person shall be prosecuted and punished for the same offence more than once.

3. No person accused of any offence shall be compelled to be a witness against himself.

21. Protection of Life and Personal Liberty. No person shall be deprived of his life or personal liberty except according to procedure established by law.

22. Protection Against Arrest and Detention in Certain Cases. 1. No person, who is arrested shall be detained in custody without being informed, as soon as may be, of the grounds for such arrest nor shall he be denied the right to consult, and to be defended by, a legal practitioner of his choice.

2. Every person who is arrested and detained in custody shall be produced before the nearest Magistrate within a period of twenty-four hours of such arrest excluding the time necessary for the journey from the place of arrest to Court of the Magistrate and no such person shall be detained in custody beyond the said period without the

authority of a Magistrate.

3. Nothing in clauses (1) and (2) shall apply—

(a) to any person who for the time being is an enemy alien; or

(b) to any person who is arrested or detained under any law providing for preventive detention.

4. No law providing for preventive detention shall authorise the detention of a person for a longer period than three months unless—

(a) an Advisory Board consisting of persons who are, or have been, or are qualified to be appointed as Judges of a High Court has reported before the expiration of the said period of three months that there is in its opinion sufficient cause for such detention:

Provided that, nothing in this sub-clause shall authorise the detention of any person beyond the maximum period prescribed by any law made by Parliament under sub-clause (b) of clause (7); or

(b) such person is detained in accordance with the provisions of any law made by Parliament under sub-clauses (a) and (b) and (7).

5. When any person is detained in pursuance of an order made under any law providing for preventive detention, the authority making the order shall, as soon as may be, communicate to such person the grounds on which the order has been made and shall afford him the earliest opportunity of making a representation against the order.

6. Nothing in clause (5) shall require the authority making any such order as it referred to in that clause to disclose facts which such authority considers to be against the public interest to disclose.

7. Parliament may by law prescribe—

(a) the circumstances under which, and the class or classes of cases in which, a person may be detained for a period longer than three months under any law providing for preventive detention without obtaining the opinion of an Advisory Board in accordance with the provisions of sub-clause (a) of clause (4);

(b) the maximum period for which any person may in any class or classes of cases be detained under any provision for preventive detention; and

(c) the procedure to be followed by an Advisory Board in an inquiry under sub-clause (a) of clause (4).

23. Prohibition of Traffic in Human Beings and Forced Labour. 1. Traffic in human beings and *begar* and other similar forms of forced labour are prohibited and any contravention of this provision shall be an offence punishable in accordance with law.

2. Nothing in this Article shall prevent the State from imposing compulsory service for public purposes, and in imposing such service the State shall not make any discrimination on grounds only of religion, race, caste or class or any of them.

24. Prohibition of Employment of Children in Factories, etc. No child below the age of fourteen years shall be employed to work in any factory or mine or engaged in any other hazardous employment.

25. Freedom of Conscience and Free Profession, Practice and Propagation of Religion. 1. Subject to public order, morality and health and to the other provisions of this Part, all persons are equally entitled to freedom of conscience and the right freely to profess, practice and propagate religion.

2. Nothing in this Article shall affect the operation of any existing law or prevent the State from making any law—

(a) regulating or restricting any economic, financial, political or other secular activity which may be associated with religious practice;

(b) providing for social welfare and reform or the throwing open of Hindu religious institutions of a public character to all classes and sections of Hindus.

Explanation I— The wearing and carrying of *kirpans* shall be deemed to be included in the profession of the Sikh religion.

Explanation II— In sub-clause (b) of clause (2), the reference to Hindus shall be construed as including a reference to persons professing the Sikh, Jaina or Buddhist religion, and the reference to Hindu religious institutions shall be construed accordingly.

26. Freedom to Manage Religious Affairs. Subject to public order, morality and health, every religious denomination or any section thereof shall have the right—

(a) to establish and maintain institutions for religious and charitable purposes;

(b) to manage its own affairs in matters of religion;

(c) to own and acquire movable and immovable property; and

(d) to administer such property in accordance with law.

27. Freedom as to Payment of Taxes for Promotion of any Particular Religion. No person shall be compelled to pay any taxes, the proceeds of which are specifically appropriate in payment of expenses for the promotion or maintenance of any particular religion or religious denomination.

28. Freedom as to Attendance at Religious Instruction or Religious Worship in Certain Educational Institutions. 1. No religious instruction shall be provided in any educational institution wholly maintained out of State funds.

2. Nothing in clause (1) shall apply to an educational institution which administered by the State but has been established under any endowment or trust which requires that religious instruction shall be imparted in such institution.

3. No person attending any educational institution recognised by the State or receiving aid out of State funds shall be required to take part in any religious instruction that may be conducted in such institution or in any premises attached thereto unless such person or, if such person is a minor his guardian has given his consent thereto.

29. Protection of Interests of Minorities. 1. Any section of the citizens residing in the territory of India or any part thereof having a distinct language, script or culture of its own shall have the right to conserve the same.

2. No citizens shall be denied admission into any educational institution maintained by the State or receiving aid out of State funds on grounds only of religion, race, caste, language or any of them.

30. Right of Minorities to Establish and Administer Educational Institutions. 1. All minorities, whether based on religion or language, shall have the right to establish and administer educational institutions of their choice.

1-A. In making any law providing for the compulsory acquisition of any property of an educational institution established and administered by a minority, referred to in clause (1), the State shall ensure that the amount fixed by or determined under such law for the acquisition of such property is such as would not restrict or abrogate the right guaranteed under that clause.

2. The State shall not, in granting aid to educational institutions, discriminate against any educational institution on the ground that it is under the management of a minority, whether based on religion or language.

31-A. Saving of Laws Providing for Acquisition of Estates, etc. 1. Notwithstanding anything contained in Article 13, no law providing for—

(a) the acquisition by the State of any estate or of any rights therein or the extinguishment or modification of any such rights, or

(b) the taking over the management of any property by the State for a limited period either in the public interest or in order to secure the proper management of the property, or

(c) the amalgamation of two or more corporations either in the public interest or in order to secure the proper management of any of the corporations, or

(d) the extinguishment or modification of any rights of managing agents, secretaries and treasurers, managing directors, directors or managers of corporations, or of any voting rights of share-holders thereof, or

(e) the extinguishment or modification of any rights accruing by virtue of any agreement, leases or licence for the purpose of searching for, or winning any mineral or mineral oil, or the premature termination or cancellation of any such agreement, leases or licence,

shall be deemed to be void on the grounds that it is inconsistent with, or takes away or abridges any of the rights conferred by Article 14 or Article 19:

Provided that where such law is a law made by the Legislature of a State, the provisions of this Article shall not apply thereto, unless such law, having been reserved for the consideration of the President, has received his assent:

Provided further that where any law makes any provision for the acquisition by the State of any estate and where any land comprised therein is held by a person under his personal cultivation, it shall not be lawful for the State to acquire any portion of such land as is within the ceiling limit application to him under any law for the time being in force or any building or structure standing thereon or appurtenant thereto, unless the law relating to the acquisition of such land, building or structure, provides for payment of compensation at a rate which shall not be less than the market value thereof.

2. In this Article—

(a) the expression "estate" shall, in relation to any local area, have the same meaning as that expression or his local equivalent has in the existing law relating to land tenures in force in that area and shall also include—

 (i) any *Jagir, Inam* or *Muafi* or other similar grant and in the States of (Tamil Nadu) and Kerala, any *janmam* right;

 (ii) any land held under *Ryotwari* settlement;

 (iii) any land held or let for purposes of agriculture or for purposes ancillary thereto, including waste land, forest land, land for pasture or sites of buildings and other structures occupied by cultivators of land, agricultural labourers and village artisans;

(b) the expression "rights", in relation to an estate, shall include any rights vesting in a proprietor, sub-proprietor, under-proprietor, tenure-holder, *raiyat* under-*raiyat* or other intermediary and any rights or privileges in respect of land revenue.

131- B, Validation of Certain Acts and Regulations. Without prejudice to the generality of the provisions contained in Article 31-A, none of the Acts and Regulations specified in the Ninth Schedule nor any of the provisions thereof, shall be deemed to be void, or ever to have become void, on the ground that such Act, Regulation or provision is inconsistent with, or takes away or abridges any of the rights conferred by, any provisions of this part, and notwithstanding any judgment, decree or order of any Court or tribunal to the contrary, each of the said Acts and Regulations shall, subject to the power of any competent. Legislature to repeal or amend it, continue in force.

31-C. Saving of Laws Giving Effect to Certain Directive Principles. Notwithstanding anything contained in Article 13, no law giving effect to the policy of the State towards securing all or any of the principles laid down in Part IV shall be deemed to be void on the ground that it is inconsistent with, or takes away or abridges any of the rights conferred by, Article 14 or Article 19; and no law containing a declaration that it is for giving effect to such policy shall be called in question in any Court on the ground that it does not give effect to such policy:

Provided that where such law is made by the Legislature of a State, the provisions of this article shall not apply thereto unless such law, having been reserved for the consideration of the President, has received his assent.

32. Remedies for Enforcement of Rights Conferred by This Part. 1. The right to move the Supreme Court by appropriate proceedings for the enforcement of the rights conferred by this Part is guaranteed.

2. The Supreme Court shall have power to issue directions or orders or writs, including writs in the nature of *habeas corpus, mandamus, prohibition, quo warranto* and *certiorari,* whichever may be appropriate, for the enforcement of any of the rights conferred by this Court.

3. Without prejudice to the powers conferred on the Supreme Court by clauses (1) and (2), Parliament may by law empower any other Court to exercise within the local limits of its jurisdiction all or any of the powers exercisable by the Supreme Court under clause (2).

4. The right guaranteed by this Article shall not be suspended except as otherwise provided for by this Constitution.

39-A. Equal Justice and Free Legal Aid. The State shall secure that the operation of the legal system promotes justice, on a basis of equal opportunity and shall, in particular, provide free legal aid, by suitable legislation or schemes or in any other way, to ensure that opportunities for securing justice are not denied to any citizen by reason of economic or other disabilities..

41. Right to Work, to Education and to Public Assistance in Certain Cases. The State shall, within the limits of its economic capacity and development, make effective provision for securing the right to work, to education and to public assistance in cases of unemployment, old age, sickness and disablement, and in other cases of undeserved want.

48-A. Protection and Improvement of Environment and Safeguarding of Forests and Wildlife. The State shall endeavour to protect and improve the environment and to safeguard the forests and wildlife of the country.

50. Separation of Judiciary from Executive. The State shall take steps to separate the judiciary from the executive in the public services of the State.

51-A. Fundamental Duties. It shall be the duty of every citizen of India—

(a) to abide by the Constitution and respect its ideals and institutions, the National Flag and the National Anthem;
(b) to cherish and follow the noble ideals which inspired our national struggle for freedom;
(c) to uphold and protect the sovereignty, unity and integrity of India;
(d) to defend the country and render national service when called upon to do so;
(e) to promote harmony and the spirit of common brotherhood amongst all the people of India transcending religious, linguistic and regional or sectional diversities, to renounce practices derogatory to the dignity of women;
(f) to value and preserve the rich heritage of our composite culture;
(g) to protect and improve the natural environment including forests, lakes, rivers and wildlife, and to have compassion for living creatures;
(h) to develop the scientific temper, humanism and the spirit of inquiry and reform;
(i) to safeguard public property and to abjure violence;
(j) to strive towards excellence in all spheres of individual and collective activity so that the nation constantly rises to higher levels of endeavour and achievement.

300-A. Persons not to be Deprived of Property Save by Authority of Law. No person shall be deprived of his properly save by authority of law.

330. Reservation of Seats for Scheduled Castes and Scheduled Tribes in the House of the People. 1. Seats shall be reserved in the House of People for—

(a) The Schedule Castes;
(b) the Scheduled Tribes except the Scheduled Tribes in the autonomous districts of Assam; and
(c) the Scheduled Tribes in the autonomous districts of Assam.

2. The number of seats reserved in any State of Union Territory

for the Scheduled Castes or the Scheduled Tribes under clause (1) shall bear, as nearly as may be, the same proportion to the total number of seats allotted to that State or Union Territory in the House of the People as the population of the Scheduled Castes in the State or Union Territory or of the Scheduled Tribes in the State or Union Territory or part of the State or Union Territory, as the case may be, in respect of which seats are so reserved bears to the total population of the State or Union Territory.

3. Notwithstanding anything contained in clause (2), the number of seats reserved in the House of the People for the Scheduled Tribes in the autonomous districts of Assam shall bear to the total number of seats allotted to that State a proportion not less than the population of the Scheduled Tribes in the autonomous districts bears to the total population of the State.

Explanation—In this Article and in Article 332, the expression "population" means the population as ascertained at the last preceding census of which the relevant figures have been published.

Provided that the reference in the *Explanation* to the last preceding census of which the relevant figures have been published shall, until the relevant figures for the first census taken after the year 2000 have been published, be construed, as a reference to the 1971 Census.

331. Representation of the Anglo-Indian Community in the House of the People. Notwithstanding anything in Article 81, the President may, if he is of opinion that Anlgo-Indian community is not adequately represented in the House of the People, nominate not more than two members of that community to the House of the People.

332. Reservation of Seats for Scheduled Castes and Scheduled Tribes in the Legislative Assemblies to the States. 1. Seats shall be reserved for the Scheduled Castes and Scheduled Tribes except the Scheduled Tribes in the autonomous districts of Assam, in the Legislative Assembly of every State.

2. Seats shall be reserved also for the autonomous districts in the Legislative Assembly of the State of Assam.

3. The number of seats reserved for the Scheduled Castes or the Scheduled Tribes in the Legislative Assembly of any State under clause (1) shall bear, as nearly as may be, the same proportion to the total number of seats in the Assembly as the population of the Scheduled Castes in the State or of the Scheduled Tribes in the State or part of the State, as the case may be, in respect of which seats are

so reserved, bears to the total population of the State.

3-A. Notwithstanding anything contained in clause (3), until the taking effect, under Article 170, of the re-adjustment, on the basis of the first census after the year 2000, of the member of seats in the Legislative Assemblies of the States of Arunachal Pradesh, Meghalaya, Mizoram and Nagaland, the seats which shall be reserved for the Scheduled Tribes in the Legislative Assembly of any such State shall be,—

(a) if all the seats in the Legislative Assembly of such State in existence on the date of coming into force of the Constitution (Fifty-seventh Amendment) Act, 1987 (hereafter in this clause referred to as the existing Assembly) are held by members of the Scheduled Tribes, all the seats except one;

(b) in any other case, such number of seats as bears to the total number of seats, a proportion not less than the number (as on the said date) of members belonging to the Scheduled Tribes in the existing Assembly bears to the total number of seats in the existing Assembly.

3-B. Notwithstanding anything contained in clause (3), until the readjustment, under Article 170, takes effect on the basis of the first census after the year 2000, of the number of seats in the Legislative Assembly of the State of Tripura, the seats which shall be reserved for the Scheduled Tribes in the Legislative Assembly shall be, such number of seats as bears to the total number of seats, a proportion not less than the number, as on the date of coming into force of the Constitution (Seventy-Second Amendment) Act, 1992, of members belonging to the Scheduled Tribes in the Legislative Assembly in existence on the said date bears to the total number of seats in that Assembly.

4. The number of seats reserved for the autonomous district in the Legislative Assembly of the State of Assam shall bear to the total number of seats in that Assembly a proportion not less than the population of the district bears to the total population of the State.

5. The constituencies for the seats reserved for any autonomous district of Assam shall not comprise any area outside that district.

6. No person who is not a member of a Scheduled Tribe of any autonomous district of the State of Assam shall be eligible for election to the Legislative Assembly of the State from any constituency of that district.

333. Representation of the Anglo-Indian Community in the

Legislative Assemblies of the States. Notwithstanding anything in Article 170, the Governor of a State may if he is of opinion that the Anglo-Indian community needs representation in the Legislative Assembly of the State and is not adequately represented therein, nominate one member of that community to the Assembly.

334. Reservation of Seats and Special Representation to Cease After Fifty Years. Notwithstanding anything in the foregoing provisions of this Part, the provisions of this Constitution relating to—

(a) the reservation of seats for the Scheduled Castes and the Scheduled Tribes in the House of the People and in the Legislative Assemblies of the States; and

(b) the representation of the Anglo-Indian community in the House of the People and in the Legislative Assemblies of the States by nomination,

shall cease to have effect on the expiration of a period of fifty years from the commencement of this Constitution:

Provided that, nothing in this Article shall effect any representation in the House of the people or in the Legislative Assembly of a State until the dissolution of the then existing House of Assembly, as the case may be.

335. Claims of Scheduled Castes and Scheduled Tribes to Services and Posts. The claims of the members of Scheduled Castes and Scheduled Tribes shall be taken into consideration, consistently with the maintenance of efficiency of administration, in the making of appointments to services and posts in connection with the affairs of the Union or of a State.

336. Special Provision for Anglo-Indian Community in Certain Services. 1. During the first two years after the commencement of this Constitution, appointments of members of the Anglo-Indian community to posts in the Railway, Customs, Postal and Telegraph Services of the Union shall be made on the same basis as immediately before the fifteenth day of August, 1947.

During every succeeding period of two years, the number of posts reserved for the members of the said community in the said services shall, as nearly as possible, be less by ten per cent than the numbers so reserved during the immediately preceding period of two years:

Provided that at the end of ten years from the commencement

of this Constitution all such reservations shall cease.

2. Nothing in clause (1) shall bar the appointment of members of the Anglo-Indian community to posts other than, or in addition to, those reserved for the community under that clause if such members are found qualified for appointment on merit as compared with the members of other communities.

337. Special Provision with Respect to Educational Grants for the Benefit of Anglo-Indian Community. During the first three financial years after the commencement of this Constitution, the same grants, if any, shall be made by the Union and by each State for the benefit of the Anglo-Indian community in respect of education as were made in the financial year ending on the thirty first day of March, 1948.

During the every succeeding period of three years the grants may be less by ten per cent than those for the immediately preceding period of three years:

Provided that at the end to ten years from the commencement of this Constitution such grants, to the extent to which they are a special concession to the Anglo-Indian community, shall cease:

Provided further that no educational institution shall be entitled to receive any grant under this Article unless at least forty per cent of the annual admissions therein are made available to members of communities other than the Anglo-Indian Community.

338. National Commission for Scheduled Castes and Scheduled Tribes. 1. There shall be a Commission for the Scheduled Castes and Scheduled Tribes to be known as the National Commission for the Scheduled Castes and Scheduled Tribes.

2. Subject to the provisions of any law made in this behalf by Parliament, the Commission shall consist of a Chairperson, Vice-Chairperson and five other Members and the conditions of the service and tenure of office of the Chairperson, Vice-Chairperson and other Members so appointed shall be such as the President may by rule determine.

3. The Chairperson, Vice-Chairperson and other Members of the Commission shall be appointed by the President by warrant under his hand and seal.

4. The Commission shall have the power to regulate its own procedure.

5. It shall be the duty of Commission—

(a) to investigate and monitor all matters relating to the safeguards provided for the Scheduled Castes and Scheduled Tribes under this Commission or under any other law for the time being in force or under any order of the Government and to evaluate the working of such safeguards;

(b) to inquire into specific complaints with respect to the deprivation of rights and safeguards of the Scheduled Castes and Scheduled Tribes;

(c) to participate and advise on the planning process of socio-economic development of the Scheduled Castes and Scheduled Tribes and to evaluate the progress of their development under the Union and any States;

(d) to present to the President, annually and at such other times as the Commission may deem fit, reports upon the working of those safeguard;

(e) to make in such reports recommendations as to the measures that should be taken by the Union or any State for the effective implementation of those safeguards and other measures for the protection, welfare and socio-economic development of the Scheduled Castes and Scheduled Tribes; and

(f) to discharge such other functions in relation to the protection, welfare and development and advancement of the Scheduled Castes and Scheduled Tribes as the President may, subject to the provisions of any law made by Parliament by rule specify.

6. The President shall cause all such reports to be laid down before such House of Parliament along with a memorandum explaining the action taken or proposed to be taken on the recommendation relating to the Union and the reasons for the non-acceptance, if any, or any such recommendations.

7. Where any such report, or any part thereof, relates to any matter with which any State Government is concerned, a copy of such report shall be forwarded to the Governor of the State who shall cause it to be laid for before the Legislature of the State along with a memorandum explaining the action taken or proposed to be taken on the recommendations relating to the States and the reasons for the non-acceptance, if any, or any of such recommendations.

8. The Commission shall, while investigating any matter referred to in sub-clause (a) or inquiring into any complaint referred to in

sub-clause (b) of clause (5), have all the powers of a civil Court trying a suit and in particular in respect of the following matters, namely—

(a) summoning and enforcing the attendance of any person from any part of India and examining him on oath;
(b) requiring the discovery and production of any document;
(c) receiving evidence of affidavits;
(d) requisitioning any public record or copy thereof from any Court or office;
(e) issuing commissions for the examination of witnesses and documents;
(f) any other matter which the President may, by rule determine.

9. The Union and every State Government shall consult the Commission on all major policy matters affecting Scheduled Castes and Scheduled Tribes.

10. In this Article, references to the Scheduled Castes and Scheduled Tribes shall be construed as including references to such other backward classes as the President may, on receipt of the report of a Commission appointed under clause (1) of Article 340, by order specify and also to the Anglo-Indian community.

339. Control of the Union over the Administration of Scheduled Areas and the Welfare of Scheduled Tribes 1. The President may at any time and shall, at the expiration of ten years from the commencement of this Constitution by order appoint a Commission to report on the administration of the Scheduled Areas and the welfare of the Scheduled Tribes in the States.

The order may define the composition, powers and procedure of the Commission and may contain such incidental or ancillary provisions as the President may consider necessary or desirable.

2. the executive power of the Union shall extend to the giving of directions to a State as to the drawing up and execution of schemes specified in the direction to be essential for the welfare of the Scheduled Tribes in the State.

340. Appointment of a Commission to Investigate the Conditions of Backward Classes. 1. The President may by order appoint a Commission consisting of such persons as he thinks fit to investigate the conditions of socially and educationally backward classes within the territory of India and the difficulties under which they labour and to make recommendations as to the steps that should be taken by the Union or any State to remove such difficulties and to improve their condition and as to the grants that should be made for the purpose by the Union or any State and the conditions subject to which such grants should be made, and the order appointing such Commission shall define the procedure to be followed by the Commission.

2. A Commission so appointed shall investigate the matters referred to them and present to the President a report setting out the facts as found by them and making such recommendations as they think proper.

3. The President shall cause a copy of the report so presented together with a memorandum explaining the action taken thereon to be laid before each House of Parliament.

341. Scheduled Castes. 1. The President may with respect to any State or Union Territory, and where it is a State, after consultation with Governorthereof by public notification, specify the castes, races or tribes or parts of or groups within castes, races or tribes which shall for the purposes of this Constitution be deemed to be Scheduled Castes in relation to that State or Union Territory, as the case may be.

2. Parliament may by law include in the, or exclude from the, list of Scheduled Castes specified in a notification issued under clause (1) and caste, race or tribe, or part or group within any castes, race or tribe, but save as aforesaid a notification issued under the said clause shall not be varied by any subsequent notification.

342. Scheduled Tribes. 1. The President (may with respect to any State, or Union Territory), and where it is a State, after consultation with the Governor (thereof by public notification, specify the tribes or tribal communities or parts of or groups within tribes or tribal communities which shall for the purposes of this Constitution be deemed to be Scheduled Tribes in relation to that State (or Union Territory, as the case may be).

2. Parliament may by law include in or exclude from the list of Scheduled Tribes specified in a notification issued under clause (1) any tribe of tribal community or part of or group within any tribe or tribal community, but, save as aforesaid a notification issued under the said clause shall not be varied by any subsequent notification.

3

The Protection of Human Rights Act, 1993

PROTECTION OF HUMAN RIGHTS ACT, 1993
No. 10 of 1994
((8th January, 1994)

An act to provide for the constitution of a National Human Rights Commission, State Human Rights Commission in States and Human Rights courts for better protection of human rights and for matters connected therewith or incidental thereto.

Be it enacted by Parliament in the Forty-fourth Year of the Republic of India as follows:

PRELIMINARY

1. ***Short Title, Extent and Commencement.*** 1. This Act may be called the Protection of Human Rights Act, 1993.

2. It extends to the whole of India:

Provided that it shall apply to the State of Jammu and Kashmir only in so far as it pertains to the matters relatable to any of the entries enumerated in List I or List III in the Seventh Schedule to the Constitution as applicable to that State.

3. It shall be deemed to have come into force on the 28th day of September, 1993.

2. ***Definitions.*** 1. In this Act, unless the context otherwise requires:

(a) "armed forces" means the naval, military and air forces and includes any other armed forces of the Union;
(b) "Chairperson" means the Chairperson of the Commission or of the State Commission, as the case may be;
(c) "Commission" means the National Human Rights Commission constituted under section 3;

(d) "Human rights" means the rights relating to life, liberty, equality and dignity of the individual guaranteed by the Constitution or embodied in the International Covenants and enforceable by courts in India;

(e) "Human Rights Court" means the Human Rights Court Specified under section 30;

(f) "International Covenants" means the International Covenant on Civil and Political Rights and The International Covenant on Economic; Social and Cultural Rights adopted by the General Assembly of the United Nations on the 16th December 1966;

(g) "Member" means a Member of the Commission or of the State Commission, as the case may be and includes the Chairperson.

(h) "National Commission for Minorities" means the National Commission for Minorities constituted under Section 3 of the National Commission for Minorities Act, 1992 (9 of 1992);

(i) "National Commission for the Scheduled Castes and Scheduled Tribes" means the National Commission for the Scheduled Castes and Scheduled Tribes referred to in Article 338 of the Constitution.

(j) "National Commission for Women" means the National Commission for Women constituted under Section 3 of the National Commission for Women Act, 1990 (20 of 1990);

(k) "Notification" means a notification published in the official Gazette;

(l) "Prescribed" means prescribed by rules made under this Act;

(m) "Public servant" shall have the meaning assigned to it in section 21 of the Indian Penal Code (45 of 1860); and

(n) "State Commissions" means a State Human Rights Commission constituted under section 21.

2. Any reference in this Act to a law which is not in force in the State of Jammu and Kashmir, shall in relation to that State, be construed as a reference to a corresponding law, if any, in force in that State.

THE NATIONAL HUMAN RIGHTS COMMISSION

3. Constitution of a National Human Rights Commission. 1. The Central Government shall constitute a body to be known as the National Human Rights Commission to exercise the powers conferred upon and to perform the functions assigned to it, under this Act,

2. The Commission shall consist of:

(a) a Chairperson who has been a Chief Justice of the Supreme Court;
(b) one member who is or has been a judge of the Supreme Court;
(c) one Member who is, or has been, the Chief Justice of a High Court; and
(d) two Members to be appointed from amongst persons having knowledge of, or practical experience in, matters relating to human rights.

3. The Chairpersons of the National Commission for Minorities, the National Commission for the Scheduled Castes and Scheduled Tribes and the National Commission for Women shall be deemed to be Member of the Commission for the discharge of functions specified in clauses (b) to (j) of section 12.

4. There shall be a Secretary-General who shall be the Chief Executive Officer of the Commission and shall exercise such powers and discharge such functions of the Commission as it may delegate to him.

5. The headquarter of the Commission shall be at Delhi and the Commission may, with the previous approval of the Central Government establish offices at other places in India.

4. Appointment of Chairperson and other Members. 1. The Chairperson and other Members shall be appointed by the President by warrant under his hand and seal:

Provided that every appointment under this sub-section shall be made after obtaining the recommendation of a Committee consisting of:

(a)	the Prime Minister	Chairperson
(b)	Speaker of the House of the People	Member
(c)	Minister-in-charge of the Ministry of Home Affairs in the Government of India	Member
(d)	Leader of the Opposition of the House of the People	Member

(e) Leader of the Opposition in the Council of States — Member

(f) Deputy Chairman of the Council of States — Member

Provided further that no sitting judge of the Supreme Court or sitting Chief Justice of a High Court shall be appointed except after consultation with the Chief Justice of India.

2. No appointment of a Chairperson or a Member shall be invalid merely by reason of any vacancy in the Committee.

5. *Removal of a Member of the Commission.* 1. Subject to the provisions of sub-section (2) the Chairperson or any other Member of the Commission shall only be removed from his office by order of the President on the ground of proved misbehaviour or incapacity after the Supreme Court, on reference being made to it by the President has, on inquiry held in accordance with the procedure prescribed in that behalf by the Supreme Court, reported that the Chairperson or such other Member as the case may be, ought on any such ground to be removed.

2. Notwithstanding anything in sub-section (1), the President may by order remove from office the Chairperson or any other Member if the Chairperson or such other Member, as the case may be—

(a) is adjudged an insolvent; or

(b) engages during his term of office in any paid employment outside the duties of his office; or

(c) is unfit to continue in office by reason of infirmity of mind or body; or

(d) is of unsound mind and stands so declared by a competent court; or

(e) is convicted and sentenced to imprisonment for an offence which in the opinion of the President involves moral turpitude.

6. *Term of Office of Members.* 1. A person appointed as Chairperson shall hold office for a term of five years from the date on which he enters upon his office or until he attains the age of seventy years, whichever is earlier.

2. A person appointed as a Member shall hold office for a term of five years from the date on which he enters upon his office and shall be eligible for re-appointment for another term of five years:

Provided that no Members shall hold office after he has attained the age of seventy years.

3. On ceasing to hold office, a Chairperson or a Member shall be ineligible for further employment under the Government of India or under the Government of any State.

7. Member to Act as Chairperson or to Discharge his Functions in Certain Circumstances. 1. In the event of the occurrence of any vacancy in the office of the Chairperson by reason of his death, resignation or otherwise, the president may by notification, authorize one of the Members to act as the Chairperson until the appointment of a new Chairperson to fill such vacancy.

2. When the Chairperson is unable to discharge his functions owing to absence on leave or otherwise, such one of the Members as the President may, by notification, authorize in this behalf, shall discharge the function of the Chairperson until the date on which the Chairperson resumes his duties.

8. Terms and Conditions of Service of Members. The salaries and allowances payable to, and other terms and conditions of service of, the Members shall be such as may be prescribed:

Provided that neither the salary and allowances nor the other terms and conditions of service of a Member shall be varied to his disadvantage after his appointment.

9. Vacancies, etc. not to Invalidate the Proceedings of the Commission. No act to proceedings of the Commission shall be questioned or shall be invalidated merely on the ground of existence of any vacancy or defect in the constitution of the Commission.

10. Procedure to be Regulated by the Commission. 1. The Commission shall meet at such time and place as the Chairperson may think fit.

2. The Commission shall regulate its own procedure.

3. All orders and decisions of the Commission shall be authenticated by the Secretary-General or any other of the Commission duly authorized by the Chairperson in this behalf.

11. Officers and other Staff of the Commission. 1. The Central Government shall make available to the commission:

(a) an officer of the rank of the Secretary to the Government of India who shall be the Secretary-General of the Commission; and

(b) such police and investigative staff under an officer not below the rank of a Director-General of Police and such other officers and staff as may necessary for the efficient performance of the functions of the Commission.

2. Subject to such rules as may be made by the Central Government in this behalf, the Commission may appoint such other administrative, technical and scientific staff as it may consider necessary.

3. The salaries, allowances and conditions of service of the officers and other staff appointed under sub-section (2) shall be such as may be prescribed.

FUNCTIONS AND POWERS OF THE COMMISSION

12. Functions of the Commission. The Commission shall perform all or any of the following functions, namely;

(a) inquire, *suo motu* or on a petition presented to it by a victim or any person on his behalf, into complaint of—

  (i) violation of human rights or abatement thereof, or
  (ii) negligence in the prevention of such violation;
  by a public servant;

(b) intervenes in any proceedings involving any allegation of violation of human rights pending before a court with the approval of such court;

(c) visit, under intimation to the State Government, any jail or any other institution under control of the State Government, where persons are detained or lodged for purposes of treatment, reformation or protection to study the living condition of the inmates and make recommendations thereon;

(d) review the safeguards provided by or under the Constitution or any law for the time being in force for the protection of human rights and recommend measures for their effective implementation;

(e) review the factors including acts of terrorism that inhibit the enjoyment of human rights and recommend appropriate remedial measures;

(f) study treaties and other international instruments on human rights and make recommendations for their effective implementation;

(g) undertake and promote research in the field of human rights;
(h) spread human rights literacy among various sections of society and promote awareness of the safeguards available for the protection of these rights through publication, the media, seminars and other available means;
(i) encourage the efforts of non-governmental organizations and institutions working in the field of human rights; and
(j) such other functions as it may consider necessary for the promotion of human rights.

13. Powers Relating to Inquiries. 1. The Commission shall, while inquiring into complaints under this Act, have all the powers of a civil court trying a suit under the Code of Civil Procedure, 1908 (5 of 1908) and in particular in respect of the following matters, namely—

(a) summoning and enforcing the attendance of witnesses and examining them on oath;
(b) discovery and production of any document;
(c) receiving evidence on affidavits;
(d) requisitioning any public record or copy thereof from any court of office;
(e) issuing commissions for the examination of witnesses or documents; and
(f) any other matter which may be prescribed.

2. The Commission shall have power to require any person, subject to any privilege which may be claimed by that person under any law for the time being in force, to furnish information on such points or matters as, in the opinion of the commission, may be useful for, or relevant to, the subject matter of the inquiry and any person so required shall be deemed to be legally bound to furnish such information within the meaning of Section 176 and Section 177 of the Indian Penal Code (45 of 1860).

3. The Commission or any other officer, not below the rank of a Gazetted Officer, specially authorized in this behalf by the Commission may enter any building or place where the Commission has reason to believe that any document relating to the subject matter of the inquiry may be found and may seize any such document or take extracts or copies therefrom subject to the

provisions of section 100 of the Code of Criminal Procedure, 1973, insofar as it may be applicable.

4. The Commission shall be deemed to be a civil court and when any offence as is described in Section 175, Section 178, Section 179, Section 180 or Section 228 of the Indian Penal Code is committed in the view or presence (45 of 1980) of the Commission, the Commission may, after recording the facts constituting the offence and the statement of the accused as provided for in the Code of Criminal Procedure, 1973, forward the case to a Magistrate having jurisdiction to try the same and the Magistrate to whom any such case is forwarded shall proceed to hear the complaint against the accused as if the case has been forwarded to him under section 346 of the Code of Criminal Procedure, 1973 (2 of 1974).

5. Every proceeding before the commission shall be deemed to be a judicial proceeding within the meaning of sections 193 and 228 and for the purposes of section 196, of the Indian Penal Code (45 of 1960) and the Commission shall be deemed to be a civil court for all the purposes of section 195 and Chapter XXVI of the Code of Criminal Procedure, 1973 (2 of 1974)

14. Investigation. 1. The Commission may, for the purpose of conducting any investigation pertaining to the inquiry, utilize the services of any officer or investigation agency of the Central Government or any State Government with the concurrence of the Central Government or the State Government, as the case may be.

2. For the purpose of investigating into any matter pertaining to the inquiry, any officer or agency whose services are utilized under sub-section (1) may, subject to the direction and control of the Commission:

(a) summon and enforce the attendance of any person and examine him;
(b) require the discovery and production of any document; and
(c) requisition any public record or copy thereof from any office.

3. The provisions of section 15 apply in relation to any statement made by a person before any officer or agency whose services are utilized under sub-section (1) as they apply in relation to any statement made by person in the course of giving evidence before the Commission.

4. The officer or agency whose services are utilized under sub-section (1) shall investigate into any matter pertaining to

the inquiry and submit a report thereon to the Commission within such period as may be specified by the Commission in this behalf.

5. The Commission shall satisfy itself about the correctness of the facts stated and the conclusion, if any, arrived at in the report submitted to it under sub-section (4) and for this purpose the Commission may make such inquiry (including the examination of the person or persons who conducted or assisted in the investigation) as it thinks fit.

15. *Statement Made by Persons to the Commission.* No Statement made by a person in the course of giving evidence before the Commission shall subject him, to or be used against him in, any civil or criminal proceedings except a prosecution for giving false evidence by such statement.

Provided that the statement:

(a) is made in reply to the question which he is required by the Commission to answer; or

(b) is relevant to the subject matter of the inquiry.

16. Persons Likely to be Prejudicially Affected to be Heard. If at any stage of the inquiry, the Commission:

(a) considers it necessary to inquire into the conduct of any person; or

(b) is of the opinion that the reputation of any person is likely to be prejudicially affected by the inquiry;

it shall give to that person a reasonable opportunity of being heard in the inquiry and to produce evidence in his defence:

Provided that nothing in this section shall apply where the credit of a witness is being impeached.

PROCEDURE

17. Inquiry into Complaints. The Commission while inquiring into the complaints of violations of human rights may:

(i) call for information or report from the Central Government or any State Government or any other authority or organisation subordinate thereto within such time as may be specified by it: provided that

(a) if the information or report is not received within the

time stipulated by the Commission, it may proceed to inquire into the complaint on its own.

(b) if, on receipt of information or report, the Commission is satisfied either that no further inquiry is required or that the required action has been initiated or taken by the concerned Government or authority, it may not proceed with the complaint and inform the complainant accordingly;

(ii) without prejudice to any thing contained in clause (i), if it considers necessary, having regard to the nature of the complaint, initiate an inquiry.

18. Steps after Inquiry. The Commission may take any of the following steps upon the completion of an inquiry held under this Act. namely:

1. Where the inquiry discloses, the Commission of violation of human rights or negligence in the prevention of violation of human rights by a public servant, it may recommend to the concerned Government or authority the initiation of proceedings for prosecution or such other action as the Commission may deem fit against the concerned person or persons.

2. Approach the Supreme Court or the High Court concerned for such directions, orders or writs as that Court may deem necessary.

3. Recommend to the concerned Government or authority for the grant of such immediate interim relief to the victim or the members of his family as the Commission may consider necessary.

4. Subject to the provision of clause (5) provide a copy of the inquiry report to the petitioner or his representative.

5. The Commission shall send a copy of its inquiry report together with its recommendations to the concerned Government or authority and the concerned Government or authority shall, within a period of one month, or such further time as the Commission may allow, forward its comments on the report, including the action taken or proposed to be taken thereon, to the Commission.

6. The Commission shall publish its inquiry report together with the comments of the concerned Government or authority, if any, and the action taken or proposed to be taken by the concerned

Government or authority on the recommendations of the Commission.

19. Procedure with Respect to Armed Forces. 1. Notwithstanding anything contained in this Act, while dealing with complaints of violation of human rights by members of the armed forces, the Commission shall adopt the following, namely:

(a) it may, either on its own motion or on receipt of a petition, seek a report from the Central Government; and

(b) after the receipt of the report, it may, either not proceed with the complaint or, as the case may be, make its recommendations to that Government.

2. The Central Government shall inform the Commission of the action taken on the recommendations within three months or such further time as the Commission may allow.

3. The Commission shall publish its report together with its recommendations made to the Central Government and the action taken by that Government on such recommendations.

4. The Commission shall provide a copy of the report published under sub-section (3) to the petitioner or his representative.

20. Annual and Special Report of the Commission. 1. The Commission shall submit an annual report to the Central government and to the State Government concerned and may at any time submit special reports on any matter which, in its opinion, is of such urgency or importance that it should not be deferred till submission of the annual report.

2. The Central Government and the State Government, as the case may be shall be annual and special reports of the Commission to be laid before each house of Parliament or the State Legislature respectively as the case may be, along with a memorandum of action taken or proposed to be taken on the recommendations of the Commission and the reasons for non-acceptance of the recommendations, if any.

NATIONAL HUMAN RIGHTS COMMISSION (PROCEDURE) REGULATIONS, 1994

In exercise of the powers conferred by sub-section (2) of Section 10 of the Protection of Human Rights Act, 1993 (No. 10 of 1994), the National Human Rights Commission hereby makes the following regulations, namely:

1. Short Title and Commencement. 1. These Regulations may be called the National Human Rights Commission (Procedure) Regulations, 1994.

2. They shall come into force with effect from the 1st day of March, 1994.

2. Definitions. In these Regulations unless the context otherwise requires,—

(a) "Act" means the Protection of Human Rights Act, 1993.
(b) "Chairperson" means the Chairperson of the Commission.
(c) "Commission" means the National Human Rights Commission.
(d) "Member" means a Member of the Commission and includes the Chairperson.

3. Headquarters of the Commission. The Headquarters of the Commission shall be located at Delhi.

4. Venue of the Meetings. The Commission shall ordinarily hold its meetings and sittings in its office located at Delhi. However, it may, in its direction, hold its meetings and sittings at any other place in India if it considers it necessary and expedient.

5. Periodicity of Meetings. The Commission shall normally have its regular sittings in the first and third weeks of every month, excepting holidays. However, the Chairperson by himself or at the instance of one or more of the members may direct a special sitting of the Commission to be convened to consider any specific matter of urgency.

6. Secretariat Assistance. The Secretary-General, along with such other officers of the Commission as may be directed by the Chairperson, or considered necessary, shall attend the meetings of the Commission.

7. Agenda. The Secretary-General shall, in consultations with the Chairperson prepare the agenda for each meeting of the Commission and shall cause notes thereon to be prepared by the Secretariat. Such notes shall, as far as possible, be self-contained.

Specific files covering the agenda items shall be made readily available to the Commission for reference. The agenda paper shall ordinarily be circulated to the Members at least two clear days in advance of every meeting; but when matters are set down only for hearing, cause list of the day of sitting shall be prepared and circulated.

*8. **Procedure for Dealing with Complaints.*** 1. All complaints in whatever form received by the Commission shall be registered and assigned a number and place for admission before a Bench of two Members constituted for the purpose not later than two weeks of receipt thereof. Ordinarily complaints of the following nature are not entertainable by the Commission.

(a) in regard to events which happened more than one year before the making of complaints;
(b) with regard to matters which are *sub judice;*
(c) which are vague, anonymous or pseudonymous;
(d) which are of frivolous nature; or
(e) those which are outside the purview of the Commission.

2. No fee is chargeable on complaints.

3. Every attempt should be made to disclose a complete picture of the matter leading to the complaint and the same may be made in English or Hindi to enable the Commission to take immediate action. To facilitate the filling of complaints, the Commission shall, however, entertain complaints in any language included in English Schedule of the Constitution. It shall be open to the Commission to ask for further information and affidavits to be filed in support of allegations whenever considered necessary.

4. The Commission may, in its discretion, accept telegraphic complaints and complaints conveyed through fax.

5. The Commission shall have power to dismiss a complaint in limini.

6. Upon admission of a complaint, the Chairperson/ Commission shall direct whether the matter would be set down for inquiry by it or should be investigated into.

7. On every complaint on which a decision is taken by the Chairperson/Commission to either hold an inquiry or investigation, the Secretariat shall call for reports/comments from the concerned Government/authority giving the latter a reasonable time therefor.

8. On receipt of the comments of the concerned authority, a detailed note on the merits of the case shall be prepared for consideration of the Commission.

9. The directions and recommendations of the Commission shall be communicated to the concerned Government/authority and the petitioner as provided for in Sections 18 and 19 of the Act.

10. The Commission may, in its discretion, afford a personal hearing to the petitioner or any other person on his behalf and such other person or persons as in the opinion of the Commission should be heard for appropriate disposal of the matter before it and, where necessary, call for records and examine witnesses in connection with it. The Commission shall afford a reasonable hearing, including opportunity of cross-examining witnesses, if any, in support of the complaint and leading of evidence in support of his stand, to a person whose conduct is enquired into by it or where in its opinion the reputation of such person is likely to be prejudicially affected.

11. Where investigation is undertaken by the team of the Commission or by any other person under its discretion, the report shall be submitted within a week of its completion of such further time as the Commission may allow. The Commission may, in its discretion, direct further investigation in a given case if it is of opinion that investigation has not been proper or the matter requires further investigation for ascertaining the truth or enabling it to properly dispose of the matter. On receipt of the report, the Commission on its own motion, or if moved in the matter, may direct inquiry to be carried by it and receive evidence in course of such inquiry.

12. The Commission or any of its Members when requested by the Chairperson may undertake visits for an on-the-spot study and where such study is undertaken by one or more Members, a report thereon shall be furnished to the Commission as early as possible.

9. *Minutes of the Meetings.*

(a) The minutes of each meeting of the Commission shall be recorded during the meeting itself or immediately thereafter by the Secretary-General or by any other officer as directed. Such minutes shall be submitted to the Chairperson for his approval and, upon approval, be circulated to all the Members of the Commission at the earliest and in any case, sufficiently before the commencement of the next morning.

(b) The conclusions of the Commission in every matter undertaken by it shall be recorded in the form of an opinion. Dissenting opinions, if given, shall also form part of and be kept on record. Action shall be taken on the basis of the majority opinion where there be any difference.

(c) Follow-up action:

Unless specifically authorised, no action shall be taken by the Secretariat of the Commission on the minutes of the meetings until the same are confirmed by the Chairperson.

10. Record of Minutes. A master copy of the minutes of every meeting and opinions of the Commission shall be maintained duly authenticated by the Secretary-General and a copy of the minutes pertaining to each item shall be added to the relevant file for appropriate action. Opinions shall be kept in the respective records and for convenience, copies thereof with appropriate indexing shall be kept in guard files.

11. Report of Action Taken. Report of follow-up action shall be submitted to the Commission at every subsequent sitting indicating therein the present stage of action on each item on which the Commission had taken a decision in any of its earlier meetings, excepting the items on which no further action is called for.

12. Transaction of Business Outside the Headquarters. The Commission or some of the Members may transact business at places outside its Headquarters as and when previously approved by the Chairperson, provided that if parties are to be heard in connection with any inquiry under the Act at least two Members shall continue the bench of the Commission for such purpose.

13. Authentication of Orders and Decisions. 1. Orders and decision of the Commission shall be authenticated by the Secretary-General or any officer of the Commission (authorised by the Chairperson) not below the rank of an Under-Secretary.

2. Copies of enquiry reports or orders passed finally disposing of matters by the Commission shall be furnished free of cost to the petitioner or his representative.

3. Unless any document is classified by the Commission as confidential, copy thereof would be available to the parties in the

matter on payment of a reasonable fee raised to meet the cost. Every effort should be made to provide the copies with utmost expedition and, in any case, not later than one week of the date of request.

14. Annual Report. The Commission shall furnish its annual report for the period commencing from 1st April of the year to 31st March of the succeeding year to the Central Government and to the State Government concerned as provided in Section 20(1) of the Act. The original report shall be signed by the Chairperson and Members of the Commission and appropriately preserved and a duly authenticated copy shall be sent to the appropriate Government by end of May of every year.

15. Special Reports. The Commission may furnish such Special Reports on specific matters as may be considered necessary in terms of Section 20(1) of the Act.

16. Reports on Complaints and Inquiries. Every report to which section 18 or 19 of the Act applies shall be sent to the concerned Government, authority or person, as the case may be, within one week of completion of the proceedings before the Commission and on receipt of the comments of the concerned Government or authority. The Commission shall publish the report in the manner provided in sections 18(6) or 19(3) of the Act, as the case may be, within one week of the receipt of the appropriate intimation.

17. Printing of the Report. The Secretariat of the Commission shall be responsible for the printing of the Annual Report and Special Reports with utmost expedition and in any case, not later than one month of finalisation of the same.

18. Investigation Team. The Commission shall have its own team of investigation to be headed by a person not below the rank of a Director-General of Police appointed by it and such team shall consist of one Deputy Inspector General of Police, 2 Superintendents of Police, 6 Deputy-Superintendents of Police and 24 Inspectors of Police and such other categories of officers as the Commission from time to time decides. The Commission may in any given case appoint an appropriate number of outsiders to be associated with the investigation either as Investigators or Observers.

19. As and when any matter which is not covered by these Regulations arises, it shall be competent for the Commission to make appropriate directions and the Commission may add, delete, amplify and amend these Regulations from time to time.

BASIC STANDARDS RECOMMENDED BY AMNESTY INTERNATIONAL RELATING TO NATIONAL HUMAN RIGHTS COMMISSION, 1994

The creation of a National Human Rights Commission can be an important mechanism to strengthen human rights protection but can never replace, nor should it in any way diminish, the safeguards inherent in comprehensive and effective legal structures enforced by an independent, impartial, adequately resourced and accessible judiciary. In India, the creation of such a human rights commission should go hand in hand with a thorough review of existing institutions and mechanism including legal aid programmes-in order to make these more effective instruments of human rights protection. These initiatives should be accompanied by a determined government policy aimed at holding the perpetrators of human rights violations fully accountable, thus ending the impunity now effectively granted to virtually all those who violate human rights.

The Commission on Human Rights adopted by consensus Resolution 1992/54 concerning the Principles relating to the status national institutions and has transmitted these through the Economic and Social Council to the 47th regular session of the General Assembly for adoption. These internationally recognised Principles should serve as the basic minimum guidelines for the establishment of a national institution for the promotion and protection of human rights. In addition, Amnesty International would like to put forward in this discussion document the following key recommendations relating to the establishment and functioning of a National Human Rights Commission.

Mandate and Composition

The Commission should be independent from Government and its Charter should reflect this. The Commission should be established by law or, preferably, by Constitutional amendment .

The Commission should consist of men and women known for their integrity and impartiality of judgment who shall decide matters before them on the basis of facts and in accordance with the law, without any restrictions, improper influences, inducements, pressures, or threats or interferences from any quarter or for any reason. Its members should be independent of Government, have a proven expertise and competence in the field of protecting and promoting human rights and should be drawn from a variety of different backgrounds, including relevant professional groups and the non-governmental sector. The method of selection of its members should be fair and transparent and should afford all necessary guarantees of independence and broad representation. Commission members should serve in their individual capacity and should be able to serve the Commission effectively. The terms of their appointment, tenure and removal should be clearly specified, laid down in the Charter and should afford the strongest possible guarantees of competence, impartiality and independence.

The Commission should be mandated to monitor and report on compliance with and implementation of relevant international human rights standards, including the Universal Declaration of Human Rights, the International Covenant on Civil and Political Rights, the UN Declaration and Convention against Torture, as well as the UN Code of Conduct for Law Enforcement Officials, the UN Body of Principles for the Protection of All Persons under Any Form of Detention or Imprisonment and the UN Principles on the Effective Prevention and Investigation of Extra-Legal Arbitrary or Summary Executions.

The Commission should be mandated to review the effectiveness of existing legislation and/or administrative provisions in protecting human rights and should be able to make recommendations for the amendment of such legislation or the introduction of new legislation as necessary. The Commission should also examine bills and proposals for new legislation put forward by the Government or Parliament to verify its conformity with international human rights standards and to ensure the State's compliance with the above international human rights instruments.

Following from the recommendation that the scope of the Commission's concerns be defined in terms of State obligations under international human rights law, Amnesty International believes that the Commission should exclude from its mandate criminal actions by criminal organisations, by political groups which have resorted to arms as a means to achieve their goals and criminal actions occurring in the context of domestic violence, to which separate mechanism can devote special attention.

The Commission should have precisely defined powers to investigate on its own initiative situations and cases of reported human rights violations and set clear priorities for its work in accordance with the seriousness of the violations alleged. Priority should be given to alleged violations of the right to life and security of the person and the right not be the tortured (rights from which no derogation can be made by any Government under any circumstances) as well as the right not to be arbitrarily arrested or detained.

The Commission should be directed to establish effective cooperation with non-governmental organisation with first-hand information about reports of human rights violations.

The Commission should also have the powers to conduct wide-ranging national inquiries on human rights concerns of fundamental importance to the nation. One critical analysis which Amnesty International recommends be made is an in-depth study of the factors which have contributed to the persistence of human rights violations in India, including the failure of existing institutions and legal mechanisms adequately to protect human rights. Such a study, which could draw upon authoritative investigations already carried out, such as by the National Police Commission, could recommend institutional and other changes necessary to bring about effective reform to halt these violations.

The Commission should be empowered to investigate the conduct of the police as well as the army and paramilitary security forces in all Indian States. In order to do this effectively, the Commission should have adequate facilities to conduct thorough investigations independent of the police and other security forces, whose conduct it will be called upon to assess.

Facilities and Methodology

The Commission should have all necessary human and material resources to examine, thoroughly, effectively, speedily and throughout the country, the evidence and other case material concerning specific allegations of violations put before it. The Commission should have its own investigative machinery and should have access to e pert assistance whenever required to verify alleges violations. It should have adequate facilities to carry out on the spot investigations. The Commission should have immediate and unhindered access to all places where detained persons are held or are suspected to be held. Officials should be obliged to co-operate with the Commission's investigations.

The Commission should have powers to initiate investigations on its own motion. It should be able to receive communications not only from the complainants themselves but also, if they themselves are unable or prevented from doing so, from lawyers, relatives or others acting on their behalf and non-governmental groups. Investigations initiated by the Commission should be adequately published especially in the state concerned to enable and encourage witnesses to come forward to testify.

The Commission should have full and effective powers to compel the attendance of witnesses and the production of documents.

The Commission should have full and effective powers to protect witnesses, complainants or others providing evidence to the Commission, including bringing about the suspension or transfer of officials allegedly involved to other duties where they would have no power over witnesses or complainants without prejudice pending completion of investigations. Victims or relatives should have access to all relevant information and documents relating to the investigation and be granted all necessary facilities to present evidence. The Commission should be able to provide financial assistance to witnesses enabling them to travel and be accommodated in order to present their evidence before the Commission.

The Commission should work in an open way with its hearings generally open to the public. Private hearings should be an exceptional measure and be resorted to only in specific pre-established circumstances. The Commission's methodology and the result of its investigations, together with official reports, including post-mortem and other expert reports as well as police and Court records, should in each case be published in full, in an easily accessible and comprehensible form. The Commission should also prepare regular reports documenting all the complaints it has received, together with the action taken in each case, as well as an account of all its other activities for and protection of human rights. The Commission's reports should be presented periodically to representative bodies such as the National and State Assemblies.

The result of the Commission's investigations should be referred to appropriate judicial bodies without delay. Anyone the Commission alleges to have been responsible for committing human rights violations or for ordering, encouraging or permitting them, should automatically be brought to justice. The Government should ensure that any prosecutions for human rights related offences are brought by authorities which are distinctly independent from the police or security forces or other bodies allegedly implicated in the human rights violations.

The Commission should have powers to ensure that superior officers are held accountable for acts committed under their authority and should be mandated to closely follow subsequent legal proceedings in the case, for example by serving as a 'watchdog' at trials, if necessary appearing before the court to make legal submission to press for appropriate legal action to be taken within a reasonable time.

The Commission should have powers to ensure that effectively remedies including interim measures to protect the life and safety of an individual and free medical treatment where necessary; it should ensure that full and prompt compensation is paid and other measures of redress and rehabilitation are taken in all cases it has taken up in which the police or the security forces are found to have perpetrated human rights violations.

The Government should undertake an obligation to respond, within a reasonable time, to the case specific as well as the more general findings, conclusions and recommendations made by the Commission. The Government's response should be made public.

FORMATION OF STATE HUMAN RIGHTS COMMISSION, 1993

21. Constitution of State Human Rights Commissions. 1. A State Government may constitute a body to be known as the . . . (name of the State) Human Rights Commission to exercise the powers conferred upon, and to perform the functions assigned to, a State Commission under this chapter.

2. The State Commission shall consist of—

(a) a chairperson who has been a Chief Justice of a High Court;
(b) one Member who is, or has been a Judge of a High Court;
(c) one Member who is, or has been, a District Judge in that State; and
(d) two Members to be appointed from amongst persons having knowledge of, or practical experience in, matters relating to human rights.

3. There shall be a Secretary who shall be the Chief Executive Officer of the State Commission and shall exercise such powers and discharge such functions of the State Commission as it may delegate to him.

4. The headquarters of the State Commission shall be at such place as the State Government may, by notification, specify.

5. A State Commission may inquire into violation of human rights only in respect of matters relatable to any of the entries enumerated in List II and List III in the Seventh Schedule to the Constitution:

Provided that if any such matter is already being inquired into by the Commission or any other Commission duly constituted under any law for the time being in force, the State Commission shall not inquire into the said matter.

Provided further that in relation to the Jammu and Kashmir Human Rights Commission, this sub-section shall have effect as if for the words and figures "List II and List III in the Seventh Schedule to the Constitution" the words and figures "List III in the Seventh Schedule to the Constitution as applicable to the State of Jammu and Kashmir and in respect of matters in relation to which the Legislature of that State has power to make laws" had been substituted.

22. Appointment of Chairperson and other Members of State Commission. 1. The Chairperson and other Member shall be appointed by the Governor by warrant under this hand and seal.

Provided that every appointment under this sub-section shall be made after obtaining the recommendation of a Committee consisting of:

(a)	the Chief Minister	Chairperson
(b)	Speaker of the Legislative Assembly	Member
(c)	Minister-in-charge of the Department of Home in that State	Member
(d)	Leader of the Opposition in the Legislative Assembly	Member

Provided further that where there is a Legislative Council in a State, the Chairman of that Council and the Leader of the Opposition in that Council shall also be members of the Committee:

Provided also that no sitting judge of a High Court or a sitting District Judge shall be appointed except after consultation with the Chief Justice of the High Court of the concerned State.

2. No appointment of a Chairperson or a Member of the State Commission shall be invalid merely by reason of any vacancy in the Committee.

23. Removal of a Member of the State Commission. 1. Subject to the provisions of sub-section (2), the Chairperson or any other member of the State Commission shall only be removed from his office by order of the President on the ground of proved misbehaviour or incapacity after the Supreme Court, on a reference being made to it by the President, has, on inquiry held in accordance with the procedure prescribed in that behalf by the Supreme Court, reported that the Chairperson or such other Member, as the case may be, ought on any such ground to be removed.

2. Notwithstanding anything in sub-section (1), the President may by order remove from office the Chairperson or any other Member if the Chairperson or such other Member, as the case may be—

(a) is adjudged an insolvent; or

(b) engages during his term of office in any paid employment outside the duties of his office; or

(c) is unfit to continue in office by reason of infirmity of mind or body; or

(d) is of unsound mind and stands so declared by a competent court; or

(e) is convicted and sentenced to imprisonment for an offence which in the opinion of the President involves moral turpitude.

24. Term of Office of Member of the State Commission. 1. A person appointed as Chairperson shall hold office for a term of five years from the date on which he enters upon his office or until he attains the age of seventy years, whichever is earlier.

2. A person appointed as a Member shall hold office for a term of five years from the date on which he enters upon his office and shall be eligible for re-appointment for another term of five years:

Provided that no Member shall hold office after he has attained the age of seventy years.

3. On ceasing to hold office, a Chairperson or a Member shall be ineligible for further employment under the Government of a State or under the Government of India.

25. Member to Act as Chairperson or to Discharge his Functions in Certain Circumstances. 1. In the event of the occurrence of any vacancy in the office of the Chairperson by reason of his death, resignation or otherwise, the Governor may by notification, authorize one of the Members to act as the Chairperson until the appointment of a new Chairperson to fill such vacancy.

2. When the Chairperson is unable to discharge his functions owing to absence on leave or otherwise, such one of the Members as the Governor may, by notification, authorize in this behalf, shall discharge the functions of the Chairperson until the date on which the Chairperson resumes his duties.

26. Terms and Conditions of Service of Members of the State Commission. The salaries and allowances payable to, and other terms and conditions of service of, the Members shall be such as may be prescribed by the State Government:

Provided that neither the salary and allowances nor the other terms and conditions of service of a Member shall be varied to his disadvantage after his appointment.

27. Officers and other Staff of the State Commission. 1. The State Government shall make available to the Commission—

(a) an officer not below the rank of a Secretary to the State Government who shall be the Secretary of the State Commission; and

(b) such police and investigative staff under an officer not below the rank of an Inspector-General of Police and such other officers and staff as may be necessary for the efficient performance of the functions of the State Commission.

2. subject to such rules as may be made by the State Government in this behalf, the State Commission may appoint such other administrative technical and scientific staff as it may consider necessary.

3. The salaries, allowances and conditions of service of the officers and other staff appointed under sub-section (2) shall be such as may be prescribed by the State Government.

28. Annual and Special Reports of State Commission. 1. The State Commission shall submit an annual report to the State Government and may at any time submit special reports on any matter which, in its opinion, is of such urgency or importance that it should not be referred till submission of the annual report.

2. The State Government shall cause the annual and special reports of the State Commission to be laid before each House of State Legislature where to consists of two Houses, or where such Legislature consists of one House, before that House along with a memorandum of action taken or proposed to be taken on the recommendations of the State Commission and the reasons for non-acceptance of the recommendations, if any.

29. Application of Certain Provisions Relating to National Human Rights Commission to State Commissions. The provisions of sections 9, 10, 12, 13, 14, 15, 16, 17 and 18 shall apply to a State Commission and shall have effect, subject to the following modifications, namely:

(a) references to "Commission" shall be construed as references to "State Commission";

(b) in Section 10, in sub-section (3), for the word "Secretary General", the word "Secretary" shall be substituted;

(c) in section 12, clause (f) shall be omitted; and

(d) in section 17, in clause (i), the words "Central Government or any" shall be omitted.

HUMAN RIGHTS COURTS

30. For the purpose of providing speedy trial of offences arising out of violation of human rights, the State Government may, with the concurrence of the Chief Justice of the High Court, by notification, specify for each district a Court of Session to be a Human Rights court to try the said offences.
Provided that nothing in this section shall apply it:

(a) a Court of Session is already specified as a special court, or
(b) a special court is already constituted, for such offences under any other law for the time being in force.

31. Special Public Prosecutor. For every Human Rights Court, the State Government shall, by notification, specify a Public Prosecutor or appoint an advocate who has been in practice as an advocate forgot less than seven years, as a Special Public Prosecutor for the purpose of conducting cases in that Court.

FINANCE, ACCOUNTS AND AUDIT

32. Grants by the Central Government. 1. The Central Government shall after due appropriation made by Parliament by law in this behalf, pay to the Commission by way of grants such sums of money as the Central Government may think fit for being utilized for the purposes of the Act.

2. The Commission may spend such sums as it thinks fit for performing the functions under this Act, and such sums shall be treated as expenditure payable out of the grants referred to in sub-section (1).

33. Grants by the State Government. 1. The State Government shall, after due appropriation made by Legislature by law in this behalf, pay to the State Commission by way of grants such sums of money as the State Government may think fit for being utilized for the purposes of this Act.

2. The State Commission may spend such sums as it thinks fit for performing the functions under Chapter V, and such sums shall be treated as expenditure payable out of the grants referred to in sub-section (1).

34. Accounts and Audit. 1. The Commission shall maintain proper accounts and other relevant records and prepare an annual statement of accounts in such form as may be prescribed by the Central Government in consultation with the Comptroller and Auditor-General of India.

2. The Accounts of the Commission shall be audited by the Comptroller and Auditor-General at such intervals as may be specified by him and any expenditure incurred in connection with such audit shall be payable by the Commission to the Comptroller and Auditor-General.

3. The Comptroller and Auditor-General and any person appointed by him in connection with the audit of the accounts of the Commission under this Act shall have the same rights and privileges and the authority in connection with such audit as the comptroller and Auditor-General generally has in connection with the audit of Government accounts and, in particular, shall have the right to demand the production of books, accounts, connected vouchers and other documents and papers and to inspect any of the offices of the Commission.

4. The accounts of the Commission as certified by the Comptroller and Auditor-General or any other person appointed him in this behalf, together with the audit report thereon shall be forwarded annually to the Central Government be the Commission and the Central Government shall cause the audit report to be laid, as soon as may be after it is received, before each House of Parliament.

35. Accounts and Audit of State Commissioner. 1. The State Commission shall maintain proper accounts and other relevant records and prepare an annual statement of accounts in such form as may be prescribed by the State Government in consultation with the Comptroller and Auditor-General of India.

2. The accounts and Audit of State commission shall be audited by the Comptroller and Auditor-General at such interval as may be specified by him and any expenditure incurred in connection with such audit shall be payable by the State Commission to the Comptroller and Auditor-General.

3. The Comptroller and Auditor-General and any person appointed by him in connection with the audit of the accounts of the State Commission under this act shall have the same rights and privileges and the authority in connection with such audit as the Comptroller and Auditor-General has in connection with the

audit of Government accounts and in particular, shall have the right to demand the production of books, accounts, connected vouchers and other documents and papers and to inspect any of the offices of the State Commission.

4. The accounts of the State Commission, as certified by the Comptroller and Auditor-General or any other person appointed by him in this behalf, together with the audit report thereon, shall be forwarded annually to the State Government by the State Commission and the State Government shall cause the audit report to be laid, as soon as may be after it is received, before the State Legislature.

MISCELLANEOUS

36. Matters not Subject to Jurisdiction of the Commission. 1. The Commission shall not inquire into any matter which is pending before a State Commission or any other Commission fully constituted under any law for the time being in force.

2. The Commission or the State Commission shall not inquire into any matter after the expiry of one year from the date on which the act constituting violation of human rights is alleged to have been committed.

37. Constitution of Special Investigation Teams. Notwithstanding any thing contained in any other law for the time being in force, where the Government considers it necessary so to do. It may constitute one or more special investigation teams, consisting of such police officers as it thinks necessary for purposes of investigation and prosecution of offences arising out of violations of human rights.

38. Protection of Action Taken in Good Faith. No suit or other legal proceeding shall lie against the Central Government, State Government, Commission, the State Commission or any Member thereof or any person acting under the direction either of the Central Government, State Government, Commission or the State Commission in respect of any thing which is in good faith done or intended to be done in pursuance of this Act or of any rules or any order made thereunder or in respect of the publication by or under the authority of the Central Government, State Government, Commission or the State Commission of any report, paper or proceedings.

39. Member and Officers to be Public Servants. Every Member of the Commission, State Commission, and every officer appointed or authorized by the Commission of the State Commission to exercise functions under this Act shall be deemed to be a public servant within the meaning the meaning of section 21 of the Indian Penal Code.

40. Power of Central Government to Make Rules. 1. The Central Government may, by notification, make rules to carry out the provisions of this Act.

2. In particular and without prejudice to the generality of the foregoing power, such rules may provide for all or any of the following matters, namely,

(a) the salaries and allowances and other terms and conditions of service of the Members under section 8;

(b) the conditions subject to which other administrative, technical and scientific staff may be appointed by the Commission and the salaries and allowances of officers and other staff under sub-section (3) of section 11;

(c) any other power of a civil court required to be prescribed under clause (f) of sub-section (1) of section 13;

(d) the form in which the annual statement of accounts is to be prepared by the Commission under sub-section (1) of section 34; and

(e) any other matter which has to be, or may be prescribed.

3. Every rule made under this Act shall be laid, as sin as may be after it is made, before each House of Parliament, while it is in session, for a total period of thirty days which may be comprised in one session or in two or more successive session, and if, before the expiry of the sessions immediately following the session or the successive sessions aforesaid both Houses agree in making any modification in the rule or both Houses agree that the rule should not be made, the rule shall thereafter have effect only in such modified form or be of no effect, as the case may be; so however that any such modification or annulment shall be without prejudice to the validity of anything previously done under that rule.

41. Power of State Government to Make Rules. 1. The State Government may, by notification, make rules to carry out the provisions of this Act.

2. In the particular and without prejudice to the generality of the foregoing power; such rules may provide for all or any of the following matters, namely:

(a) the salaries and allowances and other terms and conditions of service of the members under section 26;

(b) the conditions subject to which other administrative, technical and scientific staff may be appointed by the State Commission and the salaries and allowances of officers and other staff under sub-section (3) of section 27; and

(c) the form in which the annual statement of accounts is to be prepared under sub-section (1) of section 35.

3. Every rule made by the State Government under this section shall be laid, as soon as may be after it is made before each House of the State Legislature where it consists of two Houses, or where such Legislature consists of one House, before that House.

42. Power to Remove Difficulties. 1. If any difficulty arises in giving effect to the provisions of this Act the Central Government may by order published in the Official Gazette make such provisions, not inconsistent with the provisions of this Act as appear to it to be necessary or expedient for removing the difficulty.

Provided that no such order shall be made after the expiry of the period of two years from the date of commencement of this Act.

2. Every Order made under this section shall, as soon as may be after it is made, by laid before each House of Parliament.

43. Repeal and Savings. 1. the Protection of Human Rights Ordinance, 1993 is hereby repeated.

2. Notwithstanding such repeal, anything done or any action taken and under the said Ordinance, shall be deemed to have been done or taken under the corresponding provisions of this Act.

THE PROTECTION OF CIVIL RIGHTS ACT, 1955
(Act No. 22 of 1955)
(As amended by Act No. 106 of 1976)

An Act to prescribe punishment for the preaching and practice of "Untouchability", for the enforcement of any disability arising therefrom and for matters connected therewith.

Be it enacted by Parliament in the Sixth Year of the Republic of India as follows:

1. ***Short Title, Extent and Commencement.*** 1. This Act may be called the Protection of Civil Rights Act, 1955.

2. It extends to the whole of India.

3. It shall come into force on such date as the Central Government may, by notification in the official Gazette, appoint.

2. ***Definitions.*** In this Act, unless the context otherwise requires:

(a) "civil rights" means any right accruing to a person by reason of the abolition of untouchability by Article 17 of the Constitution;

(aa) "hotel' includes a refreshment room, a boarding house, a lodging house, a coffee house and a cafe;

(b) "place" includes a house, building and other structure and premises, and also includes a tent, vehicle and vessel;

(c) "place of public entertainment" includes any place to which the public are admitted and in which an entertainment is provided or held;

Explanation: "Entertainment" includes any exhibition, performance game, sport and any other form of amusement;

(d) "place of public worship" means a place by whatever name known, which is used as a place of public religious worship or which is dedicated generally to, or is used generally by persons professing any religion or belonging to any religious denomination or any section thereof, for the performance of any religious service or for offering prayers therein and includes—

(i) all lands and subsidiary shrines appurtenant or attached to any such place,

(ii) convately owned place of worship which is, in fact allowed by the owner thereof to be used as a place of public worship, and

(iii) such land or subsidiary shrine appurtenant to such privately owned place of worship as is allowed by the owner thereof to be used as a place of public religious worship];

[(da) "Prescribed" means prescribed by rules made under this Act;

(db) "Scheduled Castes" has the meaning assigned to it in Clause (24) of Art. 166 of the Constitution];

(e) "show" means any premises where goods are sold either wholesale or by retail or both wholesale and by retail and includes—

(i) any place from where goods are sold by a hawker or vendor or from a mobile van or cart;

(ii) a laundry and a hair-cutting saloon,

(iii) any other place where services are rendered to customers;]

3. *Punishment for Enforcing Religious.* Whoever on the ground of "untouchability" prevents any person—

(a) from entering any place of public worship which is open to other persons professing the same religion or any section thereof as such person; or

(b) from worshiping or offering prayers or performing any religious service in any place of public worship, or bathing in, or using the waters of, any sacred tank, well, spring or water-course, river or lake or bathing at any *ghat* of such tank, water course, river or lake in the same manner and to the same manner and to the same extent as is permissible to the other person professing the same religion or any section thereof, as such person

[shall be punishable with imprisonment for a term of not less than one month and not more than six months and also with fine which shall be not less than one hundred rupees and not more than five hundred rupees.]

Explanation: For the purposes of this Section and Section 4 persons professing the Buddhist, Sikh and Jaina religion or persons professing the Hindu religion in any of its forms or developments including Virashaivas, Lingayats, Adivasis, followers of Brahmo, Prarthana, Arya Samaj and the Swaminarayana Smoradaya shall be deemed to be Hindus.

4. *Punishment for Enforcing Social Disabilities.* Whoever on the ground of "untouchability" enforces against any person any disability with regard to—

(i) access to any shop, public restaurant, hotel or place of public entertainment, or
(ii) the use of any utensils, and other Articles kept in any public restaurant, hotel, *dharmasala, sarai* or *musafirkhana* for the use of the general public or of any section thereof; or
(iii) the practice of any profession or the carrying on of any occupation, trade or business or employment in any job; or
(iv) the use of or access to, any river, stream, spring, well, tank, cistern, water-tap or other watering place, or any bathing *ghat*, burial or cremation ground, any sanitary convenience, any road, or passage, or any other place of public resort which other members of the public, or any section thereof, have a right to use or have access to; or
(v) the use of or access to, any place used for a charitable or a public purpose maintained wholly or partly out of State funds or dedicated to the use of the general public or any section thereof; or
(vi) the enjoyment of the benefit under a charitable trust created for the benefit of the general public or of any section thereof; or
(vii) the use of, or access to, any public conveyance; or
(viii) the construction, acquisition, or occupation of any residential premises in any locality, whatsoever, or
(ix) the use of any *dharmasala, sarai,* or *musafirkhana* which is open to general public, or to any section thereof; or
(x) the observance of any social or religious custom, usage or ceremony or taking part in, or taking out, any religious, social or cultural processing; or
(xi) the use of jewelry and finery.

[shall be punishable with imprisonment for a term of not less than one month and not more than six months and also with fine which shall be not less than one hundred rupees and not more than five hundred rupees.]

Explanation: For the purposes of this Section, enforcement of any disability includes any discrimination on the ground of "untouchability".

5. ***Punishment for Refusing to Admit Persons to Hospitals, etc.*** Whoever on the ground of "untouchability"—

(a) refuses admission to any person to any hospital, dispensary, educational institution or any hotel [x x x] if such hospital, dispensary, educational institution or hotel is established or maintained for the benefit of the general public or any section thereof; or

(b) does any act which discriminates against any such person after admission to any of aforesaid institution;

[shall be punishable with imprisonment for a term of not less than one month and not more than six months and also with fine which shall be not less than one hundred rupees and not more than five hundred rupees.]

6. ***Punishment for Refusing to Sell Goods or Render Services.*** Whoever on the ground of "untouchability" refuses to sell any goods or refuses to render any service to any person at the same time and place and on the same terms and conditions at/on which such goods are sold or services are rendered to other persons in the ordinary course of business shall be punishable with imprisonment for a term of not less than one month and not more than six months and also with fine which shall be not less than one hundred rupees and not more than five hundred rupees.

7. ***Punishment for other Offences Arising out of "Untouchability".*** Whoever:

(a) prevents any person from exercising any rights accruing to him by reason of the abolition of "untouchability" under Article 17 of the Constitution; or

(b) molests, injures, annoys, obstructs or causes or attempts to cause obstruction to any person in the exercise of any such right or molests, injures, annoys or boycotts any person by reason of his having exercised any such rights; or

(c) by words, either spoken or written, or by signs or by visible representations or otherwise, incites or encourages any person or class of persons or the public generally to practice "untouchability" in any form whatsoever; or

(d) insults or attempts to insult on the ground of "untouchability" a member of a Scheduled Caste;

[shall be punishable with imprisonment for a term of not less than one month and not more than six months, and also with fine which shall be not less than one hundred rupees and not more than five hundred rupees.]

Explanation 1. A person shall be deemed to boycott another person who—

(a) refuses to such other person or refuses to permit such other person, to use or occupy any house or land or refuses to deal with, work for hire for, or do business with, such other person or to render to him, receive from him any customary service, or refuses to do any of the said things on the terms on which such things would be commonly done in the ordinary course of business; or

(b) abstains from such social, professional or business relations as he would ordinarily maintain with other person.

Explanation 2. For the purpose of clause (c) a person shall be deemed to incite or encourage the practice of "untouchability"—

(i) if he directly or indirectly, preaches "untouchability" or it practices in any form; or

(ii) if he justifies whether on historical, philosophical or religious grounds or on the ground of any trading of the caste system or on any other ground, the practice of "untouchability" in any form.

1-A. Whoever commits any offence against the person or property of any individual as a reprisal or revenge for his having exercised any right accruing to him by reason of the abolition of "untouchability" under Article 17 of the constitution, shall, where the offence is punishable with imprisonment for a term proceeding two years, be punishable with imprisonment for a term which shall be of less than two years and also with fine

2. Whoever:

(i) demise to any person belonging to his community or any section thereof any right or privilege to which such person would be entitled as a member of such community or section; or

(ii) takes any part in the ex-communication of such person, on the ground that such person has refused to practice "untouchability" that such person has done any act in furtherance of the objects of this Act;

shall be punishable with imprisonment for a term of not less than one month and not more than six months, and also with fine which shall be not less than one hundred rupees and not more than five hundred rupees.

7. (a) *Unlawful Compulsory Labour when to be Deemed to be a Practice of "Untouchability".* 1. Whoever compels any person, on the ground of "untouchability" to do any scavenging or sweeping or to remove any carcass or a flay any animal, or to remove the umbilical cord or to do any other job of a similar nature shall be deemed to have enforced a disability arising out of "untouchability".

2. Whoever is deemed under sub-section (1) to have enforced a disability arising out of "untouchability" shall be punishable with imprisonment for a term which shall be not less than three months and not more than six months and also with fine which shall be not less than one hundred rupees and not more than five hundred rupees.

Explanation. For the purposes of the section "compulsion" includes a threat of social or economic boycott.

8. Cancellation or Suspension of Licenses in Certain Cases. When a person who is convicted of an offence under Section 6, holds any license under any law for the time being in force in respect of any profession, trade, calling or employment in relation to which the offence is committed the court trying the offence may, without prejudice to any other penalty to which such person may be liable under that section, direct that the license shall stand cancelled or to be suspended for such period, as the Court may deem fit, and every order of the Court to cancelling or suspending a license shall have effect as if it had been passed by the authority competent to cancel or suspend the license under any such law.

Explanation. In this section, "license" includes a permit or permission.

9. Resumption or Suspension of Grants made by Government. Where the manager or trustee of a place of public worship or any educational institution or hostel which is in respect of a grant of land or money from the Government is convicted of an offence under this Act and such conviction is not reversed or quashed in any appeal or revision, the Government may, if in its opinion the circumstances of the case warrant such a course, direct the suspension or resumption of the whole or any part of such grant.

10. Abatement of Offence. Whoever abets any offence under this Act shall be punishable with the punishment provided for the offence.

Explanation. A public servant who willfully neglects the investigation of any offence punishable under this Act shall be deemed to have abetted an offence punishable under this Act.

10.A. Power to State Government to Impose Collective Fine. 1. If after an inquiry in the prescribed manner the State Government is satisfied that the inhabitants of an area are concerned in, or abetting the commission of, any offence punishable under this Act, or labouring persons concerned in the commission of such offence or failing to render all the assistance in their power to discover or apprehend the offender or offenders or suppressing material evidence of the commission of such offence, the State Government may, by notification in the Official Gazette, impose a collective fine on such inhabitants and apportion such fine amongst the inhabitants who are able collectively to pay it, and such apportionment shall be made according to the State Government's judgment of the respective means of such inhabitants and in making any such apportionment the Government may assign a portion of such fine to a Hindu undivided family to be payable by it:

Provided that the fine apportioned to an inhabitant shall not be realized until the petition, if any, filed by him under sub-section (3) is disposed of.

2. The notification made under sub-section (1) shall be proclaimed in the area by beat of drum or in such other manner as the State Government may think best in the circumstances to bring the imposition of the collective fine to the notice of the inhabitants of the said area.

3. (a) Any person aggrieved by the imposition of the collective fine under sub-section (1) or by the order of apportionment, may within the prescribed period file a petition before the State Government or such other authority as that Government may specify in this behalf for being exempted from such fine or for modification of the order of apportionment:

Provided that no fee shall be charged for filing such petition.

(b) The State Government or the authority specified by it shall, after giving to the petitioner a reasonable opportunity of being heard, pass such order as it may think fit:

Provided that the amount of the fine exempted or reduced under this section shall not be realizable from any person, and the total fine imposed on the inhabitants of an area under sub-section (1) shall be deemed to have been reduced to that extent.

4. Notwithstanding anything contained in sub-section (4), the State Government may exempt the victims of any offence punishable under this Act or any person who does not, in its opinion, fall within the category of persons specified in sub-section (1), or any portion thereof.

5. The portion of collective fine payable by any person (including a Hindu undivided family) may be recovered in the manner provided by the Code of Criminal Procedure, 1973 (2 of 1974), for the recovery of fines imposed by a Court as if such portion were a fine imposed by a Magistrate.

11. Enhanced Penalty on Subsequent Conviction. Whoever having already been convicted of an offence under this Act or of an abatement of such offence is again convicted of any such offence or abatement shall, on conviction, be punishable:

(a) for the second offence, with imprisonment for a term of not less than six months and not more than one year, and also with fine which shall be not less than two hundred rupees and not more than five hundred rupees;

(b) for the third offence subsequent to the third offence with imprisonment for a term of not less than one year and not more than two years, and also with fine which shall be not less than five hundred rupees and not more than one thousand rupees.

12. Presumption by Courts in Certain Cases. Where any act constituting an offence under this Act is committed in relation to a member of a Scheduled Caste [xx], the Court shall presume, unless the contrary is proved, that such Act was committed on the ground of "untouchability".

13. Limitation of Jurisdiction of Civil Courts. 1. No Civil Court shall entertain or continue any suit or proceeding or shall pass any decree or order or executive wholly or partially any decree or order if the claim involved in such suit or proceeding or if the passing of such decree or order or if such execution would, in any way, be contrary to the provisions of this Act.

2. No Court shall, in adjudicating any matter or executing any decree or order, recognize any custom or usage imposing any disability on any person on the ground of "untouchability".

14. Offences by Companies. 1. If the person committing an offence under this Act is a company, every person who at the time the offence was committed was in-charge of and was responsible to, the company for the conduct of the business of the company, shall be deemed to be guilty of the offences and shall be liable to be proceeded against and punished accordingly:

Provided that nothing contained in this sub-section shall render any such person liable to any punishment, if he proves that the offence was committed without his knowledge or that he exercised all due diligence to prevent the commission of such offence.

2. Notwithstanding anything contained in sub-section (1) where an offence under this Act has been committed with consent of any director or manager, secretary or other officer of the company such director, manager, secretary or other officer shall also be deemed to be guilty of that offence and shall be liable to be proceeded against and punished accordingly.

Explanation. For the purposes of this section—

(a) "company" means any body corporate and includes a firm or other association of individuals; and

(b) "director" in relation to a firm means a partner in the firm.

[***14. Protection of Action Taken in Good Faith.*** 1. No suit, prosection or other legal proceeding shall lie against the Central Government or a State Government for anything which in good faith done or intended to be done under this Act.

2. No suit or other legal proceeding shall lie against the Central Government or a State Government for any damage cause or likely to be caused by anything which is in good faith done or intended to be done under this Act.]

15. Offences to be Cognizable and Triable Summarily. 1. Notwithstanding anything contained in the Code of Criminal Procedure, 1973 (2 of 1974) every offence punishable under this Act shall be cognizable and every such offence except where it is a punishable with imprisonment for a minimum term exceeding three months may be tried summarily by a Judicial Magistrate of the first class or in a Metropolitan area by a Metropolitan Magistrate in accordance with the procedure specified in the said code.

2. Notwithstanding anything contained in the Code of Criminal Procedure, 1973 (2 of 1974) when any public servant is alleged to have committed the offence of abatement of an offence punishable under this Act while acting or purporting to act in the discharge of his official duty, no court shall take cognizance of such offence of abatement except with the previous sanction—

(a) of the Central Government, in the case of a person employed in connection with the affairs of the Union; and
(b) of the State Government, in the case of a person employed in connection with the affairs of a State.

15-A. *Duty of State Government to Ensure that the Rights Accruing from the Abolition of "Untouchability" may be Availed of by the Concerned Persons:* 1. Subject to such rules as the Central Government may make in this behalf, the State Government shall take such measures as may be necessary for ensuring that the rights from the abolition of "untouchability" or made available to and are availed of by, the persons subjected to any disability arising out of "untouchability".

2. In particular, and without prejudice to the generality of the provisions of sub-section (1) such measures may include—

(i) the provision of adequate facilities including legal aid, to the persons subjected to any disability arising out of "untouchability" to enable them to avail themselves of such rights;
(ii) the appointment of officer for initiating exercising supervision over prosecution for the contravention of the provision of this Act;
(iii) the setting up of Special Courts for the trial of offences under this Act;
(iv) the setting up of Committees at such appropriate levels as the State Government may think fit to assist the State Government in formulating or implementing such measures;
(v) provision for periodic survey of the working of the

provisions of this Act with a view to suggesting measures for the better implementation of the provisions of this Act; and

(vi) the identification of the areas where persons are under any disability arising out of "untouchability" and adoption of such disability from such areas.

3. The Central Government shall take such steps as may be necessary to co-ordinate the measures taken by the State Government under sub-Section (1).

4. The Central Government shall, every year, place on the Table of each House of Parliament, report on the measures taken by itself and by the State Governments in pursuance of the provisions of this section.

16. Act to override other laws. Save as otherwise expressly provided in this Act, the provisions of this Act shall have effect notwithstanding anything inconsistent therewith contained in any other law for the time being in force, or any custom or usage or any instrument having effect by virtue of any such law or any decree or order of any Court or other authority.

16-A. Probation of Offenders Act, 1958, not to apply to persons above the age of fourteen years. The provisions of the probation of Offenders Act, 1958, (20 of 1958) shall not apply to any person above the age of fourteen years who is found guilty of having committed any offence punishable under this Act.

16-B. Power to make rules. 1. The Central Government may by notification in the Official Gazette, make rules to carry out the provisions of this Act.

2. Every rule made by the Central Government under this Act shall be laid as soon as may be after it is made, before each House of Parliament while it is in session for a total period of thirty days which may be comprised in one session or in two or more successive sessions, and if, before the expiry of the session immediately following the session or the successive session aforesaid, both Houses agree in making any modification in the rule or both Houses agree that the rule should not be made, the rule shall thereafter have effect only in such modified form or to be of no effect, as the case may be, so however, that any such modification or annulment shall be without prejudice to the validity of anything previously done under that rule.

17. Repeal. The enactments specified in the Schedule are hereby repealed to the extent to which they or any of the provisions contained therein correspond or are repugnant to this Act or to any of the provisions contained therein.

THE PROTECTION OF CIVIL RIGHTS RULES, 1977

S.O. 3006, 15.9.1977. In exercise of the powers conferred by Section 16-B of the Protection of Civil Rights Act, 1955 (22 of 1955), the Central Government hereby makes the following rules, namely:

1. Short Title and Commencement. 1. These rules may be called the Protection of Civil Rights Rules, 1977.

2. They shall come into force on the date of their publication in the Official Gazette.

2. Definition. In these rules unless the context otherwise requires,

(a) "Act" means the Protection of Civil Rights Act, 1955 (22 of 1955);

(b) " Section" means a section of the Act.

3. Manner of Inquiry under Sub-section (1) of Section 10-A. 1. The State Government may appoint an officer not below the rank of a Sub-Divisional Magistrate for the purpose of making an inquiry referred to in sub-section (1) of Section 10-A.

2. The officer appointed under sub-rule (1) (hereinafter in this rule referred to as the inquiry officer) shall issue a public notice specifying the date, time, place and the purpose of such inquiry and calling upon all the residents of the area in respect of which the inquiry is to be held to furnish such information and materials including documents in their possession, as may be relevant for the purposes of the enquiry, or

3. The public notice referred to in sub-rule (2) shall be in the local language or languages of the area and the same shall be,-

(i) published on the notice board in the Offices of the District Magistrate, the District Superintendent of Police, The Village Panchayat or Municipal Committee of the area and such other places as the enquiry officer deems fit and at least in one daily newspaper circulating in the area; and

(ii) proclaimed in the area by beat of drum or in such other manner as the inquiry officer may think best in the circumstance to bring the contents of the public notice to the notice of the inhabitants of the area.

4. The inquiry officer, while making such inquiry shall follow as nearly as practicable, the procedure for summary trials including

the recording of evidence as laid down in Chapter XXI of Code of Criminal Procedure, 1973 (2 of 1974).

5. The inquiry officer shall complete the inquiry as expeditiously as possible and submit his report to the State Government within such period, not exceeding six weeks as may be specified by the State Government in the order appointing the inquiry officer:

Provided that the State Government may having regard to the nature of the inquiry, extend the period of submission of the report by such period not exceeding two months in total as it may consider necessary.

4. Period for Filing a Petition under Sub-section (3) of Section 10-A. Any person aggrieved by the imposition of a collective fine under sub-section (1) of Section 10-A or by the order of apportionment, may within a period of thirty days from the date of proclamation of the notification under sub-section (2) of that section file a petition before the State Government or the authority specified by it:

Provided that where the State Government or the authority, as the case may be, may entertain the petition after the expiry of the said period if it is satisfied that the petitioner was prevented by sufficient cause from filing the petition in time.

2. The State Government or the authority before which the petition is filed shall dispose of the petition as expeditiously as possible.

5. Reports by the Government.- Every State Government shall, for the purpose of enabling the Central Government, place the report referred to in sub-section (4) of Section 15-A on the Table of each house of Parliament, furnish to the Government before the 15th day of February each year, a summary of the measures taken by it under sub-sections (1) and a (2) of the section during the preceding calendar year and shall also furnish such other information as may be required by the Central Government from time to time.

4

Scheduled Castes, Scheduled Tribes, Backward Classes, *Safai Karamcharis*, Minorities and Human Rights

THE SCHEDULED CASTES AND THE SCHEDULED TRIBES (PREVENTION OF ATROCITIES) ACT, 1989

(No. 33 of 1989)
(11th September, 1989)

Received the assent of the President on September 11, 1989 and published in the Gazette of India, Extra, Part II, Section 1, Dt. 12th September, 1989, Sl. No. 39.

An act to prevent the commission of offences of atrocities against the members of the Scheduled Castes and the Scheduled Tribes, to provide for Special Courts for the trial of such offences and for the relief and rehabilitation of the victims of such offences and for matters connected therewith or incidental thereto.

Be it enacted by Parliament in the Fortieth Year of the Republic of India as follows:

The Scheduled Castes and the Scheduled Tribes (Prevention of Atrocities) Act, 1989 is an Act to prevent the Commission of offences of atrocities against the member of the Scheduled Castes and the Scheduled Tribes and to provide for special courts for the trial of such offences.

PRELIMINARY

1. ***Short Title, Extent and Commencement.*** 1. This Act may be called the Scheduled Castes and the Scheduled Tribes (Prevention of Atrocities) Act, 1989.

2. It extends to the whole of India except the State of Jammu and Kashmir.

It shall come into force on such date as the Central Government may by notification in the Official Gazette, appoint.

2. *Definitions.* 1. In this Act unless the context otherwise requires—

(a) "Atrocity" means an offence punishable under Section 3;

(b) "Code" means the Code of Criminal Procedure 1973 (2 of 1974);

(c) "Scheduled Castes and Scheduled Tribes" shall have the meanings assigned to them respectively under Clause (24) and Clause (25) of Article 366 of the Constitution;

(d) "Special Court" means a Court of Session specified as a Special Court in Section 14;

(e) "Special Public Prosecutor" means a Public Prosecutor specified as Special Public Prosecutor or an advocate referred to in Section 15;

(f) Words and expressions used but not defined in this Act, and defined in the Code or the Indian Penal Code (45 of 1860) shall have the meanings assigned to them respectively in the Code, or as the case may be, in the Indian Penal Code.

2. Any reference in this Act to any enactment or any provision thereof shall, in relation to an area in which such enactment or such provision is not in force, be construed as a reference to the corresponding law, if any, in force in that area.

OFFENCES AT ATROCITIES

3. ***Punishment for Offences of Atrocities.*** 1. Whoever, not being a member of a Scheduled Caste or a Scheduled Tribe

(i) forces a member of a Scheduled Caste or a Scheduled Tribe to drink or eat any inedible or obnoxious substance;

(ii) acts with intent to cause injury, insult or annoyance to any member of a Scheduled Caste or a Scheduled Tribe by dumping excreta, waste matter, carcasses or any other obnoxious substance in his premises or neighbourhood;

(iii) forcibly removes clothes from the person of a member of a Scheduled Caste or a Scheduled Tribe or parades him naked or with painted face or body or commits any similar act which is derogatory to Human Dignity;

(iv) wrongfully occupies or cultivates any land owned by, or allotted to, or notified by any competent authority to be allotted to, a member of a Scheduled Caste or Scheduled Tribe or gets the land allotted to him transferred;

(v) wrongfully dispossesses a member of a Scheduled Caste or a Scheduled Tribe from his land or premises or interferes with the enjoyment of his rights any land, premises or water;

(vi) compels or entices a member of a Scheduled Caste or Scheduled Tribe to do 'begging' or other similar forms of forced or bonded labour other than any, compulsory service for public purpose imposed by Government;

(vii) forces or intimidates a member of a Scheduled Caste or a Scheduled Tribe not to vote or to vote to a particular candidate or to vote in a manner other than that provided by law;

(viii) institutes false, malicious or vexatious suit or criminal or other legal proceedings against a member of a Scheduled Caste or a Scheduled Tribe;

(ix) gives any false or frivolous information to any public servant and thereby causes such public servant to use his lawful power to the injury or annoyance of a member of a Scheduled Caste or a Scheduled Tribe;

(x) internationally insults or intimidates with extent to humiliate a member of a Scheduled Caste or a Scheduled Tribe in any place within public view;

(xi) assaults or uses force to any woman belonging to a Scheduled Caste or a Scheduled Tribe with intent to dishonour or outrage her modesty;

(xii) being in a position to dominate the will of a woman belonging to Scheduled Caste or a Scheduled Tribe and uses that position to exploit her sexually to which she would not have otherwise agreed;

(xiii) corrupts or fouls the water of any spring reservoir or any other source ordinarily used by members of the Scheduled Castes or the Scheduled Tribes so as to render it less fit for the purpose for which it is ordinarily used;

(xiv) denies a member of a Scheduled Caste or a Scheduled Tribe any customary right to passage to place of public resort or obstructs such member so as to prevent him from using or having access to a place of public resort to which other members of public or any section thereof have a right to use or access to;

(xv) forces or causes a member of a Scheduled Caste of Scheduled Tribe to leave his house, village, or other place or residence;

shall be punishable with imprisonment for a term which shall not be less that six months but which may extend to five years and with fine.

2 Whoever, not being a member of a Scheduled Caste or a Scheduled Tribe.

(i) gives or fabricates false evidence intending thereby to cause, or knowing it to be likely that he will thereby cause any member of a Scheduled Caste or a Scheduled Tribe to be convicted of an offence which is capital by the law for the time being in force shall be punished with imprisonment for life and with fine and if an innocent member of a Scheduled Caste or a Scheduled Tribe be convicted and executed in consequence of such false or fabricated evidence the person who gives or fabricates such false evidence shall be punished with death.

(ii) gives or fabricates false evidence intending thereby to cause, or knowing it to be likely that he will thereby cause, any member of a Scheduled Caste or a Scheduled Tribe to be convicted of an offence which is not capital but punishable with imprisonment for a term of seven years or upwards, shall be punishable with imprisonment for a term which shall not be less than six months but which may extend to seven years or upwards and with fine;

(iii) commits mischief by fire or any explosive substance intending to cause or knowing it to be likely that he will thereby cause damage to any property belonging to a member of a Scheduled Castes or a Scheduled Tribes, shall be punishable with imprisonment for a term which shall not be less than six months but which may extend to seven years and with fine;

(iv) commits mischief by fire or any explosive substance intending to cause or knowing it to be likely that he will thereby cause destruction of any building which is ordinarily used as a place of worship or as a place for human dwelling or as a place for custody of the property by a member of a Scheduled Caste or a Scheduled Tribe, shall be punishable with imprisonment for life and with fine;

(v) commits any offence under the Indian Penal Code (45 of 1860) punishable with imprisonment for a term of 10 years or more against a person or property on the ground that such person is a member of a Scheduled Caste or a Scheduled Tribe, or such propert belongs to such member, shall be punishable with imprisonment for life and with fine;

(vi) knowingly or having reason to believe that an offence has been committed under this Chapter, causes any evidence of the commission of that offence to disappear with the intention of screening the offender from legal punishment, or with the intention gives any information respecting the offence which he knows or believes to be false, shall be punishable with the punishment provided for that offence; or

(vii) being a public servant, commits any offence under this section shall be punishable with imprisonment for a term which shall not be less than one year but which may extend to the punishment provided for their offence.

4. *Punishment for Neglect of Duties.* Whoever, being public servant but not being a member of a Scheduled Caste or a Scheduled Tribe, willfully neglects his duties required to be performed by him under this Act, shall be punishable with imprisonment for a term which shall not be less than six months but which may extend to one year.

5. *Enhanced Punishment for Subsequent Conviction.* Whoever, having already been convicted of an offence under this Chapter is convicted for the second offence or any offence subsequent to the second offence, shall be punishable with imprisonment for a term which shall not be less than one year which may extend to the punishment provided for that offence.

6. *Application of Certain Provisions of the Indian Penal Code.* Subject to the other provisions of this Act, the provisions of Sec. 34, Chapter III, Chapter IV, Chapter V, Chapter V-A, Section 149 and Chapter XXIII of the Indian Penal Code (45 of 1860), shall, so far as may be, apply for the purposes of this Act as they apply for the purposes of the Indian Penal Code.

7. *Forfeiture of Property of Certain Persons.* 1. Where a person has been convicted any offence punishable under this Chapter, the Special Court may, in addition to awarding any punishment, by order in writing, declare that any property, movable or immovable or both belonging to the person, which has been sued for the commission of that offence, shall stand forfeited to Government.

2. Where any person is accused of any offence under this Chapter, it shall be open to the Special Court trying him to pass an order that all or any of the period of such trial, be attached, and where such trial ends in conviction, the property so attached shall be liable to forfeiture to the extent it is required for the purpose of realization of any fine imposed under this Chapter.

*8. **Presumption as to Offences.*** In a prosecution for an offence under this Chapter, if it is proved that—

(a) the accused rendered any financial assistance to a person accused of, or reasonably suspected of committing an offence under this Chapter, the special Court shall presume, unless the contrary proved, that such person had abetted the offence;

(b) a group of persons committed an offence under this Chapter and if it is proved that the offence committed was a sequel to any existing dispute regarding land or any other matter, it shall be presumed that the offence was committed in furtherance of the common intention or in prosecution of the common object.

*9. **Conferment of Powers.*** 1. Notwithstanding anything contained in the Code or in any other provision of this Act, the State Government may, if it considers it necessary or expedient so to do—

(a) for the prevention of and for copying with any offence under this Act, or

(b) for any case or class or group of cases this Act, on any district or part thereof, confer by notification in the Official Gazette, on any district or part thereof, as the case may be, for such case or class or group of cases, and in particular, the powers of arrest, investigation and prosecution of persons before any Special Court.

2. All officers of police and all other officers of Government shall assist the officer referred to in sub-section (1) in the execution of the provisions of this Act or any rule, scheme or order made hereunder.

3. The provisions of the Code shall, so far as may be apply to the exercise of the powers by an officer under sub-section (1).

EXTERNMENT

10. Removal of Person Likely to Commit Offence. 1. Where the Special Court is satisfied, upon a complaint or a police report that a person is likely to commit an offence under Chapter II of this Act in any area included in 'Scheduled Area' or 'tribal areas', as referred to in Article 244 of the Constitution, it may by order in writing, direct such person to remove himself beyond the limits of such area, by such route and within such time as may be specified in the order, and not to return to that area from which he was directed to remove himself for such period, not exceeding two years, as may be specified in the order;

2. The Special Court shall, along with the order under sub-section (1), communicate to the persons directed under that sub-section the grounds on which such order has been made.

3. The Special Court may revoke or modify the order made under sub-section (1) for the reasons to be recorded in writing, on the representation made by the person against whom such order has been made or by any other person on his behalf within thirty days from the date of the order.

11. Procedure and Failure of Person to Remove Himself from Area and Enter thereon after Removal. 1. If a person to whom direction has been issued under Section 10 to remove himself from any area—

(a) fails to remove himself as directed; or
(b) having so removed himself enters such area within the period specified in the order.

Otherwise than with the permission in writing of the Special Court under sub-section (2) the Special Court may cause him to be arrested and removed in police custody to such place outside such area as the Special Court may specify.

2. The Special Court may, by order in writing, permit any person in respect of whom an order under Section 10 has been made, to return to the area from which he was directed to remove himself for such temporary period and subject to such conditions as may be specified in such order and may require him to execute a bond with or without surety for the due observation of the conditions imposed.

3. The Special Court may at any time revoke any such permission.

4. Any person who, with such permission returns to the area from which he was directed to remove himself shall observe the

conditions imposed and at the expiry of the temporary period for which he was permitted to return or on the revocation of such permission before the expiry of such temporary period, shall remove himself outside such area and shall not return thereto within the unexpired portion specified under Section 10 without a fresh permission.

5. If a person fails to observe any of the conditions imposed or to remove himself accordingly having so removed himself enters or returns to such area without fresh permission the Special Court may cause him to be arrested and removed in police custody to such place outside area as the Special Court may specify.

12. Taking Measurements and Photographs, etc. of Persons Against Whom Order Under Section 10 is Made. 1. Every person against whom an order has been made under Section 10 shall, if so required by the Special Court, allow, his measurement and photographs to be taken by a police officer.

2. If any person referred to in sub-section (1), when required to his measurements or photographs to be taken resists or refuses to allow his taking of such measurements or photographs, it shall be lawful to use all necessary means to secure the taking thereof.

3. Resistance to or refusal to allow the taking of measurements or photographs under sub-section (2) shall be deemed to an offence under Section 186 of the Indian Penal Code (45 of 1860).

4. Where an order under Section 10 is revoked, all measurements and photographs (including negatives) taken under sub-section (2) shall be destroyed or made over to the person against whom such order is made.

13. Penalty for Non-compliance with Order Under Section 10. Any person contravening an order of the Special Court made under Section 10 shall be punishable with imprisonment for a term which may extend to one year and with fine.

SPECIAL COURTS

14. Special Court. For the purpose of providing for speedy trial, the State Government shall, with the concurrence of the Chief Justice of the High Court, by notification in the Official Gazette, specify for each district a Court of Session to be a Special Court to try the offences under this Act.

15. Special Public Prosecutor. For every Special Court, the State Government shall, by notification in the Official Gazette, specify a Public Prosecutor or appoint an advocate who has been in practice as an advocate for not less than seven years, as a Special Public Prosecutor for the purpose of conducting cases in that Court.

MISCELLANEOUS

16. Power of State Government to Impose Collective Fine. The provision of Section 10-A of the Protection of Civil Rights, Act, `1955 (22 of 1955) shall so far as may, apply for the purpose of imposition and realization of collective fine and for all other matters connected therewith under this Act.

17. Preventive Action to be Taken by the Law and Order Machinery. 1. A District Magistrate or a Sub-Divisional Magistrate or any other Executive Magistrate or any Police Officer not below the rank of a Deputy Superintendent of Police may on receiving information and after such inquiry as he may think necessary has reason to believe that a person or a group of persons not belonging to the Scheduled Castes or the Scheduled Tribes, residing in or frequenting any place within the local limits of his jurisdiction is likely to commit an offence or has threatened to commit any offence under this Act and is of the opinion that there are sufficient grounds for proceeding declare such an area to be an area prone to atrocities and take necessary action for keeping the peace and good behaviour and maintenance of public order and tranquility and may take preventive action.

2. The provisions of Chapter VII, X and XI of the Code shall, so far as may be apply for the purposes of sub-section (1).

3. The State Government may, by notification, in the Official Gazette, make one or more schemes specifying the manner in which the officers referred to sub-section (1) shall take appropriate action specified in such scheme or schemes to prevent atrocities and to restore the feeling of security amongst the members of the Scheduled Castes and the Scheduled Tribes.

18. Section 438 of the Code not to Apply to Person Committing an Offence Under the Act. Nothing in Section 438 of the Code shall apply in relation to any case involving the arrest of any person on an accusation of having committed an offence under this Act.

19. Section 360 of the Code or the Provision of the Probation of Offenders Act not Apply to Persons Guilty of an Offence Under the Act. The provisions of Section 360 of the Code and the provisions of the Probation of Offenders Act, 1958 (20 of 1958) shall apply to any person above the age of eighteen years who is found guilty having committed an offence under this Act.

20. Act to Override other Laws. Save as otherwise provided in this Act, the provisions of this Act shall have effect notwithstanding anything inconsistent therein contained in any. other law for the time being in force or any custom or usage or any instrument having effect by virtue of any such law.

21. Duty of Government to Ensure Effective Implementation of the Act. 1. Subject to such rules as the Central Government may make in this behalf, the State Government shall take such measures as may be necessary for the effective implementation of this Act.

2. In particular, and without prejudice to the generality of the foregoing provisions, such measures may include—

(i) the provision for adequate facilities, including legal aid, to the persons subjected to atrocities to enable them to avail themselves of justice;

(ii) the provisions for travelling and maintenance expenses to witness, including the victims of atrocities, during investigation and trial of offences under this Act;

(iii) the provision for the economic and social rehabilitation or the victims of the atrocities;

(iv) the appointment of officers of initiating or exercising supervision over prosecution for the contravention of the provisions of this Act;

(v) the setting up of committees at such appropriate levels as the State Government may think fit to assist that Government in formulation or implementation of such measures;

(vi) provision for a periodic survey of the working of the provisions this Act with a view to suggesting measures for the better implementation of the provisions of this Act;

(vii) the identification of the areas where the members of the Scheduled Castes and the Scheduled Tribes are likely to be subjected to atrocities and adoption of such measures so as to ensure safety for such members.

3. The Central Government shall take such steps as may be necessary to co-ordinate the measures taken by the State Government under sub-section (1)

4. The Central Government shall, every year, place on the table of each House of Parliament a report on the measures taken by itself and by the State Governments in pursuance of the provisions of this section.

22. *Protection of Action Taken in Good Faith.* No suit, prosecution of other legal proceedings shall lie against the Central Government or against the State Government or any officer or authority of Government or any other person for anything which is in good faith done or intended to be done under this Act.

23. *Power to Make Rules.* 1. The Central Government may, by notification in the Official Gazette, make rules for carrying out the purposes of this Act.

2. Every rule made under this Act shall be laid, as soon as may be after it is made, before each House of Parliament, while it is in session for a total period of thirty days which may be comprised in one session or in two or more successive sessions and if, before the expiry of the session immediately following the session of successive sessions aforesaid, both Houses agree in making any modification in the rule or both Houses agree that the rule should not be made, the rule shall thereafter have effect only in such modified form or be of no effect, as the case may be; so however, that any such modification or annulment shall be without prejudice to be validity of any thing previously done under that rule.

THE SCHEDULED CASTES AND THE SCHEDULED TRIBES (PREVENTION OF ATROCITIES) RULES, 1995

G S.R. No. 316(E), dated 31st March, 1995—In exercise of the power conferred by sub-section (1) of Section 23 of the Scheduled Castes and the Scheduled Tribes (Prevention of Atrocities) Act, 1989 (33 of 1989), the Central Government hereby makes the following rules namely.

1. *Short Title and Commencement.* 1. These rules may be called the Scheduled Castes and Scheduled Tribes (Prevention of Atrocities) Rules, 1995.

2. They shall come into force on the date of their publication in the Official Gazette.

2. *Definitions.* In these rules, unless the context otherwise requires,—

(a) "Act" means the Scheduled Castes and the Scheduled Tribes (Prevention of Atrocities) Act, 1989 (33 of 1989);

(b) "dependent", with its grammatical variations and cognate expression, includes wife, children, whether married or unmarried, dependent parents, widowed sister, widow and children of predeceased son of a victim of atrocity;

(c) "identified area" means such area where State Government has reason to believe that atrocity may take place or there is an apprehension of re-occurrence of an offence under the Act or an area prone to victim of atrocity;

(d) "Non-Government Organisation" means a voluntary organisation engaged in the welfare activities relating to the Scheduled Castes and the Scheduled Tribes and registered under the Societies Registration Act, 1860 (21 of 1860) or under any law for the registration of documents or such organisation for the time being in force;

(e) "Schedule" means the Schedule annexed to these rules;

(f) "Section" means section of the Act;

(g) "State Government", in relation to a Union Territory, means the Administrator of that union Territory appointed by the President under Article 239 of the Constitution;

(h) words and expressions used herein and not defined but defined in the Act shall have the meaning, respectively, assigned to them in the Act.

3. Precautionary and Preventive Measures. 1. With a view to prevent atrocities on the Scheduled Castes and the Scheduled Tribes, the State Government shall,

(i) identify the area where it has reasons to believe that atrocity may take place or there is an apprehension of re-occurrence of an offence under the Act;

(ii) order the District Magistrate and Superintendent of Police or any other officer to visit the identified area and review the law and other situation;

(iii) if deem necessary, in the identified area cancel the arms licences of the persons, not being member of the Scheduled Castes or Scheduled Tribes, their near relations, servants or employees and family friends and get such arms deposited in the Government Armoury;

(iv) seize all illegal firearms and prohibit an illegal manufacture of firearms;

(v) with a view to ensure the safety of person and property, if deem necessary, provide arms licences to the members of the Scheduled Castes and the Scheduled Tribes;

(vi) constitute a high power State-level committee, district and divisional level committees or such number of committees as deem proper and necessary for assisting the Government in implementation of the provisions of the Act;

(vii) set-up a vigilance and monitoring committee to suggest effective measures to implement the provisions of the Act;

(viii) set-up Awareness Centres and organise Workshops in the identified area or at some other place to educate the persons belonging to the Scheduled Castes and the Scheduled Tribes about their rights and the protection available to them under the provisions of various Central and State enactments or rules, regulations and schemes framed thereunder;

(ix) encourage Non-Government Organisations for establishing and maintaining Awareness Centres and organising Workshops and provide them necessary financial and other sort of assistance;

(x) deploy special Police force in the identified area;

(xi) by the end of every quarter, review the law and order situation, functioning of different committees, performance of Special Public Prosecutors, Investigating Officers and other Officers responsible for implementing the provisions of the Act and the cases registered under the Act.

4. *Supervision of Prosecution and Submission of Report.* 1. The State Government on the recommendation to the District Magistrate shall prepare for each district a panel of such number of eminent senior advocates who have been in practice for not less than seven years, as it may deem necessary for conducting cases in the Special Courts. Similarly, in consultation with the Director of Prosecution, officer-in-charge of the prosecution, a panel of such number of Public Prosecutors as it may deem necessary for conducting cases in the Special Courts, shall also be specified. Both these panels shall be notified in the Official Gazette of the State and shall remain in force for a period of three years.

2. The District Magistrate and the Director of Prosecution, officer-in-charge of the prosecution shall review at least twice in a calendar year, in the month of January and July, the performance of Special Public Prosecutors so specified or appointed and submit a report to the State Government.

3. If the State Government is satisfied or has reason to believe that a Special Public Prosecutor so appointed as specified has not conducted the case to the best of his ability and with due care and caution, his name may be, for reasons to be recorded in writing, denotified.

4. The District Magistrate and the officer-in-charge of the prosecution at the District level, shall review the position of cases registered under the Act and submit a monthly report on or before 20th day of each subsequent month to the Director of Prosecution and the State Government. This report shall specify the actions taken/proposed to be taken in respect of investigation and prosecution of each case.

5. Notwithstanding anything contained in sub-rule (1) the District Magistrate or the Sub-Divisional Magistrate may, if deem necessary or if so desired by the victims of atrocity engage an eminent Senior Advocate for conducting cases in the Special Courts on such payment of fees as he may consider appropriate.

6. Payment of fee to the Special Public Prosecutor shall be fixed by the State Government on a scale higher than the other panel advocates in the State.

5. Information to Police Officer-in-Charge of a Police Station. 1. Every information relating to the commission of an offence under the Act, if given orally to an officer-in-charge of a Police station shall be reduced to writing by him or under his direction, and be read over to the informant, and every such information, whether given in writing or reduced to writing as aforesaid, shall be signed by the person giving it, and the substance thereof shall be entered in a book to be maintained by that police station.

2. A copy of the information as so recorded under sub-rule (1) above shall be given forthwith, free of cost, to the informant.

3. Any person aggrieved by a refusal on the part of a officer-in-charge of a Police station to record the information referred to in sub-rule (1) may send the substance of such information, in writing and by post, to the Superintendent of Police concerned who after investigation either by himself or by a Police officer not below the rank of Deputy Superintendent of Police, shall make an order in writing to the officer-in-charge of the concerned Police station to enter the substance of that information in the book to be maintained by that police station.

6. Spot Inspection by Officers. 1. Whenever the District Magistrate or the Sub-Divisional Magistrate or any other Executive Magistrate or any Police officer not below the rank of Deputy Superintendent of Police receives an information from any person or upon his own knowledge that an atrocity had been committed on the members of the Scheduled Castes or the Scheduled Tribes within his jurisdiction he shall immediately himself visit the place of occurrence to assess the extent of atrocity, loss of life, loss and damage to the property and submit a report forthwith to the State Government.

2. The District Magistrate or the Sub-Divisional Magistrate or any other Executive Magistrate and the Superintendent of Police, Deputy Superintendent of Police after inspecting the place or area shall on the spot,—

(i) draw a list of victims, their family members and dependents entitled of relief,

(ii) prepare a detailed report of the extent of atrocity loss and damage to the property of the victims;

(iii) order for intensive Police patrolling in the area;

(iv) take effective and necessary steps to provide protection to the witnesses and other sympathisers of the victims;

(v) provide immediate relief to the victims.

7. ***Investigating Officer.*** 1. An offence committed under the Act shall be investigated by a Police officer not below the rank of a Deputy Superintendent of Police. The Investigating Officer shall be appointed by the State Government, Director-General of Police, Superintendent of Police after taking into account his past experience, sense of ability and justice to perceive the implications of the case and investigate it along with right lines within the shortest possible time.

2. The Investigating Officer so appointed under sub-rule (1) shall complete the investigation on top priority within thirty days and submit the report to the Superintendent of Police who in turn will immediately forward the report to the Director-General of Police of the State Government.

3. The Home Secretary and the Social Secretary to the State Government, Director of Prosecution, the Officer-in-Charge of Prosecution and the Director General of Police shall review by the end of every quarter the position of all investigations done by the Investigating Officer.

8. ***Setting up of the Scheduled Castes and the Scheduled Tribes Protection Cell.*** 1. The State Government shall set up a Scheduled Castes and the Scheduled Tribes Protection Cell at the State headquarters under the charge of Director of Police, Inspector-General of Police. This Cell shall be responsible for,

(i) conducting survey of the identified area;

(ii) maintaining public order and tranquillity in the identified area;

(iii) recommending to the State Government for deployment of special Police force or establishment of special Police post in the identified area;

(iv) making investigations about the probable causes leading to an offence under the Act;

(v) restoring the feeling of security amongst the members of the Scheduled Castes and the Scheduled Tribes;

(vi) informing the nodal officer and special officer about the law and order situation in the identified area;

(vii) making enquiries about the investigation and spot inspections conducted by various officers;

(viii) making enquiries about the action taken by the Superintendent of Police in the cases where an officer-in-charge of the police station has refused to enter an information in a book to be maintained by that police station under sub-rule (3) of Rule 5;

(ix) making enquiries about the wilful negligence by a public servant;

(x) reviewing the position of cases registered under the Act; and

(xi) submitting a monthly report on or before 20th day of each subsequent month to the State Government nodal officer about the action taken or proposed to be taken in respect of the above.

9. Nomination of Nodal Officer. The State Government shall nominate a nodal officer of the level of a Secretary to the Government preferably belonging to the Scheduled Castes or the Scheduled Tribes, for co-ordinating the functioning of the District Magistrates and Superintendent of Police or other officers authorised by them as Investigating Officers and other officers responsible for implementing the provisions of the Act. By the end of the every quarter, the nodal officer shall review—

(i) the reports received by the State Government under sub-rules (2) and (4) of Rule 4, Rule 6, clause (xi) of rule 8;

(ii) the position of cases registered under the Act;

(iii) law and order situation in the identified area;

(iv) various kinds of measures adopted for providing immediate relief in cash or kind or both to the victim of atrocity or his or her dependent;

(v) adequacy of immediate facilities like rationing, clothing, shelter, legal aid, travelling allowance, daily allowance and transport facilities provided to the victim of atrocity or his or her dependents;

(vi) performance of non-Government organisations, the Scheduled Castes and the Schedule Tribes Protection Cell, various committees and the public servants responsible for implementing the provisions of the Act.

10. Appointment of a Special Officer. In the identified area a Special Officer not below the rank of an Additional District Magistrate shall be appointed to co-ordinate with the District Magistrate,

Superintendent of Police or other officers responsible for implementing the provisions of the Act, various committees and the Scheduled Castes and the Scheduled Tribes Protection Cell.

The Special Officer shall be responsible for—

(i) providing immediate relief and other facilities to the victims of atrocity and initiate necessary measures to prevent or avoid reoccurrence of atrocity;

(ii) setting up an awareness centre and organising workshop in the identified area or at the district headquarters to educate the persons belonging to the Scheduled Castes and the Scheduled Tribes about their rights and the protection available to them under the provisions of various Central and State enactments or rules and schemes etc., framed therein;

(iii) co-ordinating with the Non-Governmental organisations and providing necessary facilities and financial and other type of assistance to Non-Governmental Organisation for maintaining centres or organising workshops.

11. Travelling Allowance, Daily Allowance, Maintenance Expenses and Transport Facilities to the Victim of Atrocity or his or her Dependents and Witnesses. 1. Every victim of atrocity or his/her dependents and witnesses shall be paid to and fro rail fare by second class in express/mail/passenger train or actual bus or taxi fare from his/her place of residence or actual bus or taxi fare from his/her place of residence or place of stay to the place of investigation or hearing of trial of an offence under the Act.

2. The District Magistrate or the Sub-Divisional Magistrate or any other Executive Magistrate shall make necessary arrangements for providing transport facilities or reimbursement of full payment thereof to the victims of atrocity and witnesses for visiting the Investigating Officer, Superintendent of Police/Deputy Superintendent of Police, District Magistrate or any other Executive Magistrate.

3. Every woman witness the victim of atrocity or her dependent being a woman or a minor, a person more than sixty years of age and a person having 40 per cent or more disability shall be entitled to be accompanied by an attendant of her/his choice. The attendant shall also be paid travelling and maintenance expenses as applicable to the witness or the victim of atrocity when called upon during hearing, investigation and trial of an offence under the Act.

4. The witness, the victim of atrocity or his/her dependent and the attendant shall be paid daily maintenance expenses for the days he/she is away from the place of his/her residence or stay during investigation, hearing and trial of an offence, at such rates but not less than the minimum wages, as may be fixed by the State Government for the agricultural labourers.

5. In addition to daily maintenance expenses the witness, the victim of atrocity (or his/her dependent) and the attendant shall also be paid diet expenses at such rates as may be fixed by the State Government from time to time.

6. The payment of travelling allowance, daily allowance, maintenance expenses and reimbursement of transport facilities shall be made immediately or not later than three days by the District Magistrate or the Sub-Divisional Magistrate or any other Executive Magistrate to the victims, their dependents/attendants and witnesses for the days they visit the Investigating Officer or in charge of Police station or hospital authorities or Superintendent of Police, Deputy Superintendent of Police or District Magistrate or any other officer concerned or the Special Court.

7. When an offence has been committed under Section 3 of the Act, the District Magistrate or the Sub-Divisional Magistrate or any other Executive Magistrate shall reimburse the payment of medicines, special medical consultation, blood transfusion, replacement of essential clothings, meals and fruits provided to the victim(s) of atrocity.

12. Measures to be Taken by the District Administration. 1. The District Magistrate and the Superintendent of Police shall visit the place or area where the atrocity has been committed to assess the loss of life and damage to the property and draw a list of victims, their family members and dependents entitled for relief.

2. The Superintendent of Police shall ensure that the First Information Report is registered in the book of the concerned police station and effective measures for apprehending the accused are taken.

3. The Superintendent of Police, after spot inspection, shall immediately appoint an Investigation Officer and deploy such police force in the area and take such other preventive measures as he may deem proper and necessary.

4. The District Magistrate or the Sub-Divisional Magistrate or any other Executive Magistrate shall make arrangements providing

immediate relief in cash or in kind or both to the victims of atrocity, their family members and dependents according to the scale as in the Schedule annexed to these Rules (Annexure I read with Annexure II). Such immediate relief shall also include food, water, clothing, shelter, medical aid, transport facilities and other essential items necessary for human beings.

5. The relief provided to the victim of the atrocity or his/her dependent under sub-rule (4) in respect of death, or injury to, or damage to property shall be in addition to any other right to claim compensation in respect thereof under any other law for the time being in force.

6. The relief and rehabilitation facilities mentioned in sub-rule (4) above shall be provided by the District Magistrate or the Sub-Divisional Magistrate or any other Executive Magistrate in accordance with the scales provided in the Schedule annexed to these rules.

7. A report of the relief and rehabilitation facilities provided to the victims shall also be forwarded to the Special Court by the District Magistrate or the Sub-Divisional Magistrate or the Executive Magistrate or Superintendent of Police. In case the Special Court is satisfied that the payment of relief was not made to the victim or his/her dependent in time or the amount of relief or compensation was not sufficient or only a part payment of relief or compensation was made, it may order for making in full on part payment of relief or any other kind of assistance.

13. Selection of Officers and Other Staff Members for Completing the Work Relating to Atrocity. 1. The State Government shall ensure that the administrative officers and other staff members to be appointed in an area prone to atrocity shall have the right aptitude and understanding of the problems of the Scheduled Castes and Scheduled Tribes.

2. It shall also be ensured by the State Government that persons from the Scheduled Castes and the Scheduled Tribes are adequately represented in the administration and in the Police force at all levels, particularly at the level of police posts and police station.

14. Specified Responsibility of the State Government. The State Government shall make necessary provisions in its annual budget for providing relief and rehabilitation facilities to the victims of atrocity. It shall review at least twice in a calendar year, in the month of January and July the performance of the Special Public Prosecutor specified or appointed under Section 15 of the Act, various reports received, investigation made and preventive steps taken by the District Magistrate, Sub-Divisional Magistrate and Superintendent of Police, relief and rehabilitation facilities provided to the victims and the reports in respect of lapses on behalf of the concerned officers.

15. Contingency Plan by the State Government. 1. State Government shall prepare a model contingency plan for implementing the provisions of the Act and notify the same in the Official Gazette of the State Government. It should specify the role and responsibility of various departments and their officers at different levels, the role and responsibility of Rural/Urban Local Bodies and Non-Government Organisation. *Inter alia* this plan shall contain a package of relief measures including the following:

(a) scheme to provide immediate relief in cash or in kind or both;
(b) allotment of agricultural land and house-sites;
(c) the rehabilitation packages;
(d) scheme for employment in Government or Government Undertaking to the dependent or one of the family members of the victim;
(e) pension scheme for widows, dependent children of the deceased, handicapped or old age victims of atrocity;
(f) mandatory compensation for the victims;
(g) scheme for strengthening the socio-economic condition of the victim;
(h) provision for providing brick/stone masonry house to the victims;
(i) such other elements as health care, supply of essential commodities, electrification, adequate drinking water facility, burial/cremation ground and link roads to the Scheduled Castes and the Scheduled Tribes habitates.

2. The State Government shall forward a copy of contingency plan or a summary thereof and a copy of the scheme, as soon as may be, to the Central Government in the Ministry of Welfare and to all the District Magistrates, Sub-Divisional Magistrates, Inspector Generals of Police and Superintendents of Police.

16. Constitution of State Level Vigilance and Monitoring Committee. 1. The State Government shall constitute a high power vigilance and monitoring committee of not more than 25 members consisting of the following—

(i) Chief Minister/Administrator-Chairman (in case of a State under President's Rule Governor); —*Chairman*

(ii) Home Minister, Finance Minister and Welfare Minister (in case of a State under the President's Rule Advisors); —*Members*

(iii) all elected Members of Parliament and the State Legislative Assembly and Legislative Counsel from the State belonging to the Scheduled Castes and the Scheduled Tribes. —*Members*

(iv) Chief Secretary, the Home Secretary, the Director-General of Police, Director/Deputy Director of National Commission for the Scheduled Castes and the Scheduled Tribes. —*Members*

(v) the Secretary-in-Charge of the welfare and development of the Scheduled Castes and the Scheduled Tribes. —*Convenor*

2. The high power vigilance and monitoring committee shall meet at least twice in a calendar year, in the months of January and July to review the implementation of the provisions of the Act, relief and rehabilitation facilities provided to the victims and other matters connected therewith, prosecution of cases under the Act, rule of different officers/agencies responsible for implementing the provisions of the Act and various reports received by the State Government.

17. Constitution of District Level Vigilance and Monitoring Committee. 1. In each district within the State, the District Magistrate shall set up a vigilance and monitoring committee in his district to review the implementation of the provisions of the Act, relief and rehabilitation facilities provided to the victims and other matters connected therewith, prosecution of cases under the Act, role of different officers/agencies responsible for implementing the provisions of the Act and various reports received by the District Administration.

2. The district level vigilance and monitoring committee shall consist of the elected Members of the Parliament and State Legislative Assembly and Legislative Council, Superintendent of Police, three group 'A' Officers, Gazetted Officers of the State Government belonging to the Scheduled Castes and the Scheduled Tribes not more than 5 non-official members belonging to the Scheduled Castes and the Scheduled Tribes and not more than 3 members from the

categories other than the Scheduled Castes and the Scheduled Tribes having association with Non-Government Organisations. The District Magistrate and District Social Welfare Officer shall be Chairman and Member-Secretary, respectively.

3. The district level committee shall meet at least once in three months.

18. Material for Annual Report. The State Government shall, before every 31st March, forward the report to the Central Government about the measures taken for implementing provisions of the Act and various schemes/plans framed by it during the previous calendar year.

RULES OF PROCEDURE OF THE NATIONAL COMMISSION FOR SCHEDULED CASTES AND SCHEDULED TRIBES

GENERAL

1. Constitution of the Commission. The National Commission for Scheduled Castes and Scheduled Tribes (hereinafter called the Commission) has been constituted under Article 338 of the Constitution of India as amended by the Constitution (Sixty-fifth Amendment) Act, 1990. The Commission shall consist of a Chairperson, a Vice-Chairperson and five other Members.

2. Headquarters of the Commission. The Headquarters of the Commission shall be located at New Delhi.

3. State Offices of the Commission. The Commission shall have under its control the following State Offices:

Location	Jurisdiction
1. Agartala	Tripura
2. Ahmedabad	Gujarat, and UT of Dadra and Nagar Haveli
3. Bangalore	Karnataka
4. Bhopal	Madhya Pradesh
5. Bhubaneshwar	Orissa
6. Kolkata	West Bengal, Sikkim and UT of A&N Islands
7. Chandigarh	Punjab, Haryana, Himachal Predesh, J&K and UT of Chandigarh

8. Guwahati	Assam, Arunachal Pradesh, Manipur and Nagaland
9. Hyderabad	Andhra Pradesh
10. Jaipur	Rajasthan
11. Lucknow	Uttar Pradesh and Uttaranchal
12. Madras	Tamil Nadu and UT of Pondicherry
13. Patna	Bihar
14. Pune	Maharashtra, Goa, and UT of Daman and Diu
15. Shillong	Meghalaya and Mizoram
16. Thiruvananthapuram	Kerala and UT of Lakshadweep and Minicoy Islands

4. The Commission may, if considered necessary, open new offices and sub-offices and upgrade or downgrade the status and change the jurisdiction of any of its State Offices.

5. The function and responsibilities of the Commission as laid down in the Constitution are:

(a) to investigate and monitor all matters relating to the safeguards provided for the Scheduled Castes and Scheduled Tribes under the Constitution or under any other law for the time being in force or under any order of the Government and to evaluate the working of such safeguards;

(b) to inquire into specific complaints with respect to the deprivation of rights and safeguards of the Scheduled Castes and Scheduled Tribes;

(c) to participate and advise on the planning process of socio-economic development of the Scheduled Castes and Scheduled Tribes and to evaluate the progress of their development under the Union and any State;

(d) to present to the President, annually and at such other times as the Commission may deem fit, reports upon the working of those safeguards;

(e) to make in such reports recommendation as to the measures that should be taken by the Union or any State for the effective implementation of those safeguards and other measures for the protection, welfare and socio-economic development of the Scheduled Castes and Scheduled Tribes; and

(f) to discharge such other functions in relation to the protection, welfare and development and advancement of the Scheduled Castes and Scheduled Tribes as the President may, subject to the provisions of any law made by Parliament, by rule specify.

6. The Commission shall function by holding 'sittings' and 'meetings' at any place within the country and also through its officers at the Headquarters and in the State Offices. The Members of the Commission including the Chairperson and the Vice-Chairperson shall function in accordance with the procedure prescribed under these rules.

DIVISION OF RESPONSIBILITIES AND ALLOCATION OF WORK

Chairperson

7. The Chairperson shall be the head of the Commission and shall have the residuary powers to decide on all questions and matters arising in the Commission excepting such matters where specific provision has been made in these rules.

8. The Chairperson shall allocate subject and responsibilities among the Members of the Commission. The Order allocating the subjects and responsibilities shall be circulated to all concerned by the Secretariat of the Commission.

9. The Chairperson shall be the authority to sanction leave and approve tours of the Members.

10. The Chairperson shall preside over the meetings of the Commission.

11. All important decisions in the Commission pertaining to the subjects allotted to the Members shall be taken with the approval of the Chairperson.

12. The Chairperson may call for any records on any matter which he considers important any may take a decision on it himself or, if necessary, place it at the meeting of the Commission.

Vice-Chairperson

13. The Vice-Chairperson shall preside over the meetings of the Commission in the absence of the Chairperson.

14. The Vice-Chairperson shall perform such functions as are entrusted to him by the Chairperson.

Members

15. The Members of the Commission shall have collective responsibility and shall function by participating in the 'meetings' and 'sittings' of the Commission and looking after the subjects allocated to them. Important actions and decisions of a Member may be brought at a meeting of the Commission which may review for same.

16. Any Members may suggest items for inclusion in the agenda of a meeting of the Commission and the same shall be so included after obtaining the consent of the Chairperson.

17. Each member shall have overall responsibility of subjects and/or regions or State(s) as may be allocated to him.

18. The Members shall play the role of advising the State Governments under their jurisdiction on matters of planning and development relating to the welfare of Scheduled Castes and Scheduled Tribes. The Commission's Secretariat at Headquarters and the State Offices shall assist the Members in keeping them fully informed of the problems and activities of the States and subjects under their respective charge.

19. One or more Members may, in accordance with the procedure specified in the rules elsewhere, hold sittings of the Commission to give hearing to the cases or to collect evidence or information on any matter, issue or case under investigation or inquiry by the Commission.

20. The Members shall communicate their tour programmes well in advance to the State Offices indicating in detail the purpose of the visit and to the State Government Department and others concerned for discussions/inquiry, etc., during the tour/visit. The Members will observe the norms laid down by the State Governments regarding security/travel/accommodation etc., during such tours.

Secretary

21. The Secretary shall be the administrative head of the Commission and shall assist the Commission in the discharge of its functions with the assistance of the officers of the Commission.

22. All important administrative matters shall be placed before the Secretary who may pass general or specific orders on such matters.

23. The Secretary shall be responsible for having the agenda prepared for the meetings of the Commission and for circulating the minutes.

24. The Secretary shall assist the Commission in finalising the Reports.

25. The Secretary may, in his discretion, delegate any of the functions or authority to a subordinate officer of the Secretariat.

INVESTIGATION AND INQUIRY BY THE COMMISSION

Methods of Investigation and Inquiry

26. The Commission may adopt any one or more of the following methods for investigating or inquiring into the matters falling within its authority:

(a) by the Commission directly;
(b) by an Investigating Team Constituted at the Headquarters of the Commission; and
(c) through its State Offices.

Investigation and Inquiry by the Commission Directly

27. The Commission may hold sittings for investigation into matters relating to safeguards, protection, welfare and development of the Scheduled Castes and Scheduled Tribes or for inquiring into specific complaints for which the Commission decides to take up investigation or inquiry directly. Such sittings may be held either at the Headquarters of the Commission or at any other place within the country.

28. The sitting(s) of the Commission would be held after giving due notice to the parties intended to be heard and also due publicity notice to the general public. Care will be taken to see that the members of the Scheduled Castes or Scheduled Tribes who are affected in the matter under investigation or inquiry are given due information through notice or publicity.

29. When a decision for direct investigation is taken, an officer not below the rank of Research Officer/Section Officer along with necessary staff may be attached to the Member(s) entrusted with such investigation or enquiry and they shall take all steps to arrange such sittings.

30. During the course of the investigation or inquiry the Commission, acting through such a sitting, may make evidence on oath or receive affidavits. When considered necessary, the Commission, for the purpose of taking evidence in the investigation or inquiry, require the presence of any person and may issue summons to him. The summons shall provide at least fifteen days' notice to the person directed to be present before the Commission from the date of receipt of the summons.

31. Where the property, service/employment of SCs and STs and other related matters are under immediate threat and prompt attention of the Commission is required, the matter shall be taken cognizance by issue of telex/fax to the concerned authority for making it known to them that the Commission is seized of the issue. Urgent reply by telegram or fax shall be called from the concerned authority. In case no letter is received within a week, the authority concerned shall be summoned at a short notice for enquiry.

32. The Commission may issue Commission to take evidence in any matter under investigation or inquiry and for this purpose appoint any person by an order in writing. The Commission may make further rules for payment of fee and travelling and other allowances to persons appointed to take evidence on commission.

33. After holding the required sittings, the Member(s) who conducted the investigation shall make a report which shall be sent to the Secretary or any other officer authorised to receive the report. After examination, action may be initiated on the report with the approval of the Chairperson.

Investigation or Inquiry by an Investigation Team Constituted at the Headquarters of the Commission

34. The Commission may decide about the matter that is to be investigated or enquired into by an Investigating Team of officials of the Commission, provided that in case the matter is urgent, the decision for such investigation or inquiry may be taken by the Chairperson.

35. The Investigating Team shall hold the investigation or inquiry, as the case may be, promptly and for this purpose may initiate necessary correspondence including issuance of notices for production of documents in Form I.

36. The Investigating Team may visit the area concerned after observing due formalities for obtaining approval of tours and other administrative requirements and after giving information to the concerned local authorities regarding the matter, purpose, scope and procedure of the investigation or inquiry. The Investigating Team may enlist the help of the officers and staff of the concerned State Office but the responsibility of preparing and presenting the report shall rest with the head of the Investigating Team.

37. The Investigating Team shall submit the report of the investigation or enquiry, as the case may be, to the Secretary or a subordinate officer of the Commission as may be directed by general or specific orders within the stipulated time, if any. If the time limit stipulated is likely to be exceeded the head of the Investigating Team shall obtain the orders of the Secretary through the Officer-in-Charge of the matter. The report shall be examined and put up to the competent authority for decision regarding the action to be taken on the report.

38. The report shall be placed before the Chairperson of the Commission who will take appropriate action in the matter.

Investigation and Inquiry Through the State Offices

39. The Chairperson, the Vice-Chairperson, the Members having jurisdiction over the subject or the Secretary of the Commission may decide about an investigation or inquiry that may be carried out through the State Offices of the Commission. The decision will be conveyed to the Officer-in-Charge of the concerned State Office who will be asked to get the matter investigated or inquired into within a stipulated time and send the report. The State Office shall conduct the investigation or inquiry through interrogation, on the spot visit, discussions and correspondence and examination of documents as may be necessary in the case and shall follow any special or general instructions issued in the matter by the Secretariat of the Commission from time to time.

40. If the investigation or inquiry cannot be completed within the stipulated time the Officer-in-Charge of the State Office may send a communication to the Secretariat of the Commission before the expiry of the stipulated time and explain the circumstances and reasons for non-completion of the investigation or inquiry, as the case may be, within the stipulated time. The Secretary to the Commission or an officer acting under delegated functions may consider the request and communicate a revised date for the completion of the investigation or inquiry.

41. If during the course of investigation or inquiry the head of the State Office feels that it is necessary to invoke the powers of the Commission to require the production of any document or compelling the attendance of a person, he may make a special report with full facts to the Secretariat of the Commission. On receipt of such special report the matter shall be placed before the Secretary/ Member-in-Charge of the subject/State/UT who may make an order that necessary legal processes to compel attendance or to require production of any document may be issued. The summons and warrants issued for the purpose may be served on the person concerned either directly or through the Officer-in-Charge of the State Office as may be directed by the Secretary/Member authorising issue of such legal process.

42. After completion of the investigation or inquiry, as the case may be, the head of the State Office shall submit the report to the Secretary of the Commission suggesting the course of action that could be followed in the matter. The gist or findings of the report may be placed before the Secretary who may decide about further action in the matter.

Confidentiality of Certain Reports

43. The Commission may, through a decision at a meeting or otherwise, direct that the contents of any report made on any matter shall be kept confidential and shall not be revealed to any person other than those who have been authorised access to such report.

Legal Processes

44. All summons and warrants that are required to be issued in pursuance of the exercise of the powers of a Civil Court by the Commission shall be written in the prescribed form and shall bear the seal of the Commission. The legal process shall be issued from the Legal Cell of the Commission and shall bear its seal. The provisions of the Code of Civil Procedure applicable for the service of the legal processes shall be followed by the Commission.

Issue of Letters and Notices

45. Letters and notices requiring production of documents which are issued without exercising the powers of the Civil Court by the Commission may be signed by an officer not below the rank of Research Officer/Section Officer.

Form of Summons and Warrants

46. The summons and warrants shall be as provided in Forms II and III respectively, appended to these rules.

MEETINGS OF THE COMMISSION

Frequency of Meetings

47. The Commission shall meet at least once in two months. The notice for a meeting shall normally be issued two weeks in advance. Emergent meetings may also be called by the Chairperson either on his own or on the request of a Member or the Secretary for disposing of important matters requiring urgent consideration by the Commission.

Quorum

48. The Chairperson or the vice-Chairperson and two other Members shall form the quorum for holding a meeting of the Commission.

Matters Requiring Decisions by the Commission at its Meetings

49. The following matters shall be brought up before the Commission at a meeting for consideration and decision:

- (i) any amendment to these Rules of Procedure;
- (ii) matters to be investigated by the Commission directly;
- (iii) all the reports that are required to be considered by the Commission as provided in these rules;
- (iv) any matters that a Member may like to bring to the meeting, with the approval of the Chairperson;
- (v) importing matters relating to planning and development for the welfare and advancement of the Scheduled Castes and Scheduled Tribes and specially references received under Article 338(9) of the Constitution; and
- (vi) any matter that the Chairperson may direct to be placed at a meeting of the Commission.

Agenda for the Meeting

50. The agenda will normally be circulated to all the Members at least seven days before the date of the meeting, provided that for an Emergent meeting this time limit may not apply.

51. The minutes of a meeting shall be circulated as soon as possible to all the Members.

Place of Meeting of the Commission

52. Normally the place of meeting of the Commission shall be the Headquarters of the Commission at New Delhi. The Commission may, however, decide to hold a meeting at any other place in India.

Fee

53. The Chairperson, the Vice-Chairperson and the Members shall not be entitled to any fee for sitting in the meeting of the Commission. However, the entitlement of Part-time Members, if any, may be determined by the terms of appointment of such Members.

SITTINGS OF THE COMMISSION

Need for Sittings

54. Whenever a matter is to be investigated into directly by the Commission it may do so by holding sittings of the Commission. In the case of such sittings the presence of all the Members may not be necessary.

Officers to be Present

55. Whenever a Member(s) is holding a sitting, an Officer of the Commission, not below the rank of Research Officer/Section Officer, duly deputed for the purpose shall be present to assist the Member(s) holding the sitting to discharge the functions properly and promptly. It shall be the duty of the officer to assist the Member(s) in preparing the report if called upon to do so by the Member(s). The Officer shall also be responsible for assisting the Member(s) in following the prescribed procedure.

Frequency of Sitting(s)

56. Sittings of the Commission may be held as and when necessary. The Commission may hold more than one sitting simultaneously in different parts of the country with different Members functioning separately.

Programme of the Sittings

57. The programme of the sittings, both at the Headquarters and at other places, would normally be worked out each month in advance and duly circulated.

Defraying Expenses to Witnesses

58. The Commission may defray travelling expenses to persons who have been called through summons to appear before the Commission in a sitting, provided that the place of residence of one person is more than 8 kms, from the place of the sittings of the Commission. The amount so defrayed shall be limited to the actual travelling expenses plus Daily Allowance for the number of days that the person has appeared before the Commission in its sitting, provided that the person is not entitled to travelling and daily allowance from any other source. Persons who are employees of the Government/Public Sector Undertaking shall be deemed to be on duty if they are summoned to depose before the Commission or produce documents. The limit of travelling expenses shall be determined on the basis of the rail fare and road mileage calculated on the basis of the rates that may be prescribed by the Commission. In the case of any doubt regarding the entitlement of the person the decision of the Secretary of the Commission shall be final.

59. The officer attached to the Member for the purposes of the sitting shall take steps to ensure that sufficient cash amount is carried if the sitting is held at a place other than the Headquarters of the Commission. The Secretariat of the Commission may devise a suitable procedure to ensure that such claims as above are paid on the spot and in cash to the person(s) so appearing.

60. The claim for travelling expenses as above shall not be admissible in the case of a person who appears before the Commission during any investigation or enquiry on his own accord or in response to a communication or notice which is not a summon issued by the Commission.

DUTIES OF THE STATE OFFICES OF THE COMMISSION

61. It shall be the duty of the State Offices of the Commission:

(i) To act as the "eyes and ears" of the Commission in the State(s) of their jurisdiction.

(ii) To maintain effective interaction and liaison with State Government/UT Administrations on behalf of the Commission.

(iii) To serve on State Level Advisory Councils/Committees/Corporations, etc. on behalf of the Commission.

(iv) To provide information and documentation about the policies and programmes of the Union Government for the welfare and advancement of SCs and STs to the States, NGOs, Media in their respective jurisdiction. Obtain similar information and documentation from such organisation and provide to the Headquarters of the Commission information/documentation about important development, social movements, policy changes. etc. in the State affecting the interest of SCs and STs.

(v) To monitor and assist the working of voluntary and other non-governmental organisations receiving grant-in-aid from the Ministry of Social Justice and Empowerment as also other Ministries/Departments of the Central Government and the concerned State Governments, Foreign Aid Agencies, etc., for Research Studies and any other development work relating to SCs and STs.

(vi) To conduct Research Studies, Seminars, Conferences, Surveys, etc. either on their own or as entrusted to them by Headquarters from time to time.

(vii) To conduct on the spot inquiries into cases of atrocities on SCs and STs either on their own or as entrusted to them by Headquarters and interact with the concerned Administrative/Police authorities having jurisdiction and report to the Headquarters.

(viii) To deal with complaints/representations from individuals, SC/ST Welfare Associations, etc. on various matters.

(ix) To participate and advise in the planning process for socio-economic development of the SCs/STs as envisaged under Clause 5 of Article 338 of the Constitution of India.

(x) To collect, compile, analyse and monitor issues pertaining to development of SCs and STs in the States especially with reference to SCP, TSP and SCA, and prepare drafts of Reports pertaining to the State/UT under their jurisdiction.

(xi) To prepare and maintain a comprehensive and up to date

data base of SC/ST population, education, development, etc. in the State/UT; and

(xii) To perform any other duty specifically assigned/entrusted to the State Office(s) by the Commission or the Secretary or any other officer empowered in this regard.

ADVISORY ROLE OF THE COMMISSION

Interaction of the Commission with the State Governments

62. The Commission shall interact with the State Governments through its Members, Secretariat and the State Offices.

63. The Member in charge of the State/UT would interact with the State Government/UT Administration through meetings, personal contacts, visits and correspondence. The information in this regard may be sent to the concerned Department/Organisations well in advance and the State Offices should also be informed about the same. For this purpose, detailed guidelines may be formulated by the Commission. The Secretariat of the Commission through its concerned Wing(s) would provide necessary assistance and information to the Member for enabling him to discharge his functions effectively. The State Government should provide facilities for transport, security, accommodation etc., to the Member as per his entitlement.

Interaction with the Planning Commission

64. The Commission shall interact with the Planning Commission at appropriate levels through representation in the various Committees, Working Groups or other such bodies set up by the Planning Commission. The Commission shall indicate this requirement through general or specific communication to the Planning Commission.

65. The Commission may request the Planning Commission to forward copies of all the documents concerning the process of planning and development and evaluation of all programmes and schemes touching upon the Scheduled Castes and Scheduled Tribes.

66. The Commission may decide about the manner of interaction between the Chairperson/Members of the Commission and the Deputy Chairman/Members of the Planning Commission.

Interaction of the State Offices with the State Governments

67. The State Offices of the Commission shall work in a manner so as to provide a regular and effective link between the State Governments concerned and the Commission. For this purpose the Commission may send communication to the State Governments suggesting that the officers-in-charge of the State Offices of the Commission may be taken on important Planning, Evaluation and Advisory Bodies including Corporations concerned with the welfare protection and development of the Scheduled Castes and Scheduled Tribes.

68. The officer-in-charge of the State Offices may be directed or authorised by the Commission to convey to any State Authority the formal views, opinion or approach of the Commission on any specific or general matter or issue arising at any meeting or deliberation.

Research/Studies/Surveys/Evaluation

69. The Commission may undertake studies to evaluate the impact of the development schemes on the socio-economic development of the Scheduled Castes and Scheduled Tribes taken up by the Union or State Governments. For this purpose the Commission may constitute Study Teams either at the Headquarters or at the State Offices. The Study Teams may undertake investigations, survey or studies either in collaboration with the Central or State Government authorities or Universities or Research Bodies, as the case may be, or may do so independently.

70. The Commission may entrust surveys or evaluation studies to any professional body or person considered suitable and competent to undertake such work and for this purpose may make any reasonable payment to such body or person towards the cost of the study by way of fee or grant.

71. The studies so undertaken or their gists may form part of the Annual or Special Report of the Commission to be presented to the President or may be published separately by the Commission.

72. The Commission may forward a copy of such a study report to the Union or the State Government concerned, as the case may be, asking for their comments, if any. The comments or action taken reports by the Union/State Government may also form part of the Annual Report of the Commission.

MONITORING FUNCTIONS OF THE COMMISSION

The Commission to Determine Subjects for Monitoring

73. The Commission may determine from time to time the subjects or matters and areas that it would monitor relating to safeguards and other socio-economic development measures provided for the Scheduled Castes and Scheduled Tribes under the Constitution or under any other law for the time being in force or under any order of the Government.

Prescribing Returns and Reports

74. The Commission may prescribe periodical returns or reports to be furnished by any authority responsible for or having control of the subject-matter of which monitoring is being done by the Commission.

75. The Commission may from time to time issue instructions to its State Offices to collect information and data on any particular subject or matter from the State Governments. Local Bodies, Corporate Bodies or any other authorities which is charged with the implementation of the safeguards provided for the Scheduled Castes and Scheduled Tribes.

76. The Commission may direct its State Offices to process the information or data in the State Offices with a view to arriving at conclusion with regard to the deficiencies or shortcoming discovered through such processing or analysis of the data and to bring these to the notice of the concerned authority for comments and rectification, where necessary.

77. The Commission may have data, relating to the subject monitored collected to the headquarters and may prescribe returns and reports for the purpose to be sent directly to its Headquarters by the Ministries/Departments of the Central Government or a State Government or Public Sector Undertaking or any other body or authority which is charged with the responsibility of implementing safeguards relating to the Scheduled Castes and Scheduled Tribes.

Follow-up Action

78. In order to ensure that monitoring is done effectively the Commission, after getting the information as prescribed in the above rules and after reaching conclusions, may as early as possible send out communication to the concerned authority describing the shortcomings that have been noticed in the implementation of the safeguards and suggesting corrective steps. Decisions on sending out such a communication may be taken at a level not lower than that of Joint Secretary/Secretary at Headquarters. Directors-in-Charge of State Offices may take decisions on routine matter whereas they will seek approval of the Secretary and the concerned Member on complex and important matters effecting the interest of SCs and STs, as a group.

79. The Commission may ask for the comments of the concerned authority on the action taken in pursuance of the communication sent under the provisions of Rule 78.

80. The Commission may include in its Annual Report or any Special Report findings and conclusions arrived at through the process of monitoring of the subjects relating to the safeguards and socio-economic development measures provided for the Scheduled Castes and Scheduled Tribes under the Constitution or under any other law for the time being in force or under any order of the Union/State Government.

NON-FORMAL ACTIONS BY THE COMMISSION

81. The Commission may initiate correspondence in special cases in matters or cases which are not strictly covered under the law if the matter is such that the welfare of an individual person belonging to Scheduled Castes or Scheduled Tribes or that of a group of such persons is involved and it is necessary for the Commission in its inherent capacity as the protector of the interests of these classes of persons, to take action. The decision for correspondence on such matter shall be taken at the level of Director or above.

82. All routine formal communications from the Commission shall be issued under the signatures of an Officer not below the rank of Research Officer/Section Officer.

83. The Commission can sue or be sued through its Secretary.

84. The Scheduled Castes and Scheduled Tribes in these rules will have the same connotation as is given in Clause 10 of Article 338 of the Constitution.

Applicability of Rules, etc., of the Central Government

85. All rules, regulations and orders issued by the Central Government and applicable in the Ministries/Departments will also apply in the Commission.

86. The provisions relating to the delegation of financial powers in the Government of India shall apply to the corresponding officers in the Commission.

Use of Staff Cars

87. The Staff Car Rules of the Government of India shall apply for the purposes of utilisation of staff cars in the Commission.

Decision on Matters not Specified in These Rules

88. If a question arises regarding any such matter for which no provision exists in these rules, the decision of the Chairperson shall be sought. The Chairperson may, if deems fit, direct that the matter may be considered at a meeting of the Commission.

FORM I

NATIONAL COMMISSION FOR SCHEDULED CASTES AND SCHEDULED TRIBES

(A Constitutional body under Article 338 of the Constitution of India)

5th Floor, Loknayak Bhawan
New Delhi—110 003

(Notice for collecting basic facts)

To

Whereas a Petition/complaint/information has been received by the National Commission for Scheduled Castes and Scheduled Tribes from .... press news under caption ....appearing in................dated................as enclosed and the Commission has decided to investigate/inquire into the matter in pursuance of the powers conferred upon it under Article 338 of the Constitution of India, you are hereby requested to submit the facts and information on the action taken on the allegations/ matters to the undersigned within 30 days of receipt of this notice either by post or in person or by any other means of communication.

Please take notice that in case of the Commission does not receive reply from you within the stipulated time, the Commission may exercise the powers of Civil Courts conferred on it under

Article 338 of the Constitution of India and issue summons for your appearance in person or by a representative before the Commission.

Signature
Director/Under Secretary/Dy. Director/Assistant
Director/Research Officer/Section Officer
National Commission for Scheduled Castes
and Scheduled Tribes

Dated:

FORM II
BEFORE THE NATIONAL COMMISSION FOR SCHEDULED CASTES AND SCHEDULED TRIBES

(A Constitutional body exercising powers of Civil Court under Article 338 of the Constitution of India)

SUMMONS

File No.

5th Floor, Loknayak Bhawan
New Delhi—110 003

To

Whereas the National Commission has decided to investigate into the following matter in pursuance of powers conferred upon it under Article 338 of the Constitution of India, your attendance is hereby required in person to appear before the National Commission on the .... of ....2000................at................hours at................

You are required to bring with you the connected documents for examination by the National Commission.

Case reference

If you fail to comply with this order without lawful excuse, you shall be subjected to the consequences of non-attendance laid down in Rule 12 of Order XVI of Code of Civil Procedure, 1908.

Given under my hand and seal of the National Commission

for SCs & STs exercising powers of Civil Court this................of................200................

Seal **Court Officer**

FORM III

(WARRANT OF ARREST OF WITNESS)

National Commission for Scheduled Castes and Scheduled Tribes

(A Constitutional body exercising powers of Civil Court under Article 338 of the Constitution of India)

Loknayak Bhawan (Floor V)
New Delhi—110 003

To,

Whereas............................R/o............................has been duly served with a summons but has failed to attend (absconds and keeps out of the way for the purpose of avoiding service of a summons), the National Commission for Scheduled Castes and Scheduled Tribes exercising powers of a Civil Court under Article 338(8) of the Constitution of India hereby order you to arrest and bring the said....................before the National Commission at New Delhi.

You are further ordered to return this warrant on or before the ....day of....................200....................with an endorsement certifying the day and the manner in which it has been executed, or the reason why it has not been executed.

Given under my hands and the seal of the National Commission exercising powers of Civil Court, this ....day of....................200....................

Seal Signature

THE NATIONAL COMMISSION FOR BACKWARD CLASSES ACT, 1993
(Act 27 of 1993)

[2 April, 1993]

An Act to constitute a National Commission for Backward Classes other than the Scheduled Castes and Scheduled Tribes and to provide for matters connected therewith or incidental thereto.

Be it enacted by Parliament in the Forty-fourth Year of the Republic of India as follows—

Statement of Objects and Reasons. In its judgment dated 16th November, 1992 on matter arising out of Government Orders on reservation of appointments or posts under the Government of India in favour of Backward Classes of citizens under Article 16(4) of the Constitution, the Supreme Court, *inter alia* directed the Government of India to constitute a permanent body within four months from the date of judgment, i.e. by 15th March, 1993 for entertaining and examining and for recommending upon request made to it for, inclusion and complaints of over-inclusion and under-inclusion in the lists of Backward Classes of citizens. The Supreme Court observed that the body so created can also be consulted by the Government in the matter of periodic revision of lists of backward classes. The Supreme Court has also observed that the permanent body must be empowered to examine complaints relating to such matters and pass appropriate orders. Its advice/opinion should ordinarily be binding upon the Government.

As Parliament was not in session, and as the Government was required to comply with the direction of the Supreme Court within the time-frame stipulated in the judgment, the President promulgated the National Commission for Backward Classes Ordinance, 1993 on the 1st day of February, 1993.

The Bill seeks to replace the said Ordinance.

PRELIMINARY

1. Short Title, Extent and Commencement. 1. This Act may be called the National Commission for Backward Classes Act, 1993.

2. It extends to the whole of India except the State of Jammu and Kashmir.

3. It shall be deemed to have come into force on the 1st day of February, 1993.

2. *Definitions.* In this Act, unless the context otherwise requires—

(a) "backward classes" means such backward classes of citizens other than the Scheduled Castes and the Scheduled Tribes as may be specified by the Central Government in the lists;
(b) "Commission" means the National Commission for Backward Classes constituted under Section 3;
(c) "lists" means lists prepared by the Government of India from time to time for purposes of making provision for the reservation of appointments or posts in favour of backward classes of citizens which, in the opinion of that Government, are not adequately represented in the services under the Government of India and any local or other authority within the territory of India or under the control of the Government of India;
(d) "Member" means a Member of the Commission and includes the Chairperson;
(e) "prescribed" means prescribed by rules made under this Act.

THE NATIONAL COMMISSION FOR BACKWARD CLASSES

3. ***Constitution of National Commission for Backward Classes.*** 1. The Central Government shall constitute a body to be known as the National Commission for Backward Classes to exercise the powers conferred on, and to perform the functions assigned to, it under this Act.

2. The Commission, shall consist of the following Members nominated by the Central Government:

(a) a Chairperson, who is or has been a Judge of the Supreme Court or of a High Court;
(b) a social scientist;
(c) two persons, who have special knowledge in matters relating to backward classes; and
(d) a Member-Secretary, who is or has been an officer of the Central Government in the rank of a Secretary to the Government of India.

4. ***Term of Office and Conditions of Service of Chairperson and Members.*** 1. Every Member shall hold office for a term of three years from the date he assumes office.

2. A Member may, by writing under his hand addressed to the Central Government, resign from the office of Chairperson or as the case may be, of Member at any time.

3. The Central Government shall remove a person from the office of Member if that person—

(a) becomes as undischarged insolvent:

(b) is convicted and sentenced to imprisonment for an offence which, in the opinion of the Central Government, involves moral turpitude;

(c) becomes of unsound mind and stands so declared by a competent Court;

(d) refuses to act or becomes incapable of acting;

(e) is, without obtaining leave of absence from the Commission, absent from three consecutive meetings of the Commission; or

(f) has, in the opinion of the Central Government, so abused the position of Chairperson or Member as to render that person's continuance in office detrimental to the interests of backward classes or the public interest:

Provided that, no person shall be removed under this clause until that person has been given an opportunity of being heard in the matter.

4. A vacancy caused under sub-section (2) or otherwise shall be filled by fresh nomination.

5. The salaries and allowances payable to, and the other terms and conditions of service of, the Chairperson and Members shall be such as may be prescribed.

5. Officers and Other Employees of the Commission. 1. The Central Government shall provide the Commission with such officers and employees as may be necessary for the efficient performance of the functions of the Commission.

2. The salaries and allowances payable to, and the other terms and conditions of service of, the officers and other employee appointed for the purpose of the Commission shall be such as may be prescribed.

6. Salaries and Allowances to be Paid out of Grants. The salaries and allowances payable to the Chairperson and Members and the administrative expenses, including salaries, allowances and pension payable to the officers and other employees referred to in

Section 5, shall be paid out of the grants referred to in sub-section (1) of Section 12.

7. Vacancies, etc. not to Invalidate Proceedings of the Commission. No act or proceedings of the Commission shall be invalid on the ground merely of the existence of any vacancy or defect in the constitution of the Commission.

8. Procedure to be Regulated by the Commission. 1. The Commission shall meet as and when necessary at such time and place as the Chairperson may think fit.

2. The Commission shall regulate its own procedure.

3. All orders and decisions of the Commission shall be authenticated by the Member-Secretary or any other officer of the Commission duly authorised by the Members-Secretary in this behalf.

FUNCTIONS AND POWERS OF THE COMMISSION

9. Functions of the Commission. 1. The Commission shall examine requests for inclusion of any class of citizens as a backward class in such lists and hear complaints of over-inclusion or under-inclusion of any backward class in such lists and tender such advice to the Central Government as it deems appropriate.

2. The advice of the Commission shall ordinarily be binding upon the Central Government.

10. Powers of the Commission. The Commission shall, while performing its functions under sub-section (1) of Section 9, have all the power of a Civil Court trying a suit and in particular, in respect of the following matters, namely:

(a) summoning and enforcing the attendance of any person from any part of India and examining him on oath;
(b) requiring the discovery and production of any document;
(c) receiving evidence on affidavits;
(d) requisitioning any public record or copy thereof, from any court or office;
(e) issuing commissions for the examination of witnesses and documents; and
(f) any other matter which may be prescribed.

11. Periodic Revision of Lists by the Central Government. 1. The Central Government may at any time, and shall, at the expiration of ten years from the coming into force of this Act and every succeeding period of ten years thereafter, undertake revision of the lists with a view to excluding from such lists those classes who have ceased to be backward classes or for including in such lists new backward classes.

2. The Central Government shall, while undertaking any revision referred to in sub-section (1), consult the Commission.

FINANCE, ACCOUNTS AND AUDIT

12. Grants by the Central Government. 1. The Central Government shall, after due appropriation made by Parliament by law in this behalf, pay to the Commission by way of grants such sums of money as the Central Government may think fit for being utilised for the purposes of this Act.

2. The Commission may spend such sums as it thinks fit for performing the functions under this Act,, and sums shall be treated as expenditure payable out of the grants referred to in sub-section (1).

13. Accounts and Audit. 1. The Commission shall maintain proper accounts and order relevant records and prepare an annual statement of accounts in such form as may be prescribed by the Central Government in consultation with the Comptroller and Auditor-General.

2. The accounts of the Commission shall be audited by the Comptroller and Auditor-General at such intervals as may be specified by him and any expenditure incurred in connection with such audit shall be payable by the Commission to the Comptroller and Auditor-General.

3. The Comptroller and Auditor-General and any person appointed by him in connection with the audit of the accounts of the Commission under this Act shall have the same rights and privileges and the authority in connection with such audit as the Comptroller and Auditor-General generally has in connection with the audit of Government accounts and, in particular, shall have the right to demand the production of books, accounts, connected vouchers and other documents and papers and to inspect any of the offices of the Commission.

14. Annual Report. The Commission shall prepare, in such form and at such time, for each financial year, as may be prescribed, its annual report, giving a full account of its activities during the previous financial year and forward a copy thereof, to the Central Government.

15. Annual Report and Audit Report to be Laid before Parliament. The Central Government shall cause the annual report, together with memorandum of action taken on the advice tendered by the Commission under Section 9 and the reasons for the non-acceptance, if any, of any such advice, and the audit report to be laid as soon as may be after they are received before each House of Parliament.

MISCELLANEOUS

16. Chairperson, Members and Employees of the Commission to be Public Servants. The Chairperson, Members and employees of the Commission shall be deemed to be public servants within the meaning of Section 21 of the Indian Penal Code (45 of 1860).

17. Power to Make Rules. 1. The Central Government may, by notification in the official Gazette, make rules for carrying out the provisions of the Act.

2. In particular, and without prejudice to the generality of the foregoing powers, such rules may provide for all or any of the following matters, namely:

(a) salaries and allowances payable to, and the other terms and conditions of service of, the Chairperson and Members under sub-section (5) of Section 4 and the officers and other employees under sub-section (2) of Section 5;

(b) the form in which the annual statement of accounts shall be prepared under sub-section (1) of Section 13;

(c) the form in, and the time at, which the annual report shall be prepared under Section 14;

Any other matter which is required to be, or may be, prescribed.

3. Every rule made under this Act, shall be laid, as soon as may be after it is made, before each House of Parliament, while it is in session, for a total period of thirty days which may be comprised in one session or in two or more successive sessions, and if, before the expiry of the session immediately following the session or the successive session aforesaid, both houses agree in making any modification in the rule or both Houses agree that the rule should not be made, the rule shall thereafter have effect only in such modified form or be of no effect, as the case may be; so, however, that any such modification or annulment shall be without prejudice to the validity of anything previously done under that rule.

18. Power to Remove Difficulties. 1. If any difficulty arises in giving effect to the provisions of this Act, the Central Government may, by order published in the Official Gazette, make provisions, not inconsistent with the provisions of this Act as appear to it to be necessary or expedient, for removing the difficulty:

Provided that no such order shall be made after the expiry of a period of two years from the date of commencement of this Act.

2. Every order made under this section shall, as soon as may be after it is made, be laid before each House of Parliament.

19. Repeal and Saving. 1. The National Commission for Backward Classes Ordinance, 1993 (Ordinance 23 of 1993) is hereby repealed.

2. Notwithstanding such repeal, anything done or any action taken under the said Ordinance, shall be deemed to have been done or taken under the corresponding provisions of this Act.

THE NATIONAL COMMISSION FOR *SAFAI KARAMCHARIS* ACT, 1993
[Act 64 of 1993]

[4th September, 1993]

An Act to constitute a National Commission for Safai Karamcharis and to provide for matters connected therewith or incidental thereto.

Be it enacted by Parliament in the Forty-fourth year of the Republic of India as follows:

Statement of objects and reasons. 1. The Government of India have taken a number of steps for the social, economic and educational upliftment of *Safai Karamcharis*, special schemes for the liberation and rehabilitation of *Safai karamcharis* have also been formulated by the Government. In spite of these efforts, the obnoxious practice of manual scavenging still continues in many parts of the country. Since this practice is a continuing stigma on our social fabric, Government is determined to eradicate the practice within a fixed time frame, i.e. by the end of the Eighth Five Year Plan. A total plan outlay of Rs. 464 crore has been allocated in the Eighth Five Year Plan for liberation of scavengers. The total cost of the scheme including Bank loans and States' contribution is estimated to be Rs. 905 crore. The scheme is at present being implemented by the Scheduled Castes Development Corporation set up by the State Governments. There is no agency at the Central level to study, evaluate and monitor the scheme of liberation and rehabilitation of *Safai Karamcharis*. Since the scope of the national Commission for Scheduled Castes and Scheduled Tribes is restricted to Scheduled Castes and Scheduled Tribes and since persons other than those belonging to the Scheduled Castes and the Scheduled Tribes also constitute a sizable proportion of *Safai Karamcharis*, it was felt that a separate statutory National Commission needs to be established for monitoring the schemes for the liberation and rehabilitation of *Safai Karamcharies*.

2. The Bill seeks to achieve the aforesaid objects.

PRELIMINARY

1. Short Title, Extent, Application, Commencement, Duration and Savings. 1. The Act may be called the National Commission for *Safai Karamcharis* Act, 1993.

2. It extends to the whole of India except the State of Jammu and Kashmir.

3. It shall come into force on such date as the Central Government may, by notification in the Official Gazette, appoint.

4. It shall cease to have effect after [31st day of March, 2002], except as respects things done or omitted to be done before such cesser, and upon such cesser Section 6 of the General Clauses Act, 1897 (10 of 1897), shall apply as if this Act had then been repealed by a Central Act.

2. *Definitions.* In this Act, unless the context otherwise requires,:

(a) "Chairperson" means the Chairperson of the Commission;
(b) "Commission" means the National Commission for *Safai Karamcharis* constituted under Section 3;
(c) "Member" means a Member of the Commission;
(d) "Prescribed' means prescribed by rules made under this Act;
(e) " *Safai Karamcharis*" means a person engaged in, or employed for, manually carrying human excreta or any sanitation work:
(f) "Vice-Chairperson" means the Vice-Chairperson of the Commission.

THE NATIONAL COMMISSION FOR *SAFAI KARAMCHARIS*

3. Constitution of National Commission for Safai karamcharis. 1. The Central Government shall, by notification in the official Gazette, constitute a body to be known as the National Commission for *Safai Karamcharis* to exercise the powers conferred on, and to perform the functions assigned to it under this Act.

2. The Commission shall consist of—

(a) a Chairperson;
(b) a Vice-Chairperson;
(c) five members,

to be nominated from amongst the persons of eminence connected with the socio-economic development and welfare of *Safai Karamcharis*, by the Central Government:

Provided that at least one of the members shall be a woman.

4. Term of Office and Conditions of Service of Chairperson, Vice Chairperson and Members. 1. The Chairperson, Vice-Chairperson any every Member shall hold office for such period not exceeding three years as may be specified by the Central

Government in this behalf or upto the 31st day of March, 1997, whichever is earlier:

[Provided that, the Chairperson, Vice-Chairperson and every Member holding office as such immediately before the commencement of the National Commission for *Safai Karamcharis* (Amendment) Act, 1997 shall vacate their respective offices on the 31st day of March, 1997:

Provided further that the Chairperson , Vice-Chairperson and every Member appointed after commencement of the National Commission for *Safai Karamcharis* (Amendment) Act, 1997 shall hold office for such period not exceeding three years as may be specified by the Central Government in this behalf or upto the 31st day of March, 2002, whichever is earlier.]

2. The Chairperson, Vice-Chairperson or a Member may, by notice in writing addressed to the Central Government, resign from the office of Chairperson, Vice-Chairperson, or as the case may be, of the Member at any time.

3. The Central Government shall remove a person from the office of Chairperson, Vice-Chairperson, or a Member if that person,—

(a) becomes an undischarged insolvent;
(b) is convicted and sentenced to imprisonment, for an offence which, in the opinion of the Central Government, involves moral turpitude;
(c) becomes of unsound mind and stands so declared by a competent Court;
(d) refuses to act or becomes incapable of acting;
(e) is, without obtaining leave of absence from the Commission, absent from three consecutive meetings of the Commission; or
(f) in the opinion of the Central Government has so abused the position of Chairperson, Vice-Chairperson or Member as to render that persons' continuance in office detrimental to the public interest:

Provided that no person shall be removed under this clause until that person has been given a reasonable opportunity of being heard in the matter.

4. A vacancy caused under sub-section (2) or sub-section (3) or otherwise shall be filled by fresh nomination and a person so nominated shall hold office for the unexpired period of the term for

which his predecessor in office would have held office if, such vacancy has not arisen.

5. The salaries and allowances payable to, and other terms and conditions of service of, the Chairperson, Vice-Chairperson and Members shall be such as may be prescribed.

5. Officers and other Employees of the Commission. 1. The Central Government shall provide the Commission with such officers and employees as may be necessary for the efficient performance of the functions of the Commission under this Act.

2. The salaries and allowances payable to, and other terms and conditions of service of, the officers and other employees appointed for the purpose of the Commission shall be such as may be prescribed.

6. Vacancy, etc., not to Invalidate the Proceedings of the Commission. No act or proceedings of the Commission shall be questioned or shall be invalid on the ground merely of the existence of any vacancy or defect in the constitution of the Commission.

7. Procedure to be Regulated by the Commission. 1. The Commission shall meet as and when necessary and shall meet at such time and place as the Chairperson may think fit.

2. The Commission shall regulate its own procedure.

3. All orders and decisions of the Commission shall be authenticated by the Chairperson or any other officer of the Commission duly authorised by the Chairperson in this behalf.

FUNCTIONS AND POWERS OF THE COMMISSION

8. Functions and Powers of the Commission. 1. The Commission shall perform all or any of the following functions, namely:

(a) recommend to the Central Government specific programmes of action towards elimination of inequalities in status, facilities and opportunities for *Safai Karamcharis* under a time-bound action plan;

(b) study and evaluate the implementation of the programmes and schemes relating to the social and economic rehabilitation of *Safai Karamcharis* and make recommendation to the Central Government and State Governments for better co-ordination and implementation of, such programmes and schemes;

(c) investigate specific grievances and take *suo motu* notice of matter relating to non-implementation, of,—

  (i) programmes or schemes in respect of any group of *Safai Karamcharis;*
  (ii) decisions, guidelines or instructions aimed at mitigating the hardship of *Safai Karamcharis;*
  (iii) measures for the social and economic upliftment of *Safai Karamcharis;*
  (iv) the provisions of any law in its application to *Safai Karamcharis,*

and take up such matters with the concerned authorities or with the Central or State Governments;

(d) make periodical reports to Central and State Government on any matter concerning *Safai Karamcharis,* taking into account any difficulties or disabilities being encountered by *Safai Karamcharis;*
(e) any other matter which may be referred to it by the Central Government.

2. In the discharge of its functions under sub-section (1), the Commission shall have power to call for information with respect to any matter specified in that sub-section from any Government of local or other authority.

MISCELLANEOUS

9. Chairperson, Vice-Chairperson and Members and other Employees of the Commission. The Chairperson, Vice-Chairperson, Members, Officers and other employees of the Commission shall be deemed to be public servants within the meaning of Section 21 of the Indian Penal Code (45 of 1860).

10. Central Government to Consult Commission. The Central Government shall consult the Commission on all major policy matters affecting *Safai Karamcharis.*

11. Annual Report. The Commission shall prepare in such form and at such time for each financial year as may be prescribed its annual report giving a full account of its activities during the previous financial year and forward a copy thereof to the Central Government.

12. Annual Report to be Laid before Parliament or the Legislative Assembly. 1. The Central Government shall cause the annual report to be laid before each House of Parliament along with the memorandum explaining the action taken or proposed to be taken on the recommendations contained therein so far as they relate to the Central Government and the reasons for non-acceptance, if any, of such recommendation.

2. Where the said report or any part thereof relates to any matter within which a State Government is concerned, a copy of such report shall be forwarded to the Governor of the State who shall cause it to be laid before the Legislature of the State along with a memorandum explaining the action taken or proposed to be taken on the recommendations relating to the State and the reason for the non-acceptance, if any of any such recommendation or part.

13. Delegation of Powers. The Commission may, by general or special order, delegate to the Chairperson, Vice-Chairperson or any Member or to any officer of the Commission subject to such conditions and limitations, if any, as may be specified there in. Such of its powers and duties under this Act as it may deem fit.

14. Protection of Action Taken in Good Faith. No suit, prosecution or other legal proceeding shall lie against the Central Government, Commission, Chairperson, Vice-Chairperson, Members or any officer or other employee of the Commission for anything which is in good faith done or intended to be done under this Act.

15. Power to Make Rules. 1. The Central Government may, by notification in the Official Gazette, make rules for carrying out the provisions of this Act.

2. In particular, and without prejudice to the generality of the foregoing powers, such rules may provide for all or any of the following matters, namely:

(a) salaries and allowances payable to, and the other terms and conditions of service of, the Chairperson, Vice-Chairperson and Members under sub-section (5) of Section 4 and of officers and other employees of the Commission under sub-section (2) of Section 5;

(b) the form in, and the time at, which the annual report shall be prepared under Section 11;

(c) any other matter which is required to be, or may be, prescribed.

3. Every rule made under this Act shall be laid. As soon as may be after it is made, before such House of Parliament, while it is in

session for a total period of thirty days which may be comprised in one session or in two or more successive sessions, and if, before the expiry of the session immediately following the session or the successive session aforesaid, both Houses agree in making any modification in the rule or both Houses agree that the rule should not be made, the rule shall thereafter, have effect only in such modified form or be of no effect, as the case may be; so, however, that any such modification of annulment shall be without prejudice to the validity of anything previously done under that rule.

THE NATIONAL COMMISSION FOR MINORITIES ACT, 1992

[17th May 1992]

AN ACT to constitute a National Commission for Minorities and to provide for matters connected therewith or incidental thereto.

Be it enacted by Parliament in the Forty-third Year of the Republic of India as follows:

PRELIMINARY

1. *Short Title, Extent and Commencement.* 1. This Act may be called the National Commission for Minorities Act, 1992.

2. It extends to the whole of India except the State of Jammu and Kashmir.

3. It shall come into force on such date as the Central Government may, by notification in the Official Gazette, appoint.

2. *Definitions.* In this Act, unless the context otherwise requires,—

(a) "Commission" means the National Commission for Minorities constituted under section 3;

(b) "Member" means a Member of the Commission;

(c) "minority", for the purpose of this Act, means a community notified as such by the Central Government;

(d) "prescribed" means prescribed by rules made under this Act.

THE NATIONAL COMMISSION FOR MINORITIES

3. Constitution of the National Commission for Minorities. 1. The Central Government shall constitute a body to be known as the National Commission for Minorities to exercise the powers conferred on, and to perform the functions assigned to, it under this Act.

2. The Commission shall consist of a Chairperson and six Members to be nominated by the Central Government from amongst persons of eminence, ability and integrity:

Provided that five Members including the Chairperson shall be from amongst the minority communities.

4. Term of Office and Conditions of Service of Chairperson and Members. 1. The Chairperson and every Member shall hold office for a term of three years from the date he assumes office.

2. The Chairperson or a Member may, by writing under his

hand addressed to the Central Government, resign from the office of Chairperson or, as the case may be, of the Member at any time.

3. The Central Government shall remove a person from the office of Chairperson or a Member referred to in sub-section (2) if that person:

(a) becomes an undischarged insolvent;
(b) is convicted and sentenced to imprisonment for an offence which, in the opinion of the Central Government, involves moral turpitude;
(c) becomes of unsound mind and stands so declared by a competent court;
(d) refuses to act or becomes incapable of acting;
(e) is, without obtaining leave of absence from the Commission, absent from three consecutive meetings of the Commission; or
(f) has, in the opinion of the Central Government, so abused the position of Chairperson or Member as to render that person's continuance in office detrimental to the interests of minorities or the public interest:

Provided that no person shall be removed under this clause until that person has been given a reasonable opportunity of being heard in the matter.

4. A vacancy caused under sub-section (2) or otherwise shall be filled by fresh nomination

5. The salaries and allowances payable to, and the other terms and conditions of service of, the Chairperson and Members shall be such as may be prescribed.

5. Officers and other Employees of the Commission. 1. The Central Government shall provide the Commission with a Secretary and such other officers and employees as may be necessary for the efficient performance of the functions of the Commission under this Act.

2. The salaries and allowances payable to, and the other terms and conditions of service of, the officers and other employees appointed for the purpose of the Commission shall be such as may be prescribed.

6. Salaries and Allowances to be Paid out of Grants. The salaries and allowances payable to the Chairperson and Members and the administrative expenses, including salaries, allowances and pensions payable to the officers and other employees referred to in section 5, shall be paid out of the grants referred to in sub-section (1) of section 10.

7. Vacancies, etc., not to Invalidate Proceedings of the Commission. No act or proceeding of the Commission shall be questioned or shall be invalid merely on the ground of the existence of any vacancy or defect in the constitution of the Commission.

8. Procedure to be Regulated by the Commission. 1. The Commission shall meet as and when necessary at such time and place as the Chairperson may think fit.

2. The Commission shall regulate its own procedure.

3. All orders and decisions of the Commission shall be authenticated by the Secretary or any officer of the Commission duly authorised by the secretary in this behalf.

FUNCTIONS OF THE COMMISSION

9. Functions of the Commission. 1. The Commission shall perform all or any of the following functions, namely:

(a) evaluate the progress of the development of minorities under the Union and States;

(b) monitor the working of the safeguards provided in the Constitution and in laws enacted by Parliament and the State Legislatures;

(c) make recommendations for the effective implementation of safeguards for the protection of the interests of minorities by the Central Government or the State Governments;

(d) look into specific complaints regarding deprivation of rights and safeguards of the minorities and take up such matters with the appropriate authorities;

(e) cause studies to be undertaken into problems arising out of any discrimination against minorities and recommend measures for their removal;

(f) conduct studies, research and analysis on the issues relating to socio-economic and educational development of minorities;

(g) suggest appropriate measures in respect of any minority to be undertaken by the Central Government or the State Governments;

(h) make periodical or special reports to the Central Government on any matter pertaining to minorities and in particular difficulties confronted by them; and

(i) any other matter which may be referred to it by the Central Government.

2. The Central Government shall cause the recommendations referred to in clause (c) of sub-section (1) to be laid before each House of Parliament along with a memorandum explaining the action taken or proposed to be taken on the recommendations relating to the Union and the reasons for the non-acceptance, if any, of any of such recommendations.

3. Where any recommendation referred to in clause (c) of sub-section (1) or any part thereof with which any State Government is concerned, the Commission shall forward a copy of such recommendation or part to such State Government who shall cause it to be laid before the Legislature of the State along with a memorandum explaining the action taken or proposed to be taken on the recommendations relating to the State and the reasons for the non-acceptance if any, of any of such recommendation or part.

4. The Commission shall, while performing any of the functions mentioned in sub-clauses (a), (b) and (d) of sub-section (1), have all the powers of a civil court trying a suit and in particular, in respect of the following matters, namely:

(a) summoning and enforcing the attendance of any person from any part of India and examining him on oath;
(b) requiring the discovery and production of any document;
(c) receiving evidence on affidavits;
(d) requisitioning any public record or copy thereof from any court of office;
(e) issuing commissions for the examination of witnesses and documents; and
(f) any other matter which may be prescribed.

FINANCE, ACCOUNTS AND AUDIT

10. Grants by the Central Government. 1. The Central Government shall, after due appropriation made by Parliament by law in this behalf, pay to the Commission by way of grants such sums of money as the Central Government may think fit for being utilised for the purposes of this Act.

2. The Commission may spend such sums as it thinks fit for performing the functions under this Act, and such sums shall be

treated as expenditure payable out of the grants referred to in sub-section (1).

11. Accounts and Audit. 1. The Commission shall maintain proper accounts and other relevant records and prepare an annual statement of accounts in such form as may be prescribed by the Central Government in consultation with the Comptroller and Auditor-General of India.

2. The accounts of the Commission shall be audited by the Comptroller and Auditor-General at such intervals as may be specified by him and any expenditure incurred in connection with such audit shall be payable by the Commission to the Comptroller and Auditor-General.

3. The Comptroller and Auditor-General and any person appointed by him in connection with the audit of the accounts of the Commission under this Act shall have the same rights and privileges and the authority in connection with such audit as the Comptroller and Auditor-General generally has in connection with the audit of Government accounts and, in particular, shall have the right to demand the production of books, accounts, connected vouchers and other documents and papers and to inspect any of the offices of the Commission.

12. Annual Report. The Commission shall prepare, in such form and at such time, for each financial year, as may be prescribed, its annual report, giving a full account of its activities during the previous financial year and forward a copy thereof to the Central Government.

13. Annual Report and Audit Report to be Laid before Parliament. The Central Government shall cause the annual report together with a memorandum of action taken on the recommendations contained therein, in so far as they relate to the Central Government, and the reasons for the non-acceptance, if any, of any of such recommendations and the audit report to be laid as soon as may be after the reports are received, before each House of Parliament.

MISCELLANEOUS

14. Chairperson, Members and Staff of the Commission to be Public Servants. The Chairperson, Members and employees of the Commission shall be deemed to be public servants within the meaning of section 21 of the Indian Penal Code.

15. Power to Make Rules. 1. The Central Government may, by notification in the Official Gazette, make rules for carrying out the provisions of this Act.

2. In particular, and without prejudice to the generality of the foregoing powers, such rules may provide for all or any of the following matters, namely:

(a) salaries and allowances payable to, and the other terms and conditions of service of, the Chairperson and Members under sub-section (5) of section 4 and of officers and other employees under sub-section (2) of section 5;
(b) any other matter under clause (f) of sub-section (4) of section 9;
(c) the form in which the annual statement of accounts shall be maintained under sub-section (1) of section 11;
(d) the form in, and the time at, which the annual report shall be prepared under section 12;
(e) any other matter which is required to be, or may be, prescribed.

3. Every rule made under this Act shall be laid, as soon as may be after it is made, before each House of Parliament, while it is in session, for a total period of thirty days which may be comprised in one session or in two more successive sessions, and if, before the expiry of the session immediately following the session or the successive sessions aforesaid, both houses agree in making any modification in the rule or both Houses agree that the rule should not be made, the rule shall thereafter have effect only in such modified form or be of no effect, as the case may be; so, however, that any such modification or annulment shall be without prejudice to the validity of anything previously done under that rule.

16. Power to Remove Difficulties. 1. If any difficulty arises in giving effect to the provisions of this Act, the Central Government may, by order published in the Official Gazette, make such provisions, not inconsistent with the provisions of this Act as appear to it to be necessary or expedient for removing the difficulty:

Provided that no such order shall be made after the expiry of a period of two years from the date of commencement of this Act.

2. Every order made under this section shall, as soon as may be after it is made, be laid before each House of Parliament.

CHRISTIAN MARRIAGE AND MATRIMONIAL CAUSES BILL, 1994

(a) Marriage. The Bill is a consensus of the Christian people of India to update their laws pertaining to marriage and matrimonial causes bearing in mind the vast social changes that have taken place in the last century. As stated above, the law on the subject comprises of two major enactments. Of these, the Indian Christian Marriage Act 1872 is in need of urgent improvement on several points of substance. To mention the most important changes at this state (i) the conditions of marriage are nowhere set out conveniently in the Act in a manner that will give at a glance the position in that respect as regards all Christian. This has been taken care of; (ii) secondly, there is a bewildering variety of forms of marriage as envisaged by the 1872 Act. It is felt that while the parties should be allowed to enjoy, at their option, the facility of a religious or a secular marriage (as at present) there is scope for simplifying the law in this regard. Besides this, from the linguistic point of view, the provisions of the 1872 Act on marriage are very badly in need of revision. All these changes have been conveniently carried out, keeping in mind the objectives mentioned above. (iii) There are provisions for marriage for minors, which have been excluded. (iv) Marriages annulled by any Church has been declared null and void under this Act in order to avoid a double process of obtaining annulment under the existing State laws.

(b) Divorce. 1. The topic of divorce amongst Christians was in even greater need of law reform. Both from the constitutional point of view which demands that discrimination between men and women should go, and from the social point of view, substantial expansion of the grounds of divorce was needed. This did not, of course, mean that divorce at the sweet will of one party should be granted for the mere asking. However, reasonably acceptable grounds of divorce, particularly where one party has been guilty of cruelty should at least receive serious consideration. In addition, (with certain safe-guards) divorce by mutual consent of the couple should be available to Christians, as it is now available to Hindus and to persons married under the Special Marriage Act, 1994. There is a similar scope for making the law as to nullity and legitimacy more rational.

2. Several procedural aspects of the present divorce law have

also proved to be inconvenient irritants in practice, and the time has come to revise the law on those points also.

3. Apart from proposing improvements in point of substance and language, the Bill seeks to collect at one place provisions at present scattered in two enactments-and that too in a very haphazard fashion.

4. For the purpose of this Bill 'divorce' means the dissolution of the civil effects of marriage.

SPECIAL MARRIAGE ACT

The Christian Marriage Bill 1994 has been drafted to be as close to the Special Marriage Act 1954 as possible.

CHRISTIAN ADOPTION AND MAINTENANCE BILL, 1994

For the first time in the history of Indian Christians, there is a provision for adoption of children by Christians. The major points of the Bill are as follows:

1. Christian women and men should have the right to adopt children of either sex.
2. The adoption should be capable of being effected without court permission.
3. The child to be adopted should not have completed 15 years of age.
4. Sufficient protection be guaranteed for adopted child.

INDIAN SUCCESSION AMENDMENT BILL, 1994

The following changes have been made, keeping in mind also Christians belonging to the matriarchal tribal communities.

1. There should be one law of succession for all Christians, irrespective of the regions they belong to, giving equal rights to women and men in property.

2. The Succession Act should be changed, so that the wife has full right to the property of her husband, if the husband died without making a will and without leaving issue and parents. His assets should not be shared with remote kindred of the deceased and vice-versa. (See also point 5 below)

3. In case the father is dead, the mother should have the right to approve the minor's pre-marital settlement under section 22 and vice-versa.

4. The provision in section 32, depriving a widow of a share in her husband's estate if she has made pre-marriage contract to that effect should be deleted.

5. The present position (in sections 24, 33, 41, 48) under which if there are 'kindred' surviving, the widow gets only one half, should be modified and the widow should get full property.

6. The benefit of minimum guaranteed payment to the widow (section 33A) should be extended to Christians (to whom it does not, at present, apply). The amount (of Rs. 5,000) should be suitably raised and this benefit made available even if the husband has made a will.

7. Illegitimate children (section 37) should have the same rights (on intestacy), as legitimate children.

8. Where the father is alive (and there are no lineal descendants), the mother gets no share at present (section 42-46) - a position that needs to be reformed. The father and the mother should share equally.

9. Where the father is of unsound mind, the mother should have the rights to appoint a testamentary guardian and vice-versa (section 60).

10. The prohibition against death-bed bequests for religious or charitable purposes by persons having near relatives (section 118) should be deleted or substantially modified, as it is out of tune with current notions (The sections applies *inter alia* to Indian Christians).

11. The bar against a person establishing right as executor or legate without probate (section 213) should not apply to Indian Christians. Already section 370CI, allows Indian Christian to recover debts, etc. Some liberal approach should be adopted in regard to need for probate, etc.

5

Women, Children and Human Rights

THE DOWRY PROHIBITION ACT, 1961

An Act to prohibit the giving or taking of dowry

Be it enacted by Parliament in the Twelfth Year of the Republic of India as follows:

1. Short Title, Extent and Commencement. 1. This Act may be called the Dowry Prohibition Act 1961.

2. It extends to the whole of India except the State of Jammu and Kashmir.

3. It shall come into force on such date, as the Central Government may, by notification in the Official Gazette, appoint.

2. Definition of 'Dowry'. In this Act, 'dowry' means any property or valuable security given or agreed to be given either directly or indirectly—

(a) by one party to a marriage to the other party to the marriage or

(b) by the parents of either party to a marriage or by any other person, to either party to the marriage or to any other person, at or before [or any time after the marriage] in connection with the marriage of the said parties it does not include] dower or *mahr* in the case of person to whom the Muslim Personal Law *(Shariat)* applies.

State Amendments

Haryana: (Vide Haryana Act No. 38 of 1,376 the following sections shall be substituted for Sectarian 2).

2. *Definitions* : In this Act, unless the context otherwise requires,

(i) 'dowry' means any property or valuable security given or agreed to be given either directly or indirectly—

(a) by one party to a marriage to the other party to the marriage;

(b) by the parents of either party to a marriage or by any other person, to either party to the marriage or to another person;

at or before or after the marriage as consideration to the marriage of the said parties, but does not include dower or *mahr* in the case of person to whom the Muslim Personal law *(Shariat)* applies.

Explanation I. For the removal of doubts it is hereby declared that any presents made at the time of a marriage to either party to the marriage in the form of cash, ornaments, clothes, or other articles shall not be deemed to be dowry within the meaning of this section unless they are made as consideration for the marriage of the said parties.

Explanation II. The expression 'valuable securities' has the same meaning as in Section 30 of the Indian Penal Code (45 of 1860)

(ii) 'marriage expenses' shall include expenses incurred directly or indirectly at or before the marriage on—

(a) *thakka sagai, tikka shagum* and *milni* ceremonies;

(b) the gifts made by one party to a marriage to the other party to the marriage or by the parents, grandparents and brothers of either party a marriage, to either party to the marriage or their blood relations thereof.

(c) illuminations, food and the arrangements for serving food to the members of the marriage party and other expenses incidental thereto.

Explanation III. For the removal of doubts, it is hereby declared that any gifts made by a person other than those specified in sub-clause (b), at the time of the marriage either party to the marriage shall not be deemed to be marriage expenses

3. ***Penalty for Giving or Taking Dowry.*** [1. If any person, after the commencement of this Act, gives or take or abets the giving or taking of dowry, he shall be punishable with imprisonment for a term which shall not be less than five years, and with fine which shall not be less than fifteen thousand rupees or the amount of the value of such dowry, whichever is more.

Provided that the Court may, for adequate and special reasons to be recorded in the judgment, impose a sentence of imprisonment for a term of less than [five years].

2. Nothing in sub-section (1) shall apply to, or in relation to—

(a) presents which are given at the time of a marriage to the bride (without any demand having in that behalf)
Provided that such presents are entered in a list maintained in accordance with the rules made under this Act;

(b) presents which are given at the time of a marriage to the bridegroom (without any demand having been made in that behalf):
Provided that such presents are entered in a list maintained in accordance with the rules made under this Act :
Provided further that where such presents are made by or on behalf of the bride or any person related to the bride, such presents are of a customary nature and the value thereof is not excessive having regard to the financial status of the person by whom, or on whose behalf, such presents are given.

State Amendments

Bihar: (Vide Bihar Act No. 4 1976 for section 3 the following shall be substituted),

"Penalty for Giving or Taking Dowry. If any person after the commencement of this Act, gives or takes or abets the giving or taking of dowry, he shall be punishable with imprisonment which may extend to six months and with fine which may extend to five thousand rupees.

Haryana. (Vide Haryana Act No. 38 of 1976, for Section 3 the following, shall be substituted).

3. ***Bar of Certain Acts.*** No person shall

(a) give or take or abet the giving or taking of dowry
(b) demand, directly or indirectly, from the parents or guardian of a bride or bridegroom, as the case may be, any dowry:
(c) incur marriage expenses the aggregate value share of exceeds five thousand rupees:
(d) display any gifts made at or before the marriage in the form of cash, ornaments, clothes or other articles
(e) take or carry in excess of

(i) twenty-five members of the marriage party : and
(ii) eleven members of the band;

(f) deny conjugal rights to his wife on the ground that dowry has not been given or the dowry given is insufficient'.

Himachal Pradesh. (Vide H.P. Act No. 25 of 1976, the following shall be substituted for Section 3).

3. *Penalty for Giving or Taking Dowry.* If any person gives or takes or abets the giving or taking of dowry, he shall be punishable with imprisonment which may extend to one year and with fine which, may extend to five thousand rupees.

Punjab. Vide Punjab Act No. 26 of 1976 Section 3. For the words "six months or with fine which may extend to five thousand rupees:, the words "one year, and fine which may extend to five thousand" shall be substituted.

West Bengal. Vide W. B. Act of 35 of 1975 in Section 3. For the words "which may extend to five thousand rupees", the words "shall not be less than two thousand rupees, but which may extend to ten thousand rupees" shall be substituted.

4. *Penalty for Demanding Dowry.* If any person demands, directly or indirectly, from the parents or other relatives or guardian of a bride or bridegroom, as the case may be, any dowry shall be punishable with imprisonment for a term which shall not be less than six months, but which may extend to two years and with fine which may extend to ten thousand rupees;

Provided that the Court may, for adequate and special reasons to be mentioned in the judgment, impose a sentence imprisonment for a term of less than six months.

4 -A. Ban on Advertisement. If any person,

(a) offers, through any advertisement in any newspaper, periodical, journal or through any other media, any share in his property or of any money or both as a share in any business or other interest as consideration for the marriage of his son or daughter or any other relative,

(b) prints or publishes or circulates any advertisement referred to in clause (a), he shall be punishable with imprisonment for a term which shall not be less than six months, but which may extend to five years, or with fine which may extend to fifteen thousand rupees:

Provided that the Court may, for adequate and special reasons in the judgment, impose a sentence for imprisonment for a term of less than six months,

State Amendments

Bihar (Vide Bihar Act No. 4 of 1976 the following shall be substituted for Section 4)

4. Penalty for Demanding Dowry. If any person after the commencement of this Act, demands, directly or indirectly, from the parents or guardian of a bride or bridegroom, as the case may be, any dowry, he shall be punishable with imprisonment which extend to six months and with fine which may extend to five thousand rupees.

Provided that no court shall take cognizance of any offence under this section except with the previous sanction of the State Government or of such officer as the State Government may, by general order, specify in this behalf'

Haryana (Vide Haryana Act No. 38 of 1976 the following shall be substituted for Section 4)

4. Penalty. 1. If any person contravenes any of the provision of Section 3, he shall be punishable with imprisonment which may extend to six months and with fine which may extend to five thousand rupees.

2. The Court trying an offence under Clause (f) of Section 3 relating to conjugal right may, at any stage of the proceedings, on the execution of a bond by 'the husband undertaking not to demand dowry and to allow conjugal rights to the wife, drop the proceedings.

3. Any proceedings dropped under subsection (2) shall revive if the Court is satisfied on an application made by the wife, in this behalf, that the husband has failed to carry out the undertaking or has otherwise acted contrary to the terms of the bond and thereupon the Court shall proceed with the case from the stage at which it was dropped.

Provided that no application under this sub-section shall be entertained if it is made after the expiry of a period of three years from the date on which proceedings were dropped.

4. The Court may direct that the fine, if any, imposed for the coutravention of Clause (f) of Section 3 or such portion thereof, as the Court may deem proper, shall be paid to the wife.

4. Penalty for Demanding Dowry. "If any person demands dowry directly or indirectly, from the parents or guardian of a bride or bridegroom or from any other person, as the case may be, any dowry, he shall be punishable with imprisonment which may extend to one year and with fine which may extend to five thousand rupees.

4-A. Bar of Certain Acts. Any person who:

(i) displays any presents made at the time of marriage in the form of cash, ornaments, clothes or other articles, or

(ii) gives in the form of *shagun* at time of *thakka* betrothal or like anything the value of which exceeds eleven rupees, or

(iii) gives to the parents or any other relation of a party to the marriage anything on the occasion of milni or any other ceremony performed in relation to betrothal or marriage;

shall be punishable with imprisonment for a term which may extend to six months or with fine which may extend to five thousand rupees or with both.

4-B. Penalty for Depriving Any Part of any Rights and Privileges of Marriage. 1. If after the marriage, any party to the marriage or without assistance of any of other person deprives the other party of the rights, and privileges of marriage or tortures or refuses to maintain the said other party for non-payment of dowry before, during or after marriage, he shall be punishable with imprisonment which may extend to one year and with fine which may extend to five thousand rupees.

2. The provisions of this section shall be in addition to and not derogation of, any provision on the subject contained in any other law for time being in force.

Punjab. (Vide Punjab Act No. 26 of 1976 in Section 4 the following shall be substituted and Section 4-A and 4-B shall be inserted):

(a) For the words "six months or with fine which may extend to five thousand rupees" the words "one year and fine which may extend to five thousand rupees" shall be substituted; and

(b) the provison shall be omitted.

4-A. Bar of Certain Acts. Any person who:

(i) displays any presents made at the time of such marriage in the form of cash, ornaments, clothes or other articles, or

(ii) takes in a marriage party more than twenty-five persons exclusive of minors and the members of the band; or

(iii) gives in the form of *shagun* at the time of *thakka*, betrothal or marriage, anything the value of which exceeds eleven rupees, or

(iv) gives to the parents or any other relation of a party to the marriage anything on the occasion of *milni* or any other ceremony performed in relation to betrothal or marriage; or

(v) serves to the marriage party more than two principal meals,

shall be punishable with imprisonment for a term which may extend to six months or with fine which may extend to five thousand rupees or with both.

Explanation. In this section the expression "Principal meal" mean lunch or dinner.

4-B. ***Penalty for Depriving Any Party of Rights and Privileges of Marriage.*** Any party to the marriage who after the marriage, deprives the other party of the rights and privileges of marriage, or tortures or refuses to maintain the said other party, non-payment of dowry and any person who assists such party in the commission of such offence shall be punishable with imprisonment for a term which may extend to one year and fine which may extend to five thousand rupees.

West Bengal. (Vide West Bengal Act No. 36 of 1975 in Section 4 the following shall be substituted and Section 4-A shall be inserted).

(a) after the words 'bride or bridegroom' the words 'or from any other person', shall be inserted.

(b) for the words 'which may extend to six months or with fine— which may extend to five thousand rupees', the words which shall not be less than three months, but may extend to three years or with fine which shall not be less than two thousand rupees but may extend to ten thousand rupees shall be substituted.

(c) for the proviso, the following proviso shall be substituted, namely:

Provided that no Court shall take cognizance of any offence under this section except on a complaint made by any aggrieved party or his parents or by any other person with the previous sanction of the authority specified by the State Government in this behalf;

Provided further that no such previous sanction shall be necessary for taking cognizance on a complaint made by such organization for social welfare with a minimum standing of five years as may be specified by the State Government by notification in the Official Gazette or by any person duly authorised by such organisation.

4-A. Penalty for Depriving Any Party of the Rights and Privileges of Marriage. 1. If after marriage, any party to the marriage with or without assistance of his parents or guardian deprives the other party of the rights and privileges of marriage, or tortures or refuses to maintain the said other party for non-payment of dowry before, during or after marriage. He shall be punishable with imprisonment which shall not be less than three months, but may extend to one year or with fine which shall not be less than two thousand rupees, but may extend to five thousand rupees, or with both.

2. The provisions of this section shall be in addition to, and not in derogation of, any provisions on the subject contained in any other law for the time being in force.

5. Agreement for Giving or Taking Dowry to be Void. Any agreement for the giving or taking of dowry shall be void.

6. Dowry to be for the Benefit of the Wife or her Heirs. 1. Where any dowry is received by any person other than the woman in connection with whose marriage it is given that person shall transfer it to the woman:

(a) if the dowry was received before marriage, within three months after the date of marriage; or

(b) if the dowry was received at the time of or after the marriage within three months after the date of its receipt : or,

(c) if the dowry was received when the woman was a minor, within three months after she has attained the age of eighteen years and pending such transfer, shall hold it in trust for the benefit of the woman.

2. If any person fails to transfer any property as required by sub-section (1) within the time specified therefore or as required by sub-section (3), he shall be punishable with imprisonment for a term which shall not be less than six months, but which may extend to two years or with the fine which shall not be less than five thousand rupees, but which may extend to ten thousand rupees or with both.

3. Where the woman entitled to any property under sub-section

(1) (dies before receiving it, the heirs of the woman shall be entitled to claim it from the person holding it for the time being.

[Provided that whether such woman dies within seven years of her marriage, otherwise than due to natural causes, such property shall

(a) be transferred to her parents, if she has no children, or
(b) be transferred to such children and pending such transfer, be held in trust for such children, if she has children.

3A. Where a person, convicted under sub-section (2) for failure to transfer any property as required by sub-section (1) or sub-section (3) has not, before his conviction under that sub-section, transferred such property to the woman entitled thereto or, as the case may be, her heirs, parents or children, the court shall, in addition to awarding punishment under that sub-section, direct by order in writing, that such person shall transfer the property to such woman or, as the case may be, her heirs, parents or children] within such periods as may be specified in the order and if such a person fails to comply with the direction within the period so specified, an amount equal to the value of the property may be recovered from him as if it were a fine imposed by such court and paid to such woman, or as the case may be, her heirs, parents or children.

State Amendments

Haryana: In sub-section (2) of Section 6, for the words, or with fine, which may extend to five thousand rupees or with both', the words 'and with fine which may extend to five thousand rupees' shall be substituted.

Orissa. (Vide Orissa Act No. 1 of 1976, the following shall be inserted after Section 6).

6-A. Penalty for Denial of Conjugal R ights by the Husband. 1. If any person denies conjugal rights to his wife on the ground that dowry has not been given, or on the ground that the dowry given is insufficient, he shall be punishable with imprisonment which may extend to one year or with fine which may extend to ten thousand rupees or with both.

2. The Court trying an offence under this section may, at any stage of the proceedings, on the execution of a bond by the husband undertaking not to realise the dowry or any portion thereof, as the

case may be, and to allow conjugal rights to the wife, drop the proceedings.

3. Any proceeding dropped under sub-section (2) shall revive if the Court is satisfied, on an application made in that behalf by the wife that the, husband has failed to carry out the undertaking or has otherwise acted contrary to the terms of the bond, and thereupon the Court shall proceed with the case from the stage at which it was dropped.

6-B. Maintenance to be Paid by Husband on his Conviction. 1. On conviction of a person for an offence under Section 6-A, the Court trying the offence may, on a claim made, by his wife in that behalf within two months from the date of the order of the conviction, order such person to make a monthly allowance for the maintenance of his wife at such monthly rate riot exceeding five hundred rupees, as the Court deems proper :

Provided that no such order shall be made without giving the parties concerned a reasonable opportunity of being heard.

2. In determining the monthly allow under this section regard shall be held to

(a) the position and status of the parties;
(b) the reasonable wants of the wife;
The value of the wife's property and any income derived from such property, or from the wife's own earnings or from any other source;
(d) the amount of compensation awarded under Section 6-A.

3. The maintenance allow so ordered shall be a charge on the property, if any, of the husband whether, acquired before or after the date of the order.

4. Where a complaint has been filed by the wife for an offence under Section 6-A, the husband shall not transfer any of his assets till

(a) where no claim for maintenance has been preferred under this section, the date of expiry of the period of limitation specified in sub-section (1) for filing such claim; and
(b) where such claim is preferred, the disposal of the claim,

5. Notwithstanding anything contained in any other law, the wife may enforce any claim for maintenance against any property

transferred by the husband in contravention of the provisions of subsection (4) as if such transfer were null and void.

6. The provisions contained in subsection (3) of Section 125 of the Code of Criminal Procedure, 1973, shall so far as may be, apply to the recovery of the maintenance allowance ordered under this section.

7. Nothing contained in this section shall effect the provisions of Section 3 or Section 4.

7. ***Cognizance of offences.*** 1. Notwithstanding anything contained in the Code of Criminal Procedure, 1973 (2 of 1974)

(a) no court, inferior to that of Metropolitan Magistrate or a Judicial Magistrate of the first class shall try any offence under this Act.

(b) no court shall take cognizance of an offence under this Act except upon—

(i) its own knowledge or a police report of the facts which constitute such offence, or

(ii) a complaint by the person aggrieved by the offence or other relative of such person, or by any recognized welfare institution or organization.

(c) it shall be lawful for a Metropolitan Magistrate or a Judicial Magistrate of the first class to pass any sentence authorised by this Act or, any person convicted of any offence under this Act.

Explanation. For the purposes of this sub-section, recognized welfare institution or organisation means a social welfare institution or organisation recognized in the behalf by the Central or State Government.

2. Nothing in Chapter XXXVI of the Code of Criminal Procedure, 1973 (2 of 1974), shall apply to any offence punishable under this Act.

2[3] Notwithstanding anything contained any law for the time being in force, a statement made by the person aggrieved by the offence shall not subject such person to a prosecution under this Act.

Bihar. (Vide Bihar Act No. 4 of 1976 the following shall be substituted for Section 7)

'7. ***Trial of offences.*** Notwithstanding anything contained in the Code of Criminal Procedure 1973 (Act 2 of 1974) no Court inferior to that of a Metropolitan Magistrate or a Judicial Magistrate of the first class shall try any offence under this Act.

Haryana. (Vide Haryana Act No. 38 of 1,979 the following shall be substituted for Section 7)

7. Cognizance of Offences. Notwithstanding anything contained in the Code of Criminal Procedure, 1973 (2 of 1974),

(a) no Court inferior to that of a Judicial Magistrate of the first class try any offence under this Act:

(b) no Court shall take cognizance of any such offence except on a complaint made by any party to the marriage or her father, mother or brother or a Gazetted Officer specially authorised by the State Government in this behalf, within a period of one year from the date of the marriage;

(c) no Court shall take cognizance of any such offence except with the previous sanction of the District Magistrate or of such officer as the State Government may, by general or special order, specify in this behalf;

(d) no enquiry shall be got made through any Police Officer below the rank of a Deputy Superintendent of Police

(e) no woman shall be called to Police Station for the purpose of an enquiry regarding any offence under this Act."

Himachal Pradesh (vide H. P. Act No. 25 of 1976 the following shall be substituted for Section 7)

"7.Trial of Offences. Notwithstanding anything contained] in the Code of Criminal Procedure, 1973 (No, 2 of 1974), no court inferior to that of a Judicial Magistrate of the first class shall try any offence under this Act.

2. No Court shall take cognizance of any offence under this Act, except that of offence under section 4-B, except on a police report or complaint made within one year of the marriage" (H.P. Act No. 25 of 1976, Section 5).

Punjab. (Vide Punjab Act No 26 of 1976 the following shall be substituted for Section 7)

"7. Cognizance of Offences. Notwithstanding anything contained in the Code of Criminal Procedure, 1973 (2 of 1974).

1. No Court inferior to that of a Judicial Magistrate of the first class shall try any offence under this Act;

2. No court shall take cognizance of any offence punishable under Section 3, 4 and 4-B, except upon a complaint made within

one year from the date of the offence by some person aggrieved by the offence.

Provided that

(a) where such person is under the age of eighteen years, or is an idiot or a lunatic, or is from sickness or infirmity unable to make a complaint, or is a woman who, according to the local customs and manners, ought not to be compelled to appear in public, some other person may, with the leave of the Court, make a complaint on his or her behalf;

(b) where the person aggrieved by an offence is the wife, complaint may be made on, her behalf by her father, mother, brother, sister or by her father's or mother's brother, or sister, and

3. every offence under Section 4-A shall be cognizable.

Provided that no Police Officer below the rank of a Deputy Superintendent of Police shall investigate any offence punishable under this Act or make any arrest therefore.

***West Bengal*:** In Section 7 vide West Bengal Act No 35 of 1975:

(a) for the words and figures "Code of Criminal Procedure 1898 (6 of 1898), the words and figures "Code of Criminal Procedure 1971 (2 of 1974) shall be substituted;

(b) for the words "Presidency Magistrate, Magistrate of the first class" in the two places where they occur the words "Metropolitan Magistrate or a Judicial Magistrate of the first class" shall be substituted.

(c) In clause (b) for the words "one year from the, date of" the words "three years from the date of the offence" shall be substituted.

8. Offences to be Cognizable for Certain Purposes and to be Non-bailable and Non-compoundable. 1 The Code of Criminal Procedure, 1973 (2 of 1974) shall apply to offences under this Act as if they were cognizable offences.

(a) for the purposes of investigation of such offences and

(b) for the purposes of matters other man

.(i) matter referred to in Section 42 of that Code and

(ii) the arrest of a person without a warrant or without an order of a Magistrate.

2. Every offence under this Act shall be non-bailable and non-compoundable.

8A. ***Burden of Proof in Certain Cases.*** Where any person is prosecuted for taking or abetting the taking of any dowry under Section 3, or the demanding of dowry under Section 4, the burden of proving that he had not committed an offence under those sections shall be on him.

8-B. ***Dowry Prohibition Officers.*** 1. The State Government may appoint as many Dowry Prohibition Officers as it thinks fit and specify the areas in respect of which they shall exercise their jurisdiction and powers under this Act.

2. Every Dowry Prohibition Officer shall exercise and perform the following powers and functions, namely

(a) to see that the provisions of this Act are complied with

(b) to prevent as far as possible, the taking or abetting the taking of, or the demanding of, dowry.

(c) to collect such evidence as may be necessary for the prosecution of persons committing offences under the Act.

State Amendments

Bihar. The following shall be substituted for Section 8 vide Bihar Act No.4 of 1976.

8. Offences to be Cognizable, Non-bailable and Non-compoundable. Every offence under this Act shall be cognizable, non-bailable and non-compoundable

Himachal Pradesh. Section 8 shall be substituted as follows vide H.P. Act No. 25 of 1976 Section 8 A will be inserted.

"8. Offences to be Cognizable, Bailable and Non-compoundable. Notwithstanding anything contained in the Code of Criminal procedure, 1973 (Act No 2 of 1974), every offence under this Act shall be cognizable, bailable and non-compoundable,

8-A. ***Cognizance of Offences.*** No court shall take cognizance of any offence under this Act except on a police report under Section 173 of the Code of Criminal Procedure, 1973 (Act No. 2 of 1974) or a complaint made by a person aggrieved by the offence.

Provided that no police Officer of the rank lower than that of the Deputy Superintendent of Police shall investigate any case registered under this Act:

Provided further that no court shall take cognizance of any offence under this Act except with the previous sanction of the District Magistrate, having jurisdiction in the area.

Orissa **(Vide Orissa Act No. 1 of 1976 in Section 8).** For the words "Every offence", the words "save as otherwise provided every offence" shall be substituted.

Punjab. (Vide Punjab Act No. 26 of 1976 Section 8 shall be substituted and 8-A shall be inserted).

8. ***Offences to be Bailable and Non-compoundable.*** Every offence under this Act shall be bailable and non-compoundable.

8-A. ***Institution of Proceedings.*** No prosecution shall be instituted against any person in respect of any offence committed under this Act without the previous sanction of the District Magistrate or of such officer as the State Government may by special or general order appoint in this behalf.

9. ***Power to Make Rules.*** 1. The Central Government may by notification in the Official Gazette, make rules for carrying out the purposes of this Act.

In particular and without prejudice to the generality or the foregoing power, such rules may provide for:

(a) the form and manner in which, and the persons by whom, any list of presents referred to in sub-section (2) of Section 3 shall be maintained and all other matters connected therewith; and
(b) the better coordination of policy and action with respect to the administration of this Act.

2. Every rule made under this section shall be laid as soon as may be after it is made before each House of Parliament while it is in session for a total period of thirty days which may be comprised in one session or [in two or more successive sessions, and if, before the expiry of the session immediately following the session or the successive sessions aforesaid), both Houses agree in making any modification in the rule or both Houses agree that the rule should not be made, the rule shall thereafter have effect only in such modified form or be of no effect, as the case may be, so however that any such modification or annulment shall be without prejudice to the validity of anything previously done under that rule.

State Amendments

Himachal Pradesh: In Section 9 vide H.P. Act No. of 1976:

(a) after the words "Central Government", occurring in sub-section (1) the words "or the State Government with the prior approval of the Central Government" shall be inserted:

(b) in sub-section (2) after the words "every rule made" and before the words "under this section" the words "by the Central Government", shall be inserted;

(c) after sub-section (2), the following shall be inserted—

3. Every rule made by the State Government under this section shall be laid, as soon as may be, after it is made, before the State Legislature while it is in session for a total period of not less than seven days which may be comprised in one session or in two successive sessions and if before the expiry of the session in which it is as laid or the session immediately following, the Legislature requires any modification in the rule or desires that the rule should not be made, the rule snail thereafter have affect only in such modified form or be of no effect as the case may be, so, however that any such modification or annulment shall be without prejudice to the validity of anything previously one under that rule".

Punjab. In Section 9 vide Punjab Act No 28 of 1926 the following shall be substituted

(i) in sub-section (2), after the words "Central Government", the words "or the State Government" shall be inserted.

(ii) in sub-section (2), after the words "every rule made" the words "by the Central Government" shall be inserted, and

(iii) after sub-section (2) the following shall be inserted:

3. Every rule made under this section by the State Government shall be laid before the House of the State Legislature, it is in session for a total period of ten days which may be comprised in one session or in two or more successive sessions and if, before the expiry of the session in which it is so laid or the successive sessions aforesaid, the House agrees in making any modification in the rule or the House agrees that the rule should not be made, the rule shall thereafter have affect only in such modified form or be of no effect, as the case may be, so however, that any such modification or annulment shall be without prejudice to the validity or anything previously done under that rule.

10. Power of the State Government to Make Rules. 1. The State Government may, by notification in the Official Gazette, make rules for carrying out the purposes of this Act.

2. In particular, and without prejudice to the generality of the foregoing power, such rules may provide for all or any of the following matters namely:

(a) the additional functions to be performed by the Dowry Prohibition Officers under sub-section (2) of Section 813;
(b) limitations and conditions subject to which a Dowry Prohibition Officer may exercise his functions under sub-section (3) of Section 8-B.

3. Every rule made by the State Government under this section shall be laid as soon as may be after it is made before the State Legislature.

The Dowry Prohibition

G.S.R. 664 (E), in exercises of the powers conferred by Section 9 of the Dowry Prohibition Act, 1961 (28 of 1961) the Central Government hereby make the following rules, namely:

1. *Short Title and Commencement.* 1. These rules may be called the Dowry Prohibition (Maintenance of lists of Presents to the Bride and Bridegroom) Rules, 1985.

2. They shall come into force on the 2nd day of October, 1985 being the date appointed for the coming into force of the Dowry Prohibition (Amendment) Act, 1984 (63 of 1984)

2. *Rules in Accordance with which Lists of Presents are to be Maintained.* 1. The list of presents which are given at the time of the marriage to the bride shall be maintained by the bride.

2. The list of presents which are given at the time of the marriage to the bride shall be maintained by the bridegroom.

3. Every list of presents referred to in sub-rule (1) or sub-rule (2)—

(a) shall be prepared at the time of the marriage or as soon as possible after the marriage
(b) shall be in writing
(c) shall contain:

    (i) a brief description of each present;
    (ii) the approximate value of the present:
    (iii) the name of tire who has given the present; and
    (iv) where the person giving the present is related to the bride or bridegroom, a description of such relationship;

(d) shall be signed by both the bride and the bridegroom.

Explanation 1. Where the bride is unable to sign, she may affix her thumb impression in lieu of her signature after having the list read out to her and obtaining signature on the list of the person who has so read out the particulars contained in the list.

Explanation 2. Where the bridegroom is unable to sign, he may affix his thumb impression in lieu of his signature after having the list read out to him and obtaining the signature on the list, of the person who has so read out the particulars contained in the list.

4. The bride or the bridegroom may, if she or he so desires, obtained on either or both of the lists referred to in sub-rule (1) or sub-section (2) the signature or signatures of any relations of the bride or the bridegroom or of any other persons or person present at the time of the marriage.

THE COMMISSION OF SATI (PREVENTION) ACT, 1987
[ACT NO. 3 OF 1988]

3rd January, 1988

SYNOPSIS

An Act to provide for the more effective prevention of the commission of sati and its glorification and for matters connected herewith or incidental thereto.

Whereas, *sati* or the burning or burying alive of widows or women is revolting to the feelings of human nature and is nowhere enjoined by any of the religions of India as an imperative duty;

And whereas, it is necessary to take more effective measures to prevent the commission of *sati* and its glorification.

Be it enacted by Parliament in the Thirty-eighth Year of the Republic of India as follows:

PRELIMINARY

1. Short Title, Extent and Commencement. 1. This Act may be called the Commission of *Sati* (Prevention) Act, 1987.

2. It extends to the whole of India except the State of Jammu and Kashmir.

3. It shall come into force in a State on such date as the Central Government may, by notification in the Official Gazette, appoint, and different dates may be appointed for different States.

2. Definitions. 1. In this Act, unless the context otherwise requires—

(a) "Code" means the Code of Criminal Procedure, 1973 (2 of 1974);

(b) "Glorification", in relation to *sati*, whether such *sati*, was committed before or after the commencement of this Act, includes, among other things,—

  (i) The observance of any ceremony or the taking out of a procession in connection with the commission of *sati*; or

  (ii) The supporting, justifying or propagating the practice of *sati* in any manner; or

  (iii) The arranging of any function to eulogise the person, who has committed *sati*; or

  (iv) The creation of a trust, or the collection of funds, or the construction of a temple or other structure or the carrying on of any form of worship or the performance of any ceremony thereat, with a view to perpetuate the honour of, or to preserve the memory of, a person, who has committed *sati*;

(c) "*Sati*" means the burning or burying alive of—

(i) Any widow along with the body of her deceased husband or any other relative or with any article, object or thing associated with the husband or such relative; or

(ii) Any women along with the body of any of her relatives, irrespective of whether such burning or burying is claimed to be voluntary on the part of the widow or the women or otherwise;

(d) "Special Court" means a specially constituted Court under Section 9;

(e) "Temple" includes any building or other structure, whether roofed or not, constructed or made to preserve the memory of a person in respect of whom *sati* has been committed or used or intended to be used for the carrying on of any form of worship or for the observance of any ceremony in connection with such commission.

2. Words and expressions used but not defined in this Act and defined in the Indian Penal Code (45 of 1860), or in the Code shall have the same meanings as are respectively assigned to them in the Indian Penal Code or the Code.

PUNISHMENTS FOR OFFENCES RELATING TO *SATI*

3. ***Attempt to Commit Sati.*** Notwithstanding anything contained in the Indian Penal Code (45 of 1860), whoever, attempts to commit *sati* and does any act towards such commission shall be punishable with imprisonment for a term which may extend to one year or with fine or with both:

Provided that the Special Court trying an offence under this section shall, before convicting any person, take into consideration the circumstances leading to the commission of the offence, the act committed, the state of mind of the person charged of the offence at the time of the commission of the act and all other relevant factors.

4. *Abetment of Sati.* 1. Notwithstanding anything contained in the Indian Penal Code (45 of 1860), if any person commits *sati*, whoever abets the commission of such *sati*, either directly or indirectly, shall be punishable with death or imprisonment for life and shall also be liable to fine.

2. If any person attempts to commit *sati*, whoever abets such attempt, either directly or indirectly, shall be punishable with imprisonment for life and shall also be liable to fine.

Explanation. For the purposes of this section, any of the following acts, or the like shall also be deemed to be an abetment, namely—

(a) Any inducement to a widow or women to get her burnt, or buried alive along with the body of her deceased husband or with any other relative or with any article, object or thing associated with the husband or such relative irrespective of whether she is in a fit state of mind or is labouring under a state of intoxication or stupefaction or other cause impeding, the exercise of her free will;

(b) Making a widow or women believe that the commission of *sati* would result in some spiritual benefit to her or her deceased husband or relative, or the general well being of the family;

(c) Encouraging a widow or women to remain fixed in her resolve to commit *sati* and thus instigating her to commit *sati*;

(d) Participating in any procession in connection with the commission of *sati* or aiding the widow or women in her decision to commit *sati* by taking her along with the body of her deceased husband or relative to the cremation or burial ground;

(e) Being present at the place where *sati* is committed as an active participant to such commission or to any ceremony connected with it;

(f) Preventing or obstructing the widow or woman from saving herself from being burnt or buried alive;

(g) Obstructing or interfering with, the police in the discharge of its duties of taking any steps to prevent the commission of *sati*.

5. *Punishment for Glorification of Sati.* Whoever does any act for the glorification of *sati* shall be punishable with imprisonment for a term which shall not be less than one year but which may extend to seven years and with fine which shall not be less than five thousand rupees but which may extend to thirty thousand rupees.

POWERS OF COLLECTOR OR DISTRICT MAGISTRATE TO PREVENT OFFENCES RELATING TO *SATI*

6. *Power to Prohibit Certain Acts.* 1. Where the Collector or the District Magistrate is of the opinion that *sati* or any abetment thereof is being or is about to be committed, he may, by order, prohibit the doing of any act towards the commission of *sati* by any person in any area or areas specified in the order.

2. The Collector or the District Magistrate may also, by order, prohibit the glorification in any manner of *sati* by any person in any area or areas specified in the order.

3. Whoever contravenes any order made under sub-section (1) or sub-section (2) shall, if such contravention is not punishable under any other provision of this Act, be punishable with imprisonment for a term which shall not be less than one year but which may extend to seven years and with fine which shall not be less than five thousand rupees but, which may extend to thirty thousand rupees.

7. *Power to Remove Certain Temples or Other Structures.* 1. The State Government may, if it is satisfied that in any temple or other structure which has been in existence for not less than twenty years, any form or worship of the performance of any ceremony is carried on with a view to perpetuate the honour of, or to preserve the memory of, any person in respect of whom *sati* has been committed, by order, direct the removal of such temple or other structure.

2. The Collector or the District Magistrate may, if he is satisfied that in any temple or other structure, other than that referred to in sub-section (1), any form of worship or the performance of any ceremony is carried on with a view to perpetuate the honour of, or to preserve the memory of, any person in respect of whom *sati* has been committed, by order, direct the removal of such temple or other structure.

3. Where any order under sub-section (1), of sub-section (2) is not complied with, the State Government or the Collector or the District Magistrate, as the case may be, shall cause the temple or other structure to be removed through a police officer not below the rank of a Sub-Inspector at the cost of the defaulter.

8. *Power to Seize Certain Properties.* 1. Where the Collector or the District Magistrate has reason to believe that any funds or property have been collected or acquired for the purpose of glorification of the commission of any *sati* or which may be found under circumstances which create suspicion of the commission of any offence under this Act, he may seize such funds or property.

2. Every Collector or District Magistrate acting under sub-section (1) shall report the seizure to the Special Court, if any, constituted to try any offence in relation to which such funds or property were collected or acquired and shall await the orders of such Special Court as to the disposal of the same.

SPECIAL COURTS

9. Trial of Offences Under This Act. 1. Notwithstanding anything contained in the Code, all offences under this Act shall be triable only by a Special Court constituted under this section.

2. The State Government shall, by notification in the Official Gazette, constitute one or more Special Courts for the trial of offences under this Act and every Special Court shall exercise jurisdiction in respect of the whole or such part of the State as may be specified in the notification.

3. A Special Court shall be presided over by a Judge to be appointed by the State Government with the concurrence of the Chief Justice of the High Court.

4. A person shall not be qualified for appointment as a Judge of a Special Court unless he is, immediately before such appointment, a Sessions Judge or an Additional Sessions Judge in any State.

10. Special Public Prosecutors. 1. For every Special Court, the State Government shall appoint a person to be a Special Public Prosecutor.

2. A person shall be eligible to be appointed as a Special Public Prosecutor under this section only if he had been in practice as an advocate for not less than seven years or has held any post for a period of not less than seven years under the State requiring special knowledge of law.

3. Every person appointed as a Special Public Prosecutor under this section shall be deemed to be a Public Prosecutor within the meaning of clause (u) of Section 2 of the Code and the provisions of the Code shall have effect accordingly.

11. Procedure and Powers of Special Courts. 1. A Special Court may take cognizance of any offence, without the accused being committed to it for trial, upon receiving a complaint of facts which constitute such offence, or upon a police report of such facts.

2. Subject to the other provisions of this Act, a Special Court shall, for the purpose of the trial of any offence, have all the powers of a Court of Sessions and shall try such offence as if it were a Court of Session, so far as may be, in accordance with the procedure prescribed in the Code for trial before a Court of Session.

12. Power of Special Court with Respect to Other Offences. 1. When trying any offence under this Act, a Special Court may also try any other offence with which the accused may, under the Code, be charged at the same trial if the offence is connected with such other offence.

2. If, in the course of any trial of any offence under this Act, it is found that the accused person has committed any other offence under this Act or under any other law, a Special Court may convict such person also of such other offence and pass any sentence authorised by this Act or such other law for the punishment thereof.

3. In every inquiry or trial, the proceedings shall be held as expeditiously as possible, and, in particular, where the examination of witnesses has begun the same shall be continued from day to day until the witnesses in attendance have been examined, and if any Special Court finds the adjournment of the same beyond the following date to be necessary, it shall record its reasons for doing so.

13. Forfeiture of Funds or Property. Where a person has been convicted of an offence under this Act, the Special Court trying such offence may, if it is considered necessary to do so, declare that any funds or property seized under Section 8 shall stand forfeited to the State.

14. Appeal. 1. Notwithstanding anything contained in the Code, an appeal shall lie as a matter of right from any judgment, sentence or order, not being an interlocutory order, of a Special Court to the High Court both on facts and on law.

2. Every appeal under this section shall be preferred within a period of thirty days from the date of the judgment, sentence or order appealed from: Provided that the High Court may entertain an appeal after the expiry of the said period of thirty days, if it is satisfied that the appellant had sufficient cause for not preferring the appeal within the period of thirty days.

MISCELLANEOUS

15. Protection of Action Taken Under This Act. No suit, prosecution or other legal proceeding shall lie against the State Government or any officer or authority of the State Government for anything which is in good faith done or intended to be done in pursuance of this Act, or any rules or orders made under this Act.

16. Burden of Proof. Where any person is prosecuted of an offence under Section 4, the burden of proving that he had not committed the offence under the said section shall be on him.

17. Obligation of Certain Persons to Report About the Commission of Offence Under This Act. 1. All officers of Government are hereby required and empowered to assist the police in the execution of the provisions of this Act, or any rule of order made thereunder.

2. All village officers and such other officers as may be specified by the Collector or the District Magistrate in relation to any area and the inhabitants of such area shall, if they have reason to believe or have the knowledge that *sati* is about to be, or has been, committed in the area shall forthwith report such fact to the nearest police station.

3. Whoever contravenes the provisions of sub-section (1) or sub-section (2) shall be punishable with imprisonment of either description for a term which may extend to two years and shall also be liable to fine.

18. Person Convicted of an Offence Under Section 4 to be Disqualified from Inheriting Certain Properties. A person convicted of an offence under sub-section (1) of Section 4 in relation to the commission of *sati* shall be disqualified from inheriting the property of the person in respect of whom such *sati* has been committed or the property any other person which he would have been entitled to inherit on the death of the person in respect of whom such *sati* has been committed.

19. Amendment of Act 43 of 1951. In the Representation of the People Act, 1951:

(a) In Section 8, sub-section (2), after the proviso, the following proviso shall be inserted, namely:

"Provided further that a person convicted by a Special Court for the contravention of any of the provisions of the Commission of *Sati* (Prevention) Act, 1987, shall be disqualified from the date of such conviction and shall continue to be disqualified for a further period of five years since his release."

(b) In Section 123, after clause (3-A), the following clause shall be inserted, namely:

"(3-B) The propagation of the practice or the commission of *sati* or its glorification by a candidate or his agent or any other person with the consent of the candidate or his election agent for the furtherance of the prospects of the election of that candidate or for prejudicially affecting the election of any candidate."

Explanation—For the purposes of this clause, "*sati*" and "glorification" in relation to *sati* shall have the meanings respectively assigned to them in the Commission of *Sati* (Prevention) Act, 1987.

20. Act to Have Overriding Effect. The provisions of this Act or any rule or order made thereunder shall have effect notwithstanding anything inconsistent therewith contained in any enactment other than this Act or in any instrument having effect by virtue of any enactment other than this Act.

21. Power to Make Rules. 1. The Central Government may, by notification in the official Gazette, make rules for carrying out the provisions of this Act.

2. Every rule made under this section, shall be laid, as soon as may be after it is made, before each House of Parliament, while it is in session, for a total period of thirty days which may be comprised in one session or in two or more successive sessions, and if, before the expiry of the session immediately following the session or the successive sessions aforesaid, both Houses agree that the rule should not be made, the rule shall thereafter, have effect only in such modified form or be of no effect, as the case may be, so, however, that any such modification or annulment shall be without prejudice to the validity of anything previously done under that rule.

22. Repeal of Existing Laws. 1. All laws in force in any State immediately before the commencement of this Act in that State which provide for the prevention or the glorification of *sati* shall, on such commencement, stand repealed.

2. Notwithstanding such repeal, anything done or any action taken under any law repealed under sub-section (1) shall be deemed to have been done or taken under the corresponding provisions of this Act, and, in particular, any case taken cognizance of by a Special Court under the provisions of any law so repealed and pending

before it immediately before the commencement of this Act in that State shall continue to be dealt with by that Special Court after such commencement as if such Special Court had been constituted under Section 9 of this Act.

COMMISSION OF *SATI* (PREVENTION) RULES, 1988

G.S.R. 360(E), dated 21st March, 1988.—In exercise of the powers conferred by Section 21 of the Commission of *Sati* (Prevention) Act, 1987 (3 of 1988), the Central Government hereby makes the following rules, namely:

1. Short Title and Commencement. 1. These rules may be called Commission of *Sati* (Prevention) Rules, 1988.

2. They shall come into force on the date of their publication in the official Gazette.

2. Definitions. 1. In these rules, unless the context otherwise requires:

(a) "Act" means the Commission of *Sati* (Prevention) Act, 1987 (3 of 1988);

(b) "Prohibitory order" means an order issued under Section 6;

(c) "Section" means section of the Act.

2. Words and expression used but not defined in these rules and defined in the Act, shall have the same meanings as are respectively assigned to them in the Act.

3. Delegation of Power to Prohibit Certain Acts. 1. The State Government may, by order and subject to such conditions as it may deem fit to impose, direct that the powers of the Collector or the District Magistrate under Section 6, may also be exercised by such other officers, not below the rank of the village officers.

4. Prohibitory Orders Under Section 6, How Made. 1. Every prohibitory order under Section 6 shall be made by beat of drum or other customary mode, in the concerned village, or in case of town or city, in the locality in which the act prohibited as likely to occur or has taken place.

2. The prohibitory order shall be displayed at some conspicuous place in the area or areas to which such acts relate and a copy thereof, shall also be displayed in the office of the officer issuing the prohibitory order and such display shall be taken as a sufficient notice to all persons concerned in the area or areas to which such order relates.

5. Manner of Making Order for Removal of Temples or Structures

under Sub-section (1) of Section *7.* 1. Before making any order under sub-section (1) of Section 7, for removal of any temple or structure, the State Government or any other officer authorised by the State Government in this behalf, shall give at least ninety days' notice to the person or persons involved in the acts complained of, and also to the owners and occupiers of the temple or structure proposed to be removed.

2. The notice under sub-rule (1) shall specify—

(i) The temple/structure proposed to be removed, its location and other particulars,

(ii) The owners/occupiers of the temple/structure, and

(iii) The specific instance or instances of worship or ceremony contravening the provisions of Section 7.

3. The Government or the officer authorised by the State Government in this behalf shall, after giving reasonable opportunity of being heard to the persons specified in the notice, order the removal of the temple or structure through a police officer not below the rank of the Sub-Inspector.

6. Manner of Making Order for Removal of Temples or Structures under Sub-section (2) of Section *7.* 1. After issue of a prohibitory order under Section 7, the Collector or the District Magistrate, or such other officer as directed by the State Government by order under Rule 3 shall, before making any order of the removal of any temple or structure under sub-section (2) of Section 7, gives at least ninety days, notice to the person or persons involved in the acts complained of, and also to the owners and occupiers of the temple of structure proposed to be removed.

2. The Collector or the District Magistrate, or such other officer as directed by the State Government by order under Rule 3, shall follow the provisions of sub-rules (2) and (3) of Rule 4 in the case made under this rule.

7. Inventory and Forfeiture of the Property of Temple or Structure. As soon as the order of removal of the temple or structure is executed, the State Government or the Collector or the District Magistrate, or as the case may be, the officer as directed by the State Government by order under Rule 3, shall prepare an inventory of all the material and other property obtained after removal of such temple or structure specifying in it the place where it is lodged or kept. And shall forward the intimation thereof to the Special Court for declaration for forfeiture of the said material or property to the State under Section 13, if the Special Court considers it necessary to do so and shall also give a copy of the inventory to the owners/occupiers of the temple/structure removed.

THE NATIONAL COMMISSION FOR WOMEN ACT, 1990

[No. 20 of 1990]

[30th August, 1990]

An Act to constitute a National Commission for Women and to provide for matters connected therewith or incidental thereto.

Be it enacted by Parliament in the Forty-first Year of the Republic of India as follows:

PRELIMINARY

1. *Short Title, Extent and Commencement.* 1. This Act may be called the National Commission for Women Act, 1990.

2. It extends to the whole of India except the State of Jammu and Kashmir.

3. It shall come into force on such date as the Central Government may, by notification in the Official Gazette, appoint.

2. *Definitions.* In this Act, unless the context otherwise requires,

(a) "Commission" means the National Commission for Women constituted under Sections 3;

(b) "Member" means a Member of the Commission and includes the Member-Secretary;

(c) "Prescribed" means prescribed by rules made under this Act.

THE NATIONAL COMMISSION FOR WOMEN

3. Constitution of the National Commission for Women. 1. The Central Government shall constitute a body to be known as the National Commission for Women to exercise the powers conferred on, and to perform the functions assigned to it under this Act.

2. The Commission shall consist of—

(a) a chairperson, committed to the cause of women, to be nominated by the Central Government;

(b) five Members to be nominated by the Central Government from amongst persons of ability, integrity and standing who have had experience in law or legislation, trade unionism, management of an industry or organisation committed to increasing the employment potential of women, women's voluntary organizations (including women activists), administration, economic development, health, education or social welfare:

Provided that at least one Member each shall be from amongst persons belonging to the Scheduled Castes and Scheduled Tribes respectively;

(c) a Member-Secretary to be nominated by the Central Government, who shall be—

   (i) an expert in the field of management, organizational structure or sociological movement, or

   (ii) an officer who is member of a civil service of the Union or of an all-India service or holds a civil post under the Union with appropriate experience.

4. *Term of Office and Conditions of Service of Chairperson and members.* 1. The Chairperson and every Member shall hold office for such period, not exceeding three years, as may be specified by the Central Government in this behalf.

2. The Chairperson or a Member (other than the Member-Secretary who is a member of a civil service of the Union or of an All-India Service or holds a civil post under the Union) may be writing and addressed to the Central Government, resign from the office of Chairperson or, as the case may be of the member at any time.

3. The Central Government shall remove a person from the office of Chairperson or Member referred to in sub-section (2) if that person—

(a) becomes an undischarged insolvent;

(b) gets convicted and sentenced to imprisonment for an offence which in the opinion of the Central Government involves moral turpitude;

(c) becomes of unsound mind and stands so declared by a competent court;

(d) refuses to act or becomes incapable of acting;

(e) is, without obtaining leave of absence from the Commission, absent from three consecutive meetings of the Commission; or

(f) in the opinion of the Central Government has so abused the position of Chairperson or Member as to render that person's continuance in office detrimental to the public interest;

Provided that no person shall be removed under this clause until that person has been given a reasonable opportunity of being heard in the matter.

4. A vacancy caused under sub-section (2) or otherwise shall be filled by fresh nomination.

5. The salaries and allowances payable to and the other terms and conditions of service of the Chairperson and Members shall be such as may be prescribed.

5. Officers and Other Employees of the Commission. 1. The Central Government shall provide the Commission with such officers and employees as may be necessary for the efficient performance of the functions of the Commission under this Act.

2. The salaries and allowances payable to, and the other terms and conditions of service of the officers and other employees appointed for the purpose of the Commission shall be such as may be prescribed.

6. Salaries and Allowances to be Paid out of Grants. The salaries and allowances payable to the Chairperson and Members and the administrative expenses, including salaries, allowances and pensions payable to the officers and other employees referred to in Section 5 shall be paid out of the grants referred to in sub-section (1) of Section 11.

7. Vacancies, etc., Not to Invalidate Proceeding of the Commission. No act or proceeding of the Commission shall be questioned or shall be invalid on the ground merely of the existence of any vacancy of defect in the constitution of the Commission.

8. Committees of the Commission. 1. The Commission may appoint such committees as may be necessary for dealing with such special issues as may be taken up by the Commission from time to time.

2.The Commission shall have the power to co-opt. as members of any committee appointed under sub-section (1) such number of persons, who are not Members of the Commission, as it may think fit and the persons so co-opted shall have the right to attend the meetings of the committee and take part in its proceedings but shall not have the right to vote.

3. The person so co-opted shall be entitled to receive such allowances for attending the meetings of the Committee as may be prescribed.

9. Procedure to be Regulated by the Commission. 1. The Commission or a committee thereof shall meet as and when necessary and shall meet at such time and place as the Chairperson may think fit.

2. The Commission shall regulate its own procedure of the committees thereof.

3. All orders and decisions of the Commission shall be authenticated by the Member-Secretary or any other of the Commission duly authorized by the Member-Secretary in this behalf.

FUNCTIONS OF THE COMMISSION

10. Functions of the Commission. 1. The Commission shall perform all or any of the following functions, namely—

(a) investigate and examine all matters relating to the safeguards provided for women under the Constitution and other laws;

(b) present to the Central Government, annually and at such other time as the Commission may deem fit, reports upon the working of those safeguards;

(c) make in such reports recommendations for the effective implementation of those safeguards for improving the conditions of women by the Union or any State;

(d) review, from time to time, the existing provisions of the Constitution and other laws affecting women and recommend amendments thereto so as to suggest remedial legislative measures to meet any lacunae, inadequacies or shortcomings in such legislation;

(e) take up the cases of violation of the provisions of the Constitution and of other laws relating to women with the appropriate authorities;

(f) look into complaints and take *suo moto* notice of matters relating to—

(i) deprivation of women's rights;

(ii) non-implementation of laws enacted to provide protection to women and also to achieve the objective of equality and development;

(iii) non-compliance of policy decisions, guidelines or

instructions aimed at mitigating hardships and ensuring welfare and providing relief to women.

and take up the issues arising out of such matters with appropriate authorities;

(g) call for special studies or investigations into specific problems or situations arising out of discrimination and atrocities against women and identify the constraints so as to recommend strategies for their removal;

(h) undertake promotional and educational research so as to suggest ways of ensuring due representation of women in all spheres and identify factors responsible for impeding their advancement, such as, lack of access to housing and basic services, inadequate support services and technologies for reducing drudgery and occupational health hazards and for increasing their productivity;

(i) participate and advise on the planning process of socio-economic development of women;

(j) evaluate the progress of the development of women under the Union and any State;

(k) inspect or cause to be inspected a jail, remand home, women's institution or other place of custody where women are kept as prisoners or otherwise, and take up with the concerned authorities for remedial action, if found necessary;

(l) fund litigation involving issues affecting a large body of women;

(m) make periodical reports to the Government on any matter pertaining to women and in particular various difficulties under which women toil; and

(n) any other matter which may be referred to it by the Central Government.

2. The Central Government shall cause all the reports referred to in clause (b) of sub-section (1) to be laid before each House of Parliament along with a memorandum explaining the action taken or proposed to be taken on the recommendations relating to the Union and the reasons for the non-acceptance, if any, of any of such recommendations.

3. Where any such report or any part thereof relates to any matter with which any State Government is concerned, the Commission shall forward a copy of such report or part of such

State Government who shall cause it to be laid before the Legislature of the State along with a memorandum explaining the action taken or proposed to be taken on the recommendations relating to the State and the reasons for the non-acceptance, if any, of such recommendations.

4. The Commission shall, while investigating any matter referred to in clause (a) or sub-clause (i) of clause (f) of sub-section (1), have all the powers of a civil court trying a suit and, in particular, in respect of the following matters, namely—

(a) summoning and enforcing the attendance of any person from any part of India and examining him on oath;
(b) requiring the discovery and production of any document;
(c) receiving evidence on affidavits;
(d) requisitioning any public record or copy thereof from any Court or office;
(e) issuing commissions for the examination of witnesses and documents; and
(f) any other matter which may be prescribed.

FINANCE, ACCOUNTS AND AUDIT

11. Grants by the Central Government. 1. The Central Government shall, after due appropriation made by parliament by law in his behalf, pay to the Commission by way of grants such sums of money as the Central Government may think fit for being utilized for the purposes of this Act.

2. The Commission may spend such sums as it thinks fit for performing the functions under this Act, and such sums shall be treated as expenditure payable out of the grants referred to in sub-section (1).

12. Accounts and Audit. 1. The Commission shall maintain proper accounts and other relevant records and prepare an annual statement of accounts in such form as may be prescribed by the Central Government in consultation with the Comptroller and Auditor-General of India.

2. The accounts of the Commission shall be audited by the Comptroller and Auditor-General at such intervals as may be specified by him and any expenditure incurred in connection with such audit shall be payable by the Commission to the Comptroller and Auditor-General.

3. The Comptroller and Auditor-General and any person appointed by him in connection with the audit of the accounts of the Commission under this Act shall have the same right and privileges and the authority in connection with such audit as the Comptroller and Auditor-General generally has in connection with the audit of Government accounts and, in particular, shall have the right to demand the production of books, accounts, connected vouchers and other documents and papers and to inspect any of the offices of the Commission.

13. Annual Report. The Commission shall prepare, in such form and at such time, for each financial year, as may be prescribed, its annual report, giving a full account of its activities during the previous financial year and forward a copy thereof to the Central Government.

14. Annual Report and Audit Report to be Laid before Parliament. The Central Government shall cause the annual report together with a memorandum of action taken on the recommendations contained therein, in so far as they relate to the Central Government, and the reasons for the non-acceptance, if any, of any of such recommendations and the audit report to be laid as soon as may be after the reports are received, before each House of Parliament.

MISCELLANEOUS

15. Chairperson, Members and Staff of the Commission to be Public Servants. The Chairperson, the Members, officers and other employees of the Commission shall be deemed to be public servants within the meaning of Section 21 of Indian Penal Code (45 of 1860).

16. Central Government to Consult Commission. The Central Government shall consult the commission in all major policy matters effecting women.

17. Power to Make Rules. 1. The Central Government may, by notification in the Official Gazette, make rules for carrying out the provisions of this Act.

2. In particular, and without prejudice to the generality of the foregoing power such rules may provide for all or any of the following matters, namely:

(a) salaries and allowances payable to, and the other terms and conditions of service of the Chairperson and Members under sub-section (5) of Section 4 and of officers and other employees under sub-section (2) of Section 5;

(b) allowances for attending the meetings of the committee by the co-opted person under sub-section (3) of Section 8;

(c) other matters under clause (f) of sub-section (4) of Section 10;

(d) the form in which the annual statement of accounts shall be maintained under sub-section (1) of Section 12;

(e) the form in, and the time at, which the annual report shall be prepared under Section 13; and

(f) any other matter which is required to be, or may be, prescribed.

3. Every rule made under this Act shall be laid, as soon as may be after it is made, before each House of Parliament, while it is in session, for a total period of thirty days which may be comprised in one session or in two or more successive sessions, and of, before the expiry of the session immediately following the session or the successive sessions aforesaid, both Houses agree in making any modification in the rule or both Houses agree that the rule should not be made, the rule shall thereafter have effect only in such modified form or be of no effect, as the case may be; so, however, that any such modification of annulment shall be without prejudice to the validity of anything previously done under that rule.

THE CHILD LABOUR (PROHIBITION AND REGULATION) ACT, 1986
(Act No. 61 of 1986)
23rd December, 1986

An Act to prohibit the engagement of children in certain employments and to regulate the conditions of work or children in certain other employments.

Be it enacted by Parliament in the Thirty-seventh year of the Republic of India as follows:

Comments

Social and beneficial legislation—Social legislation is designed to protect the interest of a class of society who, because of their economic conditions, deserves such protection. With a view to pass the test of reasonable classification there must exist intelligible differentiation between persons or things grouped together from those who have been left out and there must be a reasonable nexus with the object to be achieved by the legislation.

The Court must strive to so interpret the statute as to protect and advance the object and purpose of the enactment. Any narrow or technical interpretation of the provisions would defeat the legislative policy. The Court must, therefore, keep the legislative policy in mind in applying the provisions of the Act to the facts of the case.

PRELIMINARY

1. Short Title, Extent and Commencement. 1. This Act may be called the Child Labour (Prohibition and Regulation) Act, 1986.

2. It extends to the whole of India.

3. The provisions of this Act, other than Part III, shall come into force at once, and Part III shall come into force on such date as the Central Government may, by notification in the official Gazette, appoint, and different dates may be appointed for different States and for different classes of establishments.

Comment

May and shall—where the Legislature uses two words "may" and "shall" in two different parts of the same provision *prima facie* it would appear that the Legislature manifested its intention to make one part directory and another mandatory. But that by itself is not decisive. The power of the Court still to ascertain the real intention of the Legislature by carefully examining the scope of the statute to find out whether the provision is directory or mandatory remains unimpaired even where both the words are used in the same provision. In interpreting the provisions the exercise undertaken by the Court is to make explicit the intention of the Legislature which enacted the legislation. It is not for the Court to reframe the legislation for the very good reason that the powers to "legislate" have not been conferred on the Court.

In order to sustain the presumption of constitutionality of a legislative measure, the Court can take into consideration matters of a common knowledge, matters of common report, the history of the times and also assume every state of facts which can be conceived existing at the time of the legislation.

2. *Definitions.* In this Act, unless the context otherwise requires,

(i) "appropriate Government" means, in relation to an establishment under the control of the Central Government or a railway administration or a major port or a control of the Central Government or a railway administration or a major port or a mine or oilfield, the Central Government, and in all other cases, the State Government;

(ii) "child" means a person who has not completed his fourteenth year of age;

(iii) "day" means a period of twenty-four hours beginning at midnight;

(iv) "establishment" includes a shop, commercial establishment, workshop, farm, residential hotel, restaurant, eating-house, theatre or other place of public amusement or entertainment;

(v) "family", in relation to an occupier, means the individual, the wife or husbands as the ease may be, of such individual, and their children, brother or sister of such individual;

(vi) "occupier", in relation to an establishment or a workshop, means the person who has the ultimate control over the affairs of the establishment or workshop;

(vii) "prescribed" means prescribed by rules made under Sec. 18;

(viii) "week" means a period of seven days beginning at midnight on Saturday night or such other night as may be approved in writing for a particular area by the Inspector;

(ix) "workshop" means any premises (including the precincts thereof) wherein any industrial process is carried on, but does not include any premises to which the provisions of Sec. 67 of the Factories Act, 1948 (63 of 1948), for the time being, apply.

Comments

This section defines the various words and expressions occurring in the Act.

Interpretation of section—The Court can merely interpret the section: it cannot re-write, re-cast or re- design the section.

Ambiguous expression—Courts must find out the literal meaning of the expression in the task of construction. In doing so if the expressions are ambiguous then the construction that fulfills the object of the legislation must provide the key to the meaning. Courts must not make mockery of legislation and should take a constructive approach to fulfill the purpose and for that purpose, if necessary, iron out the creases.

PROHIBITION OF EMPLOYMENT OF CHILDREN IN CERTAIN OCCUPATIONS AND PROCESSES

3. Prohibition of Employment of Children in Certain Occupations and Processes. No child shall be employed or permitted to work in any of the occupations set forth in Part A of the Schedule or in any workshop wherein any of the processes set forth in Part B of the Schedule is carried on.

Provided that nothing in this section shall apply to any workshop wherein any process is carried on by the occupier with aid of his family or to any school established by or receiving assistance or recognition from, Government.

Comment

This section imposes prohibition on employment of children in the occupation and processes specified in the Schedule.

Proviso. A proviso is intended to limit the enacted provision so as to except something which would have otherwise been within it or in some measure to modify the enacting clause. Sometimes proviso may be embedded in the main provision and become an integral part of it so as to amount to a substantive provision itself.

4. Power to Amend the Schedule. The Central Government, after giving by notification in the official Gazette, not less than three months notice of its intention so to do, may, be like notification, add any occupation or process to the Schedule and thereupon the Schedule shall be deemed to have been amended accordingly.

Comment

This section empowers the Central Government to amend the Schedule so as to include therein any occupation or process considered necessary.

Construction of a section —It is an elementary rule that construction of a section is to be made of all parts together. It is not permissible to omit any part of it. For, the principle that the statute must be read as a whole is equally applicable to different parts of the same section.

5. Child Labour Technical Advisory Committee. 1. The Central Government may, by notification in the official Gazette, constitute an advisory Committee to be called the child Labour Technical Advisory Committee (hereinafter in this section referred to as the Committee) to advise the Central Government for the purpose of addition or occupations and processes to the Schedule.

2. The Committee shall consist of a Chairman and such other members not exceeding ten, as may be appointed by the Central Government.

3. The Committee shall meet as often as it may consider necessary and shall have power to regulate its own procedure.

4. The Committee may, if it deems it necessary so to do, constitute one or more sub-committees and may appoint to any such sub-committee, whether generally or for the consideration of any particular matter, any person who is not a member of the Committee.

5. The term of office of, the manner of filling casual vacancies in the office of, and the allowances, if any, payable to, the Chairman and other members of the Committee, and the conditions and restrictions subject to which the Committee may appoint any person who is not a member of the Committee as a member of any of its sub-committees shall be such as may be prescribed.

Comment

This section empowers the Central Government to constitute the Child Labour Technical Advisory Committee for giving advice in the matter of inclusion of any occupation and process in the Schedule.

REGULATION OF CONDITIONS OF WORK OF CHILDREN

6. Application of Part. The provisions of this Part shall apply to an establishment or a class of establishments in which none of the occupations or processes referred to in Sec. 3 is carried on.

Comment

This section lays down that provisions of this Part shall apply to an establishment in which none of the prohibited occupation or processes is carried on.

7. Hours and Period of Work. 1. No child shall be required or permitted to work in any establishment in excess of such number of hours as may be prescribed for such establishment or class of establishment.

2. The period of work on each day shall be so fixed that no period shall exceed three hours and that no child shall work for more than three hours before he has had an interval for rest for at least one hour.

3. The period of work of a child shall be so arranged that inclusive of this interval for rest, under sub-section (2), it shall not be spread over more than six hours, including the time spent in waiting for work on any day.

4. No child shall be permitted or required to work between 7 p.m. and 8 a.m.

5. No child shall be permitted or required to work overtime.

6. No child shall be required or permitted to work in any establishment on any day on which he has already been working in another establishment.

Comment

This section prescribes working hours for a child labour.

Provision if mandatory or directory. The surest test for determination as to whether the provisions is mandatory or directory is to see as to whether the sanction is provided therein.

8. Weekly Holidays. Every child employed in an establishment shall be allowed in each week, a holiday of one whole day, which day shall be specified by the occupier in a notice permanently exhibited in a conspicuous place in the establishment and the day so specified shall not be altered by the occupier more than once in three months.

Comment

This section lays down that a weekly holiday should be allowed to every child labour.

9. Notice to Inspector. 1. Every occupier in relation to an establishment in which a child was employed or permitted to work immediately before the date of commencement of this Act in relation to such establishment shall, within a period of thirty days from such commencement, send to the Inspector within whose local limits the establishment is situated, a written notice containing the following particulars, namely:

(a) the name and situation of the establishment;

(b) the name of the person in actual management of the establishment;

(c) the address to which communication relating to establishment should be sent; and

(d) the nature of the occupation or process carried on it establishment.

2. Every occupier, in relation to an establishment, who employes, or permits to work, any child after the date of commencement of this Act in relation to such establishment, shall, within a period of thirty days from the date of such employment, send to the Inspector within whose local limits the establishment is situated, a written notice containing the particulars as are mentioned in sub-section (1).

Explanation. For the purpose of sub-section (1) and (2), "date of commencement of this Act, in relation to an establishment" means the date of bringing into force of this Act in relation to such establishment.

3. Nothing in sections 7, 8 and 9 shall apply to any establishment wherein any process is carried on by the occupier with the aid of his family or to any school establishment by, or receiving assistance or recognition from Government.

Comment

This section makes provision for furnishing regarding employment of a child labour to Inspector.

Explanation. It is now well settled that an explanation added to a statutory provision is not a substantive provision in any sense of the term but as the plain meaning of the word itself shows it is merely meant to explain or clarify certain ambiguities which may have crept in the provision.

10. Disputes As to Age. If any question arises between an Inspector and an occupier as to the age of any child who is employed or is permitted to work by him in an establishment, the question shall, in the absence of a certificate as to the age of such child granted by the prescribed medical authority, be referred by the Inspector for decision to the prescribed medical authority.

Comment

This section makes provision for settlement of disputes as to age of any child labour.

11. Maintenance of Register. A register shall be maintained by every occupier in respect of children employed or permitted to work in any establishment, which is to be available for inspection by an Inspector at all times during working hours or when work is being carried on in any such establishment showing—

(a) the name and date of birth of every child so employed or permitted to work;
(b) hours and periods of work of any such child and the intervals of rest to which he is entitled;
(c) the nature of work of any such child; and
(d) such other particulars as may be prescribed.

Comment

This section makes provision of maintenance of register in respect of child labour.

12. Display of Notice Containing Abstract of Sections 3 and 14. Every railway administration, every port authority and every occupier shall cause to be displayed in a conspicuous and accessible place at every station or its railway or within the limits of a post or at the place of work, as the case may be, a notice in the local language and in the English language containing an abstract of Sections 3 and 14.

Comment

This section makes provision for display of notice in a conspicuous place at every railway station or port of place of work regarding prohibition of employment of child labour, penalties, etc., in the local language and in the English language.

13. Health and Safety. 1. The Government may, by notification in the Official Gazette, make appropriate rules for the health and safety of the children employed or permitted to work in any establishment or class of establishments.

2. Without prejudice to the generality of the foregoing provisions, the said rules may provide for all or any of the following matters, namely;

(a) cleanliness in the place of work and its freedom from nuisance;
(b) disposal of wastes and effluents;
(c) ventilation and temperature;
(d) dust and fume;
(e) artificial humidification;
(f) lighting;
(g) drinking water;
(h) latrine and urinals;
(i) spittoons;
(j) fencing of machinery;
(k) work at or near machinery in motion;
(l) employment of children on dangerous machines;
(m) instructions, training and supervision in relation to employment of children on dangerous machines;
(n) device for cutting off power;
(o) self-acting machinery;
(p) easing of new machinery;
(q) floor, stairs and means of access;
(r) pits, sumps, opening in floors, etc.
(s) excessive weights;
(t) protection of eyes;
(u) explosive or inflammable dust, gas, etc.
(v) precautions in case of fire;
(w) maintenance of buildings; and
(x) safety of buildings and machinery.

Comment

This section lays down that the Government is required to make rules for the health and safety of the child labour.

14. Penalties. 1. Whoever employs any child or permits any child to work in contravention of the provisions of Section 3 shall be punishable with imprisonment for a term which shall not be less than three months but which may extend to one year or with fine which shall not be less than ten thousand rupees but which may extend to twenty thousand rupees or with both.

2. Whoever, having been convicted of an offence under Section 3 commits a like offence afterwards, he shall be punishable with imprisonment for a term which shall not be less than six months but which may extend to two years.

3. whoever

(a) fails to give notice as required by Section 9; or

(b) fails to maintain a register as required by Section 11 or makes any false entry in any such register; or

(c) fails to display a notice containing an abstract of Section 3 and this section as required by Section 12; or

(d) fails to comply with or contravenes any other provision of this Act or the rules made thereunder;

shall be punishable with simple imprisonment which may extend to one month or with fine which may extend to ten thousand rupees or with both.

Comments

This section makes provision for penalty for contravention of the provisions of the Act.

Penalty—*Mens rea*—Essential—Penalty proceedings are quasi-criminal proceedings. Before penalty can be imposed it has to be ensured that *mens rea* has been established.

Penal provision—Object of—The law in its wisdom seeks to punish the guilty who commits the sin, and not his son, who is innocent.

15. Modified Application of Certain Laws in Relation to Penalties. 1. Where any person is found guilty and convicted of contravention of any of the provisions mentioned in sub-section (2), he shall be liable to penalties as provided in sub-sections (1) and (2) of Section 14 of this Act and not under the Acts in which those provisions are contained.

2. The provision referred to in sub-section (1) are the provisions mentioned below:

(a) Section 67 of the Factories Act, 1948 (63 of 1948);

(b) Section 40 of the Mines Act, 1952 (35 of 1952); and

(c) Section 109 of the Merchant Shipping Act, 1958 (44 of 1958); and

(d) Section 21 of the Motor Transport Workers Act, 1961 (27 of 1961)

Comment

This Section makes provision of penalties under the Act even when any person is found guilty and convicted of contravention of any of the provisions of Section 67 of the Factories Act, 1948, Section 40 of the Mines Act, 1952, Sec. 109 of the Merchant Shipping Act, 1958 and Section 21 of the Motor Transport Workers Act, 1961.

16. Procedures Relating to Offences. 1. Any person, police officer or Inspector may file a complaint of the commission of an offence under this Act in any Court of competent jurisdiction.

2. Every certificate as to the age of a child which has been granted by a prescribed medical authority shall, for the purposes of this Act, be conclusive evidence as to the age of the child to whom it relates.

3. No court inferior to that of a Metropolitan Magistrate or a Magistrate of the first class shall try any offence under this Act.

Comment

This section lays down that any person, police officer or Inspector can make a complaint regarding commission of offences. It also lays down the procedure for disposal of such a complaint.

Court Duty of. The Court should meticulously consider all facts and circumstances of the case. The Court is not bound to grant specific performance merely because it is lawful to do so. The motive behind the litigation should also enter into the judicial verdict. The Court should take care to see that it is used as an instrument of oppression to have an unfair advantage to the plaintiff.

17. Appointment of Inspectors. The appropriate Government may appoint Inspectors for the purposes of securing compliance with the provisions of this Act and any Inspector so appointed shall be deemed to be a public servant within the meaning of the Indian Penal Code (45 of 1860).

Comment

This section empowers the appropriate Government to appoint Inspectors for securing compliance of the provisions of the Act. Such Inspector is deemed to be a public servant within the meaning of the Indian Penal Code (45 of 1860).

Public Servant. Every public officer is a trustee and in respect of the office he holds and the salary and other benefits which he draws, he is obliged to render appropriate service to the State. If an officer does not behave as required of him under the law he is certainly liable to be punished in accordance with law.

18. Power to Make Rules. 1. The Government may, by notification in the official Gazette and subject to the condition of previous publication, make appropriate rules for carrying into effect the provisions of this Act.

2. In particular and without prejudice to the generality of the foregoing power, such rules may provide for all or any of the following matters, n amely:

(a) the term of office of, the manner of filling casual vacancies of, and the allowances payable to, the Chairman and members of the Child Labour Technical Advisory Committee and the conditions and restrictions subject to which a non-member may be appointed to a sub-committee under sub-section (5) of Section 5;

(b) number of hours for which a child may be required or permitted to work under sub-section (1) cf Section 7;

(c) grant of certificates of age in respect of young persons in employment or seeking employment, the medical authorities which may issue such certificate, the form of such certificate, the charges which may be made thereunder and the manner in which such certificate mav be issued;
Provided that no charge shall be made for the issue of any such certificate if the application is accompanied by evidence of age deemed satisfactory by the authority concerned;

(d) the other particulars which a register maintained under Section 11 should contain.

Comment

This section empowers the appropriate Government to make rule for carrying out the provisions of the Act.

Rules for Effectuating the Purpose of the Act. The general power of framing rules for effectuating the purposes of the Act, would plainly authorize and sanctify the framing of such a rule.

19. Rules and Notifications to be Laid before Parliament or State Legislature. 1. Every rule made under this Act by the Central Government and every notification issued under Section 4, shall be laid, as soon as may be after it is made or issued, before each House of Parliament, while it is in session for a total period of thirty days which may be comprised in one session or in two or more successive sessions, and if, before the expiry of the session immediately following the session or the successive session aforesaid, both Houses agree in making any modification in the rule or notification or both Houses agree that the rule or notification should not be made or issued, the rule or notification shall thereafter have effect only in such modified form or be of no effect, as the case may be. So, however, that any such modification or annulment shall be without prejudice to the validity of anything previously done under that rule or notification.

2. Every rule made by a State Government under this Act shall be laid as soon as may be after it is made, before the Legislature of that State.

Comment

Under this section the rules and notification are to be laid before Parliament or State Legislature for approval.

20. Certain other Provisions of Law not Barred. Subject to the provision contained in Section 15, the provision of this Act and the rules made thereunder shall be in addition to, and not in derogation of, the provisions of the Factories Act, 1948 (63 of 1948), the Plantation Labour Act, 1951 (69 of 1951) and the Mines Act 1952 (35 of 1952).

Comment

This section lays down that the provisions of this Act shall be in addition to and not in derogation of, the provisions of the Factories Act, 1948, the Plantations Labour Act, 1951 and the Mines Act, 1952.

21. Power to Remove Difficulties. 1. If any difficulty arises in giving effect of the provision of this Act, the Central Government may, by order published in the official Gazette, make such provisions not inconsistent with the provisions of this Act as appear to it to be necessary or expedient for removal of the difficulty:

Provided that no such order shall be made after the expiry of a period of three years from the date on which this Act receives the assent of the President.

2. Every order made under this section shall, as soon as may be after it is made, before the House of Parliament.

Comment

Under the provisions of this section, the Central Government is empowered to remove difficulties which arise in giving effect to the provisions of this Act.

22. *Repeal and Savings.* 1. The Employment of Children Act, 1938 (26 of 1938) is hereby repealed.

2. Notwithstanding such repeal, anything done or any action taken or purported to have been done or taken under the Act so repealed shall, in so far as it is not inconsistent with the provisions of this Act, be deemed to have been done or taken under the corresponding provisions of this Act.

Comment

The Employment of Children Act, 1938 (26 of 1938) has been repealed by this section.

Implied Repeal. It is well settled that when a competent authority makes a new law which is totally inconsistent with the earlier law and that the two cannot stand together any longer it must be construed that the earlier law had been repealed by necessary implication by the latter law.

23. *Amendment of Act 11 of 1948.* In section 2 of the Minimum Wages Act, 1948—

(1) For Clause (a), the following clauses shall be substituted, namely; "(a) 'adolescent ' means a person who has completed his fourteenth year of age but has not completed his eighteenth year;

"(aa) 'adult' means a person who has completed his eighteenth year of age;";

(ii) after Clause (b), the following clause shall be inserted, namely:

(bb) 'child' means a person who has not completed his fourteenth year of age;".

Comment

Under this section, Section 2 of the Minimum Wages Act, 1948 has been amended so as to define the term "adolescent", "adult" and "child"

24. Amendment of Act 69 of 1951. In the Plantation Labour Act, 1951.

(a) in Section 2, in Clauses (a) and (c), for the word "fifteenth", the word "fourteenth" shall be substituted;

(b) Section 24 shall be omitted;

(c) in Section 26, in opening portion, the words "who has completed his twelfth year" shall be committed.

Comment

Under this section, Section 2 of the Plantations Labour Act, 1951, has been amended so far as it relates to the employment of child labour.

25. Amendment of Act 44 of 1958. In the Merchant Shipping Act, 1958, in section 109, for the word "fifteen", the word "fourteen" shall be substituted.

Comment

Under this section, Section 109 of the Merchant Shipping Act. 1958, has been amended so far as it relates to the employment of child labour.

26. Amendment of Act 27 of 1961. In the Motor Transport Workers Act, 1961, in section 2, in Clause (a) and (c), for the word "fifteenth", the word " fourteenth" shall be substituted.

Comment

Under this section, Section 2 of the Motor Transport Workers Act, 1961, has been amended so far as it relates to the employment of child labour.

THE SCHEDULE

(See Section 3)

Part A

Occupations

Any occupation connected with—

1. Transport of passengers, goods or mails by railway;

2. Cinder picking, clearing of an ash pit or building operation in the railway premises;

3. Work in a catering establishment at a railway station, involving the movement of a vendor or any other employee of the establishment from one platform to another or into or out of a moving train;

4. Work relating to the construction of a railway station or with any other work where such work is done in close proximity to or between the railway lines;

5. A port authority within the limits of any port.

6. Work relating to selling of crackers and fireworks in shops with temporary licences;

7. Abattoirs/Slaughter House.

Part B

Processes

1. *Beedi*-making.
2. Carpet-weaving.
3. Cement manufacture, including bagging of cement.
4. Cloth printing, dyeing and weaving.
5. Manufacturing of matches, explosives and fire-works.
6. Mica-cutting and splitting.
7. Shellac manufacture.
8. Soap manufacture.
9. Training.
10. Wool-cleaning.
11. Building and construction industry.
12. Manufacture of slate pencils (including packing)
13. Manufacture of products from agate.
14. Manufacturing processes using toxic metals and substances such as lead, mercury, manganese, chromium, cadmium, benzene, pesticides and asbestos.
15. "Hazardous processes" as defined in Section 3 (cb) and 'dangerous operations' as notified in rules made under Section 87 of the Factories Act, 1948 (63 of 1948)
16. Printing as defined in section 2 (k) (iv) of the Factories Act, 1948 (63 of 1948)
17. Cashew and cashewnut descaling and processing.
18. Soldering processes in electronic industries.

SUPPLEMENT

Child Labour (Prohibition and Regulation) Act, 1986

In exercise of the powers conferred by Section 4 of the Child Labour (Prohibition and Regulation) Act, 1986, the Central Government hereby adds the following occupation and processes in the Schedule to the said Act, namely:

In the Schedule to the said Act,—

(1) In Part A, after item (5) and the entry relating thereto, the following item and entry shall be inserted, namely:

(6) "Work relating to selling of crackers and fire works in shops with temporary licences.";

(2) In Part B, after item (11) and the entry relating thereto, the following items and entries shall be inserted, namely:

(12) Manufacture of slate pencils (including packing)

(13) Manufacture of products from agate.

(14) Manufacturing processes using toxic metals and substances such as lead, mercury, managanese, chromium, cadmium, benzene, pesticides and asbestos.

THE CHILD LABOUR (PROHIBITION AND REGULATION) RULES, 1988

G.S.R.847 (e), dated 10th August, 1988—In exercise of the powers conferred by sub-section (1) of Section 18 of the said Act, the Central Government, hereby makes the following rules, namely:

Comment

Rule-making power. The general power of framing rules for effectuating the purpose of the Act, would plainly authorize and sanctify the framing of such a rule.

1. Short Title and Commencement. 1. These rules may be called the Child Labour (Prohibition and Regulation) Rules, 1988.

2. They shall come into force on the date of their publication in the official Gazette.

Comment

These rules have been framed by the Central Government in the exercise of the powers conferred by Section 18 (1) of the Child Labour (Prohibition and Regulation) Act, 1986.

Rules—*Whether Validity Framed*—The question whether rules are validly framed to carry out the purposes of the Act can be determined on the analysis of the provisions of the Act.

2. Definitions. In these rules, unless the context otherwise requires —

(a) "Act" means the Child Labour (Prohibition and Regulation) Act, 1986 (61 of 1986)

(b) "Committee" means the Child Labour Technical Advisory Committee constituted under sub-section (1) of Section 5 of the Act;

(c) "Chairman" means the Chairman of the Committee appointed under sub-section (2) of Section 5 of Act;

(d) "Form" means a Form appended to these rules;

(e) "Register" means the register required to be maintained under section 11 of the Act;

(f) "Schedule" means the schedule appended to the Act;

(g) "Section" means a section of the Act.

Comment

This rule defines the various expressions occurring in the Rules.

Interpretation by a Court. The Court can merely interpret the section; it cannot re-write, re-cast or re-design the section.

Otherwise—What Amounts to. The word "otherwise" is not to be construed *ejusdem generis* with the word "circulars, advertisements."

3. *Term of Office of the Members of the Committee.* 1. The term of office of the members of the Committee shall be one year from the date on which their appointment is notified in the official Gazette:

Provided that the Central Government may extend the term of office of the member of the Committee for a maximum period of two years:

Provided further that the member shall, notwithstanding the expiration of his term, continue to hold office until his successor enters upon his office.

2. The member appointed under sub-rule (1) shall be eligible for re-appointment.

Comment

"shall" cannot be interpreted as "may"

Proviso—In Abdul Jabar Butt *v.* State of Jammu and Kashmir, it was held that a proviso must be considered with relation to the principal matter to which it stands as a proviso.

4. *Secretary to the Committee.* The Central Government may appoint an officer not below the rank of an Under-Secretary to the Government of India as Secretary of the Committee.

Comment

and allowance as may be admissible to the officers of the Central Government drawing a pay of rupees four thousand and five hundred or above.

6. *Resignation.* 1. A member may resign his office by writing under his hand addressed to the Chairman.

2. The Chairman may resign his office by writing under his hand addressed to the Central Government.

3. The resignation referred to in sub-rule (1) and sub-rule (2) shall take effect from the date of its acceptance or on the expiry of thirty days from the date of its receipt of such resignation, whichever is earlier, by the Chairman or the Central Government, as the case may be.

7. Removal of Chairman or Member of the Committee. The Central Government may remove the Chairman or any member of the Committee at any time before the expiry of the term of office after giving him a reasonable opportunity of showing cause against the proposed removal.

Comment

This rule lays down procedure for removal of Chairman or member of the Committee by the Central Government.

8. Cessation of Membership. If a member:

(a) is absent without leave of the Chairman for three or more consecutive meetings of the Committee; or

(b) is declared to be of unsound mind by a competent court; or

(c) is or has been convicted of any offence which, in the opinion of the Central Government, involves moral turpitude; or

(d) is, or at any time, has been adjudicated insolvent or has suspended his debts or has compounded with his creditors, shall cease to be a member of the Committee.

10. Time and Place of Meetings. The Committee shall meet at such times and places as the Chairman may fix in this behalf.

11. Notice of Meetings. The Secretary to the Committee shall give at least seven days' notice to every member of the Committee of the time and place fixed for each meeting along with the list of business to the transacted at the said meeting.

12. Presiding at Meeting. The Chairman shall preside at every meeting of the Committee at which he is present; if however, the Chairman is unable to attend a meeting, any member elected by the members present among themselves shall preside at the meeting.

Comment

"Shall"—It is well-known principal that in the interpretation of statutes that where the situation and the context warrants it, the word "shall" used in a section or rule of a statute has to be construed as "may".

13. Quorum. No business shall be transacted at a meeting of the Committee unless at least three members of the Committee other than the Chairman and the Secretary are present:

Provided that any meeting in which less than three of the total members are present, the Chairman may adjourn the meeting to a date as he deems fit and inform the members present and notify other members that the business of the scheduled meeting shall be disposed of at the adjourned meeting irrespective of the *quorum* and it shall be lawful to dispose of the business at such adjourned meeting irrespective of the member or members attending the meeting.

Comment

Scope of proviso — The scope of a proviso is well settled. In Ram Narain Sons Ltd. *v.* Assistent. Commissioner of Sales Tax, it was held:

"It is a cardinal rule of interpretation that a proviso to a particular provision of statute only embraces the field which is covered by the main provision. It carves out an exception to the main a provision to which it has been enacted as a proviso and to no other."

14. Decision by Majority. All questions considered at a meeting of the Committee shall be decided by a majority of votes of the members present and voting and in the event of equality of votes the Chairman, or in the absence of Chairman, the member presiding at the meeting, as the case may be, shall have a second or casting vote.

Comment

This rule lays down that the matters considered by the Committee in its meeting should be decided by a majority votes of the members present. The rule further lays down that the Chairman or in his absence the member presiding at the meeting shall have a casting vote.

15. Sub-Committee. The Committee may constitute one or more Sub-Committees, whether consisting only of members of the Committee or partly of members of the Committee and partly of other persons as it thinks fit, for such purposes, as it may decide and any sub-committee so constituted shall discharge such functions as may be delegated to it by the Committee.

16. Register to be Maintained under Section 11 of the Acts. 1. Every occupier of an establishment shall maintain a register in respect of children employed or permitted to work, in Form A.

2. The register shall be maintained on a yearly basis but shall be retained by employer for a period of three years after the date of the last entry made therein.

Comment

Under this rule every occupier of an establishment is required to maintain an yearly register showing the children employed or permitted to work and to retain such registers for a period of three years.

17. Certificate of Age. 1. All young persons in employment in any of the occupations set forth in Part A of the Schedule or in any workshop wherein any of the processes set forth in Part B the Schedule is carried on, shall produce a certificate of age from the appropriate medical authority, whenever required to do so by an Inspector.

2. The certificate of age referred to in sub-rule (1) shall be issued in Form 'B'.

3. The charges payable to the medical authority for the issue of such certificate shall be the same as prescribed by the State Government or the Central Government, as the case may be, for their respective Medical Boards.

4. The charges payable to the medical authority shall be borne by the employer of the young person whose age is under question.

Explanation—For the purposes of sub-rule (1), the appropriate "Medical authority" shall be Government medical doctor not below the rank of an Assistant Surgeon of a District or a regular doctor of equivalent rank employed in Employees' State Insurance Dispensaries or hospitals.

Comment

Explanation. It is not well settled that an explanation added to a statutory provision is not a substantive provision in any sense of the term but as the plain meaning of the word itself shows it is merely meant to explain and clarify certain ambiguities which may have crept in the statutory provision.

SUPPLEMENT

THE CHILD LABOUR (PROHIBITION AND REGULATION) ACT, 1986

S.O. 333 (E), dated 26th May, 1993 — In exercise of the powers conferred by sub-section (3) of Section 1 of the Child Labour (Prohibition and Regulation) Act, 1986 (61 of 1986) the Central

Government hereby appoints the 26th day of May, 1993 as the date of which the provisions of Part III of the said Act shall come into force in respect of all classes of establishments, throughout the territory of India, in which none of the occupations and processes referred to in section 3 of the said Act is carried on.

THE PRE-NATAL DIAGNOSTIC TECHNIQUES (REGULATION AND PREVENTION OF MISUSE) ACT, 1994

[Act No. 57 of 1994]

20th September, 1994

PRELIMINARY

1. Short Title, Extent and Commencement. 1. This Act may be called the Pre-natal Diagnostic Techniques (Regulation and Prevention of Misuse) Act, 1994.

2. It shall extend to the whole of India except the State of Jammu and Kashmir.

3. It shall come into force on such date as the Central Government, may, by notification in the Official Gazette, appoint.

2. *Definitions.* In this Act, unless the contrary text includes—

(a) "Appropriate Authority" means the Appropriate Authority appointed under Section 17;

(b) "Board" means the Central Supervisory Board, constituted under Section 7;

(c) "Genetic Counselling Centre" means an Institute, Hospital, Nursing Home or any place, by whatever name called, which provides for genetic counselling to patients;

(d) "Genetic Clinic" means a clinic, Institute, Hospital, Nursing Home or any place.

(f) "Gynaecologist" means a person who possesses a post graduate qualification in gynaecology and obstetrics;

(g) "Medical geneticist" means a person who possesses a degree or diploma or certificate in medical genetics in the field of pre-natal diagnostic techniques or has experience of not less than two years in such field after obtaining:

  (i) Any one of the medical qualifications recognised under Indian Medical Council Act, 1956 (102 of 1956); or

  (ii) a post-graduate degree in biological sciences;

  (h) "Paediatrician" means a person who possesses a post-graduate qualification in paediatrics

(i) "Pre-natal diagnostic procedures" means all gyncological or obsterical or medical procedures such as ultra-sonographys, foetoscopy, taking or removing samples of amniotic fluid, chorionic villi, blood or any tissue of a pregnant woman for being sent to a Genetic Laboratory or Genetic Clinic for conducting pre-natal diagnostic tests;

(j) "Pre-natal diagnostic techniques" include all pre-natal diagnostic procedures and pre-natal diagnostic tests;

(k) "Pre-natal diagnostic test" means ultrasonography or chrionic villi, blood or any tissue of a pregnant womsan conducted to detect genetic or metabolic disorders of chromosomal abnormalities or congential anomalies or haemoglobin apathies or sex-linked diseases;

(l) "Prescribed" means prescribed by rules made under this Act;

(m) "Registered medical practitioner" means a medical practitioner who possesses any recognised medical qualification as defined in clause (h) of Section 2 of the Indian Medical Council Act, 1956 (102 of 1956), and whose name has been entered in a State Medical Register;

(n) "Regulations" means regulations framed by the Board under this Act.

REGULATION OF GENETIC COUNSELLING CENTRES, GENETIC LABORATORIES AND GENETIC CLINICS

3. ***Regulation of Genetic Counselling Centres, Genetic Laboratories and Genetic Clinics.*** On and from the commencement of this Act,—

1. No Genetic Counselling Centre, Genetic Laboratory or Genetic Clinic unless registered under this Act, shall conduct or associate with, or help in, conducting activities relating to pre-natal diagnostic techniques;

2. No Genetic Counselling Centre, Genetic Laboratory or Genetic Clinic shall employ or caused to be employed any person who does not possess the prescribed qualifications:

3. No medical genaeticist, gynecologists, paediatrician, registered medical practitioner or any other person shall conduct or cause to be conducted or aid in conducting by himself or through any other person, any pre-natal diagnostic techniques at a place other than a place registered under this Act.

REGULATION OF PRE-NATAL DIAGNOSTIC TECHNIQUES

4. ***Regulation of Pre-natal Diagnostic Techniques.*** On and from commencement of this Act,—

1. No place including a registered Genetic Counselling Centre, or Genetic Laboratory or Genetic Clinic shall be used or caused to be used by any person for conducting pre-natal diagnostic techniques except for the purposes specified in clause (2) and after satisfying any of the conditions specified in clause (3);

2. No pre-natal diagnostic techniques shall be conducted except for the purposes of detection of any of the following abnormalities, namely:

(i) chromosomal abnormalities
(ii) genetic metabolic diseases;
(iii) Haemoglobinopathies;
(iv) Sex-linked genetic diseases;
(v) congenital anomalies;
(vi) cogenital anomalies;
(vii) any other abnormalities or disease as may be specified by the Central Supervisory Board.

3. No pre-natal diagnostic techniques shall be used or conducted unless the person qualified to do so is satisfied that any of the following conditions are fulfilled, namely:

(i) age of the pregnant woman is above thirty-five years;
(ii) the pregnant woman has undergone two or more spontaneous abortions or foetal loss;
(iii) the pregnant woman had been exposed to potentialy teratogenic agents such as drugs, radiation, infection or chemicals;
(iv) the pregnant woman has a family history of mental retardation or physical deformities such as spasticity or any other genetic disease;
(v) any other conditions as may be specified by the Central Supervisory Board.

4. No person, being a relative or the husband of the pregnant woman shall seek or encourage the conduct of any pre-natal diagnostic techniques on her except for the purpose specified in clause (2).

5. ***Written Consent of Pregnant Woman and Prohibition of Communicating the Sex of Foetus.*** 1. No person referred to in clause (2) of Section 3 shall conduct the pre-natal diagnostic procedures unless (a) he has explained all known side and after effects of such

procedures to the pregnant woman concerned; (b) he has obtained in the prescribed form her written consent to undergo such procedures in the language which she understands; and (c) a copy of her written consent obtained under such clause (b) is given to the pregnant woman.

2. No person conducting pre-natal diagnostic procedures shall communicate to the pregnant woman concerned or her relatives the sex of the foetus by words, signs or in any other manner.

6. Determination of Sex Prohibited. On and from commencement of this Act,—

(a) no Genetic Counselling Centre or Genetic Laboratory or Genetic Clinic shall conduct or cause to be conducted in its Centres, Laboratory or Clinic, pre-natal diagnostic techniques including ultrasonography, for the purpose of determining the sex of a foetus;

(b) no person shall conduct or cause to be conducted any pre-natal diagnostic techniques including ultrasonography for the purpose of determining the sex of a foetus.

CENTRAL SUPERVISORY BOARD

7. Constitution of Central Supervisory Board. 1. The Central Government shall constitute a Board to be known as the Central Supervisory Board to exercise the powers and perform the functions conferred on the Board under this Act.

2. The Board shall consist of—

(a) The Minister-in-charge of the Ministry or Department of Family Welfare, who shall be the Chairman, *ex-officio;*

(b) The Secretary to the Government of India incharge of the Department of Family Welfare, who shall be the Vice-Chairman, *ex officio;*

(c) Two members to be appointed by the Central Government to represent the ministries of Central Government in charge of Woman and Child Development and of Law and Justice, *ex-officio;*

(d) Director-General of Health Services of the Central Government;

(e) Ten members to be appointed by the Central Government; two each from amongst—

(i) Eminent medical geneticist;
(ii) Eminent gynaecologists and obsterians;
(iii) Eminent paediatricians;
(iv) Eminent social scientists;
(v) representatives of Women Welfare Organisations;

(f) Three women Members of Parliament of whom two shall be elected by the House of the People and one by the Council of States;
(g) Four members to be appointed by Central Government by rotation to represent the State and the Union territories, two in the alphabetical order and two in the reverse alphabetical order; Provided that no appointment under this clause shall be made except on the recommendation of the State Government or, as the case may be, the Union Territory;
(h) An officer, not below the post of Joint Secretary or equivalent of the Central Government, Officer-in-Charge of Family Welfare, who shall be Member-Secretary *ex-officio.*

8. Term of Office of Members. 1. The term of office of a member, other than an *ex-officio* member, shall be—

(a) In case of appointment under clause (e) or clause (f) of sub-section 2, of Section 7,—Three years; and
(b) in case of appointment under clause (g) of the said sub-section—one year.

2. If a casual vacancy occurs in the office of any other members, whether by reason of his death, resignation or inability to discharge his functions owing to illness or other incapacity, such vacancy shall be filled by the Central Government by making a fresh appointment and the members so appointed shall hold office for the remainder of the term of office of the person in whose place he is so appointed.

3. The Vice-Chairman shall perform such functions, as may be assigned to him by the Chairman from time to time.

4. The procedure to be followed by the members in the discharge of their functions shall be such as may be prescribed.

9. Meetings of the Board. 1. The Board shall meet at such time and place, and shall observe such rules of procedure in regard to the transaction of business at its meetings (including the quorum at such meetings) as may be provided by the regulations;

Provided that the Board shall meet at least once in six months.

2. The Chairman and in his absence the Vice-Chairman shall preside at the meetings of the Board.

3. If for any reason the Chairman or the Vice-Chairman is unable to attend any meeting of the Board, any other member chosen by the members present at the meeting shall preside at the meeting.

4. All questions which come up before any meeting of the Board shall be decided by a majority of the votes of the members present and voting, and in the event of an equality of votes, the Chairman, or in his absence, the person presiding shall have and exercise a second or casting vote.

5. Members other than *ex-officio* members, shall receive such allowance, if any, from the Board as may be prescribed.

10. Vacancies, etc. not to Invalidate Proceedings of the Board. No act of proceeding of the Board shall be invalid merely by reason of—

(a) any vacancy in, or any defect in the constitution of the Board; or

(b) any defect in the appointment of a person acting as a member of the Board; or

(c) any irregularity in the procedure of the Board not affecting the merits of the case.

11. Temporary Association of Persons with the Board for Particular Purposes. 1. The Board may associate with itself, in such manner and for such purposes as may be determined by the regulations, any person whose assistance or advice it may desire in carrying out any of the provisions of this Act.

2. A person associated with it by the Board under sub-section (1) for any purpose shall have a right to take part in the discussions relevant to that purpose, but shall not have a right to vote at a meeting of the Board and shall not be a member for any other purpose.

12. Appointment of Officers and Other Employees of the Board. 1. For the purpose of enabling it efficiently to discharge its functions under this Act, the Board, may subject to such regulations as may be made in this behalf, appoint (whether on deputation or otherwise) such number of officers and other employees as it may consider necessary:

Provided that the appointment of such category of officers, as may be specified in such regulations, shall be subject to the approval of the Central Government.

2. Every officer or other employee appointed by the Board shall be subject to such conditions of service and shall be entitled to such remuneration as may be specified in the regulations.

13. Authentication of Orders and other Instruments of the Board. All orders and decisions of the Board shall be authenticated by the signature of the Chairman or any other member authorised by the Board in this behalf, and all other instrument issued by the Board shall be authenticated by the signature of the Member-Secretary or any other Officer of the Board authorised in like manner in this behalf.

14. Disqualifications for Appointment as a Member. A person shall be disqualified for being appointed as a member if, he—

(a) has been convicted and sentenced to imprisonment for an offence which, in the opinion of the Central Government, involves moral turpitude; or

(b) is an undischarged insolvent; or

(c) is of unsound mind, and stands so declared by a competent Court; or

(d) has been removed or dismissed from the service of the Government or a Corporation owned or controlled by the Government; or

(e) has, in the opinion of the Central Government, such financial or other interest in the Board as is likely to affect pre-judicially the discharge by him of his functions as a member; or

(f) has, in the opinion of the Central Government, been associated with the use of or promotion of pre-natal technique for determination of sex.

15. Eligibility of Member for Re-appointment. Subject to the other terms and conditions of service, as may be prescribed, any person ceasing to be a member shall be eligible for reappointment as such member.

16. Functions of the Board. The Board shall have the following functions, namely:

(i) to advise the Government on policy matters relating to use of pre-natal diagnostic techniques;

(ii) to review implementation of the Act and the rules made thereunder and recommend changes in the said Act and rules to the Central Government;

(iii) to create public awareness against the practice of pre-natal determination of sex and female foeticide;

(iv) to lay down Code of Conduct to be observed by person working at genetic counselling centres, genetic laboratories and genetic clinics.

(v) any other functions as may be specified under the Act.

APPROPRIATE AUTHORITY AND ADVISORY COMMITTEE

17. Appropriate Authority and Advisory Committee. 1. The Central Government shall appoint by notification in the Official Gazette, one or more officers as appropriate authorities for each of the Union territories for the purposes of this Act.

2. The State Government shall appoint, by notification in the Official Gazette, one or more appropriate authorities for the whole or part of the State for the purposes of this Act having regard to the intensity of the problem of pre-natal sex determination leading to female foeticide.

3. The officers appointed as appropriate authorities under sub-section (1) or sub-section (2), shall be, (a) when appointed for the whole of the State or the Union Territory, of or (b) when appointed for any part of the State or the Union Territory, of such other rank as the State Government or the Central Government, as the case may be, may deem fit, to aid and advise the appropriate authority in the discharge of its functions, and shall appoint one of the members of the Advisory Committee to be its Chairman, above the rank of the Joint Director of Health and Family Welfare; and

4. The appropriate authority shall have the following functions, namely:

(a) to grant, suspend or cancel registration of a Genetic, Genetic Laboratory or Genetic Clinic;

(b) to enforce standards prescribed for the Genetic Counselling Centre, Genetic Laboratories and Genetic Clinics; or

(c) to investigate complaints of the breach of provisions of this Act or the rules made thereunder and take immediate action.

(d) to seek and consider the advice of the Advisory Committee, constituted under sub-section (5), on application for registration and on complaints for suspension or cancellation of registration.

5. (i) The Central Government or the State Government, as the case may be, shall constitute an Advisory Committee for each appropriate authority.

6. The Advisory Committee shall consist of—

(a) three medical experts from amongst gynaecologists, obstetricians, paediatricians and medical geneticists;
(b) one legal expert;
(c) one officer to represent the department dealing with information and publicity of the State Government or the Union Territory, as the case may be;
(d) three eminent social workers of whom not less than one shall be from amongst representatives of woman's organisations.

7. No person, who, in the opinion of the Central Government or the State Government, as the case may be, has been associated with the use or promotion of pre-natal diagnostic technique for determination of sex shall be appointed as a member of the Advisory Committee.

8. The Advisory Committee may meet as and when it thinks fit or on the request of the appropriate authority for consideration of any application for registration or any complaint for suspension or cancellation of registration and to give advice thereon;

Provided that the period of intervening between any two meetings shall not exceed the prescribed period.

9. The terms and conditions subject to which a person may be appointed to the Advisory Committee and the procedure to be followed by such committee in the discharge of its functions shall be such as may be prescribed.

REGISTRATION OF GENETIC COUNSELLING CENTRES, GENETIC LABORATORIES OR GENETIC CLINICS

18. Registration of Genetic Counselling Centres, Genetic Laboratories or Genetic Clinics. 1. No person shall open any Genetic Counselling Centre, Genetic Laboratory or Genetic Clinic after the commencement of this Act, unless such Centre, Laboratory or Clinic is duly registered separately or jointly under this Act.

2. Every application for registration under sub-section (1), shall

be made to the appropriate authority in such form and in such manner and shall be accompanied by such fees as may be prescribed.

3. Every Genetic Counselling Centre, Genetic Laboratory or a Genetic Clinic engaged, either partly or exclusively, in counselling or conducting pre-natal diagnostic techniques for any of the purposes mentioned in Section 4, immediately before the commencement of this Act, shall apply for registration within sixty days from the date of such commencement.

4. Subject to the provisions of Section 6, every Genetic Counselling Centre, Genetic Laboratory or Genetic Clinic engaged in counselling or conducting pre-natal diagnostic techniques shall cease to conduct any such counselling or technique on the expiry of six months from the date of commencement of this Act unless such Centre, Laboratory or Clinic has applied for registration and is so registered separately or jointly or till such application is disposed of, whichever is earlier.

5. No Genetic Counselling Centre, Genetic Laboratory or Genetic Clinic shall be registered under this Act unless the appropriate authority is satisfied that such Centre, Laboratory or Clinic is in a position to provide such facilities, maintain such equipments and standards as may be prescribed.

19. Certificate of registration. 1. The appropriate authority shall, after holding an inquiry and after satisfying itself that the applicant has complied with all the requirements of this Act and the rules made thereunder and having regard to the advice of the advisory committee in this behalf, grant a certificate of registration in the prescribed form jointly or separately to the Genetic Counselling Centre, Genetic Laboratory or Genetic Clinic, as the case may be.

2. If, after the inquiry and after giving an opportunity of being heard, to the applicant and having regard to the advice the Advisory Committee, the Appropriate Authority is satisfied that the applicant has not complied with the requirement of this Act or the rules, it shall, for reasons to be recorded in writing, reject the application for registration.

3. Every certificate of registration shall be renewed in such manner and after such period and on payment of such fees, as may be prescribed.

4. The certificate of registration shall be displayed by the registered Genetic Counselling Centre, Genetic Laboratory or Genetic Clinic in a conspicuous place at its place of business.

20. Cancellation or Suspension of Registration. 1. The appropriate authority may *suo moto*, or on complaint, issue a notice to the Genetic Counselling Centre, Genetic Laboratory or Genetic Clinic to show cause why its registration should not be suspended or cancelled for the reasons mentioned in the notice.

2. If, after giving a reasonable opportunity of being heard to the Genetic Counselling Centre, Genetic Laboratory or Genetic Clinic, and having regard to the advice of the Advisory Committee, the appropriate authority is satisfied that there has been a breach of the provisions of this Act or the rules, it may, without prejudice to any criminal action that it may take against such Centre, or Clinic, suspend its registration for such period as it may think fit or cancel its registration, as the case may be.

3. Notwithstanding anything contained in sub-sections (1) and (2), if the appropriate authority is of the opinion that it is necessary or expedient so to do in the public interest, it may for reasons to be recorded in writing, suspend the registration of any Genetic Counselling Centre, Genetic Laboratory or Genetic Clinic without issuing any such notice referred to in sub-section (1).

21. Appeal. The Genetic Counselling Centre, Genetic Laboratory or Genetic Clinic, may, within thirty days from the date of receipt of the order of the suspension or cancellation of registration passed by the appropriate authority under section 20, prefer an appeal against such order to—

(i) the Central Government, where the appeal is against the order of the Central appropriate authority; and
(ii) the State Government, where the appeal is against the order of the State appropriate authority, in the prescribed manner.

OFFENCES AND PENALTIES

22. Prohibition of Advertisement Relating to Pre-natal Determination of Sex and Punishment for Contravention. 1. No person, organisation, Genetic Counselling Centre, Genetic Laboratory or Genetic Clinic shall issue or cause to be issued any advertisement in any manner regarding facilities of pre-natal determination of sex available at such Centre, Laboratory, Clinic or any other place.

2. No person or organisation shall publish or distribute or

caused to be published or distributed any advertisement in any manner regarding facilities of pre-natal determination of sex available at any Genetic Counselling Centre, Genetic Laboratory, Genetic Clinic or any other place.

3. Any person, who contravenes the provisions of sub-section (1), or sub-section (2) shall be punishable with imprisonment for a term which may extend to three years and with a fine which may extend to ten thousand rupees:

Explanation. For the purpose of this section, "advertisement" includes any notice, circular, label, wrapper or other document and also includes any visible representation made by means of any light, sound, smoke or gas.

23. Offences and Penalties. 1. Any medical geneticist, gynaecologist, registered medical practitioner or any person who owns a Genetic Counselling Centre, a Genetic Laboratory or a Genetic Clinic or is employed in such Centre, Laboratory or Clinic and renders his professional or technical services to or at such a Centre, Laboratory or Clinic, whether on an honorary basis or otherwise, and who contravenes any of the provisions of this Act or rules made thereunder shall be punishable with imprisonment for a term which may extend to three years and with fine which may extend to ten thousand rupees and on any subsequent conviction, with imprisonment which may extend to five years and with fine which may extend to fifty thousand rupees.

2. The name of the registered medical practitioner who has been convicted by the Court under sub-section (1), shall be reported by the appropriate authority to the respective State Medical Council for taking necessary action including the removal of his name from the register of the Council for a period of two years for the first offence and permanently for the subsequent offence.

3. Any person who seeks the aid of a Genetic Counselling Centre, Genetic Laboratory or Genetic clinic or of a medical geneticist, gynaecologist or registered medical practitioner for conducting pre-natal diagnostic techniques on any pregnant woman (including such woman unless she was compelled to undergo such diagnostic techniques) for purposes other than those specified in Clause (2) of section 4, shall be punishable with imprisonment for a term which may extend to three years and with fine which may extend to ten thousand rupees and on any subsequent conviction with

imprisonment which may extend to five years and with fine which may extend to fifty thousand rupees.

24. Presumption in the Case of Conduct on Pre-natal Diagnostic Techniques. Notwithstanding anything in the Indian Evidence Act, 1872 (Act No.1 of 1872), the Court shall presume unless the contrary is proved that the pregnant woman has been compelled by her husband or the relative to undergo pre-natal diagnostic technique and such person shall be liable for abetment of offence under sub-section (3) of section 23 and shall be punishable for the offence specified under that section.

25. Penalty for Contravention of the Provisions of the Act or Rules for Which no Specific Punishment is Provided. Whoever contravenes any of the provisions of this Act or any rules made thereunder, for which no penalty has been elsewhere provided in this Act, shall be punishable to the imprisonment for a term which may extend to three months or with fine, which may extend to one thousand rupees or with both and in the case of continuing contravention with an additional fine which may extend to five hundred rupees for every day during which such contravention continues after conviction for the first such contravention.

26. Offences by Companies. 1. Where any offence, punishable under this Act, has been committed by a company, every person who, at the time the offence was committed, was in charge of , and was responsible to, the company for the conduct of the business of the company, as well as the company, shall be deemed to be guilty of the offence and shall be liable to be proceeded against and punished accordingly:

Provided that nothing contained in this sub-section shall render any such person liable to any punishment, if he proves that the offence was committed without his knowledge or that he has exercised all due diligence to prevent the commission of such offence.

2. Notwithstanding anything contained in sub-section (1), where any offence punishable under this Act has been committed by a company and it is proved that the offence has been committed with the consent or connivance of, or is attributable to any neglect on the part of, any Director, Manager, Secretary or other officer of the company such Director, Manager Secretary or other Officer shall also be deemed to be guilty of that offence and shall be liable to be proceeded against and punished accordingly.

Explanation. For the purposes of this section.

(a) "company" means any body corporate and includes a firm or other association of individuals; and

(b) "director" in relation to a firm, means a partner in the firm.

*27. **Offence to be Cognizable, Non-bailable and Non-compoundable.*** Every offence under this Act shall be cognizable, non-bailable and non-compoundable.

*28. **Cognizance of Offence.*** 1. No Court shall take cognizance of an offence under this Act except on a complaint made by—

(a) the appropriate authority concerned, or any officer authorised in this behalf by the Central Government or the State Government, as the case may be, or the appropriate authority; or

(b) a person who has given notice of not less than thirty days, in the manner prescribed, to the appropriate authority, of the alleged offence and of his intention to make a complaint to the Court.

Explanation. For the purpose of this clause "person", includes a social organisation.

2. No Court other than that of a Metropolitan Magistrate or a Judicial Magistrate of the First Class shall try any offence punishable under this Act.

3. Where a complaint has been made under clause (b) of sub-section (1), the Court may, on demand by such person, direct the appropriate authority to make available copies of the relevant records in its possession to such person.

MISCELLANEOUS

*29. **Maintenance of Records.*** 1. All records, charts, forms, reports, consent letters and all other documents required to be maintained under this Act and the rules shall be preserved for a period of two years or for such period as may be prescribed:

Provided that, if any criminal or other proceedings are instituted against any Genetic Counselling Centre, Genetic Laboratory or Genetic Clinic, the records and all other documents of such Centre, Laboratory or Clinic shall be preserved till the final disposal of such proceedings.

2. All such records shall, at all reasonable times, be made available for inspection to the appropriate authority or to any

other person authorised by the appropriate authority in this behalf.

30. Power to Search and Seize Records, etc. 1. If the appropriate authority has reason to believe that an offence under this Act has been or is being committed at any Genetic Counselling Centre, Genetic Laboratory or Genetic Clinic, such authority or any officer authorised, in this behalf thereof may, subject to such rules as may be prescribed enter and search at all reasonable times with such assistance, if any, as such authority or officer considers necessary, such Genetic Counselling Centre, Genetic Laboratory or Genetic Clinic and examine any record, register, document, book, pamphlet, advertisement or any other object found therein and seize the same if such authority or officer has reason to believe that it may furnish evidence of the commission of an offence punishable under this Act.

2. The provisions of the Code of Criminal Procedure, 1973 (2 of 1974) relating to searches and seizures, shall, so far as may be, apply to every search or seizure made under this Act.

31. Protection of Action Taken in Good Faith. No suit, prosecution or other legal proceeding shall lie against the Central or the State Government or the appropriate authority or any officer authorised by the Central or State Government, or by the Authority for anything which is in good faith done or intended to be done in pursuance of the provisions of this Act.

32. Power to Make Rules. 1. The Central Government may make rules for carrying out the provisions of this Act.

2. In particular and without prejudice to the generality of the foregoing power such rules may provide for—

(i) the minimum qualifications for persons employed at a registered Genetic Counselling Centre, Genetic Laboratory or Genetic Clinic under clause (1) of Section 3;

(ii) the form in which consent of a pregnant woman has to be obtained under section 5;

(iii) the procedure to be followed by the members of the Central Supervisory Board in the discharge of their functions under sub- section (4) of section 8;

(iv) allowances for members other than *ex officio* members admissible under sub-section (5) of Section 9;

(v) the period intervening between any two meetings of the

Advisory Committee under the proviso to sub-section (8) of Section 17;

(vi) the terms and conditions subject to which a person may be appointed to the Advisory Committee and the procedure to be followed by such committee under sub-section (9) of Section 17.

(vii) the form and manner in which an application shall be made for registration and the fee payable thereof under sub-section (2) of Section 18;

(viii) the facilities to be provided, equipment and other standards to be maintained by the Genetic Counselling Centre, Genetic Laboratory or Genetic Clinic under sub- section (5) of section 18;

(ix) the form in which a certificate of registration shall be issued under sub-section (1) of Section 19;

(x) the manner in which and the period after which a certificate of registration shall be renewed and the fee payable for such renewal under sub-section (3) of Section 19;

(xi) the manner in which an appeal may be preferred under Section 21;

(xii) the period up to which records, charts, etc., shall be preserved under sub- section (1) of Section 29;

(xiii) the manner in which the seizure of documents, records, objects etc. shall be made and the manner in which seizure list shall be prepared and delivered to the person from whose custody such documents, records or objects were seized under sub-section (1) of Section 30;

(xiv) any other matter that is required to be, or may be, prescribed.

33. ***Power to Make Regulations.*** The Board, may, with the previous sanction of the Central Government, by notification in the Official Gazette, or regulations not inconsistent with the provision of this Act and the rules made thereunder to provide for—

(a) the time and place of the meetings of the Board and the procedure to be followed for the transaction of business at such meetings and the number of members which shall form the quorum under sub-section (1) of Section 9;

(b) the manner in which a person may be temporarily associated with the Board under sub-section (1) of Section 11;

(c) the method of appointment, the conditions of service and scales of pay and allowances of the officer and other employees of the Board appointed under Section 12;

(d) generally for the efficient conduct of the affairs of the Board.

34. Rules and Regulations to be Laid before the Parliament. Every rule and regulation made under this Act shall be laid, as soon as may be after it is made, before each House of Parliament, while it is in session, for a total period of thirty days which may be comprised in one session or in two or more successive sessions, and if, before the expiry of the session immediately following the session or the successive sessions aforesaid, both Houses agree in making any modification in the rule or regulation, or both Houses agree that the rule or regulation should not be made, the rule or regulation shall thereafter have effect only in such modified form or be of no effect, as the case may be; so, however, that any such modification or annulment shall be without prejudice to the validity of anything previously done under that rule or regulation.